MznLnx

Missing Links Exam Preps

Exam Prep for

Economics

McConnell, 17th Edition

The MznLnx Exam Prep is your link from the texbook and lecture to your exams.
The MznLnx Exam Preps are unauthorized and comprehensive reviews of your textbooks.

All material provided by MznLnx and Rico Publications (c) 2010
Textbook publishers and textbook authors do not particpate in or contribute to these reviews.

MznLnx

Rico Publications

Exam Prep for Economics
17th Edition
McConnell

Publisher: Raymond Houge
Assistant Editor: Michael Rouger
Text and Cover Designer: Lisa Buckner
Marketing Manager: Sara Swagger
Project Manager, Editorial Production: Jerry Emerson
Art Director: Vernon Lowerui

Product Manager: Dave Mason
Editorial Assitant: Rachel Guzmanji
Pedagogy: Debra Long
Cover Image: Jim Reed/Getty Images
Text and Cover Printer: City Printing, Inc.
Compositor: Media Mix, Inc.

(c) 2010 Rico Publications
ALL RIGHTS RESERVED. No part of this work
covered by the copyright may be reproduced or
used in any form or by an means--graphic, electronic,
or mechanical, including photocopying, recording,
taping, Web distribution, information storage, and
retrieval systems, or in any other manner--without the
written permission of the publisher.

Printed in the United States
ISBN:

For more information about our products, contact us at:
Dave.Mason@RicoPublications.com

For permission to use material from this text or
product, submit a request online to:
Dave.Mason@RicoPublications.com

Contents

CHAPTER 1
Limits, Alternatives, and Choices — 1

CHAPTER 2
The Market System and the Circular Flow — 18

CHAPTER 3
Demand, Supply, and Market Equilibrium — 34

CHAPTER 4
The U.S. Economy: Private and Public Sectors — 48

CHAPTER 5
The United States in the Global Economy — 71

CHAPTER 6
Measuring Domestic Output and National Income — 85

CHAPTER 7
Introduction to Economic Growth and Instability — 102

CHAPTER 8
Basic Macroeconomic Relationships — 124

CHAPTER 9
The Aggregate Expenditures Model — 139

CHAPTER 10
Aggregate Demand and Aggregate Supply — 152

CHAPTER 11
Fiscal Policy, Deficits, and Debt — 169

CHAPTER 12
Money and Banking — 184

CHAPTER 13
Money Creation — 202

CHAPTER 14
Interest Rates and Monetary Policy — 209

CHAPTER 15
Extending the Analysis of Aggregate Supply — 226

CHAPTER 16
Economic Growth — 235

CHAPTER 17
Disputes over Macro Theory and Policy — 249

CHAPTER 18
Extensions of Demand and Supply Analysis — 263

CHAPTER 19
Consumer Behavior and Utility Maximization — 276

CHAPTER 20
The Costs of Production — 285

Contents (Cont.)

CHAPTER 21
Pure Competition — 295

CHAPTER 22
Pure Monopoly — 310

CHAPTER 23
Monopolistic Competition and Oligopoly — 325

CHAPTER 24
Technology, R&D, and Efficiency — 341

CHAPTER 25
The Demand for Resources — 354

CHAPTER 26
Wage Determination — 365

CHAPTER 27
Rent, Interest, and Profit — 378

CHAPTER 28
Government and Market Failure — 394

CHAPTER 29
Public Choice Theory and the Economics of Taxation — 406

CHAPTER 30
Antitrust Policy and Regulation — 416

CHAPTER 31
Agriculture: Economics and Policy — 430

CHAPTER 32
Income Inequality and Poverty — 442

CHAPTER 33
The Economics of Health Care — 458

CHAPTER 34
Labor Market Institutions and Issues: Unionism, Discrimination, Immigration — 469

CHAPTER 35
International Trade — 483

CHAPTER 36
Exchange Rates, the Balance of Payments, and Trade Deficits — 497

ANSWER KEY — 513

TO THE STUDENT

COMPREHENSIVE

The *MznLnx* Exam Prep series is designed to help you pass your exams. Editors at MznLnx review your textbooks and then prepare these practice exams to help you master the textbook material. Unlike study guides, workbooks, and practice tests provided by the texbook publisher and textbook authors, *MznLnx* gives you **all** of the material in each chapter in exam form, not just samples, so you can be sure to nail your exam.

MECHANICAL

The MznLnx Exam Prep series creates exams that will help you learn the subject matter as well as test you on your understanding. Each question is designed to help you master the concept. Just working through the exams, you gain an understanding of the subject--its a simple mechanical process that produces success.

INTEGRATED STUDY GUIDE AND REVIEW

MznLnx is not just a set of exams designed to test you, its also a comprehensive review of the subject content. Each exam question is also a review of the concept, making sure that you will get the answer correct without having to go to other sources of material. You learn as you go! Its the easiest way to pass an exam.

HUMOR

Studying can be tedious and dry. MznLnx's instructional design includes moderate humor within the exam questions on occassion, to break the tedium and revitalize the brain

Chapter 1. Limits, Alternatives, and Choices

1. In economics, _____ is the total demand for final goods and services in the economy (Y) at a given time and price level. It is the amount of goods and services in the economy that will be purchased at all possible price levels. This is the demand for the gross domestic product of a country when inventory levels are static.
   - a. Aggregation problem
   - b. Aggregate demand
   - c. Aggregate supply
   - d. Aggregate expenditure

2. In economics, a _____ is a loss of economic efficiency that can occur when equilibrium for a good or service is not Pareto optimal. In other words, either people who would have more marginal benefit than marginal cost are not buying the good or service, or people who would have more marginal cost than marginal benefit are buying the product.

   Causes of _____ can include monopoly pricing, externalities, taxes or subsidies, and binding price ceilings or floors.
   - a. Contract curve
   - b. Distributive efficiency
   - c. Leapfrogging
   - d. Deadweight loss

3. _____s is the social science that studies the production, distribution, and consumption of goods and services. The term _____s comes from the Ancient Greek οἰκονομία from οἶκος (oikos, 'house') + νόμος (nomos, 'custom' or 'law'), hence 'rules of the house(hold)'. Current _____ models developed out of the broader field of political economy in the late 19th century, owing to a desire to use an empirical approach more akin to the physical sciences.
   - a. Opportunity cost
   - b. Energy economics
   - c. Inflation
   - d. Economic

4. _____ is the increase in the amount of the goods and services produced by an economy over time. It is conventionally measured as the percent rate of increase in real gross domestic product, or real GDP. Growth is usually calculated in real terms, i.e. inflation-adjusted terms, in order to net out the effect of inflation on the price of the goods and services produced.
   - a. ACCRA Cost of Living Index
   - b. Economic growth
   - c. AD-IA Model
   - d. ACEA agreement

5. In economics, the _____ is the change in consumption resulting from a change in real income.

   Another important item that can change is the money income of the consumer. The _____ is the phenomenon observed through changes in purchasing power.
   - a. Equilibrium wage
   - b. Export subsidy
   - c. Inflation hedge
   - d. Income effect

6. A _____ is any systematic process enabling many market players to bid and ask: helping bidders and sellers interact and make deals. It is not just the price mechanism but the entire system of regulation, qualification, credentials, reputations and clearing that surrounds that mechanism and makes it operate in a social context.

   Because a _____ relies on the assumption that players are constantly involved and unequally enabled, a _____ is distinguished specifically from a voting system where candidates seek the support of voters on a less regular basis.

Chapter 1. Limits, Alternatives, and Choices

a. Contestable market
c. Price mechanism
b. Competitive equilibrium
d. Market system

7. In microeconomics, _____ is quite simply the conversion of inputs into outputs. It is an economic process that uses resources to create a good or service that is suitable for exchange. This can include manufacturing, storing, shipping, and packaging.
    a. Solved
    b. MET
    c. Red Guards
    d. Production

8. _____ in economics refers to metrics and measures of output from production processes, per unit of input. Labor _____, for example, is typically measured as a ratio of output per labor-hour, an input. _____ may be conceived of as a metrics of the technical or engineering efficiency of production.
    a. Fordism
    b. Piece work
    c. Production-possibility frontier
    d. Productivity

9. _____ or amortisation is the process of increasing an amount over a period of time. The word comes from Middle English amortisen to kill, alienate in mortmain, from Anglo-French amorteser, alteration of amortir, from Vulgar Latin admortire to kill, from Latin ad- + mort-, mors death. Particular instances of the term include:

   - _____, the allocation of a lump sum amount to different time periods, particularly for loans and other forms of finance, including related interest or other finance charges.
     - _____ schedule, a table detailing each periodic payment on a loan (typically a mortgage), as generated by an _____ calculator.
     - Negative _____, an _____ schedule where the loan amount actually increases through not paying the full interest
   - Amortized analysis, analyzing the execution cost of algorithms over a sequence of operations.
   - _____ of capital expenditures of certain assets under accounting rules, particularly intangible assets, in a manner analogous to depreciation.
   - _____ (tax law)

_____ is also used in the context of zoning regulations and describes the time in which a property owner has to relocate when the property's use constitutes a preexisting nonconforming use under zoning regulations.

   a. Augmentation
   b. Amortization
   c. Economic miracle
   d. Oslo Agreements

10. In economics, _____ is a measure of national income. Basically, it is an approach to measure GDP. It is defined as the value of planned goods and services produced in an economy.
    a. Aggregation problem
    b. Aggregate demand
    c. Aggregate supply
    d. Aggregate expenditure

Chapter 1. Limits, Alternatives, and Choices

11. Economics:

    - _____, the desire to own something and the ability to pay for it
    - _____ curve, a graphic representation of a _____ schedule
    - _____ deposit, the money in checking accounts
    - _____ pull theory, the theory that inflation occurs when _____ for goods and services exceeds existing supplies
    - _____ schedule, a table that lists the quantity of a good a person will buy it each different price
    - _____ side economics, the school of economics at believes government spending and tax cuts open economy by raising _____

    a. Production
    c. McKesson ' Robbins scandal
    b. Variability
    d. Demand

12. In economics, _____ refers to how the marginal contribution of a factor of production usually decreases as more of the factor is used. According to this relationship, in a production system with fixed and variable inputs, beyond some point, each additional unit of the variable input yields smaller and smaller increases in output. Conversely, producing one more unit of output costs more and more in variable inputs.

    a. Patent troll
    c. Diminishing returns
    b. Community property
    d. Derivatives law

13. _____, in microeconomics, are the cost advantages that a business obtains due to expansion. They are factors that cause a producere;s average cost per unit to fall as scale is increased. _____ is a long run concept and refers to reductions in unit cost as the size of a facility, or scale, increases.

    a. Isoquant
    c. Economic production quantity
    b. Underinvestment employment relationship
    d. Economies of scale

14. _____ is a procedure used in economics to measure the contribution of different factors to economic growth and to indirectly compute the rate of technological progress, measured as a residual, in an economy.

    _____ decomposes the growth rate of economy's total output into that which is due to increases in the amount of factors used - usually the increase in the amount of capital and labor - and that which cannot be accounted for by observable changes in factor utilization. The unexplained part of growth in GDP is then taken to represent increases in productivity (getting more output with the same amounts of inputs) or a measure of broadly defined technological progress.

    a. Spillover effect
    c. Reaganomics
    b. Cobb-Douglas
    d. Growth accounting

15. In calculus, a function f defined on a subset of the real numbers with real values is called _____, if for all x and y such that $x >\leq y$ one has $f(x) >\leq f(y)$, so f preserves the order. In layman's terms, the sign of the slope is always positive (the curve tending upwards) or zero (i.e., non-decreasing, or asymptotic, or depicted as a horizontal, flat line) Likewise, a function is called monotonically decreasing (non-increasing) if, whenever $x >\leq y$, then $f(x) >\geq f(y)$, so it reverses the order.

a. 100-year flood
b. 1921 recession
c. 130-30 fund
d. Monotonic

16. _____ is the term denoting either an entrance or changes which are inserted into a system and which activate/modify a process. It is an abstract concept, used in the modeling, system(s) design and system(s) exploitation. It is usually connected with other terms, e.g., _____ field, _____ variable, _____ parameter, _____ value, _____ signal, _____ device and _____ file.
   a. ACEA agreement
   b. ACCRA Cost of Living Index
   c. AD-IA Model
   d. Input

17. In economics and finance, _____ is the change in total cost that arises when the quantity produced changes by one unit. It is the cost of producing one more unit of a good. Mathematically, the _____ function is expressed as the first derivative of the total cost (TC) function with respect to quantity (Q.)
   a. Quality costs
   b. Khozraschyot
   c. Variable cost
   d. Marginal cost

18. The _____ is the apparent contradiction that although water is on the whole more useful, in terms of survival, than diamonds, diamonds command a higher price in the market. The economist Adam Smith is often considered to be the classic presenter of this paradox. Nicolaus Copernicus, John Locke, John Law and others had previously tried to explain the disparity.
   a. 130-30 fund
   b. 100-year flood
   c. St. Petersburg paradox
   d. Paradox of value

19. In economics, and cost accounting, _____ describes the total economic cost of production and is made up of variable costs, which vary according to the quantity of a good produced and include inputs such as labor and raw materials, plus fixed costs, which are independent of the quantity of a good produced and include inputs (capital) that cannot be varied in the short term, such as buildings and machinery. _____ in economics includes the total opportunity cost of each factor of production in addition to fixed and variable costs.

The rate at which _____ changes as the amount produced changes is called marginal cost.

   a. 100-year flood
   b. 1921 recession
   c. Total cost
   d. 130-30 fund

20. In economics, _____ is a measure of the relative satisfaction from consumption of various goods and services. Given this measure, one may speak meaningfully of increasing or decreasing _____, and thereby explain economic behavior in terms of attempts to increase one's _____. For illustrative purposes, changes in _____ are sometimes expressed in units called utils.
   a. Utility
   b. Utility function
   c. Ordinal utility
   d. Expected utility hypothesis

21. In economics, a model is a theoretical construct that represents economic processes by a set of variables and a set of logical and/or quantitative relationships between them. The _____ is a simplified framework designed to illustrate complex processes, often but not always using mathematical techniques. Frequently, _____s use structural parameters.

a. Economic model
b. ACCRA Cost of Living Index
c. AD-IA Model
d. ACEA agreement

22. _____ or economic opportunity loss is the value of the next best alternative foregone as the result of making a decision. _____ analysis is an important part of a company's decision-making processes but is not treated as an actual cost in any financial statement. The next best thing that a person can engage in is referred to as the _____ of doing the best thing and ignoring the next best thing to be done.
   a. Industrial organization
   b. Economic
   c. Economic ideology
   d. Opportunity cost

23. In ethical philosophy, _____ is the principle that an action is rational if and only if it maximizes one's self-interest. The view is a normative form of egoism. However, it is different from other forms of egoism, such as ethical egoism and psychological egoism.
   a. Adam Smith
   b. Adolph Fischer
   c. Rational egoism
   d. Adolf Hitler

24. _____ and Keynesian Theory) is a macroeconomic theory based on the ideas of 20th-century British economist John Maynard Keynes. _____ argues that private sector decisions sometimes lead to inefficient macroeconomic outcomes and therefore advocates active policy responses by the public sector, including monetary policy actions by the central bank and fiscal policy actions by the government to stabilize output over the business cycle.

The theories forming the basis of _____ were first presented in The General Theory of Employment, Interest and Money, published in 1936.

   a. Rational choice theory
   b. Deflation
   c. Market failure
   d. Keynesian economics

25. _____ refers to bodies of techniques for investigating phenomena, acquiring new knowledge, or correcting and integrating previous knowledge. To be termed scientific, a method of inquiry must be based on gathering observable, empirical and measurable evidence subject to specific principles of reasoning. A _____ consists of the collection of data through observation and experimentation, and the formulation and testing of hypotheses.
   a. 130-30 fund
   b. 100-year flood
   c. 1921 recession
   d. Scientific method

26. In economics, a _____ is a graph of the costs of production as a function of total quantity produced. In a free market economy, productively efficient firms use these curves to find the optimal point of production, where they make the most profits. There are a few different types of _____s, each relevant to a different area of economics.
   a. Cost curve
   b. Phillips curve
   c. Demand curve
   d. Kuznets curve

27. A statistical hypothesis test is a method of making statistical decisions using experimental data. It is sometimes called confirmatory data analysis, in contrast to exploratory data analysis. In frequency probability, these decisions are almost always made using null-hypothesis tests; that is, ones that answer the question Assuming that the null hypothesis is true, what is the probability of observing a value for the test statistic that is at least as extreme as the value that was actually observed? One use of _____ is deciding whether experimental results contain enough information to cast doubt on conventional wisdom.

a. 100-year flood
c. 130-30 fund
b. 1921 recession
d. Hypothesis testing

28. _____ is a branch of economics that deals with the performance, structure, and behavior of a national or regional economy as a whole. Along with microeconomics, _____ is one of the two most general fields in economics. It is the study of the behavior and decision-making of entire economies.

a. New Trade Theory
c. Nominal value
b. Tobit model
d. Macroeconomics

29. _____ is a branch of economics that studies how individuals, households and firms and some states make decisions to allocate limited resources, typically in markets where goods or services are being bought and sold. _____ examines how these decisions and behaviours affect the supply and demand for goods and services, which determines prices; and how prices, in turn, determine the supply and demand of goods and services.

Whereas macroeconomics involves the 'sum total of economic activity, dealing with the issues of growth, inflation and unemployment, and with national economic policies relating to these issues' and the effects of government actions on them.

a. New Keynesian economics
c. Countercyclical
b. Recession
d. Microeconomics

30. _____ is a broad label that refers to any individuals or households that use goods and services generated within the economy. The concept of a _____ is used in different contexts, so that the usage and significance of the term may vary.

Typically when business people and economists talk of _____s they are talking about person as _____, an aggregated commodity item with little individuality other than that expressed in the buy/not-buy decision.

a. Consumer
c. 1921 recession
b. 100-year flood
d. 130-30 fund

31. _____ are final goods specifically intended for the mass market. For instance, _____ do not include investment assets, like precious antiques, even though these antiques are final goods.

Manufactured goods are goods that have been processed by way of machinery.

a. Bulgarian-American trade
c. Fiscal stimulus plans
b. G-20 Leaders Summit on Financial Markets and the World Economy
d. Consumer goods

32. A _____ product is a product designed for cheapness and short-term convenience rather than medium to long-term durability, with most products only intended for single use. The term is also sometimes used for products that may last several months (ex. _____ air filters) to distinguish from similar products that last indefinitely (ex.

a. 100-year flood
b. 130-30 fund
c. 1921 recession
d. Disposable

33. _____ is gross income minus income tax on that income.

Discretionary income is income after subtracting taxes and normal expenses (such as rent or mortgage, utilities, insurance, medical, transportation, property maintenance, child support, inflation, food and sundries, 'c.) to maintain a certain standard of living.

a. Stamp Act
b. Disposable personal income
c. Taxation as theft
d. Disposable income

34. A variety of measures of _____ and output are used in economics to estimate total economic activity in a country or region, including gross domestic product (GDP), gross national product (GNP), and net _____

There are three main ways of calculating these numbers; the output approach, the income approach and the expenditure approach. In theory, the three must yield the same, because total expenditures on goods and services must equal the total income paid to the producers (Gnational income), and that must also equal the total value of the output of goods and services (GNP.)

a. GNI per capita
b. National income
c. Gross world product
d. Volume index

35. _____ is the branch of economics that incorporates value judgments (that is, normative judgements) about what the economy ought to be like or what particular policy actions ought to be recommended to achieve a desirable goal. _____ looks at the desirability of certain aspects of the economy. It underlies expressions of support for particular economic policies.

a. Double bottom line
b. Normative economics
c. Broad money
d. Nanoeconomics

36. _____ is the branch of economics that concerns the description and explanation of economic phenomena (Wong, 1987, p. 920.) It focuses on facts and cause-and-effect relationships and includes the development and testing of economics theories.

a. 100-year flood
b. 130-30 fund
c. Regulatory economics
d. Positive economics

37. In economics and business, specifically cost accounting, the _____ point (BEP) is the point at which cost or expenses and revenue are equal: there is no net loss or gain, and one has 'broken even'. A profit or a loss has not been made, although opportunity costs have been paid, and capital has received the risk-adjusted, expected return.

For example, if the business sells less than 200 tables each month, it will make a loss, if it sells more, it will be a profit.

a. Small numbers game
b. Nonmarket
c. Buffer stock scheme
d. Break-even

38. A _____ is an object whose consumption increases the utility of the consumer, for which the quantity demanded exceeds the quantity supplied at zero price. _____s are usually modeled as having diminishing marginal utility. The first individual purchase has high utility; the second has less.
   a. Composite good
   b. Pie method
   c. Merit good
   d. Good

39. _____ was a survey conducted by the U.S. Department of Justice to gauge the prevalence of alcohol and illegal drug use among prior arrestees. It was a reformulation of the prior Drug Use Forecasting (DUF) program, focused on five drugs in particular: cocaine, marijuana, methamphetamine, opiates, and PCP.

Participants were randomly selected from arrest records in major metropolitan areas; because no personally identifying information is taken from each record chosen, the resulting data can be correlated to arrest rates, but not to the total population of persons charged.

   a. ACCRA Cost of Living Index
   b. ACEA agreement
   c. AD-IA Model
   d. Arrestee Drug Abuse Monitoring

40. _____ was a Scottish moral philosopher and a pioneer of political economy. One of the key figures of the Scottish Enlightenment, Smith is the author of The Theory of Moral Sentiments and An Inquiry into the Nature and Causes of the Wealth of Nations. The latter, usually abbreviated as The Wealth of Nations, is considered his magnum opus and the first modern work of economics.
   a. Alan Greenspan
   b. Adam Smith
   c. Adolf Hitler
   d. Adolph Fischer

41. _____ is a misspelled phrase from Latin 'pro capite' phrase meaning per head with pro meaning 'per' or 'for each' and capite meaning 'head.' Both words together equate to the phrase 'for each head.'

It is usually used in the field of statistics to indicate the average per person for any given concern, such as income, crime rate, etc.

It is also used in wills to indicate that each of the named beneficiaries should receive, by devise or bequest, equal shares of the estate. This is in contrast to a per stirpes division, in which each branch of the inheriting family inherits an equal share of the estate.

   a. Sargan test
   b. False positive rate
   c. Population statistics
   d. Per capita

42. _____ means how much each individual receives, in monetary terms, of the yearly income generated in the country. This is what each citizen is to receive if the yearly national income is divided equally among everyone. _____ is usually reported in units of currency per year.
   a. Lerman ratio
   b. Real income
   c. Per capita income
   d. Family income

43. The _____ consists of a number of economic theories which describe the nature of the firm, company including its existence, its behaviour, and its relationship with the market.

Chapter 1. Limits, Alternatives, and Choices

In simplified terms, the _____ aims to answer these questions:

1. Existence - why do firms emerge, why are not all transactions in the economy mediated over the market?
2. Boundaries - why the boundary between firms and the market is located exactly there? Which transactions are performed internally and which are negotiated on the market?
3. Organization - why are firms structured in such specific way? What is the interplay of formal and informal relationships?

Despite looking simple, these questions are not answered by the established economic theory, which usually views firms as given, and treats them as black boxes without any internal structure.

The First World War period saw a change of emphasis in economic theory away from industry-level analysis which mainly included analysing markets to analysis at the level of the firm, as it became increasingly clear that perfect competition was no longer an adequate model of how firms behaved. Economic theory till then had focussed on trying to understand markets alone and there had been little study on understanding why firms or organisations exist.

a. Theory of the firm
b. Technology gap
c. Policy Ineffectiveness Proposition
d. Khazzoom-Brookes postulate

44. _____ is a specific term used in companies' financial reporting from the company-whole point of view. Because that use excludes the effects of changing ownership interest, an economic measure of _____ is necessary for financial analysis from the shareholders' point of view

_____ is defined by the Financial Accounting Standards Board, or FASB, as e;the change in equity [net assets] of a business enterprise during a period from transactions and other events and circumstances from nonowner sources. It includes all changes in equity during a period except those resulting from investments by owners and distributions to owners.e;

_____ is the sum of net income and other items that must bypass the income statement because they have not been realized, including items like an unrealized holding gain or loss from available for sale securities and foreign currency translation gains or losses.

a. Windfall gain
b. Comprehensive income
c. Net national income
d. Real income

45. A _____ is a situation that involves losing one quality or aspect of something in return for gaining another quality or aspect. It implies a decision to be made with full comprehension of both the upside and downside of a particular choice.

In economics the term is expressed as opportunity cost, referring the most preferred alternative given up.

a. Whitemail
b. Nonmarket
c. Friedman-Savage utility function
d. Trade-off

Chapter 1. Limits, Alternatives, and Choices

46. In Marxian economics, _____ originally referred to the means of production. Individuals, organizations and governments use _____ in the production of other goods or commodities. _____ include factories, machinery, tools, equipment, and various buildings which are used to produce other products for consumption.
    a. Capital goods
    b. Capital intensive
    c. Capital deepening
    d. Wealth inequality in the United States

47. The _____, sometimes called the fundamental _____, is one of the fundamental economic theories in the operation of any economy. It asserts that there is scarcity, that the finite resources available are insufficient to satisfy all human wants. The problem then becomes how to determine what is to be produced and how the factors of production (such as capital and labour) are to be allocated.
    a. Economic problem
    b. Endogenous growth theory
    c. Economic nationalism
    d. Eclectic paradigm

48. An _____ is a person who has possession of an enterprise and assumes significant accountability for the inherent risks and the outcome. It is an ambitious leader who combines land, labor, and capital to create and market new goods or services. The term is a loanword from French and was first defined by the Irish economist Richard Cantillon.
    a. ACEA agreement
    b. Expansionary policies
    c. ACCRA Cost of Living Index
    d. Entrepreneur

49. In economics, _____ are the resources employed to produce goods and services. They facilitate production but do not become part of the product (as with raw materials) or significantly transformed by the production process (as with fuel used to power machinery.) To 19th century economists, the _____ were land (natural resources, gifts from nature), labor (the ability to work), and capital goods (human-made tools and equipment.)
    a. Hicks-neutral technical change
    b. Factors of production
    c. Product Pipeline
    d. Long-run

50. The _____ or Aggregate Demand-Aggregate Supply model is a macroeconomic model that explains price level and output through the relationship of aggregate demand and aggregate supply. It was first put forth by John Maynard Keynes in his work The General Theory of Employment, Interest, and Money. It is the foundation for the modern field of macroeconomics, and is accepted by a broad array of economists, from Libertarian, Monetarist supporters of laissez-faire, such as Milton Friedman to Socialist, Post-Keynesian supporters of economic interventionism, such as Joan Robinson.
    a. Adaptive expectations
    b. Economic interdependence
    c. IS/LM model
    d. AD-AS

51. In macroeconomics, _____ is a condition of the national economy, where all or nearly all persons willing and able to work at the prevailing wages and working conditions are able to do so. It is defined either as 0% unemployment, literally, no unemployment (the rate of unemployment is the fraction of the work force unable to find work), as by James Tobin, or as the level of employment rates when there is no cyclical unemployment. It is defined by the majority of mainstream economists as being an acceptable level of natural unemployment above 0%, the discrepancy from 0% being due to non-cyclical types of unemployment.
    a. Full employment
    b. Demand shock
    c. Harrod-Johnson diagram
    d. Marginal propensity to consume

52. In economics, _____ is the total supply of goods and services produced by a national economy during a specific time period. It is the total amount of goods and services in the economy available at all possible price levels.

a. Aggregate demand
b. Aggregation problem
c. Aggregate expenditure
d. Aggregate supply

53. The term _____ refers to economy-wide fluctuations in production or economic activity over several months or years. These fluctuations occur around a long-term growth trend, and typically involve shifts over time between periods of relatively rapid economic growth (expansion or boom), and periods of relative stagnation or decline (contraction or recession.)

These fluctuations are often measured using the growth rate of real gross domestic product.

a. Tobit model
b. Nominal value
c. Consumer theory
d. Business cycle

54. In economics, _____ refers to the ability of a person or a country to produce a particular good at a lower marginal cost and opportunity cost than another person or country. It is the ability to produce a product most efficiently given all the other products that could be produced. It can be contrasted with absolute advantage which refers to the ability of a person or a country to produce a particular good at a lower absolute cost than another.
a. Gravity model of trade
b. Hot money
c. Triffin dilemma
d. Comparative advantage

55. _____ is a common concept in economics, and gives rise to derived concepts such as consumer debt. Generally _____ is defined by opposition to production. But the precise definition can vary because different schools of economists define production quite differently.
a. Federal Reserve Bank Notes
b. Foreclosure data providers
c. Consumption
d. Cash or share options

56. A _____ is:

- Rewrite _____, in generative grammar and computer science
- Standardization, a formal and widely-accepted statement, fact, definition, or qualification
- Operation, a determinate _____ for performing a mathematical operation and obtaining a certain result (Mathematics, Logic)
    - Unary operation
    - Binary operation
- _____ of inference, a function from sets of formulae to formulae (Mathematics, Logic)
- _____ of thumb, principle with broad application that is not intended to be strictly accurate or reliable for every situation. Also often simply referred to as a _____
- Moral, an atomic element of a moral code for guiding choices in human behavior
- Heuristic, a quantized '_____' which shows a tendency or probability for successful function
- A regulation, as in sports
- A Production _____, as in computer science
- Procedural law, a _____ set governing the application of laws to cases
    - A law, which may informally be called a '_____'
    - A court ruling, a decision by a court
- In the U.S. Government, a regulation mandated by Congress, but written or expanded upon by the Executive Branch.
- Norm (sociology), an informal but widely accepted _____, concept, truth, definition, or qualification (social norms, legal norms, coding norms)
- Norm (philosophy), a kind of sentence or a reason to act, feel or believe
- 'Rulership' is the concept of governance by a government:
    - Military _____, governance by a military body
    - Monastic _____, a collection of precepts that guides the life of monks or nuns in a religious order where the superior holds the place of Christ
- Slide _____

- '_____,' a song by Ayumi Hamasaki
- '_____,' a song by rapper Nas
- '_____s,' an album by the band The Whitest Boy Alive
- _____s: Pyaar Ka Superhit Formula, a 2003 Bollywood film
- ruler, an instrument for measuring lengths
- _____, a component of an astrolabe, circumferator or similar instrument
- The _____s, a bestselling self-help book
- _____ Project (Run Up-to-date Linux Everywhere), a project that aims to use up-to-date Linux software on old PCs
- _____ engine, a software system that helps managing business _____s
- Ja _____, a hip hop artist
    - R.U.L.E., a 2005 greatest hits album by rapper Ja _____
- '_____s,' a KMFDM song

a. Demand
b. Technocracy
c. Procter ' Gamble
d. Rule

57. The _____ is an international financial institution that provides financial and technical assistance to developing countries for development programs (e.g. bridges, roads, schools, etc.) with the stated goal of reducing poverty.

The _____ differs from the _____ Group, in that the _____ comprises only two institutions:

- International Bank for Reconstruction and Development (IBRD)
- International Development Association (IDA)

Whereas the latter incorporates these two in addition to three more:

- International Finance Corporation (IFC)
- Multilateral Investment Guarantee Agency (MIGA)
- International Centre for Settlement of Investment Disputes (ICSID)

John Maynard Keynes (right) represented the UK at the conference, and Harry Dexter White represented the US.

The _____ is one of two major financial institutions created as a result of the Bretton Woods Conference in 1944. The International Monetary Fund, a related but separate institution, is the second.

a. Flow to Equity-Approach
c. Financial costs of the 2003 Iraq War
b. World Bank
d. Bank-State-Branch

58. _____ is used to assign the available resources in an economic way. It is part of resource management.

In strategic planning,is a plan for using available resources, for example human resources, especially in the near term, to achieve goals for the future.

a. 100-year flood
c. 130-30 fund
b. Resource allocation
d. 1921 recession

59. _____, officially the Islamic Republic of _____, is a landlocked country that is located approximately in the center of Asia. It is variously designated as geographically located within Central Asia, South Asia, and the Middle East. It is bordered by Pakistan in the south and east, Iran in the south and west, Turkmenistan, Uzbekistan and Tajikistan in the north, and China in the far northeast.

a. ACEA agreement
c. Afghanistan
b. ACCRA Cost of Living Index
d. AD-IA Model

60. The _____ or gross domestic income (GDI), a basic measure of an economy's economic performance, is the market value of all final goods and services produced within the borders of a nation in a year. _____ can be defined in three ways, all of which are conceptually identical. First, it is equal to the total expenditures for all final goods and services produced within the country in a stipulated period of time (usually a 365-day year.)

a. Countercyclical
c. Monopolistic competition
b. Market structure
d. Gross domestic product

Chapter 1. Limits, Alternatives, and Choices

61. The _____ or the output gap is the difference between potential GDP and actual GDP or actual output. The calculation for the output gap is Y-Y* where Y* is potential output and Y is actual output. If this calculation yields a positive number it is called an expansionary gap and indicates an economy in expansion; if the calculation yields a negative number it is called a recessionary gap and indicates an economy in recession.
   - a. 1921 recession
   - b. 100-year flood
   - c. 130-30 fund
   - d. GDP gap

62. The _____ was a worldwide economic downturn starting in most places in 1929 and ending at different times in the 1930s or early 1940s for different countries. It was the largest and most important economic depression in the 20th century, and is used in the 21st century as an example of how far the world's economy can fall. The _____ originated in the United States; historians most often use as a starting date the stock market crash on October 29, 1929, known as Black Tuesday.
   - a. Jarrow March
   - b. Great Depression
   - c. Wall Street Crash of 1929
   - d. British Empire Economic Conference

63. _____ is a term used to described a tendency or preference towards a particular perspective, ideology or result, especially when the tendency interferes with the ability to be impartial, unprejudiced, or objective. The term _____ed is used to describe an action, judgment, or other outcome influenced by a prejudged perspective. It is also used to refer to a person or body of people whose actions or judgments exhibit _____.
   - a. 130-30 fund
   - b. 100-year flood
   - c. 1921 recession
   - d. Bias

64. A _____ arises when one infers that something is true of the whole from the fact that it is true of some part of the whole (or even of every proper part.) For example: 'This fragment of metal cannot be broken with a hammer, therefore the machine of which it is a part cannot be broken with a hammer.' This is clearly fallacious, because many machines can be broken into their constituent parts without any of those parts being breakable.

This fallacy is often confused with the fallacy of hasty generalization, in which an unwarranted inference is made from a statement about a sample to a statement about the population from which it is drawn.

   - a. 130-30 fund
   - b. 100-year flood
   - c. 1921 recession
   - d. Fallacy of composition

65. _____ is an online peer-reviewed magazine published by the Agricultural ' Applied Economics Association (AAEA) for readers interested in the policy and management of agriculture, the food industry, natural resources, rural communities, and the environment. _____ is published quarterly and is available free online. It is currently one of three outreach products offered by AAEA, along with the more timely Policy Issues and the forthcoming Shared Materials section of the AAEA Web site.
   - a. 130-30 fund
   - b. Choices
   - c. 100-year flood
   - d. 1921 recession

66. In statistics, _____ indicates the strength and direction of a linear relationship between two random variables. That is in contrast with the usage of the term in colloquial speech, which denotes any relationship, not necessarily linear. In general statistical usage, _____ or co-relation refers to the departure of two random variables from independence.

a. 130-30 fund
b. 1921 recession
c. 100-year flood
d. Correlation

67. A _____ is a public market for the trading of company stock and derivatives at an agreed price; these are securities listed on a stock exchange as well as those only traded privately.

The size of the world _____ was estimated at about $36.6 trillion US at the beginning of October 2008 . The total world derivatives market has been estimated at about $791 trillion face or nominal value, 11 times the size of the entire world economy.

a. Adam Smith
b. Stock market
c. Adolph Fischer
d. Adolf Hitler

68. A _____ is a type of economic bubble taking place in stock markets when price of stocks rise and become overvalued by any measure of stock valuation.

The existence of _____s is at odds with the assumptions of efficient market theory which assumes rational investor behaviour. Behavioral finance theory attribute _____s to cognitive biases that lead to groupthink and herd behavior.

a. Scrip issue
b. Fill or kill
c. Growth investing
d. Stock market bubble

69. _____ is exchange of capital, goods, and services across international borders or territories. In most countries, it represents a significant share of gross domestic product (GDP.) While _____ has been present throughout much of history , its economic, social, and political importance has been on the rise in recent centuries.

a. Import license
b. Intra-industry trade
c. International trade
d. Incoterms

70. In economics, the people in the _____ are the suppliers of labor. The _____ is all the nonmilitary people who are employed or unemployed. In 2005, the worldwide _____ was over 3 billion people.

a. Grenelle agreements
b. Labor Force
c. Distributed workforce
d. Departmentalization

71. The terms '_____' and 'independent variable' are used in similar but subtly different ways in mathematics and statistics as part of the standard terminology in those subjects. They are used to distinguish between two types of quantities being considered, separating them into those available at the start of a process and those being created by it, where the latter (_____s) are dependent on the former (independent variables.)

In traditional calculus, a function is defined as a relation between two terms called variables because their values vary.

a. 100-year flood
b. 130-30 fund
c. 1921 recession
d. Dependent variable

72. The terms 'dependent variable' and '_____' are used in similar but subtly different ways in mathematics and statistics as part of the standard terminology in those subjects. They are used to distinguish between two types of quantities being considered, separating them into those available at the start of a process and those being created by it, where the latter (dependent variables) are dependent on the former (_____s.)

The _____ is typically the variable being manipulated or changed and the dependent variable is the observed result of the _____ being manipulated.

a. Independent variable
b. ACCRA Cost of Living Index
c. ACEA agreement
d. AD-IA Model

73. _____ in economics and business is the result of an exchange and from that trade we assign a numerical monetary value to a good, service or asset. If Alice trades Bob 4 apples for an orange, the _____ of an orange is 4 apples. Inversely, the _____ of an apple is 1/4 oranges.

a. Price war
b. Premium pricing
c. Price book
d. Price

74. A _____ is a hypothetical measure of overall prices for some set of goods and services, in a given region during a given interval, normalized relative to some base set. Typically, a _____ is approximated with a price index.

The classical dichotomy is the assumption that there is a relatively clean distinction between overall increases or decreases in prices and underlying, e;reale; economic variables.

a. Price elasticity of supply
b. Price level
c. Discouraged worker
d. Discretionary spending

75. An inverse or negative relationship is a mathematical relationship in which one variable, say y, decreases as another, say x, increases. For a linear (straight-line) relation, this can be expressed as y = a-bx, where -b is a constant value less than zero and a is a constant. For example, there is an _____ between education and unemployment -- that is, as education increases, the rate of unemployment decreases.

a. Inverse relationship
b. AD-IA Model
c. ACEA agreement
d. ACCRA Cost of Living Index

76. In mathematics, a _____ system is a system which is not linear, that is, a system which does not satisfy the superposition principle, or whose output is not proportional to its input. Less technically, a _____ system is any problem where the variable(s) to be solved for cannot be written as a linear combination of independent components. A nonhomogeneous system, which is linear apart from the presence of a function of the independent variables, is _____ according to a strict definition, but such systems are usually studied alongside linear systems, because they can be transformed to a linear system of multiple variables.

a. 130-30 fund
b. 100-year flood
c. Nonlinear system
d. Nonlinear

77. _____ is the process by which money is produced or issued. There are three different ways to create money:

- manufacturing a new monetary unit, such as paper currency or metal coins (_____)
- loaning out a physical monetary unit multiple times through fractional-reserve lending (credit creation)
- buying of government securities or other financial instruments by central bank through Open market operations (electronic creation)

Coins are produced by manufacturing metal in a factory called a mint.

Banknotes and bank account balances are financial securities issued by a bank.

Similarly, money destruction, i.e., the reverse of _____, can occur in two different ways, depending on how the money was created.

a. Monetary policy of Sweden
b. Second-round effect
c. Money creation
d. Shadow Open Market Committee

78. A security is a fungible, negotiable instrument representing financial value. _____ are broadly categorized into debt _____; equity _____, e.g., common stocks; and derivative (finance) contracts such as forwards, futures, options and swaps. The company or other entity issuing the security is called the issuer.

a. Red herring prospectus
b. Pass-Through Certificates
c. Settlement risk
d. Securities

Chapter 2. The Market System and the Circular Flow

1. _____ is an economic system in which wealth, and the means of producing wealth, are privately owned. Through _____, the land, labor, and capital are owned, operated, and traded for the purpose of generating profits, without force or fraud, by private individuals either singly or jointly, and investments, distribution, income, production, pricing and supply of goods, commodities and services are determined by voluntary private decision in a market economy. A distinguishing feature of _____ is that each person owns his or her own labor and therefore is allowed to sell the use of it to employers.

   a. Creative capitalism
   b. Socialism for the rich and capitalism for the poor
   c. Late capitalism
   d. Capitalism

2. _____ is a broad label that refers to any individuals or households that use goods and services generated within the economy. The concept of a _____ is used in different contexts, so that the usage and significance of the term may vary.

   Typically when business people and economists talk of _____s they are talking about person as _____, an aggregated commodity item with little individuality other than that expressed in the buy/not-buy decision.

   a. 130-30 fund
   b. 100-year flood
   c. 1921 recession
   d. Consumer

3. _____ are final goods specifically intended for the mass market. For instance, _____ do not include investment assets, like precious antiques, even though these antiques are final goods.

   Manufactured goods are goods that have been processed by way of machinery.

   a. Fiscal stimulus plans
   b. Bulgarian-American trade
   c. G-20 Leaders Summit on Financial Markets and the World Economy
   d. Consumer goods

4. _____s is the social science that studies the production, distribution, and consumption of goods and services. The term _____s comes from the Ancient Greek oá¼°κονομῖα from oá¼¶κος (oikos, 'house') + vÏŒμος (nomos, 'custom' or 'law'), hence 'rules of the house(hold)'. Current _____ models developed out of the broader field of political economy in the late 19th century, owing to a desire to use an empirical approach more akin to the physical sciences.

   a. Economic
   b. Inflation
   c. Opportunity cost
   d. Energy economics

5. _____ is a term used in economic research and policy debates. As with freedom generally, there are various definitions, but no universally accepted concept of _____. One major approach to _____ comes from the libertarian tradition emphasizing free markets and private property, while another extends the welfare economics study of individual choice, with greater _____ coming from a 'larger' (in some technical sense) set of possible choices.

   a. Economic liberalization
   b. Investment policy
   c. Economic Freedom
   d. International sanctions

6. An _____ or Å"conomic system is a system that involves the production, distribution and consumption of goods and services between the entities in a particular society. It is the method used by society to produce and distribute goods and services. The _____ is composed of people and institutions, including their relationships to productive resources, such as through the convention of property.

a. Intention economy
c. Information economy
b. Indicative planning
d. Economic system

7. A _____ is an object whose consumption increases the utility of the consumer, for which the quantity demanded exceeds the quantity supplied at zero price. _____s are usually modeled as having diminishing marginal utility. The first individual purchase has high utility; the second has less.
   a. Merit good
   b. Composite good
   c. Pie method
   d. Good

8. _____ is a term used to describe a policy of allowing events to take their own course. The term is a French phrase literally meaning 'let do'. It is a doctrine that states that government generally should not intervene in the marketplace.
   a. Theory of Productive Forces
   b. Laissez-faire
   c. Communization
   d. Heroic capitalism

9. A _____ is any systematic process enabling many market players to bid and ask: helping bidders and sellers interact and make deals. It is not just the price mechanism but the entire system of regulation, qualification, credentials, reputations and clearing that surrounds that mechanism and makes it operate in a social context.

   Because a _____ relies on the assumption that players are constantly involved and unequally enabled, a _____ is distinguished specifically from a voting system where candidates seek the support of voters on a less regular basis.

   a. Contestable market
   b. Competitive equilibrium
   c. Price mechanism
   d. Market system

10. In economics, _____ is a measure of national income. Basically, it is an approach to measure GDP. It is defined as the value of planned goods and services produced in an economy.
    a. Aggregate expenditure
    b. Aggregation problem
    c. Aggregate supply
    d. Aggregate demand

11. The term _____ refers to economy-wide fluctuations in production or economic activity over several months or years. These fluctuations occur around a long-term growth trend, and typically involve shifts over time between periods of relatively rapid economic growth (expansion or boom), and periods of relative stagnation or decline (contraction or recession.)

    These fluctuations are often measured using the growth rate of real gross domestic product.

    a. Nominal value
    b. Consumer theory
    c. Tobit model
    d. Business cycle

12. _____ has several particular meanings:

- in mathematics
    - _____ function
    - Euler _____
    - _____
    - _____ subgroup
    - method of _____s (partial differential equations)
- in physics and engineering
    - any _____ curve that shows the relationship between certain input- and output parameters, e.g.
    - an I-V or current-voltage _____ is the current in a circuit as a function of the applied voltage
    - Receiver-Operator _____
- in fiction
    - in Dungeons ' Dragons, _____ is another name for ability score

a. Demand
b. Technocracy
c. Russian financial crisis
d. Characteristic

13. A _____ or directed economy is an economic system in which the government or workers' councils manages the economy. It is an economic system in which the central government makes all decisions on the production and consumption of goods and services. Its most extensive form is referred to as a _____, centrally planned economy, or command and control economy.

a. Subsistence economy
b. Transition economy
c. Nutritional Economics
d. Command economy

14. _____ is a socioeconomic structure and political ideology that promotes the establishment of an egalitarian, classless, stateless society based on common ownership and control of the means of production and property in general. In political science, the term '_____' is sometimes used to refer to communist states, a form of government in which the state operates under a one-party system and declares allegiance to Marxism-Leninism or a derivative thereof, even if the party does not actually claim that it has already reached _____.

Forerunners of communist ideas existed in antiquity and particularly in the 18th and early 19th century France, with thinkers such as Jean-Jacques Rousseau and the more radical Gracchus Babeuf.

a. Social fascism
b. New Communist Movement
c. Communism
d. Democratic centralism

15. In microeconomics, _____ is quite simply the conversion of inputs into outputs. It is an economic process that uses resources to create a good or service that is suitable for exchange. This can include manufacturing, storing, shipping, and packaging.

a. MET
b. Production
c. Solved
d. Red Guards

16. _____ in political thought refers to economic theories of social organization advocating collective ownership and administration of the means of production and distribution of goods, and a society characterized by equality for all individuals, with an egalitarian method of compensation. Modern _____ originated in the late 19th-century intellectual and working class political movement that criticized the effects of industrialization and private ownership on society. Karl Marx posited that _____ would be achieved via class struggle and a proletarian revolution after a transitional stage from capitalism called the dictatorship of the proletariat.

- a. Adolf Hitler
- b. Adolph Fischer
- c. Adam Smith
- d. Socialism

17. An _____ is a person who has possession of an enterprise and assumes significant accountability for the inherent risks and the outcome. It is an ambitious leader who combines land, labor, and capital to create and market new goods or services. The term is a loanword from French and was first defined by the Irish economist Richard Cantillon.

- a. ACCRA Cost of Living Index
- b. Expansionary policies
- c. ACEA agreement
- d. Entrepreneur

18. _____ are legal property rights over creations of the mind, both artistic and commercial, and the corresponding fields of law. Under _____ law, owners are granted certain exclusive rights to a variety of intangible assets, such as musical, literary, and artistic works; ideas, discoveries and inventions; and words, phrases, symbols, and designs. Common types of _____ include copyrights, trademarks, patents, industrial design rights and trade secrets.

- a. Independent contractor
- b. Expedited Funds Availability Act
- c. Ease of Doing Business Index
- d. Intellectual property

19. Bartering is a medium in which goods or services are directly exchanged for other goods and/or services, without the use of money. It can be bilateral or multilateral, and usually exists parallel to monetary systems in most developed countries, though to a very limited extent. _____ usually replaces money as the method of exchange in times of monetary crisis, when the currency is unstable and devalued by hyperinflation.

- a. Community-based economics
- b. Barter
- c. Meitheal
- d. New Economics Foundation

20. In economics, the _____ is the term economists use to describe the self-regulating nature of the marketplace. The _____ is a metaphor coined by the economist Adam Smith in The Wealth of Nations.

Adam Smith mentions the metaphor in Book IV of The Wealth of Nations, arguing that people in any society will certainly employ their capital in foreign trading only if the profits available by that method far exceed those available locally, and that in such a case it is better for society as a whole if they so did.

- a. ACCRA Cost of Living Index
- b. AD-IA Model
- c. ACEA agreement
- d. Invisible hand

21. A _____ is the exclusive authority to determine how a resource is used, whether that resource is owned by government or by individuals. All economic goods have a _____s attribute. This attribute has three broad components

1. The right to use the good
2. The right to earn income from the good
3. The right to transfer the good to others

The concept of _____s as used by economists and legal scholars are related but distinct. The distinction is largely seen in the economists' focus on the ability of an individual or collective to control the use of the good.

a. Post-sale restraint
b. High-reeve
c. Holder in due course
d. Property right

22. _____ and Keynesian Theory) is a macroeconomic theory based on the ideas of 20th-century British economist John Maynard Keynes. _____ argues that private sector decisions sometimes lead to inefficient macroeconomic outcomes and therefore advocates active policy responses by the public sector, including monetary policy actions by the central bank and fiscal policy actions by the government to stabilize output over the business cycle.

The theories forming the basis of _____ were first presented in The General Theory of Employment, Interest and Money, published in 1936.

a. Keynesian economics
b. Rational choice theory
c. Market failure
d. Deflation

23. In Marxian economics, _____ originally referred to the means of production. Individuals, organizations and governments use _____ in the production of other goods or commodities. _____ include factories, machinery, tools, equipment, and various buildings which are used to produce other products for consumption.

a. Capital intensive
b. Capital deepening
c. Wealth inequality in the United States
d. Capital goods

24. _____ in economics and business is the result of an exchange and from that trade we assign a numerical monetary value to a good, service or asset. If Alice trades Bob 4 apples for an orange, the _____ of an orange is 4 apples. Inversely, the _____ of an apple is 1/4 oranges.

a. Price
b. Price war
c. Premium pricing
d. Price book

25. _____ was a survey conducted by the U.S. Department of Justice to gauge the prevalence of alcohol and illegal drug use among prior arrestees. It was a reformulation of the prior Drug Use Forecasting (DUF) program, focused on five drugs in particular: cocaine, marijuana, methamphetamine, opiates, and PCP.

Participants were randomly selected from arrest records in major metropolitan areas; because no personally identifying information is taken from each record chosen, the resulting data can be correlated to arrest rates, but not to the total population of persons charged.

a. ACEA agreement
b. AD-IA Model
c. ACCRA Cost of Living Index
d. Arrestee Drug Abuse Monitoring

26. _____ was a Scottish moral philosopher and a pioneer of political economy. One of the key figures of the Scottish Enlightenment, Smith is the author of The Theory of Moral Sentiments and An Inquiry into the Nature and Causes of the Wealth of Nations. The latter, usually abbreviated as The Wealth of Nations, is considered his magnum opus and the first modern work of economics.

Chapter 2. The Market System and the Circular Flow

a. Adolph Fischer
b. Alan Greenspan
c. Adolf Hitler
d. Adam Smith

27. The _____ problem (often 'double _____') is an important category of transaction costs that impose severe limitations on economies lacking money and thus dominated by barter or other in-kind transactions. The problem is caused by the improbability of the wants, needs or events that cause or motivate a transaction occurring at the same time and the same place.

In-kind transactions have several problems, most notably timing constraints.

a. Coincidence of wants
b. RFM
c. Buy-sell agreement
d. Going concern

28. Economics:

- _____, the desire to own something and the ability to pay for it
- _____ curve, a graphic representation of a _____ schedule
- _____ deposit, the money in checking accounts
- _____ pull theory, the theory that inflation occurs when _____ for goods and services exceeds existing supplies
- _____ schedule, a table that lists the quantity of a good a person will buy it each different price
- _____ side economics, the school of economics at believes government spending and tax cuts open economy by raising _____

a. Variability
b. Production
c. McKesson ' Robbins scandal
d. Demand

29. The _____ is the desired holding of money balances in the form of cash or bank deposits.

Money is dominated as store of value by interest bearing assets. However, money is necessary to carry out transactions, or in other words, it provides liquidity.

a. Borrowing base
b. Demand for money
c. Market neutral
d. Conglomerate merger

30. A _____ is an intermediary used in trade to avoid the inconveniences of a pure barter system.

By contrast, as William Stanley Jevons argued, in a barter system there must be a coincidence of wants before two people can trade - one must want exactly what the other has to offer, when and where it is offered, so that the exchange can occur. A _____ permits the value of goods to be assessed and rendered in terms of the intermediary, most often, a form of money widely accepted to buy any other good.

a. Price revolution
b. Labour economics
c. Consumer theory
d. Medium of exchange

Chapter 2. The Market System and the Circular Flow

31. A _____ is a general term that describes any government policy or regulation that restricts international trade. The barriers can take many forms, including the following terms that include many restrictions in international trade within multiple countries that import and export any items of trade.

- Import duty
- Import licenses
- Export licenses
- Import quotas
- Tariffs
- Subsidies
- Non-tariff barriers to trade
- Voluntary Export Restraints
- Local Content Requirements
- Embargo

Most _____s work on the same principle: the imposition of some sort of cost on trade that raises the price of the traded products. If two or more nations repeatedly use _____s against each other, then a trade war results.

a. National Foreign Trade Council
b. Certificate of origin
c. Global financial system
d. Trade barrier

32. In economics, _____ refers to the ability of a party to produce a good or service using fewer real resources than another entity producing the same good or service..A party has an _____ when using the same input as another party, it can produce a greater output. Since _____ is determined by a simple comparison of labor productivities, it is possible for a party to have no _____ in anything. It can be contrasted with the concept of comparative advantage which refers to the ability to produce a particular good at a lower opportunity cost.

a. Index number
b. Absolute advantage
c. ACCRA Cost of Living Index
d. International economics

33. In finance, the _____ is the global financial market for short-term borrowing and lending. It provides short-term liquidity funding for the global financial system. The _____ is where short-term obligations such as Treasury bills, commercial paper and bankers' acceptances are bought and sold.

a. T-Model
b. Deferred compensation
c. Consignment stock
d. Money Market

34. _____ is money accepted for exchange of goods in an economy. The prevalence of one money over another arises, usually, when a government designates through decrees that the government shall accept only particular notes and coins in payment for taxes. Typically, money of _____ consists of stamped coins and minted paper bills.

a. Currency
b. Local currency
c. Totnes pound
d. Security thread

35. In economics, a _____ exists when the production or use of goods and services by the market is not efficient. That is, there exists another outcome where all involved can be made better off. _____s can be viewed as scenarios where individuals' pursuit of pure self-interest leads to results that are not efficient - that can be improved upon from the societal point-of-view.

a. Market failure
c. Fixed exchange rate
b. General equilibrium
d. Financial economics

36. A _____ is a kind of negotiable instrument, a promissory note made by a bank payable to the bearer on demand, used as money, and in many jurisdictions is legal tender. Along with coins, _____s make up the cash or bearer forms of all modern money. With the exception of non-circulating high-value or precious metal commemorative issues, coins are generally used for lower valued monetary units, while _____s are used for higher values.
   a. Security thread
   c. Local currency
   b. Banknote
   d. Microprinting

37. _____ is a government outline where any more than minimal governmental intervention in personal liberties and the economy is not usually allowed by law, usually in a written Constitution. It is closely related to libertarianism, classical liberalism, and some tendencies of liberalism and conservatism in the United States.

_____ is a common practice through Western culture.

   a. 1921 recession
   c. 130-30 fund
   b. 100-year flood
   d. Limited government

38. _____ is a term which is used in economics to refer to the rule or sovereignty of purchasers in markets as to production of goods. It is the power of consumers to decide what gets produced. People use the this term to describe the consumer as the 'king,' or ruler, of the market, the one who determines what products will be produced.
   a. Microeconomic reform
   c. Reservation price
   b. Schedule delay
   d. Consumer sovereignty

39. The _____ consists of a number of economic theories which describe the nature of the firm, company including its existence, its behaviour, and its relationship with the market.

In simplified terms, the _____ aims to answer these questions:

1. Existence - why do firms emerge, why are not all transactions in the economy mediated over the market?
2. Boundaries - why the boundary between firms and the market is located exactly there? Which transactions are performed internally and which are negotiated on the market?
3. Organization - why are firms structured in such specific way? What is the interplay of formal and informal relationships?

Despite looking simple, these questions are not answered by the established economic theory, which usually views firms as given, and treats them as black boxes without any internal structure.

The First World War period saw a change of emphasis in economic theory away from industry-level analysis which mainly included analysing markets to analysis at the level of the firm, as it became increasingly clear that perfect competition was no longer an adequate model of how firms behaved. Economic theory till then had focussed on trying to understand markets alone and there had been little study on understanding why firms or organisations exist.

a. Technology gap
b. Khazzoom-Brookes postulate
c. Policy Ineffectiveness Proposition
d. Theory of the firm

40. In economics, _____ is the difference between a company's total revenue and its opportunity costs. It is the increase in wealth that an investor has from making an investment, taking into consideration all costs associated with that investment including the opportunity cost of capital.

Profit is the factor income of the entrepreneur.

a. Operating profit
b. Accounting profit
c. ACCRA Cost of Living Index
d. Economic profit

41. In economics, and cost accounting, _____ describes the total economic cost of production and is made up of variable costs, which vary according to the quantity of a good produced and include inputs such as labor and raw materials, plus fixed costs, which are independent of the quantity of a good produced and include inputs (capital) that cannot be varied in the short term, such as buildings and machinery. _____ in economics includes the total opportunity cost of each factor of production in addition to fixed and variable costs.

The rate at which _____ changes as the amount produced changes is called marginal cost.

a. 1921 recession
b. 100-year flood
c. Total cost
d. 130-30 fund

42. _____ is the total money received from the sale of any given quantity of output.

The _____ is calculated by taking the price of the sale times the quantity sold, i.e.

_____ = price X quantity.

a. Market development funds
b. Small numbers game
c. Total revenue
d. Ceteris paribus

43. _____ is the difference between price and the costs of bringing to market whatever it is that is accounted as an enterprise (whether by harvest, extraction, manufacture, or purchase) in terms of the component costs of delivered goods and/or services and any operating or other expenses.

A key difficulty in measuring profit is in defining costs. Pure economic monetary profits can be zero or negative even in competitive equilibrium when accounted monetized costs exceed monetized price.

a. ACCRA Cost of Living Index
b. Operating profit
c. Economic profit
d. Accounting profit

Chapter 2. The Market System and the Circular Flow

44. _____ is used to refer to a number of related concepts. It is the using resources in such a way as to maximize the production of goods and services. A system can be called economically efficient if:

- No one can be made better off without making someone else worse off.
- More output cannot be obtained without increasing the amount of inputs.
- Production proceeds at the lowest possible per-unit cost.

These definitions of efficiency are not equivalent, but they are all encompassed by the idea that nothing more can be achieved given the resources available.

An economic system is more efficient if it can provide more goods and services for society without using more resources.

a. Efficient contract theory
b. ACCRA Cost of Living Index
c. ACEA agreement
d. Economic efficiency

45. The _____ or gross domestic income (GDI), a basic measure of an economy's economic performance, is the market value of all final goods and services produced within the borders of a nation in a year. _____ can be defined in three ways, all of which are conceptually identical. First, it is equal to the total expenditures for all final goods and services produced within the country in a stipulated period of time (usually a 365-day year.)

a. Monopolistic competition
b. Countercyclical
c. Market structure
d. Gross domestic product

46. The _____ or the output gap is the difference between potential GDP and actual GDP or actual output. The calculation for the output gap is Y-Y* where Y* is potential output and Y is actual output. If this calculation yields a positive number it is called an expansionary gap and indicates an economy in expansion; if the calculation yields a negative number it is called a recessionary gap and indicates an economy in recession.

a. 130-30 fund
b. 100-year flood
c. 1921 recession
d. GDP gap

47. _____ is a component of the firm's opportunity costs. The time that the owner spends running the firm could be spent on running another firm. This is _____: the return the entrepreneur can expect to earn or the profit that the business owners considers necessary to make running the business worth his/her while.

a. 100-year flood
b. Profit margin
c. Profit maximization
d. Normal profit

48. _____ is defined as the measure of responsiveness in the quantity demanded for a commodity as a result of change in price of the same commodity. It is a measure of how consumers react to a change in price. In other words, it is percentage change in quantity demanded as per the percentage change in price of the same commodity.

a. Price elasticity of demand
b. 100-year flood
c. 130-30 fund
d. 1921 recession

49. In economics, the _____ is defined as a numerical measure of the responsiveness of the quantity supplied of product (A) to a change in price of product (A) alone. It is the measure of the way quantity supplied reacts to a change in price.

Chapter 2. The Market System and the Circular Flow

For example, if, in response to a 10% rise in the price of a good, the quantity supplied increases by 20%, the _____ would be 20%/10% = 2.

a. Hedonimetry
c. Demand shaping
b. Passive income
d. Price elasticity of supply

50.

A _____ is a type of financial intermediary and a type of bank. Commercial banking is also known as business banking. It is a bank that provides checking accounts, savings accounts, and money market accounts and that accepts time deposits.

a. Lombard banking
c. Bought deal
b. Daylight overdraft
d. Commercial bank

51. In economics, _____ is the ratio of the percent change in one variable to the percent change in another variable. It is a tool for measuring the responsiveness of a function to changes in parameters in a relative way. Commonly analyzed are _____ of substitution, price and wealth.

a. Elasticity of demand
c. Elasticity
b. ACCRA Cost of Living Index
d. ACEA agreement

52. Price _____ is defined as the measure of responsiveness in the quantity demanded for a commodity as a result of change in price of the same commodity. It is a measure of how consumers react to a change in price. In other words, it is percentage change in quantity demanded by the percentage change in price of the same commodity.

a. Elasticity
c. ACEA agreement
b. Elasticity of demand
d. ACCRA Cost of Living Index

53. A _____ is:

- Rewrite _____, in generative grammar and computer science
- Standardization, a formal and widely-accepted statement, fact, definition, or qualification
- Operation, a determinate _____ for performing a mathematical operation and obtaining a certain result (Mathematics, Logic)
    - Unary operation
    - Binary operation
- _____ of inference, a function from sets of formulae to formulae (Mathematics, Logic)
- _____ of thumb, principle with broad application that is not intended to be strictly accurate or reliable for every situation. Also often simply referred to as a _____
- Moral, an atomic element of a moral code for guiding choices in human behavior
- Heuristic, a quantized '_____' which shows a tendency or probability for successful function
- A regulation, as in sports
- A Production _____, as in computer science
- Procedural law, a _____ set governing the application of laws to cases
    - A law, which may informally be called a '_____'
    - A court ruling, a decision by a court
- In the U.S. Government, a regulation mandated by Congress, but written or expanded upon by the Executive Branch.
- Norm (sociology), an informal but widely accepted _____, concept, truth, definition, or qualification (social norms, legal norms, coding norms)
- Norm (philosophy), a kind of sentence or a reason to act, feel or believe
- 'Rulership' is the concept of governance by a government:
    - Military _____, governance by a military body
    - Monastic _____, a collection of precepts that guides the life of monks or nuns in a religious order where the superior holds the place of Christ
- Slide _____

- '_____,' a song by Ayumi Hamasaki
- '_____,' a song by rapper Nas
- '_____s,' an album by the band The Whitest Boy Alive
- _____s: Pyaar Ka Superhit Formula, a 2003 Bollywood film
- ruler, an instrument for measuring lengths
- _____, a component of an astrolabe, circumferator or similar instrument
- The _____s, a bestselling self-help book
- _____ Project (Run Up-to-date Linux Everywhere), a project that aims to use up-to-date Linux software on old PCs
- _____ engine, a software system that helps managing business _____s
- Ja _____, a hip hop artist
    - R.U.L.E., a 2005 greatest hits album by rapper Ja _____
- '_____s,' a KMFDM song

a. Procter ' Gamble
b. Technocracy
c. Rule
d. Demand

Chapter 2. The Market System and the Circular Flow

54. The _____ or Aggregate Demand-Aggregate Supply model is a macroeconomic model that explains price level and output through the relationship of aggregate demand and aggregate supply. It was first put forth by John Maynard Keynes in his work The General Theory of Employment, Interest, and Money. It is the foundation for the modern field of macroeconomics, and is accepted by a broad array of economists, from Libertarian, Monetarist supporters of laissez-faire, such as Milton Friedman to Socialist, Post-Keynesian supporters of economic interventionism, such as Joan Robinson.

   a. Economic interdependence   b. IS/LM model
   c. AD-AS   d. Adaptive expectations

55. The notion of _____ is found in the writings of Mikhail Bakunin, Friedrich Nietzsche, and in Werner Sombart's Krieg und Kapitalismus (War and Capitalism) (1913, p. 207), where he wrote: 'again out of destruction a new spirit of creativity arises'. In Capitalism, Socialism and Democracy, the Austrian economist Joseph Schumpeter popularized and used the term to describe the process of transformation that accompanies radical innovation.

   a. 100-year flood   b. 130-30 fund
   c. 1921 recession   d. Creative destruction

56. A _____ product is a product designed for cheapness and short-term convenience rather than medium to long-term durability, with most products only intended for single use. The term is also sometimes used for products that may last several months (ex. _____ air filters) to distinguish from similar products that last indefinitely (ex.

   a. 130-30 fund   b. Disposable
   c. 100-year flood   d. 1921 recession

57. _____ is gross income minus income tax on that income.

Discretionary income is income after subtracting taxes and normal expenses (such as rent or mortgage, utilities, insurance, medical, transportation, property maintenance, child support, inflation, food and sundries, 'c.') to maintain a certain standard of living.

   a. Stamp Act   b. Disposable personal income
   c. Taxation as theft   d. Disposable income

58. A variety of measures of _____ and output are used in economics to estimate total economic activity in a country or region, including gross domestic product (GDP), gross national product (GNP), and net _____

There are three main ways of calculating these numbers; the output approach, the income approach and the expenditure approach. In theory, the three must yield the same, because total expenditures on goods and services must equal the total income paid to the producers (Gnational income), and that must also equal the total value of the output of goods and services (GNP.)

   a. Volume index   b. National income
   c. GNI per capita   d. Gross world product

59. In economics and business, specifically cost accounting, the _____ point (BEP) is the point at which cost or expenses and revenue are equal: there is no net loss or gain, and one has 'broken even'. A profit or a loss has not been made, although opportunity costs have been paid, and capital has received the risk-adjusted, expected return.

Chapter 2. The Market System and the Circular Flow 31

For example, if the business sells less than 200 tables each month, it will make a loss, if it sells more, it will be a profit.

a. Buffer stock scheme
b. Small numbers game
c. Nonmarket
d. Break-even

60. In economics, accounting and Marxian economics, _____ is often equated with investment of profit income, especially in real capital goods. The concentration and centralisation of capital are two of the results of such accumulation

But _____ can refer variously to

- working and consuming less than earned
- relying on the effects of compound interest to increase initial capital
- real investment in tangible means of production.
- financial investment in assets represented on paper.
- investment in non-productive physical assets such as residential real estate that appreciate in value.
- consuming less than produced by productive assets like farm land--saving or accumulating the residual
- 'human _____,' i.e., new education and training increasing the skills of the labour force.

Non-financial and financial _____ is usually needed for economic growth, since additional production usually requires additional funds to enlarge the scale of production. Smarter and more productive organization of production can also increase production without increased capital.

a. Productive force
b. Cultural Marxism
c. Marxian economics
d. Capital accumulation

61. In economics and sociology, an _____ is any factor (financial or non-financial) that enables or motivates a particular course of action, or counts as a reason for preferring one choice to the alternatives. It is an expectation that encourages people to behave in a certain way. Since human beings are purposeful creatures, the study of _____ structures is central to the study of all economic activity (both in terms of individual decision-making and in terms of co-operation and competition within a larger institutional structure.)

a. Epstein-Zin preferences
b. Incentive
c. Isocost
d. Economic reform

62. An Inquiry into the Nature and Causes of the _____ is the magnum opus of the Scottish economist Adam Smith. It is a clearly written account of economics at the dawn of the Industrial Revolution, as well as a rhetorical piece written for the generally educated individual of the 18th century - advocating a free market economy as more productive and more beneficial to society.

The work is credited as a watershed in history and economics due to its comprehensive, largely accurate characterization of economic mechanisms that survive in modern economics; and also for its effective use of rhetorical technique, including structuring the work to contrast real world examples of free and fettered markets.

Chapter 2. The Market System and the Circular Flow

a. Wealth of Nations
b. Black Book of Communism
c. The Bell Curve
d. The Rise and Fall of the Great Powers

63. In economics, the term _____ of income or _____ refers to a simple economic model which describes the reciprocal circulation of income between producers and consumers. In the _____ model, the inter-dependent entities of producer and consumer are referred to as 'firms' and 'households' respectively and provide each other with factors in order to facilitate the flow of income. Firms provide consumers with goods and services in exchange for consumer expenditure and 'factors of production' from households.
   a. 130-30 fund
   b. 100-year flood
   c. 1921 recession
   d. Circular flow

64. A political party described as a _____ includes those that advocate the application of the social principles of communism through a communist form of government. The name originates from the 1848 tract Manifesto of the _____ by Karl Marx, Friedrich Engels. The Leninist concept of a _____ encompasses a larger political system and includes not only an ideological orientation but also a wide set of organizational policies.
   a. Communism
   b. Criticisms of anarcho-capitalism
   c. Criticisms of Communist party rule
   d. Communist party

65. _____ is the electoral problem resulting from competition between two or more candidates or political parties from the same or approximate location in the political ideological spectrum or space against an opposing candidate or political party from the other side of the political ideological spectrum or space. The resulting fragmentation of political support may result in electoral defeat. _____s, and thus political calculations attempting to avoid them, appear most frequently in elections involving executives and representatives from single member districts.
   a. 100-year flood
   b. 130-30 fund
   c. 1921 recession
   d. Coordination failure

66. _____ is the term denoting either an entrance or changes which are inserted into a system and which activate/modify a process. It is an abstract concept, used in the modeling, system(s) design and system(s) exploitation. It is usually connected with other terms, e.g., _____ field, _____ variable, _____ parameter, _____ value, _____ signal, _____ device and _____ file.
   a. Input
   b. ACEA agreement
   c. ACCRA Cost of Living Index
   d. AD-IA Model

67. In economics, the _____ is a subset of the domestic economy excluding the economic activities of general government, private households, and nonprofit organizations serving individuals. In the United States the _____ accounted for about 78 percent of the value of gross domestic product (GDP) in 2000. .
   a. Reaganomics
   b. Social savings
   c. Business sector
   d. Happiness economics

68. The _____ is 'the basic residential unit in which economic production, consumption, inheritance, child rearing, and shelter are organized and carried out'; [the _____] 'may or may not be synonymous with family'.

The _____ is the basic unit of analysis in many social, microeconomic and government models. The term refers to all individuals who live in the same dwelling.

a. 100-year flood
b. Family economics
c. 130-30 fund
d. Household

69. In economics, the _____ market is a hypothetical market that brings savers and borrowers together, also bringing together the money available in commercial banks and lending institutions available for firms and households to finance expenditures, either investments or consumption. Savers supply the _____; for instance, buying bonds will transfer their money to the institution issuing the bond, which can be a firm or government. In return, borrowers demand _____; when an institution sells a bond, it is demanding _____.
a. Reservation wage
b. Buffer stock scheme
c. Spatial inequality
d. Loanable funds

70. A _____ is a hypothetical measure of overall prices for some set of goods and services, in a given region during a given interval, normalized relative to some base set. Typically, a _____ is approximated with a price index.

The classical dichotomy is the assumption that there is a relatively clean distinction between overall increases or decreases in prices and underlying, e;reale; economic variables.

a. Discretionary spending
b. Price level
c. Price elasticity of supply
d. Discouraged worker

71. _____ is a mechanism that allows people easily to buy and sell products. Services are often included in the scope of the term. _____ regulation is an economic term that describes restrictions in the market.
a. Product market
b. Financialization
c. Fixed exchange rate system
d. Market dominance

72. In economics, an _____ is a monetary policy that increases the money supply.
a. International free trade agreement
b. Income effect
c. Elements of economic profit
d. Easy money policy

73. _____ exists when sales of identical goods or services are transacted at different prices from the same provider. In a theoretical market with perfect information, no transaction costs or prohibition on secondary exchange (or re-selling) to prevent arbitrage, _____ can only be a feature of monopoly and oligopoly markets, where market power can be exercised. Otherwise, the moment the seller tries to sell the same good at different prices, the buyer at the lower price can arbitrage by selling to the consumer buying at the higher price but with a tiny discount.
a. Lerner Index
b. Loss leader
c. Transfer pricing
d. Price discrimination

74. In economics, a _____ exists when a specific individual or enterprise has sufficient control over a particular product or service to determine significantly the terms on which other individuals shall have access to it. Monopolies are thus characterized by a lack of economic competition for the good or service that they provide and a lack of viable substitute goods. The verb 'monopolize' refers to the process by which a firm gains persistently greater market share than what is expected under perfect competition.
a. Monopoly
b. 1921 recession
c. 100-year flood
d. 130-30 fund

Chapter 3. Demand, Supply, and Market Equilibrium

1. The _____ , established in 1848, is the world's oldest futures and options exchange. More than 50 different options and futures contracts are traded by over 3,600 _____ members through open outcry and eTrading. Volumes at the exchange in 2003 were a record breaking 454 million contracts.
   - a. Chicago Board of Trade
   - b. New York Mercantile Exchange
   - c. 100-year flood
   - d. 130-30 fund

2. Economics:
   - _____ ,the desire to own something and the ability to pay for it
   - _____ curve,a graphic representation of a _____ schedule
   - _____ deposit, the money in checking accounts
   - _____ pull theory,the theory that inflation occurs when _____ for goods and services exceeds existing supplies
   - _____ schedule,a table that lists the quantity of a good a person will buy it each different price
   - _____ side economics,the school of economics at believes government spending and tax cuts open economy by raising _____

   - a. Production
   - b. Variability
   - c. McKesson ' Robbins scandal
   - d. Demand

3. In economics, a _____ is a table that lists the quantity of a good a person will buy it each different price See Demand curve.
   - a. Free contract
   - b. Demand schedule
   - c. Federal Reserve districts
   - d. Rational irrationality

4. In economics, the _____ of demand measures the responsiveness of the demand of a good to the change in the income of the people demanding the good. It is calculated as the ratio of the percent change in demand to the percent change in income. For example, if, in response to a 10% increase in income, the demand of a good increased by 20%, the _____ of demand would be 20%/10% = 2.
   - a. AD-IA Model
   - b. ACCRA Cost of Living Index
   - c. ACEA agreement
   - d. Income elasticity

5. In economics, the _____ measures the responsiveness of the demand of a good to the change in the income of the people demanding the good. It is calculated as the ratio of the percent change in demand to the percent change in income. For example, if, in response to a 10% increase in income, the demand of a good increased by 20%, the _____ would be 20%/10% = 2.
   - a. Indifference map
   - b. Expenditure minimization problem
   - c. Elasticity of substitution
   - d. Income elasticity of demand

6. A _____ is any systematic process enabling many market players to bid and ask: helping bidders and sellers interact and make deals. It is not just the price mechanism but the entire system of regulation, qualification, credentials, reputations and clearing that surrounds that mechanism and makes it operate in a social context.

Because a _____ relies on the assumption that players are constantly involved and unequally enabled, a _____ is distinguished specifically from a voting system where candidates seek the support of voters on a less regular basis.

Chapter 3. Demand, Supply, and Market Equilibrium

a. Contestable market
b. Competitive equilibrium
c. Price mechanism
d. Market system

7. _____ is an equity (stock) exchange located at 11 Wall Street in lower Manhattan, New York, USA. It is the largest stock exchange in the world by dollar value of its listed companies' securities. As of October 2008, the combined capitalization of all domestic _____ listed companies was US$10.1 trillion.
   a. 1921 recession
   b. 130-30 fund
   c. 100-year flood
   d. New York Stock Exchange

8. _____ in economics and business is the result of an exchange and from that trade we assign a numerical monetary value to a good, service or asset. If Alice trades Bob 4 apples for an orange, the _____ of an orange is 4 apples. Inversely, the _____ of an apple is 1/4 oranges.
   a. Premium pricing
   b. Price
   c. Price war
   d. Price book

9. _____ is defined as the measure of responsiveness in the quantity demanded for a commodity as a result of change in price of the same commodity. It is a measure of how consumers react to a change in price. In other words, it is percentage change in quantity demanded as per the percentage change in price of the same commodity.
   a. 130-30 fund
   b. 100-year flood
   c. 1921 recession
   d. Price elasticity of demand

10. In economics, the _____ is defined as a numerical measure of the responsiveness of the quantity supplied of product (A) to a change in price of product (A) alone. It is the measure of the way quantity supplied reacts to a change in price.

>

For example, if, in response to a 10% rise in the price of a good, the quantity supplied increases by 20%, the _____ would be 20%/10% = 2.

   a. Hedonimetry
   b. Demand shaping
   c. Passive income
   d. Price elasticity of supply

11. In microeconomics, _____ is quite simply the conversion of inputs into outputs. It is an economic process that uses resources to create a good or service that is suitable for exchange. This can include manufacturing, storing, shipping, and packaging.
   a. Solved
   b. MET
   c. Red Guards
   d. Production

12. A _____ is a corporation or mutual organization which provides trading facilities for stock brokers and traders, to trade stocks and other securities. It may be a physical trading room where the traders gather, or a formalised communications network. Creation of a _____ is a strategy of economic development.
   a. SEAQ
   b. 100-year flood
   c. Primary shares
   d. Stock Exchange

Chapter 3. Demand, Supply, and Market Equilibrium

13. In economics, _____ is the ratio of the percent change in one variable to the percent change in another variable. It is a tool for measuring the responsiveness of a function to changes in parameters in a relative way. Commonly analyzed are _____ of substitution, price and wealth.
    a. Elasticity of demand
    b. ACCRA Cost of Living Index
    c. ACEA agreement
    d. Elasticity

14. Price _____ is defined as the measure of responsiveness in the quantity demanded for a commodity as a result of change in price of the same commodity. It is a measure of how consumers react to a change in price. In other words, it is percentage change in quantity demanded by the percentage change in price of the same commodity.
    a. Elasticity
    b. ACCRA Cost of Living Index
    c. ACEA agreement
    d. Elasticity of demand

Chapter 3. Demand, Supply, and Market Equilibrium 37

15. A _____ is:

- Rewrite _____, in generative grammar and computer science
- Standardization, a formal and widely-accepted statement, fact, definition, or qualification
- Operation, a determinate _____ for performing a mathematical operation and obtaining a certain result (Mathematics, Logic)
    - Unary operation
    - Binary operation
- _____ of inference, a function from sets of formulae to formulae (Mathematics, Logic)
- _____ of thumb, principle with broad application that is not intended to be strictly accurate or reliable for every situation. Also often simply referred to as a _____
- Moral, an atomic element of a moral code for guiding choices in human behavior
- Heuristic, a quantized '_____' which shows a tendency or probability for successful function
- A regulation, as in sports
- A Production _____, as in computer science
- Procedural law, a _____ set governing the application of laws to cases
    - A law, which may informally be called a '_____'
    - A court ruling, a decision by a court
- In the U.S. Government, a regulation mandated by Congress, but written or expanded upon by the Executive Branch.
- Norm (sociology), an informal but widely accepted _____, concept, truth, definition, or qualification (social norms, legal norms, coding norms)
- Norm (philosophy), a kind of sentence or a reason to act, feel or believe
- 'Rulership' is the concept of governance by a government:
    - Military _____, governance by a military body
    - Monastic _____, a collection of precepts that guides the life of monks or nuns in a religious order where the superior holds the place of Christ
- Slide _____

- '_____,' a song by Ayumi Hamasaki
- '_____,' a song by rapper Nas
- '_____s,' an album by the band The Whitest Boy Alive
- _____s: Pyaar Ka Superhit Formula, a 2003 Bollywood film
- ruler, an instrument for measuring lengths
- _____, a component of an astrolabe, circumferator or similar instrument
- The _____s, a bestselling self-help book
- _____ Project (Run Up-to-date Linux Everywhere), a project that aims to use up-to-date Linux software on old PCs
- _____ engine, a software system that helps managing business _____s
- Ja _____, a hip hop artist
    - R.U.L.E., a 2005 greatest hits album by rapper Ja _____
- '_____s,' a KMFDM song

a. Procter ' Gamble   b. Rule
c. Demand   d. Technocracy

Chapter 3. Demand, Supply, and Market Equilibrium

16. _____ is a common concept in economics, and gives rise to derived concepts such as consumer debt. Generally _____ is defined by opposition to production. But the precise definition can vary because different schools of economists define production quite differently.

   a. Cash or share options
   b. Foreclosure data providers
   c. Consumption
   d. Federal Reserve Bank Notes

17. In economics, the _____ can be defined as the graph depicting the relationship between the price of a certain commodity, and the amount of it that consumers are willing and able to purchase at that given price. It is a graphic representation of a demand schedule. The _____ for all consumers together follows from the _____ of every individual consumer: the individual demands at each price are added together.

   a. Cost curve
   b. Kuznets curve
   c. Wage curve
   d. Demand curve

18. In economics, the _____ is the change in consumption resulting from a change in real income.

Another important item that can change is the money income of the consumer. The _____ is the phenomenon observed through changes in purchasing power.

   a. Income effect
   b. Export subsidy
   c. Equilibrium wage
   d. Inflation hedge

19. _____ and Keynesian Theory) is a macroeconomic theory based on the ideas of 20th-century British economist John Maynard Keynes. _____ argues that private sector decisions sometimes lead to inefficient macroeconomic outcomes and therefore advocates active policy responses by the public sector, including monetary policy actions by the central bank and fiscal policy actions by the government to stabilize output over the business cycle.

The theories forming the basis of _____ were first presented in The General Theory of Employment, Interest and Money, published in 1936.

   a. Keynesian economics
   b. Market failure
   c. Deflation
   d. Rational choice theory

20. In economics, the _____ is an economic law that states that consumers buy more of a good when its price decreases and less when its price increases.

There are certain goods which do not follow this law. These include Veblen and Giffen goods

   a. Georgism
   b. Financial crisis
   c. Market failure
   d. Law of demand

21. A public utility (usually just utility) is an organization that maintains the infrastructure for a public service (often also providing a service using that infrastructure.) _____ are subject to forms of public control and regulation ranging from local community-based groups to state-wide government monopolies. Common arguments in favor of regulation include the desire to control market power, facilitate competition, promote investment or system expansion, or stabilize markets.

a. 1921 recession
b. 100-year flood
c. 130-30 fund
d. Public utilities

22. In economics, the _____ of a good or of a service is the utility of the specific use to which an agent would put a given increase in that good or service, or of the specific use that would be abandoned in response to a given decrease. In other words, _____ is the utility of the marginal use -- which, on the assumption of economic rationality, would be the least urgent use of the good or service, from the best feasible combination of actions in which its use is included. Under the mainstream assumptions, the _____ of a good or service is the posited quantified change in utility obtained by increasing or by decreasing use of that good or service.
   a. 1921 recession
   b. Marginal utility
   c. 100-year flood
   d. 130-30 fund

23. In economics, _____ is a measure of the relative satisfaction from consumption of various goods and services. Given this measure, one may speak meaningfully of increasing or decreasing _____, and thereby explain economic behavior in terms of attempts to increase one's _____. For illustrative purposes, changes in _____ are sometimes expressed in units called utils.
   a. Expected utility hypothesis
   b. Utility function
   c. Ordinal utility
   d. Utility

24. _____ is a broad label that refers to any individuals or households that use goods and services generated within the economy. The concept of a _____ is used in different contexts, so that the usage and significance of the term may vary.

Typically when business people and economists talk of _____s they are talking about person as _____, an aggregated commodity item with little individuality other than that expressed in the buy/not-buy decision.

   a. 1921 recession
   b. 130-30 fund
   c. 100-year flood
   d. Consumer

25. In algebra, a _____ is a function depending on n that associates a scalar, det(A), to an n×n square matrix A. The fundamental geometric meaning of a _____ is a scale factor for measure when A is regarded as a linear transformation. _____s are important both in calculus, where they enter the substitution rule for several variables, and in multilinear algebra.

For a fixed nonnegative integer n, there is a unique _____ function for the n×n matrices over any commutative ring R. In particular, this function exists when R is the field of real or complex numbers.

   a. Determinant
   b. 130-30 fund
   c. 100-year flood
   d. 1921 recession

26. Necessary _____s:

If x is a necessary _____ of y, then the presence of y necessarily implies the presence of x. The presence of x, however, does not imply that y will occur.

Chapter 3. Demand, Supply, and Market Equilibrium

Sufficient _____s:

If x is a sufficient _____ of y, then the presence of x necessarily implies the presence of y.

a. Materialism
b. Cause
c. Political philosophy
d. Philosophy of economics

27. _____ are final goods specifically intended for the mass market. For instance, _____ do not include investment assets, like precious antiques, even though these antiques are final goods.

Manufactured goods are goods that have been processed by way of machinery.

a. Consumer goods
b. Bulgarian-American trade
c. G-20 Leaders Summit on Financial Markets and the World Economy
d. Fiscal stimulus plans

28. A _____ product is a product designed for cheapness and short-term convenience rather than medium to long-term durability, with most products only intended for single use. The term is also sometimes used for products that may last several months (ex. _____ air filters) to distinguish from similar products that last indefinitely (ex.

a. 130-30 fund
b. 1921 recession
c. 100-year flood
d. Disposable

29. _____ is gross income minus income tax on that income.

Discretionary income is income after subtracting taxes and normal expenses (such as rent or mortgage, utilities, insurance, medical, transportation, property maintenance, child support, inflation, food and sundries, 'c.) to maintain a certain standard of living.

a. Taxation as theft
b. Stamp Act
c. Disposable personal income
d. Disposable income

30. A variety of measures of _____ and output are used in economics to estimate total economic activity in a country or region, including gross domestic product (GDP), gross national product (GNP), and net _____

There are three main ways of calculating these numbers; the output approach, the income approach and the expenditure approach. In theory, the three must yield the same, because total expenditures on goods and services must equal the total income paid to the producers (Gnational income), and that must also equal the total value of the output of goods and services (GNP.)

a. GNI per capita
b. National income
c. Volume index
d. Gross world product

31. In economics, _____s are any goods for which demand increases when income increases and falls when income decreases but price remains constant, i.e. with a positive income elasticity of demand. The term does not necessarily refer to the quality of the good.

Depending on the indifference curves, the amount of a good bought can either increase, decrease, or stay the same when income increases.

   a. Financial contagion
   b. Normative economics
   c. Bord halfpenny
   d. Normal good

32. _____ make up a larger proportion of consumption as income rises, and therefore are a type of normal goods in consumer theory. Such a good must possess two economic characteristics: it must be scarce, and, along with that, it must have a high price. The scarcity of the good can be natural or artificial; however, the general population (i.e., consumers) must recognize the good as distinguishably better.
   a. Goods and services
   b. Superior goods
   c. Durable good
   d. Merit good

33. In economics and business, specifically cost accounting, the _____ point (BEP) is the point at which cost or expenses and revenue are equal: there is no net loss or gain, and one has 'broken even'. A profit or a loss has not been made, although opportunity costs have been paid, and capital has received the risk-adjusted, expected return.

For example, if the business sells less than 200 tables each month, it will make a loss, if it sells more, it will be a profit.

   a. Nonmarket
   b. Small numbers game
   c. Buffer stock scheme
   d. Break-even

34. A _____ is an object whose consumption increases the utility of the consumer, for which the quantity demanded exceeds the quantity supplied at zero price. _____s are usually modeled as having diminishing marginal utility. The first individual purchase has high utility; the second has less.
   a. Pie method
   b. Composite good
   c. Merit good
   d. Good

35. _____ are those things that are neither used with, nor instead of, the item of interest. Their use is independent of the use of the good being considered. A person's demand of nails is independent of his or her demand for bread.
   a. Export-oriented
   b. Inferior good
   c. Information good
   d. Independent goods

36. In consumer theory, an _____ is a good that decreases in demand when consumer income rises, unlike normal goods, for which the opposite is observed. It is a good that consumers demand increases when their income increases. Inferiority, in this sense, is an observable fact relating to affordability rather than a statement about the quality of the good.
   a. Independent goods
   b. Inferior good
   c. Information good
   d. Export-oriented

Chapter 3. Demand, Supply, and Market Equilibrium

37. A _____ or complement good in economics is a good which is consumed with another good; its cross elasticity of demand is negative. - It is two goods that are bought and used together. This means that, if goods A and B were complements, more of good A being bought would result in more of good B also being bought.

   a. Complementary Good
   b. Free good
   c. Manufactured goods
   d. Final good

38. In economics, _____ are the resources employed to produce goods and services. They facilitate production but do not become part of the product (as with raw materials) or significantly transformed by the production process (as with fuel used to power machinery.) To 19th century economists, the _____ were land (natural resources, gifts from nature), labor (the ability to work), and capital goods (human-made tools and equipment.)

   a. Factors of production
   b. Product Pipeline
   c. Hicks-neutral technical change
   d. Long-run

39. In economics, the _____ is the tendency of suppliers to offer more of a good at a higher price. The relationship between price and quantity supplied is usually a positive relationship. A rise in price is associated with a rise in quantity supplied.

   a. Law of supply
   b. Market failure
   c. Heterodox economics
   d. Mathematical economics

40. In economics and finance, _____ is the change in total cost that arises when the quantity produced changes by one unit. It is the cost of producing one more unit of a good. Mathematically, the _____ function is expressed as the first derivative of the total cost (TC) function with respect to quantity (Q.)

   a. Variable cost
   b. Quality costs
   c. Marginal cost
   d. Khozraschyot

41. In economics, _____ is the total supply of goods and services produced by a national economy during a specific time period. It is the total amount of goods and services in the economy available at all possible price levels.

   a. Aggregate expenditure
   b. Aggregate demand
   c. Aggregation problem
   d. Aggregate supply

42. To _____ is to impose a financial charge or other levy upon a taxpayer by a state or the functional equivalent of a state.

_____es are also imposed by many subnational entities. _____es consist of direct _____ or indirect _____, and may be paid in money or as its labour equivalent (often but not always unpaid.)

   a. 100-year flood
   b. 1921 recession
   c. 130-30 fund
   d. Tax

43. To tax is to impose a financial charge or other levy upon a taxpayer by a state or the functional equivalent of a state.

_____ are also imposed by many subnational entities. _____ consist of direct tax or indirect tax, and may be paid in money or as its labour equivalent (often but not always unpaid.)

a. 1921 recession
b. 130-30 fund
c. 100-year flood
d. Taxes

44. In economics, economic equilibrium is simply a state of the world where economic forces are balanced and in the absence of external influences the (equilibrium) values of economic variables will not change. It is the point at which quantity demanded and quantity supplied are equal. _____, for example, refers to a condition where a market price is established through competition such that the amount of goods or services sought by buyers is equal to the amount of goods or services produced by sellers.
    a. Regulated market
    b. Marketization
    c. Product-Market Growth Matrix
    d. Market equilibrium

45. _____ is an economic model based on price, utility and quantity in a market. It predicts that in a competitive market, price will function to equalize the quantity demanded by consumers, and the quantity supplied by producers, resulting in an economic equilibrium of price and quantity. The model incorporates other factors changing equilibrium as a shift of demand and/or supply.
    a. Deferred gratification
    b. Rational addiction
    c. Joint demand
    d. Supply and demand

46. In economics, a _____ is a loss of economic efficiency that can occur when equilibrium for a good or service is not Pareto optimal. In other words, either people who would have more marginal benefit than marginal cost are not buying the good or service, or people who would have more marginal cost than marginal benefit are buying the product.

    Causes of _____ can include monopoly pricing, externalities, taxes or subsidies, and binding price ceilings or floors.

    a. Deadweight loss
    b. Contract curve
    c. Leapfrogging
    d. Distributive efficiency

47. In economics, _____ is when quantity demanded is more than quantity supplied. See Economic shortage.
    a. Excess demand
    b. ACCRA Cost of Living Index
    c. ACEA agreement
    d. AD-IA Model

48. In economics, _____ is when quantity supplied is more than quantity demanded. .
    a. Excess supply
    b. Economic Value Creation
    c. Illicit financial flows
    d. Effective unemployment rate

49. In economics, a _____ is a graph of the costs of production as a function of total quantity produced. In a free market economy, productively efficient firms use these curves to find the optimal point of production, where they make the most profits. There are a few different types of _____s, each relevant to a different area of economics.
    a. Kuznets curve
    b. Phillips curve
    c. Demand curve
    d. Cost curve

Chapter 3. Demand, Supply, and Market Equilibrium

50. In economics, and cost accounting, _____ describes the total economic cost of production and is made up of variable costs, which vary according to the quantity of a good produced and include inputs such as labor and raw materials, plus fixed costs, which are independent of the quantity of a good produced and include inputs (capital) that cannot be varied in the short term, such as buildings and machinery. _____ in economics includes the total opportunity cost of each factor of production in addition to fixed and variable costs.

The rate at which _____ changes as the amount produced changes is called marginal cost.

a. 100-year flood
c. Total cost
b. 130-30 fund
d. 1921 recession

51. _____ is a situation in which the limited resources of a firm are allocated in accordance with the wishes of consumers. An allocatively efficient economy produces an 'optimal mix' of commodities. A firm is allocatively efficient when its price is equal to its marginal costs (that is, P = MC) in a perfect market.

a. ACCRA Cost of Living Index
c. ACEA agreement
b. Economic efficiency
d. Allocative efficiency

52. In economic theory, _____ is the competitive situation in any market where the conditions necessary for perfect competition are not satisfied. It is a market structure that does not meet the conditions of perfect competition.

Forms of _____ include:

- Monopoly, in which there is only one seller of a good.
- Oligopoly, in which there is a small number of sellers.
- Monopolistic competition, in which there are many sellers producing highly differentiated goods.
- Monopsony, in which there is only one buyer of a good.
- Oligopsony, in which there is a small number of buyers.

There may also be _____ in markets due to buyers or sellers lacking information about prices and the goods being traded.

There may also be _____ due to a time lag in a market.

a. AD-IA Model
c. Imperfect competition
b. ACCRA Cost of Living Index
d. ACEA agreement

53. In economics, _____ describes the state of a market with respect to competition.

- Perfect competition, in which the market consists of a very large number of firms producing a homogeneous product.
- Monopolistic competition where there are a large number of independent firms which have a very small proportion of the market share.
- Oligopoly, in which a market is dominated by a small number of firms which own more than 40% of the market share.
- Oligopsony, a market dominated by many sellers and a few buyers.
- Monopoly, where there is only one provider of a product or service.
- Natural monopoly, a monopoly in which economies of scale cause efficiency to increase continuously with the size of the firm. A firm is a natural monopoly if it is able to serve the entire market demand at a lower cost than any combination of two or more smaller, more specialized firms.
- Monopsony, when there is only one buyer in a market.

The imperfectly competitive structure is quite identical to the realistic market conditions where some monopolistic competitors, monopolists, oligopolists, and duopolists exist and dominate the market conditions. The elements of _____ include the number and size distribution of firms, entry conditions, and the extent of differentiation.

These somewhat abstract concerns tend to determine some but not all details of a specific concrete market system where buyers and sellers actually meet and commit to trade.

a. Labour economics
c. Monopolistic competition
b. Human capital
d. Market structure

54. _____ occurs when the economy is operating at its production possibility frontier (PPF.) This takes place when production of one good is achieved at the lowest cost possible, given the production of the other good(s.) Equivalently, it is when the highest possible output of one good is produced, given the production level of the other good(s.)

a. Productive efficiency
c. Preclusive purchasing
b. Discretionary spending
d. Free contract

55. _____ is the controlled distribution of resources and scarce goods or services. _____ controls the size of the ration, one's allotted portion of the resources being distributed on a particular day or at a particular time.

In economics, it is often common to use the word '_____' to refer to one of the roles that prices play in markets, while _____ is called 'non-price _____.' Using prices to ration means that those with the most money (or other assets) and who want a product the most are first to receive it.

a. 130-30 fund
c. 1921 recession
b. 100-year flood
d. Rationing

56. In finance, a _____ is a debt security, in which the authorized issuer owes the holders a debt and, depending on the terms of the _____, is obliged to pay interest (the coupon) and/or to repay the principal at a later date, termed maturity. A _____ is a formal contract to repay borrowed money with interest at fixed intervals.

Thus a _____ is like a loan: the issuer is the borrower (debtor), the holder is the lender (creditor), and the coupon is the interest.

a. Zero-coupon
b. Callable
c. Prize Bond
d. Bond

57. _____ is money accepted for exchange of goods in an economy. The prevalence of one money over another arises, usually, when a government designates through decrees that the government shall accept only particular notes and coins in payment for taxes. Typically, money of _____ consists of stamped coins and minted paper bills.

a. Currency
b. Totnes pound
c. Security thread
d. Local currency

58. In economics, a _____ exists when a specific individual or enterprise has sufficient control over a particular product or service to determine significantly the terms on which other individuals shall have access to it. Monopolies are thus characterized by a lack of economic competition for the good or service that they provide and a lack of viable substitute goods. The verb 'monopolize' refers to the process by which a firm gains persistently greater market share than what is expected under perfect competition.

a. 100-year flood
b. 130-30 fund
c. 1921 recession
d. Monopoly

59. A _____ is a government imposed limit on how high a price can be charged on a product. For a _____ to be effective, it must differ from the free market price. In the graph at right, the supply and demand curves intersect to determine the free-market quantity and price.

a. Price ceiling
b. Product sabotage
c. Fire sale
d. Pricing

60. The underground economy or _____ is a market where all commerce is conducted without regard to taxation, law or regulations of trade. The term is also often known as the underdog, shadow economy, black economy, parallel economy or phantom trades.

In modern societies the underground economy covers a vast array of activities.

a. Black market
b. Social market economy
c. Protectionism
d. Market economy

61. A _____ is a government- or group-imposed limit on how low a price can be charged for a product. In order for a _____ to be effective, it must be greater than the equilibrium price. An ineffective _____, below equilibrium price.

A _____ can be set below the free-market equilibrium price.

a. Price markdown
b. Two-part tariff
c. Flat rate
d. Price floor

62. Economic _____ is defined as an excess distribution to any factor in a production process above that which is required to induce the factor into the process or any excess above that which is necessary to keep the factor in its current use..

Classical Factor _____ is primarily concerned with the fee paid for the use of fixed (e.g. natural) resources. The classical definition is expressed as any excess payment above that required to induce or provide for production.

a. 1921 recession
c. 130-30 fund
b. 100-year flood
d. Rent

63. _____ refers to laws or ordinances that set price controls on the renting of residential housing. It functions as a price ceiling.

_____ exists in approximately 40 countries around the world.

a. Tenant rights
c. 100-year flood
b. National Housing Conference
d. Rent control

64. _____, or a _____ is the concept of a resulting effect (cf. cause and effect, arising from another action. In general terms, it is used to indicate that all human actions, particularly crime and sin, have profound effects.

a. Rule
c. Variability
b. Solved
d. Consequence

65. _____ describes a deliberate attempt to interfere with the free and fair operation of the market and create artificial, false or misleading appearances with respect to the price of a security, commodity or currency. _____ is prohibited under Section 9(a)(2) of the Securities Exchange Act of 1934, and in Australia under Section s 1041A of the Corporations Act 2001. The Act defines _____ as transactions which create an artificial price or maintain an artificial price for a tradable security.

a. Managerial economics
c. Net domestic product
b. Legal monopoly
d. Market manipulation

66. A _____ is the procedure of systematically acquiring and recording information about the members of a given population. It is a regularly occurring and official count of a particular population. The term is used mostly in connection with national 'population and door to door _____es' (to be taken every 10 years according to United Nations recommendations), agriculture, and business _____es.

a. 100-year flood
c. 1921 recession
b. Census
d. 130-30 fund

Chapter 4. The U.S. Economy: Private and Public Sectors

1. In economics, the _____ is the change in consumption resulting from a change in real income.

Another important item that can change is the money income of the consumer. The _____ is the phenomenon observed through changes in purchasing power.

   a. Export subsidy
   b. Inflation hedge
   c. Income effect
   d. Equilibrium wage

2. In economics, _____ is a measure of the relative satisfaction from consumption of various goods and services. Given this measure, one may speak meaningfully of increasing or decreasing _____, and thereby explain economic behavior in terms of attempts to increase one's _____. For illustrative purposes, changes in _____ are sometimes expressed in units called utils.
   a. Expected utility hypothesis
   b. Ordinal utility
   c. Utility function
   d. Utility

3. _____ is the a method of technical and economic research of the systems for purpose to optimize a parity between system's consumer functions or properties and expenses to achieve those functions or properties.

This methodology for continuous perfection of production, industrial technologies, organizational structures was developed by Juryj Sobolev in 1948 at the 'Perm telephone factory'

- 1948 Juryj Sobolev - the first success in application of a method analysis at the 'Perm telephone factory' .
- 1949 - the first application for the invention as result of use of the new method.

Today in economically developed countries practically each enterprise or the company use methodology of the kind of functional-cost analysis as a practice of the quality management, most full satisfying to principles of standards of series ISO 9000.

- Interest of consumer not in products itself, but the advantage which it will receive from its usage.
- The consumer aspires to reduce his expenses
- Functions needed by consumer can be executed in the various ways, and, hence, with various efficiency and expenses. Among possible alternatives of realization of functions exist such in which the parity of quality and the price is the optimal for the consumer.

The goal of _____ is achievement of the highest consumer satisfaction of production at simultaneous decrease in all kinds of industrial expenses Classical _____ has three English synonyms - Value Engineering, Value Management, Value Analysis.

   a. Function cost analysis
   b. Monopoly wage
   c. Willingness to pay
   d. Staple financing

4. A _____ product is a product designed for cheapness and short-term convenience rather than medium to long-term durability, with most products only intended for single use. The term is also sometimes used for products that may last several months (ex. _____ air filters) to distinguish from similar products that last indefinitely (ex.

a. 100-year flood
b. 130-30 fund
c. 1921 recession
d. Disposable

5. _____ is gross income minus income tax on that income.

Discretionary income is income after subtracting taxes and normal expenses (such as rent or mortgage, utilities, insurance, medical, transportation, property maintenance, child support, inflation, food and sundries, 'c.) to maintain a certain standard of living.

a. Taxation as theft
b. Stamp Act
c. Disposable personal income
d. Disposable income

6. The _____ is 'the basic residential unit in which economic production, consumption, inheritance, child rearing, and shelter are organized and carried out'; [the _____] 'may or may not be synonomous with family'.

The _____ is the basic unit of analysis in many social, microeconomic and government models. The term refers to all individuals who live in the same dwelling.

a. Family economics
b. 100-year flood
c. 130-30 fund
d. Household

7. _____ is a fee paid on borrowed assets. It is the price paid for the use of borrowed money , or, money earned by deposited funds . Assets that are sometimes lent with _____ include money, shares, consumer goods through hire purchase, major assets such as aircraft, and even entire factories in finance lease arrangements.

a. Asset protection
b. Insolvency
c. Internal debt
d. Interest

8. A variety of measures of _____ and output are used in economics to estimate total economic activity in a country or region, including gross domestic product (GDP), gross national product (GNP), and net _____

There are three main ways of calculating these numbers; the output approach, the income approach and the expenditure approach. In theory, the three must yield the same, because total expenditures on goods and services must equal the total income paid to the producers (Gnational income), and that must also equal the total value of the output of goods and services (GNP.)

a. National income
b. Gross world product
c. Volume index
d. GNI per capita

9. The _____ was an evolution of developed countries from an industrial/manufacturing-based wealth producing economy into a service sector asset based economy, brought about by globalization and currency manipulation by governments and their central banks. Some analysts claimed that this change in the economic structure of the United States had created a state of permanent steady growth, low unemployment, and immunity to boom and bust macroeconomic cycles. They believed that the change rendered obsolete many business practices.

a. 130-30 fund
b. 100-year flood
c. 1921 recession
d. New Economy

10. In economics, the _____ is that part of the economy which is both run for private profit and is not controlled by the state. By contrast, enterprises that are part of the state are part of the public sector; private, non-profit organizations are regarded as part of the voluntary sector.

A variety of legal structures exist for _____ business organizations, depending on the jurisdiction in which they have their legal domicile.

- a. Secondary sector of the economy
- b. Standard Industrial Classification
- c. Primary products
- d. Private sector

11. In economics and business, specifically cost accounting, the _____ point (BEP) is the point at which cost or expenses and revenue are equal: there is no net loss or gain, and one has 'broken even'. A profit or a loss has not been made, although opportunity costs have been paid, and capital has received the risk-adjusted, expected return.

For example, if the business sells less than 200 tables each month, it will make a loss, if it sells more, it will be a profit.

- a. Buffer stock scheme
- b. Break-even
- c. Nonmarket
- d. Small numbers game

12. Economics:

- _____, the desire to own something and the ability to pay for it
- _____ curve, a graphic representation of a _____ schedule
- _____ deposit, the money in checking accounts
- _____ pull theory, the theory that inflation occurs when _____ for goods and services exceeds existing supplies
- _____ schedule, a table that lists the quantity of a good a person will buy it each different price
- _____ side economics, the school of economics at believes government spending and tax cuts open economy by raising _____

- a. Demand
- b. Variability
- c. McKesson ' Robbins scandal
- d. Production

13. In mathematics, an _____ is a statement about the relative size or order of two objects, or about whether they are the same or not

- The notation a < b means that a is less than b.
- The notation a > b means that a is greater than b.
- The notation a ≠ b means that a is not equal to b, but does not say that one is greater than the other or even that they can be compared in size.

In each statement above, a is not equal to b. These relations are known as strict inequalities. The notation a < b may also be read as 'a is strictly less than b'.

a. AD-IA Model
b. ACCRA Cost of Living Index
c. ACEA agreement
d. Inequality

14. In economics, the _____ market is a hypothetical market that brings savers and borrowers together, also bringing together the money available in commercial banks and lending institutions available for firms and households to finance expenditures, either investments or consumption. Savers supply the _____; for instance, buying bonds will transfer their money to the institution issuing the bond, which can be a firm or government. In return, borrowers demand _____; when an institution sells a bond, it is demanding _____.
   a. Buffer stock scheme
   b. Reservation wage
   c. Spatial inequality
   d. Loanable funds

15. The _____ is the apparent contradiction that although water is on the whole more useful, in terms of survival, than diamonds, diamonds command a higher price in the market. The economist Adam Smith is often considered to be the classic presenter of this paradox. Nicolaus Copernicus, John Locke, John Law and others had previously tried to explain the disparity.
   a. Paradox of value
   b. 100-year flood
   c. 130-30 fund
   d. St. Petersburg paradox

16. _____ is a broad label that refers to any individuals or households that use goods and services generated within the economy. The concept of a _____ is used in different contexts, so that the usage and significance of the term may vary.

Typically when business people and economists talk of _____s they are talking about person as _____, an aggregated commodity item with little individuality other than that expressed in the buy/not-buy decision.

   a. 100-year flood
   b. 130-30 fund
   c. 1921 recession
   d. Consumer

17. _____ or consumer demand or consumption is also known as personal consumption expenditure. It is the largest part of aggregate demand or effective demand at the macroeconomic level. There are two variants of consumption in the aggregate demand model, including induced consumption and autonomous consumption.
   a. Potential output
   b. Complex multiplier
   c. Consumer spending
   d. Dishoarding

18. An _____ is a tax levied on the financial income of people, corporations, or other legal entities. Various _____ systems exist, with varying degrees of tax incidence. Income taxation can be progressive, proportional, or regressive.
   a. ACCRA Cost of Living Index
   b. AD-IA Model
   c. ACEA agreement
   d. Income tax

19. In economics, the _____ is used to illustrate the idea that increases in the rate of taxation do not necessarily increase tax revenue. (For instance, whereas a 0% income tax rate will generate no revenue, neither will a 100% rate, as citizens will have no incentive to make money.) Increasing taxes beyond the peak of the curve point will decrease tax revenue.

a. 130-30 fund
b. 1921 recession
c. Laffer curve
d. 100-year flood

20. The _____ is the component statistic for consumption in GDP collected by the BEA. It consists of the actual and imputed expenditures of households and includes data pertaining to durable and non-durable goods, and services. It is essentially a measure of goods and services targeted towards individuals and consumed by individuals.
   a. Real gross domestic product
   b. State Domestic Product
   c. Personal consumption expenditure
   d. Hemline index

21. _____ in economics and business is the result of an exchange and from that trade we assign a numerical monetary value to a good, service or asset. If Alice trades Bob 4 apples for an orange, the _____ of an orange is 4 apples. Inversely, the _____ of an apple is 1/4 oranges.
   a. Premium pricing
   b. Price
   c. Price book
   d. Price war

22. _____ exists when sales of identical goods or services are transacted at different prices from the same provider. In a theoretical market with perfect information, no transaction costs or prohibition on secondary exchange (or re-selling) to prevent arbitrage, _____ can only be a feature of monopoly and oligopoly markets, where market power can be exercised. Otherwise, the moment the seller tries to sell the same good at different prices, the buyer at the lower price can arbitrage by selling to the consumer buying at the higher price but with a tiny discount.
   a. Price discrimination
   b. Transfer pricing
   c. Lerner Index
   d. Loss leader

23. In finance, _____ is a financial action that does not promise safety of the initial investment along with the return on the principal sum. _____ typically involves the lending of money or the purchase of assets, equity or debt but in a manner that has not been given thorough analysis or is deemed to have low margin of safety or a significant risk of the loss of the principal investment. The term, '_____,' which is formally defined as above in Graham and Dodd's 1934 text, Security Analysis, contrasts with the term 'investment,' which is a financial operation that, upon thorough analysis, promises safety of principal and a satisfactory return.
   a. Global Financial Centres Index
   b. Hybrid market
   c. Municipal Bond Arbitrage
   d. Speculation

24. _____ is a common concept in economics, and gives rise to derived concepts such as consumer debt. Generally _____ is defined by opposition to production. But the precise definition can vary because different schools of economists define production quite differently.
   a. Foreclosure data providers
   b. Cash or share options
   c. Federal Reserve Bank Notes
   d. Consumption

25. To _____ is to impose a financial charge or other levy upon a taxpayer by a state or the functional equivalent of a state.

_____es are also imposed by many subnational entities. _____es consist of direct _____ or indirect _____, and may be paid in money or as its labour equivalent (often but not always unpaid.)

a. Tax
b. 130-30 fund
c. 1921 recession
d. 100-year flood

26. To tax is to impose a financial charge or other levy upon a taxpayer by a state or the functional equivalent of a state.

_____ are also imposed by many subnational entities. _____ consist of direct tax or indirect tax, and may be paid in money or as its labour equivalent (often but not always unpaid.)

a. 130-30 fund
b. 1921 recession
c. Taxes
d. 100-year flood

27. _____ are final goods specifically intended for the mass market. For instance, _____ do not include investment assets, like precious antiques, even though these antiques are final goods.

Manufactured goods are goods that have been processed by way of machinery.

a. Bulgarian-American trade
b. Consumer goods
c. Fiscal stimulus plans
d. G-20 Leaders Summit on Financial Markets and the World Economy

28. The _____ consists of a number of economic theories which describe the nature of the firm, company including its existence, its behaviour, and its relationship with the market.

In simplified terms, the _____ aims to answer these questions:

1. Existence - why do firms emerge, why are not all transactions in the economy mediated over the market?
2. Boundaries - why the boundary between firms and the market is located exactly there? Which transactions are performed internally and which are negotiated on the market?
3. Organization - why are firms structured in such specific way? What is the interplay of formal and informal relationships?

Despite looking simple, these questions are not answered by the established economic theory, which usually views firms as given, and treats them as black boxes without any internal structure.

The First World War period saw a change of emphasis in economic theory away from industry-level analysis which mainly included analysing markets to analysis at the level of the firm, as it became increasingly clear that perfect competition was no longer an adequate model of how firms behaved. Economic theory till then had focussed on trying to understand markets alone and there had been little study on understanding why firms or organisations exist.

a. Khazzoom-Brookes postulate
b. Policy Ineffectiveness Proposition
c. Technology gap
d. Theory of the firm

Chapter 4. The U.S. Economy: Private and Public Sectors

29. In economics, a _____ or a hard good is a good which does not quickly wear out it yields services or utility over time rather than being completely used up when used once. Most goods are therefore _____s to a certain degree. These are goods that can last for a relatively long time, such as refrigerators, cars, and DVD players.
    a. Durable good
    b. Superior goods
    c. Search good
    d. Luxury good

30. _____ is a concept whereby a person's financial liability is limited to a fixed sum, most commonly the value of a person's investment in a company or partnership with _____. A shareholder in a limited company is not personally liable for any of the debts of the company, other than for the value of his investment in that company. The same is true for the members of a _____ partnership and the limited partners in a limited partnership.
    a. Nexus of contracts
    b. Deficiency judgment
    c. Limited liability
    d. Personal Responsibility and Work Opportunity Reconciliation Act of 1996

31. A _____ is a type of business entity in which partners (owners) share with each other the profits or losses of the business _____s are often favored over corporations for taxation purposes, as the _____ structure does not generally incur a tax on profits before it is distributed to the partners (i.e. there is no dividend tax levied.) However, depending on the _____ structure and the jurisdiction in which it operates, owners of a _____ may be exposed to greater personal liability than they would as shareholders of a corporation.

    For a country-by-country listing of types of _____s, companies, etc., see Types of business entity.

    a. Feoffee
    b. Minimum wage law
    c. Partnership
    d. Due diligence

32. A _____, or simply proprietorship is a type of business entity which legally has no separate existence from its owner. Hence, the limitations of liability enjoyed by a corporation and limited liability partnerships do not apply to sole proprietors. All debts of the business are debts of the owner.
    a. Golden hello
    b. Corporate tax
    c. Golden parachute
    d. Sole proprietorship

33. A _____ is an object whose consumption increases the utility of the consumer, for which the quantity demanded exceeds the quantity supplied at zero price. _____s are usually modeled as having diminishing marginal utility. The first individual purchase has high utility; the second has less.
    a. Composite good
    b. Merit good
    c. Pie method
    d. Good

34. A security is a fungible, negotiable instrument representing financial value. _____ are broadly categorized into debt _____; equity _____, e.g., common stocks; and derivative (finance) contracts such as forwards, futures, options and swaps. The company or other entity issuing the security is called the issuer.
    a. Securities
    b. Red herring prospectus
    c. Pass-Through Certificates
    d. Settlement risk

35. In finance, a _____ is a debt security, in which the authorized issuer owes the holders a debt and, depending on the terms of the _____, is obliged to pay interest (the coupon) and/or to repay the principal at a later date, termed maturity. A _____ is a formal contract to repay borrowed money with interest at fixed intervals.

Thus a _____ is like a loan: the issuer is the borrower (debtor), the holder is the lender (creditor), and the coupon is the interest.

a. Zero-coupon
b. Prize Bond
c. Callable
d. Bond

36. In political science and economics, the _____ or agency dilemma treats the difficulties that arise under conditions of incomplete and asymmetric information when a principal hires an agent, such as the problem that the two may not have the same interests, while the principal is, presumably, hiring the agent to pursue the interests of the former.

Various mechanisms may be used to try to align the interests of the agent with those of the principal, such as piece rates/commissions, profit sharing, efficiency wages, performance measurement (including financial statements), the agent posting a bond, or fear of firing. The _____ is found in most employer/employee relationships, for example, when stockholders hire top executives of corporations.

a. Principal-agent problem
b. 100-year flood
c. 1921 recession
d. 130-30 fund

37. _____, or corporate _____ are political and business scandals which arise with the disclosure of misdeeds by trusted executives of large public corporations. Such misdeeds typically involve complex methods for misusing or misdirecting funds, overstating revenues, understating expenses, overstating the value of corporate assets or underreporting the existence of liabilities, sometimes with the cooperation of officials in other corporations or affiliates.

In public companies, this type of 'creative accounting' can amount to fraud and investigations are typically launched by government oversight agencies, such as the Securities and Exchange Commission (SEC) in the United States.

a. ACCRA Cost of Living Index
b. Accounting scandals
c. ACEA agreement
d. AD-IA Model

38. The _____ or gross domestic income (GDI), a basic measure of an economy's economic performance, is the market value of all final goods and services produced within the borders of a nation in a year. _____ can be defined in three ways, all of which are conceptually identical. First, it is equal to the total expenditures for all final goods and services produced within the country in a stipulated period of time (usually a 365-day year.)

a. Countercyclical
b. Monopolistic competition
c. Market structure
d. Gross domestic product

39. In economics, _____ is a rise in the general level of prices of goods and services in an economy over a period of time. When the general price level rises, each unit of currency buys fewer goods and services; consequently, _____ is also a decline in the real value of money--a loss of purchasing power in the medium of exchange which is also the monetary unit of account in the economy. A chief measure of general price-level _____ is the general _____ rate, which is the percentage change in a general price index (normally the Consumer Price Index) over time.

a. Energy economics
b. Economic
c. Opportunity cost
d. Inflation

40. In economics, the _____ is a measure of inflation, the rate of increase of a price index (for example, a consumer price index.)It is the percentage rate of change in price level over time. The rate of decrease in the purchasing power of money is approximately equal.

It's used to calculate the real interest rate, as well as real increases in wages, and official measurements of this rate act as input variables to COLA adjustments and Inflation derivatives prices.

- a. Inflation rate
- b. Equity value
- c. Interest rate option
- d. Edgeworth paradox

41. An _____, in economics, is the amount by which the real Gross domestic product exceeds potential GDP. The real GDP is also known as GDP 'adjusted for inflation', 'constant prices' GDP or 'constant dollar' GDP, because it measures the aggregate output in a country's income accounts in a given year, expressed in base-year prices. On the other hand, the potential GDP is the quantity of real GDP when a country's economy is at full-employment.
- a. ACEA agreement
- b. Inflationary gap
- c. ACCRA Cost of Living Index
- d. AD-IA Model

Chapter 4. The U.S. Economy: Private and Public Sectors

42. A _____ is:

- Rewrite _____, in generative grammar and computer science
- Standardization, a formal and widely-accepted statement, fact, definition, or qualification
- Operation, a determinate _____ for performing a mathematical operation and obtaining a certain result (Mathematics, Logic)
    - Unary operation
    - Binary operation
- _____ of inference, a function from sets of formulae to formulae (Mathematics, Logic)
- _____ of thumb, principle with broad application that is not intended to be strictly accurate or reliable for every situation. Also often simply referred to as a _____
- Moral, an atomic element of a moral code for guiding choices in human behavior
- Heuristic, a quantized '_____' which shows a tendency or probability for successful function
- A regulation, as in sports
- A Production _____, as in computer science
- Procedural law, a _____ set governing the application of laws to cases
    - A law, which may informally be called a '_____'
    - A court ruling, a decision by a court
- In the U.S. Government, a regulation mandated by Congress, but written or expanded upon by the Executive Branch.
- Norm (sociology), an informal but widely accepted _____, concept, truth, definition, or qualification (social norms, legal norms, coding norms)
- Norm (philosophy), a kind of sentence or a reason to act, feel or believe
- 'Rulership' is the concept of governance by a government:
    - Military _____, governance by a military body
    - Monastic _____, a collection of precepts that guides the life of monks or nuns in a religious order where the superior holds the place of Christ
- Slide _____

- '_____,' a song by Ayumi Hamasaki
- '_____,' a song by rapper Nas
- '_____s,' an album by the band The Whitest Boy Alive
- _____s: Pyaar Ka Superhit Formula, a 2003 Bollywood film
- ruler, an instrument for measuring lengths
- _____, a component of an astrolabe, circumferator or similar instrument
- The _____s, a bestselling self-help book
- _____ Project (Run Up-to-date Linux Everywhere), a project that aims to use up-to-date Linux software on old PCs
- _____ engine, a software system that helps managing business _____s
- Ja _____, a hip hop artist
    - R.U.L.E., a 2005 greatest hits album by rapper Ja _____
- '_____s,' a KMFDM song

a. Technocracy   b. Demand
c. Rule   d. Procter ' Gamble

Chapter 4. The U.S. Economy: Private and Public Sectors

43. A _____ is a public market for the trading of company stock and derivatives at an agreed price; these are securities listed on a stock exchange as well as those only traded privately.

The size of the world _____ was estimated at about $36.6 trillion US at the beginning of October 2008. The total world derivatives market has been estimated at about $791 trillion face or nominal value, 11 times the size of the entire world economy.

a. Adam Smith
b. Adolph Fischer
c. Stock market
d. Adolf Hitler

44. A _____ is a type of economic bubble taking place in stock markets when price of stocks rise and become overvalued by any measure of stock valuation.

The existence of _____s is at odds with the assumptions of efficient market theory which assumes rational investor behaviour. Behavioral finance theory attribute _____s to cognitive biases that lead to groupthink and herd behavior.

a. Fill or kill
b. Scrip issue
c. Stock market bubble
d. Growth investing

45. In economics, _____ is the total demand for final goods and services in the economy (Y) at a given time and price level. It is the amount of goods and services in the economy that will be purchased at all possible price levels. This is the demand for the gross domestic product of a country when inventory levels are static.

a. Aggregation problem
b. Aggregate expenditure
c. Aggregate supply
d. Aggregate demand

46. A _____ is a measure of the average price of consumer goods and services purchased by households. A _____ measures a price change for a constant market basket of goods and services from one period to the next within the same area (city, region, or nation.) It is a price index determined by measuring the price of a standard group of goods meant to represent the typical market basket of a typical urban consumer.

a. Lipstick index
b. CPI
c. Cost-of-living index
d. Consumer price index

47. A _____ is a normalized average (typically a weighted average) of prices for a given class of goods or services in a given region, during a given interval of time. It is a statistic designed to help to compare how these prices, taken as a whole, differ between time periods or geographical locations.

Price indices have several potential uses.

a. Two-part tariff
b. Product sabotage
c. Transactional Net Margin Method
d. Price index

Chapter 4. The U.S. Economy: Private and Public Sectors

48. Competition law, known in the United States as _____ law, has three main elements:

- prohibiting agreements or practices that restrict free trading and competition between business entities. This includes in particular the repression of cartels.
- banning abusive behaviour by a firm dominating a market, or anti-competitive practices that tend to lead to such a dominant position. Practices controlled in this way may include predatory pricing, tying, price gouging, refusal to deal, and many others.
- supervising the mergers and acquisitions of large corporations, including some joint ventures. Transactions that are considered to threaten the competitive process can be prohibited altogether, or approved subject to 'remedies' such as an obligation to divest part of the merged business or to offer licences or access to facilities to enable other businesses to continue competing.

The substance and practice of competition law varies from jurisdiction to jurisdiction. Protecting the interests of consumers (consumer welfare) and ensuring that entrepreneurs have an opportunity to compete in the market economy are often treated as important objectives. Competition law is closely connected with law on deregulation of access to markets, state aids and subsidies, the privatisation of state owned assets and the establishment of independent sector regulators. In recent decades, competition law has been viewed as a way to provide better public services.

a. Antitrust
c. United Kingdom competition law

b. Anti-Inflation Act
d. Intellectual property law

49. In economics, _____ is the transfer of income, wealth or property from some individuals to others.

One premise of _____ is that money should be distributed to benefit the poorer members of society, and that the rich have an obligation to assist the poor, thus creating a more financially egalitarian society. Another argument is that the rich exploit the poor or otherwise gain unfair benefits.

a. 130-30 fund
c. 1921 recession

b. 100-year flood
d. Redistribution

50. A _____ is any systematic process enabling many market players to bid and ask: helping bidders and sellers interact and make deals. It is not just the price mechanism but the entire system of regulation, qualification, credentials, reputations and clearing that surrounds that mechanism and makes it operate in a social context.

Because a _____ relies on the assumption that players are constantly involved and unequally enabled, a _____ is distinguished specifically from a voting system where candidates seek the support of voters on a less regular basis.

a. Market system
c. Competitive equilibrium

b. Contestable market
d. Price mechanism

Chapter 4. The U.S. Economy: Private and Public Sectors

51. In economics, a _____ exists when a specific individual or enterprise has sufficient control over a particular product or service to determine significantly the terms on which other individuals shall have access to it. Monopolies are thus characterized by a lack of economic competition for the good or service that they provide and a lack of viable substitute goods. The verb 'monopolize' refers to the process by which a firm gains persistently greater market share than what is expected under perfect competition.

    a. 130-30 fund
    b. 1921 recession
    c. Monopoly
    d. 100-year flood

52. In economics, a _____ occurs when, due to the economies of scale of a particular industry, the maximum efficiency of production and distribution is realized through a single supplier.

Natural monopolies arise where the largest supplier in an industry, often the first supplier in a market, has an overwhelming cost advantage over other actual or potential competitors. This tends to be the case in industries where capital costs predominate, creating economies of scale which are large in relation to the size of the market, and hence high barriers to entry; examples include water services and electricity.

    a. Natural monopoly
    b. Privatizing profits and socializing losses
    c. Common-pool resource
    d. Collective goods

53. The _____ is the part of economic and administrative life that deals with the delivery of goods and services by and for the government, whether national, regional or local/municipal.

Examples of _____ activity range from delivering social security, administering urban planning and organising national defenses.

The organization of the _____ can take several forms, including:

- Direct administration funded through taxation; the delivering organization generally has no specific requirement to meet commercial success criteria, and production decisions are determined by government.
- Publicly owned corporations (in some contexts, especially manufacturing, 'state-owned enterprises'); which differ from direct administration in that they have greater commercial freedoms and are expected to operate according to commercial criteria, and production decisions are not generally taken by government (although goals may be set for them by government.)
- Partial outsourcing (of the scale many businesses do, e.g. for IT services), is considered a _____ model.

A borderline form is

- Complete outsourcing or contracting out, with a privately owned corporation delivering the entire service on behalf of government. This may be considered a mixture of private sector operations with public ownership of assets, although in some forms the private sector's control and/or risk is so great that the service may no longer be considered part of the _____.

a. Public sector
b. Policy cycle
c. 130-30 fund
d. 100-year flood

54.

The _____ was the first United States Federal statute to limit cartels and monopolies. It falls under antitrust law.

The Act provides: 'Every contract, combination in the form of trust or otherwise, or conspiracy, in restraint of trade or commerce among the several States, or with foreign nations, is declared to be illegal'. The Act also provides: 'Every person who shall monopolize, or attempt to monopolize, or combine or conspire with any other person or persons, to monopolize any part of the trade or commerce among the several States, or with foreign nations, shall be deemed guilty of a felony [. . .]' The Act put responsibility upon government attorneys and district courts to pursue and investigate trusts, companies and organizations suspected of violating the Act. The Clayton Act extended the right to sue under the antitrust laws to 'any person who shall be injured in his business or property by reason of anything forbidden in the antitrust laws.' Under the Clayton Act, private parties may sue in U.S. district court and should they prevail, they may be awarded treble damages and the cost of suit, including reasonable attorney's fees.

a. 100-year flood
b. 1921 recession
c. 130-30 fund
d. Sherman Antitrust Act

55. In economics, a _____ is a redistribution of income in the market system. These payments are considered to be nonexhaustive because they do not directly absorb resources or create output. Examples of certain _____s include welfare (financial aid), social security, and government subsidies for certain businesses (firms.)

a. 1921 recession
b. Transfer payment
c. 100-year flood
d. 130-30 fund

56. In economics, _____ is a measure of national income. Basically, it is an approach to measure GDP. It is defined as the value of planned goods and services produced in an economy.

a. Aggregate supply
b. Aggregation problem
c. Aggregate demand
d. Aggregate expenditure

57. A _____ is the transfer of wealth from one party (such as a person or company) to another. A _____ is usually made in exchange for the provision of goods, services or both, or to fulfill a legal obligation.

The simplest and oldest form of _____ is barter, the exchange of one good or service for another.

a. Soft count
b. Going concern
c. Social gravity
d. Payment

58. In law and economics, the _____, describes the economic efficiency of an economic allocation or outcome in the presence of externalities. The theorem states that when trade in an externality is possible and there are no transaction costs, bargaining will lead to an efficient outcome regardless of the initial allocation of property rights. In practice, obstacles to bargaining or poorly defined property rights can prevent Coasian bargaining.

a. General Mining Act of 1872
b. Coase theorem
c. Prior appropriation water rights
d. Means test

59. In economics, the _____ can be defined as the graph depicting the relationship between the price of a certain commodity, and the amount of it that consumers are willing and able to purchase at that given price. It is a graphic representation of a demand schedule. The _____ for all consumers together follows from the _____ of every individual consumer: the individual demands at each price are added together.

a. Wage curve
b. Cost curve
c. Kuznets curve
d. Demand curve

60. In economics, a _____ exists when the production or use of goods and services by the market is not efficient. That is, there exists another outcome where all involved can be made better off. _____s can be viewed as scenarios where individuals' pursuit of pure self-interest leads to results that are not efficient - that can be improved upon from the societal point-of-view.

a. Fixed exchange rate
b. General equilibrium
c. Market failure
d. Financial economics

61. Many _____ are related to the environmental consequences of production and use

- Systemic risk describes the risks to the overall economy arising from the risks which the banking system takes. That the private costs of banking failure may be smaller than the social costs justifies banking regulations, although regulations could create a moral hazard.

- Anthropogenic climate change is attributed to greenhouse gas emissions from burning oil, gas, and coal. Global warming has been ranked as the #1 externality of all economic activity, in the magnitude of potential harms and yet remains unmitigated.

a. Total Economic Value
b. White certificates
c. Negative externalities
d. Green certificate

62. _____ is used to assign the available resources in an economic way. It is part of resource management.

In strategic planning,is a plan for using available resources, for example human resources, especially in the near term, to achieve goals for the future.

a. 100-year flood
b. 1921 recession
c. 130-30 fund
d. Resource allocation

Chapter 4. The U.S. Economy: Private and Public Sectors

63. _____ has several particular meanings:

- in mathematics
    - _____ function
    - Euler _____
    - _____
    - _____ subgroup
    - method of _____s (partial differential equations)
- in physics and engineering
    - any _____ curve that shows the relationship between certain input- and output parameters, e.g.
    - an I-V or current-voltage _____ is the current in a circuit as a function of the applied voltage
    - Receiver-Operator _____
- in fiction
    - in Dungeons ' Dragons, _____ is another name for ability score

a. Demand
b. Russian financial crisis
c. Technocracy
d. Characteristic

64. _____s is the social science that studies the production, distribution, and consumption of goods and services. The term _____s comes from the Ancient Greek οἰκονομῖα from οἶκος (oikos, 'house') + νόμος (nomos, 'custom' or 'law'), hence 'rules of the house(hold)'. Current _____ models developed out of the broader field of political economy in the late 19th century, owing to a desire to use an empirical approach more akin to the physical sciences.

a. Inflation
b. Energy economics
c. Opportunity cost
d. Economic

65. _____ is the increase in the amount of the goods and services produced by an economy over time. It is conventionally measured as the percent rate of increase in real gross domestic product, or real GDP. Growth is usually calculated in real terms, i.e. inflation-adjusted terms, in order to net out the effect of inflation on the price of the goods and services produced.

a. ACEA agreement
b. AD-IA Model
c. ACCRA Cost of Living Index
d. Economic growth

66. In economics, an _____ or spillover of an economic transaction is an impact on a party that is not directly involved in the transaction. In such a case, prices do not reflect the full costs or benefits in production or consumption of a product or service. A positive impact is called an external benefit, while a negative impact is called an external cost.

a. Externality
b. Environmental tariff
c. Environmental impact assessment
d. Existence value

64 *Chapter 4. The U.S. Economy: Private and Public Sectors*

67. Examples of _____ include:

- A beekeeper keeps the bees for their honey. A side effect or externality associated with his activity is the pollination of surrounding crops by the bees. The value generated by the pollination may be more important than the value of the harvested honey.

- An individual planting an attractive garden in front of his house may provide benefits to others living in the area, and even financial benefits in the form of increased property values for all property owners.

- An individual buying a product that is interconnected in a network (e.g., a video cellphone) will increase the usefulness of such phones to other people who have a video cellphone. When each new user of a product increases the value of the same product owned by others, the phenomenon is called a network externality or a network effect. Network externalities often have 'tipping points' where, suddenly, the product reaches general acceptance and near-universal usage, a phenomenon which can be seen in the near universal take-up of cellphones in some Scandinavian countries.

- Knowledge spillover of inventions and information - once an invention (or most other forms of practical information) is discovered or made more easily accessible, others benefit by exploiting the invention or information. Copyright and intellectual property law are mechanisms to allow the inventor or creator to benefit from a temporary, state-protected monopoly in return for 'sharing' the information through publication or other means.

a. Negative externalities
c. Total Economic Value
b. Weighted average cost of carbon
d. Positive Externalities

68. A _____ is defined in economics as a good that exhibits these properties:

- Excludable - it is reasonably possible to prevent a class of consumers (e.g. those who have not paid for it) from consuming the good.
- Rivalrous - consumptions by one consumer prevents simultaneous consumption by other consumers. _____s satisfies an individual want while public good satisfies a collective want of the society.

A _____ is the opposite of a public good, as they are almost exclusively made for profit.

An example of the _____ is bread: bread eaten by a given person cannot be consumed by another (rivalry), and it is easy for a baker to refuse to trade a loaf (excludable

a. Positional goods
c. Pie method
b. Private good
d. Demerit good

69. In economics, a _____ is a good that is non-rivaled and non-excludable. This means, respectively, that consumption of the good by one individual does not reduce availability of the good for consumption by others; and that no one can be effectively excluded from using the good. In the real world, there may be no such thing as an absolutely non-rivaled and non-excludable good; but economists think that some goods approximate the concept closely enough for the analysis to be economically useful.

Chapter 4. The U.S. Economy: Private and Public Sectors

a. Happiness economics
b. Demand-pull theory
c. Neoclassical synthesis
d. Public good

70. In economics, _____ is the total supply of goods and services produced by a national economy during a specific time period. It is the total amount of goods and services in the economy available at all possible price levels.
    a. Aggregation problem
    b. Aggregate demand
    c. Aggregate supply
    d. Aggregate expenditure

71. In economics, economic output is divided into physical goods and intangible services. Consumption of _____ is assumed to produce utility. It is often used when referring to a _____ Tax.
    a. Composite good
    b. Private good
    c. Manufactured goods
    d. Goods and services

72. _____ is a policy or ideology of violence intended to intimidate or cause terror for the purpose of 'exerting pressure on decision making by state bodies.' The term 'terror' is largely used to indicate clandestine, low-intensity violence that targets civilians and generates public fear. Thus 'terror' is distinct from asymmetric warfare, and violates the concept of a common law of war in which civilian life is regarded. The term '-ism' is used to indicate an ideology --typically one that claims its attacks are in the domain of a 'just war' concept, though most condemn such as crimes against humanity.
    a. 100-year flood
    b. 130-30 fund
    c. 1921 recession
    d. Terrorism

73. The _____ or Aggregate Demand-Aggregate Supply model is a macroeconomic model that explains price level and output through the relationship of aggregate demand and aggregate supply. It was first put forth by John Maynard Keynes in his work The General Theory of Employment, Interest, and Money. It is the foundation for the modern field of macroeconomics, and is accepted by a broad array of economists, from Libertarian, Monetarist supporters of laissez-faire, such as Milton Friedman to Socialist, Post-Keynesian supporters of economic interventionism, such as Joan Robinson.
    a. IS/LM model
    b. Adaptive expectations
    c. Economic interdependence
    d. AD-AS

74. _____ refers to an absence of excessive fluctuations in the macroeconomy. An economy with fairly constant output growth and low and stable inflation would be considered economically stable. An economy with frequent large recessions, a pronounced business cycle, very high or variable inflation, or frequent financial crises would be considered economically unstable.
    a. Economic stability
    b. Export subsidy
    c. Export-led growth
    d. Income effect

75. The _____ is the central banking system of the United States. Created in 1913 by the enactment of the Federal Reserve Act (signed by Woodrow Wilson), it is a quasi-public and quasi-private (government entity with private components) banking system that comprises (1) the presidentially appointed Board of Governors of the _____ in Washington, D.C.; (2) the Federal Open Market Committee; (3) twelve regional Federal Reserve Banks located in major cities throughout the nation acting as fiscal agents for the U.S. Treasury, each with its own nine-member board of directors; (4) numerous other private U.S. member banks, which subscribe to required amounts of non-transferable stock in their regional Federal Reserve Banks; and (5) various advisory councils. Since February 2006, Ben Bernanke has served as the Chairman of the Board of Governors of the _____.

a. Term auction facility
b. Federal Reserve System
c. Monetary Policy Report to the Congress
d. Federal Reserve System Open Market Account

76. In macroeconomics, _____ is a condition of the national economy, where all or nearly all persons willing and able to work at the prevailing wages and working conditions are able to do so. It is defined either as 0% unemployment, literally, no unemployment (the rate of unemployment is the fraction of the work force unable to find work), as by James Tobin, or as the level of employment rates when there is no cyclical unemployment. It is defined by the majority of mainstream economists as being an acceptable level of natural unemployment above 0%, the discrepancy from 0% being due to non-cyclical types of unemployment.

a. Demand shock
b. Harrod-Johnson diagram
c. Marginal propensity to consume
d. Full employment

77. The _____ or the output gap is the difference between potential GDP and actual GDP or actual output. The calculation for the output gap is Y-Y* where Y* is potential output and Y is actual output. If this calculation yields a positive number it is called an expansionary gap and indicates an economy in expansion; if the calculation yields a negative number it is called a recessionary gap and indicates an economy in recession.

a. 1921 recession
b. 130-30 fund
c. 100-year flood
d. GDP gap

78. _____ and Keynesian Theory) is a macroeconomic theory based on the ideas of 20th-century British economist John Maynard Keynes. _____ argues that private sector decisions sometimes lead to inefficient macroeconomic outcomes and therefore advocates active policy responses by the public sector, including monetary policy actions by the central bank and fiscal policy actions by the government to stabilize output over the business cycle.

The theories forming the basis of _____ were first presented in The General Theory of Employment, Interest and Money, published in 1936.

a. Keynesian economics
b. Rational choice theory
c. Market failure
d. Deflation

79. In economics, a _____ is a monetary-policy rule that stipulates how much the central bank would or should change the nominal interest rate in response to divergences of actual inflation rates from target inflation rates and of actual Gross Domestic Product (GDP) from potential GDP. It was first proposed by the by U.S. economist John B. Taylor in 1993. The rule can be written as follows:

$$i_t = \pi_t + r_t^* + a_\pi(\pi_t - \pi_t^*) + a_y(y_t - \bar{y}_t).$$

In this equation, i_t is the target short-term nominal interest rate (e.g. the federal funds rate in the US), π_t is the rate of inflation as measured by the GDP deflator, π_t^* is the desired rate of inflation, r_t^* is the assumed equilibrium real interest rate, y_t is the logarithm of real GDP, and $\bar{y}_t$ is the logarithm of potential output, as determined by a linear trend.

Chapter 4. The U.S. Economy: Private and Public Sectors

a. Federal Reserve Banks
b. Taylor rule
c. Term Securities Lending Facility
d. Fed Funds Probability

80. _____ is a type of inflation caused by substantial increases in the cost of important goods or services where no suitable alternative is available. A situation that has been often cited of this was the oil crisis of the 1970s, which some economists see as a major cause of the inflation experienced in the Western world in that decade. It is argued that this inflation resulted from increases in the cost of petroleum imposed by the member states of OPEC.
    a. Mundell-Tobin effect
    b. Headline inflation
    c. Chronic inflation
    d. Cost-push inflation

81. In economics, the term _____ of income or _____ refers to a simple economic model which describes the reciprocal circulation of income between producers and consumers. In the _____ model, the inter-dependent entities of producer and consumer are referred to as 'firms' and 'households' respectively and provide each other with factors in order to facilitate the flow of income. Firms provide consumers with goods and services in exchange for consumer expenditure and 'factors of production' from households.
    a. 100-year flood
    b. 130-30 fund
    c. 1921 recession
    d. Circular flow

82. _____ refers to a business or organization attempting to acquire goods or services to accomplish the goals of the enterprise. Though there are several organizations that attempt to set standards in the _____ process, processes can vary greatly between organizations. Typically the word '_____' is not used interchangeably with the word 'procurement', since procurement typically includes Expediting, Supplier Quality, and Traffic and Logistics (T'L) in addition to _____.
    a. 100-year flood
    b. Purchasing
    c. Free port
    d. 130-30 fund

83. _____ or government expenditure is classified by economists into three main types. Government purchases of goods and services for current use are classed as government consumption. Government purchases of goods and services intended to create future benefits, such as infrastructure investment or research spending, are classed as government investment.
    a. 1921 recession
    b. Government spending
    c. 100-year flood
    d. 130-30 fund

84. _____ is the first day of the year in which a nation as a whole has theoretically earned enough income to fund its annual tax burden. It is annually calculated in the United States by the Tax Foundation--a Washington, D.C.-based tax research organization. Every dollar that is officially considered income by the government is counted, and every payment to the government that is officially considered a tax is counted.
    a. Tax wedge
    b. Virtual tax
    c. Tax revenue
    d. Tax Freedom Day

85. In general, a _____ is an arrangement to provide people with an income when they are no longer earning a regular income from employment.

The terms retirement plan or superannuation refer to a _____ granted upon retirement . Retirement plans may be set up by employers, insurance companies, the government or other institutions such as employer associations or trade unions.

a. Real wage
b. Pension
c. Profit-sharing agreement
d. Superannuation

86. _____ is that which is owed; usually referencing assets owed, but the term can also cover moral obligations and other interactions not requiring money. In the case of assets, _____ is a means of using future purchasing power in the present before a summation has been earned. Some companies and corporations use _____ as a part of their overall corporate finance strategy.

a. Hard money loan
b. Collateral Management
c. Debt
d. Debenture

87. _____ are the income that is gained by governments because of taxation of the people.

Just as there are different types of tax, the form in which _____ is collected also differs; furthermore, the agency that collects the tax may not be part of central government, but may be an alternative third-party licenced to collect tax which they themselves will use. For example:

- In the UK, the DVLA collects road tax, which is then passed on the treasury.

_____s on purchases can come from two forms: 'tax' itself is a percentage of the price added to the purchase (such as sales tax in US states, or VAT in the UK), while 'duty' is a fixed amount added to the purchase price (such as is commonly found on cigarettes.) In order to calculate the total tax raised from these sales, we must work out the effective tax rate multiplied by the quantity supplied.

a. Tax and spend
b. Taxable wage
c. Taxation as slavery
d. Tax revenue

88. Total _____ is defined by the United States' Bureau of Economic Analysis as

income received by persons from all sources. It includes income received from participation in production as well as from government and business transfer payments. It is the sum of compensation of employees (received), supplements to wages and salaries, proprietors' income with inventory valuation adjustment (IVA) and capital consumption adjustment (CCAdj), rental income of persons with CCAdj, _____ receipts on assets, and personal current transfer receipts, less contributions for government social insurance.

a. Dividend Discount Model
b. Bidding
c. Greater fool theory
d. Personal income

89. A _____ is a tax by which the tax rate increases as the taxable amount increases. 'Progressive' describes a distribution effect on income or expenditure, referring to the way the rate progresses from low to high, where the average tax rate is less than the marginal tax rate. It can be applied to individual taxes or to a tax system as a whole; a year, multi-year, or lifetime.

a. 130-30 fund
b. Proportional tax
c. Progressive tax
d. 100-year flood

Chapter 4. The U.S. Economy: Private and Public Sectors

90. The United States _____ is an independent agency of the United States federal government that administers Social Security, a social insurance program consisting of retirement, disability, and survivors' benefits. To qualify for these benefits, most American workers pay Social Security taxes on their earnings; future benefits are based on the employees' contributions.

The _____ was established by a law currently codified at 42 U.S.C.

a. 100-year flood
c. 1921 recession
b. Social Security Administration
d. 130-30 fund

91. The _____ is the means by which the federal government of the United States accounts for excess paid-in contributions from workers and employers to the Social Security system that are not required to fund current benefit payments to retirees, survivors, and the disabled or to pay administrative expenses. More importantly, the trust fund also contains the securities that will be redeemed to make benefit payments in the future when contributions derived from payroll taxes and self-employment contributions no longer are sufficient to fully fund then-current benefit payments. (The controversy over its meaningfulness is a topic of the sustainability of the unified Federal budget.)

a. Retirement Insurance Benefits
c. Legacy debt
b. Social Security Disability Insurance
d. Social Security trust fund

92. _____ are the divisions at which tax rates change in a progressive tax system (or an explicitly regressive tax system, although this is much rarer.) Essentially, they are the cutoff values for taxable income -- income past a certain point will be taxed at a higher rate.

a. Disposable income
c. Tax farming
b. Popiwek
d. Tax brackets

93. In economic models, the _____ time frame assumes no fixed factors of production. Firms can enter or leave the marketplace, and the cost (and availability) of land, labor, raw materials, and capital goods can be assumed to vary. In contrast, in the short-run time frame, certain factors are assumed to be fixed, because there is not sufficient time for them to change.

a. Productivity world
c. Price/performance ratio
b. Diseconomies of scale
d. Long-run

94. In a company, _____ is the sum of all financial records of salaries, wages, bonuses and deductions.

A paycheck, is traditionally a paper document issued by an employer to pay an employee for services rendered. While most commonly used in the United States, recently the physical paycheck has been increasingly replaced by electronic direct deposit to bank accounts.

a. Total Expense Ratio
c. Tax expense
b. 100-year flood
d. Payroll

95. A _____ is a consumption tax charged at the point of purchase for certain goods and services. The tax is usually set as a percentage by the government charging the tax. There is usually a list of exemptions.

a. 100-year flood
c. 1921 recession
b. Sales tax
d. 130-30 fund

96. _____ is an ad valorem tax that an owner is required to pay on the value of the property being taxed. _____ can be defined as 'generally, tax imposed by municipalities upon owners of property within their jurisdiction based on the value of such property.' There are three species or types of property: Land, Improvements to Land (immovable manmade objects; i.e., buildings), and Personal (movable manmade objects.) Real estate, real property or realty are all terms for the combination of land and improvements.
 a. Community property
 b. Bank regulation
 c. Chief Financial Officers Act of 1990
 d. Property tax

97. In economics, _____ refers to how the marginal contribution of a factor of production usually decreases as more of the factor is used. According to this relationship, in a production system with fixed and variable inputs, beyond some point, each additional unit of the variable input yields smaller and smaller increases in output. Conversely, producing one more unit of output costs more and more in variable inputs.
 a. Community property
 b. Derivatives law
 c. Patent troll
 d. Diminishing returns

98. A _____ is the procedure of systematically acquiring and recording information about the members of a given population. It is a regularly occurring and official count of a particular population. The term is used mostly in connection with national 'population and door to door _____es' (to be taken every 10 years according to United Nations recommendations), agriculture, and business _____es.
 a. 100-year flood
 b. 130-30 fund
 c. 1921 recession
 d. Census

Chapter 5. The United States in the Global Economy

1. _____ is exchange of capital, goods, and services across international borders or territories. In most countries, it represents a significant share of gross domestic product (GDP.) While _____ has been present throughout much of history, its economic, social, and political importance has been on the rise in recent centuries.
   - a. Intra-industry trade
   - b. Import license
   - c. International trade
   - d. Incoterms

2. In economics, _____ refers to how the marginal contribution of a factor of production usually decreases as more of the factor is used. According to this relationship, in a production system with fixed and variable inputs, beyond some point, each additional unit of the variable input yields smaller and smaller increases in output. Conversely, producing one more unit of output costs more and more in variable inputs.
   - a. Patent troll
   - b. Community property
   - c. Derivatives law
   - d. Diminishing returns

3. _____s is the social science that studies the production, distribution, and consumption of goods and services. The term _____s comes from the Ancient Greek οἰκονομία from οἶκος (oikos, 'house') + νόμος (nomos, 'custom' or 'law'), hence 'rules of the house(hold)'. Current _____ models developed out of the broader field of political economy in the late 19th century, owing to a desire to use an empirical approach more akin to the physical sciences.
   - a. Opportunity cost
   - b. Economic
   - c. Energy economics
   - d. Inflation

4. The _____ is 'the basic residential unit in which economic production, consumption, inheritance, child rearing, and shelter are organized and carried out'; [the _____] 'may or may not be synonomous with family'.

   The _____ is the basic unit of analysis in many social, microeconomic and government models. The term refers to all individuals who live in the same dwelling.

   - a. Family economics
   - b. 130-30 fund
   - c. 100-year flood
   - d. Household

5. _____ is the a method of technical and economic research of the systems for purpose to optimize a parity between system's consumer functions or properties and expenses to achieve those functions or properties.

   This methodology for continuous perfection of production, industrial technologies, organizational structures was developed by Juryj Sobolev in 1948 at the 'Perm telephone factory'

   - 1948 Juryj Sobolev - the first success in application of a method analysis at the 'Perm telephone factory'.
   - 1949 - the first application for the invention as result of use of the new method.

Chapter 5. The United States in the Global Economy

Today in economically developed countries practically each enterprise or the company use methodology of the kind of functional-cost analysis as a practice of the quality management, most full satisfying to principles of standards of series ISO 9000.

- Interest of consumer not in products itself, but the advantage which it will receive from its usage.
- The consumer aspires to reduce his expenses
- Functions needed by consumer can be executed in the various ways, and, hence, with various efficiency and expenses. Among possible alternatives of realization of functions exist such in which the parity of quality and the price is the optimal for the consumer.

The goal of _____ is achievement of the highest consumer satisfaction of production at simultaneous decrease in all kinds of industrial expenses Classical _____ has three English synonyms - Value Engineering, Value Management, Value Analysis.

a. Staple financing
b. Function cost analysis
c. Willingness to pay
d. Monopoly wage

6. The _____ consists of a number of economic theories which describe the nature of the firm, company including its existence, its behaviour, and its relationship with the market.

In simplified terms, the _____ aims to answer these questions:

1. Existence - why do firms emerge, why are not all transactions in the economy mediated over the market?
2. Boundaries - why the boundary between firms and the market is located exactly there? Which transactions are performed internally and which are negotiated on the market?
3. Organization - why are firms structured in such specific way? What is the interplay of formal and informal relationships?

Despite looking simple, these questions are not answered by the established economic theory, which usually views firms as given, and treats them as black boxes without any internal structure.

The First World War period saw a change of emphasis in economic theory away from industry-level analysis which mainly included analysing markets to analysis at the level of the firm, as it became increasingly clear that perfect competition was no longer an adequate model of how firms behaved. Economic theory till then had focussed on trying to understand markets alone and there had been little study on understanding why firms or organisations exist.

a. Theory of the firm
b. Technology gap
c. Khazzoom-Brookes postulate
d. Policy Ineffectiveness Proposition

7. In economics, an _____ is any good or commodity, transported from one country to another country in a legitimate fashion, typically for use in trade. _____ goods or services are provided to foreign consumers by domestic producers. _____ is an important part of international trade.

Chapter 5. The United States in the Global Economy

a. AD-IA Model
b. ACCRA Cost of Living Index
c. Export
d. ACEA agreement

8. The _____ or gross domestic income (GDI), a basic measure of an economy's economic performance, is the market value of all final goods and services produced within the borders of a nation in a year. _____ can be defined in three ways, all of which are conceptually identical. First, it is equal to the total expenditures for all final goods and services produced within the country in a stipulated period of time (usually a 365-day year.)

a. Gross domestic product
b. Market structure
c. Countercyclical
d. Monopolistic competition

9. The _____ or the output gap is the difference between potential GDP and actual GDP or actual output. The calculation for the output gap is Y-Y* where Y* is potential output and Y is actual output. If this calculation yields a positive number it is called an expansionary gap and indicates an economy in expansion; if the calculation yields a negative number it is called a recessionary gap and indicates an economy in recession.

a. 1921 recession
b. 130-30 fund
c. 100-year flood
d. GDP gap

10. A _____ is an object whose consumption increases the utility of the consumer, for which the quantity demanded exceeds the quantity supplied at zero price. _____s are usually modeled as having diminishing marginal utility. The first individual purchase has high utility; the second has less.

a. Composite good
b. Pie method
c. Merit good
d. Good

11. In economics, economic output is divided into physical goods and intangible services. Consumption of _____ is assumed to produce utility. It is often used when referring to a _____ Tax.

a. Manufactured goods
b. Composite good
c. Goods and services
d. Private good

12. _____ , as defined by the _____ Association of America (Information technologyAA), is 'the study, design, development, implementation, support or management of computer-based information systems, particularly software applications and computer hardware.' _____ deals with the use of electronic computers and computer software to convert, store, protect, process, transmit, and securely retrieve information.

Today, the term _____ has ballooned to encompass many aspects of computing and technology, and the term has become very recognizable. The _____ umbrella can be quite large, covering many fields.

a. Information technology
b. AD-IA Model
c. ACEA agreement
d. ACCRA Cost of Living Index

13. _____ is a term used in accounting, economics and finance to spread the cost of an asset over the span of several years.

In simple words we can say that _____ is the reduction in the value of an asset due to usage, passage of time, wear and tear, technological outdating or obsolescence, depletion, inadequacy, rot, rust, decay or other such factors.

In accounting, _____ is a term used to describe any method of attributing the historical or purchase cost of an asset across its useful life, roughly corresponding to normal wear and tear.

a. Salvage value
c. Net income per employee

b. Historical cost
d. Depreciation

14. _____ in economics and business is the result of an exchange and from that trade we assign a numerical monetary value to a good, service or asset. If Alice trades Bob 4 apples for an orange, the _____ of an orange is 4 apples. Inversely, the _____ of an apple is 1/4 oranges.

a. Price war
c. Price

b. Price book
d. Premium pricing

15. A _____ is a normalized average (typically a weighted average) of prices for a given class of goods or services in a given region, during a given interval of time. It is a statistic designed to help to compare how these prices, taken as a whole, differ between time periods or geographical locations.

Price indices have several potential uses.

a. Product sabotage
c. Two-part tariff

b. Transactional Net Margin Method
d. Price index

16. A _____ is a general term that describes any government policy or regulation that restricts international trade. The barriers can take many forms, including the following terms that include many restrictions in international trade within multiple countries that import and export any items of trade.

- Import duty
- Import licenses
- Export licenses
- Import quotas
- Tariffs
- Subsidies
- Non-tariff barriers to trade
- Voluntary Export Restraints
- Local Content Requirements
- Embargo

Most _____s work on the same principle: the imposition of some sort of cost on trade that raises the price of the traded products. If two or more nations repeatedly use _____s against each other, then a trade war results.

a. Certificate of origin
c. Global financial system

b. Trade barrier
d. National Foreign Trade Council

Chapter 5. The United States in the Global Economy

17. In economics, _____ refers to the ability of a party to produce a good or service using fewer real resources than another entity producing the same good or service..A party has an _____ when using the same input as another party, it can produce a greater output. Since _____ is determined by a simple comparison of labor productivities, it is possible for a a party to have no _____ in anything. It can be contrasted with the concept of comparative advantage which refers to the ability to produce a particular good at a lower opportunity cost.
    a. ACCRA Cost of Living Index
    b. International economics
    c. Index number
    d. Absolute advantage

18. In economics and finance, _____ is the change in total cost that arises when the quantity produced changes by one unit. It is the cost of producing one more unit of a good. Mathematically, the _____ function is expressed as the first derivative of the total cost (TC) function with respect to quantity (Q.)
    a. Variable cost
    b. Marginal cost
    c. Khozraschyot
    d. Quality costs

19. In microeconomics, _____ is quite simply the conversion of inputs into outputs. It is an economic process that uses resources to create a good or service that is suitable for exchange. This can include manufacturing, storing, shipping, and packaging.
    a. Solved
    b. Production
    c. Red Guards
    d. MET

20. The balance of trade (or net exports, sometimes symbolized as NX) is the difference between the monetary value of exports and imports in an economy over a certain period of time. It is the relationship between a nation's imports and exports. A favorable balance of trade is known as a trade surplus and consists of exporting more than is imported; an unfavorable balance of trade is known as a _____ or, informally, a trade gap.
    a. Computational economic
    b. Demographics of India
    c. Trade deficit
    d. Complementary asset

21. The balance of trade (or net exports, sometimes symbolized as NX) is the difference between the monetary value of exports and imports in an economy over a certain period of time. It is the relationship between a nation's imports and exports. A favorable balance of trade is known as a _____ and consists of exporting more than is imported; an unfavorable balance of trade is known as a trade deficit or, informally, a trade gap.
    a. Trade surplus
    b. Business valuation standards
    c. Black-Scholes
    d. Dividend unit

22. In economics, an _____ is any good (e.g. a commodity) or service brought into one country from another country in a legitimate fashion, typically for use in trade.It is a good that is brought in from another country for sale. _____ goods or services are provided to domestic consumers by foreign producers. An _____ in the receiving country is an export to the sending country.
    a. Economic integration
    b. Import
    c. Incoterms
    d. Import quota

23. In economics, and cost accounting, _____ describes the total economic cost of production and is made up of variable costs, which vary according to the quantity of a good produced and include inputs such as labor and raw materials, plus fixed costs, which are independent of the quantity of a good produced and include inputs (capital) that cannot be varied in the short term, such as buildings and machinery. _____ in economics includes the total opportunity cost of each factor of production in addition to fixed and variable costs.

The rate at which _____ changes as the amount produced changes is called marginal cost.

a. 1921 recession
b. 130-30 fund
c. Total cost
d. 100-year flood

24. The _____ or Aggregate Demand-Aggregate Supply model is a macroeconomic model that explains price level and output through the relationship of aggregate demand and aggregate supply. It was first put forth by John Maynard Keynes in his work The General Theory of Employment, Interest, and Money. It is the foundation for the modern field of macroeconomics, and is accepted by a broad array of economists, from Libertarian, Monetarist supporters of laissez-faire, such as Milton Friedman to Socialist, Post-Keynesian supporters of economic interventionism, such as Joan Robinson.

a. Economic interdependence
b. IS/LM model
c. Adaptive expectations
d. AD-AS

25. _____ arises when aggregate demand in an economy outpaces aggregate supply. It involves inflation rising as real gross domestic product rises and unemployment falls, as the economy moves along the Phillips curve. This is commonly described as 'too much money chasing too few goods'.

a. Kinked demand curve
b. Kinked demand
c. Marshallian demand function
d. Demand-pull inflation

26. A _____ is a duty imposed on goods when they are moved across a political boundary. They are usually associated with protectionism, the economic policy of restraining trade between nations. For political reasons, _____s are usually imposed on imported goods, although they may also be imposed on exported goods.

a. 130-30 fund
b. Tariff
c. 1921 recession
d. 100-year flood

27. In economics, _____ is a rise in the general level of prices of goods and services in an economy over a period of time. When the general price level rises, each unit of currency buys fewer goods and services; consequently, _____ is also a decline in the real value of money--a loss of purchasing power in the medium of exchange which is also the monetary unit of account in the economy. A chief measure of general price-level _____ is the general _____ rate, which is the percentage change in a general price index (normally the Consumer Price Index) over time.

a. Economic
b. Energy economics
c. Opportunity cost
d. Inflation

28. _____ was a survey conducted by the U.S. Department of Justice to gauge the prevalence of alcohol and illegal drug use among prior arrestees. It was a reformulation of the prior Drug Use Forecasting (DUF) program, focused on five drugs in particular: cocaine, marijuana, methamphetamine, opiates, and PCP.

Participants were randomly selected from arrest records in major metropolitan areas; because no personally identifying information is taken from each record chosen, the resulting data can be correlated to arrest rates, but not to the total population of persons charged.

a. AD-IA Model
b. Arrestee Drug Abuse Monitoring
c. ACEA agreement
d. ACCRA Cost of Living Index

29. _____ was a Scottish moral philosopher and a pioneer of political economy. One of the key figures of the Scottish Enlightenment, Smith is the author of The Theory of Moral Sentiments and An Inquiry into the Nature and Causes of the Wealth of Nations. The latter, usually abbreviated as The Wealth of Nations, is considered his magnum opus and the first modern work of economics.

   a. Alan Greenspan   b. Adolph Fischer
   c. Adam Smith   d. Adolf Hitler

30. _____ is a socioeconomic structure and political ideology that promotes the establishment of an egalitarian, classless, stateless society based on common ownership and control of the means of production and property in general. In political science, the term '_____' is sometimes used to refer to communist states, a form of government in which the state operates under a one-party system and declares allegiance to Marxism-Leninism or a derivative thereof, even if the party does not actually claim that it has already reached _____.

Forerunners of communist ideas existed in antiquity and particularly in the 18th and early 19th century France, with thinkers such as Jean-Jacques Rousseau and the more radical Gracchus Babeuf.

   a. New Communist Movement   b. Social fascism
   c. Democratic centralism   d. Communism

31. The _____ is the official currency of 16 of the 27 member states of the European Union (EU.) The states, known collectively as the Eurozone, are Austria, Belgium, Cyprus, Finland, France, Germany, Greece, Ireland, Italy, Luxembourg, Malta, the Netherlands, Portugal, Slovakia, Slovenia, and Spain. The currency is also used in a further five European countries, with and without formal agreements and is consequently used daily by some 327 million Europeans.

   a. IRS Code 3401   b. Import and Export Price Indices
   c. Equity capital market   d. Euro

32. The _____ is an economic and political union of 27 member states, located primarily in Europe. It was established by the Treaty of Maastricht on 1 November 1993, upon the foundations of the pre-existing European Economic Community. With a population of almost 500 million, the _____ generates an estimated 30% share (US$18.4 trillion in 2008) of the nominal gross world product.

   a. European Court of Justice   b. European Union
   c. ACCRA Cost of Living Index   d. ACEA agreement

33. A _____ or transnational corporation is a corporation or enterprise that manages production or delivers services in more than one country. It can also be referred to as an international corporation.

The first modern MNC is generally thought to be the Dutch East India Company, established in 1602.

   a. Luxembourg Income Study   b. Rakon
   c. Foreign direct investment   d. Multinational corporation

34. The _____ was an evolution of developed countries from an industrial/manufacturing-based wealth producing economy into a service sector asset based economy, brought about by globalization and currency manipulation by governments and their central banks. Some analysts claimed that this change in the economic structure of the United States had created a state of permanent steady growth, low unemployment, and immunity to boom and bust macroeconomic cycles. They believed that the change rendered obsolete many business practices.

a. 1921 recession
b. 130-30 fund
c. 100-year flood
d. New Economy

35. The Organization of the Petroleum Exporting Countries is a cartel of twelve countries made up of Algeria, Angola, Ecuador, Iran, Iraq, Kuwait, Libya, Nigeria, Qatar, Saudi Arabia, the United Arab Emirates, and Venezuela. The cartel has maintained its headquarters in Vienna since 1965, and hosts regular meetings among the oil ministers of its Member Countries. Indonesia withdrew its membership in _____ in 2008 after it became a net importer of oil, but stated it would likely return if it became a net exporter in the world.
   a. ACEA agreement
   b. ACCRA Cost of Living Index
   c. AD-IA Model
   d. OPEC

36. In economics, _____ refers to the ability of a person or a country to produce a particular good at a lower marginal cost and opportunity cost than another person or country. It is the ability to produce a product most efficiently given all the other products that could be produced. It can be contrasted with absolute advantage which refers to the ability of a person or a country to produce a particular good at a lower absolute cost than another.
   a. Hot money
   b. Gravity model of trade
   c. Triffin dilemma
   d. Comparative advantage

37. _____ is the increase in the amount of the goods and services produced by an economy over time. It is conventionally measured as the percent rate of increase in real gross domestic product, or real GDP. Growth is usually calculated in real terms, i.e. inflation-adjusted terms, in order to net out the effect of inflation on the price of the goods and services produced.
   a. AD-IA Model
   b. ACEA agreement
   c. Economic growth
   d. ACCRA Cost of Living Index

38. The term microeconomic reform (or often just _____) refers to policies directed to achieve improvements in economic efficiency, either by removing distortions in individual sectors of the economy or by reforming economy-wide policies such as tax policy and competition policy with an emphasis on economic efficiency (rather than other goals such as equity or employment growth.)

_____ usually refers to government action to improve efficiency in economic markets to overcome regulatory and statutory impediments. It may sometimes also refer to legislative efforts to reduce the size of government, in order to improve economic efficiency.

   a. Isocost
   b. Incentive
   c. Economic reform
   d. Inventory analysis

39. In finance, the _____s between two currencies specifies how much one currency is worth in terms of the other. It is the value of a foreign natione;s currency in terms of the home natione;s currency. For example an _____ of 102 Japanese yen to the United States dollar means that JPY 102 is worth the same as USD 1.
   a. Exchange rate
   b. ACEA agreement
   c. Interbank market
   d. ACCRA Cost of Living Index

40. A _____, sometimes called a pegged exchange rate, is a type of exchange rate regime wherein a currency's value is matched to the value of another single currency or to a basket of other currencies such as gold.

A _____ is usually used to stabilize the value of a currency, vis-a-vis the currency it is pegged to. This facilitates trade and investments between the two countries, and is especially useful for small economies where external trade forms a large part of their GDP.

a. Monetary economics
b. Law of supply
c. Leading indicators
d. Fixed exchange rate

41. An _____ is an economy in which people, including businesses, can trade in goods and services with other people and businesses in the international community at large. This contrasts with a closed economy in which international trade cannot take place.

The act of selling goods or services to a foreign country is called exporting.

a. Indicative planning
b. Information economy
c. Attention work
d. Open economy

42. In economics, _____ is the total supply of goods and services produced by a national economy during a specific time period. It is the total amount of goods and services in the economy available at all possible price levels.

a. Aggregate expenditure
b. Aggregation problem
c. Aggregate demand
d. Aggregate supply

43. In international economics and international trade, _____ or _____ is the relative prices of a country's export to import. '_____' are sometimes used as a proxy for the relative social welfare of a country, but this heuristic is technically questionable and should be used with extreme caution. An improvement in a nation's _____ is good for that country in the sense that it has to pay less for the products it import.

a. Commercial invoice
b. Common market
c. Kennedy Round
d. Terms of trade

44. In finance, _____ is a financial action that does not promise safety of the initial investment along with the return on the principal sum. _____ typically involves the lending of money or the purchase of assets, equity or debt but in a manner that has not been given thorough analysis or is deemed to have low margin of safety or a significant risk of the loss of the principal investment. The term, '_____,' which is formally defined as above in Graham and Dodd's 1934 text, Security Analysis, contrasts with the term 'investment,' which is a financial operation that, upon thorough analysis, promises safety of principal and a satisfactory return.

a. Municipal Bond Arbitrage
b. Hybrid market
c. Global Financial Centres Index
d. Speculation

45. The _____ is published by The Economist as an informal way of measuring the purchasing power parity (PPP) between two currencies and provides a test of the extent to which market exchange rates result in goods costing the same in different countries. It 'seeks to make exchange-rate theory a bit more digestible'.

The index takes its name from the Big Mac, a hamburger sold at McDonald's restaurants.

a. Cost-weighted activity index
b. Rank mobility index
c. Deindexation
d. Big Mac index

46. The _____ is where currency trading takes place. It is where banks and other official institutions facilitate the buying and selling of foreign currencies. FX transactions typically involve one party purchasing a quantity of one currency in exchange for paying a quantity of another.
   a. Floating currency
   b. Currency swap
   c. Covered interest arbitrage
   d. Foreign exchange market

47. _____ is money accepted for exchange of goods in an economy. The prevalence of one money over another arises, usually, when a government designates through decrees that the government shall accept only particular notes and coins in payment for taxes. Typically, money of _____ consists of stamped coins and minted paper bills.
   a. Local currency
   b. Currency
   c. Security thread
   d. Totnes pound

48. _____ is an economic model based on price, utility and quantity in a market. It predicts that in a competitive market, price will function to equalize the quantity demanded by consumers, and the quantity supplied by producers, resulting in an economic equilibrium of price and quantity. The model incorporates other factors changing equilibrium as a shift of demand and/or supply.
   a. Rational addiction
   b. Supply and demand
   c. Joint demand
   d. Deferred gratification

49. In finance, a _____ is a debt security, in which the authorized issuer owes the holders a debt and, depending on the terms of the _____, is obliged to pay interest (the coupon) and/or to repay the principal at a later date, termed maturity. A _____ is a formal contract to repay borrowed money with interest at fixed intervals.

Thus a _____ is like a loan: the issuer is the borrower (debtor), the holder is the lender (creditor), and the coupon is the interest.

   a. Zero-coupon
   b. Prize Bond
   c. Callable
   d. Bond

50. Economics:

   - _____,the desire to own something and the ability to pay for it
   - _____ curve,a graphic representation of a _____ schedule
   - _____ deposit, the money in checking accounts
   - _____ pull theory,the theory that inflation occurs when _____ for goods and services exceeds existing supplies
   - _____ schedule,a table that lists the quantity of a good a person will buy it each different price
   - _____ side economics,the school of economics at believes government spending and tax cuts open economy by raising _____

Chapter 5. The United States in the Global Economy

a. Production
b. McKesson ' Robbins scandal
c. Variability
d. Demand

51. _____ is a term used in accounting relating to the increase in value of an asset. In this sense it is the reverse of depreciation, which measures the fall in value of assets over their normal life-time.

_____ is a rise of a currency in a floating exchange rate.

a. ACEA agreement
b. ACCRA Cost of Living Index
c. Appreciation
d. AD-IA Model

52. _____ is the loss of value of a country's currency with respect to one or more foreign reference currencies, typically in a floating exchange rate system. It is most often used for the unofficial increase of the exchange rate due to market forces, though sometimes it appears interchangeably with devaluation. Its opposite is called appreciation.

a. Hero Card
b. Quote currency
c. Fed Shreds
d. Currency depreciation

53. An autarky is an economy that is self-sufficient and does not take part in international trade, or severely limits trade with the outside world. Likewise the term refers to an ecosystem not affected by influences from the outside, which relies entirely on its own resources. In the economic meaning, it is also referred to as a _____.

a. Digital economy
b. Network Economy
c. Closed economy
d. Transition economy

54. An _____ is a type of protectionist trade restriction that sets a physical limit on the quantity of a good that can be imported into a country in a given period of time. Quotas, like other trade restrictions, are used to benefit the producers of a good in a domestic economy at the expense of all consumers of the good in that economy.

Critics say quotas often lead to corruption (bribes to get a quota allocation), smuggling (circumventing a quota), and higher prices for consumers.

a. Agreement on Agriculture
b. Economic integration
c. International Monetary Systems
d. Import quota

55. _____ is the economic policy of restraining trade between states, through methods such as tariffs on imported goods, restrictive quotas, and a variety of other restrictive government regulations designed to discourage imports, and prevent foreign take-over of local markets and companies. This policy is closely aligned with anti-globalization, and contrasts with free trade, where government barriers to trade are kept to a minimum. The term is mostly used in the context of economics, where _____ refers to policies or doctrines which 'protect' businesses and workers within a country by restricting or regulating trade with foreign nations.

a. Google economy
b. Protectionism
c. Knowledge economy
d. Digital economy

56. To _____ is to impose a financial charge or other levy upon a taxpayer by a state or the functional equivalent of a state.

_____es are also imposed by many subnational entities. _____es consist of direct _____ or indirect _____, and may be paid in money or as its labour equivalent (often but not always unpaid.)

a. 1921 recession
c. 100-year flood
b. Tax
d. 130-30 fund

57. To tax is to impose a financial charge or other levy upon a taxpayer by a state or the functional equivalent of a state.

_____ are also imposed by many subnational entities. _____ consist of direct tax or indirect tax, and may be paid in money or as its labour equivalent (often but not always unpaid.)

a. 1921 recession
c. 100-year flood
b. 130-30 fund
d. Taxes

58. The _____ was an act signed into law on June 17, 1930, that raised U.S. tariffs on over 20,000 imported goods to record levels. In the United States 1,028 economists signed a petition against this legislation, and after it was passed, many countries retaliated with their own increased tariffs on U.S. goods, and American exports and imports were reduced by more than half.

Although rated capacity had increased tremendously, actual output, income, and expenditure had not.

a. Judgment summons
c. Patent Law Treaty
b. Loss of use
d. Smoot-Hawley Tariff Act

59. The General Agreement on Tariffs and Trade was the outcome of the failure of negotiating governments to create the International Trade Organization (ITO.) _____ was formed in 1947 and lasted until 1994, when it was replaced by the World Trade Organization. The Bretton Woods Conference had introduced the idea for an organization to regulate trade as part of a larger plan for economic recovery after World War II.
a. Dutch-Scandinavian Economic Pact
c. General Agreement on Tariffs and Trade
b. General Agreement on Trade in Services
d. GATT

60. The _____ was the outcome of the failure of negotiating governments to create the International Trade Organization (ITO.) GATT was formed in 1947 and lasted until 1994, when it was replaced by the World Trade Organization. The Bretton Woods Conference had introduced the idea for an organization to regulate trade as part of a larger plan for economic recovery after World War II.
a. GATT
c. General Agreement on Tariffs and Trade
b. Dutch-Scandinavian Economic Pact
d. General Agreement on Trade in Services

61. The _____ provided for the negotiation of tariff agreements between the United States and separate nations, particularly Latin American countries. It resulted in a reduction of duties.

Chapter 5. The United States in the Global Economy

President Franklin D. Roosevelt was authorized by the Act for a fixed period of time to negotiate on bilateral basis with other countries and then implement reductions in tariffs in exchange for compensating tariff reductions by the partner trading country. Roosevelt was also instructed to maximize market access abroad without jeopardizing domestic industry, and reduce tariffs only as necessary to promote exports in accord with the 'needs of various branches of American production.' A most favored nation clause was also included.

a. Patent Law Treaty
b. Long service leave
c. Kaldor-Hicks efficiency
d. Reciprocal Trade Agreements Act

62. The _____ commenced in September 1986 and continued until April 1994. The round, based on the General Agreement on Tariffs and Trade (GATT) ministerial meeting in Geneva (1982), was launched in Punta del Este in Uruguay (hence the name), followed by negotiations in Montreal, Geneva, Brussels, Washington, D.C., and Tokyo, with the 20 agreements finally being signed in Marrakech - the Marrakesh Agreement. The Round transformed the GATT into the World Trade Organization.

a. AD-IA Model
b. ACEA agreement
c. Uruguay Round
d. ACCRA Cost of Living Index

63. The _____ is an important selective, mainly private, international organization designed by its founders to supervise and liberalize international trade. The organization officially commenced on 1 January 1995, under the Marrakesh Agreement, succeeding the 1947 General Agreement on Tariffs and Trade (GATT.)

The _____ deals with regulation of trade between participating countries; it provides a framework for negotiating and formalising trade agreements, and a dispute resolution process aimed at enforcing participants' adherence to _____ agreements which are signed by representatives of member governments and ratified by their parliaments.

a. 2009 G-20 London summit protests
b. Backus-Kehoe-Kydland consumption correlation puzzle
c. Bio-energy village
d. World Trade Organization

64. The _____ is a trilateral trade bloc in North America created by the governments of the United States, Canada, and Mexico. The agreement creating the trade bloc came into force on January 1, 1994. It superseded the Canada-United States Free Trade Agreement between the U.S. and Canada.

a. Demand-side technologies
b. Federal Reserve Bank Notes
c. North American Free Trade Agreement
d. Case-Shiller Home Price Indices

65. In a _____ there is both a monopoly (a single seller) and monopsony (a single buyer) in the same market.

In such market price and output will be determined by the non economic forces like bargaining power of both buyer and seller. A _____ model is often used in situations where the switching costs of both sides are prohibitively high.

a. Market concentration
b. Revenue-cap regulation
c. Price takers
d. Bilateral monopoly

Chapter 5. The United States in the Global Economy

66. _____ is a type of trade policy that allows traders to act and transact without interference from government. Thus, the policy permits trading partners mutual gains from trade, with goods and services produced according to the theory of comparative advantage.

Under a _____ policy, prices are a reflection of true supply and demand, and are the sole determinant of resource allocation.

a. 130-30 fund
c. 1921 recession
b. 100-year flood
d. Free trade

67. A _____ is crossing the border without being taxed for it.

A _____ or export processing zone (EPZ) is one or more special areas of a country where some normal trade barriers such as tariffs and quotas are eliminated and bureaucratic requirements are lowered in hopes of attracting new business and foreign investments. It is a a region where a group of countries has agreed to reduce or eliminate trade barriers.

a. Heckscher-Ohlin model
c. Free trade zone
b. Competitiveness
d. Most favoured nation

68. In economics, a _____ exists when a specific individual or enterprise has sufficient control over a particular product or service to determine significantly the terms on which other individuals shall have access to it. Monopolies are thus characterized by a lack of economic competition for the good or service that they provide and a lack of viable substitute goods. The verb 'monopolize' refers to the process by which a firm gains persistently greater market share than what is expected under perfect competition.

a. 130-30 fund
c. 100-year flood
b. 1921 recession
d. Monopoly

69. _____ in its literal sense is the process of transformation of local or regional phenomena into global ones. It can be described as a process by which the people of the world are unified into a single society and function together.

This process is a combination of economic, technological, sociocultural and political forces.

a. Global Cosmopolitanism
c. Helsinki Process on Globalisation and Democracy
b. Globalization
d. Globally Integrated Enterprise

Chapter 6. Measuring Domestic Output and National Income

1. _____ is a broad label that refers to any individuals or households that use goods and services generated within the economy. The concept of a _____ is used in different contexts, so that the usage and significance of the term may vary.

Typically when business people and economists talk of _____s they are talking about person as _____, an aggregated commodity item with little individuality other than that expressed in the buy/not-buy decision.

a. Consumer
b. 100-year flood
c. 1921 recession
d. 130-30 fund

2. _____ are final goods specifically intended for the mass market. For instance, _____ do not include investment assets, like precious antiques, even though these antiques are final goods.

Manufactured goods are goods that have been processed by way of machinery.

a. G-20 Leaders Summit on Financial Markets and the World Economy
b. Bulgarian-American trade
c. Consumer goods
d. Fiscal stimulus plans

3. _____s is the social science that studies the production, distribution, and consumption of goods and services. The term _____s comes from the Ancient Greek oá¼°κονομῖα from oá¼¶κος (oikos, 'house') + vÏŒμος (nomos, 'custom' or 'law'), hence 'rules of the house(hold)'. Current _____ models developed out of the broader field of political economy in the late 19th century, owing to a desire to use an empirical approach more akin to the physical sciences.

a. Energy economics
b. Inflation
c. Opportunity cost
d. Economic

4. _____ refers to the actions that governments take in the economic field. It covers the systems for setting interest rates and government deficit as well as the labour market, national ownership, and many other areas of government.

Such policies are often influenced by international institutions like the International Monetary Fund or World Bank as well as political beliefs and the consequent policies of parties.

a. ACEA agreement
b. ACCRA Cost of Living Index
c. AD-IA Model
d. Economic policy

5. In economics _____s are goods that are ultimately consumed rather than used in the production of another good. For example, a car sold to a consumer is a _____; the components such as tires sold to the car manufacturer are not; they are intermediate goods used to make the _____.

When used in measures of national income and output the term _____s only includes new goods.

a. Goods and services
b. Substitute good
c. Luxury good
d. Final good

Chapter 6. Measuring Domestic Output and National Income

6. The term _____ refers to government debt, expenditures and revenues, or to finance (particularly financial revenue) in general.

- _____ deficit is the budget deficit of federal or local government
- _____ policy is the discretionary spending of governments. Contrasts with monetary policy.
- _____ year and _____ quarter are reporting periods for firms and other agencies.

a. Procter ' Gamble
c. Drawdown
b. Bucket shop
d. Fiscal

7. In economics, _____ is the use of government spending and revenue collection to influence the economy.

_____ can be contrasted with the other main type of economic policy, monetary policy, which attempts to stabilize the economy by controlling interest rates and the supply of money. The two main instruments of _____ are government spending and taxation.

a. Fiscalism
c. 100-year flood
b. Sustainable investment rule
d. Fiscal policy

8. The _____ or gross domestic income (GDI), a basic measure of an economy's economic performance, is the market value of all final goods and services produced within the borders of a nation in a year. _____ can be defined in three ways, all of which are conceptually identical. First, it is equal to the total expenditures for all final goods and services produced within the country in a stipulated period of time (usually a 365-day year.)

a. Countercyclical
c. Gross domestic product
b. Market structure
d. Monopolistic competition

9. The _____ or the output gap is the difference between potential GDP and actual GDP or actual output. The calculation for the output gap is Y-Y* where Y* is potential output and Y is actual output. If this calculation yields a positive number it is called an expansionary gap and indicates an economy in expansion; if the calculation yields a negative number it is called a recessionary gap and indicates an economy in recession.

a. 1921 recession
c. 130-30 fund
b. 100-year flood
d. GDP gap

10. _____ is an adjective used to describe an object or system consisting of multiple items having a large number of structural variations. It is the opposite of homogeneous, which means that an object or system consists of multiple identical items. The term is often used in a scientific (such as a kind of catalyst), mathematical, sociological or statistical context.

a. 100-year flood
c. 1921 recession
b. 130-30 fund
d. Heterogeneous

11. _____ or producer goods are goods used as inputs in the production of other goods, such as partly finished goods. They are goods used in production of final goods. A firm may make then use _____, or make then sell, or buy then use them.

Chapter 6. Measuring Domestic Output and National Income

a. Inflation adjustment
c. Economic forecasting
b. Income distribution
d. Intermediate goods

12. _____ is the process by which the government, central bank (ii) availability of money, and (iii) cost of money or rate of interest, in order to attain a set of objectives oriented towards the growth and stability of the economy. Monetary theory provides insight into how to craft optimal _____.

_____ is referred to as either being an expansionary policy where an expansionary policy increases the total supply of money in the economy, and a contractionary policy decreases the total money supply.

a. 130-30 fund
c. Monetary policy
b. 1921 recession
d. 100-year flood

13. A variety of measures of _____ and output are used in economics to estimate total economic activity in a country or region, including gross domestic product (GDP), gross national product (GNP), and net _____

There are three main ways of calculating these numbers; the output approach, the income approach and the expenditure approach. In theory, the three must yield the same, because total expenditures on goods and services must equal the total income paid to the producers (Gnational income), and that must also equal the total value of the output of goods and services (GNP.)

a. Volume index
c. GNI per capita
b. Gross world product
d. National Income

14. _____ use double-entry accounting to report the monetary value and sources of output produced in a country and the distribution of incomes that production generates. Data are available at the national and industry levels.

The NIPA summarizes national income on the left (debit, revenue) side and national product on the right (credit, expense) side of a two-column accounting report.

a. Net national product
c. Gross private domestic investment
b. Current account
d. National Income and Product Accounts

15. The _____ consists of a number of economic theories which describe the nature of the firm, company including its existence, its behaviour, and its relationship with the market.

In simplified terms, the _____ aims to answer these questions:

1. Existence - why do firms emerge, why are not all transactions in the economy mediated over the market?
2. Boundaries - why the boundary between firms and the market is located exactly there? Which transactions are performed internally and which are negotiated on the market?
3. Organization - why are firms structured in such specific way? What is the interplay of formal and informal relationships?

Despite looking simple, these questions are not answered by the established economic theory, which usually views firms as given, and treats them as black boxes without any internal structure.

The First World War period saw a change of emphasis in economic theory away from industry-level analysis which mainly included analysing markets to analysis at the level of the firm, as it became increasingly clear that perfect competition was no longer an adequate model of how firms behaved. Economic theory till then had focussed on trying to understand markets alone and there had been little study on understanding why firms or organisations exist.

   a. Theory of the firm
   c. Policy Ineffectiveness Proposition
   b. Technology gap
   d. Khazzoom-Brookes postulate

16. A _____ is an object whose consumption increases the utility of the consumer, for which the quantity demanded exceeds the quantity supplied at zero price. _____s are usually modeled as having diminishing marginal utility. The first individual purchase has high utility; the second has less.
   a. Good
   c. Merit good
   b. Composite good
   d. Pie method

17. _____ in economics and business is the result of an exchange and from that trade we assign a numerical monetary value to a good, service or asset. If Alice trades Bob 4 apples for an orange, the _____ of an orange is 4 apples. Inversely, the _____ of an apple is 1/4 oranges.
   a. Premium pricing
   c. Price book
   b. Price war
   d. Price

18. A _____ is a normalized average (typically a weighted average) of prices for a given class of goods or services in a given region, during a given interval of time. It is a statistic designed to help to compare how these prices, taken as a whole, differ between time periods or geographical locations.

Price indices have several potential uses.

   a. Price index
   c. Product sabotage
   b. Transactional Net Margin Method
   d. Two-part tariff

19. _____ is the a method of technical and economic research of the systems for purpose to optimize a parity between system's consumer functions or properties and expenses to achieve those functions or properties.

This methodology for continuous perfection of production, industrial technologies, organizational structures was developed by Juryj Sobolev in 1948 at the 'Perm telephone factory'

- 1948 Juryj Sobolev - the first success in application of a method analysis at the 'Perm telephone factory' .
- 1949 - the first application for the invention as result of use of the new method.

Chapter 6. Measuring Domestic Output and National Income

Today in economically developed countries practically each enterprise or the company use methodology of the kind of functional-cost analysis as a practice of the quality management, most full satisfying to principles of standards of series ISO 9000.

- Interest of consumer not in products itself, but the advantage which it will receive from its usage.
- The consumer aspires to reduce his expenses
- Functions needed by consumer can be executed in the various ways, and, hence, with various efficiency and expenses. Among possible alternatives of realization of functions exist such in which the parity of quality and the price is the optimal for the consumer.

The goal of _____ is achievement of the highest consumer satisfaction of production at simultaneous decrease in all kinds of industrial expenses Classical _____ has three English synonyms - Value Engineering, Value Management, Value Analysis.

a. Monopoly wage
c. Function cost analysis
b. Staple financing
d. Willingness to pay

20. A _____ is a public market for the trading of company stock and derivatives at an agreed price; these are securities listed on a stock exchange as well as those only traded privately.

The size of the world _____ was estimated at about $36.6 trillion US at the beginning of October 2008 . The total world derivatives market has been estimated at about $791 trillion face or nominal value, 11 times the size of the entire world economy.

a. Adolf Hitler
c. Adam Smith
b. Stock market
d. Adolph Fischer

21. _____ refers to the additional value of a commodity over the cost of commodities used to produce it from the previous stage of production. An example is the price of gasoline at the pump over the price of the oil in it. In national accounts used in macroeconomics, it refers to the contribution of the factors of production, i.e., land, labor, and capital goods, to raising the value of a product and corresponds to the incomes received by the owners of these factors.

a. Solow residual
c. Hodrick-Prescott filter
b. Value added
d. Full employment

22. A _____ is an event or condition under the contract between a buyer and a seller to exchange an asset for payment. In accounting, it is recognized by an entry in the books of account. It involves a change in the status of the finances of two or more businesses or individuals.

a. Negative gearing
c. Present value of costs
b. Financial transaction
d. Biflation

23. A _____ is the transfer of wealth from one party (such as a person or company) to another. A _____ is usually made in exchange for the provision of goods, services or both, or to fulfill a legal obligation.

The simplest and oldest form of _____ is barter, the exchange of one good or service for another.

| a. Social gravity | b. Going concern |
| c. Soft count | d. Payment |

24. In economics, a _____ is a redistribution of income in the market system. These payments are considered to be nonexhaustive because they do not directly absorb resources or create output. Examples of certain _____s include welfare (financial aid), social security, and government subsidies for certain businesses (firms.)
   a. 1921 recession
   b. 130-30 fund
   c. 100-year flood
   d. Transfer payment

25. _____ or consumer demand or consumption is also known as personal consumption expenditure. It is the largest part of aggregate demand or effective demand at the macroeconomic level. There are two variants of consumption in the aggregate demand model, including induced consumption and autonomous consumption.
   a. Consumer spending
   b. Complex multiplier
   c. Potential output
   d. Dishoarding

26. In economics, a _____ or a hard good is a good which does not quickly wear out it yields services or utility over time rather than being completely used up when used once. Most goods are therefore _____s to a certain degree. These are goods that can last for a relatively long time, such as refrigerators, cars, and DVD players.
   a. Luxury good
   b. Search good
   c. Superior goods
   d. Durable good

27. _____ is a specific term used in companies' financial reporting from the company-whole point of view. Because that use excludes the effects of changing ownership interest, an economic measure of _____ is necessary for financial analysis from the shareholders' point of view

_____ is defined by the Financial Accounting Standards Board, or FASB, as e;the change in equity [net assets] of a business enterprise during a period from transactions and other events and circumstances from nonowner sources. It includes all changes in equity during a period except those resulting from investments by owners and distributions to owners.e;

_____ is the sum of net income and other items that must bypass the income statement because they have not been realized, including items like an unrealized holding gain or loss from available for sale securities and foreign currency translation gains or losses.

   a. Windfall gain
   b. Real income
   c. Net national income
   d. Comprehensive income

28. _____ is the measure of investment used to compute GDP. This is an important component of GDP because it provides an indicator of the future productive capacity of the economy. It includes replacement purchases plus net additions to capital assets plus investments in inventories.
   a. Current account
   b. National Income and Product Accounts
   c. Compensation of employees
   d. Gross private domestic investment

29. The _____ is one of three major groups of methodologies, called valuation approaches, used by appraisers. It is particularly common in commercial real estate appraisal and in business appraisal. The fundamental math is similar to the methods used for financial valuation, securities analysis, or bond pricing.

Chapter 6. Measuring Domestic Output and National Income

a. Income approach
b. ACCRA Cost of Living Index
c. ACEA agreement
d. Urban growth boundary

30. The _____ is the component statistic for consumption in GDP collected by the BEA. It consists of the actual and imputed expenditures of households and includes data pertaining to durable and non-durable goods, and services. It is essentially a measure of goods and services targeted towards individuals and consumed by individuals.
   a. Hemline index
   b. Real gross domestic product
   c. Personal consumption expenditure
   d. State Domestic Product

31. _____ is a common concept in economics, and gives rise to derived concepts such as consumer debt. Generally _____ is defined by opposition to production. But the precise definition can vary because different schools of economists define production quite differently.
   a. Foreclosure data providers
   b. Federal Reserve Bank Notes
   c. Cash or share options
   d. Consumption

32. _____ refers to a business or organization attempting to acquire goods or services to accomplish the goals of the enterprise. Though there are several organizations that attempt to set standards in the _____ process, processes can vary greatly between organizations. Typically the word '_____' is not used interchangeably with the word 'procurement', since procurement typically includes Expediting, Supplier Quality, and Traffic and Logistics (T'L) in addition to _____.
   a. 130-30 fund
   b. Free port
   c. 100-year flood
   d. Purchasing

33. _____ is a term used in accounting, economics and finance to spread the cost of an asset over the span of several years.

In simple words we can say that _____ is the reduction in the value of an asset due to usage, passage of time, wear and tear, technological outdating or obsolescence, depletion, inadequacy, rot, rust, decay or other such factors.

In accounting, _____ is a term used to describe any method of attributing the historical or purchase cost of an asset across its useful life, roughly corresponding to normal wear and tear.

   a. Salvage value
   b. Historical cost
   c. Net income per employee
   d. Depreciation

34. The _____ was a worldwide economic downturn starting in most places in 1929 and ending at different times in the 1930s or early 1940s for different countries. It was the largest and most important economic depression in the 20th century, and is used in the 21st century as an example of how far the world's economy can fall. The _____ originated in the United States; historians most often use as a starting date the stock market crash on October 29, 1929, known as Black Tuesday.
   a. British Empire Economic Conference
   b. Jarrow March
   c. Great Depression
   d. Wall Street Crash of 1929

35. In economics, _____ refers to an activity of spending which increases the availability of fixed capital goods or means of production. It is the total spending on new fixed investment minus replacement investment, which simply replaces depreciated capital goods.

a. Lehman Formula
b. Net investment
c. Greenfield investment
d. Tangible investments

36. _____ is a social science concept used in business, economics, organizational behaviour, political science, public health and sociology that refers to connections within and between social networks. Though there are a variety of related definitions, which have been described as 'something of a cure-all' for the problems of modern society, they tend to share the core idea 'that social networks have value. Just as a screwdriver (physical capital) or a college education (human capital) can increase productivity (both individual and collective), so do social contacts affect the productivity of individuals and groups'.

a. Diversity training
b. Pre-industrial society
c. Social capital
d. Social inequality

Chapter 6. Measuring Domestic Output and National Income

37. A _____ is:

- Rewrite _____, in generative grammar and computer science
- Standardization, a formal and widely-accepted statement, fact, definition, or qualification
- Operation, a determinate _____ for performing a mathematical operation and obtaining a certain result (Mathematics, Logic)
    - Unary operation
    - Binary operation
- _____ of inference, a function from sets of formulae to formulae (Mathematics, Logic)
- _____ of thumb, principle with broad application that is not intended to be strictly accurate or reliable for every situation. Also often simply referred to as a _____
- Moral, an atomic element of a moral code for guiding choices in human behavior
- Heuristic, a quantized '_____' which shows a tendency or probability for successful function
- A regulation, as in sports
- A Production _____, as in computer science
- Procedural law, a _____ set governing the application of laws to cases
    - A law, which may informally be called a '_____'
    - A court ruling, a decision by a court
- In the U.S. Government, a regulation mandated by Congress, but written or expanded upon by the Executive Branch.
- Norm (sociology), an informal but widely accepted _____, concept, truth, definition, or qualification (social norms, legal norms, coding norms)
- Norm (philosophy), a kind of sentence or a reason to act, feel or believe
- 'Rulership' is the concept of governance by a government:
    - Military _____, governance by a military body
    - Monastic _____, a collection of precepts that guides the life of monks or nuns in a religious order where the superior holds the place of Christ
- Slide _____

- '_____,' a song by Ayumi Hamasaki
- '_____,' a song by rapper Nas
- '_____s,' an album by the band The Whitest Boy Alive
- _____s: Pyaar Ka Superhit Formula, a 2003 Bollywood film
- ruler, an instrument for measuring lengths
- _____, a component of an astrolabe, circumferator or similar instrument
- The _____s, a bestselling self-help book
- _____ Project (Run Up-to-date Linux Everywhere), a project that aims to use up-to-date Linux software on old PCs
- _____ engine, a software system that helps managing business _____s
- Ja _____, a hip hop artist
    - R.U.L.E., a 2005 greatest hits album by rapper Ja _____
- '_____s,' a KMFDM song

a. Demand
b. Technocracy
c. Procter ' Gamble
d. Rule

Chapter 6. Measuring Domestic Output and National Income

38. In economics, _____ is a measure of national income. Basically, it is an approach to measure GDP. It is defined as the value of planned goods and services produced in an economy.
   a. Aggregate expenditure
   b. Aggregate demand
   c. Aggregation problem
   d. Aggregate supply

39. In economics, an _____ is any good or commodity, transported from one country to another country in a legitimate fashion, typically for use in trade. _____ goods or services are provided to foreign consumers by domestic producers. _____ is an important part of international trade.
   a. AD-IA Model
   b. ACCRA Cost of Living Index
   c. ACEA agreement
   d. Export

40. In economics supernormal profit _____ or pure profit or excess profits, is a profit exceeding the normal profit. Normal profit equals the opportunity cost of labour and capital, while supernormal profit is the amount exceeds the normal return from these input factors in production.

   _____ is usually generated by an oligopoly or a monopoly; however, these firms often try to hide this from the market to reduce risk of competition or antitrust investigation.

   a. Accounting profit
   b. Economic profit
   c. ACCRA Cost of Living Index
   d. Abnormal profit

41. _____ is a fee paid on borrowed assets. It is the price paid for the use of borrowed money , or, money earned by deposited funds . Assets that are sometimes lent with _____ include money, shares, consumer goods through hire purchase, major assets such as aircraft, and even entire factories in finance lease arrangements.
   a. Insolvency
   b. Internal debt
   c. Asset protection
   d. Interest

42. Economic _____ is defined as an excess distribution to any factor in a production process above that which is required to induce the factor into the process or any excess above that which is necessary to keep the factor in its current use..

   Classical Factor _____ is primarily concerned with the fee paid for the use of fixed (e.g. natural) resources. The classical definition is expressed as any excess payment above that required to induce or provide for production.

   a. 1921 recession
   b. Rent
   c. 130-30 fund
   d. 100-year flood

43. _____ is the difference between price and the costs of bringing to market whatever it is that is accounted as an enterprise (whether by harvest, extraction, manufacture, or purchase) in terms of the component costs of delivered goods and/or services and any operating or other expenses.

   A key difficulty in measuring profit is in defining costs. Pure economic monetary profits can be zero or negative even in competitive equilibrium when accounted monetized costs exceed monetized price.

a. Economic profit
b. Operating profit
c. Accounting profit
d. ACCRA Cost of Living Index

44. _____ is a term used in business accounts, tax assessments and national accounts for depreciation of fixed assets. CFC is used in preference to 'depreciation' to emphasize that fixed capital is used up in the process of generating new output; CFC may include other costs incurred in using fixed assets beyond actual depreciation charges. Normally the term applies only to producing enterprises, but sometimes it applies also to real estate assets.

a. Capital goods
b. Consumption of fixed capital
c. Modigliani-Miller theorem
d. Firm-specific infrastructure

45. _____s are payments made by a corporation to its shareholders. It is the portion of corporate profits paid out to stockholders. When a corporation earns a profit or surplus, that money can be put to two uses: it can either be re-invested in the business (called retained earnings), or it can be paid to the shareholders as a _____.

a. Dividend cover
b. Dividend yield
c. Dividend puzzle
d. Dividend

46. In economics, _____ is the difference between a company's total revenue and its opportunity costs. It is the increase in wealth that an investor has from making an investment, taking into consideration all costs associated with that investment including the opportunity cost of capital.

Profit is the factor income of the entrepreneur.

a. ACCRA Cost of Living Index
b. Operating profit
c. Accounting profit
d. Economic profit

47. In economics, the _____ is used to illustrate the idea that increases in the rate of taxation do not necessarily increase tax revenue. (For instance, whereas a 0% income tax rate will generate no revenue, neither will a 100% rate, as citizens will have no incentive to make money.) Increasing taxes beyond the peak of the curve point will decrease tax revenue.

a. 100-year flood
b. 1921 recession
c. 130-30 fund
d. Laffer curve

48. _____ is a component of the firm's opportunity costs. The time that the owner spends running the firm could be spent on running another firm. This is _____: the return the entrepreneur can expect to earn or the profit that the business owners considers necessary to make running the business worth his/her while.

a. Profit maximization
b. Normal profit
c. 100-year flood
d. Profit margin

49.

A _____ is a type of financial intermediary and a type of bank. Commercial banking is also known as business banking. It is a bank that provides checking accounts, savings accounts, and money market accounts and that accepts time deposits.

a. Bought deal
b. Commercial bank
c. Daylight overdraft
d. Lombard banking

Chapter 6. Measuring Domestic Output and National Income

50. _____ is the returns received on factors of production: rent is return on land, wages on labor, interest on capital, and profit on entrepreneurship. It is also known as Net Factor Payments (NFP.)

Part of current account with balance of trade (exports minus imports of goods and services) and net transfer payments (such as foreign aid.)

a. 100-year flood
b. Redistributive justice
c. 130-30 fund
d. Factor income

51. In economics, an _____ is any good (e.g. a commodity) or service brought into one country from another country in a legitimate fashion, typically for use in trade.It is a good that is brought in from another country for sale. _____ goods or services are provided to domestic consumers by foreign producers. An _____ in the receiving country is an export to the sending country.

a. Incoterms
b. Import quota
c. Economic integration
d. Import

52. An _____ is a tax levied on the financial income of people, corporations, or other legal entities. Various _____ systems exist, with varying degrees of tax incidence. Income taxation can be progressive, proportional, or regressive.

a. Income tax
b. AD-IA Model
c. ACCRA Cost of Living Index
d. ACEA agreement

53. In microeconomics, _____ is quite simply the conversion of inputs into outputs. It is an economic process that uses resources to create a good or service that is suitable for exchange. This can include manufacturing, storing, shipping, and packaging.

a. Solved
b. Red Guards
c. Production
d. MET

54. To _____ is to impose a financial charge or other levy upon a taxpayer by a state or the functional equivalent of a state.

_____es are also imposed by many subnational entities. _____es consist of direct _____ or indirect _____, and may be paid in money or as its labour equivalent (often but not always unpaid.)

a. Tax
b. 100-year flood
c. 130-30 fund
d. 1921 recession

55. To tax is to impose a financial charge or other levy upon a taxpayer by a state or the functional equivalent of a state.

_____ are also imposed by many subnational entities. _____ consist of direct tax or indirect tax, and may be paid in money or as its labour equivalent (often but not always unpaid.)

a. 1921 recession
b. 100-year flood
c. 130-30 fund
d. Taxes

Chapter 6. Measuring Domestic Output and National Income

56. A _____ product is a product designed for cheapness and short-term convenience rather than medium to long-term durability, with most products only intended for single use. The term is also sometimes used for products that may last several months (ex. _____ air filters) to distinguish from similar products that last indefinitely (ex.
    a. 100-year flood
    b. 130-30 fund
    c. 1921 recession
    d. Disposable

57. _____ is gross income minus income tax on that income.

Discretionary income is income after subtracting taxes and normal expenses (such as rent or mortgage, utilities, insurance, medical, transportation, property maintenance, child support, inflation, food and sundries, 'c.) to maintain a certain standard of living.

   a. Taxation as theft
   b. Stamp Act
   c. Disposable personal income
   d. Disposable income

58. The _____ equals the gross domestic product (GDP) minus depreciation on a country's capital goods.

_____ accounts for capital that has been consumed over the year in the form of housing, vehicle, or machinery deterioration. The depreciation accounted for is often referred to as capital consumption allowance and represents the amount needed in order to replace those depreciated assets.

   a. Commodity price shocks
   b. Cass criterion
   c. Carrying charge
   d. Net domestic product

59. Total _____ is defined by the United States' Bureau of Economic Analysis as

income received by persons from all sources. It includes income received from participation in production as well as from government and business transfer payments. It is the sum of compensation of employees (received), supplements to wages and salaries, proprietors' income with inventory valuation adjustment (IVA) and capital consumption adjustment (CCAdj), rental income of persons with CCAdj, _____ receipts on assets, and personal current transfer receipts, less contributions for government social insurance.

   a. Greater fool theory
   b. Bidding
   c. Personal income
   d. Dividend Discount Model

60. In economics and business, specifically cost accounting, the _____ point (BEP) is the point at which cost or expenses and revenue are equal: there is no net loss or gain, and one has 'broken even'. A profit or a loss has not been made, although opportunity costs have been paid, and capital has received the risk-adjusted, expected return.

For example, if the business sells less than 200 tables each month, it will make a loss, if it sells more, it will be a profit.

   a. Nonmarket
   b. Small numbers game
   c. Buffer stock scheme
   d. Break-even

Chapter 6. Measuring Domestic Output and National Income

61. The _____ is 'the basic residential unit in which economic production, consumption, inheritance, child rearing, and shelter are organized and carried out'; [the _____] 'may or may not be synonomous with family'.

The _____ is the basic unit of analysis in many social, microeconomic and government models. The term refers to all individuals who live in the same dwelling.

a. Household
c. 130-30 fund
b. Family economics
d. 100-year flood

62. In economics, the term _____ of income or _____ refers to a simple economic model which describes the reciprocal circulation of income between producers and consumers. In the _____ model, the inter-dependent entities of producer and consumer are referred to as 'firms' and 'households' respectively and provide each other with factors in order to facilitate the flow of income. Firms provide consumers with goods and services in exchange for consumer expenditure and 'factors of production' from households.

a. 100-year flood
c. 1921 recession
b. Circular flow
d. 130-30 fund

63. The _____ was an evolution of developed countries from an industrial/manufacturing-based wealth producing economy into a service sector asset based economy, brought about by globalization and currency manipulation by governments and their central banks. Some analysts claimed that this change in the economic structure of the United States had created a state of permanent steady growth, low unemployment, and immunity to boom and bust macroeconomic cycles. They believed that the change rendered obsolete many business practices.

a. 100-year flood
c. New Economy
b. 130-30 fund
d. 1921 recession

64. The term _____ or commodity bundle refers to a fixed list of items used specifically to track the progress of inflation in an economy or specific market.

The most common type of _____ is the basket of consumer goods, used to define the Consumer Price Index (CPI.) Other types of baskets are used to define

- Producer Price Index (PPI), previously known as Wholesale Price Index (WPI)
- various commodity price indices

The term _____ analysis in the retail business refers to research that provides the retailer with information to understand the purchase behaviour of a buyer. This information will enable the retailer to understand the buyer's needs and rewrite the store's layout accordingly, develop cross-promotional programs, or even capture new buyers (much like the cross-selling concept.)

a. Cost-weighted activity index
c. Robin Hood index
b. Category Development Index
d. Market basket

65. An _____, in economics, is the amount by which the real Gross domestic product exceeds potential GDP. The real GDP is also known as GDP 'adjusted for inflation', 'constant prices' GDP or 'constant dollar' GDP, because it measures the aggregate output in a country's income accounts in a given year, expressed in base-year prices. On the other hand, the potential GDP is the quantity of real GDP when a country's economy is at full-employment.

Chapter 6. Measuring Domestic Output and National Income

a. AD-IA Model
b. Inflationary gap
c. ACEA agreement
d. ACCRA Cost of Living Index

66. In economics, _____ is the total demand for final goods and services in the economy (Y) at a given time and price level. It is the amount of goods and services in the economy that will be purchased at all possible price levels. This is the demand for the gross domestic product of a country when inventory levels are static.
a. Aggregation problem
b. Aggregate demand
c. Aggregate supply
d. Aggregate expenditure

67. A _____ is a measure of the average price of consumer goods and services purchased by households. A _____ measures a price change for a constant market basket of goods and services from one period to the next within the same area (city, region, or nation.) It is a price index determined by measuring the price of a standard group of goods meant to represent the typical market basket of a typical urban consumer.
a. Consumer price index
b. CPI
c. Cost-of-living index
d. Lipstick index

68. Economics:

- _____, the desire to own something and the ability to pay for it
- _____ curve, a graphic representation of a _____ schedule
- _____ deposit, the money in checking accounts
- _____ pull theory, the theory that inflation occurs when _____ for goods and services exceeds existing supplies
- _____ schedule, a table that lists the quantity of a good a person will buy it each different price
- _____ side economics, the school of economics at believes government spending and tax cuts open economy by raising _____

a. McKesson ' Robbins scandal
b. Production
c. Variability
d. Demand

69. In economics, economic output is divided into physical goods and intangible services. Consumption of _____ is assumed to produce utility. It is often used when referring to a _____ Tax.
a. Composite good
b. Private good
c. Manufactured goods
d. Goods and services

70. _____ is a macroeconomic measure of the size of an economy adjusted for price changes and inflation. It measures in constant prices the output of final goods and services and incomes within an economy. The formula for its definition is [(Nominal GDP)/(GDP deflator)] x 100, however, it is not calculated in this way.
a. Gross world product
b. TED spread
c. Bureau of Labor Statistics
d. Real Gross Domestic Product

71. In economics, a _____ or reference period is a point in time used as a reference point for comparison with other periods. It is generally used as a benchmark for measuring financial or economic data. _____s typically provide a point of reference for economic studies, consumer demand, and unemployment benefit claims.

a. Blue collar and service occupations
b. Cost-minimization
c. Demand for money
d. Base period

72. CÄ"terÄ«s paribus is a Latin phrase, literally translated as 'with other things the same.' It is commonly rendered in English as 'all other things being equal.' A prediction, or a statement about causal or logical connections between two states of affairs, is qualified by _____ in order to acknowledge, and to rule out, the possibility of other factors which could override the relationship between the antecedent and the consequent.

A _____ assumption is often fundamental to the predictive purpose of scientific inquiry. In order to formulate scientific laws, it is usually necessary to rule out factors which interfere with examining a specific causal relationship.

a. Dematerialization
b. Capital outflow
c. Friedman-Savage utility function
d. Ceteris paribus

73. _____ is the price at which an asset would trade in a competitive Walrasian auction setting. _____ is often used interchangeably with open _____, fair value or fair _____, although these terms have distinct definitions in different standards, and may differ in some circumstances.

International Valuation Standards defines _____ as 'the estimated amount for which a property should exchange on the date of valuation between a willing buyer and a willing seller in an arm's-length transaction after proper marketing wherein the parties had each acted knowledgeably, prudently, and without compulsion.'

_____ is a concept distinct from market price, which is 'the price at which one can transact', while _____ is 'the true underlying value' according to theoretical standards.

a. Personal financial management
b. Netting
c. Secured loan
d. Market value

74. _____ refers to internal and external organizing and correcting factors that provide order to market and other types of societal institutions and organizations - economic, political, social and cultural - so that they may function efficiently and effectively as well as repair their failures.

The expression _____ is increasingly found in the title, abstract and text of articles, chapters and papers in the business, management, organization, strategy, social-issues, political-science and sociology literatures. The ABI/Inform Global source located 1748 such uses of both expressions in October 2008, compared with 31 in 1991 and 247 in 2002.

a. Private Benefits of Control
b. Positive statement
c. Total revenue
d. Nonmarket

75. In law and economics, the _____, describes the economic efficiency of an economic allocation or outcome in the presence of externalities. The theorem states that when trade in an externality is possible and there are no transaction costs, bargaining will lead to an efficient outcome regardless of the initial allocation of property rights. In practice, obstacles to bargaining or poorly defined property rights can prevent Coasian bargaining.

a. Means test
c. General Mining Act of 1872
b. Prior appropriation water rights
d. Coase theorem

76. The _____ or black market is a market where all commerce is conducted without regard to taxation, law or regulations of trade. The term is also often known as the underdog, shadow economy, black economy, parallel economy or phantom trades.

In modern societies the _____ covers a vast array of activities.

a. Autarky
c. Information markets
b. Information economy
d. Underground economy

77. In economics, a _____ may be either a subsidy or a price control, both with the intended effect of keeping the market price of a good higher than the competitive equilibrium level.

In the case of a price control, a _____ is the minimum legal price a seller may charge, typically placed above equilibrium. It is the support of certain price levels at or above market values by the government.

a. Payment schedule
c. Labor intensity
b. Marginal profit
d. Price support

78. A _____ is the procedure of systematically acquiring and recording information about the members of a given population. It is a regularly occurring and official count of a particular population. The term is used mostly in connection with national 'population and door to door _____es' (to be taken every 10 years according to United Nations recommendations), agriculture, and business _____es.

a. Census
c. 1921 recession
b. 130-30 fund
d. 100-year flood

79. _____ refers to the number of privately owned new homes (technically housing units) on which construction has been started in a given period. This data is divided into three types: single-family houses, townhouses or small condos, and apartment buildings with 5 or more units.

Each apartment unit is considered a single start.

a. Housing Starts
c. 130-30 fund
b. 1921 recession
d. 100-year flood

Chapter 7. Introduction to Economic Growth and Instability

1. The _____ or gross domestic income (GDI), a basic measure of an economy's economic performance, is the market value of all final goods and services produced within the borders of a nation in a year. _____ can be defined in three ways, all of which are conceptually identical. First, it is equal to the total expenditures for all final goods and services produced within the country in a stipulated period of time (usually a 365-day year.)
   a. Countercyclical
   b. Monopolistic competition
   c. Gross domestic product
   d. Market structure

2. The _____ or the output gap is the difference between potential GDP and actual GDP or actual output. The calculation for the output gap is Y-Y* where Y* is potential output and Y is actual output. If this calculation yields a positive number it is called an expansionary gap and indicates an economy in expansion; if the calculation yields a negative number it is called a recessionary gap and indicates an economy in recession.
   a. GDP gap
   b. 1921 recession
   c. 130-30 fund
   d. 100-year flood

3. In economics, _____ is a rise in the general level of prices of goods and services in an economy over a period of time. When the general price level rises, each unit of currency buys fewer goods and services; consequently, _____ is also a decline in the real value of money--a loss of purchasing power in the medium of exchange which is also the monetary unit of account in the economy. A chief measure of general price-level _____ is the general _____ rate, which is the percentage change in a general price index (normally the Consumer Price Index) over time.
   a. Inflation
   b. Economic
   c. Energy economics
   d. Opportunity cost

4. In economics, the _____ is a measure of inflation, the rate of increase of a price index (for example, a consumer price index.)It is the percentage rate of change in price level over time. The rate of decrease in the purchasing power of money is approximately equal.

It's used to calculate the real interest rate, as well as real increases in wages, and official measurements of this rate act as input variables to COLA adjustments and Inflation derivatives prices.

   a. Equity value
   b. Inflation rate
   c. Interest rate option
   d. Edgeworth paradox

5. An _____, in economics, is the amount by which the real Gross domestic product exceeds potential GDP. The real GDP is also known as GDP 'adjusted for inflation', 'constant prices' GDP or 'constant dollar' GDP, because it measures the aggregate output in a country's income accounts in a given year, expressed in base-year prices. On the other hand, the potential GDP is the quantity of real GDP when a country's economy is at full-employment.
   a. ACEA agreement
   b. ACCRA Cost of Living Index
   c. AD-IA Model
   d. Inflationary gap

Chapter 7. Introduction to Economic Growth and Instability 103

6. A _____ is:

- Rewrite _____, in generative grammar and computer science
- Standardization, a formal and widely-accepted statement, fact, definition, or qualification
- Operation, a determinate _____ for performing a mathematical operation and obtaining a certain result (Mathematics, Logic)
    - Unary operation
    - Binary operation
- _____ of inference, a function from sets of formulae to formulae (Mathematics, Logic)
- _____ of thumb, principle with broad application that is not intended to be strictly accurate or reliable for every situation. Also often simply referred to as a _____
- Moral, an atomic element of a moral code for guiding choices in human behavior
- Heuristic, a quantized '_____' which shows a tendency or probability for successful function
- A regulation, as in sports
- A Production _____, as in computer science
- Procedural law, a _____ set governing the application of laws to cases
    - A law, which may informally be called a '_____'
    - A court ruling, a decision by a court
- In the U.S. Government, a regulation mandated by Congress, but written or expanded upon by the Executive Branch.
- Norm (sociology), an informal but widely accepted _____, concept, truth, definition, or qualification (social norms, legal norms, coding norms)
- Norm (philosophy), a kind of sentence or a reason to act, feel or believe
- 'Rulership' is the concept of governance by a government:
    - Military _____, governance by a military body
    - Monastic _____, a collection of precepts that guides the life of monks or nuns in a religious order where the superior holds the place of Christ
- Slide _____

- '_____,' a song by Ayumi Hamasaki
- '_____,' a song by rapper Nas
- '_____s,' an album by the band The Whitest Boy Alive
- _____s: Pyaar Ka Superhit Formula, a 2003 Bollywood film
- ruler, an instrument for measuring lengths
- _____, a component of an astrolabe, circumferator or similar instrument
- The _____s, a bestselling self-help book
- _____ Project (Run Up-to-date Linux Everywhere), a project that aims to use up-to-date Linux software on old PCs
- _____ engine, a software system that helps managing business _____s
- Ja _____, a hip hop artist
    - R.U.L.E., a 2005 greatest hits album by rapper Ja _____
- '_____s,' a KMFDM song

a. Technocracy
c. Procter ' Gamble
b. Demand
d. Rule

7. Unemployment occurs when a person is available to work and seeking work but currently without work. The prevalence of unemployment is usually measured using the _____, which is defined as the percentage of those in the labor force who are unemployed. The _____ is also used in economic studies and economic indexes such as the United States' Conference Board's Index of Leading Indicators as a measure of the state of the macroeconomics.
   a. ACEA agreement
   b. Unemployment rate
   c. AD-IA Model
   d. ACCRA Cost of Living Index

8. In economics, _____ is the total demand for final goods and services in the economy (Y) at a given time and price level. It is the amount of goods and services in the economy that will be purchased at all possible price levels. This is the demand for the gross domestic product of a country when inventory levels are static.
   a. Aggregate supply
   b. Aggregation problem
   c. Aggregate demand
   d. Aggregate expenditure

9. _____ is a broad label that refers to any individuals or households that use goods and services generated within the economy. The concept of a _____ is used in different contexts, so that the usage and significance of the term may vary.

Typically when business people and economists talk of _____s they are talking about person as _____, an aggregated commodity item with little individuality other than that expressed in the buy/not-buy decision.

   a. 130-30 fund
   b. 1921 recession
   c. 100-year flood
   d. Consumer

10. A _____ is a measure of the average price of consumer goods and services purchased by households. A _____ measures a price change for a constant market basket of goods and services from one period to the next within the same area (city, region, or nation.) It is a price index determined by measuring the price of a standard group of goods meant to represent the typical market basket of a typical urban consumer.
    a. Lipstick index
    b. Cost-of-living index
    c. CPI
    d. Consumer price index

11. Economics:

    - _____, the desire to own something and the ability to pay for it
    - _____ curve, a graphic representation of a _____ schedule
    - _____ deposit, the money in checking accounts
    - _____ pull theory, the theory that inflation occurs when _____ for goods and services exceeds existing supplies
    - _____ schedule, a table that lists the quantity of a good a person will buy it each different price
    - _____ side economics, the school of economics at believes government spending and tax cuts open economy by raising _____

    a. Production
    b. McKesson ' Robbins scandal
    c. Demand
    d. Variability

Chapter 7. Introduction to Economic Growth and Instability

12. _____ in economics and business is the result of an exchange and from that trade we assign a numerical monetary value to a good, service or asset. If Alice trades Bob 4 apples for an orange, the _____ of an orange is 4 apples. Inversely, the _____ of an apple is 1/4 oranges.
    a. Premium pricing
    b. Price book
    c. Price war
    d. Price

13. A _____ is a normalized average (typically a weighted average) of prices for a given class of goods or services in a given region, during a given interval of time. It is a statistic designed to help to compare how these prices, taken as a whole, differ between time periods or geographical locations.

    Price indices have several potential uses.

    a. Product sabotage
    b. Transactional Net Margin Method
    c. Two-part tariff
    d. Price index

14. The _____ or Aggregate Demand-Aggregate Supply model is a macroeconomic model that explains price level and output through the relationship of aggregate demand and aggregate supply. It was first put forth by John Maynard Keynes in his work The General Theory of Employment, Interest, and Money. It is the foundation for the modern field of macroeconomics, and is accepted by a broad array of economists, from Libertarian, Monetarist supporters of laissez-faire, such as Milton Friedman to Socialist, Post-Keynesian supporters of economic interventionism, such as Joan Robinson.
    a. Adaptive expectations
    b. Economic interdependence
    c. IS/LM model
    d. AD-AS

15. _____s is the social science that studies the production, distribution, and consumption of goods and services. The term _____s comes from the Ancient Greek οἰκονομία from οἶκος (oikos, 'house') + νόμος (nomos, 'custom' or 'law'), hence 'rules of the house(hold)'. Current _____ models developed out of the broader field of political economy in the late 19th century, owing to a desire to use an empirical approach more akin to the physical sciences.
    a. Energy economics
    b. Economic
    c. Inflation
    d. Opportunity cost

16. _____ is the increase in the amount of the goods and services produced by an economy over time. It is conventionally measured as the percent rate of increase in real gross domestic product, or real GDP. Growth is usually calculated in real terms, i.e. inflation-adjusted terms, in order to net out the effect of inflation on the price of the goods and services produced.
    a. AD-IA Model
    b. Economic growth
    c. ACEA agreement
    d. ACCRA Cost of Living Index

17. The term _____s refers to wages that have been adjusted for inflation. This term is used in contrast to nominal wages or unadjusted wages.

    The use of adjusted figures is in undertaking some form of economic analysis.

    a. Real wage
    b. Federal Wage System
    c. Profit sharing
    d. Living wage

Chapter 7. Introduction to Economic Growth and Instability

18. _____ is a misspelled phrase from Latin 'pro capite' phrase meaning per head with pro meaning 'per' or 'for each' and capite meaning 'head.' Both words together equate to the phrase 'for each head.'

It is usually used in the field of statistics to indicate the average per person for any given concern, such as income, crime rate, etc.

It is also used in wills to indicate that each of the named beneficiaries should receive, by devise or bequest, equal shares of the estate. This is in contrast to a per stirpes division, in which each branch of the inheriting family inherits an equal share of the estate.

a. Population statistics
b. False positive rate
c. Per capita
d. Sargan test

19. _____ is a macroeconomic measure of the size of an economy adjusted for price changes and inflation. It measures in constant prices the output of final goods and services and incomes within an economy. The formula for its definition is [(Nominal GDP)/(GDP deflator)] x 100, however, it is not calculated in this way.

a. Gross world product
b. Real Gross Domestic Product
c. Bureau of Labor Statistics
d. TED spread

20. _____ is the term denoting either an entrance or changes which are inserted into a system and which activate/modify a process. It is an abstract concept, used in the modeling, system(s) design and system(s) exploitation. It is usually connected with other terms, e.g., _____ field, _____ variable, _____ parameter, _____ value, _____ signal, _____ device and _____ file.

a. AD-IA Model
b. ACCRA Cost of Living Index
c. ACEA agreement
d. Input

21. In calculus, a function f defined on a subset of the real numbers with real values is called _____, if for all x and y such that x >≤ y one has f(x) >≤ f(y), so f preserves the order. In layman's terms, the sign of the slope is always positive (the curve tending upwards) or zero (i.e., non-decreasing, or asymptotic, or depicted as a horizontal, flat line) Likewise, a function is called monotonically decreasing (non-increasing) if, whenever x >≤ y, then f(x) >≥ f(y), so it reverses the order.

a. 130-30 fund
b. 100-year flood
c. 1921 recession
d. Monotonic

22. In statistics, _____ has two related meanings:

- the arithmetic _____
- the expected value of a random variable, which is also called the population _____.

It is sometimes stated that the '_____' _____s average. This is incorrect if '_____' is taken in the specific sense of 'arithmetic _____' as there are different types of averages: the _____, median, and mode. Other simple statistical analyses use measures of spread, such as range, interquartile range, or standard deviation. For a real-valued random variable X, the _____ is the expectation of X. Note that not every probability distribution has a defined _____ (or variance); see the Cauchy distribution for an example.

a. 1921 recession
b. Mean
c. 100-year flood
d. 130-30 fund

23. In economics, a _____ may be either a subsidy or a price control, both with the intended effect of keeping the market price of a good higher than the competitive equilibrium level.

In the case of a price control, a _____ is the minimum legal price a seller may charge, typically placed above equilibrium. It is the support of certain price levels at or above market values by the government.

a. Marginal profit
b. Labor intensity
c. Payment schedule
d. Price support

24. _____ in economics refers to metrics and measures of output from production processes, per unit of input. Labor _____, for example, is typically measured as a ratio of output per labor-hour, an input. _____ may be conceived of as a metrics of the technical or engineering efficiency of production.

a. Fordism
b. Productivity
c. Piece work
d. Production-possibility frontier

25. The term _____ refers to economy-wide fluctuations in production or economic activity over several months or years. These fluctuations occur around a long-term growth trend, and typically involve shifts over time between periods of relatively rapid economic growth (expansion or boom), and periods of relative stagnation or decline (contraction or recession.)

These fluctuations are often measured using the growth rate of real gross domestic product.

a. Tobit model
b. Business cycle
c. Consumer theory
d. Nominal value

26. _____ and Keynesian Theory) is a macroeconomic theory based on the ideas of 20th-century British economist John Maynard Keynes. _____ argues that private sector decisions sometimes lead to inefficient macroeconomic outcomes and therefore advocates active policy responses by the public sector, including monetary policy actions by the central bank and fiscal policy actions by the government to stabilize output over the business cycle.

The theories forming the basis of _____ were first presented in The General Theory of Employment, Interest and Money, published in 1936.

a. Deflation
b. Rational choice theory
c. Market failure
d. Keynesian economics

27. In economics, a _____ is a general slowdown in economic activity over a sustained period of time, or a business cycle contraction. During _____s, many macroeconomic indicators vary in a similar way. Production as measured by Gross Domestic Product (GDP), employment, investment spending, capacity utilization, household incomes and business profits all fall during _____s.

a. Recession
b. Treasury View
c. Leading indicators
d. Monetary economics

Chapter 7. Introduction to Economic Growth and Instability

28. _____ is a type of inflation caused by substantial increases in the cost of important goods or services where no suitable alternative is available. A situation that has been often cited of this was the oil crisis of the 1970s, which some economists see as a major cause of the inflation experienced in the Western world in that decade. It is argued that this inflation resulted from increases in the cost of petroleum imposed by the member states of OPEC.

   a. Chronic inflation
   b. Headline inflation
   c. Mundell-Tobin effect
   d. Cost-push inflation

29. A _____ product is a product designed for cheapness and short-term convenience rather than medium to long-term durability, with most products only intended for single use. The term is also sometimes used for products that may last several months (ex. _____ air filters) to distinguish from similar products that last indefinitely (ex.

   a. 1921 recession
   b. 100-year flood
   c. 130-30 fund
   d. Disposable

30. _____ is gross income minus income tax on that income.

Discretionary income is income after subtracting taxes and normal expenses (such as rent or mortgage, utilities, insurance, medical, transportation, property maintenance, child support, inflation, food and sundries, 'c.) to maintain a certain standard of living.

   a. Stamp Act
   b. Taxation as theft
   c. Disposable income
   d. Disposable personal income

31. In economics, a _____ or a hard good is a good which does not quickly wear out it yields services or utility over time rather than being completely used up when used once. Most goods are therefore _____s to a certain degree. These are goods that can last for a relatively long time, such as refrigerators, cars, and DVD players.

   a. Search good
   b. Luxury good
   c. Superior goods
   d. Durable good

32. The _____ was a worldwide economic downturn starting in most places in 1929 and ending at different times in the 1930s or early 1940s for different countries. It was the largest and most important economic depression in the 20th century, and is used in the 21st century as an example of how far the world's economy can fall. The _____ originated in the United States; historians most often use as a starting date the stock market crash on October 29, 1929, known as Black Tuesday.

   a. British Empire Economic Conference
   b. Great Depression
   c. Jarrow March
   d. Wall Street Crash of 1929

33. The _____ is 'the basic residential unit in which economic production, consumption, inheritance, child rearing, and shelter are organized and carried out'; [the _____] 'may or may not be synonomous with family'.

The _____ is the basic unit of analysis in many social, microeconomic and government models. The term refers to all individuals who live in the same dwelling.

   a. Household
   b. Family economics
   c. 130-30 fund
   d. 100-year flood

Chapter 7. Introduction to Economic Growth and Instability

34. In economics, _____ is the total amount of money available in an economy at a particular point in time. There are several ways to define 'money', but standard measures usually include currency in circulation and demand deposits.

_____ data are recorded and published, usually by the government or the central bank of the country.

a. Velocity of money
c. Veil of money
b. Neutrality of money
d. Money supply

35. A variety of measures of _____ and output are used in economics to estimate total economic activity in a country or region, including gross domestic product (GDP), gross national product (GNP), and net _____

There are three main ways of calculating these numbers; the output approach, the income approach and the expenditure approach. In theory, the three must yield the same, because total expenditures on goods and services must equal the total income paid to the producers (Gnational income), and that must also equal the total value of the output of goods and services (GNP.)

a. GNI per capita
c. National income
b. Volume index
d. Gross world product

36. In a _____ there is both a monopoly (a single seller) and monopsony (a single buyer) in the same market.

In such market price and output will be determined by the non economic forces like bargaining power of both buyer and seller. A _____ model is often used in situations where the switching costs of both sides are prohibitively high.

a. Market concentration
c. Bilateral monopoly
b. Revenue-cap regulation
d. Price takers

37. In economics and business, specifically cost accounting, the _____ point (BEP) is the point at which cost or expenses and revenue are equal: there is no net loss or gain, and one has 'broken even'. A profit or a loss has not been made, although opportunity costs have been paid, and capital has received the risk-adjusted, expected return.

For example, if the business sells less than 200 tables each month, it will make a loss, if it sells more, it will be a profit.

a. Small numbers game
c. Break-even
b. Nonmarket
d. Buffer stock scheme

38. Necessary _____s:

If x is a necessary _____ of y, then the presence of y necessarily implies the presence of x. The presence of x, however, does not imply that y will occur.

Sufficient _____s:

If x is a sufficient _____ of y, then the presence of x necessarily implies the presence of y.

a. Political philosophy
b. Materialism
c. Philosophy of economics
d. Cause

39. A _____ is an object whose consumption increases the utility of the consumer, for which the quantity demanded exceeds the quantity supplied at zero price. _____s are usually modeled as having diminishing marginal utility. The first individual purchase has high utility; the second has less.

a. Merit good
b. Pie method
c. Composite good
d. Good

40. In economics, the _____ market is a hypothetical market that brings savers and borrowers together, also bringing together the money available in commercial banks and lending institutions available for firms and households to finance expenditures, either investments or consumption. Savers supply the _____; for instance, buying bonds will transfer their money to the institution issuing the bond, which can be a firm or government. In return, borrowers demand _____; when an institution sells a bond, it is demanding _____.

a. Loanable funds
b. Buffer stock scheme
c. Reservation wage
d. Spatial inequality

41. In economics, a _____ exists when a specific individual or enterprise has sufficient control over a particular product or service to determine significantly the terms on which other individuals shall have access to it. Monopolies are thus characterized by a lack of economic competition for the good or service that they provide and a lack of viable substitute goods. The verb 'monopolize' refers to the process by which a firm gains persistently greater market share than what is expected under perfect competition.

a. 1921 recession
b. 100-year flood
c. 130-30 fund
d. Monopoly

42. The _____, a unit of the United States Department of Labor, is the principal fact-finding agency for the U.S. government in the broad field of labor economics and statistics. The BLS is an independent national statistical agency that collects, processes, analyzes, and disseminates essential statistical data to the American public, the U.S. Congress, other Federal agencies, State and local governments, business, and labor representatives. The BLS also serves as a statistical resource to the Department of Labor.

a. Gross world product
b. Gross national product
c. Bureau of Labor Statistics
d. Gross Regional Product

43. In economics, the people in the _____ are the suppliers of labor. The _____ is all the nonmilitary people who are employed or unemployed. In 2005, the worldwide _____ was over 3 billion people.

a. Grenelle agreements
b. Distributed workforce
c. Departmentalization
d. Labor force

Chapter 7. Introduction to Economic Growth and Instability

44. In economics, a _____ is a person of legal employment age who is not actively seeking employment. This is usually due to the fact that an individual has given up looking or has had no success in finding a job, hence the term 'discouraged.' Their belief may derive from a variety of factors including: a shortage of jobs in their locality or line of work; perceived discrimination for reasons such as age, race, sex and religion; a lack of necessary skills, training or experience; or, a chronic illness or disability. Some _____s, however, are voluntarily unemployed such as stay-at-home parents, pregnant mothers, and will beneficiaries.

   a. Hedonimetry
   b. Demand side economics
   c. Relative income hypothesis
   d. Discouraged worker

45. _____ is the a method of technical and economic research of the systems for purpose to optimize a parity between system's consumer functions or properties and expenses to achieve those functions or properties.

This methodology for continuous perfection of production, industrial technologies, organizational structures was developed by Juryj Sobolev in 1948 at the 'Perm telephone factory'

- 1948 Juryj Sobolev - the first success in application of a method analysis at the 'Perm telephone factory' .
- 1949 - the first application for the invention as result of use of the new method.

Today in economically developed countries practically each enterprise or the company use methodology of the kind of functional-cost analysis as a practice of the quality management, most full satisfying to principles of standards of series ISO 9000.

- Interest of consumer not in products itself, but the advantage which it will receive from its usage.
- The consumer aspires to reduce his expenses
- Functions needed by consumer can be executed in the various ways, and, hence, with various efficiency and expenses. Among possible alternatives of realization of functions exist such in which the parity of quality and the price is the optimal for the consumer.

The goal of _____ is achievement of the highest consumer satisfaction of production at simultaneous decrease in all kinds of industrial expenses Classical _____ has three English synonyms - Value Engineering, Value Management, Value Analysis.

   a. Willingness to pay
   b. Staple financing
   c. Monopoly wage
   d. Function cost analysis

46. Economists distinguish between various types of unemployment, including _____, frictional unemployment, structural unemployment and classical unemployment. Some additional types of unemployment that are occasionally mentioned are seasonal unemployment, hardcore unemployment, and hidden unemployment. Real-world unemployment may combine different types.

   a. Types of unemployment
   b. Structural unemployment
   c. Seasonal unemployment
   d. Cyclical unemployment

Chapter 7. Introduction to Economic Growth and Instability

47. Economists distinguish between various types of unemployment, including cyclical unemployment, _____, structural unemployment and classical unemployment. Some additional types of unemployment that are occasionally mentioned are seasonal unemployment, hardcore unemployment, and hidden unemployment. Real-world unemployment may combine different types.
   a. Types of unemployment
   b. Structural unemployment
   c. Seasonal unemployment
   d. Frictional unemployment

48. In macroeconomics, _____ is a condition of the national economy, where all or nearly all persons willing and able to work at the prevailing wages and working conditions are able to do so. It is defined either as 0% unemployment, literally, no unemployment (the rate of unemployment is the fraction of the work force unable to find work), as by James Tobin, or as the level of employment rates when there is no cyclical unemployment. It is defined by the majority of mainstream economists as being an acceptable level of natural unemployment above 0%, the discrepancy from 0% being due to non-cyclical types of unemployment.
   a. Demand shock
   b. Marginal propensity to consume
   c. Harrod-Johnson diagram
   d. Full employment

49. The _____ was an act signed into law on June 17, 1930, that raised U.S. tariffs on over 20,000 imported goods to record levels. In the United States 1,028 economists signed a petition against this legislation, and after it was passed, many countries retaliated with their own increased tariffs on U.S. goods, and American exports and imports were reduced by more than half.

   Although rated capacity had increased tremendously, actual output, income, and expenditure had not.

   a. Smoot-Hawley Tariff Act
   b. Loss of use
   c. Judgment summons
   d. Patent Law Treaty

50. _____ is long-term and chronic unemployment arising from imbalances between the skills and other characteristics of workers in the market and the needs of employers. It involves a mismatch between workers looking for jobs and the vacancies available often despite the number of vacancies being similar to the number of unemployed people. In this case, the unemployed workers lack the specific skills required for the jobs, or are located in a different geographical region to the vacant jobs.
   a. Seasonal unemployment
   b. Frictional unemployment
   c. Types of unemployment
   d. Structural unemployment

51. A _____ is a duty imposed on goods when they are moved across a political boundary. They are usually associated with protectionism, the economic policy of restraining trade between nations. For political reasons, _____s are usually imposed on imported goods, although they may also be imposed on exported goods.
   a. Tariff
   b. 100-year flood
   c. 1921 recession
   d. 130-30 fund

52. The Organization for Economic Co-operation and Development defines the _____ as the percentage of the working age population (ages 15 to 64 in most OECD countries) who are currently employed. According to the International Labour Organization, a person is considered employed if they have worked at least 1 hour in 'gainful' employment.
   a. Informational interview
   b. Employment rate
   c. Underemployment
   d. Encore career

53. _____ is the state of being which occurs when a person, object, or service is no longer wanted even though it may still be in good working order. _____ frequently occurs because a replacement has become available that is superior in one or more aspects. Videotapes making way for DVDs

Technical _____ may occur when a new product or technology supersedes the old, and it becomes preferred to utilize the new technology in place of the old.

a. ACCRA Cost of Living Index
b. ACEA agreement
c. Obsolescence
d. AD-IA Model

54. In economics, _____ refers to the highest level of real Gross Domestic Product output that can be sustained over the long term. The existence of a limit is due to natural and institutional constraints. If actual GDP rises and stays above _____, then (in the absence of wage and price controls) inflation tends to increase as demand exceeds supply.

a. Fundamental psychological law
b. Monetary policy reaction function
c. Monetary conditions index
d. Potential output

55. The _____ of a decision depends on both the cost of the alternative chosen and the benefit that the best alternative would have provided if chosen. _____ differs from accounting cost because it includes opportunity cost.

a. Isocost
b. Inventory analysis
c. Economic cost
d. Epstein-Zin preferences

56. An _____ is an easy accounted cost, such as wage, rent and materials. It can be transacted in the form of money payment and is lost directly, as opposed to monetary implicit costs.

a. Average fixed cost
b. Inventory valuation
c. Explicit cost
d. Average variable cost

57. The _____ is a concept of economic activity developed in particular by Milton Friedman and Edmund Phelps in the 1960s, both recipients of the Nobel prize in economics. In both cases, the development of the concept is cited as a main motivation behind the prize. It represents the hypothetical unemployment rate consistent with aggregate production being at the 'long-run' level.

a. Romer Model
b. Real Business Cycle Theory
c. Robertson lag
d. Natural rate of unemployment

58. _____ data refers to selected population characteristics as used in government, marketing or opinion research, or the _____ profiles used in such research. Note the distinction from the term 'demography' Commonly-used _____s include race, age, income, disabilities, mobility (in terms of travel time to work or number of vehicles available), educational attainment, home ownership, employment status, and even location.

a. Demographic
b. Demographic warfare
c. NEET
d. Generation Z

59. In finance, the _____ of a financial asset measures the sensitivity of the asset's price to interest rate movements. There are various definitions of _____ and derived quantities, discussed below. If not otherwise specified, '_____' generally means the Macaulay _____, as defined below.

a. Duration
b. Time value of money
c. Newtonian time
d. 100-year flood

Chapter 7. Introduction to Economic Growth and Instability

60. _____ was an Austrian-born German politician and the leader of the National Socialist German Workers Party, popularly known as the Nazi Party. He was the ruler of Germany from 1933 to 1945, serving as chancellor from 1933 to 1945 and as head of state (Führer und Reichskanzler) from 1934 to 1945.

A decorated veteran of World War I, Hitler joined the Nazi Party in 1920 and became its leader in 1921.

   a. Adolph Fischer
   c. Adam Smith
   b. Alan Greenspan
   d. Adolf Hitler

61. In mathematics, an _____ is a statement about the relative size or order of two objects, or about whether they are the same or not

- The notation a < b means that a is less than b.
- The notation a > b means that a is greater than b.
- The notation a ≠ b means that a is not equal to b, but does not say that one is greater than the other or even that they can be compared in size.

In each statement above, a is not equal to b. These relations are known as strict inequalities. The notation a < b may also be read as 'a is strictly less than b'.

   a. AD-IA Model
   c. ACCRA Cost of Living Index
   b. Inequality
   d. ACEA agreement

62. _____ refers to the actions that governments take in the economic field. It covers the systems for setting interest rates and government deficit as well as the labour market, national ownership, and many other areas of government.

Such policies are often influenced by international institutions like the International Monetary Fund or World Bank as well as political beliefs and the consequent policies of parties.

   a. Economic policy
   c. AD-IA Model
   b. ACCRA Cost of Living Index
   d. ACEA agreement

63. The term _____ refers to government debt, expenditures and revenues, or to finance (particularly financial revenue) in general.

- _____ deficit is the budget deficit of federal or local government
- _____ policy is the discretionary spending of governments. Contrasts with monetary policy.
- _____ year and _____ quarter are reporting periods for firms and other agencies.

   a. Drawdown
   c. Procter ' Gamble
   b. Fiscal
   d. Bucket shop

64. In economics, _____ is the use of government spending and revenue collection to influence the economy.

Chapter 7. Introduction to Economic Growth and Instability

_____ can be contrasted with the other main type of economic policy, monetary policy, which attempts to stabilize the economy by controlling interest rates and the supply of money. The two main instruments of _____ are government spending and taxation.

a. Sustainable investment rule
b. Fiscalism
c. 100-year flood
d. Fiscal policy

65. A _____ is the lowest hourly, daily or monthly wage that employers may legally pay to employees or workers. Equivalently, it is the lowest wage at which workers may sell their labor. Although _____ laws are in effect in a great many jurisdictions, there are differences of opinion about the benefits and drawbacks of a _____.

a. Microfoundations
b. Marginal propensity to consume
c. Permanent war economy
d. Minimum wage

66. _____ is the process by which the government, central bank (ii) availability of money, and (iii) cost of money or rate of interest, in order to attain a set of objectives oriented towards the growth and stability of the economy. Monetary theory provides insight into how to craft optimal _____.

_____ is referred to as either being an expansionary policy where an expansionary policy increases the total supply of money in the economy, and a contractionary policy decreases the total money supply.

a. 100-year flood
b. 1921 recession
c. 130-30 fund
d. Monetary policy

67. A public utility (usually just utility) is an organization that maintains the infrastructure for a public service (often also providing a service using that infrastructure.) _____ are subject to forms of public control and regulation ranging from local community-based groups to state-wide government monopolies. Common arguments in favor of regulation include the desire to control market power, facilitate competition, promote investment or system expansion, or stabilize markets.

a. 1921 recession
b. Public utilities
c. 100-year flood
d. 130-30 fund

68. _____ is exchange of capital, goods, and services across international borders or territories. In most countries, it represents a significant share of gross domestic product (GDP.) While _____ has been present throughout much of history, its economic, social, and political importance has been on the rise in recent centuries.

a. Incoterms
b. Import license
c. Intra-industry trade
d. International trade

69. The term _____ or commodity bundle refers to a fixed list of items used specifically to track the progress of inflation in an economy or specific market.

The most common type of _____ is the basket of consumer goods, used to define the Consumer Price Index (CPI.) Other types of baskets are used to define

- Producer Price Index (PPI), previously known as Wholesale Price Index (WPI)
- various commodity price indices

The term _____ analysis in the retail business refers to research that provides the retailer with information to understand the purchase behaviour of a buyer. This information will enable the retailer to understand the buyer's needs and rewrite the store's layout accordingly, develop cross-promotional programs, or even capture new buyers (much like the cross-selling concept.)

a. Cost-weighted activity index
b. Category Development Index
c. Robin Hood index
d. Market basket

70. In economics, economic output is divided into physical goods and intangible services. Consumption of _____ is assumed to produce utility. It is often used when referring to a _____ Tax.
a. Private good
b. Composite good
c. Manufactured goods
d. Goods and services

71. _____ arises when aggregate demand in an economy outpaces aggregate supply. It involves inflation rising as real gross domestic product rises and unemployment falls, as the economy moves along the Phillips curve. This is commonly described as 'too much money chasing too few goods'.
a. Demand-pull inflation
b. Kinked demand
c. Kinked demand curve
d. Marshallian demand function

72. The Federal Reserve System (also the Federal Reserve; informally The Fed) is the central banking system of the United States. Created in 1913 by the enactment of the Federal Reserve Act (signed by Woodrow Wilson), it is a quasi-public and quasi-private (government entity with private components) banking system that comprises (1) the presidentially appointed Board of Governors of the Federal Reserve System in Washington, D.C.; (2) the Federal Open Market Committee; (3) twelve regional _____ located in major cities throughout the nation acting as fiscal agents for the U.S. Treasury, each with its own nine-member board of directors; (4) numerous other private U.S. member banks, which subscribe to required amounts of non-transferable stock in their regional _____; and (5) various advisory councils. Since February 2006, Ben Bernanke has served as the Chairman of the Board of Governors of the Federal Reserve System.
a. Federal funds
b. Fed Funds Probability
c. Federal Open Market Committee
d. Federal Reserve Banks

73. A _____ is a hypothetical measure of overall prices for some set of goods and services, in a given region during a given interval, normalized relative to some base set. Typically, a _____ is approximated with a price index.

The classical dichotomy is the assumption that there is a relatively clean distinction between overall increases or decreases in prices and underlying, e;reale; economic variables.

a. Price elasticity of supply
b. Discouraged worker
c. Discretionary spending
d. Price level

74. A _____ is an event that suddenly changes the price of a commodity or service. It may be caused by a sudden increase or decrease in the supply of a particular good. This sudden change affects the equilibrium price.
a. Friedman rule
b. Demand shock
c. Supply shock
d. SIMIC

Chapter 7. Introduction to Economic Growth and Instability

75. In economics, _____ is the total supply of goods and services produced by a national economy during a specific time period. It is the total amount of goods and services in the economy available at all possible price levels.
   a. Aggregate demand
   b. Aggregation problem
   c. Aggregate expenditure
   d. Aggregate supply

76. In microeconomics, _____ is quite simply the conversion of inputs into outputs. It is an economic process that uses resources to create a good or service that is suitable for exchange. This can include manufacturing, storing, shipping, and packaging.
   a. Production
   b. Solved
   c. MET
   d. Red Guards

77. _____ is the income of individuals or nations after adjusting for inflation. It is calculated by subtracting inflation from the nominal income. Real variables, such as _____, real GDP, and real interest rate are variables that are measured in physical units, while nominal variables such as nominal income, nominal GDP, and nominal interest rate are measured in monetary units.
   a. Real income
   b. Net national income
   c. Windfall gain
   d. Family income

78. In economics, _____ is the transfer of income, wealth or property from some individuals to others.

One premise of _____ is that money should be distributed to benefit the poorer members of society, and that the rich have an obligation to assist the poor, thus creating a more financially egalitarian society. Another argument is that the rich exploit the poor or otherwise gain unfair benefits.

   a. 130-30 fund
   b. Redistribution
   c. 100-year flood
   d. 1921 recession

79. In economics, _____ is a sustained decrease in the general price level of goods and services. _____ occurs when the annual inflation rate falls below zero percent, resulting in an increase in the real value of money -- a negative inflation rate. This should not be confused with disinflation, a slow-down in the inflation rate (i.e. when the inflation decreases, but still remains positive.)
   a. Deflation
   b. Literacy rate
   c. Tobit model
   d. Price revolution

80. In economics a _____ is an entity that owes a debt to someone else. The entity may be an individual, a firm, a government, a company or other legal person. The counterparty is called a creditor.
   a. Decision process tool
   b. Senior stretch loan
   c. Duration gap
   d. Debtor

81. The _____ is the desired holding of money balances in the form of cash or bank deposits.

Money is dominated as store of value by interest bearing assets. However, money is necessary to carry out transactions, or in other words, it provides liquidity.

Chapter 7. Introduction to Economic Growth and Instability

a. Demand for money
b. Market neutral
c. Conglomerate merger
d. Borrowing base

82. In economics, the _____ is used to illustrate the idea that increases in the rate of taxation do not necessarily increase tax revenue. (For instance, whereas a 0% income tax rate will generate no revenue, neither will a 100% rate, as citizens will have no incentive to make money.) Increasing taxes beyond the peak of the curve point will decrease tax revenue.
a. Laffer curve
b. 100-year flood
c. 1921 recession
d. 130-30 fund

83. In finance and economics _____ or nominal rate of interest refers to the rate of interest before adjustment for inflation (in contrast with the real interest rate); or, for interest rates 'as stated' without adjustment for the full effect of compounding (also referred to as the nominal annual rate.) An interest rate is called nominal if the frequency of compounding (e.g. a month) is not identical to the basic time unit (normally a year.)

The real interest rate includes compensation for the lender's lost value due to inflation, whereas the _____ excludes inflation.

a. London Interbank Offered Rate
b. Fixed interest
c. Risk-free interest rate
d. Nominal interest rate

84. The '_____' is approximately the nominal interest rate minus the inflation rate Since the inflation rate over the course of a loan is not known initially, volatility in inflation represents a risk to both the lender and the borrower.

In economics and finance, an individual who lends money for repayment at a later point in time expects to be compensated for the time value of money, or not having the use of that money while it is lent.

a. Reflation
b. Real interest rate
c. Core inflation
d. Cost-push inflation

85. Bartering is a medium in which goods or services are directly exchanged for other goods and/or services, without the use of money. It can be bilateral or multilateral, and usually exists parallel to monetary systems in most developed countries, though to a very limited extent. _____ usually replaces money as the method of exchange in times of monetary crisis, when the currency is unstable and devalued by hyperinflation.
a. Meitheal
b. Community-based economics
c. New Economics Foundation
d. Barter

86. _____ is that which is owed; usually referencing assets owed, but the term can also cover moral obligations and other interactions not requiring money. In the case of assets, _____ is a means of using future purchasing power in the present before a summation has been earned. Some companies and corporations use _____ as a part of their overall corporate finance strategy.
a. Collateral Management
b. Debenture
c. Debt
d. Hard money loan

87. _____ is a fee paid on borrowed assets. It is the price paid for the use of borrowed money , or, money earned by deposited funds . Assets that are sometimes lent with _____ include money, shares, consumer goods through hire purchase, major assets such as aircraft, and even entire factories in finance lease arrangements.

Chapter 7. Introduction to Economic Growth and Instability 119

a. Asset protection
c. Internal debt

b. Insolvency
d. Interest

88. An _____ is the price a borrower pays for the use of money they do not own, for instance a small company might borrow from a bank to kick start their business, and the return a lender receives for deferring the use of funds, by lending it to the borrower. _____s are normally expressed as a percentage rate over the period of one year.

_____s targets are also a vital tool of monetary policy and are used to control variables like investment, inflation, and unemployment.

a. ACCRA Cost of Living Index
c. Enterprise value

b. Interest rate
d. Arrow-Debreu model

89. A _____ is an expression that compares quantities relative to each other. The most common examples involve two quantities, but any number of quantities can be compared. _____s are represented mathematically by separating each quantity with a colon, for example the _____ 2:3, which is read as the _____ 'two to three'.

a. Y-intercept
c. 100-year flood

b. 130-30 fund
d. Ratio

90. The reserve requirement (or required _____) is a bank regulation that sets the minimum reserves each bank must hold to customer deposits and notes. It would normally be in the form of fiat currency stored in a bank vault (vault cash), or with a central bank.

The _____ is sometimes used as a tool in the monetary policy, influencing the country's economy, borrowing, and interest rates.

a. Bank-State-Branch
c. Dividend unit

b. Reserve ratio
d. First player wins

91. The _____ is published by The Economist as an informal way of measuring the purchasing power parity (PPP) between two currencies and provides a test of the extent to which market exchange rates result in goods costing the same in different countries. It 'seeks to make exchange-rate theory a bit more digestible'.

The index takes its name from the Big Mac, a hamburger sold at McDonald's restaurants.

a. Cost-weighted activity index
c. Rank mobility index

b. Big Mac index
d. Deindexation

92. _____ or consumer demand or consumption is also known as personal consumption expenditure. It is the largest part of aggregate demand or effective demand at the macroeconomic level. There are two variants of consumption in the aggregate demand model, including induced consumption and autonomous consumption.

a. Dishoarding
c. Complex multiplier

b. Potential output
d. Consumer spending

93. In economics, _____ is inflation that is very high or 'out of control', a condition in which prices increase rapidly as a currency loses its value. Definitions used by the media vary from a cumulative inflation rate over three years approaching 100% to 'inflation exceeding 50% a month.' In informal usage the term is often applied to much lower rates. As a rule of thumb, normal inflation is reported per year, but _____ is often reported for much shorter intervals, often per month.
   a. Hyperinflation
   b. 1921 recession
   c. 100-year flood
   d. 130-30 fund

94. The _____ consists of a number of economic theories which describe the nature of the firm, company including its existence, its behaviour, and its relationship with the market.

In simplified terms, the _____ aims to answer these questions:

1. Existence - why do firms emerge, why are not all transactions in the economy mediated over the market?
2. Boundaries - why the boundary between firms and the market is located exactly there? Which transactions are performed internally and which are negotiated on the market?
3. Organization - why are firms structured in such specific way? What is the interplay of formal and informal relationships?

Despite looking simple, these questions are not answered by the established economic theory, which usually views firms as given, and treats them as black boxes without any internal structure.

The First World War period saw a change of emphasis in economic theory away from industry-level analysis which mainly included analysing markets to analysis at the level of the firm, as it became increasingly clear that perfect competition was no longer an adequate model of how firms behaved. Economic theory till then had focussed on trying to understand markets alone and there had been little study on understanding why firms or organisations exist.

   a. Technology gap
   b. Theory of the firm
   c. Policy Ineffectiveness Proposition
   d. Khazzoom-Brookes postulate

95. _____ is a common concept in economics, and gives rise to derived concepts such as consumer debt. Generally _____ is defined by opposition to production. But the precise definition can vary because different schools of economists define production quite differently.
   a. Federal Reserve Bank Notes
   b. Foreclosure data providers
   c. Cash or share options
   d. Consumption

Chapter 7. Introduction to Economic Growth and Instability 121

96. _____ is a term used to refer to certain events which occur on a Monday. It has been used in the following cases:

- _____, Dublin, 1209 - when a group of 500 recently arrived settlers from Bristol were massacred by warriors of the Gaelic O'Byrne clan. The group had left the safety of the walled city of Dublin to celebrate Easter Monday near a wood at Ranelagh, when they were attacked without warning. For centuries afterwards, this event was commemorated by a mustering of soldiers on the day as a challenge to the native tribes.
- _____, 14 April 1360 - the army of Edward III during the Hundred Years' War was struck by hailstorms, lightning and panic, causing considerable loss of life on Easter Monday.
- _____, 27 February 1865 - a 'sirocco' wind brought sandstorms to Melbourne, Australia affecting Sandhurst and Castlemaine.
- _____, 8 February 1886 - when a major protest over unemployment led to a riot in Pall Mall, London.
- _____, December 10, 1894 - when both banks of Newfoundland, Britaine;s oldest colony, had closed their doors, thus rendering that colonye;s main medium of exchange worthless.
- _____, 28 October 1929 - a day in the Wall Street Crash of 1929, which also saw major stock market upheaval.
- _____, 27 May 1935 - US Supreme Court Justices overturned multiple Acts including National Industrial Recovery Act.
- _____, September 19, 1977 - when Youngstown Sheet and Tube Company, one of America's largest regional steel-manufacturing firms, announced that it would shut down most of its operations in the vicinity of Youngstown, Ohio. This development presaged the collapse of that community's industrial economy.
- _____, 27 November 1978 - when former San Francisco Supervisor Dan White assassinated Mayor George Moscone and openly gay Supervisor Harvey Milk.
- _____, Malta, 15 October 1979 - the offices of the The Times of Malta were set on fire during a political rally. It was also on this day that supporters of the Malta Labour Party broke into the house of Dr. Edward Fenech Adami.
- _____, 19 October 1987 - the largest one-day percentage decline in recorded stock market history.
- The day following the final Sunday of the National Football League season (Week 17) in which coaches and administration are fired or resign their position. The term is also attributed to the day following the annual NFL Draft where players contracts may be terminated once new players are added to a roster.
- The Monday of Match Week when 4th year medical students find out if but not where they matched to a residency position through the National Residency Matching Program.

a. Black Monday
b. 100-year flood
c. 1921 recession
d. 130-30 fund

97. The _____ is an American economic index intended to estimate future economic activity. It is calculated by The Conference Board, a non-governmental organization, which determines the value of the index from the values of ten key variables. These variables have historically turned downward before a recession and upward before an expansion.
a. Index of diversity
b. Index of dissimilarity
c. Index of leading indicators
d. Atkinson index

98. A _____ is a public market for the trading of company stock and derivatives at an agreed price; these are securities listed on a stock exchange as well as those only traded privately.

The size of the world _____ was estimated at about $36.6 trillion US at the beginning of October 2008 . The total world derivatives market has been estimated at about $791 trillion face or nominal value, 11 times the size of the entire world economy.

a. Stock market
b. Adolf Hitler
c. Adam Smith
d. Adolph Fischer

99. A _____ is a type of economic bubble taking place in stock markets when price of stocks rise and become overvalued by any measure of stock valuation.

The existence of _____s is at odds with the assumptions of efficient market theory which assumes rational investor behaviour. Behavioral finance theory attribute _____s to cognitive biases that lead to groupthink and herd behavior.

a. Scrip issue
b. Stock market bubble
c. Fill or kill
d. Growth investing

100. The _____ is an economic term, referring to an increase in spending that accompanies an increase or perceived increase in wealth.

The effect would cause changes in the amounts and composition of consumer consumption caused by changes in consumer wealth. People should spend more when one of two things is true: when people actually are richer (by objective measurement, for example, a bonus or a pay raise at work, which would be an income effect), or when people perceive themselves to be 'richer' (for example, the assessed value of their home increases, or a stock they own has gone up in price recently.)

a. 100-year flood
b. 130-30 fund
c. Wealth effect
d. Wealth condensation

101. In economics, _____ are key economic variables that economists used to predict a new phase of the business cycle. A leading indicator is one that changes before the economy does; a lagging indicator is one that changes after the economy has changed. Examples of _____ include stock prices, which often improve or worsen before a similar change in the economy.
a. Macroeconomics
b. Gross domestic product
c. Medium of exchange
d. Leading indicators

102. _____ is the price at which an asset would trade in a competitive Walrasian auction setting. _____ is often used interchangeably with open _____, fair value or fair _____, although these terms have distinct definitions in different standards, and may differ in some circumstances.

International Valuation Standards defines _____ as 'the estimated amount for which a property should exchange on the date of valuation between a willing buyer and a willing seller in an arm's-length transaction after proper marketing wherein the parties had each acted knowledgeably, prudently, and without compulsion.'

_____ is a concept distinct from market price, which is 'the price at which one can transact', while _____ is 'the true underlying value' according to theoretical standards.

a. Personal financial management
b. Secured loan
c. Netting
d. Market value

Chapter 8. Basic Macroeconomic Relationships

1. In economics, _____ is a measure of national income. Basically, it is an approach to measure GDP. It is defined as the value of planned goods and services produced in an economy.
   a. Aggregate supply
   b. Aggregate expenditure
   c. Aggregate demand
   d. Aggregation problem

2. _____ is a common concept in economics, and gives rise to derived concepts such as consumer debt. Generally _____ is defined by opposition to production. But the precise definition can vary because different schools of economists define production quite differently.
   a. Consumption
   b. Foreclosure data providers
   c. Federal Reserve Bank Notes
   d. Cash or share options

3. A _____ product is a product designed for cheapness and short-term convenience rather than medium to long-term durability, with most products only intended for single use. The term is also sometimes used for products that may last several months (ex. _____ air filters) to distinguish from similar products that last indefinitely (ex.
   a. 130-30 fund
   b. Disposable
   c. 1921 recession
   d. 100-year flood

4. _____ is gross income minus income tax on that income.

Discretionary income is income after subtracting taxes and normal expenses (such as rent or mortgage, utilities, insurance, medical, transportation, property maintenance, child support, inflation, food and sundries, 'c.) to maintain a certain standard of living.

   a. Stamp Act
   b. Taxation as theft
   c. Disposable personal income
   d. Disposable income

5. In economics and business, specifically cost accounting, the _____ point (BEP) is the point at which cost or expenses and revenue are equal: there is no net loss or gain, and one has 'broken even'. A profit or a loss has not been made, although opportunity costs have been paid, and capital has received the risk-adjusted, expected return.

For example, if the business sells less than 200 tables each month, it will make a loss, if it sells more, it will be a profit.

   a. Break-even
   b. Nonmarket
   c. Buffer stock scheme
   d. Small numbers game

6. _____ is a broad label that refers to any individuals or households that use goods and services generated within the economy. The concept of a _____ is used in different contexts, so that the usage and significance of the term may vary.

Typically when business people and economists talk of _____s they are talking about person as _____, an aggregated commodity item with little individuality other than that expressed in the buy/not-buy decision.

   a. 100-year flood
   b. 130-30 fund
   c. 1921 recession
   d. Consumer

Chapter 8. Basic Macroeconomic Relationships

7. _____ or consumer demand or consumption is also known as personal consumption expenditure. It is the largest part of aggregate demand or effective demand at the macroeconomic level. There are two variants of consumption in the aggregate demand model, including induced consumption and autonomous consumption.
   a. Complex multiplier
   b. Consumer spending
   c. Dishoarding
   d. Potential output

8. In economics, the _____ is a single mathematical function used to express consumer spending. It was developed by John Maynard Keynes and detailed most famously in his book The General Theory of Employment, Interest, and Money. The function is used to calculate the amount of total consumption in an economy.
   a. DAD-SAS model
   b. Consumption function
   c. Liquidity preference
   d. Procyclical

9. A variety of measures of _____ and output are used in economics to estimate total economic activity in a country or region, including gross domestic product (GDP), gross national product (GNP), and net _____

There are three main ways of calculating these numbers; the output approach, the income approach and the expenditure approach. In theory, the three must yield the same, because total expenditures on goods and services must equal the total income paid to the producers (Gnational income), and that must also equal the total value of the output of goods and services (GNP.)

   a. Gross world product
   b. Volume index
   c. GNI per capita
   d. National income

10. The _____ or Aggregate Demand-Aggregate Supply model is a macroeconomic model that explains price level and output through the relationship of aggregate demand and aggregate supply. It was first put forth by John Maynard Keynes in his work The General Theory of Employment, Interest, and Money. It is the foundation for the modern field of macroeconomics, and is accepted by a broad array of economists, from Libertarian, Monetarist supporters of laissez-faire, such as Milton Friedman to Socialist, Post-Keynesian supporters of economic interventionism, such as Joan Robinson.
    a. Economic interdependence
    b. IS/LM model
    c. Adaptive expectations
    d. AD-AS

11. _____ in economics and business is the result of an exchange and from that trade we assign a numerical monetary value to a good, service or asset. If Alice trades Bob 4 apples for an orange, the _____ of an orange is 4 apples. Inversely, the _____ of an apple is 1/4 oranges.
    a. Price war
    b. Price book
    c. Premium pricing
    d. Price

12. A _____ is a hypothetical measure of overall prices for some set of goods and services, in a given region during a given interval, normalized relative to some base set. Typically, a _____ is approximated with a price index.

The classical dichotomy is the assumption that there is a relatively clean distinction between overall increases or decreases in prices and underlying, e;reale; economic variables.

   a. Price elasticity of supply
   b. Discouraged worker
   c. Discretionary spending
   d. Price level

Chapter 8. Basic Macroeconomic Relationships

13. _____ is the percentage of income spent. To find the percentage of income spent, one needs to divide consumption by income, or $APC = \dfrac{C}{Y}$. In an economy in which each individual consumer saves lots of money, there is a tendency of people losing their jobs because demand for goods and services will be low.
   - a. Operating leverage
   - b. Equity ratio
   - c. Average propensity to consume
   - d. Inventory turnover

14. The _____ is an economics term that refers to the proportion of income which is saved, usually expressed for household savings as a percentage of total household disposable income. The ratio differs considerably over time and between countries. The savings ratio can be affected by: the proportion of older people, as they have less motivation and capability to save; the rate of inflation, as expectations of rising prices encourage can encourage people to spend now rather than later
   - a. Aggregate income
   - b. Independent income
   - c. Unearned income
   - d. Average propensity to save

15. In economics, the _____ is an empirical metric that quantifies induced consumption, the concept that the increase in personal consumer spending (consumption) that occurs with an increase in disposable income (income after taxes and transfers.) For example, if a household earns one extra dollar of disposable income, and the _____ is 0.65, then of that dollar, the household will spend 65 cents and save 35 cents.

    Mathematically, the _____ (MPC) function is expressed as the derivative of the consumption (C) function with respect to disposable income (Y.)
    - a. Supply shock
    - b. Marginal propensity to consume
    - c. Technology shock
    - d. Marginal propensity to import

16. The _____ refers to the increase in saving (non-purchase of current goods and services) that results from an increase in income. For example, if a household earns one extra dollar, and the _____ is 0.35, then of that dollar, the household will spend 65 cents and save 35 cents. It can also go the other way, referring to the decrease in saving that results from a decrease in income.
    - a. Marginal propensity to save
    - b. Robertson lag
    - c. Solow residual
    - d. Real business cycle

17. The _____ is 'the basic residential unit in which economic production, consumption, inheritance, child rearing, and shelter are organized and carried out'; [the _____] 'may or may not be synonymous with family'.

    The _____ is the basic unit of analysis in many social, microeconomic and government models. The term refers to all individuals who live in the same dwelling.
    - a. 130-30 fund
    - b. 100-year flood
    - c. Family economics
    - d. Household

18. _____ is an assumption used in many contemporary macroeconomic models, and also in other areas of contemporary economics and game theory and in other applications of rational choice theory.

Chapter 8. Basic Macroeconomic Relationships

Since most macroeconomic models today study decisions over many periods, the expectations of workers, consumers, and firms about future economic conditions are an essential part of the model. How to model these expectations has long been controversial, and it is well known that the macroeconomic predictions of the model may differ depending on the assumptions made about expectations

   a. Potential output
   c. Minimum wage

   b. Balanced-growth equilibrium
   d. Rational expectations

19. The '_____' is approximately the nominal interest rate minus the inflation rate Since the inflation rate over the course of a loan is not known initially, volatility in inflation represents a risk to both the lender and the borrower.

In economics and finance, an individual who lends money for repayment at a later point in time expects to be compensated for the time value of money, or not having the use of that money while it is lent.

   a. Core inflation
   c. Real interest rate

   b. Reflation
   d. Cost-push inflation

20. Economics:

   - _____,the desire to own something and the ability to pay for it
   - _____ curve,a graphic representation of a _____ schedule
   - _____ deposit, the money in checking accounts
   - _____ pull theory,the theory that inflation occurs when _____ for goods and services exceeds existing supplies
   - _____ schedule,a table that lists the quantity of a good a person will buy it each different price
   - _____ side economics,the school of economics at believes government spending and tax cuts open economy by raising _____

   a. Variability
   c. McKesson ' Robbins scandal

   b. Production
   d. Demand

21. In algebra, a _____ is a function depending on n that associates a scalar, det(A), to an n×n square matrix A. The fundamental geometric meaning of a _____ is a scale factor for measure when A is regarded as a linear transformation. _____s are important both in calculus, where they enter the substitution rule for several variables, and in multilinear algebra.

For a fixed nonnegative integer n, there is a unique _____ function for the n×n matrices over any commutative ring R. In particular, this function exists when R is the field of real or complex numbers.

   a. Determinant
   c. 100-year flood

   b. 130-30 fund
   d. 1921 recession

Chapter 8. Basic Macroeconomic Relationships

22. _____ is a fee paid on borrowed assets. It is the price paid for the use of borrowed money, or, money earned by deposited funds. Assets that are sometimes lent with _____ include money, shares, consumer goods through hire purchase, major assets such as aircraft, and even entire factories in finance lease arrangements.
    a. Interest
    b. Asset protection
    c. Internal debt
    d. Insolvency

23. An _____ is the price a borrower pays for the use of money they do not own, for instance a small company might borrow from a bank to kick start their business, and the return a lender receives for deferring the use of funds, by lending it to the borrower. _____s are normally expressed as a percentage rate over the period of one year.

    _____s targets are also a vital tool of monetary policy and are used to control variables like investment, inflation, and unemployment.

    a. ACCRA Cost of Living Index
    b. Enterprise value
    c. Interest rate
    d. Arrow-Debreu model

24. In economics, the _____ market is a hypothetical market that brings savers and borrowers together, also bringing together the money available in commercial banks and lending institutions available for firms and households to finance expenditures, either investments or consumption. Savers supply the _____; for instance, buying bonds will transfer their money to the institution issuing the bond, which can be a firm or government. In return, borrowers demand _____; when an institution sells a bond, it is demanding _____.
    a. Reservation wage
    b. Spatial inequality
    c. Buffer stock scheme
    d. Loanable funds

25. _____ is the a method of technical and economic research of the systems for purpose to optimize a parity between system's consumer functions or properties and expenses to achieve those functions or properties.

This methodology for continuous perfection of production, industrial technologies, organizational structures was developed by Juryj Sobolev in 1948 at the 'Perm telephone factory'

- 1948 Juryj Sobolev - the first success in application of a method analysis at the 'Perm telephone factory'.
- 1949 - the first application for the invention as result of use of the new method.

Today in economically developed countries practically each enterprise or the company use methodology of the kind of functional-cost analysis as a practice of the quality management, most full satisfying to principles of standards of series ISO 9000.

- Interest of consumer not in products itself, but the advantage which it will receive from its usage.
- The consumer aspires to reduce his expenses
- Functions needed by consumer can be executed in the various ways, and, hence, with various efficiency and expenses. Among possible alternatives of realization of functions exist such in which the parity of quality and the price is the optimal for the consumer.

Chapter 8. Basic Macroeconomic Relationships

129

The goal of _____ is achievement of the highest consumer satisfaction of production at simultaneous decrease in all kinds of industrial expenses Classical _____ has three English synonyms - Value Engineering, Value Management, Value Analysis.

a. Monopoly wage
c. Staple financing
b. Willingness to pay
d. Function cost analysis

26. The _____ or gross domestic income (GDI), a basic measure of an economy's economic performance, is the market value of all final goods and services produced within the borders of a nation in a year. _____ can be defined in three ways, all of which are conceptually identical. First, it is equal to the total expenditures for all final goods and services produced within the country in a stipulated period of time (usually a 365-day year.)

a. Countercyclical
c. Market structure
b. Monopolistic competition
d. Gross domestic product

27. An _____, in economics, is the amount by which the real Gross domestic product exceeds potential GDP. The real GDP is also known as GDP 'adjusted for inflation', 'constant prices' GDP or 'constant dollar' GDP, because it measures the aggregate output in a country's income accounts in a given year, expressed in base-year prices. On the other hand, the potential GDP is the quantity of real GDP when a country's economy is at full-employment.

a. ACEA agreement
c. AD-IA Model
b. ACCRA Cost of Living Index
d. Inflationary gap

28. In economics, _____ is the total demand for final goods and services in the economy (Y) at a given time and price level. It is the amount of goods and services in the economy that will be purchased at all possible price levels. This is the demand for the gross domestic product of a country when inventory levels are static.

a. Aggregate expenditure
c. Aggregate demand
b. Aggregate supply
d. Aggregation problem

29. _____ is that which is owed; usually referencing assets owed, but the term can also cover moral obligations and other interactions not requiring money. In the case of assets, _____ is a means of using future purchasing power in the present before a summation has been earned. Some companies and corporations use _____ as a part of their overall corporate finance strategy.

a. Hard money loan
c. Collateral Management
b. Debenture
d. Debt

30. To _____ is to impose a financial charge or other levy upon a taxpayer by a state or the functional equivalent of a state.

_____es are also imposed by many subnational entities. _____es consist of direct _____ or indirect _____, and may be paid in money or as its labour equivalent (often but not always unpaid.)

a. 130-30 fund
c. 100-year flood
b. 1921 recession
d. Tax

31. To tax is to impose a financial charge or other levy upon a taxpayer by a state or the functional equivalent of a state.

_____ are also imposed by many subnational entities. _____ consist of direct tax or indirect tax, and may be paid in money or as its labour equivalent (often but not always unpaid.)

a. 100-year flood
b. 130-30 fund
c. Taxes
d. 1921 recession

32. _____ is the difference between price and the costs of bringing to market whatever it is that is accounted as an enterprise (whether by harvest, extraction, manufacture, or purchase) in terms of the component costs of delivered goods and/or services and any operating or other expenses.

A key difficulty in measuring profit is in defining costs. Pure economic monetary profits can be zero or negative even in competitive equilibrium when accounted monetized costs exceed monetized price.

a. ACCRA Cost of Living Index
b. Economic profit
c. Operating profit
d. Accounting profit

33. _____s is the social science that studies the production, distribution, and consumption of goods and services. The term _____s comes from the Ancient Greek οá¼°κονομῖα from οá¼¶κος (oikos, 'house') + vÏŒμος (nomos, 'custom' or 'law'), hence 'rules of the house(hold)'. Current _____ models developed out of the broader field of political economy in the late 19th century, owing to a desire to use an empirical approach more akin to the physical sciences.

a. Inflation
b. Opportunity cost
c. Energy economics
d. Economic

34. In economics, _____ is the difference between a company's total revenue and its opportunity costs. It is the increase in wealth that an investor has from making an investment, taking into consideration all costs associated with that investment including the opportunity cost of capital.

Profit is the factor income of the entrepreneur.

a. ACCRA Cost of Living Index
b. Economic profit
c. Operating profit
d. Accounting profit

35. _____ is a component of the firm's opportunity costs. The time that the owner spends running the firm could be spent on running another firm. This is _____: the return the entrepreneur can expect to earn or the profit that the business owners considers necessary to make running the business worth his/her while.

a. 100-year flood
b. Normal profit
c. Profit maximization
d. Profit margin

36.

A _____ is a type of financial intermediary and a type of bank. Commercial banking is also known as business banking. It is a bank that provides checking accounts, savings accounts, and money market accounts and that accepts time deposits.

a. Bought deal	b. Daylight overdraft
c. Lombard banking	d. Commercial bank

37. In economics, the _____ can be defined as the graph depicting the relationship between the price of a certain commodity, and the amount of it that consumers are willing and able to purchase at that given price. It is a graphic representation of a demand schedule. The _____ for all consumers together follows from the _____ of every individual consumer: the individual demands at each price are added together.

a. Kuznets curve	b. Cost curve
c. Wage curve	d. Demand curve

38. In finance, _____ rate of profit or sometimes just return, is the ratio of money gained or lost on an investment relative to the amount of money invested. The amount of money gained or lost may be referred to as interest, profit/loss, gain/loss, or net income/loss. The money invested may be referred to as the asset, capital, principal, or the cost basis of the investment.

a. Current ratio	b. Sortino ratio
c. Cost accrual ratio	d. Rate of return

Chapter 8. Basic Macroeconomic Relationships

39. A _____ is:

- Rewrite _____, in generative grammar and computer science
- Standardization, a formal and widely-accepted statement, fact, definition, or qualification
- Operation, a determinate _____ for performing a mathematical operation and obtaining a certain result (Mathematics, Logic)
    - Unary operation
    - Binary operation
- _____ of inference, a function from sets of formulae to formulae (Mathematics, Logic)
- _____ of thumb, principle with broad application that is not intended to be strictly accurate or reliable for every situation. Also often simply referred to as a _____
- Moral, an atomic element of a moral code for guiding choices in human behavior
- Heuristic, a quantized '_____' which shows a tendency or probability for successful function
- A regulation, as in sports
- A Production _____, as in computer science
- Procedural law, a _____ set governing the application of laws to cases
    - A law, which may informally be called a '_____'
    - A court ruling, a decision by a court
- In the U.S. Government, a regulation mandated by Congress, but written or expanded upon by the Executive Branch.
- Norm (sociology), an informal but widely accepted _____, concept, truth, definition, or qualification (social norms, legal norms, coding norms)
- Norm (philosophy), a kind of sentence or a reason to act, feel or believe
- 'Rulership' is the concept of governance by a government:
    - Military _____, governance by a military body
    - Monastic _____, a collection of precepts that guides the life of monks or nuns in a religious order where the superior holds the place of Christ
- Slide _____

- '_____,' a song by Ayumi Hamasaki
- '_____,' a song by rapper Nas
- '_____s,' an album by the band The Whitest Boy Alive
- _____s: Pyaar Ka Superhit Formula, a 2003 Bollywood film
- ruler, an instrument for measuring lengths
- _____, a component of an astrolabe, circumferator or similar instrument
- The _____s, a bestselling self-help book
- _____ Project (Run Up-to-date Linux Everywhere), a project that aims to use up-to-date Linux software on old PCs
- _____ engine, a software system that helps managing business _____s
- Ja _____, a hip hop artist
    - R.U.L.E., a 2005 greatest hits album by rapper Ja _____
- '_____s,' a KMFDM song

a. Demand
b. Procter ' Gamble
c. Rule
d. Technocracy

Chapter 8. Basic Macroeconomic Relationships

40. In economics, and cost accounting, _____ describes the total economic cost of production and is made up of variable costs, which vary according to the quantity of a good produced and include inputs such as labor and raw materials, plus fixed costs, which are independent of the quantity of a good produced and include inputs (capital) that cannot be varied in the short term, such as buildings and machinery. _____ in economics includes the total opportunity cost of each factor of production in addition to fixed and variable costs.

The rate at which _____ changes as the amount produced changes is called marginal cost.

a. 100-year flood
b. 130-30 fund
c. 1921 recession
d. Total cost

41. _____ is the process by which money is produced or issued. There are three different ways to create money:

- manufacturing a new monetary unit, such as paper currency or metal coins (_____)
- loaning out a physical monetary unit multiple times through fractional-reserve lending (credit creation)
- buying of government securities or other financial instruments by central bank through Open market operations (electronic creation)

Coins are produced by manufacturing metal in a factory called a mint.

Banknotes and bank account balances are financial securities issued by a bank.

Similarly, money destruction, i.e., the reverse of _____, can occur in two different ways, depending on how the money was created.

a. Second-round effect
b. Monetary policy of Sweden
c. Money creation
d. Shadow Open Market Committee

42. In finance and economics _____ or nominal rate of interest refers to the rate of interest before adjustment for inflation (in contrast with the real interest rate); or, for interest rates 'as stated' without adjustment for the full effect of compounding (also referred to as the nominal annual rate.) An interest rate is called nominal if the frequency of compounding (e.g. a month) is not identical to the basic time unit (normally a year.)

The real interest rate includes compensation for the lender's lost value due to inflation, whereas the _____ excludes inflation.

a. London Interbank Offered Rate
b. Risk-free interest rate
c. Fixed interest
d. Nominal interest rate

43. The _____ consists of a number of economic theories which describe the nature of the firm, company including its existence, its behaviour, and its relationship with the market.

In simplified terms, the _____ aims to answer these questions:

1. Existence - why do firms emerge, why are not all transactions in the economy mediated over the market?
2. Boundaries - why the boundary between firms and the market is located exactly there? Which transactions are performed internally and which are negotiated on the market?
3. Organization - why are firms structured in such specific way? What is the interplay of formal and informal relationships?

Despite looking simple, these questions are not answered by the established economic theory, which usually views firms as given, and treats them as black boxes without any internal structure.

The First World War period saw a change of emphasis in economic theory away from industry-level analysis which mainly included analysing markets to analysis at the level of the firm, as it became increasingly clear that perfect competition was no longer an adequate model of how firms behaved. Economic theory till then had focussed on trying to understand markets alone and there had been little study on understanding why firms or organisations exist.

- a. Technology gap
- b. Policy Ineffectiveness Proposition
- c. Khazzoom-Brookes postulate
- d. Theory of the firm

44. A security is a fungible, negotiable instrument representing financial value. _____ are broadly categorized into debt _____; equity _____, e.g., common stocks; and derivative (finance) contracts such as forwards, futures, options and swaps. The company or other entity issuing the security is called the issuer.
    - a. Red herring prospectus
    - b. Pass-Through Certificates
    - c. Settlement risk
    - d. Securities

45. _____ refers to the movement of cash into or out of a business or financial product. It is usually measured during a specified, finite period of time. Measurement of _____ can be used

    - to determine a project's rate of return or value. The time of _____s into and out of projects are used as inputs in financial models such as internal rate of return, and net present value.
    - to determine problems with a business's liquidity. Being profitable does not necessarily mean being liquid. A company can fail because of a shortage of cash, even while profitable.
    - as an alternate measure of a business's profits when it is believed that accrual accounting concepts do not represent economic realities. For example, a company may be notionally profitable but generating little operational cash (as may be the case for a company that barters its products rather than selling for cash.) In such a case, the company may be deriving additional operating cash by issuing shares evaluating default risk, re-investment requirements, etc.

_____ is a generic term used differently depending on the context. It may be defined by users for their own purposes.

- a. Second lien loan
- b. Strip financing
- c. Restricted stock
- d. Cash flow

Chapter 8. Basic Macroeconomic Relationships

46. In economics, the _____ is used to illustrate the idea that increases in the rate of taxation do not necessarily increase tax revenue. (For instance, whereas a 0% income tax rate will generate no revenue, neither will a 100% rate, as citizens will have no incentive to make money.) Increasing taxes beyond the peak of the curve point will decrease tax revenue.
   a. 130-30 fund
   b. 1921 recession
   c. 100-year flood
   d. Laffer curve

47. In economics, _____ is the total supply of goods and services produced by a national economy during a specific time period. It is the total amount of goods and services in the economy available at all possible price levels.
   a. Aggregate expenditure
   b. Aggregation problem
   c. Aggregate supply
   d. Aggregate demand

48. The term _____ refers to economy-wide fluctuations in production or economic activity over several months or years. These fluctuations occur around a long-term growth trend, and typically involve shifts over time between periods of relatively rapid economic growth (expansion or boom), and periods of relative stagnation or decline (contraction or recession.)

These fluctuations are often measured using the growth rate of real gross domestic product.

   a. Consumer theory
   b. Business cycle
   c. Nominal value
   d. Tobit model

49. In Marxian economics, _____ originally referred to the means of production. Individuals, organizations and governments use _____ in the production of other goods or commodities. _____ include factories, machinery, tools, equipment, and various buildings which are used to produce other products for consumption.
   a. Capital goods
   b. Capital intensive
   c. Capital deepening
   d. Wealth inequality in the United States

50. A _____ is an object whose consumption increases the utility of the consumer, for which the quantity demanded exceeds the quantity supplied at zero price. _____s are usually modeled as having diminishing marginal utility. The first individual purchase has high utility; the second has less.
   a. Pie method
   b. Composite good
   c. Merit good
   d. Good

51. The _____ is published by The Economist as an informal way of measuring the purchasing power parity (PPP) between two currencies and provides a test of the extent to which market exchange rates result in goods costing the same in different countries. It 'seeks to make exchange-rate theory a bit more digestible'.

The index takes its name from the Big Mac, a hamburger sold at McDonald's restaurants.

   a. Cost-weighted activity index
   b. Big Mac index
   c. Rank mobility index
   d. Deindexation

52. _____ is a term used in accounting, economics and finance to spread the cost of an asset over the span of several years.

In simple words we can say that _____ is the reduction in the value of an asset due to usage, passage of time, wear and tear, technological outdating or obsolescence, depletion, inadequacy, rot, rust, decay or other such factors.

In accounting, _____ is a term used to describe any method of attributing the historical or purchase cost of an asset across its useful life, roughly corresponding to normal wear and tear.

a. Historical cost
b. Salvage value
c. Depreciation
d. Net income per employee

53. The _____ or the output gap is the difference between potential GDP and actual GDP or actual output. The calculation for the output gap is Y-Y* where Y* is potential output and Y is actual output. If this calculation yields a positive number it is called an expansionary gap and indicates an economy in expansion; if the calculation yields a negative number it is called a recessionary gap and indicates an economy in recession.

a. 130-30 fund
b. 1921 recession
c. 100-year flood
d. GDP gap

54. _____ is exchange of capital, goods, and services across international borders or territories. In most countries, it represents a significant share of gross domestic product (GDP.) While _____ has been present throughout much of history, its economic, social, and political importance has been on the rise in recent centuries.

a. Import license
b. Incoterms
c. Intra-industry trade
d. International trade

55. A _____ is a normalized average (typically a weighted average) of prices for a given class of goods or services in a given region, during a given interval of time. It is a statistic designed to help to compare how these prices, taken as a whole, differ between time periods or geographical locations.

Price indices have several potential uses.

a. Product sabotage
b. Transactional Net Margin Method
c. Two-part tariff
d. Price index

56. In economics, the _____ or spending multiplier is the idea that an initial amount of spending (usually by the government) leads to increased consumption spending and so results in an increase in national income greater than the initial amount of spending. In other words, an initial change in aggregate demand causes a change in aggregate output for the economy that is a multiple of the initial change.

The existence of a _____ was initially proposed by Ralph George Hawtrey in 1931.

a. Spending multiplier
b. Keynesian cross
c. Magical triangle
d. Multiplier effect

57. A _____ is a public market for the trading of company stock and derivatives at an agreed price; these are securities listed on a stock exchange as well as those only traded privately.

Chapter 8. Basic Macroeconomic Relationships

The size of the world _____ was estimated at about $36.6 trillion US at the beginning of October 2008 . The total world derivatives market has been estimated at about $791 trillion face or nominal value, 11 times the size of the entire world economy.

a. Adam Smith
c. Stock market

b. Adolf Hitler
d. Adolph Fischer

58. A _____ is a type of economic bubble taking place in stock markets when price of stocks rise and become overvalued by any measure of stock valuation.

The existence of _____s is at odds with the assumptions of efficient market theory which assumes rational investor behaviour. Behavioral finance theory attribute _____s to cognitive biases that lead to groupthink and herd behavior.

a. Growth investing
c. Fill or kill

b. Scrip issue
d. Stock market bubble

59. The term _____, 'the state or characteristic of being variable',_____ describes how spread out or closely clustered a set of data is. may be applied to many different subjects:

- Climate _____
- Genetic _____
- Heart rate _____
- Human _____
- Solar van
- Spatial _____
- Statistical _____
- _____

a. Total product
c. Demand

b. Characteristic
d. Variability

60. _____ is the process by which the government, central bank (ii) availability of money, and (iii) cost of money or rate of interest, in order to attain a set of objectives oriented towards the growth and stability of the economy. Monetary theory provides insight into how to craft optimal _____.

_____ is referred to as either being an expansionary policy where an expansionary policy increases the total supply of money in the economy, and a contractionary policy decreases the total money supply.

a. 1921 recession
c. 100-year flood

b. 130-30 fund
d. Monetary policy

61. In microeconomics, _____ is quite simply the conversion of inputs into outputs. It is an economic process that uses resources to create a good or service that is suitable for exchange. This can include manufacturing, storing, shipping, and packaging.
   a. Production
   b. Red Guards
   c. Solved
   d. MET

62. The _____ is a group of three respected economists who advise the President of the United States on economic policy. It is a part of the Executive Office of the President of the United States, and provides much of the economic policy of the White House. The council prepares the annual Economic Report of the President.
   a. Hybrid renewable energy systems
   b. Constrained Pareto optimality
   c. Federal Reserve Bank Notes
   d. Council of Economic Advisers

63. The _____, more formally called the Summary of Commentary on Current Economic Conditions, is a report published by the Federal Reserve Board eight times a year. Each is a gathering of 'anecdotal information on current economic conditions' by each Federal Reserve Bank in its district from 'Bank and Branch directors and interviews with key business contacts, economists, market experts, and other.'

Federal Reserve Board _____ website

   a. Federal Reserve Note
   b. Term auction facility
   c. Beige Book
   d. Federal Reserve System

Chapter 9. The Aggregate Expenditures Model

1. In economics, _____ is a measure of national income. Basically, it is an approach to measure GDP. It is defined as the value of planned goods and services produced in an economy.
   a. Aggregation problem
   b. Aggregate expenditure
   c. Aggregate demand
   d. Aggregate supply

2. _____, 1st Baron Keynes was a renowned economist from Britain whose many ideas on economic and political theories as well as on many governments' monetary policies influenced America. He advocated a government that played an active role in the lives of people regarding business, economy, etc. In this role, the government would use fiscal measures to reduce the consequences of recessions, economic depressions and booms.
   a. John Maynard Keynes
   b. Adam Smith
   c. Adolph Fischer
   d. Adolf Hitler

3. _____ and Keynesian Theory) is a macroeconomic theory based on the ideas of 20th-century British economist John Maynard Keynes. _____ argues that private sector decisions sometimes lead to inefficient macroeconomic outcomes and therefore advocates active policy responses by the public sector, including monetary policy actions by the central bank and fiscal policy actions by the government to stabilize output over the business cycle.

   The theories forming the basis of _____ were first presented in The General Theory of Employment, Interest and Money, published in 1936.

   a. Rational choice theory
   b. Market failure
   c. Keynesian economics
   d. Deflation

4. In the _____ diagram, a desired total spending (or aggregate expenditure which increases with total national output. This increase is due to the positive relationship between consumption and consumers' disposable income in the consumption function. Aggregate demand may also rise due to increases in investment (due to the accelerator effect), while this rise is reduced if imports and tax revenues rise with income.
   a. Keynesian Revolution
   b. Keynesian formula
   c. Keynesian cross
   d. Paradox of thrift

5. An autarky is an economy that is self-sufficient and does not take part in international trade, or severely limits trade with the outside world. Likewise the term refers to an ecosystem not affected by influences from the outside, which relies entirely on its own resources. In the economic meaning, it is also referred to as a _____.
   a. Transition economy
   b. Digital economy
   c. Network Economy
   d. Closed economy

6. _____ is a common concept in economics, and gives rise to derived concepts such as consumer debt. Generally _____ is defined by opposition to production. But the precise definition can vary because different schools of economists define production quite differently.
   a. Cash or share options
   b. Federal Reserve Bank Notes
   c. Consumption
   d. Foreclosure data providers

7. Economics:

- _____ ,the desire to own something and the ability to pay for it
- _____ curve,a graphic representation of a _____ schedule
- _____ deposit, the money in checking accounts
- _____ pull theory,the theory that inflation occurs when _____ for goods and services exceeds existing supplies
- _____ schedule,a table that lists the quantity of a good a person will buy it each different price
- _____ side economics,the school of economics at believes government spending and tax cuts open economy by raising _____

a. McKesson ' Robbins scandal
b. Demand
c. Production
d. Variability

8. In economics, the _____ can be defined as the graph depicting the relationship between the price of a certain commodity, and the amount of it that consumers are willing and able to purchase at that given price. It is a graphic representation of a demand schedule. The _____ for all consumers together follows from the _____ of every individual consumer: the individual demands at each price are added together.

a. Cost curve
b. Kuznets curve
c. Wage curve
d. Demand curve

Chapter 9. The Aggregate Expenditures Model 141

9. A _____ is:

- Rewrite _____, in generative grammar and computer science
- Standardization, a formal and widely-accepted statement, fact, definition, or qualification
- Operation, a determinate _____ for performing a mathematical operation and obtaining a certain result (Mathematics, Logic)
    - Unary operation
    - Binary operation
- _____ of inference, a function from sets of formulae to formulae (Mathematics, Logic)
- _____ of thumb, principle with broad application that is not intended to be strictly accurate or reliable for every situation. Also often simply referred to as a _____
- Moral, an atomic element of a moral code for guiding choices in human behavior
- Heuristic, a quantized '_____' which shows a tendency or probability for successful function
- A regulation, as in sports
- A Production _____, as in computer science
- Procedural law, a _____ set governing the application of laws to cases
    - A law, which may informally be called a '_____'
    - A court ruling, a decision by a court
- In the U.S. Government, a regulation mandated by Congress, but written or expanded upon by the Executive Branch.
- Norm (sociology), an informal but widely accepted _____, concept, truth, definition, or qualification (social norms, legal norms, coding norms)
- Norm (philosophy), a kind of sentence or a reason to act, feel or believe
- 'Rulership' is the concept of governance by a government:
    - Military _____, governance by a military body
    - Monastic _____, a collection of precepts that guides the life of monks or nuns in a religious order where the superior holds the place of Christ
- Slide _____

- '_____,' a song by Ayumi Hamasaki
- '_____,' a song by rapper Nas
- '_____s,' an album by the band The Whitest Boy Alive
- _____s: Pyaar Ka Superhit Formula, a 2003 Bollywood film
- ruler, an instrument for measuring lengths
- _____, a component of an astrolabe, circumferator or similar instrument
- The _____s, a bestselling self-help book
- _____ Project (Run Up-to-date Linux Everywhere), a project that aims to use up-to-date Linux software on old PCs
- _____ engine, a software system that helps managing business _____s
- Ja _____, a hip hop artist
    - R.U.L.E., a 2005 greatest hits album by rapper Ja _____
- '_____s,' a KMFDM song

a. Technocracy
c. Procter ' Gamble
b. Demand
d. Rule

10. The _____ or gross domestic income (GDI), a basic measure of an economy's economic performance, is the market value of all final goods and services produced within the borders of a nation in a year. _____ can be defined in three ways, all of which are conceptually identical. First, it is equal to the total expenditures for all final goods and services produced within the country in a stipulated period of time (usually a 365-day year.)
   a. Gross domestic product
   b. Countercyclical
   c. Market structure
   d. Monopolistic competition

11. In economics, a _____ is a general slowdown in economic activity over a sustained period of time, or a business cycle contraction. During _____s, many macroeconomic indicators vary in a similar way. Production as measured by Gross Domestic Product (GDP), employment, investment spending, capacity utilization, household incomes and business profits all fall during _____s.
   a. Monetary economics
   b. Treasury View
   c. Leading indicators
   d. Recession

12. The _____ or Aggregate Demand-Aggregate Supply model is a macroeconomic model that explains price level and output through the relationship of aggregate demand and aggregate supply. It was first put forth by John Maynard Keynes in his work The General Theory of Employment, Interest, and Money. It is the foundation for the modern field of macroeconomics, and is accepted by a broad array of economists, from Libertarian, Monetarist supporters of laissez-faire, such as Milton Friedman to Socialist, Post-Keynesian supporters of economic interventionism, such as Joan Robinson.
   a. IS/LM model
   b. AD-AS
   c. Economic interdependence
   d. Adaptive expectations

13. _____ in economics and business is the result of an exchange and from that trade we assign a numerical monetary value to a good, service or asset. If Alice trades Bob 4 apples for an orange, the _____ of an orange is 4 apples. Inversely, the _____ of an apple is 1/4 oranges.
   a. Price war
   b. Premium pricing
   c. Price book
   d. Price

14. A _____ is a hypothetical measure of overall prices for some set of goods and services, in a given region during a given interval, normalized relative to some base set. Typically, a _____ is approximated with a price index.

The classical dichotomy is the assumption that there is a relatively clean distinction between overall increases or decreases in prices and underlying, e;reale; economic variables.

   a. Price elasticity of supply
   b. Discretionary spending
   c. Discouraged worker
   d. Price level

Chapter 9. The Aggregate Expenditures Model 143

15. _____ has several particular meanings:

- in mathematics
    - _____ function
    - Euler _____
    - _____
    - _____ subgroup
    - method of _____s (partial differential equations)
- in physics and engineering
    - any _____ curve that shows the relationship between certain input- and output parameters, e.g.
    - an I-V or current-voltage _____ is the current in a circuit as a function of the applied voltage
    - Receiver-Operator _____
- in fiction
    - in Dungeons ' Dragons, _____ is another name for ability score

a. Technocracy
b. Characteristic
c. Russian financial crisis
d. Demand

16. The _____ or the output gap is the difference between potential GDP and actual GDP or actual output. The calculation for the output gap is Y-Y* where Y* is potential output and Y is actual output. If this calculation yields a positive number it is called an expansionary gap and indicates an economy in expansion; if the calculation yields a negative number it is called a recessionary gap and indicates an economy in recession.

a. 130-30 fund
b. 100-year flood
c. 1921 recession
d. GDP gap

17. A _____ is a normalized average (typically a weighted average) of prices for a given class of goods or services in a given region, during a given interval of time. It is a statistic designed to help to compare how these prices, taken as a whole, differ between time periods or geographical locations.

Price indices have several potential uses.

a. Transactional Net Margin Method
b. Product sabotage
c. Two-part tariff
d. Price index

18. The Organization of the Petroleum Exporting Countries is a cartel of twelve countries made up of Algeria, Angola, Ecuador, Iran, Iraq, Kuwait, Libya, Nigeria, Qatar, Saudi Arabia, the United Arab Emirates, and Venezuela. The cartel has maintained its headquarters in Vienna since 1965, and hosts regular meetings among the oil ministers of its Member Countries. Indonesia withdrew its membership in _____ in 2008 after it became a net importer of oil, but stated it would likely return if it became a net exporter in the world.

a. ACEA agreement
b. OPEC
c. AD-IA Model
d. ACCRA Cost of Living Index

Chapter 9. The Aggregate Expenditures Model

19. A _____ is a general term that describes any government policy or regulation that restricts international trade. The barriers can take many forms, including the following terms that include many restrictions in international trade within multiple countries that import and export any items of trade.

- Import duty
- Import licenses
- Export licenses
- Import quotas
- Tariffs
- Subsidies
- Non-tariff barriers to trade
- Voluntary Export Restraints
- Local Content Requirements
- Embargo

Most _____s work on the same principle: the imposition of some sort of cost on trade that raises the price of the traded products. If two or more nations repeatedly use _____s against each other, then a trade war results.

a. Trade barrier
b. Global financial system
c. National Foreign Trade Council
d. Certificate of origin

20. In economics, _____ refers to the ability of a party to produce a good or service using fewer real resources than another entity producing the same good or service..A party has an _____ when using the same input as another party, it can produce a greater output. Since _____ is determined by a simple comparison of labor productivities, it is possible for a party to have no _____ in anything. It can be contrasted with the concept of comparative advantage which refers to the ability to produce a particular good at a lower opportunity cost.

a. International economics
b. ACCRA Cost of Living Index
c. Index number
d. Absolute advantage

21. In economics, an _____ is any good or commodity, transported from one country to another country in a legitimate fashion, typically for use in trade. _____ goods or services are provided to foreign consumers by domestic producers. _____ is an important part of international trade.

a. ACCRA Cost of Living Index
b. AD-IA Model
c. Export
d. ACEA agreement

22. _____ is exchange of capital, goods, and services across international borders or territories. In most countries, it represents a significant share of gross domestic product (GDP.) While _____ has been present throughout much of history , its economic, social, and political importance has been on the rise in recent centuries.

a. Incoterms
b. Intra-industry trade
c. Import license
d. International trade

23. An _____ is an economy in which people, including businesses, can trade in goods and services with other people and businesses in the international community at large. This contrasts with a closed economy in which international trade cannot take place.

Chapter 9. The Aggregate Expenditures Model 145

The act of selling goods or services to a foreign country is called exporting.

a. Information economy
b. Attention work
c. Indicative planning
d. Open economy

24. The _____ is the part of economic and administrative life that deals with the delivery of goods and services by and for the government, whether national, regional or local/municipal.

Examples of _____ activity range from delivering social security, administering urban planning and organising national defenses.

The organization of the _____ can take several forms, including:

- Direct administration funded through taxation; the delivering organization generally has no specific requirement to meet commercial success criteria, and production decisions are determined by government.
- Publicly owned corporations (in some contexts, especially manufacturing, 'state-owned enterprises'); which differ from direct administration in that they have greater commercial freedoms and are expected to operate according to commercial criteria, and production decisions are not generally taken by government (although goals may be set for them by government.)
- Partial outsourcing (of the scale many businesses do, e.g. for IT services), is considered a _____ model.

A borderline form is

- Complete outsourcing or contracting out, with a privately owned corporation delivering the entire service on behalf of government. This may be considered a mixture of private sector operations with public ownership of assets, although in some forms the private sector's control and/or risk is so great that the service may no longer be considered part of the _____.

a. 100-year flood
b. 130-30 fund
c. Policy cycle
d. Public sector

25. A _____ is a duty imposed on goods when they are moved across a political boundary. They are usually associated with protectionism, the economic policy of restraining trade between nations. For political reasons, _____s are usually imposed on imported goods, although they may also be imposed on exported goods.

a. 130-30 fund
b. Tariff
c. 100-year flood
d. 1921 recession

26. _____ is a term used in accounting, economics and finance to spread the cost of an asset over the span of several years.

In simple words we can say that _____ is the reduction in the value of an asset due to usage, passage of time, wear and tear, technological outdating or obsolescence, depletion, inadequacy, rot, rust, decay or other such factors.

In accounting, _____ is a term used to describe any method of attributing the historical or purchase cost of an asset across its useful life, roughly corresponding to normal wear and tear.

    a. Historical cost
    c. Salvage value
    b. Net income per employee
    d. Depreciation

27. _____s is the social science that studies the production, distribution, and consumption of goods and services. The term _____s comes from the Ancient Greek oá¼°κονομῖα from oá¼¶κος (oikos, 'house') + vΌμος (nomos, 'custom' or 'law'), hence 'rules of the house(hold)'. Current _____ models developed out of the broader field of political economy in the late 19th century, owing to a desire to use an empirical approach more akin to the physical sciences.

    a. Energy economics
    c. Inflation
    b. Opportunity cost
    d. Economic

28. In finance, the _____s between two currencies specifies how much one currency is worth in terms of the other. It is the value of a foreign natione;s currency in terms of the home natione;s currency. For example an _____ of 102 Japanese yen to the United States dollar means that JPY 102 is worth the same as USD 1.

    a. ACCRA Cost of Living Index
    c. Interbank market
    b. ACEA agreement
    d. Exchange rate

29. A _____ is an object whose consumption increases the utility of the consumer, for which the quantity demanded exceeds the quantity supplied at zero price. _____s are usually modeled as having diminishing marginal utility. The first individual purchase has high utility; the second has less.

    a. Merit good
    c. Pie method
    b. Good
    d. Composite good

30. The _____ is 'the basic residential unit in which economic production, consumption, inheritance, child rearing, and shelter are organized and carried out'; [the _____] 'may or may not be synonomous with family'.

The _____ is the basic unit of analysis in many social, microeconomic and government models. The term refers to all individuals who live in the same dwelling.

    a. 100-year flood
    c. 130-30 fund
    b. Household
    d. Family economics

31. _____ is the a method of technical and economic research of the systems for purpose to optimize a parity between system's consumer functions or properties and expenses to achieve those functions or properties.

This methodology for continuous perfection of production, industrial technologies, organizational structures was developed by Juryj Sobolev in 1948 at the 'Perm telephone factory'

- 1948 Juryj Sobolev - the first success in application of a method analysis at the 'Perm telephone factory' .
- 1949 - the first application for the invention as result of use of the new method.

Chapter 9. The Aggregate Expenditures Model

Today in economically developed countries practically each enterprise or the company use methodology of the kind of functional-cost analysis as a practice of the quality management, most full satisfying to principles of standards of series ISO 9000.

- Interest of consumer not in products itself, but the advantage which it will receive from its usage.
- The consumer aspires to reduce his expenses
- Functions needed by consumer can be executed in the various ways, and, hence, with various efficiency and expenses. Among possible alternatives of realization of functions exist such in which the parity of quality and the price is the optimal for the consumer.

The goal of _____ is achievement of the highest consumer satisfaction of production at simultaneous decrease in all kinds of industrial expenses Classical _____ has three English synonyms - Value Engineering, Value Management, Value Analysis.

a. Willingness to pay
b. Function cost analysis
c. Staple financing
d. Monopoly wage

32. In economics, the _____ is used to illustrate the idea that increases in the rate of taxation do not necessarily increase tax revenue. (For instance, whereas a 0% income tax rate will generate no revenue, neither will a 100% rate, as citizens will have no incentive to make money.) Increasing taxes beyond the peak of the curve point will decrease tax revenue.

a. 1921 recession
b. Laffer curve
c. 100-year flood
d. 130-30 fund

33. A _____ is a tax that is a fixed amount no matter what the change in circumstance of the taxed entity. (A lump-sum subsidy or lump-sum redistribution is defined similarly.) It is a regressive tax, such that the lower income is, the higher percentage of income applicable to the tax.

a. Budget deficit
b. Grant-in-aid
c. Funding body
d. Lump-sum tax

34. _____ refers to a business or organization attempting to acquire goods or services to accomplish the goals of the enterprise. Though there are several organizations that attempt to set standards in the _____ process, processes can vary greatly between organizations. Typically the word '_____' is not used interchangeably with the word 'procurement', since procurement typically includes Expediting, Supplier Quality, and Traffic and Logistics (T'L) in addition to _____.

a. Free port
b. Purchasing
c. 130-30 fund
d. 100-year flood

35. To _____ is to impose a financial charge or other levy upon a taxpayer by a state or the functional equivalent of a state.

_____es are also imposed by many subnational entities. _____es consist of direct _____ or indirect _____, and may be paid in money or as its labour equivalent (often but not always unpaid).

a. 1921 recession
c. 100-year flood
b. 130-30 fund
d. Tax

36. A _____ product is a product designed for cheapness and short-term convenience rather than medium to long-term durability, with most products only intended for single use. The term is also sometimes used for products that may last several months (ex. _____ air filters) to distinguish from similar products that last indefinitely (ex.
   a. 100-year flood
   c. 1921 recession
   b. 130-30 fund
   d. Disposable

37. _____ is gross income minus income tax on that income.

Discretionary income is income after subtracting taxes and normal expenses (such as rent or mortgage, utilities, insurance, medical, transportation, property maintenance, child support, inflation, food and sundries, 'c.) to maintain a certain standard of living.

   a. Disposable income
   c. Taxation as theft
   b. Disposable personal income
   d. Stamp Act

38. A variety of measures of _____ and output are used in economics to estimate total economic activity in a country or region, including gross domestic product (GDP), gross national product (GNP), and net _____

There are three main ways of calculating these numbers; the output approach, the income approach and the expenditure approach. In theory, the three must yield the same, because total expenditures on goods and services must equal the total income paid to the producers (Gnational income), and that must also equal the total value of the output of goods and services (GNP.)

   a. GNI per capita
   c. Gross world product
   b. Volume index
   d. National income

39. In a _____ there is both a monopoly (a single seller) and monopsony (a single buyer) in the same market.

In such market price and output will be determined by the non economic forces like bargaining power of both buyer and seller. A _____ model is often used in situations where the switching costs of both sides are prohibitively high.

   a. Market concentration
   c. Price takers
   b. Revenue-cap regulation
   d. Bilateral monopoly

40. In economics and business, specifically cost accounting, the _____ point (BEP) is the point at which cost or expenses and revenue are equal: there is no net loss or gain, and one has 'broken even'. A profit or a loss has not been made, although opportunity costs have been paid, and capital has received the risk-adjusted, expected return.

For example, if the business sells less than 200 tables each month, it will make a loss, if it sells more, it will be a profit.

Chapter 9. The Aggregate Expenditures Model

a. Small numbers game
b. Break-even
c. Nonmarket
d. Buffer stock scheme

41. In economics, a _____ exists when a specific individual or enterprise has sufficient control over a particular product or service to determine significantly the terms on which other individuals shall have access to it. Monopolies are thus characterized by a lack of economic competition for the good or service that they provide and a lack of viable substitute goods. The verb 'monopolize' refers to the process by which a firm gains persistently greater market share than what is expected under perfect competition.
a. 100-year flood
b. 130-30 fund
c. 1921 recession
d. Monopoly

42. In economics, an _____ is any good (e.g. a commodity) or service brought into one country from another country in a legitimate fashion, typically for use in trade. It is a good that is brought in from another country for sale. _____ goods or services are provided to domestic consumers by foreign producers. An _____ in the receiving country is an export to the sending country.
a. Economic integration
b. Import
c. Incoterms
d. Import quota

43. _____ is a broad label that refers to any individuals or households that use goods and services generated within the economy. The concept of a _____ is used in different contexts, so that the usage and significance of the term may vary.

Typically when business people and economists talk of _____s they are talking about person as _____, an aggregated commodity item with little individuality other than that expressed in the buy/not-buy decision.

a. 1921 recession
b. Consumer
c. 100-year flood
d. 130-30 fund

44. _____ or consumer demand or consumption is also known as personal consumption expenditure. It is the largest part of aggregate demand or effective demand at the macroeconomic level. There are two variants of consumption in the aggregate demand model, including induced consumption and autonomous consumption.
a. Complex multiplier
b. Potential output
c. Dishoarding
d. Consumer spending

45. In economics, _____ is a rise in the general level of prices of goods and services in an economy over a period of time. When the general price level rises, each unit of currency buys fewer goods and services; consequently, _____ is also a decline in the real value of money--a loss of purchasing power in the medium of exchange which is also the monetary unit of account in the economy. A chief measure of general price-level _____ is the general _____ rate, which is the percentage change in a general price index (normally the Consumer Price Index) over time.
a. Economic
b. Opportunity cost
c. Energy economics
d. Inflation

46. A _____ is a public market for the trading of company stock and derivatives at an agreed price; these are securities listed on a stock exchange as well as those only traded privately.

The size of the world _____ was estimated at about $36.6 trillion US at the beginning of October 2008 . The total world derivatives market has been estimated at about $791 trillion face or nominal value, 11 times the size of the entire world economy.

   a. Adolf Hitler
   b. Adolph Fischer
   c. Adam Smith
   d. Stock market

47. A _____ is a type of economic bubble taking place in stock markets when price of stocks rise and become overvalued by any measure of stock valuation.

The existence of _____s is at odds with the assumptions of efficient market theory which assumes rational investor behaviour. Behavioral finance theory attribute _____s to cognitive biases that lead to groupthink and herd behavior.

   a. Fill or kill
   b. Scrip issue
   c. Growth investing
   d. Stock market bubble

48. _____ was written by the English economist John Maynard Keynes. The book, generally considered to be his magnum opus, is largely credited with creating the terminology and shape of modern macroeconomics. Published in February 1936 it sought to bring about a revolution, commonly referred to as the 'Keynesian Revolution', in the way economists thought - especially in relation to the proposition that a market economy tends naturally to restore itself to full employment after temporary shocks.

   a. The General Theory of Employment, Interest and Money
   b. Wealth of Nations
   c. General Theory of Employment, Interest and Money
   d. Principles of Political Economy

49. The _____ was a worldwide economic downturn starting in most places in 1929 and ending at different times in the 1930s or early 1940s for different countries. It was the largest and most important economic depression in the 20th century, and is used in the 21st century as an example of how far the world's economy can fall. The _____ originated in the United States; historians most often use as a starting date the stock market crash on October 29, 1929, known as Black Tuesday.

   a. Great Depression
   b. British Empire Economic Conference
   c. Wall Street Crash of 1929
   d. Jarrow March

50. _____ is a fee paid on borrowed assets. It is the price paid for the use of borrowed money , or, money earned by deposited funds . Assets that are sometimes lent with _____ include money, shares, consumer goods through hire purchase, major assets such as aircraft, and even entire factories in finance lease arrangements.

   a. Interest
   b. Insolvency
   c. Asset protection
   d. Internal debt

51. A _____ is any systematic process enabling many market players to bid and ask: helping bidders and sellers interact and make deals. It is not just the price mechanism but the entire system of regulation, qualification, credentials, reputations and clearing that surrounds that mechanism and makes it operate in a social context.

Because a _____ relies on the assumption that players are constantly involved and unequally enabled, a _____ is distinguished specifically from a voting system where candidates seek the support of voters on a less regular basis.

   a. Price mechanism
   b. Contestable market
   c. Market system
   d. Competitive equilibrium

52. _____ is an economic model based on price, utility and quantity in a market. It predicts that in a competitive market, price will function to equalize the quantity demanded by consumers, and the quantity supplied by producers, resulting in an economic equilibrium of price and quantity. The model incorporates other factors changing equilibrium as a shift of demand and/or supply.
   a. Deferred gratification
   b. Joint demand
   c. Rational addiction
   d. Supply and demand

53. _____ is widely regarded as the first modern school of economic thought. It is the idea that free markets can regulate themselves. Its major developers include Adam Smith, David Ricardo, Thomas Malthus and John Stuart Mill. Sometimes the definition of _____ is expanded to include William Petty, Johann Heinrich von Thünen.
   a. Classical economics
   b. Tendency of the rate of profit to fall
   c. Marginalism
   d. Schools of economic thought

54. _____ arises when aggregate demand in an economy outpaces aggregate supply. It involves inflation rising as real gross domestic product rises and unemployment falls, as the economy moves along the Phillips curve. This is commonly described as 'too much money chasing too few goods'.
   a. Kinked demand curve
   b. Marshallian demand function
   c. Kinked demand
   d. Demand-pull inflation

55. An _____, in economics, is the amount by which the real Gross domestic product exceeds potential GDP. The real GDP is also known as GDP 'adjusted for inflation', 'constant prices' GDP or 'constant dollar' GDP, because it measures the aggregate output in a country's income accounts in a given year, expressed in base-year prices. On the other hand, the potential GDP is the quantity of real GDP when a country's economy is at full-employment.
   a. AD-IA Model
   b. ACEA agreement
   c. Inflationary gap
   d. ACCRA Cost of Living Index

56. In economics, _____ is the total demand for final goods and services in the economy (Y) at a given time and price level. It is the amount of goods and services in the economy that will be purchased at all possible price levels. This is the demand for the gross domestic product of a country when inventory levels are static.
   a. Aggregate expenditure
   b. Aggregate supply
   c. Aggregation problem
   d. Aggregate demand

57. In economics, _____ is the total supply of goods and services produced by a national economy during a specific time period. It is the total amount of goods and services in the economy available at all possible price levels.
   a. Aggregation problem
   b. Aggregate supply
   c. Aggregate expenditure
   d. Aggregate demand

Chapter 10. Aggregate Demand and Aggregate Supply

1. The _____ is the central banking system of the United States. Created in 1913 by the enactment of the Federal Reserve Act (signed by Woodrow Wilson), it is a quasi-public and quasi-private (government entity with private components) banking system that comprises (1) the presidentially appointed Board of Governors of the _____ in Washington, D.C.; (2) the Federal Open Market Committee; (3) twelve regional Federal Reserve Banks located in major cities throughout the nation acting as fiscal agents for the U.S. Treasury, each with its own nine-member board of directors; (4) numerous other private U.S. member banks, which subscribe to required amounts of non-transferable stock in their regional Federal Reserve Banks; and (5) various advisory councils. Since February 2006, Ben Bernanke has served as the Chairman of the Board of Governors of the _____.
    a. Term auction facility
    b. Monetary Policy Report to the Congress
    c. Federal Reserve System Open Market Account
    d. Federal Reserve System

2. _____ is an American economist and was the Chairman of the Federal Reserve of the United States from 1987 to 2006. He currently works as a private advisor and providing consulting for firms through his company, Greenspan Associates LLC.

First appointed Federal Reserve chairman by President Ronald Reagan in August 1987, he was reappointed at successive four-year intervals until retiring on January 31, 2006 after the second-longest tenure in the position.
    a. Alan Greenspan
    b. Adolph Fischer
    c. Adam Smith
    d. Adolf Hitler

3. In economics, a _____ is a general slowdown in economic activity over a sustained period of time, or a business cycle contraction. During _____s, many macroeconomic indicators vary in a similar way. Production as measured by Gross Domestic Product (GDP), employment, investment spending, capacity utilization, household incomes and business profits all fall during _____s.
    a. Monetary economics
    b. Recession
    c. Treasury View
    d. Leading indicators

4. The _____ or Aggregate Demand-Aggregate Supply model is a macroeconomic model that explains price level and output through the relationship of aggregate demand and aggregate supply. It was first put forth by John Maynard Keynes in his work The General Theory of Employment, Interest, and Money. It is the foundation for the modern field of macroeconomics, and is accepted by a broad array of economists, from Libertarian, Monetarist supporters of laissez-faire, such as Milton Friedman to Socialist, Post-Keynesian supporters of economic interventionism, such as Joan Robinson.
    a. Economic interdependence
    b. IS/LM model
    c. Adaptive expectations
    d. AD-AS

5. In economics, _____ is the total demand for final goods and services in the economy (Y) at a given time and price level. It is the amount of goods and services in the economy that will be purchased at all possible price levels. This is the demand for the gross domestic product of a country when inventory levels are static.
    a. Aggregation problem
    b. Aggregate supply
    c. Aggregate demand
    d. Aggregate expenditure

6. _____ is a broad label that refers to any individuals or households that use goods and services generated within the economy. The concept of a _____ is used in different contexts, so that the usage and significance of the term may vary.

Chapter 10. Aggregate Demand and Aggregate Supply

Typically when business people and economists talk of _____s they are talking about person as _____, an aggregated commodity item with little individuality other than that expressed in the buy/not-buy decision.

a. 100-year flood
c. 1921 recession
b. Consumer
d. 130-30 fund

7. _____ or consumer demand or consumption is also known as personal consumption expenditure. It is the largest part of aggregate demand or effective demand at the macroeconomic level. There are two variants of consumption in the aggregate demand model, including induced consumption and autonomous consumption.
   a. Consumer spending
   c. Complex multiplier
   b. Potential output
   d. Dishoarding

8. The _____ or gross domestic income (GDI), a basic measure of an economy's economic performance, is the market value of all final goods and services produced within the borders of a nation in a year. _____ can be defined in three ways, all of which are conceptually identical. First, it is equal to the total expenditures for all final goods and services produced within the country in a stipulated period of time (usually a 365-day year.)
   a. Gross domestic product
   c. Countercyclical
   b. Monopolistic competition
   d. Market structure

9. In economics, the _____ is the change in consumption resulting from a change in real income.

Another important item that can change is the money income of the consumer. The _____ is the phenomenon observed through changes in purchasing power.

   a. Income effect
   c. Inflation hedge
   b. Export subsidy
   d. Equilibrium wage

10. _____ and Keynesian Theory) is a macroeconomic theory based on the ideas of 20th-century British economist John Maynard Keynes. _____ argues that private sector decisions sometimes lead to inefficient macroeconomic outcomes and therefore advocates active policy responses by the public sector, including monetary policy actions by the central bank and fiscal policy actions by the government to stabilize output over the business cycle.

The theories forming the basis of _____ were first presented in The General Theory of Employment, Interest and Money, published in 1936.

   a. Market failure
   c. Deflation
   b. Rational choice theory
   d. Keynesian economics

11. _____ in economics and business is the result of an exchange and from that trade we assign a numerical monetary value to a good, service or asset. If Alice trades Bob 4 apples for an orange, the _____ of an orange is 4 apples. Inversely, the _____ of an apple is 1/4 oranges.
   a. Premium pricing
   c. Price book
   b. Price war
   d. Price

Chapter 10. Aggregate Demand and Aggregate Supply

12. A _____ is a hypothetical measure of overall prices for some set of goods and services, in a given region during a given interval, normalized relative to some base set. Typically, a _____ is approximated with a price index.

The classical dichotomy is the assumption that there is a relatively clean distinction between overall increases or decreases in prices and underlying, e;reale; economic variables.

   a. Discouraged worker
   c. Price elasticity of supply
   b. Price level
   d. Discretionary spending

13. A public utility (usually just utility) is an organization that maintains the infrastructure for a public service (often also providing a service using that infrastructure.) _____ are subject to forms of public control and regulation ranging from local community-based groups to state-wide government monopolies. Common arguments in favor of regulation include the desire to control market power, facilitate competition, promote investment or system expansion, or stabilize markets.
   a. 130-30 fund
   c. 100-year flood
   b. 1921 recession
   d. Public utilities

14. An _____, in economics, is the amount by which the real Gross domestic product exceeds potential GDP. The real GDP is also known as GDP 'adjusted for inflation', 'constant prices' GDP or 'constant dollar' GDP, because it measures the aggregate output in a country's income accounts in a given year, expressed in base-year prices. On the other hand, the potential GDP is the quantity of real GDP when a country's economy is at full-employment.
   a. ACCRA Cost of Living Index
   c. Inflationary gap
   b. AD-IA Model
   d. ACEA agreement

15. Economics:

   - _____,the desire to own something and the ability to pay for it
   - _____ curve,a graphic representation of a _____ schedule
   - _____ deposit, the money in checking accounts
   - _____ pull theory,the theory that inflation occurs when _____ for goods and services exceeds existing supplies
   - _____ schedule,a table that lists the quantity of a good a person will buy it each different price
   - _____ side economics,the school of economics at believes government spending and tax cuts open economy by raising _____

   a. McKesson ' Robbins scandal
   c. Variability
   b. Production
   d. Demand

16. In economics, the _____ can be defined as the graph depicting the relationship between the price of a certain commodity, and the amount of it that consumers are willing and able to purchase at that given price. It is a graphic representation of a demand schedule. The _____ for all consumers together follows from the _____ of every individual consumer: the individual demands at each price are added together.
   a. Cost curve
   c. Wage curve
   b. Demand curve
   d. Kuznets curve

17. _____ is a common concept in economics, and gives rise to derived concepts such as consumer debt. Generally _____ is defined by opposition to production. But the precise definition can vary because different schools of economists define production quite differently.

a. Cash or share options
b. Federal Reserve Bank Notes
c. Foreclosure data providers
d. Consumption

18. In algebra, a _____ is a function depending on n that associates a scalar, det(A), to an n×n square matrix A. The fundamental geometric meaning of a _____ is a scale factor for measure when A is regarded as a linear transformation. _____s are important both in calculus, where they enter the substitution rule for several variables, and in multilinear algebra.

For a fixed nonnegative integer n, there is a unique _____ function for the n×n matrices over any commutative ring R. In particular, this function exists when R is the field of real or complex numbers.

a. 1921 recession
b. 130-30 fund
c. 100-year flood
d. Determinant

19. In economics, an _____ is any good or commodity, transported from one country to another country in a legitimate fashion, typically for use in trade. _____ goods or services are provided to foreign consumers by domestic producers. _____ is an important part of international trade.

a. ACCRA Cost of Living Index
b. ACEA agreement
c. AD-IA Model
d. Export

20. In economics, an _____ is any good (e.g. a commodity) or service brought into one country from another country in a legitimate fashion, typically for use in trade. It is a good that is brought in from another country for sale. _____ goods or services are provided to domestic consumers by foreign producers. An _____ in the receiving country is an export to the sending country.

a. Economic integration
b. Import quota
c. Import
d. Incoterms

21. In economics, the _____ is an empirical metric that quantifies induced consumption, the concept that the increase in personal consumer spending (consumption) that occurs with an increase in disposable income (income after taxes and transfers.) For example, if a household earns one extra dollar of disposable income, and the _____ is 0.65, then of that dollar, the household will spend 65 cents and save 35 cents.

Mathematically, the _____ (MPC) function is expressed as the derivative of the consumption (C) function with respect to disposable income (Y.)

a. Supply shock
b. Marginal propensity to import
c. Marginal propensity to consume
d. Technology shock

22. In economics, _____ is the total amount of money available in an economy at a particular point in time. There are several ways to define 'money', but standard measures usually include currency in circulation and demand deposits.

_____ data are recorded and published, usually by the government or the central bank of the country.

a. Money supply
b. Velocity of money
c. Neutrality of money
d. Veil of money

23. In economics, _____ is a measure of national income. Basically, it is an approach to measure GDP. It is defined as the value of planned goods and services produced in an economy.
   a. Aggregation problem
   b. Aggregate expenditure
   c. Aggregate demand
   d. Aggregate supply

24. _____ is a term used in accounting, economics and finance to spread the cost of an asset over the span of several years.

In simple words we can say that _____ is the reduction in the value of an asset due to usage, passage of time, wear and tear, technological outdating or obsolescence, depletion, inadequacy, rot, rust, decay or other such factors.

In accounting, _____ is a term used to describe any method of attributing the historical or purchase cost of an asset across its useful life, roughly corresponding to normal wear and tear.

   a. Historical cost
   b. Salvage value
   c. Net income per employee
   d. Depreciation

25. _____ is a fee paid on borrowed assets. It is the price paid for the use of borrowed money, or, money earned by deposited funds. Assets that are sometimes lent with _____ include money, shares, consumer goods through hire purchase, major assets such as aircraft, and even entire factories in finance lease arrangements.
   a. Insolvency
   b. Internal debt
   c. Asset protection
   d. Interest

26. An _____ is the price a borrower pays for the use of money they do not own, for instance a small company might borrow from a bank to kick start their business, and the return a lender receives for deferring the use of funds, by lending it to the borrower. _____s are normally expressed as a percentage rate over the period of one year.

_____s targets are also a vital tool of monetary policy and are used to control variables like investment, inflation, and unemployment.

   a. Enterprise value
   b. ACCRA Cost of Living Index
   c. Interest rate
   d. Arrow-Debreu model

27. _____ refers to a business or organization attempting to acquire goods or services to accomplish the goals of the enterprise. Though there are several organizations that attempt to set standards in the _____ process, processes can vary greatly between organizations. Typically the word '_____' is not used interchangeably with the word 'procurement', since procurement typically includes Expediting, Supplier Quality, and Traffic and Logistics (T'L) in addition to _____.
   a. 100-year flood
   b. 130-30 fund
   c. Purchasing
   d. Free port

Chapter 10. Aggregate Demand and Aggregate Supply

28. A _____ is a duty imposed on goods when they are moved across a political boundary. They are usually associated with protectionism, the economic policy of restraining trade between nations. For political reasons, _____s are usually imposed on imported goods, although they may also be imposed on exported goods.
    a. 100-year flood
    b. 130-30 fund
    c. Tariff
    d. 1921 recession

29. A _____ product is a product designed for cheapness and short-term convenience rather than medium to long-term durability, with most products only intended for single use. The term is also sometimes used for products that may last several months (ex. _____ air filters) to distinguish from similar products that last indefinitely (ex.
    a. 130-30 fund
    b. Disposable
    c. 1921 recession
    d. 100-year flood

30. _____ is gross income minus income tax on that income.

Discretionary income is income after subtracting taxes and normal expenses (such as rent or mortgage, utilities, insurance, medical, transportation, property maintenance, child support, inflation, food and sundries, 'c.') to maintain a certain standard of living.

    a. Disposable income
    b. Disposable personal income
    c. Taxation as theft
    d. Stamp Act

31. The _____ is 'the basic residential unit in which economic production, consumption, inheritance, child rearing, and shelter are organized and carried out'; [the _____] 'may or may not be synonomous with family'.

The _____ is the basic unit of analysis in many social, microeconomic and government models. The term refers to all individuals who live in the same dwelling.

    a. 100-year flood
    b. 130-30 fund
    c. Family economics
    d. Household

32. In economics, _____ is a rise in the general level of prices of goods and services in an economy over a period of time. When the general price level rises, each unit of currency buys fewer goods and services; consequently, _____ is also a decline in the real value of money--a loss of purchasing power in the medium of exchange which is also the monetary unit of account in the economy. A chief measure of general price-level _____ is the general _____ rate, which is the percentage change in a general price index (normally the Consumer Price Index) over time.
    a. Inflation
    b. Economic
    c. Energy economics
    d. Opportunity cost

33. A variety of measures of _____ and output are used in economics to estimate total economic activity in a country or region, including gross domestic product (GDP), gross national product (GNP), and net _____

There are three main ways of calculating these numbers; the output approach, the income approach and the expenditure approach. In theory, the three must yield the same, because total expenditures on goods and services must equal the total income paid to the producers (Gnational income), and that must also equal the total value of the output of goods and services (GNP.)

Chapter 10. Aggregate Demand and Aggregate Supply

- a. Volume index
- b. GNI per capita
- c. Gross world product
- d. National income

34. The '_____' is approximately the nominal interest rate minus the inflation rate Since the inflation rate over the course of a loan is not known initially, volatility in inflation represents a risk to both the lender and the borrower.

In economics and finance, an individual who lends money for repayment at a later point in time expects to be compensated for the time value of money, or not having the use of that money while it is lent.

- a. Cost-push inflation
- b. Reflation
- c. Core inflation
- d. Real interest rate

35. The _____ is an economic term, referring to an increase in spending that accompanies an increase or perceived increase in wealth.

The effect would cause changes in the amounts and composition of consumer consumption caused by changes in consumer wealth. People should spend more when one of two things is true: when people actually are richer (by objective measurement, for example, a bonus or a pay raise at work, which would be an income effect), or when people perceive themselves to be 'richer' (for example, the assessed value of their home increases, or a stock they own has gone up in price recently.)

- a. Wealth condensation
- b. 130-30 fund
- c. 100-year flood
- d. Wealth effect

36. In economics and business, specifically cost accounting, the _____ point (BEP) is the point at which cost or expenses and revenue are equal: there is no net loss or gain, and one has 'broken even'. A profit or a loss has not been made, although opportunity costs have been paid, and capital has received the risk-adjusted, expected return.

For example, if the business sells less than 200 tables each month, it will make a loss, if it sells more, it will be a profit.

- a. Nonmarket
- b. Break-even
- c. Buffer stock scheme
- d. Small numbers game

37. _____ is that which is owed; usually referencing assets owed, but the term can also cover moral obligations and other interactions not requiring money. In the case of assets, _____ is a means of using future purchasing power in the present before a summation has been earned. Some companies and corporations use _____ as a part of their overall corporate finance strategy.
- a. Collateral Management
- b. Debenture
- c. Hard money loan
- d. Debt

38. To _____ is to impose a financial charge or other levy upon a taxpayer by a state or the functional equivalent of a state.

_____es are also imposed by many subnational entities. _____es consist of direct _____ or indirect _____, and may be paid in money or as its labour equivalent (often but not always unpaid.)

Chapter 10. Aggregate Demand and Aggregate Supply

a. 1921 recession
c. 100-year flood
b. Tax
d. 130-30 fund

39. To tax is to impose a financial charge or other levy upon a taxpayer by a state or the functional equivalent of a state.

_____ are also imposed by many subnational entities. _____ consist of direct tax or indirect tax, and may be paid in money or as its labour equivalent (often but not always unpaid.)

a. Taxes
c. 100-year flood
b. 1921 recession
d. 130-30 fund

40. The _____ is published by The Economist as an informal way of measuring the purchasing power parity (PPP) between two currencies and provides a test of the extent to which market exchange rates result in goods costing the same in different countries. It 'seeks to make exchange-rate theory a bit more digestible'.

The index takes its name from the Big Mac, a hamburger sold at McDonald's restaurants.

a. Rank mobility index
c. Cost-weighted activity index
b. Big Mac index
d. Deindexation

41. The _____ is the weighted-average most likely outcome in gambling, probability theory, economics or finance.

What Does _____ Mean? The average of a probability distribution of possible returns, calculated by using the following formula:

E(R)= Sum: probability (in scenario i) * the return (in scenario i)

How do you calculate the average of a probability distribution? As denoted by the above formula, simply take the probability of each possible return outcome and multiply it by the return outcome itself. For example, if you knew a given investment had a 50% chance of earning a 10% return, a 25% chance of earning 20% and a 25% chance of earning -10%, the _____ would be equal to 7.5%:

= (0.5) (0.1) + (0.25) (0.2) + (0.25) (-0.1) = 0.075 = 7.5%

Although this is what you expect the return to be, there is no guarantee that it will be the actual return.

a. ACEA agreement
c. AD-IA Model
b. ACCRA Cost of Living Index
d. Expected return

42. _____ or government expenditure is classified by economists into three main types. Government purchases of goods and services for current use are classed as government consumption. Government purchases of goods and services intended to create future benefits, such as infrastructure investment or research spending, are classed as government investment.

a. 100-year flood
c. 130-30 fund
b. 1921 recession
d. Government spending

43. In economics, the _____ of demand measures the responsiveness of the demand of a good to the change in the income of the people demanding the good. It is calculated as the ratio of the percent change in demand to the percent change in income. For example, if, in response to a 10% increase in income, the demand of a good increased by 20%, the _____ of demand would be 20%/10% = 2.
   a. ACEA agreement
   c. AD-IA Model
   b. ACCRA Cost of Living Index
   d. Income elasticity

44. In economics, the _____ measures the responsiveness of the demand of a good to the change in the income of the people demanding the good. It is calculated as the ratio of the percent change in demand to the percent change in income. For example, if, in response to a 10% increase in income, the demand of a good increased by 20%, the _____ would be 20%/10% = 2.
   a. Elasticity of substitution
   c. Income elasticity of demand
   b. Expenditure minimization problem
   d. Indifference map

45. _____ is defined as the measure of responsiveness in the quantity demanded for a commodity as a result of change in price of the same commodity. It is a measure of how consumers react to a change in price. In other words, it is percentage change in quantity demanded as per the percentage change in price of the same commodity.
   a. 130-30 fund
   c. Price elasticity of demand
   b. 100-year flood
   d. 1921 recession

46. In economics, _____ is the total supply of goods and services produced by a national economy during a specific time period. It is the total amount of goods and services in the economy available at all possible price levels.
   a. Aggregate expenditure
   c. Aggregation problem
   b. Aggregate demand
   d. Aggregate supply

47. In economics, _____ is the ratio of the percent change in one variable to the percent change in another variable. It is a tool for measuring the responsiveness of a function to changes in parameters in a relative way. Commonly analyzed are _____ of substitution, price and wealth.
   a. ACCRA Cost of Living Index
   c. ACEA agreement
   b. Elasticity of demand
   d. Elasticity

48. Price _____ is defined as the measure of responsiveness in the quantity demanded for a commodity as a result of change in price of the same commodity. It is a measure of how consumers react to a change in price. In other words, it is percentage change in quantity demanded by the percentage change in price of the same commodity.
   a. ACCRA Cost of Living Index
   c. Elasticity
   b. ACEA agreement
   d. Elasticity of demand

49. In finance, the _____s between two currencies specifies how much one currency is worth in terms of the other. It is the value of a foreign natione;s currency in terms of the home natione;s currency. For example an _____ of 102 Japanese yen to the United States dollar means that JPY 102 is worth the same as USD 1.
   a. ACEA agreement
   c. Interbank market
   b. ACCRA Cost of Living Index
   d. Exchange rate

Chapter 10. Aggregate Demand and Aggregate Supply

50. _____ is the difference between price and the costs of bringing to market whatever it is that is accounted as an enterprise (whether by harvest, extraction, manufacture, or purchase) in terms of the component costs of delivered goods and/or services and any operating or other expenses.

A key difficulty in measuring profit is in defining costs. Pure economic monetary profits can be zero or negative even in competitive equilibrium when accounted monetized costs exceed monetized price.

a. Operating profit
b. Economic profit
c. ACCRA Cost of Living Index
d. Accounting profit

51. _____s is the social science that studies the production, distribution, and consumption of goods and services. The term _____s comes from the Ancient Greek oá¼°κονομῖα from oá¼¶κος (oikos, 'house') + vÏŒμος (nomos, 'custom' or 'law'), hence 'rules of the house(hold)'. Current _____ models developed out of the broader field of political economy in the late 19th century, owing to a desire to use an empirical approach more akin to the physical sciences.

a. Inflation
b. Opportunity cost
c. Energy economics
d. Economic

52. In economics, _____ is the difference between a company's total revenue and its opportunity costs. It is the increase in wealth that an investor has from making an investment, taking into consideration all costs associated with that investment including the opportunity cost of capital.

Profit is the factor income of the entrepreneur.

a. Operating profit
b. Accounting profit
c. ACCRA Cost of Living Index
d. Economic profit

53. The _____ or the output gap is the difference between potential GDP and actual GDP or actual output. The calculation for the output gap is Y-Y* where Y* is potential output and Y is actual output. If this calculation yields a positive number it is called an expansionary gap and indicates an economy in expansion; if the calculation yields a negative number it is called a recessionary gap and indicates an economy in recession.

a. 1921 recession
b. 100-year flood
c. 130-30 fund
d. GDP gap

54. In economic models, the _____ time frame assumes no fixed factors of production. Firms can enter or leave the marketplace, and the cost (and availability) of land, labor, raw materials, and capital goods can be assumed to vary. In contrast, in the short-run time frame, certain factors are assumed to be fixed, because there is not sufficient time for them to change.

a. Price/performance ratio
b. Productivity world
c. Diseconomies of scale
d. Long-run

55. _____ is a component of the firm's opportunity costs. The time that the owner spends running the firm could be spent on running another firm. This is _____: the return the entrepreneur can expect to earn or the profit that the business owners considers necessary to make running the business worth his/her while.

a. 100-year flood
b. Normal profit
c. Profit margin
d. Profit maximization

56.

A _____ is a type of financial intermediary and a type of bank. Commercial banking is also known as business banking. It is a bank that provides checking accounts, savings accounts, and money market accounts and that accepts time deposits.

a. Lombard banking
c. Daylight overdraft
b. Bought deal
d. Commercial bank

57. _____ is a type of inflation caused by substantial increases in the cost of important goods or services where no suitable alternative is available. A situation that has been often cited of this was the oil crisis of the 1970s, which some economists see as a major cause of the inflation experienced in the Western world in that decade. It is argued that this inflation resulted from increases in the cost of petroleum imposed by the member states of OPEC.

a. Headline inflation
c. Chronic inflation
b. Mundell-Tobin effect
d. Cost-push inflation

58. In economics, _____ are the resources employed to produce goods and services. They facilitate production but do not become part of the product (as with raw materials) or significantly transformed by the production process (as with fuel used to power machinery.) To 19th century economists, the _____ were land (natural resources, gifts from nature), labor (the ability to work), and capital goods (human-made tools and equipment.)

a. Factors of production
c. Hicks-neutral technical change
b. Long-run
d. Product Pipeline

59. The term _____s refers to wages that have been adjusted for inflation. This term is used in contrast to nominal wages or unadjusted wages.

The use of adjusted figures is in undertaking some form of economic analysis.

a. Real wage
c. Federal Wage System
b. Profit sharing
d. Living wage

60. In economics, the concept of the _____ refers to the decision-making time frame of a firm in which at least one factor of production is fixed. Costs which are fixed in the _____ have no impact on a firms decisions. For example a firm can raise output by increasing the amount of labour through overtime.

a. Short-run
c. Productivity model
b. Hicks-neutral technical change
d. Product Pipeline

61. The term _____ refers to economy-wide fluctuations in production or economic activity over several months or years. These fluctuations occur around a long-term growth trend, and typically involve shifts over time between periods of relatively rapid economic growth (expansion or boom), and periods of relative stagnation or decline (contraction or recession.)

These fluctuations are often measured using the growth rate of real gross domestic product.

Chapter 10. Aggregate Demand and Aggregate Supply

a. Consumer theory
c. Tobit model
b. Nominal value
d. Business cycle

62. Necessary _____s:

If x is a necessary _____ of y, then the presence of y necessarily implies the presence of x. The presence of x, however, does not imply that y will occur.

Sufficient _____s:

If x is a sufficient _____ of y, then the presence of x necessarily implies the presence of y.

a. Political philosophy
c. Philosophy of economics
b. Materialism
d. Cause

63. In microeconomics, _____ is quite simply the conversion of inputs into outputs. It is an economic process that uses resources to create a good or service that is suitable for exchange. This can include manufacturing, storing, shipping, and packaging.

a. Production
c. MET
b. Red Guards
d. Solved

64. _____ is the term denoting either an entrance or changes which are inserted into a system and which activate/modify a process. It is an abstract concept, used in the modeling, system(s) design and system(s) exploitation. It is usually connected with other terms, e.g., _____ field, _____ variable, _____ parameter, _____ value, _____ signal, _____ device and _____ file.

a. ACEA agreement
c. AD-IA Model
b. ACCRA Cost of Living Index
d. Input

65. The supply of labor is the number of total hours that workers wish to work at a given real wage rate.

_____ curves are derived from the 'labor-leisure' trade-off. More hours worked earn higher incomes but necessitate a cut in the amount of leisure that workers enjoy.

a. Late capitalism
c. Creative capitalism
b. Human trafficking
d. Labor supply

66. In economics, the _____ is defined as a numerical measure of the responsiveness of the quantity supplied of product (A) to a change in price of product (A) alone. It is the measure of the way quantity supplied reacts to a change in price.

>

For example, if, in response to a 10% rise in the price of a good, the quantity supplied increases by 20%, the _____ would be 20%/10% = 2.

Chapter 10. Aggregate Demand and Aggregate Supply

a. Demand shaping
b. Price elasticity of supply
c. Passive income
d. Hedonimetry

67. A _____ is:

- Rewrite _____, in generative grammar and computer science
- Standardization, a formal and widely-accepted statement, fact, definition, or qualification
- Operation, a determinate _____ for performing a mathematical operation and obtaining a certain result (Mathematics, Logic)
    - Unary operation
    - Binary operation
- _____ of inference, a function from sets of formulae to formulae (Mathematics, Logic)
- _____ of thumb, principle with broad application that is not intended to be strictly accurate or reliable for every situation. Also often simply referred to as a _____
- Moral, an atomic element of a moral code for guiding choices in human behavior
- Heuristic, a quantized '_____' which shows a tendency or probability for successful function
- A regulation, as in sports
- A Production _____, as in computer science
- Procedural law, a _____ set governing the application of laws to cases
    - A law, which may informally be called a '_____'
    - A court ruling, a decision by a court
- In the U.S. Government, a regulation mandated by Congress, but written or expanded upon by the Executive Branch.
- Norm (sociology), an informal but widely accepted _____, concept, truth, definition, or qualification (social norms, legal norms, coding norms)
- Norm (philosophy), a kind of sentence or a reason to act, feel or believe
- 'Rulership' is the concept of governance by a government:
    - Military _____, governance by a military body
    - Monastic _____, a collection of precepts that guides the life of monks or nuns in a religious order where the superior holds the place of Christ
- Slide _____

- '_____,' a song by Ayumi Hamasaki
- '_____,' a song by rapper Nas
- '_____s,' an album by the band The Whitest Boy Alive
- _____s: Pyaar Ka Superhit Formula, a 2003 Bollywood film
- ruler, an instrument for measuring lengths
- _____, a component of an astrolabe, circumferator or similar instrument
- The _____s, a bestselling self-help book
- _____ Project (Run Up-to-date Linux Everywhere), a project that aims to use up-to-date Linux software on old PCs
- _____ engine, a software system that helps managing business _____s
- Ja _____, a hip hop artist
    - R.U.L.E., a 2005 greatest hits album by rapper Ja _____
- '_____s,' a KMFDM song

Chapter 10. Aggregate Demand and Aggregate Supply

a. Demand
c. Procter ' Gamble
b. Technocracy
d. Rule

68. In economics, _____ is the ability of a firm to alter the market price of a good or service. A firm with _____ can raise prices without losing all customers to competitors.

When a firm has _____ it faces a downward-sloping demand curve.

a. Revenue-cap regulation
c. Pacman conjecture
b. Market power
d. Price makers

69. The _____ consists of a number of economic theories which describe the nature of the firm, company including its existence, its behaviour, and its relationship with the market.

In simplified terms, the _____ aims to answer these questions:

1. Existence - why do firms emerge, why are not all transactions in the economy mediated over the market?
2. Boundaries - why the boundary between firms and the market is located exactly there? Which transactions are performed internally and which are negotiated on the market?
3. Organization - why are firms structured in such specific way? What is the interplay of formal and informal relationships?

Despite looking simple, these questions are not answered by the established economic theory, which usually views firms as given, and treats them as black boxes without any internal structure.

The First World War period saw a change of emphasis in economic theory away from industry-level analysis which mainly included analysing markets to analysis at the level of the firm, as it became increasingly clear that perfect competition was no longer an adequate model of how firms behaved. Economic theory till then had focussed on trying to understand markets alone and there had been little study on understanding why firms or organisations exist.

a. Policy Ineffectiveness Proposition
c. Khazzoom-Brookes postulate
b. Technology gap
d. Theory of the firm

70. _____ in economics refers to metrics and measures of output from production processes, per unit of input. Labor _____, for example, is typically measured as a ratio of output per labor-hour, an input. _____ may be conceived of as a metrics of the technical or engineering efficiency of production.

a. Fordism
c. Piece work
b. Production-possibility frontier
d. Productivity

71. _____ arises when aggregate demand in an economy outpaces aggregate supply. It involves inflation rising as real gross domestic product rises and unemployment falls, as the economy moves along the Phillips curve. This is commonly described as 'too much money chasing too few goods'.

a. Demand-pull inflation
b. Kinked demand curve
c. Marshallian demand function
d. Kinked demand

72. In macroeconomics, _____ is a condition of the national economy, where all or nearly all persons willing and able to work at the prevailing wages and working conditions are able to do so. It is defined either as 0% unemployment, literally, no unemployment (the rate of unemployment is the fraction of the work force unable to find work), as by James Tobin, or as the level of employment rates when there is no cyclical unemployment. It is defined by the majority of mainstream economists as being an acceptable level of natural unemployment above 0%, the discrepancy from 0% being due to non-cyclical types of unemployment.
a. Marginal propensity to consume
b. Harrod-Johnson diagram
c. Demand shock
d. Full employment

73. In economics, a _____ occurs when, due to the economies of scale of a particular industry, the maximum efficiency of production and distribution is realized through a single supplier.

Natural monopolies arise where the largest supplier in an industry, often the first supplier in a market, has an overwhelming cost advantage over other actual or potential competitors. This tends to be the case in industries where capital costs predominate, creating economies of scale which are large in relation to the size of the market, and hence high barriers to entry; examples include water services and electricity.

a. Common-pool resource
b. Collective goods
c. Privatizing profits and socializing losses
d. Natural monopoly

74. In economics, a _____ exists when a specific individual or enterprise has sufficient control over a particular product or service to determine significantly the terms on which other individuals shall have access to it. Monopolies are thus characterized by a lack of economic competition for the good or service that they provide and a lack of viable substitute goods. The verb 'monopolize' refers to the process by which a firm gains persistently greater market share than what is expected under perfect competition.
a. Monopoly
b. 100-year flood
c. 130-30 fund
d. 1921 recession

75. Economists distinguish between various types of unemployment, including _____, frictional unemployment, structural unemployment and classical unemployment. Some additional types of unemployment that are occasionally mentioned are seasonal unemployment, hardcore unemployment, and hidden unemployment. Real-world unemployment may combine different types.
a. Seasonal unemployment
b. Types of unemployment
c. Structural unemployment
d. Cyclical unemployment

76. In economics, _____ is a sustained decrease in the general price level of goods and services. _____ occurs when the annual inflation rate falls below zero percent, resulting in an increase in the real value of money -- a negative inflation rate. This should not be confused with disinflation, a slow-down in the inflation rate (i.e. when the inflation decreases, but still remains positive.)
a. Tobit model
b. Literacy rate
c. Price revolution
d. Deflation

Chapter 10. Aggregate Demand and Aggregate Supply

77. In labor economics, the _____ hypothesis argues that wages, at least in some markets, are determined by more than simply supply and demand. Specifically, it points to the incentive for managers to pay their employees more than the market-clearing wage in order to increase their productivity or efficiency. This increased labor productivity pays for the relatively higher wages.
   a. Exogenous growth model
   b. Inflatable rats
   c. Earnings calls
   d. Efficiency wage

78. A _____ is the lowest hourly, daily or monthly wage that employers may legally pay to employees or workers. Equivalently, it is the lowest wage at which workers may sell their labor. Although _____ laws are in effect in a great many jurisdictions, there are differences of opinion about the benefits and drawbacks of a _____.
   a. Permanent war economy
   b. Marginal propensity to consume
   c. Microfoundations
   d. Minimum wage

79. _____ is a term used in business to indicate a state of intense competitive rivalry accompanied by a multi-lateral series of price reduction. One competitor will lower its price, then others will lower their prices to match. If one of them reduces their price again, a new round of reductions starts.
   a. Transactional Net Margin Method
   b. Big ticket item
   c. Discounts and allowances
   d. Price war

80. The _____ is the commonly observed phenomenon that some processes cannot go backwards once certain things have happened, by analogy with the mechanical ratchet that holds the spring tight as a clock is wound up. It is related to the phenomena of featuritis and scope creep in the manufacture of various consumer goods, and of mission creep in military planning.

Garrett Hardin, a biologist and environmentalist who also wrote of the 'tragedy of the commons', used the phrase to describe how food aid keeps alive people who would otherwise die in a famine.

   a. Non-credible threat
   b. Purification theorem
   c. Partnership game
   d. Ratchet effect

81. _____ is the increase in the amount of the goods and services produced by an economy over time. It is conventionally measured as the percent rate of increase in real gross domestic product, or real GDP. Growth is usually calculated in real terms, i.e. inflation-adjusted terms, in order to net out the effect of inflation on the price of the goods and services produced.
   a. AD-IA Model
   b. Economic growth
   c. ACCRA Cost of Living Index
   d. ACEA agreement

82. A _____ is a normalized average (typically a weighted average) of prices for a given class of goods or services in a given region, during a given interval of time. It is a statistic designed to help to compare how these prices, taken as a whole, differ between time periods or geographical locations.

Price indices have several potential uses.

   a. Two-part tariff
   b. Price index
   c. Product sabotage
   d. Transactional Net Margin Method

Chapter 10. Aggregate Demand and Aggregate Supply

83. A _____ is an event that suddenly changes the price of a commodity or service. It may be caused by a sudden increase or decrease in the supply of a particular good. This sudden change affects the equilibrium price.
    a. SIMIC
    b. Friedman rule
    c. Demand shock
    d. Supply shock

84. The _____ was an evolution of developed countries from an industrial/manufacturing-based wealth producing economy into a service sector asset based economy, brought about by globalization and currency manipulation by governments and their central banks. Some analysts claimed that this change in the economic structure of the United States had created a state of permanent steady growth, low unemployment, and immunity to boom and bust macroeconomic cycles. They believed that the change rendered obsolete many business practices.
    a. New Economy
    b. 1921 recession
    c. 100-year flood
    d. 130-30 fund

85. _____ is a theory of aesthetics based on the theories of Karl Marx. It involves a dialectical approach to the application of Marxism to the cultural sphere, specifically areas related to taste such as art, beauty, etc. Marxists believe that economic and social conditions affect every aspect of an individual's life, from religious beliefs to legal systems to cultural frameworks.
    a. 1921 recession
    b. Marxist aesthetics
    c. 100-year flood
    d. 130-30 fund

Chapter 11. Fiscal Policy, Deficits, and Debt

1. Economists distinguish between various types of unemployment, including _____, frictional unemployment, structural unemployment and classical unemployment. Some additional types of unemployment that are occasionally mentioned are seasonal unemployment, hardcore unemployment, and hidden unemployment. Real-world unemployment may combine different types.
   a. Structural unemployment
   b. Types of unemployment
   c. Seasonal unemployment
   d. Cyclical unemployment

2. The term _____ refers to government debt, expenditures and revenues, or to finance (particularly financial revenue) in general.

   • _____ deficit is the budget deficit of federal or local government
   • _____ policy is the discretionary spending of governments. Contrasts with monetary policy.
   • _____ year and _____ quarter are reporting periods for firms and other agencies.

   a. Procter ' Gamble
   b. Bucket shop
   c. Drawdown
   d. Fiscal

3. In economics, _____ is the use of government spending and revenue collection to influence the economy.

   _____ can be contrasted with the other main type of economic policy, monetary policy, which attempts to stabilize the economy by controlling interest rates and the supply of money. The two main instruments of _____ are government spending and taxation.
   a. Fiscal policy
   b. 100-year flood
   c. Sustainable investment rule
   d. Fiscalism

4. _____ is a term used in economics to describe how an economic quantity is related to economic fluctuations. It is the opposite of procyclical. However, it has more than one meaning.
   a. Law of comparative advantage
   b. Countercyclical
   c. Price revolution
   d. Mathematical economics

5. The _____ or Aggregate Demand-Aggregate Supply model is a macroeconomic model that explains price level and output through the relationship of aggregate demand and aggregate supply. It was first put forth by John Maynard Keynes in his work The General Theory of Employment, Interest, and Money. It is the foundation for the modern field of macroeconomics, and is accepted by a broad array of economists, from Libertarian, Monetarist supporters of laissez-faire, such as Milton Friedman to Socialist, Post-Keynesian supporters of economic interventionism, such as Joan Robinson.
   a. Adaptive expectations
   b. Economic interdependence
   c. AD-AS
   d. IS/LM model

6. In economics, _____ is the total demand for final goods and services in the economy (Y) at a given time and price level. It is the amount of goods and services in the economy that will be purchased at all possible price levels. This is the demand for the gross domestic product of a country when inventory levels are static.
   a. Aggregate expenditure
   b. Aggregate supply
   c. Aggregation problem
   d. Aggregate demand

Chapter 11. Fiscal Policy, Deficits, and Debt

7. A _____ represents the combinations of goods and services that a consumer can purchase given current prices and his income. Consumer theory uses the concepts of a _____ and a preference map to analyze consumer choices. Both concepts have a ready graphical representation in the two-good case.
   - a. Budget constraint
   - b. Quality bias
   - c. Joint demand
   - d. Revealed preference

8. The _____ is a group of three respected economists who advise the President of the United States on economic policy. It is a part of the Executive Office of the President of the United States, and provides much of the economic policy of the White House. The council prepares the annual Economic Report of the President.
   - a. Hybrid renewable energy systems
   - b. Constrained Pareto optimality
   - c. Federal Reserve Bank Notes
   - d. Council of Economic Advisers

9. _____s is the social science that studies the production, distribution, and consumption of goods and services. The term _____s comes from the Ancient Greek οἰκονομῖα from οἶκος (oikos, 'house') + νόμος (nomos, 'custom' or 'law'), hence 'rules of the house(hold)'. Current _____ models developed out of the broader field of political economy in the late 19th century, owing to a desire to use an empirical approach more akin to the physical sciences.
   - a. Inflation
   - b. Economic
   - c. Opportunity cost
   - d. Energy economics

10. _____ or government expenditure is classified by economists into three main types. Government purchases of goods and services for current use are classed as government consumption. Government purchases of goods and services intended to create future benefits, such as infrastructure investment or research spending, are classed as government investment.
    - a. 130-30 fund
    - b. 1921 recession
    - c. 100-year flood
    - d. Government spending

11. _____ and Keynesian Theory) is a macroeconomic theory based on the ideas of 20th-century British economist John Maynard Keynes. _____ argues that private sector decisions sometimes lead to inefficient macroeconomic outcomes and therefore advocates active policy responses by the public sector, including monetary policy actions by the central bank and fiscal policy actions by the government to stabilize output over the business cycle.

    The theories forming the basis of _____ were first presented in The General Theory of Employment, Interest and Money, published in 1936.

    - a. Keynesian economics
    - b. Rational choice theory
    - c. Market failure
    - d. Deflation

12. In economics, the _____ is an empirical metric that quantifies induced consumption, the concept that the increase in personal consumer spending (consumption) that occurs with an increase in disposable income (income after taxes and transfers.) For example, if a household earns one extra dollar of disposable income, and the _____ is 0.65, then of that dollar, the household will spend 65 cents and save 35 cents.

    Mathematically, the _____ (MPC) function is expressed as the derivative of the consumption (C) function with respect to disposable income (Y.)

a. Marginal propensity to import	b. Supply shock
c. Technology shock	d. Marginal propensity to consume

13. _____ in economics and business is the result of an exchange and from that trade we assign a numerical monetary value to a good, service or asset. If Alice trades Bob 4 apples for an orange, the _____ of an orange is 4 apples. Inversely, the _____ of an apple is 1/4 oranges.

a. Price	b. Price book
c. Premium pricing	d. Price war

14. A _____ is a hypothetical measure of overall prices for some set of goods and services, in a given region during a given interval, normalized relative to some base set. Typically, a _____ is approximated with a price index.

The classical dichotomy is the assumption that there is a relatively clean distinction between overall increases or decreases in prices and underlying, e;reale; economic variables.

a. Price level	b. Discretionary spending
c. Price elasticity of supply	d. Discouraged worker

15. In economics, a _____ is a general slowdown in economic activity over a sustained period of time, or a business cycle contraction. During _____s, many macroeconomic indicators vary in a similar way. Production as measured by Gross Domestic Product (GDP), employment, investment spending, capacity utilization, household incomes and business profits all fall during _____s.

a. Leading indicators	b. Treasury View
c. Monetary economics	d. Recession

16. A _____ occurs when an entity spends more money than it takes in. The opposite of a _____ is a budget surplus. Debt is essentially an accumulated flow of deficits.

a. Public Financial Management	b. Lump-sum tax
c. Funding body	d. Budget deficit

17. _____ is a type of inflation caused by substantial increases in the cost of important goods or services where no suitable alternative is available. A situation that has been often cited of this was the oil crisis of the 1970s, which some economists see as a major cause of the inflation experienced in the Western world in that decade. It is argued that this inflation resulted from increases in the cost of petroleum imposed by the member states of OPEC.

a. Mundell-Tobin effect	b. Chronic inflation
c. Headline inflation	d. Cost-push inflation

Chapter 11. Fiscal Policy, Deficits, and Debt

18. Economics:

    - _____, the desire to own something and the ability to pay for it
    - _____ curve, a graphic representation of a _____ schedule
    - _____ deposit, the money in checking accounts
    - _____ pull theory, the theory that inflation occurs when _____ for goods and services exceeds existing supplies
    - _____ schedule, a table that lists the quantity of a good a person will buy it each different price
    - _____ side economics, the school of economics at believes government spending and tax cuts open economy by raising _____

    a. Variability
    b. McKesson ' Robbins scandal
    c. Production
    d. Demand

19. In economics, the _____ can be defined as the graph depicting the relationship between the price of a certain commodity, and the amount of it that consumers are willing and able to purchase at that given price. It is a graphic representation of a demand schedule. The _____ for all consumers together follows from the _____ of every individual consumer: the individual demands at each price are added together.
    a. Wage curve
    b. Kuznets curve
    c. Cost curve
    d. Demand curve

20. In economics, _____ is a rise in the general level of prices of goods and services in an economy over a period of time. When the general price level rises, each unit of currency buys fewer goods and services; consequently, _____ is also a decline in the real value of money--a loss of purchasing power in the medium of exchange which is also the monetary unit of account in the economy. A chief measure of general price-level _____ is the general _____ rate, which is the percentage change in a general price index (normally the Consumer Price Index) over time.
    a. Opportunity cost
    b. Inflation
    c. Economic
    d. Energy economics

21. _____ is a common concept in economics, and gives rise to derived concepts such as consumer debt. Generally _____ is defined by opposition to production. But the precise definition can vary because different schools of economists define production quite differently.
    a. Foreclosure data providers
    b. Federal Reserve Bank Notes
    c. Cash or share options
    d. Consumption

22. _____ is a broad label that refers to any individuals or households that use goods and services generated within the economy. The concept of a _____ is used in different contexts, so that the usage and significance of the term may vary.

Typically when business people and economists talk of _____s they are talking about person as _____, an aggregated commodity item with little individuality other than that expressed in the buy/not-buy decision.

Chapter 11. Fiscal Policy, Deficits, and Debt

a. Consumer
b. 1921 recession
c. 100-year flood
d. 130-30 fund

23. _____ or consumer demand or consumption is also known as personal consumption expenditure. It is the largest part of aggregate demand or effective demand at the macroeconomic level. There are two variants of consumption in the aggregate demand model, including induced consumption and autonomous consumption.
a. Dishoarding
b. Consumer spending
c. Complex multiplier
d. Potential output

24. _____ arises when aggregate demand in an economy outpaces aggregate supply. It involves inflation rising as real gross domestic product rises and unemployment falls, as the economy moves along the Phillips curve. This is commonly described as 'too much money chasing too few goods'.
a. Kinked demand
b. Demand-pull inflation
c. Kinked demand curve
d. Marshallian demand function

25. The _____ or gross domestic income (GDI), a basic measure of an economy's economic performance, is the market value of all final goods and services produced within the borders of a nation in a year. _____ can be defined in three ways, all of which are conceptually identical. First, it is equal to the total expenditures for all final goods and services produced within the country in a stipulated period of time (usually a 365-day year.)
a. Gross domestic product
b. Countercyclical
c. Market structure
d. Monopolistic competition

26. The _____ or the output gap is the difference between potential GDP and actual GDP or actual output. The calculation for the output gap is Y-Y* where Y* is potential output and Y is actual output. If this calculation yields a positive number it is called an expansionary gap and indicates an economy in expansion; if the calculation yields a negative number it is called a recessionary gap and indicates an economy in recession.
a. GDP gap
b. 1921 recession
c. 100-year flood
d. 130-30 fund

27. To _____ is to impose a financial charge or other levy upon a taxpayer by a state or the functional equivalent of a state.

_____es are also imposed by many subnational entities. _____es consist of direct _____ or indirect _____, and may be paid in money or as its labour equivalent (often but not always unpaid.)

a. 130-30 fund
b. 1921 recession
c. 100-year flood
d. Tax

28. A _____ is a reduction in taxes. Economic stimulus via _____s, along with interest rate intervention and deficit spending, are one of the central tenets of Keynesian economics.

The immediate effects of a _____ are, generally, a decrease in the real income of the government and an increase in the real income of those whose tax rate has been lowered.

a. Popiwek
b. Direct taxes
c. Withholding tax
d. Tax cut

29. A _____ is a situation in which the government takes in more than it spends.
a. 100-year flood
b. Budget set
c. Budget surplus
d. 130-30 fund

30. In economics, the _____ is used to illustrate the idea that increases in the rate of taxation do not necessarily increase tax revenue. (For instance, whereas a 0% income tax rate will generate no revenue, neither will a 100% rate, as citizens will have no incentive to make money.) Increasing taxes beyond the peak of the curve point will decrease tax revenue.
a. 100-year flood
b. 1921 recession
c. 130-30 fund
d. Laffer curve

31. The _____ is the commonly observed phenomenon that some processes cannot go backwards once certain things have happened, by analogy with the mechanical ratchet that holds the spring tight as a clock is wound up. It is related to the phenomena of featuritis and scope creep in the manufacture of various consumer goods, and of mission creep in military planning.

Garrett Hardin, a biologist and environmentalist who also wrote of the 'tragedy of the commons', used the phrase to describe how food aid keeps alive people who would otherwise die in a famine.

a. Purification theorem
b. Partnership game
c. Non-credible threat
d. Ratchet effect

32. In economics, _____ is a measure of national income. Basically, it is an approach to measure GDP. It is defined as the value of planned goods and services produced in an economy.
a. Aggregate demand
b. Aggregate supply
c. Aggregation problem
d. Aggregate expenditure

33. Competition law, known in the United States as _____ law, has three main elements:

- prohibiting agreements or practices that restrict free trading and competition between business entities. This includes in particular the repression of cartels.
- banning abusive behaviour by a firm dominating a market, or anti-competitive practices that tend to lead to such a dominant position. Practices controlled in this way may include predatory pricing, tying, price gouging, refusal to deal, and many others.
- supervising the mergers and acquisitions of large corporations, including some joint ventures. Transactions that are considered to threaten the competitive process can be prohibited altogether, or approved subject to 'remedies' such as an obligation to divest part of the merged business or to offer licences or access to facilities to enable other businesses to continue competing.

The substance and practice of competition law varies from jurisdiction to jurisdiction. Protecting the interests of consumers (consumer welfare) and ensuring that entrepreneurs have an opportunity to compete in the market economy are often treated as important objectives. Competition law is closely connected with law on deregulation of access to markets, state aids and subsidies, the privatisation of state owned assets and the establishment of independent sector regulators. In recent decades, competition law has been viewed as a way to provide better public services.

a. Antitrust
b. United Kingdom competition law
c. Anti-Inflation Act
d. Intellectual property law

34. The term _____ refers to economy-wide fluctuations in production or economic activity over several months or years. These fluctuations occur around a long-term growth trend, and typically involve shifts over time between periods of relatively rapid economic growth (expansion or boom), and periods of relative stagnation or decline (contraction or recession.)

These fluctuations are often measured using the growth rate of real gross domestic product.

a. Consumer theory
b. Business cycle
c. Nominal value
d. Tobit model

35. _____ refers to the actions that governments take in the economic field. It covers the systems for setting interest rates and government deficit as well as the labour market, national ownership, and many other areas of government.

Such policies are often influenced by international institutions like the International Monetary Fund or World Bank as well as political beliefs and the consequent policies of parties.

a. AD-IA Model
b. Economic policy
c. ACCRA Cost of Living Index
d. ACEA agreement

36. _____ is the process by which the government, central bank (ii) availability of money, and (iii) cost of money or rate of interest, in order to attain a set of objectives oriented towards the growth and stability of the economy. Monetary theory provides insight into how to craft optimal _____.

_____ is referred to as either being an expansionary policy where an expansionary policy increases the total supply of money in the economy, and a contractionary policy decreases the total money supply.

a. 1921 recession
b. Monetary policy
c. 100-year flood
d. 130-30 fund

37. A _____ is a tax by which the tax rate increases as the taxable amount increases. 'Progressive' describes a distribution effect on income or expenditure, referring to the way the rate progresses from low to high, where the average tax rate is less than the marginal tax rate. It can be applied to individual taxes or to a tax system as a whole; a year, multi-year, or lifetime.

Chapter 11. Fiscal Policy, Deficits, and Debt

a. 100-year flood
b. Proportional tax
c. 130-30 fund
d. Progressive tax

38. A variety of measures of _____ and output are used in economics to estimate total economic activity in a country or region, including gross domestic product (GDP), gross national product (GNP), and net _____

There are three main ways of calculating these numbers; the output approach, the income approach and the expenditure approach. In theory, the three must yield the same, because total expenditures on goods and services must equal the total income paid to the producers (Gnational income), and that must also equal the total value of the output of goods and services (GNP.)

a. Volume index
b. Gross world product
c. National income
d. GNI per capita

39. A _____ is a normalized average (typically a weighted average) of prices for a given class of goods or services in a given region, during a given interval of time. It is a statistic designed to help to compare how these prices, taken as a whole, differ between time periods or geographical locations.

Price indices have several potential uses.

a. Transactional Net Margin Method
b. Two-part tariff
c. Product sabotage
d. Price index

40. _____ are the income that is gained by governments because of taxation of the people.

Just as there are different types of tax, the form in which _____ is collected also differs; furthermore, the agency that collects the tax may not be part of central government, but may be an alternative third-party licenced to collect tax which they themselves will use. For example:

- In the UK, the DVLA collects road tax, which is then passed on the treasury.

_____s on purchases can come from two forms: 'tax' itself is a percentage of the price added to the purchase (such as sales tax in US states, or VAT in the UK), while 'duty' is a fixed amount added to the purchase price (such as is commonly found on cigarettes.) In order to calculate the total tax raised from these sales, we must work out the effective tax rate multiplied by the quantity supplied.

a. Taxable wage
b. Tax and spend
c. Taxation as slavery
d. Tax revenue

41. To tax is to impose a financial charge or other levy upon a taxpayer by a state or the functional equivalent of a state.

_____ are also imposed by many subnational entities. _____ consist of direct tax or indirect tax, and may be paid in money or as its labour equivalent (often but not always unpaid.)

a. 130-30 fund
b. 1921 recession
c. 100-year flood
d. Taxes

42. A _____ is a tax imposed so that the tax rate is fixed as the amount subject to taxation increases. In simple terms, it imposes an equal burden (relative to resources) on the rich and poor. 'Proportional' describes a distribution effect on income or expenditure, referring to the way the rate remains consistent (does not progress from 'low to high' or 'high to low' as income or consumption changes), where the marginal tax rate is equal to the average tax rate.
a. 100-year flood
b. Regressive tax
c. 130-30 fund
d. Proportional tax

43. A _____ is a tax imposed in such a manner that the tax rate decreases as the amount subject to taxation increases. In simple terms, a _____ imposes a greater burden (relative to resources) on the poor than on the rich -- there is an inverse relationship between the tax rate and the taxpayer's ability to pay as measured by assets, consumption, or income. 'Regressive' describes a distribution effect on income or expenditure, referring to the way the rate progresses from high to low, where the average tax rate exceeds the marginal tax rate.
a. 100-year flood
b. 130-30 fund
c. Proportional tax
d. Regressive tax

44. In macroeconomics, _____ is a condition of the national economy, where all or nearly all persons willing and able to work at the prevailing wages and working conditions are able to do so. It is defined either as 0% unemployment, literally, no unemployment (the rate of unemployment is the fraction of the work force unable to find work), as by James Tobin, or as the level of employment rates when there is no cyclical unemployment. It is defined by the majority of mainstream economists as being an acceptable level of natural unemployment above 0%, the discrepancy from 0% being due to non-cyclical types of unemployment.
a. Harrod-Johnson diagram
b. Demand shock
c. Marginal propensity to consume
d. Full employment

45. The _____ is the means by which the federal government of the United States accounts for excess paid-in contributions from workers and employers to the Social Security system that are not required to fund current benefit payments to retirees, survivors, and the disabled or to pay administrative expenses. More importantly, the trust fund also contains the securities that will be redeemed to make benefit payments in the future when contributions derived from payroll taxes and self-employment contributions no longer are sufficient to fully fund then-current benefit payments. (The controversy over its meaningfulness is a topic of the sustainability of the unified Federal budget.)
a. Legacy debt
b. Social Security Disability Insurance
c. Social Security trust fund
d. Retirement Insurance Benefits

46. _____ is an economic concept which refers to balancing out spending and saving to attain and maintain the highest possible living standard over the course of one's life. This idea is notable because of its difference in approach to common knowledge about preparing for retirement, in which individuals are encouraged to save a particular % of their income throughout their life. Some believe that this approach is flawed and typically leads to one of two outcomes: over-saving or over-spending.
a. Conspicuous consumption
b. Rule Developing Experimentation
c. Multidimensional scaling
d. Consumption smoothing

Chapter 11. Fiscal Policy, Deficits, and Debt

47. The _____ was a worldwide economic downturn starting in most places in 1929 and ending at different times in the 1930s or early 1940s for different countries. It was the largest and most important economic depression in the 20th century, and is used in the 21st century as an example of how far the world's economy can fall. The _____ originated in the United States; historians most often use as a starting date the stock market crash on October 29, 1929, known as Black Tuesday.
   a. Great Depression
   b. Wall Street Crash of 1929
   c. Jarrow March
   d. British Empire Economic Conference

48. In statistics and image processing, to smooth a data set is to create an approximating function that attempts to capture important patterns in the data, while leaving out noise or other fine-scale structures/rapid phenomena. Many different algorithms are used in _____. One of the most common algorithms is the 'moving average', often used to try to capture important trends in repeated statistical surveys.
   a. Partial residual plot
   b. Partial regression plot
   c. X-bar chart
   d. Smoothing

49. In economics, a _____ is a monetary-policy rule that stipulates how much the central bank would or should change the nominal interest rate in response to divergences of actual inflation rates from target inflation rates and of actual Gross Domestic Product (GDP) from potential GDP. It was first proposed by the by U.S. economist John B. Taylor in 1993. The rule can be written as follows:

$$i_t = \pi_t + r_t^* + a_\pi(\pi_t - \pi_t^*) + a_y(y_t - \bar{y}_t).$$

In this equation, i_t is the target short-term nominal interest rate (e.g. the federal funds rate in the US), π_t is the rate of inflation as measured by the GDP deflator, π_t^* is the desired rate of inflation, r_t^* is the assumed equilibrium real interest rate, y_t is the logarithm of real GDP, and $\bar{y}_t$ is the logarithm of potential output, as determined by a linear trend.

   a. Fed Funds Probability
   b. Federal Reserve Banks
   c. Taylor rule
   d. Term Securities Lending Facility

50. _____ is that which is owed; usually referencing assets owed, but the term can also cover moral obligations and other interactions not requiring money. In the case of assets, _____ is a means of using future purchasing power in the present before a summation has been earned. Some companies and corporations use _____ as a part of their overall corporate finance strategy.
   a. Collateral Management
   b. Debenture
   c. Hard money loan
   d. Debt

Chapter 11. Fiscal Policy, Deficits, and Debt

51. A _____ is:

- Rewrite _____, in generative grammar and computer science
- Standardization, a formal and widely-accepted statement, fact, definition, or qualification
- Operation, a determinate _____ for performing a mathematical operation and obtaining a certain result (Mathematics, Logic)
    - Unary operation
    - Binary operation
- _____ of inference, a function from sets of formulae to formulae (Mathematics, Logic)
- _____ of thumb, principle with broad application that is not intended to be strictly accurate or reliable for every situation. Also often simply referred to as a _____
- Moral, an atomic element of a moral code for guiding choices in human behavior
- Heuristic, a quantized '_____' which shows a tendency or probability for successful function
- A regulation, as in sports
- A Production _____, as in computer science
- Procedural law, a _____ set governing the application of laws to cases
    - A law, which may informally be called a '_____'
    - A court ruling, a decision by a court
- In the U.S. Government, a regulation mandated by Congress, but written or expanded upon by the Executive Branch.
- Norm (sociology), an informal but widely accepted _____, concept, truth, definition, or qualification (social norms, legal norms, coding norms)
- Norm (philosophy), a kind of sentence or a reason to act, feel or believe
- 'Rulership' is the concept of governance by a government:
    - Military _____, governance by a military body
    - Monastic _____, a collection of precepts that guides the life of monks or nuns in a religious order where the superior holds the place of Christ
- Slide _____

- '_____,' a song by Ayumi Hamasaki
- '_____,' a song by rapper Nas
- '_____s,' an album by the band The Whitest Boy Alive
- _____s: Pyaar Ka Superhit Formula, a 2003 Bollywood film
- ruler, an instrument for measuring lengths
- _____, a component of an astrolabe, circumferator or similar instrument
- The _____s, a bestselling self-help book
- _____ Project (Run Up-to-date Linux Everywhere), a project that aims to use up-to-date Linux software on old PCs
- _____ engine, a software system that helps managing business _____s
- Ja _____, a hip hop artist
    - R.U.L.E., a 2005 greatest hits album by rapper Ja _____
- '_____s,' a KMFDM song

a. Procter ' Gamble
b. Rule
c. Demand
d. Technocracy

Chapter 11. Fiscal Policy, Deficits, and Debt

52. The Organization of the Petroleum Exporting Countries is a cartel of twelve countries made up of Algeria, Angola, Ecuador, Iran, Iraq, Kuwait, Libya, Nigeria, Qatar, Saudi Arabia, the United Arab Emirates, and Venezuela. The cartel has maintained its headquarters in Vienna since 1965, and hosts regular meetings among the oil ministers of its Member Countries. Indonesia withdrew its membership in _____ in 2008 after it became a net importer of oil, but stated it would likely return if it became a net exporter in the world.
    a. ACCRA Cost of Living Index
    b. ACEA agreement
    c. OPEC
    d. AD-IA Model

53. A United States Treasury security is a government debt issued by the United States Department of the Treasury through the Bureau of the Public Debt. Treasury securities are the debt financing instruments of the United States Federal government, and they are often referred to simply as Treasuries. There are four types of marketable treasury securities: _____, Treasury notes, Treasury bonds, and Treasury Inflation Protected Securities (TIPS.)
    a. Treasury bills
    b. Lawcards
    c. Labour battalions
    d. Debt to Assets

54. In finance, a _____ is a debt security, in which the authorized issuer owes the holders a debt and, depending on the terms of the _____, is obliged to pay interest (the coupon) and/or to repay the principal at a later date, termed maturity. A _____ is a formal contract to repay borrowed money with interest at fixed intervals.

    Thus a _____ is like a loan: the issuer is the borrower (debtor), the holder is the lender (creditor), and the coupon is the interest.

    a. Prize Bond
    b. Callable
    c. Bond
    d. Zero-coupon

55. A security is a fungible, negotiable instrument representing financial value. _____ are broadly categorized into debt _____; equity _____, e.g., common stocks; and derivative (finance) contracts such as forwards, futures, options and swaps. The company or other entity issuing the security is called the issuer.
    a. Securities
    b. Pass-Through Certificates
    c. Red herring prospectus
    d. Settlement risk

56. _____ is a legally declared inability or impairment of ability of an individual or organization to pay its creditors. Creditors may file a _____ petition against a debtor ('involuntary _____') in an effort to recoup a portion of what they are owed or initiate a restructuring. In the majority of cases, however, _____ is initiated by the debtor (a 'voluntary _____' that is filed by the insolvent individual or organization.)
    a. Liquidation
    b. Bankruptcy in the United Kingdom
    c. Bankruptcy
    d. Petition mill

57. _____ is a fee paid on borrowed assets. It is the price paid for the use of borrowed money , or, money earned by deposited funds . Assets that are sometimes lent with _____ include money, shares, consumer goods through hire purchase, major assets such as aircraft, and even entire factories in finance lease arrangements.
    a. Insolvency
    b. Internal debt
    c. Asset protection
    d. Interest

58. _____ is the formal declaration of a government to not (repudiation) or only partially pay/meet its debts (due receivables) or the de facto cessation of due payments.

The _____ historically was caused by three reasons:

- insolvency/over-indebtedness of the state
- political motivated refusal to take over the debt of the old administration after a change of government
- ruin/decline of the state

If a state for economic reasons defaults on its treasury obligations/is not anymore able to handle its debt/liabilities or to pay the interest on this debt it faces _____. To declare insolvency it is sufficient if this state is only able to pay part of its due interest or to clear off only part of the debt.

Reasons for this were mostly:

- a lost war or
- decade-long public budget mismanagement/maladministration

The _____ caused by insolvency historically always appeared at the end of long years or decades of budget emergency, in which the state has spent more money than it received. This budget balance/margin was covered through new indebtedness with national and foreign citizens, banks and states.

a. Liquidation
c. Petition mill
b. Stalking horse offer
d. National bankruptcy

59. _____ is a misspelled phrase from Latin 'pro capite' phrase meaning per head with pro meaning 'per' or 'for each' and capite meaning 'head.' Both words together equate to the phrase 'for each head.'

It is usually used in the field of statistics to indicate the average per person for any given concern, such as income, crime rate, etc.

It is also used in wills to indicate that each of the named beneficiaries should receive, by devise or bequest, equal shares of the estate. This is in contrast to a per stirpes division, in which each branch of the inheriting family inherits an equal share of the estate.

a. Per capita
c. False positive rate
b. Sargan test
d. Population statistics

60. In economics and sociology, an _____ is any factor (financial or non-financial) that enables or motivates a particular course of action, or counts as a reason for preferring one choice to the alternatives. It is an expectation that encourages people to behave in a certain way. Since human beings are purposeful creatures, the study of _____ structures is central to the study of all economic activity (both in terms of individual decision-making and in terms of co-operation and competition within a larger institutional structure.)

a. Epstein-Zin preferences
c. Incentive
b. Isocost
d. Economic reform

Chapter 11. Fiscal Policy, Deficits, and Debt

61. In economics, _____ is how a natione;s total economy is distributed among its population. _____ has always been a central concern of economic theory and economic policy. Classical economists such as Adam Smith, Thomas Malthus and David Ricardo were mainly concerned with factor _____, that is, the distribution of income between the main factors of production, land, labour and capital.
   a. Eco commerce
   b. Equipment trust certificate
   c. Income distribution
   d. Authorised capital

62. _____ was a global military conflict which involved a majority of the world's nations, including all of the great powers, organized into two opposing military alliances: the Allies and the Axis. The war involved the mobilization of over 100 million military personnel, making it the most widespread war in history. In a state of 'total war', the major participants placed their entire economic, industrial, and scientific capabilities at the service of the war effort, erasing the distinction between civilian and military resources.
   a. World War II
   b. 100-year flood
   c. 1921 recession
   d. 130-30 fund

63. _____ refers to the complete or majority ownership/control of a business or resource in a country by individuals who are not citizens of that country, or by companies whose headquarters are not in that country.
   a. Givers Gain
   b. Foreign ownership
   c. No-bid contract
   d. Captive supply

64. A _____ is an object whose consumption increases the utility of the consumer, for which the quantity demanded exceeds the quantity supplied at zero price. _____s are usually modeled as having diminishing marginal utility. The first individual purchase has high utility; the second has less.
   a. Merit good
   b. Composite good
   c. Pie method
   d. Good

65. The _____ is an American economic index intended to estimate future economic activity. It is calculated by The Conference Board, a non-governmental organization, which determines the value of the index from the values of ten key variables. These variables have historically turned downward before a recession and upward before an expansion.
   a. Index of dissimilarity
   b. Index of diversity
   c. Index of leading indicators
   d. Atkinson index

66. In economics, _____ is the total amount of money available in an economy at a particular point in time. There are several ways to define 'money', but standard measures usually include currency in circulation and demand deposits.

   _____ data are recorded and published, usually by the government or the central bank of the country.
   a. Money supply
   b. Velocity of money
   c. Neutrality of money
   d. Veil of money

67. An _____, in economics, is the amount by which the real Gross domestic product exceeds potential GDP. The real GDP is also known as GDP 'adjusted for inflation', 'constant prices' GDP or 'constant dollar' GDP, because it measures the aggregate output in a country's income accounts in a given year, expressed in base-year prices. On the other hand, the potential GDP is the quantity of real GDP when a country's economy is at full-employment.

Chapter 11. Fiscal Policy, Deficits, and Debt

a. Inflationary gap
b. ACCRA Cost of Living Index
c. AD-IA Model
d. ACEA agreement

68. _____, in law and economics, is a form of risk management primarily used to hedge against the risk of a contingent loss. _____ is defined as the equitable transfer of the risk of a loss, from one entity to another, in exchange for a premium, and can be thought of as a guaranteed small loss to prevent a large, possibly devastating loss. An insurer is a company selling the _____; an insured or policyholder is the person or entity buying the _____.
   a. ACCRA Cost of Living Index
   b. Insurance
   c. AD-IA Model
   d. ACEA agreement

69. In economics, _____ are key economic variables that economists used to predict a new phase of the business cycle. A leading indicator is one that changes before the economy does; a lagging indicator is one that changes after the economy has changed. Examples of _____ include stock prices, which often improve or worsen before a similar change in the economy.
   a. Gross domestic product
   b. Macroeconomics
   c. Leading indicators
   d. Medium of exchange

70. Wisconsin originated the idea of _____ in the U.S. in 1932. In the United States, there are 50 state _____ programs plus one each in the District of Columbia and Puerto Rico. Through the Social Security Act of 1935, the Federal Government of the United States effectively coerced the individual states into adopting _____ plans.
   a. ACCRA Cost of Living Index
   b. ACEA agreement
   c. AD-IA Model
   d. Unemployment insurance

Chapter 12. Money and Banking

1. _____ is money accepted for exchange of goods in an economy. The prevalence of one money over another arises, usually, when a government designates through decrees that the government shall accept only particular notes and coins in payment for taxes. Typically, money of _____ consists of stamped coins and minted paper bills.
    - a. Totnes pound
    - b. Security thread
    - c. Local currency
    - d. Currency

2. Economics:
    - _____, the desire to own something and the ability to pay for it
    - _____ curve, a graphic representation of a _____ schedule
    - _____ deposit, the money in checking accounts
    - _____ pull theory, the theory that inflation occurs when _____ for goods and services exceeds existing supplies
    - _____ schedule, a table that lists the quantity of a good a person will buy it each different price
    - _____ side economics, the school of economics at believes government spending and tax cuts open economy by raising _____

    - a. Variability
    - b. McKesson ' Robbins scandal
    - c. Production
    - d. Demand

3. The _____ is the desired holding of money balances in the form of cash or bank deposits.

    Money is dominated as store of value by interest bearing assets. However, money is necessary to carry out transactions, or in other words, it provides liquidity.

    - a. Conglomerate merger
    - b. Borrowing base
    - c. Market neutral
    - d. Demand for money

4. _____ and Keynesian Theory) is a macroeconomic theory based on the ideas of 20th-century British economist John Maynard Keynes. _____ argues that private sector decisions sometimes lead to inefficient macroeconomic outcomes and therefore advocates active policy responses by the public sector, including monetary policy actions by the central bank and fiscal policy actions by the government to stabilize output over the business cycle.

    The theories forming the basis of _____ were first presented in The General Theory of Employment, Interest and Money, published in 1936.

    - a. Market failure
    - b. Rational choice theory
    - c. Deflation
    - d. Keynesian economics

5. A _____ is an intermediary used in trade to avoid the inconveniences of a pure barter system.

    By contrast, as William Stanley Jevons argued, in a barter system there must be a coincidence of wants before two people can trade - one must want exactly what the other has to offer, when and where it is offered, so that the exchange can occur. A _____ permits the value of goods to be assessed and rendered in terms of the intermediary, most often, a form of money widely accepted to buy any other good.

a. Consumer theory
b. Labour economics
c. Price revolution
d. Medium of exchange

6. A _____ is a kind of negotiable instrument, a promissory note made by a bank payable to the bearer on demand, used as money, and in many jurisdictions is legal tender. Along with coins, _____s make up the cash or bearer forms of all modern money. With the exception of non-circulating high-value or precious metal commemorative issues, coins are generally used for lower valued monetary units, while _____s are used for higher values.
a. Local currency
b. Microprinting
c. Security thread
d. Banknote

7. To act as a _____, a commodity, a form of money stored, and retrieved - and be predictably useful when it is so retrieved.

This is distinct from the standard of deferred payment function which requires acceptability to parties one owes a debt to and a minimum of opportunity to cheat others.

a. World currency
b. Fiat money
c. Petrodollar
d. Store of value

8. A _____ is a standard monetary unit of measurement of the market value/cost of goods, services, or assets. It is one of three well-known functions of money. It lends meaning to profits, losses, liability, or assets.
a. AD-IA Model
b. ACCRA Cost of Living Index
c. Unit of account
d. ACEA agreement

9. In business and accounting, _____ are everything of value that is owned by a person or company. It is a claim on the property your income of a borrower. The balance sheet of a firm records the monetary value of the _____ owned by the firm.
a. Amortization schedule
b. ACCRA Cost of Living Index
c. ACEA agreement
d. Assets

10. Bartering is a medium in which goods or services are directly exchanged for other goods and/or services, without the use of money. It can be bilateral or multilateral, and usually exists parallel to monetary systems in most developed countries, though to a very limited extent. _____ usually replaces money as the method of exchange in times of monetary crisis, when the currency is unstable and devalued by hyperinflation.
a. Meitheal
b. Barter
c. New Economics Foundation
d. Community-based economics

11. To _____ is to impose a financial charge or other levy upon a taxpayer by a state or the functional equivalent of a state.

_____es are also imposed by many subnational entities. _____es consist of direct _____ or indirect _____, and may be paid in money or as its labour equivalent (often but not always unpaid.)

a. 100-year flood
b. 1921 recession
c. 130-30 fund
d. Tax

Chapter 12. Money and Banking

12. _____ is the a method of technical and economic research of the systems for purpose to optimize a parity between system's consumer functions or properties and expenses to achieve those functions or properties.

This methodology for continuous perfection of production, industrial technologies, organizational structures was developed by Juryj Sobolev in 1948 at the 'Perm telephone factory'

- 1948 Juryj Sobolev - the first success in application of a method analysis at the 'Perm telephone factory' .
- 1949 - the first application for the invention as result of use of the new method.

Today in economically developed countries practically each enterprise or the company use methodology of the kind of functional-cost analysis as a practice of the quality management, most full satisfying to principles of standards of series ISO 9000.

- Interest of consumer not in products itself, but the advantage which it will receive from its usage.
- The consumer aspires to reduce his expenses
- Functions needed by consumer can be executed in the various ways, and, hence, with various efficiency and expenses. Among possible alternatives of realization of functions exist such in which the parity of quality and the price is the optimal for the consumer.

The goal of _____ is achievement of the highest consumer satisfaction of production at simultaneous decrease in all kinds of industrial expenses Classical _____ has three English synonyms - Value Engineering, Value Management, Value Analysis.

   a. Monopoly wage
   c. Willingness to pay
   b. Staple financing
   d. Function cost analysis

13.

A _____ is a type of financial intermediary and a type of bank. Commercial banking is also known as business banking. It is a bank that provides checking accounts, savings accounts, and money market accounts and that accepts time deposits.

   a. Bought deal
   c. Commercial bank
   b. Lombard banking
   d. Daylight overdraft

14. A _____ is a type of banknote issued by the Federal Reserve System and is the only type of U.S. banknote that is still produced today.

_____s are fiat currency, with the words 'this note is legal tender for all debts, public and private' printed on each bill. (See generally 31 U.S.C.

   a. Term Securities Lending Facility
   c. Federal Reserve Transparency Act
   b. Term auction facility
   d. Federal Reserve Note

Chapter 12. Money and Banking

15. A _____ is a time deposit, a financial product commonly offered to consumers by banks, thrift institutions, and credit unions.

CDs are similar to savings accounts in that they are insured and thus virtually risk-free; they are 'money in the bank' (CDs are insured by the FDIC for banks or by the NCUA for credit unions.) They are different from savings accounts in that the CD has a specific, fixed term (often three months, six months, or one to five years), and, usually, a fixed interest rate.

   a. Probability of default   b. Time deposit
   c. Mzansi Account   d. Certificate of deposit

16. A _____ refers to any type debt instrument, such as a loan, bond, mortgage that does not have a fixed rate of interest over the life of the instrument. Such debt typically uses an index or other base rate for establishing the interest rate for each relevant period. One of the most common rates to use as the basis for applying interest rates is the London Inter-bank Offered Rate, or LIBOR

   a. Floating interest rate   b. Moneylender
   c. Money market   d. Disposal tax effect

17. _____ is a type of bank account where the money in the account is legally able to be withdrawn immediately upon demand (or 'at call'.) This type of bank account can also be referred to as a 'cheque' or 'checking' or transactional account.

This type of bank account, allowing immediate conversion of the account balance into cash or withdrawal to another account, can be contrasted with a time deposit (also known as a certificate of deposit or term deposit), where the funds are not legally available for immediate withdrawal by the depositor.

   a. Tangible Common Equity   b. Clawbacks in economic development
   c. Debt rescheduling   d. Demand deposit

18. The Federal Reserve System (also the Federal Reserve; informally The Fed) is the central banking system of the United States. Created in 1913 by the enactment of the Federal Reserve Act (signed by Woodrow Wilson), it is a quasi-public and quasi-private (government entity with private components) banking system that comprises (1) the presidentially appointed Board of Governors of the Federal Reserve System in Washington, D.C.; (2) the Federal Open Market Committee; (3) twelve regional _____ located in major cities throughout the nation acting as fiscal agents for the U.S. Treasury, each with its own nine-member board of directors; (4) numerous other private U.S. member banks, which subscribe to required amounts of non-transferable stock in their regional _____; and (5) various advisory councils. Since February 2006, Ben Bernanke has served as the Chairman of the Board of Governors of the Federal Reserve System.

   a. Fed Funds Probability   b. Federal Open Market Committee
   c. Federal funds   d. Federal Reserve Banks

19. The _____ was a worldwide economic downturn starting in most places in 1929 and ending at different times in the 1930s or early 1940s for different countries. It was the largest and most important economic depression in the 20th century, and is used in the 21st century as an example of how far the world's economy can fall. The _____ originated in the United States; historians most often use as a starting date the stock market crash on October 29, 1929, known as Black Tuesday.

a. Great Depression
b. Wall Street Crash of 1929
c. British Empire Economic Conference
d. Jarrow March

20. In finance, the _____ is the global financial market for short-term borrowing and lending. It provides short-term liquidity funding for the global financial system. The _____ is where short-term obligations such as Treasury bills, commercial paper and bankers' acceptances are bought and sold.
    a. T-Model
    b. Deferred compensation
    c. Consignment stock
    d. Money market

21. A _____ is a professionally managed type of collective investment scheme that pools money from many investors and invests it in stocks, bonds, short-term money market instruments, and/or other securities. The _____ will have a fund manager that trades the pooled money on a regular basis. As of early 2008, the worldwide value of all _____s totals more than $26 trillion.
    a. Dark pools of liquidity
    b. Mutual fund
    c. Self-invested personal pension
    d. Participating policy

22. _____s are accounts maintained by retail financial institutions that pay interest but can not be used directly as money (for example, by writing a cheque.) These accounts let customers set aside a portion of their liquid assets while earning a monetary return.

    _____s are offered by commercial banks, savings and loan associations, credit unions, building societies and mutual savings banks.

    a. Fractional-reserve banking
    b. Lombard Club
    c. Fair Finance Watch
    d. Savings account

23. A _____ association is a financial institution that specializes in accepting savings deposits and making mortgage and other loans. The S'L or thrift term is mainly used in the United States; similar institutions in the United Kingdom, Ireland and some Commonwealth countries include building societies and trustee savings banks.

    They are often mutually held, meaning that the depositors and borrowers are members with voting rights, and have the ability to direct the financial and managerial goals of the organization, similar to the policyholders of a mutual insurance company.

    a. Participating policy
    b. Fonds commun de placement
    c. Savings and loan
    d. Collective investment scheme

24. A _____ is a money deposit at a banking institution that cannot be withdrawn for a certain 'term' or period of time. When the term is over it can be withdrawn or it can be held for another term. Generally speaking, the longer the term the better the yield on the money.
    a. Time deposit
    b. Finance charge
    c. Fractional-reserve banking
    d. Deposit market share

25. A _____ is a current account at a banking institution that allows money to be deposited and withdrawn by the account holder, with the transactions and resulting balance being recorded on the bank's books. Some banks charge a fee for this service, while others may pay the customer interest on the funds deposited.

Although restrictions placed on access depend upon the terms and conditions of the account and the provider, the account holder retains rights to have their funds repaid on demand.

a. Bank statement
b. Large Value Transfer System
c. Stated income loan
d. Deposit account

26. _____ is the revenue to a brokerage firm when commissioned securities and insurance salespeople sell a product, whether it is an investment like stocks, bonds or insurance like life insurance or long term care insurance. The commission that the agent receives is usually a percentage of this figure, although some firms like Merrill Lynch use figures called Production Credits, usually smaller than _____, to determine payouts and retain more revenue.

For example, a mutual fund with a 5.75% sales charge is sold to someone who invests $10,000.

a. Number of Shares
b. Monopoly price
c. Gross Dealer Concession
d. Discretionary policy

27. A _____ or labor union is an organization of workers who have banded together to achieve common goals in key areas and working conditions. The _____, through its leadership, bargains with the employer on behalf of union members (rank and file members) and negotiates labor contracts (Collective bargaining) with employers. This may include the negotiation of wages, work rules, complaint procedures, rules governing hiring, firing and promotion of workers, benefits, workplace safety and policies.

a. Case-Shiller Home Price Indices
b. Guaranteed investment contracts
c. Consumer goods
d. Trade union

28. In economics, _____ is the total amount of money available in an economy at a particular point in time. There are several ways to define 'money', but standard measures usually include currency in circulation and demand deposits.

_____ data are recorded and published, usually by the government or the central bank of the country.

a. Velocity of money
b. Veil of money
c. Neutrality of money
d. Money supply

29. _____ is that which is owed; usually referencing assets owed, but the term can also cover moral obligations and other interactions not requiring money. In the case of assets, _____ is a means of using future purchasing power in the present before a summation has been earned. Some companies and corporations use _____ as a part of their overall corporate finance strategy.

a. Collateral Management
b. Debenture
c. Hard money loan
d. Debt

30. The _____ is published by The Economist as an informal way of measuring the purchasing power parity (PPP) between two currencies and provides a test of the extent to which market exchange rates result in goods costing the same in different countries. It 'seeks to make exchange-rate theory a bit more digestible'.

The index takes its name from the Big Mac, a hamburger sold at McDonald's restaurants.

a. Big Mac index
b. Cost-weighted activity index
c. Deindexation
d. Rank mobility index

31. The _____ consists of a number of economic theories which describe the nature of the firm, company including its existence, its behaviour, and its relationship with the market.

In simplified terms, the _____ aims to answer these questions:

1. Existence - why do firms emerge, why are not all transactions in the economy mediated over the market?
2. Boundaries - why the boundary between firms and the market is located exactly there? Which transactions are performed internally and which are negotiated on the market?
3. Organization - why are firms structured in such specific way? What is the interplay of formal and informal relationships?

Despite looking simple, these questions are not answered by the established economic theory, which usually views firms as given, and treats them as black boxes without any internal structure.

The First World War period saw a change of emphasis in economic theory away from industry-level analysis which mainly included analysing markets to analysis at the level of the firm, as it became increasingly clear that perfect competition was no longer an adequate model of how firms behaved. Economic theory till then had focussed on trying to understand markets alone and there had been little study on understanding why firms or organisations exist.

a. Technology gap
b. Khazzoom-Brookes postulate
c. Policy Ineffectiveness Proposition
d. Theory of the firm

32. The _____ is a United States government corporation created by the Glass-Steagall Act of 1933. It provides deposit insurance, which guarantees the safety of deposits in member banks, currently up to $250,000 per depositor per bank. Funds in non-interest bearing transaction accounts are fully insured, with no limit, under the temporary Transaction Account Guarantee Program.

a. Great Leap Forward
b. Foreign direct investment
c. Federal Deposit Insurance Corporation
d. Luxembourg Income Study

33. _____, in law and economics, is a form of risk management primarily used to hedge against the risk of a contingent loss. _____ is defined as the equitable transfer of the risk of a loss, from one entity to another, in exchange for a premium, and can be thought of as a guaranteed small loss to prevent a large, possibly devastating loss. An insurer is a company selling the _____; an insured or policyholder is the person or entity buying the _____.

a. AD-IA Model
b. ACEA agreement
c. ACCRA Cost of Living Index
d. Insurance

34. _____ or forced tender is payment that, by law, cannot be refused in settlement of a debt.

_____ is variously defined in different jurisdictions. Formally, it is anything which when offered in payment extinguishes the debt.

a. Leave of absence
b. Patent portfolio
c. Landsbanki Freezing Order 2008
d. Legal tender

35. _____ in economics and business is the result of an exchange and from that trade we assign a numerical monetary value to a good, service or asset. If Alice trades Bob 4 apples for an orange, the _____ of an orange is 4 apples. Inversely, the _____ of an apple is 1/4 oranges.
   a. Price
   b. Price war
   c. Premium pricing
   d. Price book

36. A _____ is a hypothetical measure of overall prices for some set of goods and services, in a given region during a given interval, normalized relative to some base set. Typically, a _____ is approximated with a price index.

The classical dichotomy is the assumption that there is a relatively clean distinction between overall increases or decreases in prices and underlying, e;reale; economic variables.

   a. Discouraged worker
   b. Discretionary spending
   c. Price level
   d. Price elasticity of supply

37. A public utility (usually just utility) is an organization that maintains the infrastructure for a public service (often also providing a service using that infrastructure.) _____ are subject to forms of public control and regulation ranging from local community-based groups to state-wide government monopolies. Common arguments in favor of regulation include the desire to control market power, facilitate competition, promote investment or system expansion, or stabilize markets.
   a. 130-30 fund
   b. 100-year flood
   c. 1921 recession
   d. Public utilities

38. _____ is an economic model based on price, utility and quantity in a market. It predicts that in a competitive market, price will function to equalize the quantity demanded by consumers, and the quantity supplied by producers, resulting in an economic equilibrium of price and quantity. The model incorporates other factors changing equilibrium as a shift of demand and/or supply.
   a. Rational addiction
   b. Supply and demand
   c. Deferred gratification
   d. Joint demand

39. In economics, _____ is a measure of national income. Basically, it is an approach to measure GDP. It is defined as the value of planned goods and services produced in an economy.
   a. Aggregate supply
   b. Aggregation problem
   c. Aggregate demand
   d. Aggregate expenditure

40. In economics, the _____ of a good or of a service is the utility of the specific use to which an agent would put a given increase in that good or service, or of the specific use that would be abandoned in response to a given decrease. In other words, _____ is the utility of the marginal use -- which, on the assumption of economic rationality, would be the least urgent use of the good or service, from the best feasible combination of actions in which its use is included. Under the mainstream assumptions, the _____ of a good or service is the posited quantified change in utility obtained by increasing or by decreasing use of that good or service.
   a. 130-30 fund
   b. 1921 recession
   c. Marginal utility
   d. 100-year flood

Chapter 12. Money and Banking

41. _____ refers to a business or organization attempting to acquire goods or services to accomplish the goals of the enterprise. Though there are several organizations that attempt to set standards in the _____ process, processes can vary greatly between organizations. Typically the word '_____' is not used interchangeably with the word 'procurement', since procurement typically includes Expediting, Supplier Quality, and Traffic and Logistics (T'L) in addition to _____.
   - a. Free port
   - b. Purchasing
   - c. 130-30 fund
   - d. 100-year flood

42. _____ is the number of goods/services that can be purchased with a unit of currency. For example, if you had taken one dollar to a store in the 1950s, you would have been able to buy a greater number of items than you would today, indicating that you would have had a greater _____ in the 1950s. Currency can be either a commodity money, like gold or silver, or fiat currency like US dollars.
   - a. Human Poverty Index
   - b. Compliance cost
   - c. Genuine progress indicator
   - d. Purchasing power

43. In economics, _____ is a measure of the relative satisfaction from consumption of various goods and services. Given this measure, one may speak meaningfully of increasing or decreasing _____, and thereby explain economic behavior in terms of attempts to increase one's _____. For illustrative purposes, changes in _____ are sometimes expressed in units called utils.
   - a. Utility
   - b. Utility function
   - c. Ordinal utility
   - d. Expected utility hypothesis

44. _____ is a term used in accounting, economics and finance to spread the cost of an asset over the span of several years.

   In simple words we can say that _____ is the reduction in the value of an asset due to usage, passage of time, wear and tear, technological outdating or obsolescence, depletion, inadequacy, rot, rust, decay or other such factors.

   In accounting, _____ is a term used to describe any method of attributing the historical or purchase cost of an asset across its useful life, roughly corresponding to normal wear and tear.
   - a. Net income per employee
   - b. Salvage value
   - c. Depreciation
   - d. Historical cost

45. In economics, _____ is inflation that is very high or 'out of control', a condition in which prices increase rapidly as a currency loses its value. Definitions used by the media vary from a cumulative inflation rate over three years approaching 100% to 'inflation exceeding 50% a month.' In informal usage the term is often applied to much lower rates. As a rule of thumb, normal inflation is reported per year, but _____ is often reported for much shorter intervals, often per month.
   - a. 1921 recession
   - b. 130-30 fund
   - c. Hyperinflation
   - d. 100-year flood

46. In economics, _____ is a rise in the general level of prices of goods and services in an economy over a period of time. When the general price level rises, each unit of currency buys fewer goods and services; consequently, _____ is also a decline in the real value of money--a loss of purchasing power in the medium of exchange which is also the monetary unit of account in the economy. A chief measure of general price-level _____ is the general _____ rate, which is the percentage change in a general price index (normally the Consumer Price Index) over time.

a. Inflation
b. Energy economics
c. Opportunity cost
d. Economic

47. _____s is the social science that studies the production, distribution, and consumption of goods and services. The term _____s comes from the Ancient Greek oá¼°κονομῖα from oá¼¶κος (oikos, 'house') + vÏŒμος (nomos, 'custom' or 'law'), hence 'rules of the house(hold)'. Current _____ models developed out of the broader field of political economy in the late 19th century, owing to a desire to use an empirical approach more akin to the physical sciences.
   a. Opportunity cost
   b. Inflation
   c. Energy economics
   d. Economic

48. _____ is the increase in the amount of the goods and services produced by an economy over time. It is conventionally measured as the percent rate of increase in real gross domestic product, or real GDP. Growth is usually calculated in real terms, i.e. inflation-adjusted terms, in order to net out the effect of inflation on the price of the goods and services produced.
   a. ACEA agreement
   b. Economic growth
   c. AD-IA Model
   d. ACCRA Cost of Living Index

49. _____ is a generic term in finance and economics for the entity which controls the money supply of a given currency, and has the right to set interest rates, and other parameters which control the cost and availability of money. Generally a _____ is a central bank, though often the executive branch of a government has de facto control over monetary policy by controlling the central bank. There are other arrangements, for example a central bank for several nations, a currency board which restricts currency issuance to the amount of another currency or free banking where a broad range of entities can issue notes or coin.
   a. 1921 recession
   b. Monetary authority
   c. 100-year flood
   d. 130-30 fund

50. The _____ is the central bank of the United Kingdom and is the model on which most modern, large central banks have been based. Since 1946 it has been a state-owned institution. It was established in 1694 to act as the English Government's banker, and to this day it still acts as the banker for the UK Government.
   a. Bank of England
   b. 1921 recession
   c. 100-year flood
   d. 130-30 fund

51. A _____, reserve bank, or monetary authority is the entity responsible for the monetary policy of a country or of a group of member states. It is a bank that can lend money to other banks in times of need. Its primary responsibility is to maintain the stability of the national currency and money supply, but more active duties include controlling subsidized-loan interest rates, and acting as a lender of last resort to the banking sector during times of financial crisis (private banks often being integral to the national financial system.)
   a. 1921 recession
   b. 130-30 fund
   c. 100-year flood
   d. Central bank

Chapter 12. Money and Banking

52. The _____ is the central banking system of the United States. Created in 1913 by the enactment of the Federal Reserve Act (signed by Woodrow Wilson), it is a quasi-public and quasi-private (government entity with private components) banking system that comprises (1) the presidentially appointed Board of Governors of the _____ in Washington, D.C.; (2) the Federal Open Market Committee; (3) twelve regional Federal Reserve Banks located in major cities throughout the nation acting as fiscal agents for the U.S. Treasury, each with its own nine-member board of directors; (4) numerous other private U.S. member banks, which subscribe to required amounts of non-transferable stock in their regional Federal Reserve Banks; and (5) various advisory councils. Since February 2006, Ben Bernanke has served as the Chairman of the Board of Governors of the _____.

a. Term auction facility
b. Monetary Policy Report to the Congress
c. Federal Reserve System Open Market Account
d. Federal Reserve System

53. _____ is an assumption used in many contemporary macroeconomic models, and also in other areas of contemporary economics and game theory and in other applications of rational choice theory.

Since most macroeconomic models today study decisions over many periods, the expectations of workers, consumers, and firms about future economic conditions are an essential part of the model. How to model these expectations has long been controversial, and it is well known that the macroeconomic predictions of the model may differ depending on the assumptions made about expectations

a. Potential output
b. Balanced-growth equilibrium
c. Minimum wage
d. Rational expectations

54. The _____ , a component of the Federal Reserve System, is charged under United States law with overseeing the nation's open market operations. It is the Federal Reserve Committee that makes key decisions about interest rates and the growth jam of the United States money supply. It is the principal organ of United States national monetary policy.

a. Federal Reserve Transparency Act
b. Fed Funds Probability
c. Federal Open Market Committee
d. Primary Dealer Credit Facility

55. In the United States, the _____ also known as the Federal Reserve Banks are the twelve banking districts created by the Federal Reserve Act.

The twelve _____

The _____ are as follows:

1. Boston
2. New York
3. Philadelphia
4. Cleveland
5. Richmond
6. Atlanta
7. Chicago
8. St Louis
9. Minneapolis
10. Kansas City
11. Dallas
12. San Francisco

a. Lean consumption
b. Residual claimant
c. Free contract
d. Federal Reserve districts

56. A _____ is an institution willing to extend credit when no one else will.

Originally the term referred to a reserve financial institution that secured other banks or eligible institutions, as a last resort; most often the central bank of a country. The purpose of this loan and lender is to prevent the collapse of institutions that are experiencing financial difficulty, most often near collapse.

a. Capital requirement
b. Transactional account
c. Time deposit
d. Lender of last resort

57. In economics, the _____ is the term used to refer to the environment in which bonds are bought and sold between a central bank ' its regulated banks. It is not a free market process.

- To intervene in the 'business cycle', a central bank may choose to go into the _____ and buy or sell government bonds, which is known as _____ operations to increase reserves.

a. Inside money
b. Outside money
c. Open Market
d. ACCRA Cost of Living Index

58. _____ are the means of implementing monetary policy by which a central bank controls its national money supply by buying and selling government securities, or other financial instruments. Monetary targets, such as interest rates or exchange rates, are used to guide this implementation.

Since most money is now in the form of electronic records, rather than paper records such as banknotes, _____ are conducted simply by electronically increasing or decreasing ('crediting' or 'debiting') the amount of money that a bank has, e.g., in its reserve account at the central bank, in exchange for a bank selling or buying a financial instrument.

a. Open market operations
b. ACEA agreement
c. ACCRA Cost of Living Index
d. AD-IA Model

59. _____s are a type of administrative division, in some countries managed by a local government. They vary greatly in size, spanning entire regions or counties, several municipalities, or subdivisions of municipalities.

In Austria, a _____ or Bezirk is an administrative division normally encompassing several municipalities, roughly equivalent to the Landkreis in Germany.

a. 100-year flood
b. 1921 recession
c. District
d. 130-30 fund

60. _____ AG is an international Universal bank with its headquarters in Frankfurt, Germany. The bank employs more than 81,000 people in 76 countries, and has a large presence in Europe, the Americas, Asia Pacific and the emerging markets.

_____ has offices in major financial centers, such as London, Moscow, New York, São Paulo, Singapore, Sydney, Hong Kong and Tokyo.

a. Paris Club
b. Chinese correction
c. Federal Deposit Insurance Corporation
d. Deutsche Bank

61. Discounting is a financial mechanism in which a debtor obtains the right to delay payments to a creditor, for a defined period of time, in exchange for a charge or fee. Essentially, the party that owes money in the present purchases the right to delay the payment until some future date. The _____, or charge, is simply the difference between the original amount owed in the present and the amount that has to be paid in the future to settle the debt.

a. Reinsurance
b. Discount
c. Certified Risk Manager
d. Reliability theory

62. The _____ is an interest rate a central bank charges depository institutions that borrow reserves from it.

The term _____ has two meanings:

- the same as interest rate; the term 'discount' does not refer to the meaning of the word, but to the purpose of using the quantity, such as computations of present value, e.g. net present value or discounted cash flow

- the annual effective _____, which is the annual interest divided by the capital including that interest; this rate is lower than the interest rate; it corresponds to using the value after a year as the nominal value, and seeing the initial value as the nominal value minus a discount; it is used for Treasury Bills and similar financial instruments

The annual effective _____ is the annual interest divided by the capital including that interest, which is the interest rate divided by 100% plus the interest rate. It is the annual discount factor to be applied to the future cash flow, to find the discount, subtracted from a future value to find the value one year earlier.

For example, suppose there is a government bond that sells for $95 and pays $100 in a year's time.

a. Perpetuity
b. Johansen test
c. Discount rate
d. Stochastic volatility

63. The term _____ refers to government debt, expenditures and revenues, or to finance (particularly financial revenue) in general.

- _____ deficit is the budget deficit of federal or local government
- _____ policy is the discretionary spending of governments. Contrasts with monetary policy.
- _____ year and _____ quarter are reporting periods for firms and other agencies.

a. Drawdown
b. Bucket shop
c. Procter ' Gamble
d. Fiscal

64. _____ is a fee paid on borrowed assets. It is the price paid for the use of borrowed money , or, money earned by deposited funds . Assets that are sometimes lent with _____ include money, shares, consumer goods through hire purchase, major assets such as aircraft, and even entire factories in finance lease arrangements.

a. Asset protection
b. Interest
c. Internal debt
d. Insolvency

65. An _____ is the price a borrower pays for the use of money they do not own, for instance a small company might borrow from a bank to kick start their business, and the return a lender receives for deferring the use of funds, by lending it to the borrower. _____s are normally expressed as a percentage rate over the period of one year.

_____s targets are also a vital tool of monetary policy and are used to control variables like investment, inflation, and unemployment.

a. Arrow-Debreu model
b. ACCRA Cost of Living Index
c. Enterprise value
d. Interest rate

66. The _____, an agency of the United States Department of the Treasury, is the primary regulator of federal savings associations (sometimes referred to as federal thrifts.) Federal savings associations include both federal savings banks and federal savings and loans. The OTS is also responsible for supervising savings and loan holding companies (SLHCs) and some state-chartered institutions.
a. ACCRA Cost of Living Index
b. Interstate Commerce Commission
c. ACEA agreement
d. Office of Thrift Supervision

67. The _____ is a bank regulation that sets the minimum reserves each bank must hold to customer deposits and notes. It would normally be in the form of fiat currency stored in a bank vault (vault cash), or with a central bank.

The reserve ratio is sometimes used as a tool in the monetary policy, influencing the country's economy, borrowing, and interest rates.

a. Probability of default
b. Reserve requirement
c. Fractional-reserve banking
d. Private money

68. _____ refer to services provided by the finance industry. The finance industry encompasses a broad range of organizations that deal with the management of money. Among these organizations are banks, credit card companies, insurance companies, consumer finance companies, stock brokerages, investment funds and some government sponsored enterprises.
a. Virtual Bidding
b. Delta neutral
c. Minimum acceptable rate of return
d. Financial services

69. _____ was an American economist, statistician and public intellectual, and a recipient of the Nobel Memorial Prize in Economic Sciences. He is best known among scholars for his theoretical and empirical research, especially consumption analysis, monetary history and theory, and for his demonstration of the complexity of stabilization policy. A global public followed his restatement of a political philosophy that insisted on minimizing the role of government in favor of the private sector.
a. Adolf Hitler
b. Milton Friedman
c. Adolph Fischer
d. Adam Smith

70. In general, a _____ is an arrangement to provide people with an income when they are no longer earning a regular income from employment.

The terms retirement plan or superannuation refer to a _____ granted upon retirement . Retirement plans may be set up by employers, insurance companies, the government or other institutions such as employer associations or trade unions.

a. Profit-sharing agreement
b. Pension
c. Superannuation
d. Real wage

Chapter 12. Money and Banking

71. A security is a fungible, negotiable instrument representing financial value. _____ are broadly categorized into debt _____; equity _____, e.g., common stocks; and derivative (finance) contracts such as forwards, futures, options and swaps. The company or other entity issuing the security is called the issuer.
    a. Red herring prospectus
    b. Pass-Through Certificates
    c. Settlement risk
    d. Securities

72. The _____ is a labor union in the United States and Canada. Formed in 1903 by the merger of several local and regional locals of teamsters, the union now represents a diverse membership of blue-collar and professional workers in both the public and private sectors. The union had approximately 1.4 million members in 2007.
    a. International Brotherhood of Teamsters
    b. AD-IA Model
    c. ACEA agreement
    d. ACCRA Cost of Living Index

73. The _____ is 'the basic residential unit in which economic production, consumption, inheritance, child rearing, and shelter are organized and carried out'; [the _____] 'may or may not be synonymous with family'.

    The _____ is the basic unit of analysis in many social, microeconomic and government models. The term refers to all individuals who live in the same dwelling.

    a. Family economics
    b. Household
    c. 130-30 fund
    d. 100-year flood

74. _____ in its literal sense is the process of transformation of local or regional phenomena into global ones. It can be described as a process by which the people of the world are unified into a single society and function together.

    This process is a combination of economic, technological, sociocultural and political forces.

    a. Globally Integrated Enterprise
    b. Global Cosmopolitanism
    c. Globalization
    d. Helsinki Process on Globalisation and Democracy

75. The phrase _____ and acquisitions refers to the aspect of corporate strategy, corporate finance and management dealing with the buying, selling and combining of different companies that can aid, finance, or help a growing company in a given industry grow rapidly without having to create another business entity.

    An acquisition, also known as a takeover or a buyout, is the buying of one company (the 'target') by another. An acquisition may be friendly or hostile.

    a. Differential accumulation
    b. Political economy
    c. Peace dividend
    d. Mergers

76. The phrase _____ refers to the aspect of corporate strategy, corporate finance and management dealing with the buying, selling and combining of different companies that can aid, finance, or help a growing company in a given industry grow rapidly without having to create another business entity.

    An acquisition, also known as a takeover or a buyout, is the buying of one company (the 'target') by another. An acquisition may be friendly or hostile.

Chapter 12. Money and Banking

a. Productive and unproductive labour
b. Peace dividend
c. Political economy
d. Mergers and acquisitions

77. In economics, a _____ is a mechanism that allows people to easily buy and sell (trade) financial securities (such as stocks and bonds), commodities (such as precious metals or agricultural goods), and other fungible items of value at low transaction costs and at prices that reflect the efficient-market hypothesis.

_____s have evolved significantly over several hundred years and are undergoing constant innovation to improve liquidity.

Both general markets (where many commodities are traded) and specialized markets (where only one commodity is traded) exist.

a. Convertible arbitrage
b. Financial market
c. Market anomaly
d. Noise trader

78. A _____ is the transfer of wealth from one party (such as a person or company) to another. A _____ is usually made in exchange for the provision of goods, services or both, or to fulfill a legal obligation.

The simplest and oldest form of _____ is barter, the exchange of one good or service for another.

a. Soft count
b. Going concern
c. Payment
d. Social gravity

79. In economics, an _____ is a monetary policy that increases the money supply.
a. International free trade agreement
b. Income effect
c. Elements of economic profit
d. Easy money policy

80. _____ refers to money or scrip which is exchanged only electronically. Typically, this involves use of computer networks, the internet and digital stored value systems. Electronic Funds Transfer and direct deposit are examples of _____.

a. ACCRA Cost of Living Index
b. ACEA agreement
c. Electronic money
d. AD-IA Model

81. The underground economy or _____ is a market where all commerce is conducted without regard to taxation, law or regulations of trade. The term is also often known as the underdog, shadow economy, black economy, parallel economy or phantom trades.

In modern societies the underground economy covers a vast array of activities.

a. Protectionism
b. Market economy
c. Social market economy
d. Black market

82. In economics, _____ refers to the ability of a person or a country to produce a particular good at a lower marginal cost and opportunity cost than another person or country. It is the ability to produce a product most efficiently given all the other products that could be produced. It can be contrasted with absolute advantage which refers to the ability of a person or a country to produce a particular good at a lower absolute cost than another.
 a. Triffin dilemma
 b. Comparative advantage
 c. Gravity model of trade
 d. Hot money

83. _____ describes a deliberate attempt to interfere with the free and fair operation of the market and create artificial, false or misleading appearances with respect to the price of a security, commodity or currency. _____ is prohibited under Section 9(a)(2) of the Securities Exchange Act of 1934, and in Australia under Section s 1041A of the Corporations Act 2001. The Act defines _____ as transactions which create an artificial price or maintain an artificial price for a tradable security.
 a. Net domestic product
 b. Legal monopoly
 c. Managerial economics
 d. Market manipulation

Chapter 13. Money Creation

1. A _____ is a type of banknote issued by the Federal Reserve System and is the only type of U.S. banknote that is still produced today.

   _____s are fiat currency, with the words 'this note is legal tender for all debts, public and private' printed on each bill. (See generally 31 U.S.C.

   a. Federal Reserve Note
   b. Term auction facility
   c. Federal Reserve Transparency Act
   d. Term Securities Lending Facility

2. In business and accounting, _____ are everything of value that is owned by a person or company. It is a claim on the property your income of a borrower. The balance sheet of a firm records the monetary value of the _____ owned by the firm.
   a. ACCRA Cost of Living Index
   b. Amortization schedule
   c. ACEA agreement
   d. Assets

3.

   A _____ is a type of financial intermediary and a type of bank. Commercial banking is also known as business banking. It is a bank that provides checking accounts, savings accounts, and money market accounts and that accepts time deposits.

   a. Lombard banking
   b. Bought deal
   c. Daylight overdraft
   d. Commercial bank

4. _____ is money accepted for exchange of goods in an economy. The prevalence of one money over another arises, usually, when a government designates through decrees that the government shall accept only particular notes and coins in payment for taxes. Typically, money of _____ consists of stamped coins and minted paper bills.
   a. Totnes pound
   b. Currency
   c. Security thread
   d. Local currency

5. Fractional-reserve banking is the banking practice in which banks keep only a fraction of their deposits in reserve (as cash and other highly liquid assets) and lend out the remainder, while maintaining the simultaneous obligation to redeem all these deposits upon demand. _____ necessarily occurs when banks lend out any fraction of the funds received from demand deposits. This practice is universal in modern banking.
   a. Narrow banking
   b. Private money
   c. Prime rate
   d. Fractional reserve banking

6. The accounting equation relates assets, _____, and owner's equity:

   Assets = _____ + Owner's Equity

The accounting equation is the mathematical structure of the balance sheet.

The Australian Accounting Research Foundation defines _____ as: 'future sacrifice of economic benefits that the entity is presently obliged to make to other entities as a result of past transactions and other past events.'

Chapter 13. Money Creation

Probably the most accepted accounting definition of liability is the one used by the International Accounting Standards Board (IASB.) The following is a quotation from IFRS Framework:

A liability is a present obligation of the enterprise arising from past events, the settlement of which is expected to result in an outflow from the enterprise of resources embodying economic benefits

-

Regulations as to the recognition of _____ are different all over the world, but are roughly similar to those of the IASB.

a. Competition law theory
b. Coase theorem
c. Liabilities
d. Community property

7. _____ is the process by which money is produced or issued. There are three different ways to create money:

- manufacturing a new monetary unit, such as paper currency or metal coins (_____)
- loaning out a physical monetary unit multiple times through fractional-reserve lending (credit creation)
- buying of government securities or other financial instruments by central bank through Open market operations (electronic creation)

Coins are produced by manufacturing metal in a factory called a mint.

Banknotes and bank account balances are financial securities issued by a bank.

Similarly, money destruction, i.e., the reverse of _____, can occur in two different ways, depending on how the money was created.

a. Shadow Open Market Committee
b. Monetary policy of Sweden
c. Second-round effect
d. Money creation

8. In business, _____ is the total liabilitiess minus total outside assets of an individual or a company. For a company, this is called shareholders' prefernce and may be referred to as book value. _____ is stated as at a particular year in time.

a. Post earnings announcement drift
b. Net worth
c. Sinking fund
d. Bond credit rating

9. In financial accounting, a _____ or statement of financial position is a summary of a person's or organization's balances. Assets, liabilities and ownership equity are listed as of a specific date, such as the end of its financial year. A _____ is often described as a snapshot of a company's financial condition.

a. 1921 recession
b. 130-30 fund
c. 100-year flood
d. Balance sheet

10. _____ are banks' holdings of deposits in accounts with their central bank (for instance the European Central Bank or the Federal Reserve, in the latter case including federal funds), plus currency that is physically held in bank vaults (vault cash.) The central banks of some nations set minimum reserve requirements. Even when no requirements are set, banks commonly wish to hold some reserves, called desired reserves, against unexpected events.
   a. Bank reserves
   b. Bilateral netting
   c. Sweep account
   d. Structuring

11. A security is a fungible, negotiable instrument representing financial value. _____ are broadly categorized into debt _____; equity _____, e.g., common stocks; and derivative (finance) contracts such as forwards, futures, options and swaps. The company or other entity issuing the security is called the issuer.
   a. Pass-Through Certificates
   b. Red herring prospectus
   c. Settlement risk
   d. Securities

12. The _____ was a worldwide economic downturn starting in most places in 1929 and ending at different times in the 1930s or early 1940s for different countries. It was the largest and most important economic depression in the 20th century, and is used in the 21st century as an example of how far the world's economy can fall. The _____ originated in the United States; historians most often use as a starting date the stock market crash on October 29, 1929, known as Black Tuesday.
   a. British Empire Economic Conference
   b. Great Depression
   c. Jarrow March
   d. Wall Street Crash of 1929

13. The reserve requirement (or required _____) is a bank regulation that sets the minimum reserves each bank must hold to customer deposits and notes. It would normally be in the form of fiat currency stored in a bank vault (vault cash), or with a central bank.

   The _____ is sometimes used as a tool in the monetary policy, influencing the country's economy, borrowing, and interest rates.

   a. First player wins
   b. Dividend unit
   c. Bank-State-Branch
   d. Reserve ratio

14. A _____ is an expression that compares quantities relative to each other. The most common examples involve two quantities, but any number of quantities can be compared. _____s are represented mathematically by separating each quantity with a colon, for example the _____ 2:3, which is read as the _____ 'two to three'.
   a. Y-intercept
   b. 130-30 fund
   c. Ratio
   d. 100-year flood

15. The _____ consists of a number of economic theories which describe the nature of the firm, company including its existence, its behaviour, and its relationship with the market.

In simplified terms, the _____ aims to answer these questions:

1. Existence - why do firms emerge, why are not all transactions in the economy mediated over the market?
2. Boundaries - why the boundary between firms and the market is located exactly there? Which transactions are performed internally and which are negotiated on the market?
3. Organization - why are firms structured in such specific way? What is the interplay of formal and informal relationships?

Despite looking simple, these questions are not answered by the established economic theory, which usually views firms as given, and treats them as black boxes without any internal structure.

The First World War period saw a change of emphasis in economic theory away from industry-level analysis which mainly included analysing markets to analysis at the level of the firm, as it became increasingly clear that perfect competition was no longer an adequate model of how firms behaved. Economic theory till then had focussed on trying to understand markets alone and there had been little study on understanding why firms or organisations exist.

a. Khazzoom-Brookes postulate
c. Technology gap
b. Policy Ineffectiveness Proposition
d. Theory of the firm

16. A _____ refers to any type debt instrument, such as a loan, bond, mortgage that does not have a fixed rate of interest over the life of the instrument. Such debt typically uses an index or other base rate for establishing the interest rate for each relevant period. One of the most common rates to use as the basis for applying interest rates is the London Inter-bank Offered Rate, or LIBOR

a. Floating interest rate
c. Moneylender
b. Money market
d. Disposal tax effect

17. In banking, _____ are bank reserves in excess of the reserve requirement set by a central bank (in the United States, the Federal Reserve System, called the Fed; in Canada, the Bank of Canada.) They are reserves of cash more than the required amounts. Holding _____ is generally considered costly and uneconomical as no interest is earned on the excess amount.

a. Universal bank
c. Excess reserves
b. Origination fee
d. Annual percentage rate

18. The _____ is a United States government corporation created by the Glass-Steagall Act of 1933. It provides deposit insurance, which guarantees the safety of deposits in member banks, currently up to $250,000 per depositor per bank. Funds in non-interest bearing transaction accounts are fully insured, with no limit, under the temporary Transaction Account Guarantee Program.

a. Foreign direct investment
c. Luxembourg Income Study
b. Great Leap Forward
d. Federal Deposit Insurance Corporation

19. The Federal Reserve System (also the Federal Reserve; informally The Fed) is the central banking system of the United States. Created in 1913 by the enactment of the Federal Reserve Act (signed by Woodrow Wilson), it is a quasi-public and quasi-private (government entity with private components) banking system that comprises (1) the presidentially appointed Board of Governors of the Federal Reserve System in Washington, D.C.; (2) the Federal Open Market Committee; (3) twelve regional _____ located in major cities throughout the nation acting as fiscal agents for the U.S. Treasury, each with its own nine-member board of directors; (4) numerous other private U.S. member banks, which subscribe to required amounts of non-transferable stock in their regional _____; and (5) various advisory councils. Since February 2006, Ben Bernanke has served as the Chairman of the Board of Governors of the Federal Reserve System.
   a. Federal Open Market Committee
   b. Federal Reserve Banks
   c. Fed Funds Probability
   d. Federal funds

20. _____, in law and economics, is a form of risk management primarily used to hedge against the risk of a contingent loss. _____ is defined as the equitable transfer of the risk of a loss, from one entity to another, in exchange for a premium, and can be thought of as a guaranteed small loss to prevent a large, possibly devastating loss. An insurer is a company selling the _____; an insured or policyholder is the person or entity buying the _____.
   a. Insurance
   b. ACEA agreement
   c. ACCRA Cost of Living Index
   d. AD-IA Model

21. In finance, a _____ is a debt security, in which the authorized issuer owes the holders a debt and, depending on the terms of the _____, is obliged to pay interest (the coupon) and/or to repay the principal at a later date, termed maturity. A _____ is a formal contract to repay borrowed money with interest at fixed intervals.

Thus a _____ is like a loan: the issuer is the borrower (debtor), the holder is the lender (creditor), and the coupon is the interest.

   a. Prize Bond
   b. Zero-coupon
   c. Callable
   d. Bond

22. _____ is the difference between price and the costs of bringing to market whatever it is that is accounted as an enterprise (whether by harvest, extraction, manufacture, or purchase) in terms of the component costs of delivered goods and/or services and any operating or other expenses.

A key difficulty in measuring profit is in defining costs. Pure economic monetary profits can be zero or negative even in competitive equilibrium when accounted monetized costs exceed monetized price.

   a. Economic profit
   b. ACCRA Cost of Living Index
   c. Accounting profit
   d. Operating profit

23. _____s is the social science that studies the production, distribution, and consumption of goods and services. The term _____s comes from the Ancient Greek οἰκονομῐ́α from οἶκος (oikos, 'house') + νόμος (nomos, 'custom' or 'law'), hence 'rules of the house(hold)'. Current _____ models developed out of the broader field of political economy in the late 19th century, owing to a desire to use an empirical approach more akin to the physical sciences.
   a. Inflation
   b. Opportunity cost
   c. Energy economics
   d. Economic

Chapter 13. Money Creation

24. In economics, _____ is the difference between a company's total revenue and its opportunity costs. It is the increase in wealth that an investor has from making an investment, taking into consideration all costs associated with that investment including the opportunity cost of capital.

Profit is the factor income of the entrepreneur.

a. Accounting profit
c. ACCRA Cost of Living Index
b. Operating profit
d. Economic profit

25. In the United States, _____ are overnight borrowings by banks to maintain their bank reserves at the Federal Reserve. Banks keep reserves at Federal Reserve Banks to meet their reserve requirements and to clear financial transactions. Transactions in the _____ market enable depository institutions with reserve balances in excess of reserve requirements to lend reserves to institutions with reserve deficiencies.

a. Federal funds
c. Federal Reserve Transparency Act
b. Term auction facility
d. Federal funds rate

26. In the United States, the _____ is the interest rate at which private depository institutions (mostly banks) lend balances (federal funds) at the Federal Reserve to other depository institutions, usually overnight. It is the interest rate banks charge each other for loans. Changing the target rate is one way the Chairman of the Federal Reserve can influence the supply of money in the U.S. economy..

a. Federal funds rate
c. Monetary Policy Report to the Congress
b. Term auction facility
d. Federal banking

27. Market _____ is a business, economics or investment term that refers to an asset's ability to be easily converted through an act of buying or selling without causing a significant movement in the price and with minimum loss of value. Money, or cash on hand, is the most liquid asset. An act of exchange of a less liquid asset with a more liquid asset is called liquidation.

a. 1921 recession
c. 100-year flood
b. 130-30 fund
d. Liquidity

28. _____ is a component of the firm's opportunity costs. The time that the owner spends running the firm could be spent on running another firm. This is _____: the return the entrepreneur can expect to earn or the profit that the business owners considers necessary to make running the business worth his/her while.

a. 100-year flood
c. Profit margin
b. Profit maximization
d. Normal profit

29. In economics, _____ is the total amount of money available in an economy at a particular point in time. There are several ways to define 'money', but standard measures usually include currency in circulation and demand deposits.

_____ data are recorded and published, usually by the government or the central bank of the country.

a. Velocity of money
c. Neutrality of money
b. Veil of money
d. Money supply

30. The most common mechanism used to measure this increase in the money supply is typically called the _____. It calculates the maximum amount of money that an initial deposit can be expanded to with a given reserve ratio - such a factor is called a multiplier.

The _____, m, is the inverse of the reserve requirement, R:

$$m = \frac{1}{R}$$

This formula stems from the fact that the sum of the 'amount loaned out' column above can be expressed mathematically as a geometric series with a common ratio of 1 − R.

a. Kibbutz volunteers
b. Money multiplier
c. Flow to Equity-Approach
d. Fixed-income arbitrage

31. _____, often referred to by his initials _____, was the 32nd President of the United States. He was a central figure of the 20th century during a time of worldwide economic crisis and world war. Elected to four terms in office, he served from 1933 to 1945 and is the only U.S. president to have served more than two terms.

a. Adolf Hitler
b. Adolph Fischer
c. Franklin Delano Roosevelt
d. Adam Smith

32. A _____ is a public holiday in both the United Kingdom and Ireland. There is some automatic right to time off on these days, although the majority of the population not employed in essential services (e.g. utilities, fire, ambulance, police, health-care workers, London Underground) receive them as holidays; those employed in essential services usually receive extra pay for working on these days. _____s are often assumed to be so called because they are days upon which banks are shut, but this is not in fact the case.

a. 130-30 fund
b. 100-year flood
c. Bank holiday
d. 1921 recession

Chapter 14. Interest Rates and Monetary Policy

1. _____ is an American economist and was the Chairman of the Federal Reserve of the United States from 1987 to 2006. He currently works as a private advisor and providing consulting for firms through his company, Greenspan Associates LLC.

First appointed Federal Reserve chairman by President Ronald Reagan in August 1987, he was reappointed at successive four-year intervals until retiring on January 31, 2006 after the second-longest tenure in the position.

a. Alan Greenspan
b. Adolph Fischer
c. Adolf Hitler
d. Adam Smith

2. _____ is the process by which the government, central bank (ii) availability of money, and (iii) cost of money or rate of interest, in order to attain a set of objectives oriented towards the growth and stability of the economy. Monetary theory provides insight into how to craft optimal _____.

_____ is referred to as either being an expansionary policy where an expansionary policy increases the total supply of money in the economy, and a contractionary policy decreases the total money supply.

a. Monetary policy
b. 130-30 fund
c. 1921 recession
d. 100-year flood

3. The term _____ refers to government debt, expenditures and revenues, or to finance (particularly financial revenue) in general.

- _____ deficit is the budget deficit of federal or local government
- _____ policy is the discretionary spending of governments. Contrasts with monetary policy.
- _____ year and _____ quarter are reporting periods for firms and other agencies.

a. Procter ' Gamble
b. Drawdown
c. Bucket shop
d. Fiscal

4. In economics, _____ is the use of government spending and revenue collection to influence the economy.

_____ can be contrasted with the other main type of economic policy, monetary policy, which attempts to stabilize the economy by controlling interest rates and the supply of money. The two main instruments of _____ are government spending and taxation.

a. Fiscalism
b. 100-year flood
c. Sustainable investment rule
d. Fiscal policy

5. In business and accounting, _____ are everything of value that is owned by a person or company. It is a claim on the property your income of a borrower. The balance sheet of a firm records the monetary value of the _____ owned by the firm.

a. ACEA agreement
b. ACCRA Cost of Living Index
c. Amortization schedule
d. Assets

6. In finance, a _____ is a debt security, in which the authorized issuer owes the holders a debt and, depending on the terms of the _____, is obliged to pay interest (the coupon) and/or to repay the principal at a later date, termed maturity. A _____ is a formal contract to repay borrowed money with interest at fixed intervals.

Thus a _____ is like a loan: the issuer is the borrower (debtor), the holder is the lender (creditor), and the coupon is the interest.

a. Prize Bond
c. Bond
b. Zero-coupon
d. Callable

7. _____ is the difference between a lower selling price and a higher purchase price, resulting in a financial loss for the seller. Pursuant to IRS TAX TIP 2009-35 'If your _____es exceed your capital gains, the excess can be deducted on your tax return, up to an annual limit of $3,000 ($1,500 if you are married filing separately.)' .

a. 100-year flood
c. Capital loss
b. 130-30 fund
d. 1921 recession

8. Economics:

- _____,the desire to own something and the ability to pay for it
- _____ curve,a graphic representation of a _____ schedule
- _____ deposit, the money in checking accounts
- _____ pull theory,the theory that inflation occurs when _____ for goods and services exceeds existing supplies
- _____ schedule,a table that lists the quantity of a good a person will buy it each different price
- _____ side economics,the school of economics at believes government spending and tax cuts open economy by raising _____

a. McKesson ' Robbins scandal
c. Demand
b. Production
d. Variability

9. The _____ is the desired holding of money balances in the form of cash or bank deposits.

Money is dominated as store of value by interest bearing assets. However, money is necessary to carry out transactions, or in other words, it provides liquidity.

a. Demand for money
c. Borrowing base
b. Conglomerate merger
d. Market neutral

10. The _____ or gross domestic income (GDI), a basic measure of an economy's economic performance, is the market value of all final goods and services produced within the borders of a nation in a year. _____ can be defined in three ways, all of which are conceptually identical. First, it is equal to the total expenditures for all final goods and services produced within the country in a stipulated period of time (usually a 365-day year.)

a. Monopolistic competition
c. Countercyclical
b. Market structure
d. Gross domestic product

11. _____ is a fee paid on borrowed assets. It is the price paid for the use of borrowed money, or, money earned by deposited funds. Assets that are sometimes lent with _____ include money, shares, consumer goods through hire purchase, major assets such as aircraft, and even entire factories in finance lease arrangements.

   a. Internal debt
   b. Asset protection
   c. Interest
   d. Insolvency

12. An _____ is the price a borrower pays for the use of money they do not own, for instance a small company might borrow from a bank to kick start their business, and the return a lender receives for deferring the use of funds, by lending it to the borrower. _____s are normally expressed as a percentage rate over the period of one year.

_____s targets are also a vital tool of monetary policy and are used to control variables like investment, inflation, and unemployment.

   a. Arrow-Debreu model
   b. ACCRA Cost of Living Index
   c. Enterprise value
   d. Interest rate

13. A _____ is an intermediary used in trade to avoid the inconveniences of a pure barter system.

By contrast, as William Stanley Jevons argued, in a barter system there must be a coincidence of wants before two people can trade - one must want exactly what the other has to offer, when and where it is offered, so that the exchange can occur. A _____ permits the value of goods to be assessed and rendered in terms of the intermediary, most often, a form of money widely accepted to buy any other good.

   a. Consumer theory
   b. Price revolution
   c. Labour economics
   d. Medium of exchange

14. To act as a _____, a commodity, a form of money stored, and retrieved - and be predictably useful when it is so retrieved.

This is distinct from the standard of deferred payment function which requires acceptability to parties one owes a debt to and a minimum of opportunity to cheat others.

   a. Petrodollar
   b. Store of value
   c. World currency
   d. Fiat money

15. _____ is the demand for financial assets, e.g., securities, money or foreign currency. It is used for purposes of business transactions and personal consumption.

The need to accommodate a firm's expected cash transactions.

   a. Multiplier effect
   b. Keynesian cross
   c. Spending multiplier
   d. Transactions demand

16. Bartering is a medium in which goods or services are directly exchanged for other goods and/or services, without the use of money. It can be bilateral or multilateral, and usually exists parallel to monetary systems in most developed countries, though to a very limited extent. _____ usually replaces money as the method of exchange in times of monetary crisis, when the currency is unstable and devalued by hyperinflation.

a. New Economics Foundation
b. Meitheal
c. Community-based economics
d. Barter

17. In algebra, a _____ is a function depending on n that associates a scalar, det(A), to an n×n square matrix A. The fundamental geometric meaning of a _____ is a scale factor for measure when A is regarded as a linear transformation. _____s are important both in calculus, where they enter the substitution rule for several variables, and in multilinear algebra.

For a fixed nonnegative integer n, there is a unique _____ function for the n×n matrices over any commutative ring R. In particular, this function exists when R is the field of real or complex numbers.

a. 1921 recession
b. 130-30 fund
c. Determinant
d. 100-year flood

18. _____ in economics and business is the result of an exchange and from that trade we assign a numerical monetary value to a good, service or asset. If Alice trades Bob 4 apples for an orange, the _____ of an orange is 4 apples. Inversely, the _____ of an apple is 1/4 oranges.

a. Price book
b. Price
c. Premium pricing
d. Price war

19. A _____ is a normalized average (typically a weighted average) of prices for a given class of goods or services in a given region, during a given interval of time. It is a statistic designed to help to compare how these prices, taken as a whole, differ between time periods or geographical locations.

Price indices have several potential uses.

a. Two-part tariff
b. Transactional Net Margin Method
c. Product sabotage
d. Price index

20. _____ is the a method of technical and economic research of the systems for purpose to optimize a parity between system's consumer functions or properties and expenses to achieve those functions or properties.

This methodology for continuous perfection of production, industrial technologies, organizational structures was developed by Juryj Sobolev in 1948 at the 'Perm telephone factory'

- 1948 Juryj Sobolev - the first success in application of a method analysis at the 'Perm telephone factory' .
- 1949 - the first application for the invention as result of use of the new method.

Today in economically developed countries practically each enterprise or the company use methodology of the kind of functional-cost analysis as a practice of the quality management, most full satisfying to principles of standards of series ISO 9000.

- Interest of consumer not in products itself, but the advantage which it will receive from its usage.
- The consumer aspires to reduce his expenses
- Functions needed by consumer can be executed in the various ways, and, hence, with various efficiency and expenses. Among possible alternatives of realization of functions exist such in which the parity of quality and the price is the optimal for the consumer.

The goal of _____ is achievement of the highest consumer satisfaction of production at simultaneous decrease in all kinds of industrial expenses Classical _____ has three English synonyms - Value Engineering, Value Management, Value Analysis.

a. Willingness to pay
c. Monopoly wage
b. Staple financing
d. Function cost analysis

21. The _____ or Aggregate Demand-Aggregate Supply model is a macroeconomic model that explains price level and output through the relationship of aggregate demand and aggregate supply. It was first put forth by John Maynard Keynes in his work The General Theory of Employment, Interest, and Money. It is the foundation for the modern field of macroeconomics, and is accepted by a broad array of economists, from Libertarian, Monetarist supporters of laissez-faire, such as Milton Friedman to Socialist, Post-Keynesian supporters of economic interventionism, such as Joan Robinson.

a. Adaptive expectations
c. AD-AS
b. Economic interdependence
d. IS/LM model

22. In economics, the _____ can be defined as the graph depicting the relationship between the price of a certain commodity, and the amount of it that consumers are willing and able to purchase at that given price. It is a graphic representation of a demand schedule. The _____ for all consumers together follows from the _____ of every individual consumer: the individual demands at each price are added together.

a. Cost curve
c. Wage curve
b. Kuznets curve
d. Demand curve

23. A _____ is a hypothetical measure of overall prices for some set of goods and services, in a given region during a given interval, normalized relative to some base set. Typically, a _____ is approximated with a price index.

The classical dichotomy is the assumption that there is a relatively clean distinction between overall increases or decreases in prices and underlying, e;reale; economic variables.

a. Discretionary spending
c. Price elasticity of supply
b. Discouraged worker
d. Price level

24. The Federal Reserve System (also the Federal Reserve; informally The Fed) is the central banking system of the United States. Created in 1913 by the enactment of the Federal Reserve Act (signed by Woodrow Wilson), it is a quasi-public and quasi-private (government entity with private components) banking system that comprises (1) the presidentially appointed Board of Governors of the Federal Reserve System in Washington, D.C.; (2) the Federal Open Market Committee; (3) twelve regional _____ located in major cities throughout the nation acting as fiscal agents for the U.S. Treasury, each with its own nine-member board of directors; (4) numerous other private U.S. member banks, which subscribe to required amounts of non-transferable stock in their regional _____; and (5) various advisory councils. Since February 2006, Ben Bernanke has served as the Chairman of the Board of Governors of the Federal Reserve System.

   a. Fed Funds Probability
   b. Federal Reserve Banks
   c. Federal Open Market Committee
   d. Federal funds

25. _____ is an economic model based on price, utility and quantity in a market. It predicts that in a competitive market, price will function to equalize the quantity demanded by consumers, and the quantity supplied by producers, resulting in an economic equilibrium of price and quantity. The model incorporates other factors changing equilibrium as a shift of demand and/or supply.

   a. Joint demand
   b. Rational addiction
   c. Supply and demand
   d. Deferred gratification

26. In financial accounting, a _____ or statement of financial position is a summary of a person's or organization's balances. Assets, liabilities and ownership equity are listed as of a specific date, such as the end of its financial year. A _____ is often described as a snapshot of a company's financial condition.

   a. 1921 recession
   b. 130-30 fund
   c. 100-year flood
   d. Balance sheet

27. A _____, reserve bank, or monetary authority is the entity responsible for the monetary policy of a country or of a group of member states. It is a bank that can lend money to other banks in times of need. Its primary responsibility is to maintain the stability of the national currency and money supply, but more active duties include controlling subsidized-loan interest rates, and acting as a lender of last resort to the banking sector during times of financial crisis (private banks often being integral to the national financial system.)

   a. 130-30 fund
   b. 1921 recession
   c. 100-year flood
   d. Central bank

28. A _____ is a type of banknote issued by the Federal Reserve System and is the only type of U.S. banknote that is still produced today.

_____s are fiat currency, with the words 'this note is legal tender for all debts, public and private' printed on each bill. (See generally 31 U.S.C.

   a. Term auction facility
   b. Term Securities Lending Facility
   c. Federal Reserve Transparency Act
   d. Federal Reserve Note

29. The _____ was a worldwide economic downturn starting in most places in 1929 and ending at different times in the 1930s or early 1940s for different countries. It was the largest and most important economic depression in the 20th century, and is used in the 21st century as an example of how far the world's economy can fall. The _____ originated in the United States; historians most often use as a starting date the stock market crash on October 29, 1929, known as Black Tuesday.

a. Jarrow March
b. Wall Street Crash of 1929
c. British Empire Economic Conference
d. Great Depression

30. The accounting equation relates assets, _____, and owner's equity:

    Assets = _____ + Owner's Equity

The accounting equation is the mathematical structure of the balance sheet.

The Australian Accounting Research Foundation defines _____ as: 'future sacrifice of economic benefits that the entity is presently obliged to make to other entities as a result of past transactions and other past events.'

Probably the most accepted accounting definition of liability is the one used by the International Accounting Standards Board (IASB.) The following is a quotation from IFRS Framework:

A liability is a present obligation of the enterprise arising from past events, the settlement of which is expected to result in an outflow from the enterprise of resources embodying economic benefits

-

Regulations as to the recognition of _____ are different all over the world, but are roughly similar to those of the IASB.

a. Community property
b. Coase theorem
c. Competition law theory
d. Liabilities

31. _____ are banks' holdings of deposits in accounts with their central bank (for instance the European Central Bank or the Federal Reserve, in the latter case including federal funds), plus currency that is physically held in bank vaults (vault cash.) The central banks of some nations set minimum reserve requirements. Even when no requirements are set, banks commonly wish to hold some reserves, called desired reserves, against unexpected events.

a. Bilateral netting
b. Structuring
c. Sweep account
d. Bank reserves

32.

A _____ is a type of financial intermediary and a type of bank. Commercial banking is also known as business banking. It is a bank that provides checking accounts, savings accounts, and money market accounts and that accepts time deposits.

a. Bought deal
b. Daylight overdraft
c. Commercial bank
d. Lombard banking

33. A security is a fungible, negotiable instrument representing financial value. _____ are broadly categorized into debt _____; equity _____, e.g., common stocks; and derivative (finance) contracts such as forwards, futures, options and swaps. The company or other entity issuing the security is called the issuer.

Chapter 14. Interest Rates and Monetary Policy

a. Settlement risk
c. Pass-Through Certificates
b. Red herring prospectus
d. Securities

34. _____ is a broad label that refers to any individuals or households that use goods and services generated within the economy. The concept of a _____ is used in different contexts, so that the usage and significance of the term may vary.

Typically when business people and economists talk of _____s they are talking about person as _____, an aggregated commodity item with little individuality other than that expressed in the buy/not-buy decision.

a. 1921 recession
c. 100-year flood
b. Consumer
d. 130-30 fund

35. In economics, the _____ is the term used to refer to the environment in which bonds are bought and sold between a central bank ' its regulated banks. It is not a free market process.

- To intervene in the 'business cycle', a central bank may choose to go into the _____ and buy or sell government bonds, which is known as _____ operations to increase reserves.

a. Outside money
c. ACCRA Cost of Living Index
b. Inside money
d. Open market

36. _____ are the means of implementing monetary policy by which a central bank controls its national money supply by buying and selling government securities, or other financial instruments. Monetary targets, such as interest rates or exchange rates, are used to guide this implementation.

Since most money is now in the form of electronic records, rather than paper records such as banknotes, _____ are conducted simply by electronically increasing or decreasing ('crediting' or 'debiting') the amount of money that a bank has, e.g., in its reserve account at the central bank, in exchange for a bank selling or buying a financial instrument.

a. ACCRA Cost of Living Index
c. ACEA agreement
b. Open market operations
d. AD-IA Model

37. A _____ is a bank or securities broker-dealer that may trade directly with the Federal Reserve System of the United States ('the Fed'.) Such firms are required to make bids or offers when the Fed conducts open market operations, provide information to the Fed's open market trading desk, and to participate actively in U.S. Treasury securities auctions. They consult with both the U.S. Treasury and the Fed about funding the budget deficit and implementing monetary policy.

a. 100-year flood
c. 1921 recession
b. 130-30 fund
d. Primary dealer

38. In economics, a _____ is a monetary-policy rule that stipulates how much the central bank would or should change the nominal interest rate in response to divergences of actual inflation rates from target inflation rates and of actual Gross Domestic Product (GDP) from potential GDP. It was first proposed by the by U.S. economist John B. Taylor in 1993. The rule can be written as follows:

$$i_t = \pi_t + r_t^* + a_\pi(\pi_t - \pi_t^*) + a_y(y_t - \bar{y}_t).$$

In this equation, i_t is the target short-term nominal interest rate (e.g. the federal funds rate in the US), π_t is the rate of inflation as measured by the GDP deflator, π_t^* is the desired rate of inflation, r_t^* is the assumed equilibrium real interest rate, y_t is the logarithm of real GDP, and $\bar{y}_t$ is the logarithm of potential output, as determined by a linear trend.

a. Federal Reserve Banks
b. Fed Funds Probability
c. Term Securities Lending Facility
d. Taylor rule

39. _____ refers to a business or organization attempting to acquire goods or services to accomplish the goals of the enterprise. Though there are several organizations that attempt to set standards in the _____ process, processes can vary greatly between organizations. Typically the word '_____' is not used interchangeably with the word 'procurement', since procurement typically includes Expediting, Supplier Quality, and Traffic and Logistics (T'L) in addition to _____.

a. Free port
b. 100-year flood
c. Purchasing
d. 130-30 fund

218 Chapter 14. Interest Rates and Monetary Policy

40. A _____ is:

- Rewrite _____, in generative grammar and computer science
- Standardization, a formal and widely-accepted statement, fact, definition, or qualification
- Operation, a determinate _____ for performing a mathematical operation and obtaining a certain result (Mathematics, Logic)
    - Unary operation
    - Binary operation
- _____ of inference, a function from sets of formulae to formulae (Mathematics, Logic)
- _____ of thumb, principle with broad application that is not intended to be strictly accurate or reliable for every situation. Also often simply referred to as a _____
- Moral, an atomic element of a moral code for guiding choices in human behavior
- Heuristic, a quantized '_____' which shows a tendency or probability for successful function
- A regulation, as in sports
- A Production _____, as in computer science
- Procedural law, a _____ set governing the application of laws to cases
    - A law, which may informally be called a '_____'
    - A court ruling, a decision by a court
- In the U.S. Government, a regulation mandated by Congress, but written or expanded upon by the Executive Branch.
- Norm (sociology), an informal but widely accepted _____, concept, truth, definition, or qualification (social norms, legal norms, coding norms)
- Norm (philosophy), a kind of sentence or a reason to act, feel or believe
- 'Rulership' is the concept of governance by a government:
    - Military _____, governance by a military body
    - Monastic _____, a collection of precepts that guides the life of monks or nuns in a religious order where the superior holds the place of Christ
- Slide _____

- '_____,' a song by Ayumi Hamasaki
- '_____,' a song by rapper Nas
- '_____s,' an album by the band The Whitest Boy Alive
- _____s: Pyaar Ka Superhit Formula, a 2003 Bollywood film
- ruler, an instrument for measuring lengths
- _____, a component of an astrolabe, circumferator or similar instrument
- The _____s, a bestselling self-help book
- _____ Project (Run Up-to-date Linux Everywhere), a project that aims to use up-to-date Linux software on old PCs
- _____ engine, a software system that helps managing business _____s
- Ja _____, a hip hop artist
    - R.U.L.E., a 2005 greatest hits album by rapper Ja _____
- '_____s,' a KMFDM song

a. Demand
b. Procter ' Gamble
c. Technocracy
d. Rule

Chapter 14. Interest Rates and Monetary Policy

41. In economics, _____ is the total amount of money available in an economy at a particular point in time. There are several ways to define 'money', but standard measures usually include currency in circulation and demand deposits.

_____ data are recorded and published, usually by the government or the central bank of the country.

a. Veil of money
b. Money supply
c. Neutrality of money
d. Velocity of money

42. Discounting is a financial mechanism in which a debtor obtains the right to delay payments to a creditor, for a defined period of time, in exchange for a charge or fee. Essentially, the party that owes money in the present purchases the right to delay the payment until some future date. The _____, or charge, is simply the difference between the original amount owed in the present and the amount that has to be paid in the future to settle the debt.

a. Certified Risk Manager
b. Reliability theory
c. Reinsurance
d. Discount

43. The _____ is an interest rate a central bank charges depository institutions that borrow reserves from it.

The term _____ has two meanings:

- the same as interest rate; the term 'discount' does not refer to the meaning of the word, but to the purpose of using the quantity, such as computations of present value, e.g. net present value or discounted cash flow

- the annual effective _____, which is the annual interest divided by the capital including that interest; this rate is lower than the interest rate; it corresponds to using the value after a year as the nominal value, and seeing the initial value as the nominal value minus a discount; it is used for Treasury Bills and similar financial instruments

The annual effective _____ is the annual interest divided by the capital including that interest, which is the interest rate divided by 100% plus the interest rate. It is the annual discount factor to be applied to the future cash flow, to find the discount, subtracted from a future value to find the value one year earlier.

For example, suppose there is a government bond that sells for $95 and pays $100 in a year's time.

a. Perpetuity
b. Johansen test
c. Stochastic volatility
d. Discount rate

44. A _____ is an institution willing to extend credit when no one else will.

Originally the term referred to a reserve financial institution that secured other banks or eligible institutions, as a last resort; most often the central bank of a country. The purpose of this loan and lender is to prevent the collapse of institutions that are experiencing financial difficulty, most often near collapse.

a. Lender of last resort
b. Time deposit
c. Capital requirement
d. Transactional account

Chapter 14. Interest Rates and Monetary Policy

45. The reserve requirement (or required _____) is a bank regulation that sets the minimum reserves each bank must hold to customer deposits and notes. It would normally be in the form of fiat currency stored in a bank vault (vault cash), or with a central bank.

The _____ is sometimes used as a tool in the monetary policy, influencing the country's economy, borrowing, and interest rates.

　a. Dividend unit
　c. Bank-State-Branch
　b. First player wins
　d. Reserve ratio

46. A _____ is an expression that compares quantities relative to each other. The most common examples involve two quantities, but any number of quantities can be compared. _____s are represented mathematically by separating each quantity with a colon, for example the _____ 2:3, which is read as the _____ 'two to three'.
　a. Y-intercept
　c. 130-30 fund
　b. 100-year flood
　d. Ratio

47. _____ is the process by which money is produced or issued. There are three different ways to create money:

- manufacturing a new monetary unit, such as paper currency or metal coins (_____)
- loaning out a physical monetary unit multiple times through fractional-reserve lending (credit creation)
- buying of government securities or other financial instruments by central bank through Open market operations (electronic creation)

Coins are produced by manufacturing metal in a factory called a mint.

Banknotes and bank account balances are financial securities issued by a bank.

Similarly, money destruction, i.e., the reverse of _____, can occur in two different ways, depending on how the money was created.

　a. Second-round effect
　c. Money creation
　b. Monetary policy of Sweden
　d. Shadow Open Market Committee

48. The _____, a component of the Federal Reserve System, is charged under United States law with overseeing the nation's open market operations. It is the Federal Reserve Committee that makes key decisions about interest rates and the growth jam of the United States money supply. It is the principal organ of United States national monetary policy.
　a. Fed Funds Probability
　c. Primary Dealer Credit Facility
　b. Federal Reserve Transparency Act
　d. Federal Open Market Committee

49. In the United States, _____ are overnight borrowings by banks to maintain their bank reserves at the Federal Reserve. Banks keep reserves at Federal Reserve Banks to meet their reserve requirements and to clear financial transactions. Transactions in the _____ market enable depository institutions with reserve balances in excess of reserve requirements to lend reserves to institutions with reserve deficiencies.
　a. Federal funds
　c. Term auction facility
　b. Federal Reserve Transparency Act
　d. Federal funds rate

Chapter 14. Interest Rates and Monetary Policy

50. In the United States, the _____ is the interest rate at which private depository institutions (mostly banks) lend balances (federal funds) at the Federal Reserve to other depository institutions, usually overnight. It is the interest rate banks charge each other for loans. Changing the target rate is one way the Chairman of the Federal Reserve can influence the supply of money in the U.S. economy..
   a. Federal funds rate
   b. Monetary Policy Report to the Congress
   c. Federal banking
   d. Term auction facility

51. _____ and Keynesian Theory) is a macroeconomic theory based on the ideas of 20th-century British economist John Maynard Keynes. _____ argues that private sector decisions sometimes lead to inefficient macroeconomic outcomes and therefore advocates active policy responses by the public sector, including monetary policy actions by the central bank and fiscal policy actions by the government to stabilize output over the business cycle.

The theories forming the basis of _____ were first presented in The General Theory of Employment, Interest and Money, published in 1936.

   a. Deflation
   b. Market failure
   c. Rational choice theory
   d. Keynesian economics

52. In banking, _____ are bank reserves in excess of the reserve requirement set by a central bank (in the United States, the Federal Reserve System, called the Fed; in Canada, the Bank of Canada.) They are reserves of cash more than the required amounts. Holding _____ is generally considered costly and uneconomical as no interest is earned on the excess amount.
   a. Origination fee
   b. Excess reserves
   c. Annual percentage rate
   d. Universal bank

53. In economics, _____ is the total demand for final goods and services in the economy (Y) at a given time and price level. It is the amount of goods and services in the economy that will be purchased at all possible price levels. This is the demand for the gross domestic product of a country when inventory levels are static.
   a. Aggregation problem
   b. Aggregate expenditure
   c. Aggregate demand
   d. Aggregate supply

54. In economics, an _____ is a monetary policy that increases the money supply.
   a. Easy money policy
   b. Elements of economic profit
   c. Income effect
   d. International free trade agreement

55. The _____ or the output gap is the difference between potential GDP and actual GDP or actual output. The calculation for the output gap is Y-Y* where Y* is potential output and Y is actual output. If this calculation yields a positive number it is called an expansionary gap and indicates an economy in expansion; if the calculation yields a negative number it is called a recessionary gap and indicates an economy in recession.
   a. 130-30 fund
   b. 1921 recession
   c. 100-year flood
   d. GDP gap

56. In economics, _____ is a rise in the general level of prices of goods and services in an economy over a period of time. When the general price level rises, each unit of currency buys fewer goods and services; consequently, _____ is also a decline in the real value of money--a loss of purchasing power in the medium of exchange which is also the monetary unit of account in the economy. A chief measure of general price-level _____ is the general _____ rate, which is the percentage change in a general price index (normally the Consumer Price Index) over time.
   a. Energy economics
   b. Economic
   c. Opportunity cost
   d. Inflation

57. In economics, a _____ is a general slowdown in economic activity over a sustained period of time, or a business cycle contraction. During _____s, many macroeconomic indicators vary in a similar way. Production as measured by Gross Domestic Product (GDP), employment, investment spending, capacity utilization, household incomes and business profits all fall during _____s.
   a. Monetary economics
   b. Treasury View
   c. Leading indicators
   d. Recession

58. In economics, _____ is a measure of national income. Basically, it is an approach to measure GDP. It is defined as the value of planned goods and services produced in an economy.
   a. Aggregate supply
   b. Aggregate demand
   c. Aggregation problem
   d. Aggregate expenditure

59. _____ is a type of inflation caused by substantial increases in the cost of important goods or services where no suitable alternative is available. A situation that has been often cited of this was the oil crisis of the 1970s, which some economists see as a major cause of the inflation experienced in the Western world in that decade. It is argued that this inflation resulted from increases in the cost of petroleum imposed by the member states of OPEC.
   a. Mundell-Tobin effect
   b. Headline inflation
   c. Chronic inflation
   d. Cost-push inflation

60. _____ is monetary policy that seeks to increase the size of the money supply. In most nations, monetary policy is controlled by either a central bank or a finance ministry

Neoclassical and Keynesian economics significantly differ on the effects and effectiveness of monetary policy on influencing the real economy; there is no clear consensus on how monetary policy affects real economic variables (aggregate output or income, employment.) Both economic schools accept that monetary policy affects monetary variables (price levels, interest rates.)

   a. ACEA agreement
   b. ACCRA Cost of Living Index
   c. Expansionary Monetary policy
   d. AD-IA Model

61. _____ is a term applied in many countries to a reference interest rate used by banks. The term originally indicated the rate of interest at which banks lent to favored customers, i.e., those with high credibility, though this is no longer always the case. Some variable interest rates may be expressed as a percentage above or below _____.
   a. Capital requirement
   b. Repo Rate
   c. Transactional account
   d. Prime rate

Chapter 14. Interest Rates and Monetary Policy

62. The _____ was an evolution of developed countries from an industrial/manufacturing-based wealth producing economy into a service sector asset based economy, brought about by globalization and currency manipulation by governments and their central banks. Some analysts claimed that this change in the economic structure of the United States had created a state of permanent steady growth, low unemployment, and immunity to boom and bust macroeconomic cycles. They believed that the change rendered obsolete many business practices.

   a. 100-year flood
   b. 130-30 fund
   c. New Economy
   d. 1921 recession

63. An _____, in economics, is the amount by which the real Gross domestic product exceeds potential GDP. The real GDP is also known as GDP 'adjusted for inflation', 'constant prices' GDP or 'constant dollar' GDP, because it measures the aggregate output in a country's income accounts in a given year, expressed in base-year prices. On the other hand, the potential GDP is the quantity of real GDP when a country's economy is at full-employment.

   a. ACCRA Cost of Living Index
   b. AD-IA Model
   c. ACEA agreement
   d. Inflationary gap

64. _____ describes a deliberate attempt to interfere with the free and fair operation of the market and create artificial, false or misleading appearances with respect to the price of a security, commodity or currency. _____ is prohibited under Section 9(a)(2) of the Securities Exchange Act of 1934, and in Australia under Section s 1041A of the Corporations Act 2001. The Act defines _____ as transactions which create an artificial price or maintain an artificial price for a tradable security.

   a. Legal monopoly
   b. Net domestic product
   c. Managerial economics
   d. Market manipulation

65. In calculus, a function f defined on a subset of the real numbers with real values is called _____, if for all x and y such that x >≤ y one has f(x) >≤ f(y), so f preserves the order. In layman's terms, the sign of the slope is always positive (the curve tending upwards) or zero (i.e., non-decreasing, or asymptotic, or depicted as a horizontal, flat line) Likewise, a function is called monotonically decreasing (non-increasing) if, whenever x >≤ y, then f(x) >≥ f(y), so it reverses the order.

   a. 130-30 fund
   b. 1921 recession
   c. Monotonic
   d. 100-year flood

66. In statistics, _____ has two related meanings:

   - the arithmetic _____
   - the expected value of a random variable, which is also called the population _____.

   It is sometimes stated that the '_____' _____s average. This is incorrect if '_____' is taken in the specific sense of 'arithmetic _____' as there are different types of averages: the _____, median, and mode. Other simple statistical analyses use measures of spread, such as range, interquartile range, or standard deviation. For a real-valued random variable X, the _____ is the expectation of X. Note that not every probability distribution has a defined _____ (or variance); see the Cauchy distribution for an example.

   a. Mean
   b. 1921 recession
   c. 100-year flood
   d. 130-30 fund

67. _____ is a common concept in economics, and gives rise to derived concepts such as consumer debt. Generally _____ is defined by opposition to production. But the precise definition can vary because different schools of economists define production quite differently.
   a. Cash or share options
   b. Federal Reserve Bank Notes
   c. Foreclosure data providers
   d. Consumption

68. _____ arises when aggregate demand in an economy outpaces aggregate supply. It involves inflation rising as real gross domestic product rises and unemployment falls, as the economy moves along the Phillips curve. This is commonly described as 'too much money chasing too few goods'.
   a. Kinked demand curve
   b. Marshallian demand function
   c. Demand-pull inflation
   d. Kinked demand

69. _____ is an economic policy in which a central bank estimates and makes public a projected, or 'target,' inflation rate and then attempts to steer actual inflation towards the target through the use of interest rate changes and other monetary tools.

Because interest rates and the inflation rate tend to be inversely related, the likely moves of the central bank to raise or lower interest rates become more transparent under the policy of _____. Examples:

- if inflation appears to be above the target, the bank is likely to raise interest rates. This usually (but not always) has the effect over time of cooling the economy and bringing down inflation.

- if inflation appears to be below the target, the bank is likely to lower interest rates. This usually (again, not always) has the effect over time of accelerating the economy and raising inflation.

   a. Inflation swap
   b. Incomes policies
   c. Inflation targeting
   d. Employment Cost Index

70. Competition law, known in the United States as _____ law, has three main elements:

- prohibiting agreements or practices that restrict free trading and competition between business entities. This includes in particular the repression of cartels.
- banning abusive behaviour by a firm dominating a market, or anti-competitive practices that tend to lead to such a dominant position. Practices controlled in this way may include predatory pricing, tying, price gouging, refusal to deal, and many others.
- supervising the mergers and acquisitions of large corporations, including some joint ventures. Transactions that are considered to threaten the competitive process can be prohibited altogether, or approved subject to 'remedies' such as an obligation to divest part of the merged business or to offer licences or access to facilities to enable other businesses to continue competing.

The substance and practice of competition law varies from jurisdiction to jurisdiction. Protecting the interests of consumers (consumer welfare) and ensuring that entrepreneurs have an opportunity to compete in the market economy are often treated as important objectives. Competition law is closely connected with law on deregulation of access to markets, state aids and subsidies, the privatisation of state owned assets and the establishment of independent sector regulators. In recent decades, competition law has been viewed as a way to provide better public services.

a. Anti-Inflation Act
b. United Kingdom competition law
c. Intellectual property law
d. Antitrust

71. _____s is the social science that studies the production, distribution, and consumption of goods and services. The term _____s comes from the Ancient Greek oá¼°κονομῖα from oá¼¶κος (oikos, 'house') + vĺŒµος (nomos, 'custom' or 'law'), hence 'rules of the house(hold)'. Current _____ models developed out of the broader field of political economy in the late 19th century, owing to a desire to use an empirical approach more akin to the physical sciences.
    a. Energy economics
    b. Economic
    c. Opportunity cost
    d. Inflation

72. _____ is the increase in the amount of the goods and services produced by an economy over time. It is conventionally measured as the percent rate of increase in real gross domestic product, or real GDP. Growth is usually calculated in real terms, i.e. inflation-adjusted terms, in order to net out the effect of inflation on the price of the goods and services produced.
    a. ACEA agreement
    b. AD-IA Model
    c. ACCRA Cost of Living Index
    d. Economic growth

73. The term _____ indicates economic growth so low that it creates net unemployment. The term was created by Dr. Solomon Fabricant (New York University, National Bureau of Economic Research) and is recognized and cited more recently by business economists. Note that the term also has slightly different secondary meanings including a more general one that growth is below potential.
    a. Post-World War I recession
    b. Recession of 1953
    c. Growth recession
    d. Recession index

74. A _____ is a package or set of measures introduced to stabilise a financial system or economy. The term can refer to policies in two distinct sets of circumstances: business cycle stabilization and crisis stabilization.

Stabilization can refer to correcting the normal behavior of the business cycle.

   a. Volunteers for Economic Growth Alliance
   b. New International Economic Order
   c. Stabilization policy
   d. Capacity Development

Chapter 15. Extending the Analysis of Aggregate Supply

1. The _____ or Aggregate Demand-Aggregate Supply model is a macroeconomic model that explains price level and output through the relationship of aggregate demand and aggregate supply. It was first put forth by John Maynard Keynes in his work The General Theory of Employment, Interest, and Money. It is the foundation for the modern field of macroeconomics, and is accepted by a broad array of economists, from Libertarian, Monetarist supporters of laissez-faire, such as Milton Friedman to Socialist, Post-Keynesian supporters of economic interventionism, such as Joan Robinson.
    a. Adaptive expectations
    b. IS/LM model
    c. AD-AS
    d. Economic interdependence

2. The _____ was a worldwide economic downturn starting in most places in 1929 and ending at different times in the 1930s or early 1940s for different countries. It was the largest and most important economic depression in the 20th century, and is used in the 21st century as an example of how far the world's economy can fall. The _____ originated in the United States; historians most often use as a starting date the stock market crash on October 29, 1929, known as Black Tuesday.
    a. Jarrow March
    b. Wall Street Crash of 1929
    c. Great Depression
    d. British Empire Economic Conference

3. _____, 1st Baron Keynes was a renowned economist from Britain whose many ideas on economic and political theories as well as on many governments' monetary policies influenced America. He advocated a government that played an active role in the lives of people regarding business, economy, etc. In this role, the government would use fiscal measures to reduce the consequences of recessions, economic depressions and booms.
    a. Adolf Hitler
    b. Adolph Fischer
    c. Adam Smith
    d. John Maynard Keynes

4. _____ and Keynesian Theory) is a macroeconomic theory based on the ideas of 20th-century British economist John Maynard Keynes. _____ argues that private sector decisions sometimes lead to inefficient macroeconomic outcomes and therefore advocates active policy responses by the public sector, including monetary policy actions by the central bank and fiscal policy actions by the government to stabilize output over the business cycle.

    The theories forming the basis of _____ were first presented in The General Theory of Employment, Interest and Money, published in 1936.

    a. Rational choice theory
    b. Keynesian economics
    c. Market failure
    d. Deflation

5. In economics, the concept of the _____ refers to the decision-making time frame of a firm in which at least one factor of production is fixed. Costs which are fixed in the _____ have no impact on a firms decisions. For example a firm can raise output by increasing the amount of labour through overtime.
    a. Productivity model
    b. Hicks-neutral technical change
    c. Product Pipeline
    d. Short-run

6. In economics, _____ is a sustained decrease in the general price level of goods and services. _____ occurs when the annual inflation rate falls below zero percent, resulting in an increase in the real value of money -- a negative inflation rate. This should not be confused with disinflation, a slow-down in the inflation rate (i.e. when the inflation decreases, but still remains positive.)
    a. Tobit model
    b. Deflation
    c. Price revolution
    d. Literacy rate

Chapter 15. Extending the Analysis of Aggregate Supply

7. In economics, _____ is a rise in the general level of prices of goods and services in an economy over a period of time. When the general price level rises, each unit of currency buys fewer goods and services; consequently, _____ is also a decline in the real value of money--a loss of purchasing power in the medium of exchange which is also the monetary unit of account in the economy. A chief measure of general price-level _____ is the general _____ rate, which is the percentage change in a general price index (normally the Consumer Price Index) over time.
   a. Opportunity cost
   b. Energy economics
   c. Economic
   d. Inflation

8. In economics, _____ refers to the highest level of real Gross Domestic Product output that can be sustained over the long term. The existence of a limit is due to natural and institutional constraints. If actual GDP rises and stays above _____, then (in the absence of wage and price controls) inflation tends to increase as demand exceeds supply.
   a. Monetary policy reaction function
   b. Monetary conditions index
   c. Fundamental psychological law
   d. Potential output

9. _____ in economics and business is the result of an exchange and from that trade we assign a numerical monetary value to a good, service or asset. If Alice trades Bob 4 apples for an orange, the _____ of an orange is 4 apples. Inversely, the _____ of an apple is 1/4 oranges.
   a. Price book
   b. Price war
   c. Premium pricing
   d. Price

10. A _____ is a hypothetical measure of overall prices for some set of goods and services, in a given region during a given interval, normalized relative to some base set. Typically, a _____ is approximated with a price index.

    The classical dichotomy is the assumption that there is a relatively clean distinction between overall increases or decreases in prices and underlying, e;reale; economic variables.

    a. Price level
    b. Price elasticity of supply
    c. Discretionary spending
    d. Discouraged worker

11. In economics, _____ is the total supply of goods and services produced by a national economy during a specific time period. It is the total amount of goods and services in the economy available at all possible price levels.
    a. Aggregate expenditure
    b. Aggregation problem
    c. Aggregate demand
    d. Aggregate supply

12. In economic models, the _____ time frame assumes no fixed factors of production. Firms can enter or leave the marketplace, and the cost (and availability) of land, labor, raw materials, and capital goods can be assumed to vary. In contrast, in the short-run time frame, certain factors are assumed to be fixed, because there is not sufficient time for them to change.
    a. Diseconomies of scale
    b. Price/performance ratio
    c. Productivity world
    d. Long-run

13. _____ is a type of inflation caused by substantial increases in the cost of important goods or services where no suitable alternative is available. A situation that has been often cited of this was the oil crisis of the 1970s, which some economists see as a major cause of the inflation experienced in the Western world in that decade. It is argued that this inflation resulted from increases in the cost of petroleum imposed by the member states of OPEC.

Chapter 15. Extending the Analysis of Aggregate Supply

a. Cost-push inflation
b. Headline inflation
c. Chronic inflation
d. Mundell-Tobin effect

14. The _____ or gross domestic income (GDI), a basic measure of an economy's economic performance, is the market value of all final goods and services produced within the borders of a nation in a year. _____ can be defined in three ways, all of which are conceptually identical. First, it is equal to the total expenditures for all final goods and services produced within the country in a stipulated period of time (usually a 365-day year.)
a. Market structure
b. Monopolistic competition
c. Countercyclical
d. Gross domestic product

15. The _____ or the output gap is the difference between potential GDP and actual GDP or actual output. The calculation for the output gap is Y-Y* where Y* is potential output and Y is actual output. If this calculation yields a positive number it is called an expansionary gap and indicates an economy in expansion; if the calculation yields a negative number it is called a recessionary gap and indicates an economy in recession.
a. 100-year flood
b. 130-30 fund
c. 1921 recession
d. GDP gap

16. _____ arises when aggregate demand in an economy outpaces aggregate supply. It involves inflation rising as real gross domestic product rises and unemployment falls, as the economy moves along the Phillips curve. This is commonly described as 'too much money chasing too few goods'.
a. Marshallian demand function
b. Kinked demand
c. Kinked demand curve
d. Demand-pull inflation

17. _____s is the social science that studies the production, distribution, and consumption of goods and services. The term _____s comes from the Ancient Greek οἰκονομία from οἶκος (oikos, 'house') + νόμος (nomos, 'custom' or 'law'), hence 'rules of the house(hold)'. Current _____ models developed out of the broader field of political economy in the late 19th century, owing to a desire to use an empirical approach more akin to the physical sciences.
a. Economic
b. Energy economics
c. Opportunity cost
d. Inflation

18. In economics, a _____ is a general slowdown in economic activity over a sustained period of time, or a business cycle contraction. During _____s, many macroeconomic indicators vary in a similar way. Production as measured by Gross Domestic Product (GDP), employment, investment spending, capacity utilization, household incomes and business profits all fall during _____s.
a. Treasury View
b. Monetary economics
c. Leading indicators
d. Recession

19. In microeconomics, _____ is quite simply the conversion of inputs into outputs. It is an economic process that uses resources to create a good or service that is suitable for exchange. This can include manufacturing, storing, shipping, and packaging.
a. Red Guards
b. Solved
c. Production
d. MET

20. In economics, the _____ is a historical inverse relation between the rate of unemployment and the rate of inflation in an economy. Stated simply, the lower the unemployment in an economy, the higher the rate of increase in nominal wages in the economy. Rate of Change of Wages against Unemployment, United Kingdom 1913-1948 from Phillips (1958)

Chapter 15. Extending the Analysis of Aggregate Supply

William Phillips, a New Zealand born economist, wrote a paper in 1958 titled The Relationship between Unemployment and the Rate of Change of Money Wages in the United Kingdom 1861-1957, which was published in the quarterly journal Economica.

a. Demand curve
b. Cost curve
c. Lorenz curve
d. Phillips curve

21. The term _____s refers to wages that have been adjusted for inflation. This term is used in contrast to nominal wages or unadjusted wages.

The use of adjusted figures is in undertaking some form of economic analysis.

a. Living wage
b. Profit sharing
c. Real wage
d. Federal Wage System

22. A _____ is an event that suddenly changes the price of a commodity or service. It may be caused by a sudden increase or decrease in the supply of a particular good. This sudden change affects the equilibrium price.

a. Friedman rule
b. Demand shock
c. SIMIC
d. Supply shock

23. A _____ is a situation that involves losing one quality or aspect of something in return for gaining another quality or aspect. It implies a decision to be made with full comprehension of both the upside and downside of a particular choice.

In economics the term is expressed as opportunity cost, referring the most preferred alternative given up.

a. Friedman-Savage utility function
b. Nonmarket
c. Whitemail
d. Trade-off

24. In economics, the _____ is a measure of inflation, the rate of increase of a price index (for example, a consumer price index.)It is the percentage rate of change in price level over time. The rate of decrease in the purchasing power of money is approximately equal.

It's used to calculate the real interest rate, as well as real increases in wages, and official measurements of this rate act as input variables to COLA adjustments and Inflation derivatives prices.

a. Inflation rate
b. Edgeworth paradox
c. Equity value
d. Interest rate option

Chapter 15. Extending the Analysis of Aggregate Supply

25. Competition law, known in the United States as _____ law, has three main elements:

- prohibiting agreements or practices that restrict free trading and competition between business entities. This includes in particular the repression of cartels.
- banning abusive behaviour by a firm dominating a market, or anti-competitive practices that tend to lead to such a dominant position. Practices controlled in this way may include predatory pricing, tying, price gouging, refusal to deal, and many others.
- supervising the mergers and acquisitions of large corporations, including some joint ventures. Transactions that are considered to threaten the competitive process can be prohibited altogether, or approved subject to 'remedies' such as an obligation to divest part of the merged business or to offer licences or access to facilities to enable other businesses to continue competing.

The substance and practice of competition law varies from jurisdiction to jurisdiction. Protecting the interests of consumers (consumer welfare) and ensuring that entrepreneurs have an opportunity to compete in the market economy are often treated as important objectives. Competition law is closely connected with law on deregulation of access to markets, state aids and subsidies, the privatisation of state owned assets and the establishment of independent sector regulators. In recent decades, competition law has been viewed as a way to provide better public services.

a. United Kingdom competition law
c. Antitrust
b. Intellectual property law
d. Anti-Inflation Act

26. _____ is a broad label that refers to any individuals or households that use goods and services generated within the economy. The concept of a _____ is used in different contexts, so that the usage and significance of the term may vary.

Typically when business people and economists talk of _____s they are talking about person as _____, an aggregated commodity item with little individuality other than that expressed in the buy/not-buy decision.

a. 130-30 fund
c. Consumer
b. 1921 recession
d. 100-year flood

27. A _____ is a measure of the average price of consumer goods and services purchased by households. A _____ measures a price change for a constant market basket of goods and services from one period to the next within the same area (city, region, or nation.) It is a price index determined by measuring the price of a standard group of goods meant to represent the typical market basket of a typical urban consumer.

a. Lipstick index
c. Cost-of-living index
b. CPI
d. Consumer price index

28. The _____ is 'the basic residential unit in which economic production, consumption, inheritance, child rearing, and shelter are organized and carried out'; [the _____] 'may or may not be synonymous with family'.

The _____ is the basic unit of analysis in many social, microeconomic and government models. The term refers to all individuals who live in the same dwelling.

Chapter 15. Extending the Analysis of Aggregate Supply

a. Household
b. 100-year flood
c. Family economics
d. 130-30 fund

29. A _____ is a normalized average (typically a weighted average) of prices for a given class of goods or services in a given region, during a given interval of time. It is a statistic designed to help to compare how these prices, taken as a whole, differ between time periods or geographical locations.

Price indices have several potential uses.

a. Two-part tariff
b. Transactional Net Margin Method
c. Product sabotage
d. Price index

30. Unemployment occurs when a person is available to work and seeking work but currently without work. The prevalence of unemployment is usually measured using the _____, which is defined as the percentage of those in the labor force who are unemployed. The _____ is also used in economic studies and economic indexes such as the United States' Conference Board's Index of Leading Indicators as a measure of the state of the macroeconomics.

a. Unemployment rate
b. ACCRA Cost of Living Index
c. AD-IA Model
d. ACEA agreement

31. _____ is the a method of technical and economic research of the systems for purpose to optimize a parity between system's consumer functions or properties and expenses to achieve those functions or properties.

This methodology for continuous perfection of production, industrial technologies, organizational structures was developed by Juryj Sobolev in 1948 at the 'Perm telephone factory'

- 1948 Juryj Sobolev - the first success in application of a method analysis at the 'Perm telephone factory'.
- 1949 - the first application for the invention as result of use of the new method.

Today in economically developed countries practically each enterprise or the company use methodology of the kind of functional-cost analysis as a practice of the quality management, most full satisfying to principles of standards of series ISO 9000.

- Interest of consumer not in products itself, but the advantage which it will receive from its usage.
- The consumer aspires to reduce his expenses
- Functions needed by consumer can be executed in the various ways, and, hence, with various efficiency and expenses. Among possible alternatives of realization of functions exist such in which the parity of quality and the price is the optimal for the consumer.

The goal of _____ is achievement of the highest consumer satisfaction of production at simultaneous decrease in all kinds of industrial expenses Classical _____ has three English synonyms - Value Engineering, Value Management, Value Analysis.

a. Staple financing
b. Willingness to pay
c. Monopoly wage
d. Function cost analysis

32. _____ is the removal or simplification of government rules and regulations that constrain the operation of market forces. _____ does not mean elimination of laws against fraud, but eliminating or reducing government control of how business is done, thereby moving toward a more free market.

The stated rationale for '_____' is often that fewer and simpler regulations will lead to a raised level of competitiveness, therefore higher productivity, more efficiency and lower prices overall.

   a. Secular basis
   b. Macroeconomic policy instruments
   c. Fundamental psychological law
   d. Deregulation

33. _____ is an economic situation in which inflation and economic stagnation occur simultaneously and remain unchecked for a period of time. The portmanteau _____ is generally attributed to British politician Iain Macleod, who coined the term in a speech to Parliament in 1965. The concept is notable partly because, in postwar macroeconomic theory, inflation and recession were regarded as mutually exclusive, and also because _____ has generally proven to be difficult and costly to eradicate once it gets started.

   a. Price/wage spiral
   b. Chronic inflation
   c. Real interest rate
   d. Stagflation

34. _____ is the increase in the amount of the goods and services produced by an economy over time. It is conventionally measured as the percent rate of increase in real gross domestic product, or real GDP. Growth is usually calculated in real terms, i.e. inflation-adjusted terms, in order to net out the effect of inflation on the price of the goods and services produced.

   a. ACCRA Cost of Living Index
   b. ACEA agreement
   c. AD-IA Model
   d. Economic growth

35. In economics, an _____ is any good or commodity, transported from one country to another country in a legitimate fashion, typically for use in trade. _____ goods or services are provided to foreign consumers by domestic producers. _____ is an important part of international trade.

   a. Export
   b. AD-IA Model
   c. ACCRA Cost of Living Index
   d. ACEA agreement

36. The _____ is an economic indicator, created by economist Arthur Okun, and found by adding the unemployment rate to the inflation rate. It is assumed that both a higher rate of unemployment and a worsening of inflation create economic and social costs for a country. It is often incorrectly attributed to Chicago economist Robert Barro in the 1970s, due to the Barro _____ that additionally includes GDP and the bank rate.

   a. 100-year flood
   b. 1921 recession
   c. Misery index
   d. 130-30 fund

37. _____ is a decrease in the rate of inflation. This phase of the business cycle, in which retailers can no longer pass on higher prices to their customers, often occurs during a recession. In contrast, deflation occurs when prices are actually dropping.

   a. Disinflation
   b. Stealth inflation
   c. Reflation
   d. Mundell-Tobin effect

Chapter 15. Extending the Analysis of Aggregate Supply

38. _____ is a school of macroeconomic thought that argues that economic growth can be most effectively created using incentives for people to produce (supply) goods and services, such as adjusting income tax and capital gains tax rates, and by allowing greater flexibility by reducing regulation. Consumers will then benefit from a greater supply of goods and services at lower prices.

The term _____ was coined by journalist Jude Wanniski in 1975, and popularized the ideas of economists Robert Mundell and Arthur Laffer.

   a. Clap note
   b. Commodity trading advisors
   c. Fiscal stimulus plans
   d. Supply-side economics

39. In economics and sociology, an _____ is any factor (financial or non-financial) that enables or motivates a particular course of action, or counts as a reason for preferring one choice to the alternatives. It is an expectation that encourages people to behave in a certain way. Since human beings are purposeful creatures, the study of _____ structures is central to the study of all economic activity (both in terms of individual decision-making and in terms of co-operation and competition within a larger institutional structure.)

   a. Epstein-Zin preferences
   b. Isocost
   c. Economic reform
   d. Incentive

40. In economics, the _____ is used to illustrate the idea that increases in the rate of taxation do not necessarily increase tax revenue. (For instance, whereas a 0% income tax rate will generate no revenue, neither will a 100% rate, as citizens will have no incentive to make money.) Increasing taxes beyond the peak of the curve point will decrease tax revenue.

   a. 130-30 fund
   b. Laffer curve
   c. 1921 recession
   d. 100-year flood

41. _____ or economic opportunity loss is the value of the next best alternative foregone as the result of making a decision. _____ analysis is an important part of a company's decision-making processes but is not treated as an actual cost in any financial statement. The next best thing that a person can engage in is referred to as the _____ of doing the best thing and ignoring the next best thing to be done.

   a. Economic ideology
   b. Industrial organization
   c. Opportunity cost
   d. Economic

42. To _____ is to impose a financial charge or other levy upon a taxpayer by a state or the functional equivalent of a state.

_____es are also imposed by many subnational entities. _____es consist of direct _____ or indirect _____, and may be paid in money or as its labour equivalent (often but not always unpaid.)

   a. 1921 recession
   b. 130-30 fund
   c. Tax
   d. 100-year flood

43. To tax is to impose a financial charge or other levy upon a taxpayer by a state or the functional equivalent of a state.

_____ are also imposed by many subnational entities. _____ consist of direct tax or indirect tax, and may be paid in money or as its labour equivalent (often but not always unpaid.)

a. 130-30 fund
c. 100-year flood
b. Taxes
d. 1921 recession

44. The Demand side is a term used in economics to refer to a number of things:

- The demand element of a supply and demand partial equilibrium diagram, in microeconomics
- The aggregate demand in an economy, in macroeconomics
- Economic policy actions which are designed to affect aggregate demand.
- _____ learning referring to the incentive to learn how to use and modify free software as opposed to buying conventional software.

The term is also used broadly to distinguish supply-side economics from other schools, for instance Keynesian economics.

a. Delayed differentiation
c. Demand-side
b. Reverse auction
d. CPFR

Chapter 16. Economic Growth

1. Economics:

    - _____, the desire to own something and the ability to pay for it
    - _____ curve, a graphic representation of a _____ schedule
    - _____ deposit, the money in checking accounts
    - _____ pull theory, the theory that inflation occurs when _____ for goods and services exceeds existing supplies
    - _____ schedule, a table that lists the quantity of a good a person will buy it each different price
    - _____ side economics, the school of economics at believes government spending and tax cuts open economy by raising _____

    a. Variability
    c. McKesson ' Robbins scandal
    b. Production
    d. Demand

2. _____s is the social science that studies the production, distribution, and consumption of goods and services. The term _____s comes from the Ancient Greek oá¼°κονομΓ α from oá¼¶κος (oikos, 'house') + vΐŒμος (nomos, 'custom' or 'law'), hence 'rules of the house(hold)'. Current _____ models developed out of the broader field of political economy in the late 19th century, owing to a desire to use an empirical approach more akin to the physical sciences.
    a. Inflation
    b. Energy economics
    c. Economic
    d. Opportunity cost

3. _____ is the increase in the amount of the goods and services produced by an economy over time. It is conventionally measured as the percent rate of increase in real gross domestic product, or real GDP. Growth is usually calculated in real terms, i.e. inflation-adjusted terms, in order to net out the effect of inflation on the price of the goods and services produced.
    a. ACEA agreement
    b. AD-IA Model
    c. ACCRA Cost of Living Index
    d. Economic growth

4. The _____ or gross domestic income (GDI), a basic measure of an economy's economic performance, is the market value of all final goods and services produced within the borders of a nation in a year. _____ can be defined in three ways, all of which are conceptually identical. First, it is equal to the total expenditures for all final goods and services produced within the country in a stipulated period of time (usually a 365-day year.)
    a. Monopolistic competition
    b. Countercyclical
    c. Market structure
    d. Gross domestic product

5. The _____ or the output gap is the difference between potential GDP and actual GDP or actual output. The calculation for the output gap is Y-Y* where Y* is potential output and Y is actual output. If this calculation yields a positive number it is called an expansionary gap and indicates an economy in expansion; if the calculation yields a negative number it is called a recessionary gap and indicates an economy in recession.
    a. 1921 recession
    b. 130-30 fund
    c. GDP gap
    d. 100-year flood

6. An _____, in economics, is the amount by which the real Gross domestic product exceeds potential GDP. The real GDP is also known as GDP 'adjusted for inflation', 'constant prices' GDP or 'constant dollar' GDP, because it measures the aggregate output in a country's income accounts in a given year, expressed in base-year prices. On the other hand, the potential GDP is the quantity of real GDP when a country's economy is at full-employment.

a. ACEA agreement
c. AD-IA Model
b. ACCRA Cost of Living Index
d. Inflationary gap

7. In economics, _____ is the total demand for final goods and services in the economy (Y) at a given time and price level. It is the amount of goods and services in the economy that will be purchased at all possible price levels. This is the demand for the gross domestic product of a country when inventory levels are static.
   a. Aggregate expenditure
   b. Aggregation problem
   c. Aggregate supply
   d. Aggregate demand

8. _____ in economics and business is the result of an exchange and from that trade we assign a numerical monetary value to a good, service or asset. If Alice trades Bob 4 apples for an orange, the _____ of an orange is 4 apples. Inversely, the _____ of an apple is 1/4 oranges.
   a. Price
   b. Price book
   c. Premium pricing
   d. Price war

9. A _____ is a normalized average (typically a weighted average) of prices for a given class of goods or services in a given region, during a given interval of time. It is a statistic designed to help to compare how these prices, taken as a whole, differ between time periods or geographical locations.

Price indices have several potential uses.

   a. Price index
   b. Two-part tariff
   c. Product sabotage
   d. Transactional Net Margin Method

10. In microeconomics, _____ is quite simply the conversion of inputs into outputs. It is an economic process that uses resources to create a good or service that is suitable for exchange. This can include manufacturing, storing, shipping, and packaging.
    a. Solved
    b. Red Guards
    c. MET
    d. Production

11. The _____ or Aggregate Demand-Aggregate Supply model is a macroeconomic model that explains price level and output through the relationship of aggregate demand and aggregate supply. It was first put forth by John Maynard Keynes in his work The General Theory of Employment, Interest, and Money. It is the foundation for the modern field of macroeconomics, and is accepted by a broad array of economists, from Libertarian, Monetarist supporters of laissez-faire, such as Milton Friedman to Socialist, Post-Keynesian supporters of economic interventionism, such as Joan Robinson.
    a. AD-AS
    b. Economic interdependence
    c. IS/LM model
    d. Adaptive expectations

12. In economics, _____ is the total supply of goods and services produced by a national economy during a specific time period. It is the total amount of goods and services in the economy available at all possible price levels.
    a. Aggregate demand
    b. Aggregate expenditure
    c. Aggregation problem
    d. Aggregate supply

13. _____ is the period of time that an individual spends at paid occupational labor. Unpaid labors such as housework are not considered part of the working week. Many countries regulate the work week by law, such as stipulating minimum daily rest periods, annual holidays and a maximum number of working hours per week.

Chapter 16. Economic Growth

a. 100-year flood
c. Working time
b. 130-30 fund
d. 1921 recession

14. _____ and Keynesian Theory) is a macroeconomic theory based on the ideas of 20th-century British economist John Maynard Keynes. _____ argues that private sector decisions sometimes lead to inefficient macroeconomic outcomes and therefore advocates active policy responses by the public sector, including monetary policy actions by the central bank and fiscal policy actions by the government to stabilize output over the business cycle.

The theories forming the basis of _____ were first presented in The General Theory of Employment, Interest and Money, published in 1936.

a. Market failure
c. Rational choice theory
b. Keynesian economics
d. Deflation

15. In economics, the people in the _____ are the suppliers of labor. The _____ is all the nonmilitary people who are employed or unemployed. In 2005, the worldwide _____ was over 3 billion people.

a. Labor force
c. Grenelle agreements
b. Distributed workforce
d. Departmentalization

16. A _____ is any systematic process enabling many market players to bid and ask: helping bidders and sellers interact and make deals. It is not just the price mechanism but the entire system of regulation, qualification, credentials, reputations and clearing that surrounds that mechanism and makes it operate in a social context.

Because a _____ relies on the assumption that players are constantly involved and unequally enabled, a _____ is distinguished specifically from a voting system where candidates seek the support of voters on a less regular basis.

a. Market system
c. Contestable market
b. Price mechanism
d. Competitive equilibrium

17. _____ in economics refers to metrics and measures of output from production processes, per unit of input. Labor _____, for example, is typically measured as a ratio of output per labor-hour, an input. _____ may be conceived of as a metrics of the technical or engineering efficiency of production.

a. Fordism
c. Production-possibility frontier
b. Piece work
d. Productivity

18. In algebra, a _____ is a function depending on n that associates a scalar, det(A), to an n×n square matrix A. The fundamental geometric meaning of a _____ is a scale factor for measure when A is regarded as a linear transformation. _____s are important both in calculus, where they enter the substitution rule for several variables, and in multilinear algebra.

For a fixed nonnegative integer n, there is a unique _____ function for the n×n matrices over any commutative ring R. In particular, this function exists when R is the field of real or complex numbers.

Chapter 16. Economic Growth

a. 1921 recession
b. 130-30 fund
c. 100-year flood
d. Determinant

19. The _____ is 'the basic residential unit in which economic production, consumption, inheritance, child rearing, and shelter are organized and carried out'; [the _____] 'may or may not be synonomous with family'.

The _____ is the basic unit of analysis in many social, microeconomic and government models. The term refers to all individuals who live in the same dwelling.

a. 130-30 fund
b. Family economics
c. Household
d. 100-year flood

20. _____ occurs when the economy is operating at its production possibility frontier (PPF.) This takes place when production of one good is achieved at the lowest cost possible, given the production of the other good(s.) Equivalently, it is when the highest possible output of one good is produced, given the production level of the other good(s.)

a. Productive efficiency
b. Free contract
c. Preclusive purchasing
d. Discretionary spending

21. _____ is the a method of technical and economic research of the systems for purpose to optimize a parity between system's consumer functions or properties and expenses to achieve those functions or properties.

This methodology for continuous perfection of production, industrial technologies, organizational structures was developed by Juryj Sobolev in 1948 at the 'Perm telephone factory'

- 1948 Juryj Sobolev - the first success in application of a method analysis at the 'Perm telephone factory'.
- 1949 - the first application for the invention as result of use of the new method.

Today in economically developed countries practically each enterprise or the company use methodology of the kind of functional-cost analysis as a practice of the quality management, most full satisfying to principles of standards of series ISO 9000.

- Interest of consumer not in products itself, but the advantage which it will receive from its usage.
- The consumer aspires to reduce his expenses
- Functions needed by consumer can be executed in the various ways, and, hence, with various efficiency and expenses. Among possible alternatives of realization of functions exist such in which the parity of quality and the price is the optimal for the consumer.

The goal of _____ is achievement of the highest consumer satisfaction of production at simultaneous decrease in all kinds of industrial expenses Classical _____ has three English synonyms - Value Engineering, Value Management, Value Analysis.

a. Staple financing
b. Monopoly wage
c. Willingness to pay
d. Function cost analysis

Chapter 16. Economic Growth

22. _____ is a type of inflation caused by substantial increases in the cost of important goods or services where no suitable alternative is available. A situation that has been often cited of this was the oil crisis of the 1970s, which some economists see as a major cause of the inflation experienced in the Western world in that decade. It is argued that this inflation resulted from increases in the cost of petroleum imposed by the member states of OPEC.
    a. Mundell-Tobin effect
    b. Chronic inflation
    c. Headline inflation
    d. Cost-push inflation

23. In economics, _____ is a rise in the general level of prices of goods and services in an economy over a period of time. When the general price level rises, each unit of currency buys fewer goods and services; consequently, _____ is also a decline in the real value of money--a loss of purchasing power in the medium of exchange which is also the monetary unit of account in the economy. A chief measure of general price-level _____ is the general _____ rate, which is the percentage change in a general price index (normally the Consumer Price Index) over time.
    a. Opportunity cost
    b. Energy economics
    c. Economic
    d. Inflation

24. The _____ is a group of three respected economists who advise the President of the United States on economic policy. It is a part of the Executive Office of the President of the United States, and provides much of the economic policy of the White House. The council prepares the annual Economic Report of the President.
    a. Constrained Pareto optimality
    b. Federal Reserve Bank Notes
    c. Hybrid renewable energy systems
    d. Council of Economic Advisers

25. _____ is a procedure used in economics to measure the contribution of different factors to economic growth and to indirectly compute the rate of technological progress, measured as a residual, in an economy.

    _____ decomposes the growth rate of economy's total output into that which is due to increases in the amount of factors used - usually the increase in the amount of capital and labor - and that which cannot be accounted for by observable changes in factor utilization. The unexplained part of growth in GDP is then taken to represent increases in productivity (getting more output with the same amounts of inputs) or a measure of broadly defined technological progress.

    a. Reaganomics
    b. Growth accounting
    c. Cobb-Douglas
    d. Spillover effect

26. In economics, _____ is a measure of national income. Basically, it is an approach to measure GDP. It is defined as the value of planned goods and services produced in an economy.
    a. Aggregate demand
    b. Aggregate supply
    c. Aggregation problem
    d. Aggregate expenditure

27. _____, in microeconomics, are the cost advantages that a business obtains due to expansion. They are factors that cause a producere;s average cost per unit to fall as scale is increased. _____ is a long run concept and refers to reductions in unit cost as the size of a facility, or scale, increases.
    a. Isoquant
    b. Economic production quantity
    c. Underinvestment employment relationship
    d. Economies of scale

28. _____ is the term denoting either an entrance or changes which are inserted into a system and which activate/modify a process. It is an abstract concept, used in the modeling, system(s) design and system(s) exploitation. It is usually connected with other terms, e.g., _____ field, _____ variable, _____ parameter, _____ value, _____ signal, _____ device and _____ file.

   a. ACCRA Cost of Living Index   b. AD-IA Model
   c. Input   d. ACEA agreement

29. _____ is a term used in national accounts statistics and macroeconomics. It basically refers to the net additions to the (physical) capital stock in an accounting period, or, to the value of the increase of the capital stock; though it may occasionally also refer to the (growth of the) total stock of capital formed.

Thus, in UNSNA, _____ equals fixed capital investment, the increase in the value of inventories held, plus (net) lending to foreign countries, during an accounting period.

   a. Capital flight   b. Capital formation
   c. Capital intensity   d. Consumption of fixed capital

30. A _____ is:

- Rewrite _____, in generative grammar and computer science
- Standardization, a formal and widely-accepted statement, fact, definition, or qualification
- Operation, a determinate _____ for performing a mathematical operation and obtaining a certain result (Mathematics, Logic)
    - Unary operation
    - Binary operation
- _____ of inference, a function from sets of formulae to formulae (Mathematics, Logic)
- _____ of thumb, principle with broad application that is not intended to be strictly accurate or reliable for every situation. Also often simply referred to as a _____
- Moral, an atomic element of a moral code for guiding choices in human behavior
- Heuristic, a quantized '_____' which shows a tendency or probability for successful function
- A regulation, as in sports
- A Production _____, as in computer science
- Procedural law, a _____ set governing the application of laws to cases
    - A law, which may informally be called a '_____'
    - A court ruling, a decision by a court
- In the U.S. Government, a regulation mandated by Congress, but written or expanded upon by the Executive Branch.
- Norm (sociology), an informal but widely accepted _____, concept, truth, definition, or qualification (social norms, legal norms, coding norms)
- Norm (philosophy), a kind of sentence or a reason to act, feel or believe
- 'Rulership' is the concept of governance by a government:
    - Military _____, governance by a military body
    - Monastic _____, a collection of precepts that guides the life of monks or nuns in a religious order where the superior holds the place of Christ
- Slide _____

- '_____,' a song by Ayumi Hamasaki
- '_____,' a song by rapper Nas
- '_____s,' an album by the band The Whitest Boy Alive
- _____s: Pyaar Ka Superhit Formula, a 2003 Bollywood film
- ruler, an instrument for measuring lengths
- _____, a component of an astrolabe, circumferator or similar instrument
- The _____s, a bestselling self-help book
- _____ Project (Run Up-to-date Linux Everywhere), a project that aims to use up-to-date Linux software on old PCs
- _____ engine, a software system that helps managing business _____s
- Ja _____, a hip hop artist
    - R.U.L.E., a 2005 greatest hits album by rapper Ja _____
- '_____s,' a KMFDM song

a. Procter ' Gamble
b. Rule
c. Demand
d. Technocracy

31. _____ is a system of training a new generation of practitioners of a skill. Apprentices (or in early modern usage 'prentices') or protégés build their careers from _____s. Most of their training is done on the job while working for an employer who helps the apprentices learn their trade, in exchange for their continuing labour for an agreed period after they become skilled.

   a. AD-IA Model
   b. ACCRA Cost of Living Index
   c. Apprenticeship
   d. ACEA agreement

32. _____ refers to the stock of skills and knowledge embodied in the ability to perform labor so as to produce economic value. It is the skills and knowledge gained by a worker through education and experience. Many early economic theories refer to it simply as labor, one of three factors of production, and consider it to be a fungible resource -- homogeneous and easily interchangeable. Other conceptions of labor dispense with these assumptions.

   a. General equilibrium
   b. Price theory
   c. Law of increasing costs
   d. Human capital

33. The term _____ refers to economy-wide fluctuations in production or economic activity over several months or years. These fluctuations occur around a long-term growth trend, and typically involve shifts over time between periods of relatively rapid economic growth (expansion or boom), and periods of relative stagnation or decline (contraction or recession.)

These fluctuations are often measured using the growth rate of real gross domestic product.

   a. Consumer theory
   b. Nominal value
   c. Tobit model
   d. Business cycle

34. In economics, a _____ is a person of legal employment age who is not actively seeking employment. This is usually due to the fact that an individual has given up looking or has had no success in finding a job, hence the term 'discouraged.' Their belief may derive from a variety of factors including: a shortage of jobs in their locality or line of work; perceived discrimination for reasons such as age, race, sex and religion; a lack of necessary skills, training or experience; or, a chronic illness or disability. Some _____s, however, are voluntarily unemployed such as stay-at-home parents, pregnant mothers, and will beneficiaries.

   a. Hedonimetry
   b. Relative income hypothesis
   c. Demand side economics
   d. Discouraged worker

35. _____ is a type of private equity investment, most often a minority investment, in relatively mature companies that are looking for capital to expand or restructure operations, enter new markets or finance a significant acquisition without a change of control of the business.

Companies that seek _____, will often do so in order to finance a transformational event in their lifecycle. These companies are likely to be more mature than venture capital funded companies, able to generate revenue and operating profits but unable to generate sufficient cash to fund major expansions, acquisitions or other investments.

   a. Startup company
   b. Seed money
   c. Club deal
   d. Growth Capital

36. _____ is used to assign the available resources in an economic way. It is part of resource management.

Chapter 16. Economic Growth

In strategic planning, is a plan for using available resources, for example human resources, especially in the near term, to achieve goals for the future.

a. 1921 recession
c. 100-year flood
b. 130-30 fund
d. Resource allocation

37. In economics and sociology, an _____ is any factor (financial or non-financial) that enables or motivates a particular course of action, or counts as a reason for preferring one choice to the alternatives. It is an expectation that encourages people to behave in a certain way. Since human beings are purposeful creatures, the study of _____ structures is central to the study of all economic activity (both in terms of individual decision-making and in terms of co-operation and competition within a larger institutional structure.)

a. Incentive
c. Epstein-Zin preferences
b. Isocost
d. Economic reform

38. The _____ was an evolution of developed countries from an industrial/manufacturing-based wealth producing economy into a service sector asset based economy, brought about by globalization and currency manipulation by governments and their central banks. Some analysts claimed that this change in the economic structure of the United States had created a state of permanent steady growth, low unemployment, and immunity to boom and bust macroeconomic cycles. They believed that the change rendered obsolete many business practices.

a. 100-year flood
c. 130-30 fund
b. New Economy
d. 1921 recession

39. The _____ consists of a number of economic theories which describe the nature of the firm, company including its existence, its behaviour, and its relationship with the market.

In simplified terms, the _____ aims to answer these questions:

1. Existence - why do firms emerge, why are not all transactions in the economy mediated over the market?
2. Boundaries - why the boundary between firms and the market is located exactly there? Which transactions are performed internally and which are negotiated on the market?
3. Organization - why are firms structured in such specific way? What is the interplay of formal and informal relationships?

Despite looking simple, these questions are not answered by the established economic theory, which usually views firms as given, and treats them as black boxes without any internal structure.

The First World War period saw a change of emphasis in economic theory away from industry-level analysis which mainly included analysing markets to analysis at the level of the firm, as it became increasingly clear that perfect competition was no longer an adequate model of how firms behaved. Economic theory till then had focussed on trying to understand markets alone and there had been little study on understanding why firms or organisations exist.

a. Theory of the firm
b. Technology gap
c. Khazzoom-Brookes postulate
d. Policy Ineffectiveness Proposition

40. In economics, an _____ is a monetary policy that increases the money supply.
   a. Easy money policy
   b. International free trade agreement
   c. Elements of economic profit
   d. Income effect

41. In calculus, a function f defined on a subset of the real numbers with real values is called _____, if for all x and y such that x >≤ y one has f(x) >≤ f(y), so f preserves the order. In layman's terms, the sign of the slope is always positive (the curve tending upwards) or zero (i.e., non-decreasing, or asymptotic, or depicted as a horizontal, flat line) Likewise, a function is called monotonically decreasing (non-increasing) if, whenever x >≤ y, then f(x) >≥ f(y), so it reverses the order.
   a. 130-30 fund
   b. 100-year flood
   c. 1921 recession
   d. Monotonic

42. _____, as defined by the _____ Association of America (Information technologyAA), is 'the study, design, development, implementation, support or management of computer-based information systems, particularly software applications and computer hardware.' _____ deals with the use of electronic computers and computer software to convert, store, protect, process, transmit, and securely retrieve information.

Today, the term _____ has ballooned to encompass many aspects of computing and technology, and the term has become very recognizable. The _____ umbrella can be quite large, covering many fields.

   a. ACCRA Cost of Living Index
   b. Information technology
   c. AD-IA Model
   d. ACEA agreement

43. _____ is a common concept in economics, and gives rise to derived concepts such as consumer debt. Generally _____ is defined by opposition to production. But the precise definition can vary because different schools of economists define production quite differently.
   a. Federal Reserve Bank Notes
   b. Cash or share options
   c. Foreclosure data providers
   d. Consumption

44. The _____ is an economic and political union of 27 member states, located primarily in Europe. It was established by the Treaty of Maastricht on 1 November 1993, upon the foundations of the pre-existing European Economic Community. With a population of almost 500 million, the _____ generates an estimated 30% share (US$18.4 trillion in 2008) of the nominal gross world product.
   a. ACCRA Cost of Living Index
   b. European Court of Justice
   c. European Union
   d. ACEA agreement

45. _____ is a type of trade policy that allows traders to act and transact without interference from government. Thus, the policy permits trading partners mutual gains from trade, with goods and services produced according to the theory of comparative advantage.

Under a _____ policy, prices are a reflection of true supply and demand, and are the sole determinant of resource allocation.

Chapter 16. Economic Growth

a. 1921 recession
c. Free Trade
b. 130-30 fund
d. 100-year flood

46. In economics and business, a _____ is the effect that one user of a good or service has on the value of that product to other people.

The classic example is the telephone. The more people own telephones, the more valuable the telephone is to each owner.

a. Network effect
c. Cluster effect
b. Penn effect
d. Pigou effect

47. The _____ is a trilateral trade bloc in North America created by the governments of the United States, Canada, and Mexico. The agreement creating the trade bloc came into force on January 1, 1994. It superseded the Canada-United States Free Trade Agreement between the U.S. and Canada.

a. North American Free Trade Agreement
c. Federal Reserve Bank Notes
b. Case-Shiller Home Price Indices
d. Demand-side technologies

48. The _____ is an important selective, mainly private, international organization designed by its founders to supervise and liberalize international trade. The organization officially commenced on 1 January 1995, under the Marrakesh Agreement, succeeding the 1947 General Agreement on Tariffs and Trade (GATT.)

The _____ deals with regulation of trade between participating countries; it provides a framework for negotiating and formalising trade agreements, and a dispute resolution process aimed at enforcing participants' adherence to _____ agreements which are signed by representatives of member governments and ratified by their parliaments.

a. Backus-Kehoe-Kydland consumption correlation puzzle
c. Bio-energy village
b. 2009 G-20 London summit protests
d. World Trade Organization

49. The _____ in Davos, Switzerland (January, 2003) triggered anti-globalization protests across Switzerland. Access to the town of Davos was blocked by the police of Grisons, with reinforcements from other cantons, and even Austrian police, which was unprecedented. On Saturday January 25, the day scheduled for a protest march in Davos, only selected protesters were allowed to pass.

a. World Economic Forum
c. 130-30 fund
b. 1921 recession
d. 100-year flood

50. _____ is a comparative concept of the ability and performance of a firm, sub-sector or country to sell and supply goods and/or services in a given market. Although widely used in economics and business management, the usefulness of the concept, particularly in the context of national _____, is vigorously disputed by economists, such as Paul Krugman.

The term may also be applied to markets, where it is used to refer to the extent to which the market structure may be regarded as perfectly competitive.

a. Quota share
b. Countervailing duties
c. Competitiveness
d. Debt moratorium

51. The term '_____' refers to the concept of collecting information and attempting to spot a pattern in the information. In some fields of study, the term '_____' has more formally-defined meanings.

In project management _____ is a mathematical technique that uses historical results to predict future outcome.

a. Trend analysis
b. Coefficient of determination
c. Quantile regression
d. Probit model

52. In economics, a _____ may be either a subsidy or a price control, both with the intended effect of keeping the market price of a good higher than the competitive equilibrium level.

In the case of a price control, a _____ is the minimum legal price a seller may charge, typically placed above equilibrium. It is the support of certain price levels at or above market values by the government.

a. Marginal profit
b. Payment schedule
c. Labor intensity
d. Price support

53. A _____ product is a product designed for cheapness and short-term convenience rather than medium to long-term durability, with most products only intended for single use. The term is also sometimes used for products that may last several months (ex. _____ air filters) to distinguish from similar products that last indefinitely (ex.

a. 130-30 fund
b. 1921 recession
c. 100-year flood
d. Disposable

54. _____ is gross income minus income tax on that income.

Discretionary income is income after subtracting taxes and normal expenses (such as rent or mortgage, utilities, insurance, medical, transportation, property maintenance, child support, inflation, food and sundries, 'c.) to maintain a certain standard of living.

a. Taxation as theft
b. Stamp Act
c. Disposable personal income
d. Disposable income

55. _____ are legal property rights over creations of the mind, both artistic and commercial, and the corresponding fields of law. Under _____ law, owners are granted certain exclusive rights to a variety of intangible assets, such as musical, literary, and artistic works; ideas, discoveries and inventions; and words, phrases, symbols, and designs. Common types of _____ include copyrights, trademarks, patents, industrial design rights and trade secrets.

a. Intellectual property
b. Ease of Doing Business Index
c. Independent contractor
d. Expedited Funds Availability Act

56. A variety of measures of _____ and output are used in economics to estimate total economic activity in a country or region, including gross domestic product (GDP), gross national product (GNP), and net _____

There are three main ways of calculating these numbers; the output approach, the income approach and the expenditure approach. In theory, the three must yield the same, because total expenditures on goods and services must equal the total income paid to the producers (Gnational income), and that must also equal the total value of the output of goods and services (GNP.)

a. National income
b. Gross world product
c. Volume index
d. GNI per capita

57. _____ is a misspelled phrase from Latin 'pro capite' phrase meaning per head with pro meaning 'per' or 'for each' and capite meaning 'head.' Both words together equate to the phrase 'for each head.'

It is usually used in the field of statistics to indicate the average per person for any given concern, such as income, crime rate, etc.

It is also used in wills to indicate that each of the named beneficiaries should receive, by devise or bequest, equal shares of the estate. This is in contrast to a per stirpes division, in which each branch of the inheriting family inherits an equal share of the estate.

a. Sargan test
b. Per capita
c. False positive rate
d. Population statistics

58. _____ means how much each individual receives, in monetary terms, of the yearly income generated in the country. This is what each citizen is to receive if the yearly national income is divided equally among everyone. _____ is usually reported in units of currency per year.

a. Family income
b. Real income
c. Lerman ratio
d. Per capita income

59. A _____ is a general term that describes any government policy or regulation that restricts international trade. The barriers can take many forms, including the following terms that include many restrictions in international trade within multiple countries that import and export any items of trade.

- Import duty
- Import licenses
- Export licenses
- Import quotas
- Tariffs
- Subsidies
- Non-tariff barriers to trade
- Voluntary Export Restraints
- Local Content Requirements
- Embargo

Most _____s work on the same principle: the imposition of some sort of cost on trade that raises the price of the traded products. If two or more nations repeatedly use _____s against each other, then a trade war results.

a. Global financial system
b. National Foreign Trade Council
c. Certificate of origin
d. Trade barrier

60. In economics, _____ refers to the ability of a party to produce a good or service using fewer real resources than another entity producing the same good or service..A party has an _____ when using the same input as another party, it can produce a greater output. Since _____ is determined by a simple comparison of labor productivities, it is possible for a a party to have no _____ in anything. It can be contrasted with the concept of comparative advantage which refers to the ability to produce a particular good at a lower opportunity cost.

a. ACCRA Cost of Living Index
b. International economics
c. Index number
d. Absolute advantage

61. In economics and business, specifically cost accounting, the _____ point (BEP) is the point at which cost or expenses and revenue are equal: there is no net loss or gain, and one has 'broken even'. A profit or a loss has not been made, although opportunity costs have been paid, and capital has received the risk-adjusted, expected return.

For example, if the business sells less than 200 tables each month, it will make a loss, if it sells more, it will be a profit.

a. Small numbers game
b. Nonmarket
c. Buffer stock scheme
d. Break-even

62. A _____ is the exclusive authority to determine how a resource is used, whether that resource is owned by government or by individuals. All economic goods have a _____s attribute. This attribute has three broad components

1. The right to use the good
2. The right to earn income from the good
3. The right to transfer the good to others

The concept of _____s as used by economists and legal scholars are related but distinct. The distinction is largely seen in the economists' focus on the ability of an individual or collective to control the use of the good.

a. High-reeve
b. Property right
c. Holder in due course
d. Post-sale restraint

Chapter 17. Disputes over Macro Theory and Policy

1. _____s is the social science that studies the production, distribution, and consumption of goods and services. The term _____s comes from the Ancient Greek οἰκονομία from οἶκος (oikos, 'house') + νόμος (nomos, 'custom' or 'law'), hence 'rules of the house(hold)'. Current _____ models developed out of the broader field of political economy in the late 19th century, owing to a desire to use an empirical approach more akin to the physical sciences.

   a. Energy economics
   c. Inflation
   b. Opportunity cost
   d. Economic

2. _____ and Keynesian Theory) is a macroeconomic theory based on the ideas of 20th-century British economist John Maynard Keynes. _____ argues that private sector decisions sometimes lead to inefficient macroeconomic outcomes and therefore advocates active policy responses by the public sector, including monetary policy actions by the central bank and fiscal policy actions by the government to stabilize output over the business cycle.

   The theories forming the basis of _____ were first presented in The General Theory of Employment, Interest and Money, published in 1936.

   a. Market failure
   c. Rational choice theory
   b. Deflation
   d. Keynesian economics

250   Chapter 17. Disputes over Macro Theory and Policy

3. A _____ is:

- Rewrite _____, in generative grammar and computer science
- Standardization, a formal and widely-accepted statement, fact, definition, or qualification
- Operation, a determinate _____ for performing a mathematical operation and obtaining a certain result (Mathematics, Logic)
    - Unary operation
    - Binary operation
- _____ of inference, a function from sets of formulae to formulae (Mathematics, Logic)
- _____ of thumb, principle with broad application that is not intended to be strictly accurate or reliable for every situation. Also often simply referred to as a _____
- Moral, an atomic element of a moral code for guiding choices in human behavior
- Heuristic, a quantized '_____' which shows a tendency or probability for successful function
- A regulation, as in sports
- A Production _____, as in computer science
- Procedural law, a _____ set governing the application of laws to cases
    - A law, which may informally be called a '_____'
    - A court ruling, a decision by a court
- In the U.S. Government, a regulation mandated by Congress, but written or expanded upon by the Executive Branch.
- Norm (sociology), an informal but widely accepted _____, concept, truth, definition, or qualification (social norms, legal norms, coding norms)
- Norm (philosophy), a kind of sentence or a reason to act, feel or believe
- 'Rulership' is the concept of governance by a government:
    - Military _____, governance by a military body
    - Monastic _____, a collection of precepts that guides the life of monks or nuns in a religious order where the superior holds the place of Christ
- Slide _____

- '_____,' a song by Ayumi Hamasaki
- '_____,' a song by rapper Nas
- '_____s,' an album by the band The Whitest Boy Alive
- _____s: Pyaar Ka Superhit Formula, a 2003 Bollywood film
- ruler, an instrument for measuring lengths
- _____, a component of an astrolabe, circumferator or similar instrument
- The _____s, a bestselling self-help book
- _____ Project (Run Up-to-date Linux Everywhere), a project that aims to use up-to-date Linux software on old PCs
- _____ engine, a software system that helps managing business _____s
- Ja _____, a hip hop artist
    - R.U.L.E., a 2005 greatest hits album by rapper Ja _____
- '_____s,' a KMFDM song

a. Procter ' Gamble   b. Technocracy
c. Demand   d. Rule

4. _____ was a survey conducted by the U.S. Department of Justice to gauge the prevalence of alcohol and illegal drug use among prior arrestees. It was a reformulation of the prior Drug Use Forecasting (DUF) program, focused on five drugs in particular: cocaine, marijuana, methamphetamine, opiates, and PCP.

Participants were randomly selected from arrest records in major metropolitan areas; because no personally identifying information is taken from each record chosen, the resulting data can be correlated to arrest rates, but not to the total population of persons charged.

 a. ACCRA Cost of Living Index
 b. Arrestee Drug Abuse Monitoring
 c. AD-IA Model
 d. ACEA agreement

5. In economics, _____ is the total demand for final goods and services in the economy (Y) at a given time and price level. It is the amount of goods and services in the economy that will be purchased at all possible price levels. This is the demand for the gross domestic product of a country when inventory levels are static.
 a. Aggregate expenditure
 b. Aggregate demand
 c. Aggregate supply
 d. Aggregation problem

6. In economics, _____ is the total supply of goods and services produced by a national economy during a specific time period. It is the total amount of goods and services in the economy available at all possible price levels.
 a. Aggregate expenditure
 b. Aggregate supply
 c. Aggregation problem
 d. Aggregate demand

7. Economics:

  - _____,the desire to own something and the ability to pay for it
  - _____ curve,a graphic representation of a _____ schedule
  - _____ deposit, the money in checking accounts
  - _____ pull theory,the theory that inflation occurs when _____ for goods and services exceeds existing supplies
  - _____ schedule,a table that lists the quantity of a good a person will buy it each different price
  - _____ side economics,the school of economics at believes government spending and tax cuts open economy by raising _____

 a. Variability
 b. McKesson ' Robbins scandal
 c. Production
 d. Demand

8. The _____ is the desired holding of money balances in the form of cash or bank deposits.

Money is dominated as store of value by interest bearing assets. However, money is necessary to carry out transactions, or in other words, it provides liquidity.

 a. Conglomerate merger
 b. Borrowing base
 c. Demand for money
 d. Market neutral

9. _____ is the term denoting either an entrance or changes which are inserted into a system and which activate/modify a process. It is an abstract concept, used in the modeling, system(s) design and system(s) exploitation. It is usually connected with other terms, e.g., _____ field, _____ variable, _____ parameter, _____ value, _____ signal, _____ device and _____ file.
   a. AD-IA Model
   b. ACEA agreement
   c. ACCRA Cost of Living Index
   d. Input

10. _____, 1st Baron Keynes was a renowned economist from Britain whose many ideas on economic and political theories as well as on many governments' monetary policies influenced America. He advocated a government that played an active role in the lives of people regarding business, economy, etc. In this role, the government would use fiscal measures to reduce the consequences of recessions, economic depressions and booms.
    a. Adolph Fischer
    b. Adolf Hitler
    c. Adam Smith
    d. John Maynard Keynes

11. _____ is a term used to describe a policy of allowing events to take their own course. The term is a French phrase literally meaning 'let do'. It is a doctrine that states that government generally should not intervene in the marketplace.
    a. Heroic capitalism
    b. Theory of Productive Forces
    c. Communization
    d. Laissez-faire

12. _____ in economics and business is the result of an exchange and from that trade we assign a numerical monetary value to a good, service or asset. If Alice trades Bob 4 apples for an orange, the _____ of an orange is 4 apples. Inversely, the _____ of an apple is 1/4 oranges.
    a. Premium pricing
    b. Price war
    c. Price book
    d. Price

13. _____ is defined as the measure of responsiveness in the quantity demanded for a commodity as a result of change in price of the same commodity. It is a measure of how consumers react to a change in price. In other words, it is percentage change in quantity demanded as per the percentage change in price of the same commodity.
    a. 130-30 fund
    b. 1921 recession
    c. 100-year flood
    d. Price elasticity of demand

14. In economics, the _____ is defined as a numerical measure of the responsiveness of the quantity supplied of product (A) to a change in price of product (A) alone. It is the measure of the way quantity supplied reacts to a change in price.

For example, if, in response to a 10% rise in the price of a good, the quantity supplied increases by 20%, the _____ would be 20%/10% = 2.

   a. Price elasticity of supply
   b. Passive income
   c. Hedonimetry
   d. Demand shaping

Chapter 17. Disputes over Macro Theory and Policy

15. A public utility (usually just utility) is an organization that maintains the infrastructure for a public service (often also providing a service using that infrastructure.) _____ are subject to forms of public control and regulation ranging from local community-based groups to state-wide government monopolies. Common arguments in favor of regulation include the desire to control market power, facilitate competition, promote investment or system expansion, or stabilize markets.
    a. 100-year flood
    b. 1921 recession
    c. 130-30 fund
    d. Public utilities

16. _____ was a Scottish moral philosopher and a pioneer of political economy. One of the key figures of the Scottish Enlightenment, Smith is the author of The Theory of Moral Sentiments and An Inquiry into the Nature and Causes of the Wealth of Nations. The latter, usually abbreviated as The Wealth of Nations, is considered his magnum opus and the first modern work of economics.
    a. Adolf Hitler
    b. Adolph Fischer
    c. Alan Greenspan
    d. Adam Smith

17. Bartering is a medium in which goods or services are directly exchanged for other goods and/or services, without the use of money. It can be bilateral or multilateral, and usually exists parallel to monetary systems in most developed countries, though to a very limited extent. _____ usually replaces money as the method of exchange in times of monetary crisis, when the currency is unstable and devalued by hyperinflation.
    a. New Economics Foundation
    b. Meitheal
    c. Community-based economics
    d. Barter

18. The term _____ refers to economy-wide fluctuations in production or economic activity over several months or years. These fluctuations occur around a long-term growth trend, and typically involve shifts over time between periods of relatively rapid economic growth (expansion or boom), and periods of relative stagnation or decline (contraction or recession.)

These fluctuations are often measured using the growth rate of real gross domestic product.

    a. Consumer theory
    b. Nominal value
    c. Business cycle
    d. Tobit model

19. _____ is an economic system in which wealth, and the means of producing wealth, are privately owned. Through _____, the land, labor, and capital are owned, operated, and traded for the purpose of generating profits, without force or fraud, by private individuals either singly or jointly, and investments, distribution, income, production, pricing and supply of goods, commodities and services are determined by voluntary private decision in a market economy. A distinguishing feature of _____ is that each person owns his or her own labor and therefore is allowed to sell the use of it to employers.
    a. Late capitalism
    b. Capitalism
    c. Creative capitalism
    d. Socialism for the rich and capitalism for the poor

20. Necessary _____s:

If x is a necessary _____ of y, then the presence of y necessarily implies the presence of x. The presence of x, however, does not imply that y will occur.

Sufficient _____s:

If x is a sufficient _____ of y, then the presence of x necessarily implies the presence of y.

   a. Cause
   c. Materialism
   b. Political philosophy
   d. Philosophy of economics

21. _____ is widely regarded as the first modern school of economic thought. It is the idea that free markets can regulate themselves. Its major developers include Adam Smith, David Ricardo, Thomas Malthus and John Stuart Mill. Sometimes the definition of _____ is expanded to include William Petty, Johann Heinrich von Thünen.

   a. Tendency of the rate of profit to fall
   c. Marginalism
   b. Schools of economic thought
   d. Classical economics

22. In economics, the _____ can be defined as the graph depicting the relationship between the price of a certain commodity, and the amount of it that consumers are willing and able to purchase at that given price. It is a graphic representation of a demand schedule. The _____ for all consumers together follows from the _____ of every individual consumer: the individual demands at each price are added together.

   a. Wage curve
   c. Kuznets curve
   b. Cost curve
   d. Demand curve

23. In economics, _____ is the ratio of the percent change in one variable to the percent change in another variable. It is a tool for measuring the responsiveness of a function to changes in parameters in a relative way. Commonly analyzed are _____ of substitution, price and wealth.

   a. Elasticity of demand
   c. ACCRA Cost of Living Index
   b. ACEA agreement
   d. Elasticity

24. Price _____ is defined as the measure of responsiveness in the quantity demanded for a commodity as a result of change in price of the same commodity. It is a measure of how consumers react to a change in price. In other words, it is percentage change in quantity demanded by the percentage change in price of the same commodity.

   a. ACEA agreement
   c. ACCRA Cost of Living Index
   b. Elasticity
   d. Elasticity of demand

25. A _____ is any systematic process enabling many market players to bid and ask: helping bidders and sellers interact and make deals. It is not just the price mechanism but the entire system of regulation, qualification, credentials, reputations and clearing that surrounds that mechanism and makes it operate in a social context.

Because a _____ relies on the assumption that players are constantly involved and unequally enabled, a _____ is distinguished specifically from a voting system where candidates seek the support of voters on a less regular basis.

   a. Competitive equilibrium
   c. Price mechanism
   b. Contestable market
   d. Market system

26. The _____ or gross domestic income (GDI), a basic measure of an economy's economic performance, is the market value of all final goods and services produced within the borders of a nation in a year. _____ can be defined in three ways, all of which are conceptually identical. First, it is equal to the total expenditures for all final goods and services produced within the country in a stipulated period of time (usually a 365-day year).

a. Gross Domestic Product
b. Market structure
c. Monopolistic competition
d. Countercyclical

27. A _____ is a hypothetical measure of overall prices for some set of goods and services, in a given region during a given interval, normalized relative to some base set. Typically, a _____ is approximated with a price index.

The classical dichotomy is the assumption that there is a relatively clean distinction between overall increases or decreases in prices and underlying, e;reale; economic variables.

a. Discretionary spending
b. Price elasticity of supply
c. Discouraged worker
d. Price level

28. _____ is the electoral problem resulting from competition between two or more candidates or political parties from the same or approximate location in the political ideological spectrum or space against an opposing candidate or political party from the other side of the political ideological spectrum or space. The resulting fragmentation of political support may result in electoral defeat. _____s, and thus political calculations attempting to avoid them, appear most frequently in elections involving executives and representatives from single member districts.

a. 100-year flood
b. 1921 recession
c. 130-30 fund
d. Coordination failure

29. In economics, _____ is a measure of national income. Basically, it is an approach to measure GDP. It is defined as the value of planned goods and services produced in an economy.

a. Aggregation problem
b. Aggregate supply
c. Aggregate expenditure
d. Aggregate demand

30. In economics, the _____ is the relation:

$$M \cdot V = P \cdot Q$$

where, for a given period,

M is the total amount of money in circulation on average in an economy.
V is the velocity of money, that is the average frequency with which a unit of money is spent.
P is the price level.

a. ACCRA Cost of Living Index
b. Outside money
c. Open market
d. Equation of exchange

31. _____ is the view within monetary economics that variation in the money supply has major influences on national output in the short run and the price level over longer periods and that objectives of monetary policy are best met by targeting the growth rate of the money supply.

Chapter 17. Disputes over Macro Theory and Policy

_____ today is mainly associated with the work of Milton Friedman, who was among the generation of economists to accept Keynesian economics and then criticize it on his own terms. Friedman and Anna Schwartz wrote an influential book, Monetary History of the United States 1867-1960, and argued that 'inflation is always and everywhere a monetary phenomenon.' Friedman advocated a central bank policy aimed at keeping the supply and demand for money at equilibrium, as measured by growth in productivity and demand.

a. Marginal revenue productivity theory of wages
b. Complexity economics
c. Monetarism
d. Historical school of economics

32. In economics, _____ is the total amount of money available in an economy at a particular point in time. There are several ways to define 'money', but standard measures usually include currency in circulation and demand deposits.

_____ data are recorded and published, usually by the government or the central bank of the country.

a. Velocity of money
b. Veil of money
c. Neutrality of money
d. Money supply

33. The _____ is the average frequency with which a unit of money is spent in a specific period of time. Velocity associates the amount of economic activity associated with a given money supply. When the period is understood, the velocity may be present as a pure number; otherwise it should be given as a pure number over time.

a. Chartalism
b. Velocity of money
c. Money supply
d. Neutrality of money

34. In economics, _____ means that people form their expectations about what will happen in the future based on what has happened in the past. For example, if inflation has been higher than expected in the past, people would revise expectations for the future.

One simple version of _____ is stated in the following equation, where p^e is the next year's rate of inflation that is currently expected; p^e_{-1} is this year's rate of inflation that was expected last year; and p is this year's actual rate of inflation:

$$p^e = p^e_{-1} + \lambda(p_{-1} - p^e_{-1})$$

With λ is between 0 and 1, this says that current expectations of future inflation reflect past expectations and an 'error-adjustment' term, in which current expectations are raised (or lowered) according to the gap between actual inflation and previous expectations.

a. Economic interdependence
b. AD-IA Model
c. Investment-specific technological progress
d. Adaptive expectations

35. _____ is a common concept in economics, and gives rise to derived concepts such as consumer debt. Generally _____ is defined by opposition to production. But the precise definition can vary because different schools of economists define production quite differently.

Chapter 17. Disputes over Macro Theory and Policy

a. Cash or share options
c. Federal Reserve Bank Notes
b. Foreclosure data providers
d. Consumption

36. A _____ is an event that suddenly changes the price of a commodity or service. It may be caused by a sudden increase or decrease in the supply of a particular good. This sudden change affects the equilibrium price.
   a. Friedman rule
   c. SIMIC
   b. Demand shock
   d. Supply shock

37. _____ is the a method of technical and economic research of the systems for purpose to optimize a parity between system's consumer functions or properties and expenses to achieve those functions or properties.

This methodology for continuous perfection of production, industrial technologies, organizational structures was developed by Juryj Sobolev in 1948 at the 'Perm telephone factory'

- 1948 Juryj Sobolev - the first success in application of a method analysis at the 'Perm telephone factory' .
- 1949 - the first application for the invention as result of use of the new method.

Today in economically developed countries practically each enterprise or the company use methodology of the kind of functional-cost analysis as a practice of the quality management, most full satisfying to principles of standards of series ISO 9000.

- Interest of consumer not in products itself, but the advantage which it will receive from its usage.
- The consumer aspires to reduce his expenses
- Functions needed by consumer can be executed in the various ways, and, hence, with various efficiency and expenses. Among possible alternatives of realization of functions exist such in which the parity of quality and the price is the optimal for the consumer.

The goal of _____ is achievement of the highest consumer satisfaction of production at simultaneous decrease in all kinds of industrial expenses Classical _____ has three English synonyms - Value Engineering, Value Management, Value Analysis.

   a. Monopoly wage
   c. Staple financing
   b. Willingness to pay
   d. Function cost analysis

38. The _____ or the output gap is the difference between potential GDP and actual GDP or actual output. The calculation for the output gap is Y-Y* where Y* is potential output and Y is actual output. If this calculation yields a positive number it is called an expansionary gap and indicates an economy in expansion; if the calculation yields a negative number it is called a recessionary gap and indicates an economy in recession.
   a. 1921 recession
   c. 100-year flood
   b. GDP gap
   d. 130-30 fund

Chapter 17. Disputes over Macro Theory and Policy

39. The _____ was a worldwide economic downturn starting in most places in 1929 and ending at different times in the 1930s or early 1940s for different countries. It was the largest and most important economic depression in the 20th century, and is used in the 21st century as an example of how far the world's economy can fall. The _____ originated in the United States; historians most often use as a starting date the stock market crash on October 29, 1929, known as Black Tuesday.

a. British Empire Economic Conference
b. Great Depression
c. Jarrow March
d. Wall Street Crash of 1929

40. _____ is the process by which the government, central bank (ii) availability of money, and (iii) cost of money or rate of interest, in order to attain a set of objectives oriented towards the growth and stability of the economy. Monetary theory provides insight into how to craft optimal _____.

_____ is referred to as either being an expansionary policy where an expansionary policy increases the total supply of money in the economy, and a contractionary policy decreases the total money supply.

a. 1921 recession
b. 100-year flood
c. 130-30 fund
d. Monetary policy

41. The term _____ refers to government debt, expenditures and revenues, or to finance (particularly financial revenue) in general.

- _____ deficit is the budget deficit of federal or local government
- _____ policy is the discretionary spending of governments. Contrasts with monetary policy.
- _____ year and _____ quarter are reporting periods for firms and other agencies.

a. Bucket shop
b. Drawdown
c. Procter ' Gamble
d. Fiscal

42. In economics, _____ is the use of government spending and revenue collection to influence the economy.

_____ can be contrasted with the other main type of economic policy, monetary policy, which attempts to stabilize the economy by controlling interest rates and the supply of money. The two main instruments of _____ are government spending and taxation.

a. Fiscal policy
b. Fiscalism
c. 100-year flood
d. Sustainable investment rule

43. A _____ is a normalized average (typically a weighted average) of prices for a given class of goods or services in a given region, during a given interval of time. It is a statistic designed to help to compare how these prices, taken as a whole, differ between time periods or geographical locations.

Price indices have several potential uses.

Chapter 17. Disputes over Macro Theory and Policy

a. Product sabotage
b. Transactional Net Margin Method
c. Two-part tariff
d. Price index

44. _____ is a type of inflation caused by substantial increases in the cost of important goods or services where no suitable alternative is available. A situation that has been often cited of this was the oil crisis of the 1970s, which some economists see as a major cause of the inflation experienced in the Western world in that decade. It is argued that this inflation resulted from increases in the cost of petroleum imposed by the member states of OPEC.
 a. Mundell-Tobin effect
 b. Headline inflation
 c. Cost-push inflation
 d. Chronic inflation

45. In economics, _____ is a rise in the general level of prices of goods and services in an economy over a period of time. When the general price level rises, each unit of currency buys fewer goods and services; consequently, _____ is also a decline in the real value of money--a loss of purchasing power in the medium of exchange which is also the monetary unit of account in the economy. A chief measure of general price-level _____ is the general _____ rate, which is the percentage change in a general price index (normally the Consumer Price Index) over time.
 a. Energy economics
 b. Economic
 c. Opportunity cost
 d. Inflation

46. _____ is an assumption used in many contemporary macroeconomic models, and also in other areas of contemporary economics and game theory and in other applications of rational choice theory.

Since most macroeconomic models today study decisions over many periods, the expectations of workers, consumers, and firms about future economic conditions are an essential part of the model. How to model these expectations has long been controversial, and it is well known that the macroeconomic predictions of the model may differ depending on the assumptions made about expectations

 a. Balanced-growth equilibrium
 b. Minimum wage
 c. Potential output
 d. Rational expectations

47. _____ is a broad label that refers to any individuals or households that use goods and services generated within the economy. The concept of a _____ is used in different contexts, so that the usage and significance of the term may vary.

Typically when business people and economists talk of _____s they are talking about person as _____, an aggregated commodity item with little individuality other than that expressed in the buy/not-buy decision.

 a. Consumer
 b. 130-30 fund
 c. 1921 recession
 d. 100-year flood

48. _____ is a loose term used to refer to the non-heterodox economics taught in prominent universities. It is most closely associated with neoclassical economics. Mainstream economists are not generally separated into schools, but two major contemporary orthodox economic schools of thought are the Saltwater school of the US coastal universities, notably including MIT, Berkeley, and Harvard, and the Freshwater school of the University of Chicago, which is associated with the Chicago school of economics.

Chapter 17. Disputes over Macro Theory and Policy

a. Market structure
c. Gross domestic product
b. Mercantilism
d. Mainstream economics

49. In labor economics, the _____ hypothesis argues that wages, at least in some markets, are determined by more than simply supply and demand. Specifically, it points to the incentive for managers to pay their employees more than the market-clearing wage in order to increase their productivity or efficiency. This increased labor productivity pays for the relatively higher wages.
   a. Inflatable rats
   c. Exogenous growth model
   b. Earnings calls
   d. Efficiency wage

50. In economics, a _____ is a general slowdown in economic activity over a sustained period of time, or a business cycle contraction. During _____s, many macroeconomic indicators vary in a similar way. Production as measured by Gross Domestic Product (GDP), employment, investment spending, capacity utilization, household incomes and business profits all fall during _____s.
   a. Treasury View
   c. Leading indicators
   b. Recession
   d. Monetary economics

51. In a _____ there is both a monopoly (a single seller) and monopsony (a single buyer) in the same market.

In such market price and output will be determined by the non economic forces like bargaining power of both buyer and seller. A _____ model is often used in situations where the switching costs of both sides are prohibitively high.

   a. Market concentration
   c. Revenue-cap regulation
   b. Price takers
   d. Bilateral monopoly

52. In economics, a _____ exists when a specific individual or enterprise has sufficient control over a particular product or service to determine significantly the terms on which other individuals shall have access to it. Monopolies are thus characterized by a lack of economic competition for the good or service that they provide and a lack of viable substitute goods. The verb 'monopolize' refers to the process by which a firm gains persistently greater market share than what is expected under perfect competition.
   a. 100-year flood
   c. 1921 recession
   b. 130-30 fund
   d. Monopoly

53. The _____ or Aggregate Demand-Aggregate Supply model is a macroeconomic model that explains price level and output through the relationship of aggregate demand and aggregate supply. It was first put forth by John Maynard Keynes in his work The General Theory of Employment, Interest, and Money. It is the foundation for the modern field of macroeconomics, and is accepted by a broad array of economists, from Libertarian, Monetarist supporters of laissez-faire, such as Milton Friedman to Socialist, Post-Keynesian supporters of economic interventionism, such as Joan Robinson.
   a. AD-AS
   c. Adaptive expectations
   b. Economic interdependence
   d. IS/LM model

54. _____ is an economic policy in which a central bank estimates and makes public a projected, or 'target,' inflation rate and then attempts to steer actual inflation towards the target through the use of interest rate changes and other monetary tools.

Chapter 17. Disputes over Macro Theory and Policy

Because interest rates and the inflation rate tend to be inversely related, the likely moves of the central bank to raise or lower interest rates become more transparent under the policy of _____. Examples:

- if inflation appears to be above the target, the bank is likely to raise interest rates. This usually (but not always) has the effect over time of cooling the economy and bringing down inflation.

- if inflation appears to be below the target, the bank is likely to lower interest rates. This usually (again, not always) has the effect over time of accelerating the economy and raising inflation.

a. Inflation swap
b. Incomes policies
c. Inflation targeting
d. Employment Cost Index

55. In economics, a _____ is a monetary-policy rule that stipulates how much the central bank would or should change the nominal interest rate in response to divergences of actual inflation rates from target inflation rates and of actual Gross Domestic Product (GDP) from potential GDP. It was first proposed by the by U.S. economist John B. Taylor in 1993. The rule can be written as follows:

$$i_t = \pi_t + r_t^* + a_\pi(\pi_t - \pi_t^*) + a_y(y_t - \bar{y}_t).$$

In this equation, i_t is the target short-term nominal interest rate (e.g. the federal funds rate in the US), π_t is the rate of inflation as measured by the GDP deflator, π_t^* is the desired rate of inflation, r_t^* is the assumed equilibrium real interest rate, y_t is the logarithm of real GDP, and $\bar{y}_t$ is the logarithm of potential output, as determined by a linear trend.

a. Fed Funds Probability
b. Federal Reserve Banks
c. Term Securities Lending Facility
d. Taylor rule

56. From a Keynesian point of view, a _____ in the public sector is achieved when the government equates the revenues with expenditure over the business cycles. In other words, a government's budget is balanced if its income is equal to its expenditure. It is a budget in which revenues are equal to spending.

a. Budget crisis
b. Budget theory
c. Budget support
d. Balanced budget

57. A _____ represents the combinations of goods and services that a consumer can purchase given current prices and his income. Consumer theory uses the concepts of a _____ and a preference map to analyze consumer choices. Both concepts have a ready graphical representation in the two-good case.

a. Joint demand
b. Revealed preference
c. Quality bias
d. Budget constraint

58. A _____ occurs when an entity spends more money than it takes in. The opposite of a _____ is a budget surplus. Debt is essentially an accumulated flow of deficits.

a. Public Financial Management
b. Lump-sum tax
c. Funding body
d. Budget deficit

59. In economics, an _____ is a monetary policy that increases the money supply.
   a. Elements of economic profit
   b. International free trade agreement
   c. Income effect
   d. Easy money policy

60. _____ is monetary policy that seeks to increase the size of the money supply. In most nations, monetary policy is controlled by either a central bank or a finance ministry

Neoclassical and Keynesian economics significantly differ on the effects and effectiveness of monetary policy on influencing the real economy; there is no clear consensus on how monetary policy affects real economic variables (aggregate output or income, employment.) Both economic schools accept that monetary policy affects monetary variables (price levels, interest rates.)

   a. ACEA agreement
   b. AD-IA Model
   c. ACCRA Cost of Living Index
   d. Expansionary monetary policy

Chapter 18. Extensions of Demand and Supply Analysis

1. In mathematics, a _____ is a constant multiplicative factor of a certain object. For example, in the expression $9x^2$, the _____ of x^2 is 9.

The object can be such things as a variable, a vector, a function, etc.

   a. Coefficient
   b. 1921 recession
   c. 130-30 fund
   d. 100-year flood

2. _____ is a broad label that refers to any individuals or households that use goods and services generated within the economy. The concept of a _____ is used in different contexts, so that the usage and significance of the term may vary.

   Typically when business people and economists talk of _____s they are talking about person as _____, an aggregated commodity item with little individuality other than that expressed in the buy/not-buy decision.

   a. 1921 recession
   b. 100-year flood
   c. 130-30 fund
   d. Consumer

3. In economics, the _____ of demand measures the responsiveness of the demand of a good to the change in the income of the people demanding the good. It is calculated as the ratio of the percent change in demand to the percent change in income. For example, if, in response to a 10% increase in income, the demand of a good increased by 20%, the _____ of demand would be 20%/10% = 2.

   a. ACEA agreement
   b. AD-IA Model
   c. ACCRA Cost of Living Index
   d. Income elasticity

4. In economics, the _____ measures the responsiveness of the demand of a good to the change in the income of the people demanding the good. It is calculated as the ratio of the percent change in demand to the percent change in income. For example, if, in response to a 10% increase in income, the demand of a good increased by 20%, the _____ would be 20%/10% = 2.

   a. Indifference map
   b. Elasticity of substitution
   c. Expenditure minimization problem
   d. Income elasticity of demand

5. In economics, _____ describes demand that is not very sensitive to a change in price.
   a. Inflation hedge
   b. Export-led growth
   c. Effective unemployment rate
   d. Inelastic

6. _____ and Keynesian Theory) is a macroeconomic theory based on the ideas of 20th-century British economist John Maynard Keynes. _____ argues that private sector decisions sometimes lead to inefficient macroeconomic outcomes and therefore advocates active policy responses by the public sector, including monetary policy actions by the central bank and fiscal policy actions by the government to stabilize output over the business cycle.

The theories forming the basis of _____ were first presented in The General Theory of Employment, Interest and Money, published in 1936.

Chapter 18. Extensions of Demand and Supply Analysis

a. Deflation
c. Market failure

b. Rational choice theory
d. Keynesian economics

7. In economics, the _____ is an economic law that states that consumers buy more of a good when its price decreases and less when its price increases.

There are certain goods which do not follow this law. These include Veblen and Giffen goods

a. Georgism
c. Law of demand

b. Financial crisis
d. Market failure

8. _____ in economics and business is the result of an exchange and from that trade we assign a numerical monetary value to a good, service or asset. If Alice trades Bob 4 apples for an orange, the _____ of an orange is 4 apples. Inversely, the _____ of an apple is 1/4 oranges.

a. Price book
c. Price

b. Price war
d. Premium pricing

9. _____ is defined as the measure of responsiveness in the quantity demanded for a commodity as a result of change in price of the same commodity. It is a measure of how consumers react to a change in price. In other words, it is percentage change in quantity demanded as per the percentage change in price of the same commodity.

a. Price elasticity of demand
c. 130-30 fund

b. 1921 recession
d. 100-year flood

10. Economics:

- _____, the desire to own something and the ability to pay for it
- _____ curve, a graphic representation of a _____ schedule
- _____ deposit, the money in checking accounts
- _____ pull theory, the theory that inflation occurs when _____ for goods and services exceeds existing supplies
- _____ schedule, a table that lists the quantity of a good a person will buy it each different price
- _____ side economics, the school of economics at believes government spending and tax cuts open economy by raising _____

a. Variability
c. McKesson ' Robbins scandal

b. Production
d. Demand

11. In economics, _____ is the ratio of the percent change in one variable to the percent change in another variable. It is a tool for measuring the responsiveness of a function to changes in parameters in a relative way. Commonly analyzed are _____ of substitution, price and wealth.

a. Elasticity of demand
c. Elasticity

b. ACCRA Cost of Living Index
d. ACEA agreement

Chapter 18. Extensions of Demand and Supply Analysis

12. Price _____ is defined as the measure of responsiveness in the quantity demanded for a commodity as a result of change in price of the same commodity. It is a measure of how consumers react to a change in price. In other words, it is percentage change in quantity demanded by the percentage change in price of the same commodity.
   a. Elasticity of demand
   b. Elasticity
   c. ACEA agreement
   d. ACCRA Cost of Living Index

13. In economics, the _____ can be defined as the graph depicting the relationship between the price of a certain commodity, and the amount of it that consumers are willing and able to purchase at that given price. It is a graphic representation of a demand schedule. The _____ for all consumers together follows from the _____ of every individual consumer: the individual demands at each price are added together.
   a. Demand curve
   b. Wage curve
   c. Kuznets curve
   d. Cost curve

14. In economics, the _____ of a good or of a service is the utility of the specific use to which an agent would put a given increase in that good or service, or of the specific use that would be abandoned in response to a given decrease. In other words, _____ is the utility of the marginal use -- which, on the assumption of economic rationality, would be the least urgent use of the good or service, from the best feasible combination of actions in which its use is included. Under the mainstream assumptions, the _____ of a good or service is the posited quantified change in utility obtained by increasing or by decreasing use of that good or service.
   a. 100-year flood
   b. 1921 recession
   c. Marginal utility
   d. 130-30 fund

15. In economics, _____ is a measure of the relative satisfaction from consumption of various goods and services. Given this measure, one may speak meaningfully of increasing or decreasing _____, and thereby explain economic behavior in terms of attempts to increase one's _____. For illustrative purposes, changes in _____ are sometimes expressed in units called utils.
   a. Utility function
   b. Expected utility hypothesis
   c. Ordinal utility
   d. Utility

16. _____ is the total money received from the sale of any given quantity of output.

    The _____ is calculated by taking the price of the sale times the quantity sold, i.e.

    _____ = price X quantity.

   a. Total revenue
   b. Small numbers game
   c. Ceteris paribus
   d. Market development funds

17. In economics, the _____ is a means for determining whether demand is elastic or inelastic. If an increase in price causes an increase in total revenue, then demand can be said to be inelastic, since the increase in price does not have a large impact on quantity demanded. If an increase in price causes a decrease in total revenue, then demand can be said to be elastic, since the increase in price has a large impact on quantity demanded.
   a. 100-year flood
   b. Total revenue test
   c. 130-30 fund
   d. 1921 recession

Chapter 18. Extensions of Demand and Supply Analysis

18. _____ exists when sales of identical goods or services are transacted at different prices from the same provider. In a theoretical market with perfect information, no transaction costs or prohibition on secondary exchange (or re-selling) to prevent arbitrage, _____ can only be a feature of monopoly and oligopoly markets, where market power can be exercised. Otherwise, the moment the seller tries to sell the same good at different prices, the buyer at the lower price can arbitrage by selling to the consumer buying at the higher price but with a tiny discount.

   a. Price discrimination
   b. Loss leader
   c. Lerner Index
   d. Transfer pricing

19. In algebra, a _____ is a function depending on n that associates a scalar, det(A), to an n×n square matrix A. The fundamental geometric meaning of a _____ is a scale factor for measure when A is regarded as a linear transformation. _____s are important both in calculus, where they enter the substitution rule for several variables, and in multilinear algebra.

   For a fixed nonnegative integer n, there is a unique _____ function for the n×n matrices over any commutative ring R. In particular, this function exists when R is the field of real or complex numbers.

   a. 100-year flood
   b. 130-30 fund
   c. 1921 recession
   d. Determinant

20. _____ are final goods specifically intended for the mass market. For instance, _____ do not include investment assets, like precious antiques, even though these antiques are final goods.

   Manufactured goods are goods that have been processed by way of machinery.

   a. Bulgarian-American trade
   b. G-20 Leaders Summit on Financial Markets and the World Economy
   c. Fiscal stimulus plans
   d. Consumer goods

21. A _____ product is a product designed for cheapness and short-term convenience rather than medium to long-term durability, with most products only intended for single use. The term is also sometimes used for products that may last several months (ex. _____ air filters) to distinguish from similar products that last indefinitely (ex.

   a. 100-year flood
   b. 130-30 fund
   c. Disposable
   d. 1921 recession

22. _____ is gross income minus income tax on that income.

   Discretionary income is income after subtracting taxes and normal expenses (such as rent or mortgage, utilities, insurance, medical, transportation, property maintenance, child support, inflation, food and sundries, 'c.) to maintain a certain standard of living.

   a. Stamp Act
   b. Taxation as theft
   c. Disposable personal income
   d. Disposable income

23. A variety of measures of _____ and output are used in economics to estimate total economic activity in a country or region, including gross domestic product (GDP), gross national product (GNP), and net _____

There are three main ways of calculating these numbers; the output approach, the income approach and the expenditure approach. In theory, the three must yield the same, because total expenditures on goods and services must equal the total income paid to the producers (Gnational income), and that must also equal the total value of the output of goods and services (GNP.)

a. Volume index
b. GNI per capita
c. Gross world product
d. National income

24. In economics and business, specifically cost accounting, the _____ point (BEP) is the point at which cost or expenses and revenue are equal: there is no net loss or gain, and one has 'broken even'. A profit or a loss has not been made, although opportunity costs have been paid, and capital has received the risk-adjusted, expected return.

For example, if the business sells less than 200 tables each month, it will make a loss, if it sells more, it will be a profit.

a. Buffer stock scheme
b. Nonmarket
c. Break-even
d. Small numbers game

25. In economics, the _____ and cross price elasticity of demand measures the responsiveness of the demand of a good to a change in the price of another good.

It is measured as the percentage change in demand for the first good that occurs in response to a percentage change in price of the second good. For example, if, in response to a 10% increase in the price of fuel, the demand of new cars that are fuel inefficient decreased by 20%, the _____ would be −20%/10% = −2.

a. Snob effect
b. Convex preferences
c. Quality bias
d. Cross elasticity of demand

26. A _____ is an object whose consumption increases the utility of the consumer, for which the quantity demanded exceeds the quantity supplied at zero price. _____s are usually modeled as having diminishing marginal utility. The first individual purchase has high utility; the second has less.
a. Merit good
b. Pie method
c. Good
d. Composite good

27. In microeconomics, _____ is quite simply the conversion of inputs into outputs. It is an economic process that uses resources to create a good or service that is suitable for exchange. This can include manufacturing, storing, shipping, and packaging.
a. MET
b. Red Guards
c. Solved
d. Production

28. To _____ is to impose a financial charge or other levy upon a taxpayer by a state or the functional equivalent of a state.

_____es are also imposed by many subnational entities. _____es consist of direct _____ or indirect _____, and may be paid in money or as its labour equivalent (often but not always unpaid.)

Chapter 18. Extensions of Demand and Supply Analysis

a. 130-30 fund
b. 1921 recession
c. 100-year flood
d. Tax

29. To tax is to impose a financial charge or other levy upon a taxpayer by a state or the functional equivalent of a state. _____ are also imposed by many subnational entities. _____ consist of direct tax or indirect tax, and may be paid in money or as its labour equivalent (often but not always unpaid.)

a. 1921 recession
b. 100-year flood
c. 130-30 fund
d. Taxes

30. In economics, the _____ is defined as a numerical measure of the responsiveness of the quantity supplied of product (A) to a change in price of product (A) alone. It is the measure of the way quantity supplied reacts to a change in price.

For example, if, in response to a 10% rise in the price of a good, the quantity supplied increases by 20%, the _____ would be 20%/10% = 2.

a. Passive income
b. Price elasticity of supply
c. Demand shaping
d. Hedonimetry

31. _____ are those things that are neither used with, nor instead of, the item of interest. Their use is independent of the use of the good being considered. A person's demand of nails is independent of his or her demand for bread.

a. Inferior good
b. Export-oriented
c. Independent goods
d. Information good

32. A _____ or complement good in economics is a good which is consumed with another good; its cross elasticity of demand is negative. - It is two goods that are bought and used together. This means that, if goods A and B were complements, more of good A being bought would result in more of good B also being bought.

a. Final good
b. Free good
c. Manufactured goods
d. Complementary good

33. In economics, one kind of good (or service) is said to be a _____ for another kind in so far as the two kinds of goods can be consumed or used in place of one another in at least some of their possible uses.

Classic examples of _____s include margarine and butter, or petroleum and natural gas (used for heating or electricity.) The fact that one good is substitutable for another has immediate economic consequences: insofar as one good can be substituted for another, the demand for the two kinds of good will be bound together by the fact that customers can trade off one good for the other if it becomes advantageous to do so.

a. Veblen goods
b. Substitute good
c. Private good
d. Merit good

Chapter 18. Extensions of Demand and Supply Analysis

34. The _____ or gross domestic income (GDI), a basic measure of an economy's economic performance, is the market value of all final goods and services produced within the borders of a nation in a year. _____ can be defined in three ways, all of which are conceptually identical. First, it is equal to the total expenditures for all final goods and services produced within the country in a stipulated period of time (usually a 365-day year.)
   a. Countercyclical
   b. Monopolistic competition
   c. Gross Domestic Product
   d. Market structure

35. In economic theory, _____ is the competitive situation in any market where the conditions necessary for perfect competition are not satisfied. It is a market structure that does not meet the conditions of perfect competition.

Forms of _____ include:

- Monopoly, in which there is only one seller of a good.
- Oligopoly, in which there is a small number of sellers.
- Monopolistic competition, in which there are many sellers producing highly differentiated goods.
- Monopsony, in which there is only one buyer of a good.
- Oligopsony, in which there is a small number of buyers.

There may also be _____ in markets due to buyers or sellers lacking information about prices and the goods being traded.

There may also be _____ due to a time lag in a market.

   a. Imperfect competition
   b. AD-IA Model
   c. ACCRA Cost of Living Index
   d. ACEA agreement

36. In consumer theory, an _____ is a good that decreases in demand when consumer income rises, unlike normal goods, for which the opposite is observed. It is a good that consumers demand increases when their income increases. Inferiority, in this sense, is an observable fact relating to affordability rather than a statement about the quality of the good.
   a. Independent goods
   b. Inferior good
   c. Information good
   d. Export-oriented

37. In economics, _____ describes the state of a market with respect to competition.

- Perfect competition, in which the market consists of a very large number of firms producing a homogeneous product.
- Monopolistic competition where there are a large number of independent firms which have a very small proportion of the market share.
- Oligopoly, in which a market is dominated by a small number of firms which own more than 40% of the market share.
- Oligopsony, a market dominated by many sellers and a few buyers.
- Monopoly, where there is only one provider of a product or service.
- Natural monopoly, a monopoly in which economies of scale cause efficiency to increase continuously with the size of the firm. A firm is a natural monopoly if it is able to serve the entire market demand at a lower cost than any combination of two or more smaller, more specialized firms.
- Monopsony, when there is only one buyer in a market.

Chapter 18. Extensions of Demand and Supply Analysis

The imperfectly competitive structure is quite identical to the realistic market conditions where some monopolistic competitors, monopolists, oligopolists, and duopolists exist and dominate the market conditions. The elements of _____ include the number and size distribution of firms, entry conditions, and the extent of differentiation.

These somewhat abstract concerns tend to determine some but not all details of a specific concrete market system where buyers and sellers actually meet and commit to trade.

a. Market structure
c. Monopolistic competition
b. Labour economics
d. Human capital

38. The phrase _____ and acquisitions refers to the aspect of corporate strategy, corporate finance and management dealing with the buying, selling and combining of different companies that can aid, finance, or help a growing company in a given industry grow rapidly without having to create another business entity.

An acquisition, also known as a takeover or a buyout, is the buying of one company (the 'target') by another. An acquisition may be friendly or hostile.

a. Differential accumulation
c. Peace dividend
b. Political economy
d. Mergers

39. The phrase _____ refers to the aspect of corporate strategy, corporate finance and management dealing with the buying, selling and combining of different companies that can aid, finance, or help a growing company in a given industry grow rapidly without having to create another business entity.

An acquisition, also known as a takeover or a buyout, is the buying of one company (the 'target') by another. An acquisition may be friendly or hostile.

a. Political economy
c. Peace dividend
b. Productive and unproductive labour
d. Mergers and acquisitions

40. In economics, _____s are any goods for which demand increases when income increases and falls when income decreases but price remains constant, i.e. with a positive income elasticity of demand. The term does not necessarily refer to the quality of the good.

Depending on the indifference curves, the amount of a good bought can either increase, decrease, or stay the same when income increases.

a. Normative economics
c. Bord halfpenny
b. Financial contagion
d. Normal good

41. In economics, a _____ is a general slowdown in economic activity over a sustained period of time, or a business cycle contraction. During _____s, many macroeconomic indicators vary in a similar way. Production as measured by Gross Domestic Product (GDP), employment, investment spending, capacity utilization, household incomes and business profits all fall during _____s.

a. Monetary economics
b. Leading indicators
c. Treasury View
d. Recession

42. In economics, _____ is a measure of national income. Basically, it is an approach to measure GDP. It is defined as the value of planned goods and services produced in an economy.
   a. Aggregate supply
   b. Aggregate demand
   c. Aggregation problem
   d. Aggregate expenditure

43. _____ is a type of inflation caused by substantial increases in the cost of important goods or services where no suitable alternative is available. A situation that has been often cited of this was the oil crisis of the 1970s, which some economists see as a major cause of the inflation experienced in the Western world in that decade. It is argued that this inflation resulted from increases in the cost of petroleum imposed by the member states of OPEC.
   a. Chronic inflation
   b. Headline inflation
   c. Cost-push inflation
   d. Mundell-Tobin effect

44. In economics, _____ is a rise in the general level of prices of goods and services in an economy over a period of time. When the general price level rises, each unit of currency buys fewer goods and services; consequently, _____ is also a decline in the real value of money--a loss of purchasing power in the medium of exchange which is also the monetary unit of account in the economy. A chief measure of general price-level _____ is the general _____ rate, which is the percentage change in a general price index (normally the Consumer Price Index) over time.
   a. Energy economics
   b. Economic
   c. Opportunity cost
   d. Inflation

45. The term surplus is used in economics for several related quantities. The _____ is the amount that consumers benefit by being able to purchase a product for a price that is less than they would be willing to pay. The producer surplus is the amount that producers benefit by selling at a market price mechanism that is higher than they would be willing to sell for.
   a. Consumer surplus
   b. Microeconomic reform
   c. Necessity good
   d. Marginal rate of technical substitution

46. The _____ was a worldwide economic downturn starting in most places in 1929 and ending at different times in the 1930s or early 1940s for different countries. It was the largest and most important economic depression in the 20th century, and is used in the 21st century as an example of how far the world's economy can fall. The _____ originated in the United States; historians most often use as a starting date the stock market crash on October 29, 1929, known as Black Tuesday.
   a. British Empire Economic Conference
   b. Great Depression
   c. Wall Street Crash of 1929
   d. Jarrow March

47. _____ is the process by which money is produced or issued. There are three different ways to create money:

   - manufacturing a new monetary unit, such as paper currency or metal coins (_____)
   - loaning out a physical monetary unit multiple times through fractional-reserve lending (credit creation)
   - buying of government securities or other financial instruments by central bank through Open market operations (electronic creation)

Coins are produced by manufacturing metal in a factory called a mint.

Banknotes and bank account balances are financial securities issued by a bank.

Similarly, money destruction, i.e., the reverse of _____, can occur in two different ways, depending on how the money was created.

a. Shadow Open Market Committee
c. Monetary policy of Sweden
b. Second-round effect
d. Money creation

Chapter 18. Extensions of Demand and Supply Analysis 273

48. A _____ is:

- Rewrite _____, in generative grammar and computer science
- Standardization, a formal and widely-accepted statement, fact, definition, or qualification
- Operation, a determinate _____ for performing a mathematical operation and obtaining a certain result (Mathematics, Logic)
    - Unary operation
    - Binary operation
- _____ of inference, a function from sets of formulae to formulae (Mathematics, Logic)
- _____ of thumb, principle with broad application that is not intended to be strictly accurate or reliable for every situation. Also often simply referred to as a _____
- Moral, an atomic element of a moral code for guiding choices in human behavior
- Heuristic, a quantized '_____' which shows a tendency or probability for successful function
- A regulation, as in sports
- A Production _____, as in computer science
- Procedural law, a _____ set governing the application of laws to cases
    - A law, which may informally be called a '_____'
    - A court ruling, a decision by a court
- In the U.S. Government, a regulation mandated by Congress, but written or expanded upon by the Executive Branch.
- Norm (sociology), an informal but widely accepted _____, concept, truth, definition, or qualification (social norms, legal norms, coding norms)
- Norm (philosophy), a kind of sentence or a reason to act, feel or believe
- 'Rulership' is the concept of governance by a government:
    - Military _____, governance by a military body
    - Monastic _____, a collection of precepts that guides the life of monks or nuns in a religious order where the superior holds the place of Christ
- Slide _____

- '_____,' a song by Ayumi Hamasaki
- '_____,' a song by rapper Nas
- '_____s,' an album by the band The Whitest Boy Alive
- _____s: Pyaar Ka Superhit Formula, a 2003 Bollywood film
- ruler, an instrument for measuring lengths
- _____, a component of an astrolabe, circumferator or similar instrument
- The _____s, a bestselling self-help book
- _____ Project (Run Up-to-date Linux Everywhere), a project that aims to use up-to-date Linux software on old PCs
- _____ engine, a software system that helps managing business _____s
- Ja _____, a hip hop artist
    - R.U.L.E., a 2005 greatest hits album by rapper Ja _____
- '_____s,' a KMFDM song

a. Demand
c. Technocracy
b. Rule
d. Procter ' Gamble

Chapter 18. Extensions of Demand and Supply Analysis

49. A security is a fungible, negotiable instrument representing financial value. _____ are broadly categorized into debt _____; equity _____, e.g., common stocks; and derivative (finance) contracts such as forwards, futures, options and swaps. The company or other entity issuing the security is called the issuer.
   a. Pass-Through Certificates
   b. Securities
   c. Settlement risk
   d. Red herring prospectus

50. The term surplus is used in economics for several related quantities. The consumer surplus is the amount that consumers benefit by being able to purchase a product for a price that is less than they would be willing to pay. The _____ is the amount that producers benefit by selling at a market price mechanism that is higher than they would be willing to sell for.
   a. Producer surplus
   b. Schedule delay
   c. Returns to scale
   d. Long term

51. _____ is a situation in which the limited resources of a firm are allocated in accordance with the wishes of consumers. An allocatively efficient economy produces an 'optimal mix' of commodities. A firm is allocatively efficient when its price is equal to its marginal costs (that is, P = MC) in a perfect market.
   a. Economic efficiency
   b. ACCRA Cost of Living Index
   c. ACEA agreement
   d. Allocative efficiency

52. _____ occurs when the economy is operating at its production possibility frontier (PPF.) This takes place when production of one good is achieved at the lowest cost possible, given the production of the other good(s.) Equivalently, it is when the highest possible output of one good is produced, given the production level of the other good(s.)
   a. Preclusive purchasing
   b. Free contract
   c. Discretionary spending
   d. Productive efficiency

53. _____s is the social science that studies the production, distribution, and consumption of goods and services. The term _____s comes from the Ancient Greek oá¼°κονομῖ α from oá¼¶κος (oikos, 'house') + vÍŒμος (nomos, 'custom' or 'law'), hence 'rules of the house(hold)'. Current _____ models developed out of the broader field of political economy in the late 19th century, owing to a desire to use an empirical approach more akin to the physical sciences.
   a. Inflation
   b. Economic
   c. Opportunity cost
   d. Energy economics

54. In economics, _____ is the ability of a firm to alter the market price of a good or service. A firm with _____ can raise prices without losing all customers to competitors.

When a firm has _____ it faces a downward-sloping demand curve.

   a. Price makers
   b. Revenue-cap regulation
   c. Market power
   d. Pacman conjecture

55. _____ is one of the four Ps of the marketing mix. The other three aspects are product, promotion, and place. It is also a key variable in microeconomic price allocation theory.
   a. Guaranteed Maximum Price
   b. Premium pricing
   c. Pricing
   d. Point of total assumption

Chapter 18. Extensions of Demand and Supply Analysis

56. _____ is the removal or simplification of government rules and regulations that constrain the operation of market forces. _____ does not mean elimination of laws against fraud, but eliminating or reducing government control of how business is done, thereby moving toward a more free market.

The stated rationale for '_____' is often that fewer and simpler regulations will lead to a raised level of competitiveness, therefore higher productivity, more efficiency and lower prices overall.

- a. Macroeconomic policy instruments
- b. Deregulation
- c. Secular basis
- d. Fundamental psychological law

57. _____ is a specific term used in companies' financial reporting from the company-whole point of view. Because that use excludes the effects of changing ownership interest, an economic measure of _____ is necessary for financial analysis from the shareholders' point of view

_____ is defined by the Financial Accounting Standards Board, or FASB, as e;the change in equity [net assets] of a business enterprise during a period from transactions and other events and circumstances from nonowner sources. It includes all changes in equity during a period except those resulting from investments by owners and distributions to owners.e;

_____ is the sum of net income and other items that must bypass the income statement because they have not been realized, including items like an unrealized holding gain or loss from available for sale securities and foreign currency translation gains or losses.

- a. Windfall gain
- b. Comprehensive income
- c. Net national income
- d. Real income

58. The _____ is a US private, nonprofit research organization dedicated to studying the science and empirics of economics, especially the American economy. It is 'committed to undertaking and disseminating unbiased economic research among public policymakers, business professionals, and the academic community.' It publishes NBER Working Papers and books. The NBER is located in Cambridge, Massachusetts with branch offices in Palo Alto, California, and New York City.
- a. CEFTA
- b. Non-governmental organization
- c. Deutsche Bank
- d. National Bureau of Economic Research

Chapter 19. Consumer Behavior and Utility Maximization

1. _____ is a broad label that refers to any individuals or households that use goods and services generated within the economy. The concept of a _____ is used in different contexts, so that the usage and significance of the term may vary.

Typically when business people and economists talk of _____s they are talking about person as _____, an aggregated commodity item with little individuality other than that expressed in the buy/not-buy decision.

   a. 130-30 fund
   b. 1921 recession
   c. Consumer
   d. 100-year flood

2. _____ are final goods specifically intended for the mass market. For instance, _____ do not include investment assets, like precious antiques, even though these antiques are final goods.

Manufactured goods are goods that have been processed by way of machinery.

   a. Fiscal stimulus plans
   b. G-20 Leaders Summit on Financial Markets and the World Economy
   c. Bulgarian-American trade
   d. Consumer goods

3. In economics, a _____ or a hard good is a good which does not quickly wear out it yields services or utility over time rather than being completely used up when used once. Most goods are therefore _____s to a certain degree. These are goods that can last for a relatively long time, such as refrigerators, cars, and DVD players.
   a. Search good
   b. Luxury good
   c. Superior goods
   d. Durable good

4. In economics, the _____ of a good or of a service is the utility of the specific use to which an agent would put a given increase in that good or service, or of the specific use that would be abandoned in response to a given decrease. In other words, _____ is the utility of the marginal use -- which, on the assumption of economic rationality, would be the least urgent use of the good or service, from the best feasible combination of actions in which its use is included. Under the mainstream assumptions, the _____ of a good or service is the posited quantified change in utility obtained by increasing or by decreasing use of that good or service.
   a. 1921 recession
   b. 100-year flood
   c. 130-30 fund
   d. Marginal utility

5. In economics, _____ is a measure of the relative satisfaction from consumption of various goods and services. Given this measure, one may speak meaningfully of increasing or decreasing _____, and thereby explain economic behavior in terms of attempts to increase one's _____. For illustrative purposes, changes in _____ are sometimes expressed in units called utils.
   a. Ordinal utility
   b. Utility function
   c. Utility
   d. Expected utility hypothesis

Chapter 19. Consumer Behavior and Utility Maximization

6. Economics:

    - _____, the desire to own something and the ability to pay for it
    - _____ curve, a graphic representation of a _____ schedule
    - _____ deposit, the money in checking accounts
    - _____ pull theory, the theory that inflation occurs when _____ for goods and services exceeds existing supplies
    - _____ schedule, a table that lists the quantity of a good a person will buy it each different price
    - _____ side economics, the school of economics at believes government spending and tax cuts open economy by raising _____

    a. Demand
    c. McKesson ' Robbins scandal
    b. Production
    d. Variability

7. A _____ is an object whose consumption increases the utility of the consumer, for which the quantity demanded exceeds the quantity supplied at zero price. _____ s are usually modeled as having diminishing marginal utility. The first individual purchase has high utility; the second has less.
    a. Merit good
    c. Composite good
    b. Pie method
    d. Good

8. The _____ is a system for calculating margin requirements for futures and options on futures. It was developed by the Chicago Mercantile Exchange in 1988.

    SPAN is a portfolio margining method that uses grid simulation.

    a. Callable bull/bear contract
    c. Volatility swap
    b. Repurchase agreement
    d. Standard Portfolio Analysis of Risk

9. In economics, the _____ can be defined as the graph depicting the relationship between the price of a certain commodity, and the amount of it that consumers are willing and able to purchase at that given price. It is a graphic representation of a demand schedule. The _____ for all consumers together follows from the _____ of every individual consumer: the individual demands at each price are added together.
    a. Wage curve
    c. Cost curve
    b. Kuznets curve
    d. Demand curve

10. A _____ product is a product designed for cheapness and short-term convenience rather than medium to long-term durability, with most products only intended for single use. The term is also sometimes used for products that may last several months (ex. _____ air filters) to distinguish from similar products that last indefinitely (ex.
    a. 130-30 fund
    c. Disposable
    b. 100-year flood
    d. 1921 recession

11. _____ is gross income minus income tax on that income.

Chapter 19. Consumer Behavior and Utility Maximization

Discretionary income is income after subtracting taxes and normal expenses (such as rent or mortgage, utilities, insurance, medical, transportation, property maintenance, child support, inflation, food and sundries, 'c.) to maintain a certain standard of living.

a. Stamp Act
b. Disposable personal income
c. Disposable income
d. Taxation as theft

12. A variety of measures of _____ and output are used in economics to estimate total economic activity in a country or region, including gross domestic product (GDP), gross national product (GNP), and net _____.

There are three main ways of calculating these numbers; the output approach, the income approach and the expenditure approach. In theory, the three must yield the same, because total expenditures on goods and services must equal the total income paid to the producers (Gnational income), and that must also equal the total value of the output of goods and services (GNP.)

a. GNI per capita
b. Gross world product
c. Volume index
d. National income

13. _____ in economics and business is the result of an exchange and from that trade we assign a numerical monetary value to a good, service or asset. If Alice trades Bob 4 apples for an orange, the _____ of an orange is 4 apples. Inversely, the _____ of an apple is 1/4 oranges.

a. Premium pricing
b. Price war
c. Price book
d. Price

14. _____ is defined as the measure of responsiveness in the quantity demanded for a commodity as a result of change in price of the same commodity. It is a measure of how consumers react to a change in price. In other words, it is percentage change in quantity demanded as per the percentage change in price of the same commodity.

a. 130-30 fund
b. 100-year flood
c. 1921 recession
d. Price elasticity of demand

15. In economics, the _____ is defined as a numerical measure of the responsiveness of the quantity supplied of product (A) to a change in price of product (A) alone. It is the measure of the way quantity supplied reacts to a change in price.

For example, if, in response to a 10% rise in the price of a good, the quantity supplied increases by 20%, the _____ would be 20%/10% = 2.

a. Hedonimetry
b. Passive income
c. Demand shaping
d. Price elasticity of supply

16. In economics and business, specifically cost accounting, the _____ point (BEP) is the point at which cost or expenses and revenue are equal: there is no net loss or gain, and one has 'broken even'. A profit or a loss has not been made, although opportunity costs have been paid, and capital has received the risk-adjusted, expected return.

Chapter 19. Consumer Behavior and Utility Maximization

For example, if the business sells less than 200 tables each month, it will make a loss, if it sells more, it will be a profit.

a. Break-even
b. Nonmarket
c. Buffer stock scheme
d. Small numbers game

17. A _____ represents the combinations of goods and services that a consumer can purchase given current prices and his income. Consumer theory uses the concepts of a _____ and a preference map to analyze consumer choices. Both concepts have a ready graphical representation in the two-good case.

a. Joint demand
b. Revealed preference
c. Quality bias
d. Budget constraint

18. _____ is the study of when, why, how, where and what people do or do not buy products. It blends elements from psychology, sociology, social psychology, anthropology and economics. It attempts to understand the buyer decision making process, both individually and in groups.

a. Situational theory of publics
b. Consumption smoothing
c. Shopping Neutral
d. Consumer behavior

19. In economics, _____ is the ratio of the percent change in one variable to the percent change in another variable. It is a tool for measuring the responsiveness of a function to changes in parameters in a relative way. Commonly analyzed are _____ of substitution, price and wealth.

a. ACCRA Cost of Living Index
b. ACEA agreement
c. Elasticity of demand
d. Elasticity

20. Price _____ is defined as the measure of responsiveness in the quantity demanded for a commodity as a result of change in price of the same commodity. It is a measure of how consumers react to a change in price. In other words, it is percentage change in quantity demanded by the percentage change in price of the same commodity.

a. Elasticity
b. ACCRA Cost of Living Index
c. ACEA agreement
d. Elasticity of demand

21. A _____ is:

- Rewrite _____, in generative grammar and computer science
- Standardization, a formal and widely-accepted statement, fact, definition, or qualification
- Operation, a determinate _____ for performing a mathematical operation and obtaining a certain result (Mathematics, Logic)
    - Unary operation
    - Binary operation
- _____ of inference, a function from sets of formulae to formulae (Mathematics, Logic)
- _____ of thumb, principle with broad application that is not intended to be strictly accurate or reliable for every situation. Also often simply referred to as a _____
- Moral, an atomic element of a moral code for guiding choices in human behavior
- Heuristic, a quantized '_____' which shows a tendency or probability for successful function
- A regulation, as in sports
- A Production _____, as in computer science
- Procedural law, a _____ set governing the application of laws to cases
    - A law, which may informally be called a '_____'
    - A court ruling, a decision by a court
- In the U.S. Government, a regulation mandated by Congress, but written or expanded upon by the Executive Branch.
- Norm (sociology), an informal but widely accepted _____, concept, truth, definition, or qualification (social norms, legal norms, coding norms)
- Norm (philosophy), a kind of sentence or a reason to act, feel or believe
- 'Rulership' is the concept of governance by a government:
    - Military _____, governance by a military body
    - Monastic _____, a collection of precepts that guides the life of monks or nuns in a religious order where the superior holds the place of Christ
- Slide _____

- '_____,' a song by Ayumi Hamasaki
- '_____,' a song by rapper Nas
- '_____s,' an album by the band The Whitest Boy Alive
- _____s: Pyaar Ka Superhit Formula, a 2003 Bollywood film
- ruler, an instrument for measuring lengths
- _____, a component of an astrolabe, circumferator or similar instrument
- The _____s, a bestselling self-help book
- _____ Project (Run Up-to-date Linux Everywhere), a project that aims to use up-to-date Linux software on old PCs
- _____ engine, a software system that helps managing business _____s
- Ja _____, a hip hop artist
    - R.U.L.E., a 2005 greatest hits album by rapper Ja _____
- '_____s,' a KMFDM song

a. Technocracy
c. Rule

b. Procter ' Gamble
d. Demand

Chapter 19. Consumer Behavior and Utility Maximization

22. The _____ is published by The Economist as an informal way of measuring the purchasing power parity (PPP) between two currencies and provides a test of the extent to which market exchange rates result in goods costing the same in different countries. It 'seeks to make exchange-rate theory a bit more digestible'.

The index takes its name from the Big Mac, a hamburger sold at McDonald's restaurants.

a. Rank mobility index
c. Cost-weighted activity index
b. Big Mac index
d. Deindexation

23. In consumer theory, an _____ is a good that decreases in demand when consumer income rises, unlike normal goods, for which the opposite is observed. It is a good that consumers demand increases when their income increases. Inferiority, in this sense, is an observable fact relating to affordability rather than a statement about the quality of the good.

a. Export-oriented
c. Information good
b. Inferior good
d. Independent goods

24. In algebra, a _____ is a function depending on n that associates a scalar, det(A), to an n×n square matrix A. The fundamental geometric meaning of a _____ is a scale factor for measure when A is regarded as a linear transformation. _____s are important both in calculus, where they enter the substitution rule for several variables, and in multilinear algebra.

For a fixed nonnegative integer n, there is a unique _____ function for the n×n matrices over any commutative ring R. In particular, this function exists when R is the field of real or complex numbers.

a. Determinant
c. 1921 recession
b. 100-year flood
d. 130-30 fund

25. In economics, the _____ is the change in consumption resulting from a change in real income.

Another important item that can change is the money income of the consumer. The _____ is the phenomenon observed through changes in purchasing power.

a. Equilibrium wage
c. Inflation hedge
b. Income effect
d. Export subsidy

26. _____ was a survey conducted by the U.S. Department of Justice to gauge the prevalence of alcohol and illegal drug use among prior arrestees. It was a reformulation of the prior Drug Use Forecasting (DUF) program, focused on five drugs in particular: cocaine, marijuana, methamphetamine, opiates, and PCP.

Participants were randomly selected from arrest records in major metropolitan areas; because no personally identifying information is taken from each record chosen, the resulting data can be correlated to arrest rates, but not to the total population of persons charged.

a. AD-IA Model
c. Arrestee Drug Abuse Monitoring
b. ACCRA Cost of Living Index
d. ACEA agreement

Chapter 19. Consumer Behavior and Utility Maximization

27. _____ was a Scottish moral philosopher and a pioneer of political economy. One of the key figures of the Scottish Enlightenment, Smith is the author of The Theory of Moral Sentiments and An Inquiry into the Nature and Causes of the Wealth of Nations. The latter, usually abbreviated as The Wealth of Nations, is considered his magnum opus and the first modern work of economics.
   a. Adolf Hitler
   b. Adolph Fischer
   c. Alan Greenspan
   d. Adam Smith

28. _____ is an economic model based on price, utility and quantity in a market. It predicts that in a competitive market, price will function to equalize the quantity demanded by consumers, and the quantity supplied by producers, resulting in an economic equilibrium of price and quantity. The model incorporates other factors changing equilibrium as a shift of demand and/or supply.
   a. Supply and demand
   b. Rational addiction
   c. Joint demand
   d. Deferred gratification

29. In finance, a _____ is a debt security, in which the authorized issuer owes the holders a debt and, depending on the terms of the _____, is obliged to pay interest (the coupon) and/or to repay the principal at a later date, termed maturity. A _____ is a formal contract to repay borrowed money with interest at fixed intervals.

   Thus a _____ is like a loan: the issuer is the borrower (debtor), the holder is the lender (creditor), and the coupon is the interest.

   a. Zero-coupon
   b. Callable
   c. Bond
   d. Prize Bond

30. The _____ is the apparent contradiction that although water is on the whole more useful, in terms of survival, than diamonds, diamonds command a higher price in the market. The economist Adam Smith is often considered to be the classic presenter of this paradox. Nicolaus Copernicus, John Locke, John Law and others had previously tried to explain the disparity.
   a. 100-year flood
   b. 130-30 fund
   c. St. Petersburg paradox
   d. Paradox of value

31. In microeconomics, _____ is quite simply the conversion of inputs into outputs. It is an economic process that uses resources to create a good or service that is suitable for exchange. This can include manufacturing, storing, shipping, and packaging.
   a. Production
   b. Solved
   c. Red Guards
   d. MET

32. _____ refers to a business or organization attempting to acquire goods or services to accomplish the goals of the enterprise. Though there are several organizations that attempt to set standards in the _____ process, processes can vary greatly between organizations. Typically the word '_____' is not used interchangeably with the word 'procurement', since procurement typically includes Expediting, Supplier Quality, and Traffic and Logistics (T'L) in addition to _____.
   a. 130-30 fund
   b. 100-year flood
   c. Free port
   d. Purchasing

33. _____ is the a method of technical and economic research of the systems for purpose to optimize a parity between system's consumer functions or properties and expenses to achieve those functions or properties.

Chapter 19. Consumer Behavior and Utility Maximization

This methodology for continuous perfection of production, industrial technologies, organizational structures was developed by Juryj Sobolev in 1948 at the 'Perm telephone factory'

- 1948 Juryj Sobolev - the first success in application of a method analysis at the 'Perm telephone factory' .
- 1949 - the first application for the invention as result of use of the new method.

Today in economically developed countries practically each enterprise or the company use methodology of the kind of functional-cost analysis as a practice of the quality management, most full satisfying to principles of standards of series ISO 9000.

- Interest of consumer not in products itself, but the advantage which it will receive from its usage.
- The consumer aspires to reduce his expenses
- Functions needed by consumer can be executed in the various ways, and, hence, with various efficiency and expenses. Among possible alternatives of realization of functions exist such in which the parity of quality and the price is the optimal for the consumer.

The goal of _____ is achievement of the highest consumer satisfaction of production at simultaneous decrease in all kinds of industrial expenses Classical _____ has three English synonyms - Value Engineering, Value Management, Value Analysis.

a. Staple financing
c. Willingness to pay
b. Monopoly wage
d. Function cost analysis

34. In microeconomic theory, an _____ is a graph showing different bundles of goods, each measured as to quantity, between which a consumer is indifferent. That is, at each point on the curve, the consumer has no preference for one bundle over another. In other words, they are all equally preferred.
a. Expenditure minimization problem
c. Engel curve
b. Indifference map
d. Indifference curve

35. In economics, the _____ is the rate at which a consumer is ready to give up one good in exchange for another good while maintaining the same level of satisfaction.

Under the standard assumption of neoclassical economics that goods and services are continuously divisible, the marginal rates of substitution will be the same regardless of the direction of exchange, and will correspond to the slope of an indifference curve (more precisely, to the slope multiplied by -1) passing through the consumption bundle in question, at that point: mathematically, it is the implicit derivative. MRS of Y for X is the amount of Y for which a consumer is willing to exchange for X locally.

a. Marginal rate of substitution
c. Quality bias
b. Demand vacuum
d. Supply and demand

Chapter 19. Consumer Behavior and Utility Maximization

36. The term _____ refers to government debt, expenditures and revenues, or to finance (particularly financial revenue) in general.

- _____ deficit is the budget deficit of federal or local government
- _____ policy is the discretionary spending of governments. Contrasts with monetary policy.
- _____ year and _____ quarter are reporting periods for firms and other agencies.

a. Bucket shop
c. Procter ' Gamble

b. Drawdown
d. Fiscal

37. In economics, _____ is the use of government spending and revenue collection to influence the economy.

_____ can be contrasted with the other main type of economic policy, monetary policy, which attempts to stabilize the economy by controlling interest rates and the supply of money. The two main instruments of _____ are government spending and taxation.

a. Sustainable investment rule
c. 100-year flood

b. Fiscalism
d. Fiscal policy

38. In microeconomic theory a preference map or _____ is the collection of indifference curves possessed by an individual. Similar in nature to a topographical map, the contour lines of such a map demonstrating progressively more desirable options as they move upward or to the right. Because of the nature of indifference curves they cannot intersect and are effectively infinite in number, their sum defining all possible combinations of values.

a. Indifference map
c. Expenditure minimization problem

b. Elasticity of substitution
d. Engel curve

39. In economics, the _____ is an economic law that states that consumers buy more of a good when its price decreases and less when its price increases.

There are certain goods which do not follow this law. These include Veblen and Giffen goods

a. Financial crisis
c. Georgism

b. Market failure
d. Law of demand

Chapter 20. The Costs of Production

1. The _____ consists of a number of economic theories which describe the nature of the firm, company including its existence, its behaviour, and its relationship with the market.

In simplified terms, the _____ aims to answer these questions:

1. Existence - why do firms emerge, why are not all transactions in the economy mediated over the market?
2. Boundaries - why the boundary between firms and the market is located exactly there? Which transactions are performed internally and which are negotiated on the market?
3. Organization - why are firms structured in such specific way? What is the interplay of formal and informal relationships?

Despite looking simple, these questions are not answered by the established economic theory, which usually views firms as given, and treats them as black boxes without any internal structure.

The First World War period saw a change of emphasis in economic theory away from industry-level analysis which mainly included analysing markets to analysis at the level of the firm, as it became increasingly clear that perfect competition was no longer an adequate model of how firms behaved. Economic theory till then had focussed on trying to understand markets alone and there had been little study on understanding why firms or organisations exist.

a. Technology gap
b. Khazzoom-Brookes postulate
c. Theory of the firm
d. Policy Ineffectiveness Proposition

2. In microeconomics, _____ is quite simply the conversion of inputs into outputs. It is an economic process that uses resources to create a good or service that is suitable for exchange. This can include manufacturing, storing, shipping, and packaging.

a. MET
b. Solved
c. Red Guards
d. Production

3. _____ is the difference between price and the costs of bringing to market whatever it is that is accounted as an enterprise (whether by harvest, extraction, manufacture, or purchase) in terms of the component costs of delivered goods and/or services and any operating or other expenses.

A key difficulty in measuring profit is in defining costs. Pure economic monetary profits can be zero or negative even in competitive equilibrium when accounted monetized costs exceed monetized price.

a. Operating profit
b. Economic profit
c. ACCRA Cost of Living Index
d. Accounting profit

4. _____s is the social science that studies the production, distribution, and consumption of goods and services. The term _____s comes from the Ancient Greek οá¼°κονομῐα from οá¼¶κος (oikos, 'house') + vĺŒμος (nomos, 'custom' or 'law'), hence 'rules of the house(hold)'. Current _____ models developed out of the broader field of political economy in the late 19th century, owing to a desire to use an empirical approach more akin to the physical sciences.

a. Energy economics
b. Opportunity cost
c. Inflation
d. Economic

5. The _____ of a decision depends on both the cost of the alternative chosen and the benefit that the best alternative would have provided if chosen. _____ differs from accounting cost because it includes opportunity cost.
   a. Isocost
   b. Inventory analysis
   c. Economic cost
   d. Epstein-Zin preferences

6. In economics, _____ is the difference between a company's total revenue and its opportunity costs. It is the increase in wealth that an investor has from making an investment, taking into consideration all costs associated with that investment including the opportunity cost of capital.

Profit is the factor income of the entrepreneur.

   a. Accounting profit
   b. ACCRA Cost of Living Index
   c. Operating profit
   d. Economic profit

7. An _____ is an easy accounted cost, such as wage, rent and materials. It can be transacted in the form of money payment and is lost directly, as opposed to monetary implicit costs.
   a. Average fixed cost
   b. Average variable cost
   c. Inventory valuation
   d. Explicit cost

8. In economics, an _____ occurs when one foregoes an alternative action but does not make an actual payment. (For instance, the explicit cost of a night at the movies includes the moviegoer's ticket and soda, but the _____ includes the pay he would have earned if he had chosen to work instead.) _____s are related to forgone benefits of any single transaction.
   a. Overnight trade
   b. External sector
   c. Ostrich strategy
   d. Implicit cost

9. _____ is a component of the firm's opportunity costs. The time that the owner spends running the firm could be spent on running another firm. This is _____: the return the entrepreneur can expect to earn or the profit that the business owners considers necessary to make running the business worth his/her while.
   a. Normal profit
   b. Profit maximization
   c. Profit margin
   d. 100-year flood

10. _____ or economic opportunity loss is the value of the next best alternative foregone as the result of making a decision. _____ analysis is an important part of a company's decision-making processes but is not treated as an actual cost in any financial statement. The next best thing that a person can engage in is referred to as the _____ of doing the best thing and ignoring the next best thing to be done.
    a. Opportunity cost
    b. Industrial organization
    c. Economic
    d. Economic ideology

11. _____ is the difference between efficient behavior of firms assumed or implied by economic theory and their observed behavior in practice.

Chapter 20. The Costs of Production

Economic theory assumes that the management of firms act to maximize owners' wealth by minimizing risk and maximizing economic profits -- which is accomplished by simultaneously maximizing revenues and minimizing costs, usually through the adjustment of output. In perfect competition, the free entry and exit of firms tends toward firms producing at the point where price equals long run average costs and long run average costs are minimized.

a. Revelation principle
b. X-efficiency
c. 100-year flood
d. X-inefficiency

12.

A _____ is a type of financial intermediary and a type of bank. Commercial banking is also known as business banking. It is a bank that provides checking accounts, savings accounts, and money market accounts and that accepts time deposits.

a. Lombard banking
b. Bought deal
c. Daylight overdraft
d. Commercial bank

13. In economic models, the _____ time frame assumes no fixed factors of production. Firms can enter or leave the marketplace, and the cost (and availability) of land, labor, raw materials, and capital goods can be assumed to vary. In contrast, in the short-run time frame, certain factors are assumed to be fixed, because there is not sufficient time for them to change.

a. Productivity world
b. Long-run
c. Price/performance ratio
d. Diseconomies of scale

14. In economics, the concept of the _____ refers to the decision-making time frame of a firm in which at least one factor of production is fixed. Costs which are fixed in the _____ have no impact on a firms decisions. For example a firm can raise output by increasing the amount of labour through overtime.

a. Productivity model
b. Hicks-neutral technical change
c. Product Pipeline
d. Short-run

15. In economics, _____ refers to how the marginal contribution of a factor of production usually decreases as more of the factor is used. According to this relationship, in a production system with fixed and variable inputs, beyond some point, each additional unit of the variable input yields smaller and smaller increases in output. Conversely, producing one more unit of output costs more and more in variable inputs.

a. Patent troll
b. Community property
c. Derivatives law
d. Diminishing returns

16. In economics, the _____ or marginal physical product is the extra output produced by one more unit of an input (for instance, the difference in output when a firm's labour is increased from five to six units.) Assuming that no other inputs to production change, the _____ of a given input (X) can be expressed as:

Chapter 20. The Costs of Production

_____ = ΔY/ΔX = (the change of Y)/(the change of X.)

-
  - ○
    - Pending approval by Thomas Sowell***

In neoclassical economics, this is the mathematical derivative of the production function.... Note that the 'product' (Y) is typically defined ignoring external costs and benefits.

a. Labor problem
c. Factor prices
b. Productive capacity
d. Marginal product

17. The _____ of a variable factor of Production identifies what outputs are possible using various levels of the variable input. This can be displayed in either a chart that lists the output level corresponding to various levels of input, or a graph that summarizes the data into a '_____ curve'. The diagram shows a typical _____ curve. In this example, output increases as more inputs are employed up until point A. The maximum output possible with this Production process is Qm. (If there are other inputs used in the process, they are assumed to be fixed).

a. Tightness
c. Convexity
b. Total product
d. Consequence

18. _____ is an economics term to describe a firms variable costs (labor, electricity, etc.) divided by the quantity (Q) of total units of output.

$$AVC = \frac{TVC}{Q}$$

Where:

- TVC = Total Variable Cost
- _____ = Average variable cost
- Q = Quantity of Units Produced

_____ plus average fixed cost equals average total cost:

_____ + AFC = ATC.

a. Explicit cost
c. Average variable cost
b. Inventory valuation
d. Average fixed cost

19. _____s are expenses that change in proportion to the activity of a business. In other words, _____ is the sum of marginal costs. It can also be considered normal costs.

Chapter 20. The Costs of Production

a. Quality costs
c. Cost-Volume-Profit Analysis
b. Cost allocation
d. Variable cost

20. In economics, _____ are business expenses that are not dependent on the activities of the business They tend to be time-related, such as salaries or rents being paid per month. This is in contrast to variable costs, which are volume-related (and are paid per quantity.)

In management accounting, _____ are defined as expenses that do not change in proportion to the activity of a business, within the relevant period or scale of production.

a. Fixed costs
c. Cost-Volume-Profit Analysis
b. Cost of poor quality
d. Quality costs

21. In economics, _____ is equal to total cost divided by the number of goods produced (the output quantity, Q.) It is also equal to the sum of average variable costs (total variable costs divided by Q) plus average fixed costs (total fixed costs divided by Q.) _____s may be dependent on the time period considered (increasing production may be expensive or impossible in the short term, for example.)

a. Average cost
c. Average variable cost
b. Average fixed cost
d. Explicit cost

22. _____ is an economics term used to describe the total fixed costs (TFC) divided by the quantity (Q) of units produced.

$$AFC = \frac{TFC}{Q}$$

_____ is a per-unit measure of fixed costs. As the total number of goods produced increases, the _____ decreases because the same amount of fixed costs are being spread over a larger number of units.

a. Inventory valuation
c. Average variable cost
b. Explicit cost
d. Average fixed cost

23. In economics, and cost accounting, _____ describes the total economic cost of production and is made up of variable costs, which vary according to the quantity of a good produced and include inputs such as labor and raw materials, plus fixed costs, which are independent of the quantity of a good produced and include inputs (capital) that cannot be varied in the short term, such as buildings and machinery. _____ in economics includes the total opportunity cost of each factor of production in addition to fixed and variable costs.

The rate at which _____ changes as the amount produced changes is called marginal cost.

a. 130-30 fund
c. 100-year flood
b. Total cost
d. 1921 recession

24. In economics, a _____ is a graph of the costs of production as a function of total quantity produced. In a free market economy, productively efficient firms use these curves to find the optimal point of production, where they make the most profits. There are a few different types of _____s, each relevant to a different area of economics.

   a. Cost curve
   b. Demand curve
   c. Phillips curve
   d. Kuznets curve

25. In economics and finance, _____ is the change in total cost that arises when the quantity produced changes by one unit. It is the cost of producing one more unit of a good. Mathematically, the _____ function is expressed as the first derivative of the total cost (TC) function with respect to quantity (Q.)

   a. Quality costs
   b. Variable cost
   c. Khozraschyot
   d. Marginal cost

26. _____ is subcontracting a process, such as product design or manufacturing, to a third-party company. The decision to outsource is often made in the interest of lowering cost or making better use of time and energy costs, redirecting or conserving energy directed at the competencies of a particular business, or to make more efficient use of land, labor, capital, (information) technology and resources. _____ became part of the business lexicon during the 1980s.

   a. Averch-Johnson effect
   b. Additional Funds Needed
   c. Electronic business
   d. Outsourcing

27. In business, _____, Overhead cost or _____ expense refers to an ongoing expense of operating a business. The term _____ is usually used to group expenses that are necessary to the continued functioning of the business, but do not directly generate profits.

   _____ expenses are all costs on the income statement except for direct labor and direct materials.

   a. ACCRA Cost of Living Index
   b. ACEA agreement
   c. Overhead
   d. AD-IA Model

28. A _____ is:

- Rewrite _____, in generative grammar and computer science
- Standardization, a formal and widely-accepted statement, fact, definition, or qualification
- Operation, a determinate _____ for performing a mathematical operation and obtaining a certain result (Mathematics, Logic)
    - Unary operation
    - Binary operation
- _____ of inference, a function from sets of formulae to formulae (Mathematics, Logic)
- _____ of thumb, principle with broad application that is not intended to be strictly accurate or reliable for every situation. Also often simply referred to as a _____
- Moral, an atomic element of a moral code for guiding choices in human behavior
- Heuristic, a quantized '_____' which shows a tendency or probability for successful function
- A regulation, as in sports
- A Production _____, as in computer science
- Procedural law, a _____ set governing the application of laws to cases
    - A law, which may informally be called a '_____'
    - A court ruling, a decision by a court
- In the U.S. Government, a regulation mandated by Congress, but written or expanded upon by the Executive Branch.
- Norm (sociology), an informal but widely accepted _____, concept, truth, definition, or qualification (social norms, legal norms, coding norms)
- Norm (philosophy), a kind of sentence or a reason to act, feel or believe
- 'Rulership' is the concept of governance by a government:
    - Military _____, governance by a military body
    - Monastic _____, a collection of precepts that guides the life of monks or nuns in a religious order where the superior holds the place of Christ
- Slide _____

- '_____,' a song by Ayumi Hamasaki
- '_____,' a song by rapper Nas
- '_____s,' an album by the band The Whitest Boy Alive
- _____s: Pyaar Ka Superhit Formula, a 2003 Bollywood film
- ruler, an instrument for measuring lengths
- _____, a component of an astrolabe, circumferator or similar instrument
- The _____s, a bestselling self-help book
- _____ Project (Run Up-to-date Linux Everywhere), a project that aims to use up-to-date Linux software on old PCs
- _____ engine, a software system that helps managing business _____s
- Ja _____, a hip hop artist
    - R.U.L.E., a 2005 greatest hits album by rapper Ja _____
- '_____s,' a KMFDM song

a. Demand
b. Technocracy
c. Procter ' Gamble
d. Rule

29. In production, returns to scale refers to changes in output subsequent to a proportional change in all inputs (where all inputs increase by a constant factor.) If output increases by that same proportional change then there are _____ If output increases by less than that proportional change, there are decreasing returns to scale (DRS.)
   a. Long term
   b. Consumer sovereignty
   c. Constant returns to scale
   d. Lexicographic preferences

30. _____ are the forces that cause larger firms to produce goods and services at increased per-unit costs. They are less well known than what economists have long understood as 'economies of scale', the forces which enable larger firms to produce goods and services at reduced per-unit costs.

Some of the forces which cause a diseconomy of scale are listed below:

Ideally, all employees of a firm would have one-on-one communication with each other so they know exactly what the other workers are doing.

   a. Diseconomies of scale
   b. Factors of production
   c. Productive capacity
   d. Marginal physical product

31. _____, in microeconomics, are the cost advantages that a business obtains due to expansion. They are factors that cause a producere;s average cost per unit to fall as scale is increased. _____ is a long run concept and refers to reductions in unit cost as the size of a facility, or scale, increases.
   a. Economic production quantity
   b. Isoquant
   c. Economies of scale
   d. Underinvestment employment relationship

32. _____ in economics refers to metrics and measures of output from production processes, per unit of input. Labor _____, for example, is typically measured as a ratio of output per labor-hour, an input. _____ may be conceived of as a metrics of the technical or engineering efficiency of production.
   a. Fordism
   b. Production-possibility frontier
   c. Piece work
   d. Productivity

33. In economics, _____ and economies of scale are related terms that describe what happens as the scale of production increases. They are different terms and should not be used interchangeably.

_____ refers to a technical property of production that examines changes in output subsequent to a proportional change in all inputs (where all inputs increase by a constant factor.)

   a. Constant returns to scale
   b. Necessity good
   c. Customer equity
   d. Returns to scale

34. Network externalities resemble economies of scale, but they are not considered such because they are a function of the number of users of a good or service in an industry, not of the production efficiency within a business. _____ are only considered examples of network externalities if they are driven by demand side economies.

Chapter 20. The Costs of Production

Formally, a production function $F(K, L)$ is defined to have:

- constant returns to scale if (for any constant a greater than or equal to 0) $F(aK, aL) = aF(K, L)$
- increasing returns to scale if (for any constant a greater than 1) $F(aK, aL) > aF(K, L)$,
- decreasing returns to scale if (for any constant a greater than 1) $F(aK, aL) < aF(K, L)$

where K and L are factors of production, capital and labour, respectively.

As an example, the Cobb-Douglas functional form has constant returns to scale when the sum of the exponents adds up to one.

a. ACEA agreement
c. ACCRA Cost of Living Index
b. AD-IA Model
d. Economies of scale external to the firm

35. _____ is the increase in the amount of the goods and services produced by an economy over time. It is conventionally measured as the percent rate of increase in real gross domestic product, or real GDP. Growth is usually calculated in real terms, i.e. inflation-adjusted terms, in order to net out the effect of inflation on the price of the goods and services produced.

a. ACEA agreement
c. AD-IA Model
b. Economic growth
d. ACCRA Cost of Living Index

36. In economics, a _____ exists when a specific individual or enterprise has sufficient control over a particular product or service to determine significantly the terms on which other individuals shall have access to it. Monopolies are thus characterized by a lack of economic competition for the good or service that they provide and a lack of viable substitute goods. The verb 'monopolize' refers to the process by which a firm gains persistently greater market share than what is expected under perfect competition.

a. 100-year flood
c. 130-30 fund
b. Monopoly
d. 1921 recession

37. In economics, a _____ occurs when, due to the economies of scale of a particular industry, the maximum efficiency of production and distribution is realized through a single supplier.

Natural monopolies arise where the largest supplier in an industry, often the first supplier in a market, has an overwhelming cost advantage over other actual or potential competitors. This tends to be the case in industries where capital costs predominate, creating economies of scale which are large in relation to the size of the market, and hence high barriers to entry; examples include water services and electricity.

a. Collective goods
c. Privatizing profits and socializing losses
b. Common-pool resource
d. Natural monopoly

Chapter 20. The Costs of Production

38. _____, in law and economics, is a form of risk management primarily used to hedge against the risk of a contingent loss. _____ is defined as the equitable transfer of the risk of a loss, from one entity to another, in exchange for a premium, and can be thought of as a guaranteed small loss to prevent a large, possibly devastating loss. An insurer is a company selling the _____; an insured or policyholder is the person or entity buying the _____.

   a. AD-IA Model
   b. Insurance
   c. ACCRA Cost of Living Index
   d. ACEA agreement

39. The phrase _____, according to the Organization for Economic Co-operation and Development, refers to 'creative work undertaken on a systematic basis in order to increase the stock of knowledge, including knowledge of man, culture and society, and the use of this stock of knowledge to devise new applications [sic]'

New product design and development is more than often a crucial factor in the survival of a company. In an industry that is fast changing, firms must continually revise their design and range of products. This is necessary due to continuous technology change and development as well as other competitors and the changing preference of customers.

   a. 130-30 fund
   b. 1921 recession
   c. 100-year flood
   d. Research and development

40. In economics and business decision-making, _____ are costs that cannot be recovered once they have been incurred. _____ are sometimes contrasted with variable costs, which are the costs that will change due to the proposed course of action, and prospective costs which are costs that will be incurred if an action is taken.

In traditional microeconomic theory, only variable costs are relevant to a decision.

   a. Post-purchase rationalization
   b. Hyperbolic discounting
   c. Halo effect
   d. Sunk costs

Chapter 21. Pure Competition

1. In economic theory, _____ is the competitive situation in any market where the conditions necessary for perfect competition are not satisfied. It is a market structure that does not meet the conditions of perfect competition.

Forms of _____ include:

- Monopoly, in which there is only one seller of a good.
- Oligopoly, in which there is a small number of sellers.
- Monopolistic competition, in which there are many sellers producing highly differentiated goods.
- Monopsony, in which there is only one buyer of a good.
- Oligopsony, in which there is a small number of buyers.

There may also be _____ in markets due to buyers or sellers lacking information about prices and the goods being traded.

There may also be _____ due to a time lag in a market.

a. AD-IA Model
b. ACEA agreement
c. ACCRA Cost of Living Index
d. Imperfect competition

2. In economics, _____ describes the state of a market with respect to competition.

- Perfect competition, in which the market consists of a very large number of firms producing a homogeneous product.
- Monopolistic competition where there are a large number of independent firms which have a very small proportion of the market share.
- Oligopoly, in which a market is dominated by a small number of firms which own more than 40% of the market share.
- Oligopsony, a market dominated by many sellers and a few buyers.
- Monopoly, where there is only one provider of a product or service.
- Natural monopoly, a monopoly in which economies of scale cause efficiency to increase continuously with the size of the firm. A firm is a natural monopoly if it is able to serve the entire market demand at a lower cost than any combination of two or more smaller, more specialized firms.
- Monopsony, when there is only one buyer in a market.

The imperfectly competitive structure is quite identical to the realistic market conditions where some monopolistic competitors, monopolists, oligopolists, and duopolists exist and dominate the market conditions. The elements of _____ include the number and size distribution of firms, entry conditions, and the extent of differentiation.

These somewhat abstract concerns tend to determine some but not all details of a specific concrete market system where buyers and sellers actually meet and commit to trade.

a. Monopolistic competition
b. Market structure
c. Human capital
d. Labour economics

3. _____ is a common market structure where many competing producers sell products that are differentiated from one another (ie. the products are substitutes, but are not exactly alike.) Many markets are monopolistically competitive, common examples include the markets for restaurants, cereal, clothing, shoes and service industries in large cities.

a. Financial crisis
b. Mathematical economics
c. Monopolistic competition
d. Perfect competition

4. In economics, a _____ occurs when, due to the economies of scale of a particular industry, the maximum efficiency of production and distribution is realized through a single supplier.

Natural monopolies arise where the largest supplier in an industry, often the first supplier in a market, has an overwhelming cost advantage over other actual or potential competitors. This tends to be the case in industries where capital costs predominate, creating economies of scale which are large in relation to the size of the market, and hence high barriers to entry; examples include water services and electricity.

a. Privatizing profits and socializing losses
b. Natural monopoly
c. Common-pool resource
d. Collective goods

5. An _____ is a market form in which a market or industry is dominated by a small number of sellers (oligopolists.) Because there are few participants in this type of market, each oligopolist is aware of the actions of the others. The decisions of one firm influence, and are influenced by, the decisions of other firms.

a. Oligopoly
b. ACCRA Cost of Living Index
c. Oligopsony
d. ACEA agreement

6. In marketing, _____ is the process of distinguishing the differences of a product or offering from others, to make it more attractive to a particular target market. This involves differentiating it from competitors' products as well as one's own product offerings.

Differentiation is a source of competitive advantage.

a. Pricing science
b. Market segment
c. Product differentiation
d. Technology acceptance model

7. _____ is a situation in which the limited resources of a firm are allocated in accordance with the wishes of consumers. An allocatively efficient economy produces an 'optimal mix' of commodities. A firm is allocatively efficient when its price is equal to its marginal costs (that is, P = MC) in a perfect market.

a. ACCRA Cost of Living Index
b. Economic efficiency
c. ACEA agreement
d. Allocative efficiency

8. _____ has several particular meanings:

- in mathematics
    - _____ function
    - Euler _____
    - _____
    - _____ subgroup
    - method of _____ s (partial differential equations)
- in physics and engineering
    - any _____ curve that shows the relationship between certain input- and output parameters, e.g.
    - an I-V or current-voltage _____ is the current in a circuit as a function of the applied voltage
    - Receiver-Operator _____
- in fiction
    - in Dungeons ' Dragons, _____ is another name for ability score

a. Characteristic
b. Technocracy
c. Russian financial crisis
d. Demand

9. _____ are the forces that cause larger firms to produce goods and services at increased per-unit costs. They are less well known than what economists have long understood as 'economies of scale', the forces which enable larger firms to produce goods and services at reduced per-unit costs.

Some of the forces which cause a diseconomy of scale are listed below:

Ideally, all employees of a firm would have one-on-one communication with each other so they know exactly what the other workers are doing.

a. Factors of production
b. Marginal physical product
c. Productive capacity
d. Diseconomies of scale

10. In economics, a _____ exists when a specific individual or enterprise has sufficient control over a particular product or service to determine significantly the terms on which other individuals shall have access to it. Monopolies are thus characterized by a lack of economic competition for the good or service that they provide and a lack of viable substitute goods. The verb 'monopolize' refers to the process by which a firm gains persistently greater market share than what is expected under perfect competition.

a. 1921 recession
b. 100-year flood
c. 130-30 fund
d. Monopoly

298 Chapter 21. Pure Competition

11. A _____ is:

- Rewrite _____, in generative grammar and computer science
- Standardization, a formal and widely-accepted statement, fact, definition, or qualification
- Operation, a determinate _____ for performing a mathematical operation and obtaining a certain result (Mathematics, Logic)
    - Unary operation
    - Binary operation
- _____ of inference, a function from sets of formulae to formulae (Mathematics, Logic)
- _____ of thumb, principle with broad application that is not intended to be strictly accurate or reliable for every situation. Also often simply referred to as a _____
- Moral, an atomic element of a moral code for guiding choices in human behavior
- Heuristic, a quantized '_____' which shows a tendency or probability for successful function
- A regulation, as in sports
- A Production _____, as in computer science
- Procedural law, a _____ set governing the application of laws to cases
    - A law, which may informally be called a '_____'
    - A court ruling, a decision by a court
- In the U.S. Government, a regulation mandated by Congress, but written or expanded upon by the Executive Branch.
- Norm (sociology), an informal but widely accepted _____, concept, truth, definition, or qualification (social norms, legal norms, coding norms)
- Norm (philosophy), a kind of sentence or a reason to act, feel or believe
- 'Rulership' is the concept of governance by a government:
    - Military _____, governance by a military body
    - Monastic _____, a collection of precepts that guides the life of monks or nuns in a religious order where the superior holds the place of Christ
- Slide _____

- '_____,' a song by Ayumi Hamasaki
- '_____,' a song by rapper Nas
- '_____s,' an album by the band The Whitest Boy Alive
- _____s: Pyaar Ka Superhit Formula, a 2003 Bollywood film
- ruler, an instrument for measuring lengths
- _____, a component of an astrolabe, circumferator or similar instrument
- The _____s, a bestselling self-help book
- _____ Project (Run Up-to-date Linux Everywhere), a project that aims to use up-to-date Linux software on old PCs
- _____ engine, a software system that helps managing business _____s
- Ja _____, a hip hop artist
    - R.U.L.E., a 2005 greatest hits album by rapper Ja _____
- '_____s,' a KMFDM song

a. Procter ' Gamble
c. Rule

b. Technocracy
d. Demand

Chapter 21. Pure Competition

12. In economics and especially in the theory of competition, _____ are obstacles in the path of a firm that make it difficult to enter a given market.

_____ are the source of a firm's pricing power - the ability of a firm to raise prices without losing all its customers.

The term refers to hindrances that an individual may face while trying to gain entrance into a profession or trade.

a. Group boycott
b. Limit price
c. Social dumping
d. Barriers to entry

13. Economics:

- _____, the desire to own something and the ability to pay for it
- _____ curve, a graphic representation of a _____ schedule
- _____ deposit, the money in checking accounts
- _____ pull theory, the theory that inflation occurs when _____ for goods and services exceeds existing supplies
- _____ schedule, a table that lists the quantity of a good a person will buy it each different price
- _____ side economics, the school of economics at believes government spending and tax cuts open economy by raising _____

a. McKesson ' Robbins scandal
b. Variability
c. Production
d. Demand

14. In economics, a _____ is a table that lists the quantity of a good a person will buy it each different price See Demand curve.

a. Free contract
b. Rational irrationality
c. Federal Reserve districts
d. Demand schedule

15. _____ is a term used by economists to describe a condition in which firms can freely enter the market for an economic good by establishing production and beginning to sell the product.

_____ is implied by the perfect competition condition that there is an unlimited number of buyers and sellers in a market. In comparison to perfect competition, however, _____ is a condition often more applicable to real world conditions.

a. 130-30 fund
b. 1921 recession
c. 100-year flood
d. Free entry

16. In microeconomics, _____ is the extra revenue that an additional unit of product will bring. It is the additional income from selling one more unit of a good; sometimes equal to price. It can also be described as the change in total revenue/change in number of units sold.

a. Market demand schedule
b. Marginal revenue
c. Long term
d. Reservation price

17. _____ in economics and business is the result of an exchange and from that trade we assign a numerical monetary value to a good, service or asset. If Alice trades Bob 4 apples for an orange, the _____ of an orange is 4 apples. Inversely, the _____ of an apple is 1/4 oranges.

a. Price war
b. Premium pricing
c. Price book
d. Price

18. Monopoly power is an example of market failure which occurs when one or more of the participants has the ability to influence the price or other outcomes in some general or specialized market. The most commonly discussed form of market power is that of a monopoly, but other forms such as monopsony, and more moderate versions of these two extremes, exist. Market participants that have market power are sometimes referred to as 'price makers', while those without are sometimes called '_____'.

a. Market concentration
b. Price takers
c. Monopolization
d. Market power

19. _____ is the total money received from the sale of any given quantity of output.

The _____ is calculated by taking the price of the sale times the quantity sold, i.e.

_____ = price X quantity.

a. Small numbers game
b. Market development funds
c. Ceteris paribus
d. Total revenue

20. In economics, the _____ of a good or of a service is the utility of the specific use to which an agent would put a given increase in that good or service, or of the specific use that would be abandoned in response to a given decrease. In other words, _____ is the utility of the marginal use -- which, on the assumption of economic rationality, would be the least urgent use of the good or service, from the best feasible combination of actions in which its use is included. Under the mainstream assumptions, the _____ of a good or service is the posited quantified change in utility obtained by increasing or by decreasing use of that good or service.

a. 130-30 fund
b. Marginal utility
c. 1921 recession
d. 100-year flood

21. In economics, _____ is a measure of the relative satisfaction from consumption of various goods and services. Given this measure, one may speak meaningfully of increasing or decreasing _____, and thereby explain economic behavior in terms of attempts to increase one's _____. For illustrative purposes, changes in _____ are sometimes expressed in units called utils.

a. Ordinal utility
b. Expected utility hypothesis
c. Utility function
d. Utility

22. In economics, the concept of the _____ refers to the decision-making time frame of a firm in which at least one factor of production is fixed. Costs which are fixed in the _____ have no impact on a firms decisions. For example a firm can raise output by increasing the amount of labour through overtime.

Chapter 21. Pure Competition

a. Productivity model
c. Hicks-neutral technical change
b. Product Pipeline
d. Short-run

23. In economics, _____ is the process by which a firm determines the price and output level that returns the greatest profit. There are several approaches to this problem. The total revenue--total cost method relies on the fact that profit equals revenue minus cost, and the marginal revenue--marginal cost method is based on the fact that total profit in a perfectly competitive market reaches its maximum point where marginal revenue equals marginal cost.

a. Profit maximization
c. 100-year flood
b. Normal profit
d. Profit margin

24. In economics and business, specifically cost accounting, the _____ point (BEP) is the point at which cost or expenses and revenue are equal: there is no net loss or gain, and one has 'broken even'. A profit or a loss has not been made, although opportunity costs have been paid, and capital has received the risk-adjusted, expected return.

For example, if the business sells less than 200 tables each month, it will make a loss, if it sells more, it will be a profit.

a. Buffer stock scheme
c. Nonmarket
b. Small numbers game
d. Break-even

25. _____ is a component of the firm's opportunity costs. The time that the owner spends running the firm could be spent on running another firm. This is _____: the return the entrepreneur can expect to earn or the profit that the business owners considers necessary to make running the business worth his/her while.

a. Normal profit
c. Profit margin
b. 100-year flood
d. Profit maximization

26. _____ is an economics term used to describe the total fixed costs (TFC) divided by the quantity (Q) of units produced.

$$AFC = \frac{TFC}{Q}$$

_____ is a per-unit measure of fixed costs. As the total number of goods produced increases, the _____ decreases because the same amount of fixed costs are being spread over a larger number of units.

a. Average variable cost
c. Explicit cost
b. Inventory valuation
d. Average fixed cost

27. _____ is an economics term to describe a firms variable costs (labor, electricity, etc.) divided by the quantity (Q) of total units of output.

$$AVC = \frac{TVC}{Q}$$

Where:

- TVC = Total Variable Cost
- _____ = Average variable cost
- Q = Quantity of Units Produced

_____ plus average fixed cost equals average total cost:

    _____ + AFC = ATC.

a. Inventory valuation
c. Explicit cost
b. Average fixed cost
d. Average variable cost

28. Competition law, known in the United States as _____ law, has three main elements:

- prohibiting agreements or practices that restrict free trading and competition between business entities. This includes in particular the repression of cartels.
- banning abusive behaviour by a firm dominating a market, or anti-competitive practices that tend to lead to such a dominant position. Practices controlled in this way may include predatory pricing, tying, price gouging, refusal to deal, and many others.
- supervising the mergers and acquisitions of large corporations, including some joint ventures. Transactions that are considered to threaten the competitive process can be prohibited altogether, or approved subject to 'remedies' such as an obligation to divest part of the merged business or to offer licences or access to facilities to enable other businesses to continue competing.

The substance and practice of competition law varies from jurisdiction to jurisdiction. Protecting the interests of consumers (consumer welfare) and ensuring that entrepreneurs have an opportunity to compete in the market economy are often treated as important objectives. Competition law is closely connected with law on deregulation of access to markets, state aids and subsidies, the privatisation of state owned assets and the establishment of independent sector regulators. In recent decades, competition law has been viewed as a way to provide better public services.

a. Anti-Inflation Act
c. Intellectual property law
b. United Kingdom competition law
d. Antitrust

29. In economics, _____ are business expenses that are not dependent on the activities of the business They tend to be time-related, such as salaries or rents being paid per month. This is in contrast to variable costs, which are volume-related (and are paid per quantity.)

In management accounting, _____ are defined as expenses that do not change in proportion to the activity of a business, within the relevant period or scale of production.

a. Cost of poor quality
c. Quality costs
b. Cost-Volume-Profit Analysis
d. Fixed costs

30. In economics, and cost accounting, _____ describes the total economic cost of production and is made up of variable costs, which vary according to the quantity of a good produced and include inputs such as labor and raw materials, plus fixed costs, which are independent of the quantity of a good produced and include inputs (capital) that cannot be varied in the short term, such as buildings and machinery. _____ in economics includes the total opportunity cost of each factor of production in addition to fixed and variable costs.

The rate at which _____ changes as the amount produced changes is called marginal cost.

a. 100-year flood
c. 1921 recession
b. 130-30 fund
d. Total cost

31. _____s are expenses that change in proportion to the activity of a business. In other words, _____ is the sum of marginal costs. It can also be considered normal costs.
a. Cost-Volume-Profit Analysis
c. Cost allocation
b. Variable cost
d. Quality costs

32. _____s is the social science that studies the production, distribution, and consumption of goods and services. The term _____s comes from the Ancient Greek oá¼°κονομΓ¯α from oá¼¶κος (oikos, 'house') + vÏŒμος (nomos, 'custom' or 'law'), hence 'rules of the house(hold)'. Current _____ models developed out of the broader field of political economy in the late 19th century, owing to a desire to use an empirical approach more akin to the physical sciences.
a. Energy economics
c. Inflation
b. Opportunity cost
d. Economic

33. In economics, _____ is the difference between a company's total revenue and its opportunity costs. It is the increase in wealth that an investor has from making an investment, taking into consideration all costs associated with that investment including the opportunity cost of capital.

Profit is the factor income of the entrepreneur.

a. Accounting profit
c. ACCRA Cost of Living Index
b. Operating profit
d. Economic profit

34. _____ is the term denoting either an entrance or changes which are inserted into a system and which activate/modify a process. It is an abstract concept, used in the modeling, system(s) design and system(s) exploitation. It is usually connected with other terms, e.g., _____ field, _____ variable, _____ parameter, _____ value, _____ signal, _____ device and _____ file.
a. ACEA agreement
c. ACCRA Cost of Living Index
b. AD-IA Model
d. Input

35. _____ and Keynesian Theory) is a macroeconomic theory based on the ideas of 20th-century British economist John Maynard Keynes. _____ argues that private sector decisions sometimes lead to inefficient macroeconomic outcomes and therefore advocates active policy responses by the public sector, including monetary policy actions by the central bank and fiscal policy actions by the government to stabilize output over the business cycle.

The theories forming the basis of _____ were first presented in The General Theory of Employment, Interest and Money, published in 1936.

a. Market failure
b. Keynesian economics
c. Rational choice theory
d. Deflation

36. In economics, _____ is the total supply of goods and services produced by a national economy during a specific time period. It is the total amount of goods and services in the economy available at all possible price levels.

a. Aggregate expenditure
b. Aggregate demand
c. Aggregation problem
d. Aggregate supply

37. In economics and finance, _____ is the change in total cost that arises when the quantity produced changes by one unit. It is the cost of producing one more unit of a good. Mathematically, the _____ function is expressed as the first derivative of the total cost (TC) function with respect to quantity (Q.)

a. Khozraschyot
b. Marginal cost
c. Variable cost
d. Quality costs

38. _____ is the difference between price and the costs of bringing to market whatever it is that is accounted as an enterprise (whether by harvest, extraction, manufacture, or purchase) in terms of the component costs of delivered goods and/or services and any operating or other expenses.

A key difficulty in measuring profit is in defining costs. Pure economic monetary profits can be zero or negative even in competitive equilibrium when accounted monetized costs exceed monetized price.

a. Economic profit
b. Operating profit
c. ACCRA Cost of Living Index
d. Accounting profit

39. In economics, _____ refers to how the marginal contribution of a factor of production usually decreases as more of the factor is used. According to this relationship, in a production system with fixed and variable inputs, beyond some point, each additional unit of the variable input yields smaller and smaller increases in output. Conversely, producing one more unit of output costs more and more in variable inputs.

a. Patent troll
b. Community property
c. Derivatives law
d. Diminishing returns

40. In economics, the _____ is defined as a numerical measure of the responsiveness of the quantity supplied of product (A) to a change in price of product (A) alone. It is the measure of the way quantity supplied reacts to a change in price.

For example, if, in response to a 10% rise in the price of a good, the quantity supplied increases by 20%, the _____ would be 20%/10% = 2.

Chapter 21. Pure Competition

a. Passive income
c. Hedonimetry
b. Demand shaping
d. Price elasticity of supply

41.

A _____ is a type of financial intermediary and a type of bank. Commercial banking is also known as business banking. It is a bank that provides checking accounts, savings accounts, and money market accounts and that accepts time deposits.

a. Lombard banking
c. Bought deal
b. Daylight overdraft
d. Commercial bank

42. _____, known in the United States as antitrust law, has three main elements:

- prohibiting agreements or practices that restrict free trading and competition between business entities. This includes in particular the repression of cartels.
- banning abusive behaviour by a firm dominating a market, or anti-competitive practices that tend to lead to such a dominant position. Practices controlled in this way may include predatory pricing, tying, price gouging, refusal to deal, and many others.
- supervising the mergers and acquisitions of large corporations, including some joint ventures. Transactions that are considered to threaten the competitive process can be prohibited altogether, or approved subject to 'remedies' such as an obligation to divest part of the merged business or to offer licences or access to facilities to enable other businesses to continue competing.

The substance and practice of _____ varies from jurisdiction to jurisdiction. Protecting the interests of consumers (consumer welfare) and ensuring that entrepreneurs have an opportunity to compete in the market economy are often treated as important objectives. _____ is closely connected with law on deregulation of access to markets, state aids and subsidies, the privatisation of state owned assets and the establishment of independent sector regulators. In recent decades, _____ has been viewed as a way to provide better public services.

a. Hostile work environment
c. Fee simple
b. Due diligence
d. Competition Law

43. In economics, _____ is the ratio of the percent change in one variable to the percent change in another variable. It is a tool for measuring the responsiveness of a function to changes in parameters in a relative way. Commonly analyzed are _____ of substitution, price and wealth.

a. Elasticity
c. ACCRA Cost of Living Index
b. ACEA agreement
d. Elasticity of demand

44. _____ is an economic concept with commonplace familiarity. It is the price that a good or service is offered at, or will fetch, in the marketplace. It is of interest mainly in the study of microeconomics.

a. Paper trading
c. Noisy market hypothesis
b. Market anomaly
d. Market price

45. A _____ arises when one infers that something is true of the whole from the fact that it is true of some part of the whole (or even of every proper part.) For example: 'This fragment of metal cannot be broken with a hammer, therefore the machine of which it is a part cannot be broken with a hammer.' This is clearly fallacious, because many machines can be broken into their constituent parts without any of those parts being breakable.

This fallacy is often confused with the fallacy of hasty generalization, in which an unwarranted inference is made from a statement about a sample to a statement about the population from which it is drawn.

   a. 130-30 fund
   c. 100-year flood
   b. 1921 recession
   d. Fallacy of composition

46. A _____ is a counterfeit agreement among industries. It is an informal organization of producers that agree to coordinate prices and production. _____s usually occur in an oligopolistic industry, where there is a small number of sellers and usually involve homogeneous products.
   a. Shill
   c. Shanzhai
   b. 100-year flood
   d. Cartel

47. _____ is the transition of a national economy from monopoly control by groups of large businesses to a free market economy. This change rarely arises naturally, and is generally the result of regulation by a governing body.

A modern example of _____ is the economic restructuring of Germany after the fall of the Third Reich in 1945.

   a. Complementary monopoly
   c. Market power
   b. Monopolization
   d. Decartelization

48. In economic models, the _____ time frame assumes no fixed factors of production. Firms can enter or leave the marketplace, and the cost (and availability) of land, labor, raw materials, and capital goods can be assumed to vary. In contrast, in the short-run time frame, certain factors are assumed to be fixed, because there is not sufficient time for them to change.
   a. Long-run
   c. Price/performance ratio
   b. Diseconomies of scale
   d. Productivity world

49. In economics, a _____ is a graph of the costs of production as a function of total quantity produced. In a free market economy, productively efficient firms use these curves to find the optimal point of production, where they make the most profits. There are a few different types of _____s, each relevant to a different area of economics.
   a. Kuznets curve
   c. Demand curve
   b. Phillips curve
   d. Cost curve

50. _____ is a broad label that refers to any individuals or households that use goods and services generated within the economy. The concept of a _____ is used in different contexts, so that the usage and significance of the term may vary.

Typically when business people and economists talk of _____s they are talking about person as _____, an aggregated commodity item with little individuality other than that expressed in the buy/not-buy decision.

a. 1921 recession
b. Consumer
c. 100-year flood
d. 130-30 fund

51. A _____ is an object whose consumption increases the utility of the consumer, for which the quantity demanded exceeds the quantity supplied at zero price. _____s are usually modeled as having diminishing marginal utility. The first individual purchase has high utility; the second has less.
  a. Composite good
  b. Pie method
  c. Good
  d. Merit good

52. The _____ or gross domestic income (GDI), a basic measure of an economy's economic performance, is the market value of all final goods and services produced within the borders of a nation in a year. _____ can be defined in three ways, all of which are conceptually identical. First, it is equal to the total expenditures for all final goods and services produced within the country in a stipulated period of time (usually a 365-day year.)
  a. Gross domestic product
  b. Market structure
  c. Countercyclical
  d. Monopolistic competition

53. The _____ or the output gap is the difference between potential GDP and actual GDP or actual output. The calculation for the output gap is Y-Y* where Y* is potential output and Y is actual output. If this calculation yields a positive number it is called an expansionary gap and indicates an economy in expansion; if the calculation yields a negative number it is called a recessionary gap and indicates an economy in recession.
  a. 1921 recession
  b. GDP gap
  c. 100-year flood
  d. 130-30 fund

54. _____ is defined as the measure of responsiveness in the quantity demanded for a commodity as a result of change in price of the same commodity. It is a measure of how consumers react to a change in price. In other words, it is percentage change in quantity demanded as per the percentage change in price of the same commodity.
  a. 130-30 fund
  b. 100-year flood
  c. 1921 recession
  d. Price elasticity of demand

55. _____ is the difference between efficient behavior of firms assumed or implied by economic theory and their observed behavior in practice.

Economic theory assumes that the management of firms act to maximize owners' wealth by minimizing risk and maximizing economic profits -- which is accomplished by simultaneously maximizing revenues and minimizing costs, usually through the adjustment of output. In perfect competition, the free entry and exit of firms tends toward firms producing at the point where price equals long run average costs and long run average costs are minimized.

  a. X-inefficiency
  b. Revelation principle
  c. X-efficiency
  d. 100-year flood

56. Price _____ is defined as the measure of responsiveness in the quantity demanded for a commodity as a result of change in price of the same commodity. It is a measure of how consumers react to a change in price. In other words, it is percentage change in quantity demanded by the percentage change in price of the same commodity.

a. Elasticity
b. ACEA agreement
c. Elasticity of demand
d. ACCRA Cost of Living Index

57. _____ occurs when the economy is operating at its production possibility frontier (PPF.) This takes place when production of one good is achieved at the lowest cost possible, given the production of the other good(s.) Equivalently, it is when the highest possible output of one good is produced, given the production level of the other good(s.)
   a. Free contract
   b. Preclusive purchasing
   c. Productive efficiency
   d. Discretionary spending

58. The term surplus is used in economics for several related quantities. The _____ is the amount that consumers benefit by being able to purchase a product for a price that is less than they would be willing to pay. The producer surplus is the amount that producers benefit by selling at a market price mechanism that is higher than they would be willing to sell for.
   a. Marginal rate of technical substitution
   b. Consumer surplus
   c. Necessity good
   d. Microeconomic reform

59. _____ or economic opportunity loss is the value of the next best alternative foregone as the result of making a decision. _____ analysis is an important part of a company's decision-making processes but is not treated as an actual cost in any financial statement. The next best thing that a person can engage in is referred to as the _____ of doing the best thing and ignoring the next best thing to be done.
   a. Economic
   b. Opportunity cost
   c. Industrial organization
   d. Economic ideology

60. The term surplus is used in economics for several related quantities. The consumer surplus is the amount that consumers benefit by being able to purchase a product for a price that is less than they would be willing to pay. The _____ is the amount that producers benefit by selling at a market price mechanism that is higher than they would be willing to sell for.
   a. Long term
   b. Schedule delay
   c. Producer surplus
   d. Returns to scale

61. In microeconomics, _____ is quite simply the conversion of inputs into outputs. It is an economic process that uses resources to create a good or service that is suitable for exchange. This can include manufacturing, storing, shipping, and packaging.
   a. Production
   b. Solved
   c. MET
   d. Red Guards

62. A _____ is a set of exclusive rights granted by a state to an inventor or his assignee for a limited period of time in exchange for a disclosure of an invention.

The procedure for granting _____s, the requirements placed on the _____ee and the extent of the exclusive rights vary widely between countries according to national laws and international agreements. Typically, however, a _____ application must include one or more claims defining the invention which must be new, inventive, and useful or industrially applicable.

   a. Bank regulation
   b. Patent
   c. Long service leave
   d. Bona fide occupational qualification

63. In economics, the _____ is the term economists use to describe the self-regulating nature of the marketplace. The _____ is a metaphor coined by the economist Adam Smith in The Wealth of Nations.

Adam Smith mentions the metaphor in Book IV of The Wealth of Nations, arguing that people in any society will certainly employ their capital in foreign trading only if the profits available by that method far exceed those available locally, and that in such a case it is better for society as a whole if they so did.

a. ACCRA Cost of Living Index
c. AD-IA Model
b. ACEA agreement
d. Invisible hand

Chapter 22. Pure Monopoly

1. The _____ consists of a number of economic theories which describe the nature of the firm, company including its existence, its behaviour, and its relationship with the market.

In simplified terms, the _____ aims to answer these questions:

1. Existence - why do firms emerge, why are not all transactions in the economy mediated over the market?
2. Boundaries - why the boundary between firms and the market is located exactly there? Which transactions are performed internally and which are negotiated on the market?
3. Organization - why are firms structured in such specific way? What is the interplay of formal and informal relationships?

Despite looking simple, these questions are not answered by the established economic theory, which usually views firms as given, and treats them as black boxes without any internal structure.

The First World War period saw a change of emphasis in economic theory away from industry-level analysis which mainly included analysing markets to analysis at the level of the firm, as it became increasingly clear that perfect competition was no longer an adequate model of how firms behaved. Economic theory till then had focussed on trying to understand markets alone and there had been little study on understanding why firms or organisations exist.

a. Khazzoom-Brookes postulate
b. Technology gap
c. Policy Ineffectiveness Proposition
d. Theory of the firm

2. In economics, _____ describes the state of a market with respect to competition.

- Perfect competition, in which the market consists of a very large number of firms producing a homogeneous product.
- Monopolistic competition where there are a large number of independent firms which have a very small proportion of the market share.
- Oligopoly, in which a market is dominated by a small number of firms which own more than 40% of the market share.
- Oligopsony, a market dominated by many sellers and a few buyers.
- Monopoly, where there is only one provider of a product or service.
- Natural monopoly, a monopoly in which economies of scale cause efficiency to increase continuously with the size of the firm. A firm is a natural monopoly if it is able to serve the entire market demand at a lower cost than any combination of two or more smaller, more specialized firms.
- Monopsony, when there is only one buyer in a market.

The imperfectly competitive structure is quite identical to the realistic market conditions where some monopolistic competitors, monopolists, oligopolists, and duopolists exist and dominate the market conditions. The elements of _____ include the number and size distribution of firms, entry conditions, and the extent of differentiation.

These somewhat abstract concerns tend to determine some but not all details of a specific concrete market system where buyers and sellers actually meet and commit to trade.

a. Human capital
b. Monopolistic competition
c. Labour economics
d. Market structure

Chapter 22. Pure Monopoly

3. In economics, a _____ exists when a specific individual or enterprise has sufficient control over a particular product or service to determine significantly the terms on which other individuals shall have access to it. Monopolies are thus characterized by a lack of economic competition for the good or service that they provide and a lack of viable substitute goods. The verb 'monopolize' refers to the process by which a firm gains persistently greater market share than what is expected under perfect competition.

   a. 1921 recession
   b. 130-30 fund
   c. Monopoly
   d. 100-year flood

4. _____ has several particular meanings:

   - in mathematics
     - _____ function
     - Euler _____
     - _____
     - _____ subgroup
     - method of _____s (partial differential equations)
   - in physics and engineering
     - any _____ curve that shows the relationship between certain input- and output parameters, e.g.
     - an I-V or current-voltage _____ is the current in a circuit as a function of the applied voltage
     - Receiver-Operator _____
   - in fiction
     - in Dungeons ' Dragons, _____ is another name for ability score

   a. Demand
   b. Russian financial crisis
   c. Characteristic
   d. Technocracy

5. In economics and especially in the theory of competition, _____ are obstacles in the path of a firm that make it difficult to enter a given market.

   _____ are the source of a firm's pricing power - the ability of a firm to raise prices without losing all its customers.

   The term refers to hindrances that an individual may face while trying to gain entrance into a profession or trade.

   a. Social dumping
   b. Barriers to entry
   c. Group boycott
   d. Limit price

6. In economics, a _____ occurs when, due to the economies of scale of a particular industry, the maximum efficiency of production and distribution is realized through a single supplier.

   Natural monopolies arise where the largest supplier in an industry, often the first supplier in a market, has an overwhelming cost advantage over other actual or potential competitors. This tends to be the case in industries where capital costs predominate, creating economies of scale which are large in relation to the size of the market, and hence high barriers to entry; examples include water services and electricity.

a. Privatizing profits and socializing losses
c. Common-pool resource
b. Natural monopoly
d. Collective goods

7. _____ in economics and business is the result of an exchange and from that trade we assign a numerical monetary value to a good, service or asset. If Alice trades Bob 4 apples for an orange, the _____ of an orange is 4 apples. Inversely, the _____ of an apple is 1/4 oranges.
   a. Premium pricing
   b. Price book
   c. Price war
   d. Price

8. Monopoly power is an example of market failure which occurs when one or more of the participants has the ability to influence the price or other outcomes in some general or specialized market. The most commonly discussed form of market power is that of a monopoly, but other forms such as monopsony, and more moderate versions of these two extremes, exist. Market participants that have market power are sometimes referred to as '_____', while those without are sometimes called 'price takers'.
   a. Rate-of-return regulation
   b. Pacman conjecture
   c. Revenue-cap regulation
   d. Price makers

9. _____ is a common market structure where many competing producers sell products that are differentiated from one another (ie. the products are substitutes, but are not exactly alike.) Many markets are monopolistically competitive, common examples include the markets for restaurants, cereal, clothing, shoes and service industries in large cities.
   a. Financial crisis
   b. Perfect competition
   c. Mathematical economics
   d. Monopolistic competition

10. In economic models, the _____ time frame assumes no fixed factors of production. Firms can enter or leave the marketplace, and the cost (and availability) of land, labor, raw materials, and capital goods can be assumed to vary. In contrast, in the short-run time frame, certain factors are assumed to be fixed, because there is not sufficient time for them to change.
    a. Productivity world
    b. Long-run
    c. Diseconomies of scale
    d. Price/performance ratio

11. A _____ is a set of exclusive rights granted by a state to an inventor or his assignee for a limited period of time in exchange for a disclosure of an invention.

The procedure for granting _____s, the requirements placed on the _____ee and the extent of the exclusive rights vary widely between countries according to national laws and international agreements. Typically, however, a _____ application must include one or more claims defining the invention which must be new, inventive, and useful or industrially applicable.

   a. Patent
   b. Long service leave
   c. Bona fide occupational qualification
   d. Bank regulation

12. The phrase _____, according to the Organization for Economic Co-operation and Development, refers to 'creative work undertaken on a systematic basis in order to increase the stock of knowledge, including knowledge of man, culture and society, and the use of this stock of knowledge to devise new applications [sic]'

Chapter 22. Pure Monopoly

New product design and development is more than often a crucial factor in the survival of a company. In an industry that is fast changing, firms must continually revise their design and range of products. This is necessary due to continuous technology change and development as well as other competitors and the changing preference of customers.

a. 1921 recession
b. 100-year flood
c. 130-30 fund
d. Research and development

13. In economics, a _____ is a graph of the costs of production as a function of total quantity produced. In a free market economy, productively efficient firms use these curves to find the optimal point of production, where they make the most profits. There are a few different types of _____s, each relevant to a different area of economics.
   a. Cost curve
   b. Phillips curve
   c. Demand curve
   d. Kuznets curve

14. Economics:

- _____,the desire to own something and the ability to pay for it
- _____ curve,a graphic representation of a _____ schedule
- _____ deposit, the money in checking accounts
- _____ pull theory,the theory that inflation occurs when _____ for goods and services exceeds existing supplies
- _____ schedule,a table that lists the quantity of a good a person will buy it each different price
- _____ side economics,the school of economics at believes government spending and tax cuts open economy by raising _____

a. Variability
b. McKesson ' Robbins scandal
c. Production
d. Demand

15. In economics, the _____ can be defined as the graph depicting the relationship between the price of a certain commodity, and the amount of it that consumers are willing and able to purchase at that given price. It is a graphic representation of a demand schedule. The _____ for all consumers together follows from the _____ of every individual consumer: the individual demands at each price are added together.
   a. Cost curve
   b. Wage curve
   c. Kuznets curve
   d. Demand curve

16. _____, in microeconomics, are the cost advantages that a business obtains due to expansion. They are factors that cause a producere;s average cost per unit to fall as scale is increased. _____ is a long run concept and refers to reductions in unit cost as the size of a facility, or scale, increases.
   a. Isoquant
   b. Underinvestment employment relationship
   c. Economies of scale
   d. Economic production quantity

17. In economics, and cost accounting, _____ describes the total economic cost of production and is made up of variable costs, which vary according to the quantity of a good produced and include inputs such as labor and raw materials, plus fixed costs, which are independent of the quantity of a good produced and include inputs (capital) that cannot be varied in the short term, such as buildings and machinery. _____ in economics includes the total opportunity cost of each factor of production in addition to fixed and variable costs.

The rate at which _____ changes as the amount produced changes is called marginal cost.

a. 130-30 fund
c. 100-year flood
b. 1921 recession
d. Total cost

18. _____s is the social science that studies the production, distribution, and consumption of goods and services. The term _____s comes from the Ancient Greek oá¼°κονομῖα from oá¼¶κος (oikos, 'house') + νΐŒμος (nomos, 'custom' or 'law'), hence 'rules of the house(hold)'. Current _____ models developed out of the broader field of political economy in the late 19th century, owing to a desire to use an empirical approach more akin to the physical sciences.
a. Economic
c. Inflation
b. Energy economics
d. Opportunity cost

19. In economics, _____ is the difference between a company's total revenue and its opportunity costs. It is the increase in wealth that an investor has from making an investment, taking into consideration all costs associated with that investment including the opportunity cost of capital.

Profit is the factor income of the entrepreneur.

a. Operating profit
c. ACCRA Cost of Living Index
b. Economic profit
d. Accounting profit

20.

The _____ is an independent agency of the United States government, created, directed, and empowered by Congressional statute , and with the majority of its commissioners appointed by the current President. The _____ works towards six strategic goals in the areas of broadband, competition, the spectrum, the media, public safety and homeland security, and modernizing the _____.

a. 1921 recession
c. 100-year flood
b. Federal Communications Commission
d. 130-30 fund

21. _____ is one of the four Ps of the marketing mix. The other three aspects are product, promotion, and place. It is also a key variable in microeconomic price allocation theory.
a. Point of total assumption
c. Guaranteed Maximum Price
b. Pricing
d. Premium pricing

22. In economics, a _____ arises because one firm owns all of the resources necessary to produce the good or service.

An example of a resource monopoly is De Beers, a diamond mining company. De Beers owns the mines where diamonds are found.

a. Resources monopoly
b. 130-30 fund
c. 1921 recession
d. 100-year flood

23. _____ is a situation in which the limited resources of a firm are allocated in accordance with the wishes of consumers. An allocatively efficient economy produces an 'optimal mix' of commodities. A firm is allocatively efficient when its price is equal to its marginal costs (that is, P = MC) in a perfect market.

a. Economic efficiency
b. ACCRA Cost of Living Index
c. ACEA agreement
d. Allocative efficiency

24. Competition law, known in the United States as _____ law, has three main elements:

- prohibiting agreements or practices that restrict free trading and competition between business entities. This includes in particular the repression of cartels.
- banning abusive behaviour by a firm dominating a market, or anti-competitive practices that tend to lead to such a dominant position. Practices controlled in this way may include predatory pricing, tying, price gouging, refusal to deal, and many others.
- supervising the mergers and acquisitions of large corporations, including some joint ventures. Transactions that are considered to threaten the competitive process can be prohibited altogether, or approved subject to 'remedies' such as an obligation to divest part of the merged business or to offer licences or access to facilities to enable other businesses to continue competing.

The substance and practice of competition law varies from jurisdiction to jurisdiction. Protecting the interests of consumers (consumer welfare) and ensuring that entrepreneurs have an opportunity to compete in the market economy are often treated as important objectives. Competition law is closely connected with law on deregulation of access to markets, state aids and subsidies, the privatisation of state owned assets and the establishment of independent sector regulators. In recent decades, competition law has been viewed as a way to provide better public services.

a. Intellectual property law
b. Anti-Inflation Act
c. United Kingdom competition law
d. Antitrust

25. In economics, the _____ of a good or of a service is the utility of the specific use to which an agent would put a given increase in that good or service, or of the specific use that would be abandoned in response to a given decrease. In other words, _____ is the utility of the marginal use -- which, on the assumption of economic rationality, would be the least urgent use of the good or service, from the best feasible combination of actions in which its use is included. Under the mainstream assumptions, the _____ of a good or service is the posited quantified change in utility obtained by increasing or by decreasing use of that good or service.

a. 100-year flood
b. 130-30 fund
c. 1921 recession
d. Marginal utility

26. In economics, _____ is a measure of the relative satisfaction from consumption of various goods and services. Given this measure, one may speak meaningfully of increasing or decreasing _____, and thereby explain economic behavior in terms of attempts to increase one's _____. For illustrative purposes, changes in _____ are sometimes expressed in units called utils.

   a. Ordinal utility   b. Utility function
   c. Utility   d. Expected utility hypothesis

27. _____ and Keynesian Theory) is a macroeconomic theory based on the ideas of 20th-century British economist John Maynard Keynes. _____ argues that private sector decisions sometimes lead to inefficient macroeconomic outcomes and therefore advocates active policy responses by the public sector, including monetary policy actions by the central bank and fiscal policy actions by the government to stabilize output over the business cycle.

The theories forming the basis of _____ were first presented in The General Theory of Employment, Interest and Money, published in 1936.

   a. Rational choice theory   b. Market failure
   c. Deflation   d. Keynesian economics

28. In microeconomics, _____ is the extra revenue that an additional unit of product will bring. It is the additional income from selling one more unit of a good; sometimes equal to price. It can also be described as the change in total revenue/change in number of units sold.

   a. Long term   b. Market demand schedule
   c. Reservation price   d. Marginal revenue

29. A _____ is a counterfeit agreement among industries. It is an informal organization of producers that agree to coordinate prices and production. _____s usually occur in an oligopolistic industry, where there is a small number of sellers and usually involve homogeneous products.

   a. 100-year flood   b. Shill
   c. Cartel   d. Shanzhai

30. _____ is the transition of a national economy from monopoly control by groups of large businesses to a free market economy. This change rarely arises naturally, and is generally the result of regulation by a governing body.

A modern example of _____ is the economic restructuring of Germany after the fall of the Third Reich in 1945.

   a. Market power   b. Complementary monopoly
   c. Monopolization   d. Decartelization

31. A _____ is:

- Rewrite _____, in generative grammar and computer science
- Standardization, a formal and widely-accepted statement, fact, definition, or qualification
- Operation, a determinate _____ for performing a mathematical operation and obtaining a certain result (Mathematics, Logic)
    - Unary operation
    - Binary operation
- _____ of inference, a function from sets of formulae to formulae (Mathematics, Logic)
- _____ of thumb, principle with broad application that is not intended to be strictly accurate or reliable for every situation. Also often simply referred to as a _____
- Moral, an atomic element of a moral code for guiding choices in human behavior
- Heuristic, a quantized '_____' which shows a tendency or probability for successful function
- A regulation, as in sports
- A Production _____, as in computer science
- Procedural law, a _____ set governing the application of laws to cases
    - A law, which may informally be called a '_____'
    - A court ruling, a decision by a court
- In the U.S. Government, a regulation mandated by Congress, but written or expanded upon by the Executive Branch.
- Norm (sociology), an informal but widely accepted _____, concept, truth, definition, or qualification (social norms, legal norms, coding norms)
- Norm (philosophy), a kind of sentence or a reason to act, feel or believe
- 'Rulership' is the concept of governance by a government:
    - Military _____, governance by a military body
    - Monastic _____, a collection of precepts that guides the life of monks or nuns in a religious order where the superior holds the place of Christ
- Slide _____

- '_____,' a song by Ayumi Hamasaki
- '_____,' a song by rapper Nas
- '_____s,' an album by the band The Whitest Boy Alive
- _____s: Pyaar Ka Superhit Formula, a 2003 Bollywood film
- ruler, an instrument for measuring lengths
- _____, a component of an astrolabe, circumferator or similar instrument
- The _____s, a bestselling self-help book
- _____ Project (Run Up-to-date Linux Everywhere), a project that aims to use up-to-date Linux software on old PCs
- _____ engine, a software system that helps managing business _____s
- Ja _____, a hip hop artist
    - R.U.L.E., a 2005 greatest hits album by rapper Ja _____
- '_____s,' a KMFDM song

a. Technocracy
b. Procter ' Gamble
c. Demand
d. Rule

Chapter 22. Pure Monopoly

32. In economic theory, _____ is the competitive situation in any market where the conditions necessary for perfect competition are not satisfied. It is a market structure that does not meet the conditions of perfect competition.

Forms of _____ include:

- Monopoly, in which there is only one seller of a good.
- Oligopoly, in which there is a small number of sellers.
- Monopolistic competition, in which there are many sellers producing highly differentiated goods.
- Monopsony, in which there is only one buyer of a good.
- Oligopsony, in which there is a small number of buyers.

There may also be _____ in markets due to buyers or sellers lacking information about prices and the goods being traded.

There may also be _____ due to a time lag in a market.

a. ACEA agreement
b. Imperfect competition
c. ACCRA Cost of Living Index
d. AD-IA Model

33. _____ is the total money received from the sale of any given quantity of output.

The _____ is calculated by taking the price of the sale times the quantity sold, i.e.

_____ = price X quantity.

a. Ceteris paribus
b. Small numbers game
c. Market development funds
d. Total revenue

34. The _____ or gross domestic income (GDI), a basic measure of an economy's economic performance, is the market value of all final goods and services produced within the borders of a nation in a year. _____ can be defined in three ways, all of which are conceptually identical. First, it is equal to the total expenditures for all final goods and services produced within the country in a stipulated period of time (usually a 365-day year.)

a. Countercyclical
b. Monopolistic competition
c. Gross domestic product
d. Market structure

35. The _____ or the output gap is the difference between potential GDP and actual GDP or actual output. The calculation for the output gap is Y-Y* where Y* is potential output and Y is actual output. If this calculation yields a positive number it is called an expansionary gap and indicates an economy in expansion; if the calculation yields a negative number it is called a recessionary gap and indicates an economy in recession.

a. GDP gap
b. 1921 recession
c. 130-30 fund
d. 100-year flood

Chapter 22. Pure Monopoly

36. _____ is defined as the measure of responsiveness in the quantity demanded for a commodity as a result of change in price of the same commodity. It is a measure of how consumers react to a change in price. In other words, it is percentage change in quantity demanded as per the percentage change in price of the same commodity.
   a. 130-30 fund
   b. Price elasticity of demand
   c. 1921 recession
   d. 100-year flood

37. In economics, _____ is the process by which a firm determines the price and output level that returns the greatest profit. There are several approaches to this problem. The total revenue--total cost method relies on the fact that profit equals revenue minus cost, and the marginal revenue--marginal cost method is based on the fact that total profit in a perfectly competitive market reaches its maximum point where marginal revenue equals marginal cost.
   a. 100-year flood
   b. Profit maximization
   c. Normal profit
   d. Profit margin

38. In economics, the _____ is a means for determining whether demand is elastic or inelastic. If an increase in price causes an increase in total revenue, then demand can be said to be inelastic, since the increase in price does not have a large impact on quantity demanded. If an increase in price causes a decrease in total revenue, then demand can be said to be elastic, since the increase in price has a large impact on quantity demanded.
   a. 1921 recession
   b. 130-30 fund
   c. 100-year flood
   d. Total revenue test

39. In economics, _____ is the ratio of the percent change in one variable to the percent change in another variable. It is a tool for measuring the responsiveness of a function to changes in parameters in a relative way. Commonly analyzed are _____ of substitution, price and wealth.
   a. Elasticity of demand
   b. ACEA agreement
   c. ACCRA Cost of Living Index
   d. Elasticity

40. Price _____ is defined as the measure of responsiveness in the quantity demanded for a commodity as a result of change in price of the same commodity. It is a measure of how consumers react to a change in price. In other words, it is percentage change in quantity demanded by the percentage change in price of the same commodity.
   a. ACCRA Cost of Living Index
   b. Elasticity
   c. Elasticity of demand
   d. ACEA agreement

41. In economics, a firm is said to reap monopoly profits when a lack of viable market competition allows it to set its prices above the equilibrium price for a good or service without losing profits to competitors. Monopoly profit is a type of economic profit, that is, it is a profit greater than the normal profit that is typical in a perfectly competitive industry. The resulting price is known as the _____.
   a. Monopoly Price
   b. Payment schedule
   c. Gross national income
   d. Gross Dealer Concession

42. In economics, a firm is said to reap _____s when a lack of viable market competition allows it to set its prices above the equilibrium price for a good or service without losing profits to competitors. _____ is a type of economic profit, that is, it is a profit greater than the normal profit that is typical in a perfectly competitive industry. The resulting price is known as the monopoly price.
   a. Borrowing base
   b. Cleanup clause
   c. First-price sealed-bid auction
   d. Monopoly profit

43. _____ is the structure and set of regulations in place to control activity, usually in large organizations and government. As opposed to adhocracy, it is represented by standardized procedure (rule-following) that dictates the execution of most or all processes within the body, formal division of powers, hierarchy, and relationships. In practice the interpretation and execution of policy can lead to informal influence.

a. 1921 recession
b. 130-30 fund
c. 100-year flood
d. Bureaucracy

44. _____ occurs when the economy is operating at its production possibility frontier (PPF.) This takes place when production of one good is achieved at the lowest cost possible, given the production of the other good(s.) Equivalently, it is when the highest possible output of one good is produced, given the production level of the other good(s.)

a. Discretionary spending
b. Free contract
c. Preclusive purchasing
d. Productive efficiency

45. _____ is a broad label that refers to any individuals or households that use goods and services generated within the economy. The concept of a _____ is used in different contexts, so that the usage and significance of the term may vary.

Typically when business people and economists talk of _____s they are talking about person as _____, an aggregated commodity item with little individuality other than that expressed in the buy/not-buy decision.

a. 100-year flood
b. 1921 recession
c. 130-30 fund
d. Consumer

46. The term surplus is used in economics for several related quantities. The _____ is the amount that consumers benefit by being able to purchase a product for a price that is less than they would be willing to pay. The producer surplus is the amount that producers benefit by selling at a market price mechanism that is higher than they would be willing to sell for.

a. Necessity good
b. Marginal rate of technical substitution
c. Microeconomic reform
d. Consumer surplus

47. In economics, a _____ is a loss of economic efficiency that can occur when equilibrium for a good or service is not Pareto optimal. In other words, either people who would have more marginal benefit than marginal cost are not buying the good or service, or people who would have more marginal cost than marginal benefit are buying the product.

Causes of _____ can include monopoly pricing, externalities, taxes or subsidies, and binding price ceilings or floors.

a. Leapfrogging
b. Distributive efficiency
c. Contract curve
d. Deadweight loss

48. In economics and finance, _____ is the change in total cost that arises when the quantity produced changes by one unit. It is the cost of producing one more unit of a good. Mathematically, the _____ function is expressed as the first derivative of the total cost (TC) function with respect to quantity (Q.)

a. Variable cost
b. Marginal cost
c. Khozraschyot
d. Quality costs

Chapter 22. Pure Monopoly

49. In economics, _____ is the ability of a firm to alter the market price of a good or service. A firm with _____ can raise prices without losing all customers to competitors.

When a firm has _____ it faces a downward-sloping demand curve.

a. Pacman conjecture
c. Price makers
b. Revenue-cap regulation
d. Market power

50. The term surplus is used in economics for several related quantities. The consumer surplus is the amount that consumers benefit by being able to purchase a product for a price that is less than they would be willing to pay. The _____ is the amount that producers benefit by selling at a market price mechanism that is higher than they would be willing to sell for.

a. Returns to scale
c. Schedule delay
b. Long term
d. Producer surplus

51. In microeconomics, _____ is quite simply the conversion of inputs into outputs. It is an economic process that uses resources to create a good or service that is suitable for exchange. This can include manufacturing, storing, shipping, and packaging.

a. Red Guards
c. Solved
b. MET
d. Production

52. _____ , as defined by the _____ Association of America (Information technologyAA), is 'the study, design, development, implementation, support or management of computer-based information systems, particularly software applications and computer hardware.' _____ deals with the use of electronic computers and computer software to convert, store, protect, process, transmit, and securely retrieve information.

Today, the term _____ has ballooned to encompass many aspects of computing and technology, and the term has become very recognizable. The _____ umbrella can be quite large, covering many fields.

a. ACCRA Cost of Living Index
c. AD-IA Model
b. ACEA agreement
d. Information technology

53. In economics and business, a _____ is the effect that one user of a good or service has on the value of that product to other people.

The classic example is the telephone. The more people own telephones, the more valuable the telephone is to each owner.

a. Pigou effect
c. Cluster effect
b. Penn effect
d. Network effect

54. _____ is the difference between efficient behavior of firms assumed or implied by economic theory and their observed behavior in practice.

Economic theory assumes that the management of firms act to maximize owners' wealth by minimizing risk and maximizing economic profits -- which is accomplished by simultaneously maximizing revenues and minimizing costs, usually through the adjustment of output. In perfect competition, the free entry and exit of firms tends toward firms producing at the point where price equals long run average costs and long run average costs are minimized.

a. Revelation principle
b. X-efficiency
c. 100-year flood
d. X-inefficiency

55. _____ is a common concept in economics, and gives rise to derived concepts such as consumer debt. Generally _____ is defined by opposition to production. But the precise definition can vary because different schools of economists define production quite differently.

a. Cash or share options
b. Foreclosure data providers
c. Federal Reserve Bank Notes
d. Consumption

56. _____ is the difference between price and the costs of bringing to market whatever it is that is accounted as an enterprise (whether by harvest, extraction, manufacture, or purchase) in terms of the component costs of delivered goods and/or services and any operating or other expenses.

A key difficulty in measuring profit is in defining costs. Pure economic monetary profits can be zero or negative even in competitive equilibrium when accounted monetized costs exceed monetized price.

a. Operating profit
b. Economic profit
c. Accounting profit
d. ACCRA Cost of Living Index

57. _____ is a component of the firm's opportunity costs. The time that the owner spends running the firm could be spent on running another firm. This is _____: the return the entrepreneur can expect to earn or the profit that the business owners considers necessary to make running the business worth his/her while.

a. Profit maximization
b. 100-year flood
c. Profit margin
d. Normal profit

58. In economics, _____ is a measure of national income. Basically, it is an approach to measure GDP. It is defined as the value of planned goods and services produced in an economy.

a. Aggregate supply
b. Aggregate demand
c. Aggregation problem
d. Aggregate expenditure

59.

A _____ is a type of financial intermediary and a type of bank. Commercial banking is also known as business banking. It is a bank that provides checking accounts, savings accounts, and money market accounts and that accepts time deposits.

a. Bought deal
b. Daylight overdraft
c. Lombard banking
d. Commercial bank

Chapter 22. Pure Monopoly

60. The _____ is an independent agency of the United States government, established in 1914 by the _____ Act. Its principal mission is the promotion of 'consumer protection' and the elimination and prevention of what regulators perceive to be harmfully 'anti-competitive' business practices, such as coercive monopoly.

The _____ Act was one of President Wilson's major acts against trusts.

   a. 130-30 fund
   b. 1921 recession
   c. 100-year flood
   d. Federal Trade Commission

61. The _____ of 1914 (15 U.S.C §§ 41-58, as amended) established the Federal Trade Commission (FTC), a bipartisan body of five members appointed by the President of the United States for seven year terms. This Commission was authorized to issue Cease and Desist orders to large corporations to curb unfair trade practices. This Act also gave more flexibility to the US congress for judicial matters.
   a. Minimum wage law
   b. Buydown
   c. Competition law theory
   d. Federal Trade Commission Act

62. A _____ or transnational corporation is a corporation or enterprise that manages production or delivers services in more than one country. It can also be referred to as an international corporation.

The first modern MNC is generally thought to be the Dutch East India Company, established in 1602.

   a. Luxembourg Income Study
   b. Foreign direct investment
   c. Rakon
   d. Multinational corporation

63. _____ exists when sales of identical goods or services are transacted at different prices from the same provider. In a theoretical market with perfect information, no transaction costs or prohibition on secondary exchange (or re-selling) to prevent arbitrage, _____ can only be a feature of monopoly and oligopoly markets, where market power can be exercised. Otherwise, the moment the seller tries to sell the same good at different prices, the buyer at the lower price can arbitrage by selling to the consumer buying at the higher price but with a tiny discount.
   a. Price discrimination
   b. Loss leader
   c. Lerner Index
   d. Transfer pricing

64. _____ was a predominant American integrated oil producing, transporting, refining, and marketing company. Established in 1870 as an Ohio Corporation, it was the largest oil refiner in the world and operated as a major company trust and was one of the world's first and largest multinational corporations until it was broken up by the United States Supreme Court in 1911. John D. Rockefeller was a founder, chairman and major shareholder, and the company made him a billionaire and eventually the richest man in history.
   a. Standard Oil
   b. 1921 recession
   c. 130-30 fund
   d. 100-year flood

65. _____ is the removal or simplification of government rules and regulations that constrain the operation of market forces. _____ does not mean elimination of laws against fraud, but eliminating or reducing government control of how business is done, thereby moving toward a more free market.

The stated rationale for '_____' is often that fewer and simpler regulations will lead to a raised level of competitiveness, therefore higher productivity, more efficiency and lower prices overall.

a. Fundamental psychological law
b. Secular basis
c. Macroeconomic policy instruments
d. Deregulation

66. In economics and sociology, an _____ is any factor (financial or non-financial) that enables or motivates a particular course of action, or counts as a reason for preferring one choice to the alternatives. It is an expectation that encourages people to behave in a certain way. Since human beings are purposeful creatures, the study of _____ structures is central to the study of all economic activity (both in terms of individual decision-making and in terms of co-operation and competition within a larger institutional structure.)

a. Economic reform
b. Incentive
c. Epstein-Zin preferences
d. Isocost

Chapter 23. Monopolistic Competition and Oligopoly 325

1. In economics, _____ describes the state of a market with respect to competition.

   - Perfect competition, in which the market consists of a very large number of firms producing a homogeneous product.
   - Monopolistic competition where there are a large number of independent firms which have a very small proportion of the market share.
   - Oligopoly, in which a market is dominated by a small number of firms which own more than 40% of the market share.
   - Oligopsony, a market dominated by many sellers and a few buyers.
   - Monopoly, where there is only one provider of a product or service.
   - Natural monopoly, a monopoly in which economies of scale cause efficiency to increase continuously with the size of the firm. A firm is a natural monopoly if it is able to serve the entire market demand at a lower cost than any combination of two or more smaller, more specialized firms.
   - Monopsony, when there is only one buyer in a market.

The imperfectly competitive structure is quite identical to the realistic market conditions where some monopolistic competitors, monopolists, oligopolists, and duopolists exist and dominate the market conditions. The elements of _____ include the number and size distribution of firms, entry conditions, and the extent of differentiation.

These somewhat abstract concerns tend to determine some but not all details of a specific concrete market system where buyers and sellers actually meet and commit to trade.

   a. Labour economics   b. Monopolistic competition
   c. Human capital   d. Market structure

2. An _____ is a market form in which a market or industry is dominated by a small number of sellers (oligopolists.) Because there are few participants in this type of market, each oligopolist is aware of the actions of the others. The decisions of one firm influence, and are influenced by, the decisions of other firms.
   a. ACCRA Cost of Living Index   b. ACEA agreement
   c. Oligopsony   d. Oligopoly

3. _____ has several particular meanings:

   - in mathematics
     - _____ function
     - Euler _____
     - _____
     - _____ subgroup
     - method of _____ s (partial differential equations)
   - in physics and engineering
     - any _____ curve that shows the relationship between certain input- and output parameters, e.g.
     - an I-V or current-voltage _____ is the current in a circuit as a function of the applied voltage
     - Receiver-Operator _____
   - in fiction
     - in Dungeons ' Dragons, _____ is another name for ability score

a. Demand
b. Technocracy
c. Russian financial crisis
d. Characteristic

4. _____ is a common market structure where many competing producers sell products that are differentiated from one another (ie. the products are substitutes, but are not exactly alike.) Many markets are monopolistically competitive, common examples include the markets for restaurants, cereal, clothing, shoes and service industries in large cities.

a. Mathematical economics
b. Perfect competition
c. Financial crisis
d. Monopolistic competition

5. _____ is an agreement, usually secretive, which occurs between two or more persons to deceive, mislead or to obtain an objective forbidden by law typically involving fraud or gaining an unfair advantage. It is an agreement among firms to divide the market, set prices kickbacks, or misrepresenting the independence of the relationship between the colluding parties.' All acts effected by _____ are considered void.

a. Bid rigging
b. Dividing territories
c. Net Book Agreement
d. Collusion

6. The _____ is a measure of the size of firms in relation to the industry and an indicator of the amount of competition among them. Named after economists Orris C. Herfindahl and Albert O. Hirschman, it is an economic concept, widely applied in competition law, antitrust and also technology management. It is defined as the sum of the squares of the market shares of the 50 largest firms within the industry, where the market shares are expressed as percentages.

a. Reduced form
b. Herfindahl index
c. Panel data
d. Vector autoregression

7. _____ and Keynesian Theory) is a macroeconomic theory based on the ideas of 20th-century British economist John Maynard Keynes. _____ argues that private sector decisions sometimes lead to inefficient macroeconomic outcomes and therefore advocates active policy responses by the public sector, including monetary policy actions by the central bank and fiscal policy actions by the government to stabilize output over the business cycle.

The theories forming the basis of _____ were first presented in The General Theory of Employment, Interest and Money, published in 1936.

a. Rational choice theory
b. Deflation
c. Market failure
d. Keynesian economics

8. In marketing, _____ is the process of distinguishing the differences of a product or offering from others, to make it more attractive to a particular target market. This involves differentiating it from competitors' products as well as one's own product offerings.

Differentiation is a source of competitive advantage.

a. Pricing science
b. Market segment
c. Product differentiation
d. Technology acceptance model

Chapter 23. Monopolistic Competition and Oligopoly

9. _____, in strategic management and marketing is, according to Carlton O'Neal, the percentage or proportion of the total available market or market segment that is being serviced by a company. It can be expressed as a company's sales revenue (from that market) divided by the total sales revenue available in that market. It can also be expressed as a company's unit sales volume (in a market) divided by the total volume of units sold in that market.

   a. Product differentiation   b. Customer to customer
   c. Pricing science   d. Market share

10. _____ in economics and business is the result of an exchange and from that trade we assign a numerical monetary value to a good, service or asset. If Alice trades Bob 4 apples for an orange, the _____ of an orange is 4 apples. Inversely, the _____ of an apple is 1/4 oranges.

   a. Price war   b. Price
   c. Premium pricing   d. Price book

11. In economics and especially in the theory of competition, _____ are obstacles in the path of a firm that make it difficult to enter a given market.

_____ are the source of a firm's pricing power - the ability of a firm to raise prices without losing all its customers.

The term refers to hindrances that an individual may face while trying to gain entrance into a profession or trade.

   a. Social dumping   b. Limit price
   c. Group boycott   d. Barriers to entry

12. Economics:

- _____,the desire to own something and the ability to pay for it
- _____ curve,a graphic representation of a _____ schedule
- _____ deposit, the money in checking accounts
- _____ pull theory,the theory that inflation occurs when _____ for goods and services exceeds existing supplies
- _____ schedule,a table that lists the quantity of a good a person will buy it each different price
- _____ side economics,the school of economics at believes government spending and tax cuts open economy by raising _____

   a. Variability   b. Demand
   c. McKesson ' Robbins scandal   d. Production

13. In economics, the _____ can be defined as the graph depicting the relationship between the price of a certain commodity, and the amount of it that consumers are willing and able to purchase at that given price. It is a graphic representation of a demand schedule. The _____ for all consumers together follows from the _____ of every individual consumer: the individual demands at each price are added together.

   a. Cost curve   b. Kuznets curve
   c. Wage curve   d. Demand curve

14. The _____ or gross domestic income (GDI), a basic measure of an economy's economic performance, is the market value of all final goods and services produced within the borders of a nation in a year. _____ can be defined in three ways, all of which are conceptually identical. First, it is equal to the total expenditures for all final goods and services produced within the country in a stipulated period of time (usually a 365-day year.)

   a. Countercyclical
   b. Gross domestic product
   c. Market structure
   d. Monopolistic competition

15. The _____ or the output gap is the difference between potential GDP and actual GDP or actual output. The calculation for the output gap is Y-Y* where Y* is potential output and Y is actual output. If this calculation yields a positive number it is called an expansionary gap and indicates an economy in expansion; if the calculation yields a negative number it is called a recessionary gap and indicates an economy in recession.

   a. 100-year flood
   b. GDP gap
   c. 1921 recession
   d. 130-30 fund

16. _____ is defined as the measure of responsiveness in the quantity demanded for a commodity as a result of change in price of the same commodity. It is a measure of how consumers react to a change in price. In other words, it is percentage change in quantity demanded as per the percentage change in price of the same commodity.

   a. 130-30 fund
   b. 100-year flood
   c. 1921 recession
   d. Price elasticity of demand

17. In economics, _____ is the ratio of the percent change in one variable to the percent change in another variable. It is a tool for measuring the responsiveness of a function to changes in parameters in a relative way. Commonly analyzed are _____ of substitution, price and wealth.

   a. ACCRA Cost of Living Index
   b. ACEA agreement
   c. Elasticity of demand
   d. Elasticity

18. Price _____ is defined as the measure of responsiveness in the quantity demanded for a commodity as a result of change in price of the same commodity. It is a measure of how consumers react to a change in price. In other words, it is percentage change in quantity demanded by the percentage change in price of the same commodity.

   a. ACCRA Cost of Living Index
   b. Elasticity
   c. ACEA agreement
   d. Elasticity of demand

19. The _____ are a set of internal rules promulgated by the Antitrust Division of the United States Department of Justice (DOJ) in conjunction with the Federal Trade Commission (FTC.) These rules, which have been revised a number of times in the past four decades, govern the extent to which these two regulatory bodies will scrutinize and/or challenge a potential merger on grounds of market concentration or threat to competition within a relevant market.

The _____ have sections governing both horizontal integration and vertical integration.

   a. Law of increasing relative cost
   b. Business valuation
   c. Merger guidelines
   d. No-FEAR Act

Chapter 23. Monopolistic Competition and Oligopoly

20. In economics, a _____ exists when a specific individual or enterprise has sufficient control over a particular product or service to determine significantly the terms on which other individuals shall have access to it. Monopolies are thus characterized by a lack of economic competition for the good or service that they provide and a lack of viable substitute goods. The verb 'monopolize' refers to the process by which a firm gains persistently greater market share than what is expected under perfect competition.
   a. Monopoly
   b. 100-year flood
   c. 1921 recession
   d. 130-30 fund

21. To _____ is to impose a financial charge or other levy upon a taxpayer by a state or the functional equivalent of a state.

   _____es are also imposed by many subnational entities. _____es consist of direct _____ or indirect _____, and may be paid in money or as its labour equivalent (often but not always unpaid.)

   a. 100-year flood
   b. 130-30 fund
   c. 1921 recession
   d. Tax

22. To tax is to impose a financial charge or other levy upon a taxpayer by a state or the functional equivalent of a state.

   _____ are also imposed by many subnational entities. _____ consist of direct tax or indirect tax, and may be paid in money or as its labour equivalent (often but not always unpaid.)

   a. 130-30 fund
   b. 1921 recession
   c. 100-year flood
   d. Taxes

23. In economics, a _____ is a graph of the costs of production as a function of total quantity produced. In a free market economy, productively efficient firms use these curves to find the optimal point of production, where they make the most profits. There are a few different types of _____s, each relevant to a different area of economics.
   a. Cost curve
   b. Demand curve
   c. Phillips curve
   d. Kuznets curve

24. _____s is the social science that studies the production, distribution, and consumption of goods and services. The term _____s comes from the Ancient Greek oá¼°κονομῖα from oá¼¶κος (oikos, 'house') + vĺŒμος (nomos, 'custom' or 'law'), hence 'rules of the house(hold)'. Current _____ models developed out of the broader field of political economy in the late 19th century, owing to a desire to use an empirical approach more akin to the physical sciences.
   a. Opportunity cost
   b. Energy economics
   c. Inflation
   d. Economic

25. In economics, _____ is the difference between a company's total revenue and its opportunity costs. It is the increase in wealth that an investor has from making an investment, taking into consideration all costs associated with that investment including the opportunity cost of capital.

Profit is the factor income of the entrepreneur.

a. ACCRA Cost of Living Index
b. Economic profit
c. Accounting profit
d. Operating profit

26. In economics and finance, _____ is the change in total cost that arises when the quantity produced changes by one unit. It is the cost of producing one more unit of a good. Mathematically, the _____ function is expressed as the first derivative of the total cost (TC) function with respect to quantity (Q.)
   a. Marginal cost
   b. Khozraschyot
   c. Variable cost
   d. Quality costs

27. In microeconomics, _____ is the extra revenue that an additional unit of product will bring. It is the additional income from selling one more unit of a good; sometimes equal to price. It can also be described as the change in total revenue/change in number of units sold.
   a. Market demand schedule
   b. Long term
   c. Reservation price
   d. Marginal revenue

28. Competition law, known in the United States as _____ law, has three main elements:

- prohibiting agreements or practices that restrict free trading and competition between business entities. This includes in particular the repression of cartels.
- banning abusive behaviour by a firm dominating a market, or anti-competitive practices that tend to lead to such a dominant position. Practices controlled in this way may include predatory pricing, tying, price gouging, refusal to deal, and many others.
- supervising the mergers and acquisitions of large corporations, including some joint ventures. Transactions that are considered to threaten the competitive process can be prohibited altogether, or approved subject to 'remedies' such as an obligation to divest part of the merged business or to offer licences or access to facilities to enable other businesses to continue competing.

The substance and practice of competition law varies from jurisdiction to jurisdiction. Protecting the interests of consumers (consumer welfare) and ensuring that entrepreneurs have an opportunity to compete in the market economy are often treated as important objectives. Competition law is closely connected with law on deregulation of access to markets, state aids and subsidies, the privatisation of state owned assets and the establishment of independent sector regulators. In recent decades, competition law has been viewed as a way to provide better public services.

   a. United Kingdom competition law
   b. Intellectual property law
   c. Anti-Inflation Act
   d. Antitrust

Chapter 23. Monopolistic Competition and Oligopoly   331

29. A _____ is:

- Rewrite _____, in generative grammar and computer science
- Standardization, a formal and widely-accepted statement, fact, definition, or qualification
- Operation, a determinate _____ for performing a mathematical operation and obtaining a certain result (Mathematics, Logic)
    - Unary operation
    - Binary operation
- _____ of inference, a function from sets of formulae to formulae (Mathematics, Logic)
- _____ of thumb, principle with broad application that is not intended to be strictly accurate or reliable for every situation. Also often simply referred to as a _____
- Moral, an atomic element of a moral code for guiding choices in human behavior
- Heuristic, a quantized '_____' which shows a tendency or probability for successful function
- A regulation, as in sports
- A Production _____, as in computer science
- Procedural law, a _____ set governing the application of laws to cases
    - A law, which may informally be called a '_____'
    - A court ruling, a decision by a court
- In the U.S. Government, a regulation mandated by Congress, but written or expanded upon by the Executive Branch.
- Norm (sociology), an informal but widely accepted _____, concept, truth, definition, or qualification (social norms, legal norms, coding norms)
- Norm (philosophy), a kind of sentence or a reason to act, feel or believe
- 'Rulership' is the concept of governance by a government:
    - Military _____, governance by a military body
    - Monastic _____, a collection of precepts that guides the life of monks or nuns in a religious order where the superior holds the place of Christ
- Slide _____

- '_____,' a song by Ayumi Hamasaki
- '_____,' a song by rapper Nas
- '_____s,' an album by the band The Whitest Boy Alive
- _____s: Pyaar Ka Superhit Formula, a 2003 Bollywood film
- ruler, an instrument for measuring lengths
- _____, a component of an astrolabe, circumferator or similar instrument
- The _____s, a bestselling self-help book
- _____ Project (Run Up-to-date Linux Everywhere), a project that aims to use up-to-date Linux software on old PCs
- _____ engine, a software system that helps managing business _____s
- Ja _____, a hip hop artist
    - R.U.L.E., a 2005 greatest hits album by rapper Ja _____
- '_____s,' a KMFDM song

a. Demand
b. Technocracy
c. Procter ' Gamble
d. Rule

30. In economics, and cost accounting, _____ describes the total economic cost of production and is made up of variable costs, which vary according to the quantity of a good produced and include inputs such as labor and raw materials, plus fixed costs, which are independent of the quantity of a good produced and include inputs (capital) that cannot be varied in the short term, such as buildings and machinery. _____ in economics includes the total opportunity cost of each factor of production in addition to fixed and variable costs.

The rate at which _____ changes as the amount produced changes is called marginal cost.

a. 100-year flood
b. 130-30 fund
c. 1921 recession
d. Total cost

31. _____ is the difference between price and the costs of bringing to market whatever it is that is accounted as an enterprise (whether by harvest, extraction, manufacture, or purchase) in terms of the component costs of delivered goods and/or services and any operating or other expenses.

A key difficulty in measuring profit is in defining costs. Pure economic monetary profits can be zero or negative even in competitive equilibrium when accounted monetized costs exceed monetized price.

a. Economic profit
b. Accounting profit
c. ACCRA Cost of Living Index
d. Operating profit

32. In economics, a _____ occurs when, due to the economies of scale of a particular industry, the maximum efficiency of production and distribution is realized through a single supplier.

Natural monopolies arise where the largest supplier in an industry, often the first supplier in a market, has an overwhelming cost advantage over other actual or potential competitors. This tends to be the case in industries where capital costs predominate, creating economies of scale which are large in relation to the size of the market, and hence high barriers to entry; examples include water services and electricity.

a. Collective goods
b. Privatizing profits and socializing losses
c. Natural monopoly
d. Common-pool resource

33. _____ is a component of the firm's opportunity costs. The time that the owner spends running the firm could be spent on running another firm. This is _____: the return the entrepreneur can expect to earn or the profit that the business owners considers necessary to make running the business worth his/her while.
a. Profit margin
b. Profit maximization
c. Normal profit
d. 100-year flood

34. _____ is a situation in which the limited resources of a firm are allocated in accordance with the wishes of consumers. An allocatively efficient economy produces an 'optimal mix' of commodities. A firm is allocatively efficient when its price is equal to its marginal costs (that is, P = MC) in a perfect market.
a. Economic efficiency
b. ACCRA Cost of Living Index
c. Allocative efficiency
d. ACEA agreement

35.

Chapter 23. Monopolistic Competition and Oligopoly

A _____ is a type of financial intermediary and a type of bank. Commercial banking is also known as business banking. It is a bank that provides checking accounts, savings accounts, and money market accounts and that accepts time deposits.

a. Commercial bank
c. Lombard banking
b. Daylight overdraft
d. Bought deal

36. In economic models, the _____ time frame assumes no fixed factors of production. Firms can enter or leave the marketplace, and the cost (and availability) of land, labor, raw materials, and capital goods can be assumed to vary. In contrast, in the short-run time frame, certain factors are assumed to be fixed, because there is not sufficient time for them to change.

a. Price/performance ratio
c. Productivity world
b. Diseconomies of scale
d. Long-run

37. _____ is the structure and set of regulations in place to control activity, usually in large organizations and government. As opposed to adhocracy, it is represented by standardized procedure (rule-following) that dictates the execution of most or all processes within the body, formal division of powers, hierarchy, and relationships. In practice the interpretation and execution of policy can lead to informal influence.

a. 100-year flood
c. 1921 recession
b. 130-30 fund
d. Bureaucracy

38. _____ describes a deliberate attempt to interfere with the free and fair operation of the market and create artificial, false or misleading appearances with respect to the price of a security, commodity or currency. _____ is prohibited under Section 9(a)(2) of the Securities Exchange Act of 1934, and in Australia under Section s 1041A of the Corporations Act 2001. The Act defines _____ as transactions which create an artificial price or maintain an artificial price for a tradable security.

a. Legal monopoly
c. Net domestic product
b. Managerial economics
d. Market manipulation

39. _____ occurs when the economy is operating at its production possibility frontier (PPF.) This takes place when production of one good is achieved at the lowest cost possible, given the production of the other good(s.) Equivalently, it is when the highest possible output of one good is produced, given the production level of the other good(s.)

a. Free contract
c. Preclusive purchasing
b. Discretionary spending
d. Productive efficiency

40. The _____ consists of a number of economic theories which describe the nature of the firm, company including its existence, its behaviour, and its relationship with the market.

In simplified terms, the _____ aims to answer these questions:

1. Existence - why do firms emerge, why are not all transactions in the economy mediated over the market?
2. Boundaries - why the boundary between firms and the market is located exactly there? Which transactions are performed internally and which are negotiated on the market?
3. Organization - why are firms structured in such specific way? What is the interplay of formal and informal relationships?

Despite looking simple, these questions are not answered by the established economic theory, which usually views firms as given, and treats them as black boxes without any internal structure.

The First World War period saw a change of emphasis in economic theory away from industry-level analysis which mainly included analysing markets to analysis at the level of the firm, as it became increasingly clear that perfect competition was no longer an adequate model of how firms behaved. Economic theory till then had focussed on trying to understand markets alone and there had been little study on understanding why firms or organisations exist.

a. Policy Ineffectiveness Proposition
b. Khazzoom-Brookes postulate
c. Technology gap
d. Theory of the firm

41. Monopoly power is an example of market failure which occurs when one or more of the participants has the ability to influence the price or other outcomes in some general or specialized market. The most commonly discussed form of market power is that of a monopoly, but other forms such as monopsony, and more moderate versions of these two extremes, exist. Market participants that have market power are sometimes referred to as '_____', while those without are sometimes called 'price takers'.

a. Revenue-cap regulation
b. Rate-of-return regulation
c. Price makers
d. Pacman conjecture

42. A _____ is an object whose consumption increases the utility of the consumer, for which the quantity demanded exceeds the quantity supplied at zero price. _____s are usually modeled as having diminishing marginal utility. The first individual purchase has high utility; the second has less.

a. Merit good
b. Composite good
c. Pie method
d. Good

43. The phrase _____ and acquisitions refers to the aspect of corporate strategy, corporate finance and management dealing with the buying, selling and combining of different companies that can aid, finance, or help a growing company in a given industry grow rapidly without having to create another business entity.

An acquisition, also known as a takeover or a buyout, is the buying of one company (the 'target') by another. An acquisition may be friendly or hostile.

a. Peace dividend
b. Political economy
c. Differential accumulation
d. Mergers

Chapter 23. Monopolistic Competition and Oligopoly

44. In economics, the _____ of an industry is used as an indicator of the relative size of firms in relation to the industry as a whole. It is calculated as the sum of the percent market share of the top n industries. This may also assist in determining the market structure of the industry.
   a. Concentration ratio
   b. Quasi-rent
   c. Monopolization
   d. Pacman conjecture

45. In economics, an _____ is any good (e.g. a commodity) or service brought into one country from another country in a legitimate fashion, typically for use in trade.It is a good that is brought in from another country for sale. _____ goods or services are provided to domestic consumers by foreign producers. An _____ in the receiving country is an export to the sending country.
   a. Import
   b. Import quota
   c. Economic integration
   d. Incoterms

46. _____ are the forces that cause larger firms to produce goods and services at increased per-unit costs. They are less well known than what economists have long understood as 'economies of scale', the forces which enable larger firms to produce goods and services at reduced per-unit costs.

Some of the forces which cause a diseconomy of scale are listed below:

Ideally, all employees of a firm would have one-on-one communication with each other so they know exactly what the other workers are doing.

   a. Productive capacity
   b. Factors of production
   c. Marginal physical product
   d. Diseconomies of scale

47. In finance, the _____s between two currencies specifies how much one currency is worth in terms of the other. It is the value of a foreign natione;s currency in terms of the home natione;s currency. For example an _____ of 102 Japanese yen to the United States dollar means that JPY 102 is worth the same as USD 1.
   a. ACCRA Cost of Living Index
   b. ACEA agreement
   c. Interbank market
   d. Exchange rate

48. A _____, sometimes called a pegged exchange rate, is a type of exchange rate regime wherein a currency's value is matched to the value of another single currency or to a basket of other currencies such as gold.

A _____ is usually used to stabilize the value of a currency, vis-a-vis the currency it is pegged to. This facilitates trade and investments between the two countries, and is especially useful for small economies where external trade forms a large part of their GDP.

   a. Monetary economics
   b. Fixed exchange rate
   c. Leading indicators
   d. Law of supply

49. A _____ is an expression that compares quantities relative to each other. The most common examples involve two quantities, but any number of quantities can be compared. _____s are represented mathematically by separating each quantity with a colon, for example the _____ 2:3, which is read as the _____ 'two to three'.

Chapter 23. Monopolistic Competition and Oligopoly

a. 100-year flood
b. 130-30 fund
c. Y-intercept
d. Ratio

50. _____ is a branch of applied mathematics that is used in the social sciences (most notably economics), biology, engineering, political science, international relations, computer science, and philosophy. _____ attempts to mathematically capture behavior in strategic situations, in which an individual's success in making choices depends on the choices of others. While initially developed to analyze competitions in which one individual does better at another's expense (zero sum games), it has been expanded to treat a wide class of interactions, which are classified according to several criteria.

a. Game theory
b. Dollar auction
c. Proper equilibrium
d. Discriminatory price auction

51. A _____ is a counterfeit agreement among industries. It is an informal organization of producers that agree to coordinate prices and production. _____s usually occur in an oligopolistic industry, where there is a small number of sellers and usually involve homogeneous products.

a. Cartel
b. Shill
c. 100-year flood
d. Shanzhai

52. _____ is the transition of a national economy from monopoly control by groups of large businesses to a free market economy. This change rarely arises naturally, and is generally the result of regulation by a governing body.

A modern example of _____ is the economic restructuring of Germany after the fall of the Third Reich in 1945.

a. Decartelization
b. Monopolization
c. Complementary monopoly
d. Market power

53. _____ is one of the four Ps of the marketing mix. The other three aspects are product, promotion, and place. It is also a key variable in microeconomic price allocation theory.

a. Guaranteed Maximum Price
b. Point of total assumption
c. Pricing
d. Premium pricing

54. In economics and sociology, an _____ is any factor (financial or non-financial) that enables or motivates a particular course of action, or counts as a reason for preferring one choice to the alternatives. It is an expectation that encourages people to behave in a certain way. Since human beings are purposeful creatures, the study of _____ structures is central to the study of all economic activity (both in terms of individual decision-making and in terms of co-operation and competition within a larger institutional structure.)

a. Isocost
b. Economic reform
c. Epstein-Zin preferences
d. Incentive

55. The _____ curve theory is an economic theory regarding oligopoly and monopolistic competition. When it was created, the idea fundamentally challenged classical economic tenets such as efficient markets and rapidly-changing prices, ideas that underly basic supply and demand models. _____ was an initial attempt to explain sticky prices.

a. Kinked demand curve
b. Marginal demand
c. Kinked demand
d. Precautionary demand

Chapter 23. Monopolistic Competition and Oligopoly

56. The _____ theory is an economic theory regarding oligopoly and monopolistic competition. When it was created, the idea fundamentally challenged classical economic tenets such as efficient markets and rapidly-changing prices, ideas that underly basic supply and demand models. Kinked demand was an initial attempt to explain sticky prices.
   a. Precautionary demand
   b. Hicksian demand function
   c. Kinked demand
   d. Kinked demand curve

57. _____ is a term used in business to indicate a state of intense competitive rivalry accompanied by a multi-lateral series of price reduction. One competitor will lower its price, then others will lower their prices to match. If one of them reduces their price again, a new round of reductions starts.
   a. Price war
   b. Discounts and allowances
   c. Transactional Net Margin Method
   d. Big ticket item

58. The term _____ refers to economy-wide fluctuations in production or economic activity over several months or years. These fluctuations occur around a long-term growth trend, and typically involve shifts over time between periods of relatively rapid economic growth (expansion or boom), and periods of relative stagnation or decline (contraction or recession.)

These fluctuations are often measured using the growth rate of real gross domestic product.

   a. Consumer theory
   b. Tobit model
   c. Nominal value
   d. Business cycle

59. Necessary _____ s:

If x is a necessary _____ of y, then the presence of y necessarily implies the presence of x. The presence of x, however, does not imply that y will occur.

Sufficient _____ s:

If x is a sufficient _____ of y, then the presence of x necessarily implies the presence of y.

   a. Political philosophy
   b. Materialism
   c. Philosophy of economics
   d. Cause

60. In economics, _____ is the process by which a firm determines the price and output level that returns the greatest profit. There are several approaches to this problem. The total revenue--total cost method relies on the fact that profit equals revenue minus cost, and the marginal revenue--marginal cost method is based on the fact that total profit in a perfectly competitive market reaches its maximum point where marginal revenue equals marginal cost.
   a. Profit margin
   b. Normal profit
   c. 100-year flood
   d. Profit maximization

61. The Organization of the Petroleum Exporting Countries is a cartel of twelve countries made up of Algeria, Angola, Ecuador, Iran, Iraq, Kuwait, Libya, Nigeria, Qatar, Saudi Arabia, the United Arab Emirates, and Venezuela. The cartel has maintained its headquarters in Vienna since 1965, and hosts regular meetings among the oil ministers of its Member Countries. Indonesia withdrew its membership in _____ in 2008 after it became a net importer of oil, but stated it would likely return if it became a net exporter in the world.

a. ACEA agreement
b. AD-IA Model
c. ACCRA Cost of Living Index
d. OPEC

62. In microeconomics, _____ is quite simply the conversion of inputs into outputs. It is an economic process that uses resources to create a good or service that is suitable for exchange. This can include manufacturing, storing, shipping, and packaging.
   a. MET
   b. Solved
   c. Red Guards
   d. Production

63. In economics, a _____ is a general slowdown in economic activity over a sustained period of time, or a business cycle contraction. During _____s, many macroeconomic indicators vary in a similar way. Production as measured by Gross Domestic Product (GDP), employment, investment spending, capacity utilization, household incomes and business profits all fall during _____s.
   a. Monetary economics
   b. Leading indicators
   c. Treasury View
   d. Recession

64. The _____ is an independent agency of the United States government, established in 1914 by the _____ Act. Its principal mission is the promotion of 'consumer protection' and the elimination and prevention of what regulators perceive to be harmfully 'anti-competitive' business practices, such as coercive monopoly.

The _____ Act was one of President Wilson's major acts against trusts.

   a. Federal Trade Commission
   b. 100-year flood
   c. 1921 recession
   d. 130-30 fund

65. The _____ of 1914 (15 U.S.C §§ 41-58, as amended) established the Federal Trade Commission (FTC), a bipartisan body of five members appointed by the President of the United States for seven year terms. This Commission was authorized to issue Cease and Desist orders to large corporations to curb unfair trade practices. This Act also gave more flexibility to the US congress for judicial matters.
   a. Minimum wage law
   b. Federal Trade Commission Act
   c. Buydown
   d. Competition law theory

66. A limit price is the price set by a monopolist to discourage economic entry into a market, and is illegal in many countries. The limit price is the price that the entrant would face upon entering as long as the incumbent firm did not decrease output. The limit price is often lower than the average cost of production or just low enough to make entering not profitable. The quantity produced by the incumbent firm to act as a deterrent to entry is usually larger than would be optimal for a monopolist, but might still produce higher economic profits than would be earned under perfect competition. The problem with _____ as strategic behavior is that once the entrant has entered the market, the quantity used as a threat to deter entry is no longer the incumbent firm's best response.
   a. Third line forcing
   b. Predatory pricing
   c. Conscious parallelism
   d. Limit pricing

67. Procter is a surname, and may also refer to:

- Bryan Waller Procter (pseud. Barry Cornwall), English poet
- Goodwin Procter, American law firm
- _____, consumer products multinational

a. Tightness
c. Drawdown
b. Bucket shop
d. Procter ' Gamble

68. The phrase _____, according to the Organization for Economic Co-operation and Development, refers to 'creative work undertaken on a systematic basis in order to increase the stock of knowledge, including knowledge of man, culture and society, and the use of this stock of knowledge to devise new applications [sic]'

New product design and development is more than often a crucial factor in the survival of a company. In an industry that is fast changing, firms must continually revise their design and range of products. This is necessary due to continuous technology change and development as well as other competitors and the changing preference of customers.

a. 100-year flood
c. 1921 recession
b. Research and development
d. 130-30 fund

69. _____ is a broad label that refers to any individuals or households that use goods and services generated within the economy. The concept of a _____ is used in different contexts, so that the usage and significance of the term may vary.

Typically when business people and economists talk of _____s they are talking about person as _____, an aggregated commodity item with little individuality other than that expressed in the buy/not-buy decision.

a. 130-30 fund
c. 1921 recession
b. 100-year flood
d. Consumer

70. In economics, the _____ of demand measures the responsiveness of the demand of a good to the change in the income of the people demanding the good. It is calculated as the ratio of the percent change in demand to the percent change in income. For example, if, in response to a 10% increase in income, the demand of a good increased by 20%, the _____ of demand would be 20%/10% = 2.

a. AD-IA Model
c. ACCRA Cost of Living Index
b. ACEA agreement
d. Income elasticity

71. In economics, the _____ measures the responsiveness of the demand of a good to the change in the income of the people demanding the good. It is calculated as the ratio of the percent change in demand to the percent change in income. For example, if, in response to a 10% increase in income, the demand of a good increased by 20%, the _____ would be 20%/10% = 2.

a. Indifference map
b. Elasticity of substitution
c. Expenditure minimization problem
d. Income elasticity of demand

72. The phrase _____ refers to the aspect of corporate strategy, corporate finance and management dealing with the buying, selling and combining of different companies that can aid, finance, or help a growing company in a given industry grow rapidly without having to create another business entity.

An acquisition, also known as a takeover or a buyout, is the buying of one company (the 'target') by another. An acquisition may be friendly or hostile.

a. Mergers and acquisitions
b. Productive and unproductive labour
c. Peace dividend
d. Political economy

73. In economics, the _____ is defined as a numerical measure of the responsiveness of the quantity supplied of product (A) to a change in price of product (A) alone. It is the measure of the way quantity supplied reacts to a change in price.

For example, if, in response to a 10% rise in the price of a good, the quantity supplied increases by 20%, the _____ would be 20%/10% = 2.

a. Passive income
b. Hedonimetry
c. Demand shaping
d. Price elasticity of supply

74. _____ was a survey conducted by the U.S. Department of Justice to gauge the prevalence of alcohol and illegal drug use among prior arrestees. It was a reformulation of the prior Drug Use Forecasting (DUF) program, focused on five drugs in particular: cocaine, marijuana, methamphetamine, opiates, and PCP.

Participants were randomly selected from arrest records in major metropolitan areas; because no personally identifying information is taken from each record chosen, the resulting data can be correlated to arrest rates, but not to the total population of persons charged.

a. AD-IA Model
b. ACEA agreement
c. ACCRA Cost of Living Index
d. Arrestee Drug Abuse Monitoring

Chapter 24. Technology, R&D, and Efficiency

1. The _____ consists of a number of economic theories which describe the nature of the firm, company including its existence, its behaviour, and its relationship with the market.

In simplified terms, the _____ aims to answer these questions:

1. Existence - why do firms emerge, why are not all transactions in the economy mediated over the market?
2. Boundaries - why the boundary between firms and the market is located exactly there? Which transactions are performed internally and which are negotiated on the market?
3. Organization - why are firms structured in such specific way? What is the interplay of formal and informal relationships?

Despite looking simple, these questions are not answered by the established economic theory, which usually views firms as given, and treats them as black boxes without any internal structure.

The First World War period saw a change of emphasis in economic theory away from industry-level analysis which mainly included analysing markets to analysis at the level of the firm, as it became increasingly clear that perfect competition was no longer an adequate model of how firms behaved. Economic theory till then had focussed on trying to understand markets alone and there had been little study on understanding why firms or organisations exist.

   a. Policy Ineffectiveness Proposition
   b. Khazzoom-Brookes postulate
   c. Theory of the firm
   d. Technology gap

2. The _____ is an international organization that oversees the global financial system by following the macroeconomic policies of its member countries, in particular those with an impact on exchange rates and the balance of payments. It is an organization formed to stabilize international exchange rates and facilitate development. It also offers financial and technical assistance to its members, making it an international lender of last resort.
   a. ACCRA Cost of Living Index
   b. ACEA agreement
   c. International Monetary Fund
   d. Office of Thrift Supervision

3. A _____ is a set of exclusive rights granted by a state to an inventor or his assignee for a limited period of time in exchange for a disclosure of an invention.

The procedure for granting _____s, the requirements placed on the _____ee and the extent of the exclusive rights vary widely between countries according to national laws and international agreements. Typically, however, a _____ application must include one or more claims defining the invention which must be new, inventive, and useful or industrially applicable.

   a. Long service leave
   b. Bank regulation
   c. Bona fide occupational qualification
   d. Patent

4. The process of _____ involves the introduction of a good or service that is new or substantially improved. This includes, but is not limited to, improvements in functional characteristics, technical abilities, or ease of use.
   a. Refusal to deal
   b. Dogs of the Dow
   c. Microcap stock
   d. Product innovation

5. The phrase _____, according to the Organization for Economic Co-operation and Development, refers to 'creative work undertaken on a systematic basis in order to increase the stock of knowledge, including knowledge of man, culture and society, and the use of this stock of knowledge to devise new applications [sic]'

New product design and development is more than often a crucial factor in the survival of a company. In an industry that is fast changing, firms must continually revise their design and range of products. This is necessary due to continuous technology change and development as well as other competitors and the changing preference of customers.

a. 130-30 fund
b. 100-year flood
c. 1921 recession
d. Research and development

6. _____s is the social science that studies the production, distribution, and consumption of goods and services. The term _____s comes from the Ancient Greek οἰκονομία from οἶκος (oikos, 'house') + νόμος (nomos, 'custom' or 'law'), hence 'rules of the house(hold)'. Current _____ models developed out of the broader field of political economy in the late 19th century, owing to a desire to use an empirical approach more akin to the physical sciences.

a. Energy economics
b. Inflation
c. Economic
d. Opportunity cost

7. _____ is an economic system in which wealth, and the means of producing wealth, are privately owned. Through _____, the land, labor, and capital are owned, operated, and traded for the purpose of generating profits, without force or fraud, by private individuals either singly or jointly, and investments, distribution, income, production, pricing and supply of goods, commodities and services are determined by voluntary private decision in a market economy. A distinguishing feature of _____ is that each person owns his or her own labor and therefore is allowed to sell the use of it to employers.

a. Creative capitalism
b. Late capitalism
c. Socialism for the rich and capitalism for the poor
d. Capitalism

8. _____ and Keynesian Theory) is a macroeconomic theory based on the ideas of 20th-century British economist John Maynard Keynes. _____ argues that private sector decisions sometimes lead to inefficient macroeconomic outcomes and therefore advocates active policy responses by the public sector, including monetary policy actions by the central bank and fiscal policy actions by the government to stabilize output over the business cycle.

The theories forming the basis of _____ were first presented in The General Theory of Employment, Interest and Money, published in 1936.

a. Market failure
b. Rational choice theory
c. Deflation
d. Keynesian economics

Chapter 24. Technology, R&D, and Efficiency

9. Competition law, known in the United States as _____ law, has three main elements:

   - prohibiting agreements or practices that restrict free trading and competition between business entities. This includes in particular the repression of cartels.
   - banning abusive behaviour by a firm dominating a market, or anti-competitive practices that tend to lead to such a dominant position. Practices controlled in this way may include predatory pricing, tying, price gouging, refusal to deal, and many others.
   - supervising the mergers and acquisitions of large corporations, including some joint ventures. Transactions that are considered to threaten the competitive process can be prohibited altogether, or approved subject to 'remedies' such as an obligation to divest part of the merged business or to offer licences or access to facilities to enable other businesses to continue competing.

   The substance and practice of competition law varies from jurisdiction to jurisdiction. Protecting the interests of consumers (consumer welfare) and ensuring that entrepreneurs have an opportunity to compete in the market economy are often treated as important objectives. Competition law is closely connected with law on deregulation of access to markets, state aids and subsidies, the privatisation of state owned assets and the establishment of independent sector regulators. In recent decades, competition law has been viewed as a way to provide better public services.

   a. United Kingdom competition law
   b. Intellectual property law
   c. Anti-Inflation Act
   d. Antitrust

10. _____ was a Scottish-born American industrialist, businessman, and a major philanthropist. He was an immigrant as a child with his parents. He built Pittsburgh's Carnegie Steel Company, which was later merged with Elbert H. Gary's Federal Steel Company and several smaller companies to create U.S. Steel.
    a. Andrew Carnegie
    b. Eli Whitney
    c. Oskar Morgenstern
    d. Alfred Marshall

11. An _____ is a person who has possession of an enterprise and assumes significant accountability for the inherent risks and the outcome. It is an ambitious leader who combines land, labor, and capital to create and market new goods or services. The term is a loanword from French and was first defined by the Irish economist Richard Cantillon.
    a. ACEA agreement
    b. Entrepreneur
    c. Expansionary policies
    d. ACCRA Cost of Living Index

12. _____ was the American founder of the Ford Motor Company and father of modern assembly lines used in mass production. His introduction of the Model T automobile revolutionized transportation and American industry. He was a prolific inventor and was awarded 161 U.S. patents.
    a. George Cabot Lodge II
    b. Werner Sombart
    c. Maximilian Carl Emil Weber
    d. Henry Ford

13. In finance, a _____ is a debt security, in which the authorized issuer owes the holders a debt and, depending on the terms of the _____, is obliged to pay interest (the coupon) and/or to repay the principal at a later date, termed maturity. A _____ is a formal contract to repay borrowed money with interest at fixed intervals.

    Thus a _____ is like a loan: the issuer is the borrower (debtor), the holder is the lender (creditor), and the coupon is the interest.

a. Prize Bond
c. Callable
b. Zero-coupon
d. Bond

14. _____ is a fee paid on borrowed assets. It is the price paid for the use of borrowed money , or, money earned by deposited funds . Assets that are sometimes lent with _____ include money, shares, consumer goods through hire purchase, major assets such as aircraft, and even entire factories in finance lease arrangements.
   a. Asset protection
   c. Interest
   b. Internal debt
   d. Insolvency

15. An _____ is the price a borrower pays for the use of money they do not own, for instance a small company might borrow from a bank to kick start their business, and the return a lender receives for deferring the use of funds, by lending it to the borrower. _____s are normally expressed as a percentage rate over the period of one year.

_____s targets are also a vital tool of monetary policy and are used to control variables like investment, inflation, and unemployment.

   a. Arrow-Debreu model
   c. Enterprise value
   b. ACCRA Cost of Living Index
   d. Interest rate

16. _____ is a type of private equity capital typically provided to early-stage, high-potential, growth companies in the interest of generating a return through an eventual realization event such as an IPO or trade sale of the company. _____ investments are generally made as cash in exchange for shares in the invested company. It is typical for _____ investors to identify and back companies in high technology industries such as biotechnology and ICT.
   a. Collateralized Fund Obligation
   c. Club deal
   b. Startup company
   d. Venture capital

17. _____ is a specific term used in companies' financial reporting from the company-whole point of view. Because that use excludes the effects of changing ownership interest, an economic measure of _____ is necessary for financial analysis from the shareholders' point of view

_____ is defined by the Financial Accounting Standards Board, or FASB, as e;the change in equity [net assets] of a business enterprise during a period from transactions and other events and circumstances from nonowner sources. It includes all changes in equity during a period except those resulting from investments by owners and distributions to owners.e;

_____ is the sum of net income and other items that must bypass the income statement because they have not been realized, including items like an unrealized holding gain or loss from available for sale securities and foreign currency translation gains or losses.

   a. Real income
   c. Comprehensive income
   b. Windfall gain
   d. Net national income

Chapter 24. Technology, R&D, and Efficiency

18. A _____ is:

- Rewrite _____, in generative grammar and computer science
- Standardization, a formal and widely-accepted statement, fact, definition, or qualification
- Operation, a determinate _____ for performing a mathematical operation and obtaining a certain result (Mathematics, Logic)
    - Unary operation
    - Binary operation
- _____ of inference, a function from sets of formulae to formulae (Mathematics, Logic)
- _____ of thumb, principle with broad application that is not intended to be strictly accurate or reliable for every situation. Also often simply referred to as a _____
- Moral, an atomic element of a moral code for guiding choices in human behavior
- Heuristic, a quantized '_____' which shows a tendency or probability for successful function
- A regulation, as in sports
- A Production _____, as in computer science
- Procedural law, a _____ set governing the application of laws to cases
    - A law, which may informally be called a '_____'
    - A court ruling, a decision by a court
- In the U.S. Government, a regulation mandated by Congress, but written or expanded upon by the Executive Branch.
- Norm (sociology), an informal but widely accepted _____, concept, truth, definition, or qualification (social norms, legal norms, coding norms)
- Norm (philosophy), a kind of sentence or a reason to act, feel or believe
- 'Rulership' is the concept of governance by a government:
    - Military _____, governance by a military body
    - Monastic _____, a collection of precepts that guides the life of monks or nuns in a religious order where the superior holds the place of Christ
- Slide _____

- '_____,' a song by Ayumi Hamasaki
- '_____,' a song by rapper Nas
- '_____s,' an album by the band The Whitest Boy Alive
- _____s: Pyaar Ka Superhit Formula, a 2003 Bollywood film
- ruler, an instrument for measuring lengths
- _____, a component of an astrolabe, circumferator or similar instrument
- The _____s, a bestselling self-help book
- _____ Project (Run Up-to-date Linux Everywhere), a project that aims to use up-to-date Linux software on old PCs
- _____ engine, a software system that helps managing business _____s
- Ja _____, a hip hop artist
    - R.U.L.E., a 2005 greatest hits album by rapper Ja _____
- '_____s,' a KMFDM song

a. Demand
c. Technocracy
b. Procter ' Gamble
d. Rule

19. In economics, and cost accounting, _____ describes the total economic cost of production and is made up of variable costs, which vary according to the quantity of a good produced and include inputs such as labor and raw materials, plus fixed costs, which are independent of the quantity of a good produced and include inputs (capital) that cannot be varied in the short term, such as buildings and machinery. _____ in economics includes the total opportunity cost of each factor of production in addition to fixed and variable costs.

The rate at which _____ changes as the amount produced changes is called marginal cost.

a. 130-30 fund
b. 100-year flood
c. Total cost
d. 1921 recession

20. In finance, _____ rate of profit or sometimes just return, is the ratio of money gained or lost on an investment relative to the amount of money invested. The amount of money gained or lost may be referred to as interest, profit/loss, gain/loss, or net income/loss. The money invested may be referred to as the asset, capital, principal, or the cost basis of the investment.

a. Cost accrual ratio
b. Sortino ratio
c. Rate of return
d. Current ratio

21. A _____ is an expression that compares quantities relative to each other. The most common examples involve two quantities, but any number of quantities can be compared. _____s are represented mathematically by separating each quantity with a colon, for example the _____ 2:3, which is read as the _____ 'two to three'.

a. 130-30 fund
b. 100-year flood
c. Y-intercept
d. Ratio

22. _____ is the difference between price and the costs of bringing to market whatever it is that is accounted as an enterprise (whether by harvest, extraction, manufacture, or purchase) in terms of the component costs of delivered goods and/or services and any operating or other expenses.

A key difficulty in measuring profit is in defining costs. Pure economic monetary profits can be zero or negative even in competitive equilibrium when accounted monetized costs exceed monetized price.

a. Operating profit
b. ACCRA Cost of Living Index
c. Economic profit
d. Accounting profit

23. In economics, _____ is the difference between a company's total revenue and its opportunity costs. It is the increase in wealth that an investor has from making an investment, taking into consideration all costs associated with that investment including the opportunity cost of capital.

Profit is the factor income of the entrepreneur.

a. Operating profit
b. Accounting profit
c. ACCRA Cost of Living Index
d. Economic profit

24. _____ is a component of the firm's opportunity costs. The time that the owner spends running the firm could be spent on running another firm. This is _____: the return the entrepreneur can expect to earn or the profit that the business owners considers necessary to make running the business worth his/her while.

a. Profit maximization
b. Profit margin
c. 100-year flood
d. Normal profit

25. In economics, _____ is a measure of the relative satisfaction from consumption of various goods and services. Given this measure, one may speak meaningfully of increasing or decreasing _____, and thereby explain economic behavior in terms of attempts to increase one's _____. For illustrative purposes, changes in _____ are sometimes expressed in units called utils.

a. Utility function
b. Utility
c. Ordinal utility
d. Expected utility hypothesis

26.

A _____ is a type of financial intermediary and a type of bank. Commercial banking is also known as business banking. It is a bank that provides checking accounts, savings accounts, and money market accounts and that accepts time deposits.

a. Lombard banking
b. Daylight overdraft
c. Bought deal
d. Commercial bank

27. Economics:

- _____, the desire to own something and the ability to pay for it
- _____ curve, a graphic representation of a _____ schedule
- _____ deposit, the money in checking accounts
- _____ pull theory, the theory that inflation occurs when _____ for goods and services exceeds existing supplies
- _____ schedule, a table that lists the quantity of a good a person will buy it each different price
- _____ side economics, the school of economics at believes government spending and tax cuts open economy by raising _____

a. Variability
b. Production
c. McKesson ' Robbins scandal
d. Demand

28. In algebra, a _____ is a function depending on n that associates a scalar, det(A), to an n×n square matrix A. The fundamental geometric meaning of a _____ is a scale factor for measure when A is regarded as a linear transformation. _____s are important both in calculus, where they enter the substitution rule for several variables, and in multilinear algebra.

For a fixed nonnegative integer n, there is a unique _____ function for the n×n matrices over any commutative ring R. In particular, this function exists when R is the field of real or complex numbers.

a. 1921 recession
b. 130-30 fund
c. Determinant
d. 100-year flood

29. The _____ is the weighted-average most likely outcome in gambling, probability theory, economics or finance.

What Does _____ Mean? The average of a probability distribution of possible returns, calculated by using the following formula:

E(R)= Sum: probability (in scenario i) * the return (in scenario i)

How do you calculate the average of a probability distribution? As denoted by the above formula, simply take the probability of each possible return outcome and multiply it by the return outcome itself. For example, if you knew a given investment had a 50% chance of earning a 10% return, a 25% chance of earning 20% and a 25% chance of earning -10%, the _____ would be equal to 7.5%:

= (0.5) (0.1) + (0.25) (0.2) + (0.25) (-0.1) = 0.075 = 7.5%

Although this is what you expect the return to be, there is no guarantee that it will be the actual return.

a. ACEA agreement
b. AD-IA Model
c. Expected return
d. ACCRA Cost of Living Index

30. In economics, _____ is how a natione;s total economy is distributed among its population. ._____ has always been a central concern of economic theory and economic policy. Classical economists such as Adam Smith, Thomas Malthus and David Ricardo were mainly concerned with factor _____, that is, the distribution of income between the main factors of production, land, labour and capital.
a. Equipment trust certificate
b. Eco commerce
c. Authorised capital
d. Income distribution

31. In economics, a _____ exists when a specific individual or enterprise has sufficient control over a particular product or service to determine significantly the terms on which other individuals shall have access to it. Monopolies are thus characterized by a lack of economic competition for the good or service that they provide and a lack of viable substitute goods. The verb 'monopolize' refers to the process by which a firm gains persistently greater market share than what is expected under perfect competition.
a. 100-year flood
b. Monopoly
c. 1921 recession
d. 130-30 fund

32. _____ in economics and business is the result of an exchange and from that trade we assign a numerical monetary value to a good, service or asset. If Alice trades Bob 4 apples for an orange, the _____ of an orange is 4 apples. Inversely, the _____ of an apple is 1/4 oranges.
a. Premium pricing
b. Price book
c. Price war
d. Price

33. In economics, the _____ is the term economists use to describe the self-regulating nature of the marketplace. The _____ is a metaphor coined by the economist Adam Smith in The Wealth of Nations.

Adam Smith mentions the metaphor in Book IV of The Wealth of Nations, arguing that people in any society will certainly employ their capital in foreign trading only if the profits available by that method far exceed those available locally, and that in such a case it is better for society as a whole if they so did.

a. AD-IA Model
b. Invisible hand
c. ACCRA Cost of Living Index
d. ACEA agreement

34. In economics and sociology, an _____ is any factor (financial or non-financial) that enables or motivates a particular course of action, or counts as a reason for preferring one choice to the alternatives. It is an expectation that encourages people to behave in a certain way. Since human beings are purposeful creatures, the study of _____ structures is central to the study of all economic activity (both in terms of individual decision-making and in terms of co-operation and competition within a larger institutional structure.)
a. Isocost
b. Epstein-Zin preferences
c. Economic reform
d. Incentive

35. _____ exists when sales of identical goods or services are transacted at different prices from the same provider. In a theoretical market with perfect information, no transaction costs or prohibition on secondary exchange (or re-selling) to prevent arbitrage, _____ can only be a feature of monopoly and oligopoly markets, where market power can be exercised. Otherwise, the moment the seller tries to sell the same good at different prices, the buyer at the lower price can arbitrage by selling to the consumer buying at the higher price but with a tiny discount.
a. Transfer pricing
b. Lerner Index
c. Loss leader
d. Price discrimination

36. In economics and especially in the theory of competition, _____ are obstacles in the path of a firm that make it difficult to enter a given market.

_____ are the source of a firm's pricing power - the ability of a firm to raise prices without losing all its customers.

The term refers to hindrances that an individual may face while trying to gain entrance into a profession or trade.

a. Social dumping
b. Group boycott
c. Limit price
d. Barriers to entry

37. The _____ is a measure of the size of firms in relation to the industry and an indicator of the amount of competition among them. Named after economists Orris C. Herfindahl and Albert O. Hirschman, it is an economic concept, widely applied in competition law, antitrust and also technology management. It is defined as the sum of the squares of the market shares of the 50 largest firms within the industry, where the market shares are expressed as percentages.
a. Vector autoregression
b. Reduced form
c. Panel data
d. Herfindahl index

38. A _____ is an investment transaction by which an entire company or a controlling part of the stock of a company is sold. A firm 'buys out' a company to take control of it. A _____ can take the form of a leveraged _____, a venture capital _____ or a management _____.
a. High yield stock
b. Clap note
c. Lawcards
d. Buyout

39. _____ is a common market structure where many competing producers sell products that are differentiated from one another (ie. the products are substitutes, but are not exactly alike.) Many markets are monopolistically competitive, common examples include the markets for restaurants, cereal, clothing, shoes and service industries in large cities.

a. Monopolistic competition
c. Financial crisis
b. Perfect competition
d. Mathematical economics

40. The _____ or gross domestic income (GDI), a basic measure of an economy's economic performance, is the market value of all final goods and services produced within the borders of a nation in a year. _____ can be defined in three ways, all of which are conceptually identical. First, it is equal to the total expenditures for all final goods and services produced within the country in a stipulated period of time (usually a 365-day year.)

a. Monopolistic competition
c. Countercyclical
b. Market structure
d. Gross domestic product

41. In economics, _____ describes the state of a market with respect to competition.

- Perfect competition, in which the market consists of a very large number of firms producing a homogeneous product.
- Monopolistic competition where there are a large number of independent firms which have a very small proportion of the market share.
- Oligopoly, in which a market is dominated by a small number of firms which own more than 40% of the market share.
- Oligopsony, a market dominated by many sellers and a few buyers.
- Monopoly, where there is only one provider of a product or service.
- Natural monopoly, a monopoly in which economies of scale cause efficiency to increase continuously with the size of the firm. A firm is a natural monopoly if it is able to serve the entire market demand at a lower cost than any combination of two or more smaller, more specialized firms.
- Monopsony, when there is only one buyer in a market.

The imperfectly competitive structure is quite identical to the realistic market conditions where some monopolistic competitors, monopolists, oligopolists, and duopolists exist and dominate the market conditions. The elements of _____ include the number and size distribution of firms, entry conditions, and the extent of differentiation.

These somewhat abstract concerns tend to determine some but not all details of a specific concrete market system where buyers and sellers actually meet and commit to trade.

a. Labour economics
c. Human capital
b. Monopolistic competition
d. Market structure

42. An _____ is a market form in which a market or industry is dominated by a small number of sellers (oligopolists.) Because there are few participants in this type of market, each oligopolist is aware of the actions of the others. The decisions of one firm influence, and are influenced by, the decisions of other firms.

a. ACCRA Cost of Living Index
c. ACEA agreement
b. Oligopsony
d. Oligopoly

43. In marketing, _____ is the process of distinguishing the differences of a product or offering from others, to make it more attractive to a particular target market. This involves differentiating it from competitors' products as well as one's own product offerings.

Differentiation is a source of competitive advantage.

a. Technology acceptance model
b. Pricing science
c. Market segment
d. Product differentiation

44. _____ has several particular meanings:

- in mathematics
    - _____ function
    - Euler _____
    - _____
    - _____ subgroup
    - method of _____s (partial differential equations)
- in physics and engineering
    - any _____ curve that shows the relationship between certain input- and output parameters, e.g.
    - an I-V or current-voltage _____ is the current in a circuit as a function of the applied voltage
    - Receiver-Operator _____
- in fiction
    - in Dungeons ' Dragons, _____ is another name for ability score

a. Demand
b. Characteristic
c. Technocracy
d. Russian financial crisis

45. In economics, the _____ of an industry is used as an indicator of the relative size of firms in relation to the industry as a whole. It is calculated as the sum of the percent market share of the top n industries. This may also assist in determining the market structure of the industry.
a. Concentration ratio
b. Monopolization
c. Pacman conjecture
d. Quasi-rent

46. _____ are the forces that cause larger firms to produce goods and services at increased per-unit costs. They are less well known than what economists have long understood as 'economies of scale', the forces which enable larger firms to produce goods and services at reduced per-unit costs.

Some of the forces which cause a diseconomy of scale are listed below:

Ideally, all employees of a firm would have one-on-one communication with each other so they know exactly what the other workers are doing.

a. Marginal physical product
b. Factors of production
c. Diseconomies of scale
d. Productive capacity

47. _____ is a situation in which the limited resources of a firm are allocated in accordance with the wishes of consumers. An allocatively efficient economy produces an 'optimal mix' of commodities. A firm is allocatively efficient when its price is equal to its marginal costs (that is, P = MC) in a perfect market.
a. ACCRA Cost of Living Index
b. Economic efficiency
c. ACEA agreement
d. Allocative efficiency

Chapter 24. Technology, R&D, and Efficiency

48. The notion of _____ is found in the writings of Mikhail Bakunin, Friedrich Nietzsche, and in Werner Sombart's Krieg und Kapitalismus (War and Capitalism) (1913, p. 207), where he wrote: 'again out of destruction a new spirit of creativity arises'. In Capitalism, Socialism and Democracy, the Austrian economist Joseph Schumpeter popularized and used the term to describe the process of transformation that accompanies radical innovation.

    a. 100-year flood
    b. Creative destruction
    c. 1921 recession
    d. 130-30 fund

49. _____ occurs when the economy is operating at its production possibility frontier (PPF.) This takes place when production of one good is achieved at the lowest cost possible, given the production of the other good(s.) Equivalently, it is when the highest possible output of one good is produced, given the production level of the other good(s.)

    a. Discretionary spending
    b. Preclusive purchasing
    c. Free contract
    d. Productive efficiency

50. The Office of the _____ is a US federal agency established by the National Currency Act of 1863 and serves to charter, regulate, and supervise all national banks and the federal branches and agencies of foreign banks in the United States. Currently, the _____ is John Dugan.

Headquartered in Washington, D.C., it has four district offices located in New York City, Chicago, Dallas and Denver.

    a. 130-30 fund
    b. Comptroller of the Currency
    c. 100-year flood
    d. 1921 recession

51. _____ is money accepted for exchange of goods in an economy. The prevalence of one money over another arises, usually, when a government designates through decrees that the government shall accept only particular notes and coins in payment for taxes. Typically, money of _____ consists of stamped coins and minted paper bills.

    a. Local currency
    b. Security thread
    c. Totnes pound
    d. Currency

52. _____, short for _____, was the first general-purpose electronic computer. It was a Turing-complete, digital computer capable of being reprogrammed to solve a full range of computing problems. _____ was designed and built to calculate artillery firing tables for the U.S. Army's Ballistic Research Laboratory.

    a. AD-IA Model
    b. ACCRA Cost of Living Index
    c. ENIAC
    d. ACEA agreement

53. _____ was a survey conducted by the U.S. Department of Justice to gauge the prevalence of alcohol and illegal drug use among prior arrestees. It was a reformulation of the prior Drug Use Forecasting (DUF) program, focused on five drugs in particular: cocaine, marijuana, methamphetamine, opiates, and PCP.

Participants were randomly selected from arrest records in major metropolitan areas; because no personally identifying information is taken from each record chosen, the resulting data can be correlated to arrest rates, but not to the total population of persons charged.

    a. ACCRA Cost of Living Index
    b. AD-IA Model
    c. ACEA agreement
    d. Arrestee Drug Abuse Monitoring

54. The _____ is a trilateral trade bloc in North America created by the governments of the United States, Canada, and Mexico. The agreement creating the trade bloc came into force on January 1, 1994. It superseded the Canada-United States Free Trade Agreement between the U.S. and Canada.
   a. Federal Reserve Bank Notes
   b. Demand-side technologies
   c. Case-Shiller Home Price Indices
   d. North American Free Trade Agreement

55. The _____ is a United States government agency that supports fundamental research and education in all the non-medical fields of science and engineering. Its medical counterpart is the National Institutes of Health. With an annual budget of about $6.02 billion (fiscal year 2008), _____ funds approximately 20 percent of all federally supported basic research conducted by the United States' colleges and universities.
   a. 130-30 fund
   b. 1921 recession
   c. 100-year flood
   d. National Science Foundation

Chapter 25. The Demand for Resources

1. _____ is a term in economics, where demand for one good or service occurs as a result of demand for another. This may occur as the former is a part of production of the second. For example, demand for coal leads to _____ for mining, as coal must be mined for coal to be consumed.
   a. Derived demand
   b. Leontief production function
   c. Days Sales Outstanding
   d. Rate risk

2. In economics, the _____ of demand measures the responsiveness of the demand of a good to the change in the income of the people demanding the good. It is calculated as the ratio of the percent change in demand to the percent change in income. For example, if, in response to a 10% increase in income, the demand of a good increased by 20%, the _____ of demand would be 20%/10% = 2.
   a. AD-IA Model
   b. ACEA agreement
   c. ACCRA Cost of Living Index
   d. Income elasticity

3. In economics, the _____ measures the responsiveness of the demand of a good to the change in the income of the people demanding the good. It is calculated as the ratio of the percent change in demand to the percent change in income. For example, if, in response to a 10% increase in income, the demand of a good increased by 20%, the _____ would be 20%/10% = 2.
   a. Income elasticity of demand
   b. Indifference map
   c. Elasticity of substitution
   d. Expenditure minimization problem

4. In microeconomics, _____ is the extra revenue that an additional unit of product will bring. It is the additional income from selling one more unit of a good; sometimes equal to price. It can also be described as the change in total revenue/change in number of units sold.
   a. Long term
   b. Market demand schedule
   c. Reservation price
   d. Marginal revenue

5. The marginal revenue productivity theory of wages, also referred to as the _____ of labor, is the change in total revenue earned by a firm that results from employing one more unit of labor. It is a neoclassical model that determines, under some conditions, the optimal number of workers to employ at an exogenously determined market wage rate.

   The _____ of a worker is equal to the product of the marginal product of labor (MP) and the marginal revenue (MR), given by MR×MP = _____.

   a. Real prices and ideal prices
   b. Marginal revenue product
   c. Marginal revenue productivity theory of wages
   d. Coal depletion

6. _____ in economics and business is the result of an exchange and from that trade we assign a numerical monetary value to a good, service or asset. If Alice trades Bob 4 apples for an orange, the _____ of an orange is 4 apples. Inversely, the _____ of an apple is 1/4 oranges.
   a. Price war
   b. Price book
   c. Price
   d. Premium pricing

7. _____ is defined as the measure of responsiveness in the quantity demanded for a commodity as a result of change in price of the same commodity. It is a measure of how consumers react to a change in price. In other words, it is percentage change in quantity demanded as per the percentage change in price of the same commodity.

Chapter 25. The Demand for Resources

a. Price elasticity of demand
b. 1921 recession
c. 130-30 fund
d. 100-year flood

8. Monopoly power is an example of market failure which occurs when one or more of the participants has the ability to influence the price or other outcomes in some general or specialized market. The most commonly discussed form of market power is that of a monopoly, but other forms such as monopsony, and more moderate versions of these two extremes, exist. Market participants that have market power are sometimes referred to as 'price makers', while those without are sometimes called '_____'.

a. Price takers
b. Market concentration
c. Market power
d. Monopolization

9. _____ is used to assign the available resources in an economic way. It is part of resource management.

In strategic planning, is a plan for using available resources, for example human resources, especially in the near term, to achieve goals for the future.

a. 130-30 fund
b. 1921 recession
c. 100-year flood
d. Resource allocation

10. Economics:

- _____, the desire to own something and the ability to pay for it
- _____ curve, a graphic representation of a _____ schedule
- _____ deposit, the money in checking accounts
- _____ pull theory, the theory that inflation occurs when _____ for goods and services exceeds existing supplies
- _____ schedule, a table that lists the quantity of a good a person will buy it each different price
- _____ side economics, the school of economics at believes government spending and tax cuts open economy by raising _____

a. McKesson ' Robbins scandal
b. Variability
c. Production
d. Demand

11. In economics, _____ is the ratio of the percent change in one variable to the percent change in another variable. It is a tool for measuring the responsiveness of a function to changes in parameters in a relative way. Commonly analyzed are _____ of substitution, price and wealth.

a. ACCRA Cost of Living Index
b. ACEA agreement
c. Elasticity of demand
d. Elasticity

12. Price _____ is defined as the measure of responsiveness in the quantity demanded for a commodity as a result of change in price of the same commodity. It is a measure of how consumers react to a change in price. In other words, it is percentage change in quantity demanded by the percentage change in price of the same commodity.

a. ACCRA Cost of Living Index
b. ACEA agreement
c. Elasticity
d. Elasticity of demand

13. In economics, _____ is how a natione;s total economy is distributed among its population. ._____ has always been a central concern of economic theory and economic policy. Classical economists such as Adam Smith, Thomas Malthus and David Ricardo were mainly concerned with factor _____, that is, the distribution of income between the main factors of production, land, labour and capital.
   a. Authorised capital
   b. Equipment trust certificate
   c. Eco commerce
   d. Income distribution

14. In economics, a _____ exists when a specific individual or enterprise has sufficient control over a particular product or service to determine significantly the terms on which other individuals shall have access to it. Monopolies are thus characterized by a lack of economic competition for the good or service that they provide and a lack of viable substitute goods. The verb 'monopolize' refers to the process by which a firm gains persistently greater market share than what is expected under perfect competition.
   a. 1921 recession
   b. 130-30 fund
   c. 100-year flood
   d. Monopoly

15. _____ in economics refers to metrics and measures of output from production processes, per unit of input. Labor _____, for example, is typically measured as a ratio of output per labor-hour, an input. _____ may be conceived of as a metrics of the technical or engineering efficiency of production.
   a. Productivity
   b. Production-possibility frontier
   c. Fordism
   d. Piece work

16. A _____ is:

- Rewrite _____, in generative grammar and computer science
- Standardization, a formal and widely-accepted statement, fact, definition, or qualification
- Operation, a determinate _____ for performing a mathematical operation and obtaining a certain result (Mathematics, Logic)
    - Unary operation
    - Binary operation
- _____ of inference, a function from sets of formulae to formulae (Mathematics, Logic)
- _____ of thumb, principle with broad application that is not intended to be strictly accurate or reliable for every situation. Also often simply referred to as a _____
- Moral, an atomic element of a moral code for guiding choices in human behavior
- Heuristic, a quantized '_____' which shows a tendency or probability for successful function
- A regulation, as in sports
- A Production _____, as in computer science
- Procedural law, a _____ set governing the application of laws to cases
    - A law, which may informally be called a '_____'
    - A court ruling, a decision by a court
- In the U.S. Government, a regulation mandated by Congress, but written or expanded upon by the Executive Branch.
- Norm (sociology), an informal but widely accepted _____, concept, truth, definition, or qualification (social norms, legal norms, coding norms)
- Norm (philosophy), a kind of sentence or a reason to act, feel or believe
- 'Rulership' is the concept of governance by a government:
    - Military _____, governance by a military body
    - Monastic _____, a collection of precepts that guides the life of monks or nuns in a religious order where the superior holds the place of Christ
- Slide _____

- '_____,' a song by Ayumi Hamasaki
- '_____,' a song by rapper Nas
- '_____s,' an album by the band The Whitest Boy Alive
- _____s: Pyaar Ka Superhit Formula, a 2003 Bollywood film
- ruler, an instrument for measuring lengths
- _____, a component of an astrolabe, circumferator or similar instrument
- The _____s, a bestselling self-help book
- _____ Project (Run Up-to-date Linux Everywhere), a project that aims to use up-to-date Linux software on old PCs
- _____ engine, a software system that helps managing business _____s
- Ja _____, a hip hop artist
    - R.U.L.E., a 2005 greatest hits album by rapper Ja _____
- '_____s,' a KMFDM song

a. Rule
b. Procter ' Gamble
c. Demand
d. Technocracy

17. In economics, the _____ can be defined as the graph depicting the relationship between the price of a certain commodity, and the amount of it that consumers are willing and able to purchase at that given price. It is a graphic representation of a demand schedule. The _____ for all consumers together follows from the _____ of every individual consumer: the individual demands at each price are added together.
   a. Kuznets curve
   b. Cost curve
   c. Wage curve
   d. Demand curve

18. _____ and Keynesian Theory) is a macroeconomic theory based on the ideas of 20th-century British economist John Maynard Keynes. _____ argues that private sector decisions sometimes lead to inefficient macroeconomic outcomes and therefore advocates active policy responses by the public sector, including monetary policy actions by the central bank and fiscal policy actions by the government to stabilize output over the business cycle.

The theories forming the basis of _____ were first presented in The General Theory of Employment, Interest and Money, published in 1936.

   a. Deflation
   b. Market failure
   c. Keynesian economics
   d. Rational choice theory

19. In economics, the _____ or marginal physical product is the extra output produced by one more unit of an input (for instance, the difference in output when a firm's labour is increased from five to six units.) Assuming that no other inputs to production change, the _____ of a given input (X) can be expressed as:

   _____ = ΔY/ΔX = (the change of Y)/(the change of X.)

   - ○
     - Pending approval by Thomas Sowell***

In neoclassical economics, this is the mathematical derivative of the production function.... Note that the 'product' (Y) is typically defined ignoring external costs and benefits.

   a. Factor prices
   b. Productive capacity
   c. Marginal product
   d. Labor problem

20. In economics, _____ is a measure of national income. Basically, it is an approach to measure GDP. It is defined as the value of planned goods and services produced in an economy.
   a. Aggregation problem
   b. Aggregate demand
   c. Aggregate supply
   d. Aggregate expenditure

21. In economics, a _____ is a table that lists the quantity of a good a person will buy it each different price See Demand curve.
   a. Federal Reserve districts
   b. Demand schedule
   c. Rational irrationality
   d. Free contract

22. In economic theory, _____ is the competitive situation in any market where the conditions necessary for perfect competition are not satisfied. It is a market structure that does not meet the conditions of perfect competition.

Chapter 25. The Demand for Resources

Forms of _____ include:

- Monopoly, in which there is only one seller of a good.
- Oligopoly, in which there is a small number of sellers.
- Monopolistic competition, in which there are many sellers producing highly differentiated goods.
- Monopsony, in which there is only one buyer of a good.
- Oligopsony, in which there is a small number of buyers.

There may also be _____ in markets due to buyers or sellers lacking information about prices and the goods being traded.

There may also be _____ due to a time lag in a market.

a. ACEA agreement
c. ACCRA Cost of Living Index
b. AD-IA Model
d. Imperfect competition

23. _____ is one of the four Ps of the marketing mix. The other three aspects are product, promotion, and place. It is also a key variable in microeconomic price allocation theory.

a. Premium pricing
c. Point of total assumption
b. Pricing
d. Guaranteed Maximum Price

24. Monopoly power is an example of market failure which occurs when one or more of the participants has the ability to influence the price or other outcomes in some general or specialized market. The most commonly discussed form of market power is that of a monopoly, but other forms such as monopsony, and more moderate versions of these two extremes, exist. Market participants that have market power are sometimes referred to as '_____', while those without are sometimes called 'price takers'.

a. Pacman conjecture
c. Rate-of-return regulation
b. Revenue-cap regulation
d. Price makers

25. In algebra, a _____ is a function depending on n that associates a scalar, det(A), to an n×n square matrix A. The fundamental geometric meaning of a _____ is a scale factor for measure when A is regarded as a linear transformation. _____s are important both in calculus, where they enter the substitution rule for several variables, and in multilinear algebra.

For a fixed nonnegative integer n, there is a unique _____ function for the n×n matrices over any commutative ring R. In particular, this function exists when R is the field of real or complex numbers.

a. 100-year flood
c. 130-30 fund
b. 1921 recession
d. Determinant

26. In the theory of artificial neural networks _____ networks are a case of competitive learning in recurrent neural networks. Output nodes in the network inhibit each other and activate themselves through reflexive connections. After some time, only one node in the output layer will be active.

Chapter 25. The Demand for Resources

a. 130-30 fund
b. 1921 recession
c. 100-year flood
d. Winner-take-all

27. The term _____s refers to wages that have been adjusted for inflation. This term is used in contrast to nominal wages or unadjusted wages.

The use of adjusted figures is in undertaking some form of economic analysis.

a. Federal Wage System
b. Profit sharing
c. Living wage
d. Real wage

28. In a _____ there is both a monopoly (a single seller) and monopsony (a single buyer) in the same market.

In such market price and output will be determined by the non economic forces like bargaining power of both buyer and seller. A _____ model is often used in situations where the switching costs of both sides are prohibitively high.

a. Market concentration
b. Price takers
c. Revenue-cap regulation
d. Bilateral monopoly

29. The term '_____' refers to the concept of collecting information and attempting to spot a pattern in the information. In some fields of study, the term '_____' has more formally-defined meanings.

In project management _____ is a mathematical technique that uses historical results to predict future outcome.

a. Quantile regression
b. Trend analysis
c. Coefficient of determination
d. Probit model

30. The Office of the _____ is a US federal agency established by the National Currency Act of 1863 and serves to charter, regulate, and supervise all national banks and the federal branches and agencies of foreign banks in the United States. Currently, the _____ is John Dugan.

Headquartered in Washington, D.C., it has four district offices located in New York City, Chicago, Dallas and Denver.

a. 100-year flood
b. Comptroller of the Currency
c. 1921 recession
d. 130-30 fund

31. _____ is money accepted for exchange of goods in an economy. The prevalence of one money over another arises, usually, when a government designates through decrees that the government shall accept only particular notes and coins in payment for taxes. Typically, money of _____ consists of stamped coins and minted paper bills.

a. Security thread
b. Totnes pound
c. Local currency
d. Currency

Chapter 25. The Demand for Resources

32. The _____ was an evolution of developed countries from an industrial/manufacturing-based wealth producing economy into a service sector asset based economy, brought about by globalization and currency manipulation by governments and their central banks. Some analysts claimed that this change in the economic structure of the United States had created a state of permanent steady growth, low unemployment, and immunity to boom and bust macroeconomic cycles. They believed that the change rendered obsolete many business practices.
   a. New Economy
   b. 100-year flood
   c. 130-30 fund
   d. 1921 recession

33. _____ is the term denoting either an entrance or changes which are inserted into a system and which activate/modify a process. It is an abstract concept, used in the modeling, system(s) design and system(s) exploitation. It is usually connected with other terms, e.g., _____ field, _____ variable, _____ parameter, _____ value, _____ signal, _____ device and _____ file.
   a. Input
   b. ACEA agreement
   c. ACCRA Cost of Living Index
   d. AD-IA Model

34. In economics, and cost accounting, _____ describes the total economic cost of production and is made up of variable costs, which vary according to the quantity of a good produced and include inputs such as labor and raw materials, plus fixed costs, which are independent of the quantity of a good produced and include inputs (capital) that cannot be varied in the short term, such as buildings and machinery. _____ in economics includes the total opportunity cost of each factor of production in addition to fixed and variable costs.

The rate at which _____ changes as the amount produced changes is called marginal cost.

   a. 100-year flood
   b. Total cost
   c. 1921 recession
   d. 130-30 fund

35. In mathematics, a _____ is a constant multiplicative factor of a certain object. For example, in the expression $9x^2$, the _____ of x^2 is 9.

The object can be such things as a variable, a vector, a function, etc.

   a. 100-year flood
   b. Coefficient
   c. 1921 recession
   d. 130-30 fund

36. In economics, the _____ and cross price elasticity of demand measures the responsiveness of the demand of a good to a change in the price of another good.

It is measured as the percentage change in demand for the first good that occurs in response to a percentage change in price of the second good. For example, if, in response to a 10% increase in the price of fuel, the demand of new cars that are fuel inefficient decreased by 20%, the _____ would be −20%/10% = −2.

   a. Quality bias
   b. Cross elasticity of demand
   c. Snob effect
   d. Convex preferences

Chapter 25. The Demand for Resources

37. In microeconomics, _____ is quite simply the conversion of inputs into outputs. It is an economic process that uses resources to create a good or service that is suitable for exchange. This can include manufacturing, storing, shipping, and packaging.
    a. Solved
    b. Red Guards
    c. Production
    d. MET

38. A _____ is an expression that compares quantities relative to each other. The most common examples involve two quantities, but any number of quantities can be compared. _____s are represented mathematically by separating each quantity with a colon, for example the _____ 2:3, which is read as the _____ 'two to three'.
    a. 100-year flood
    b. Y-intercept
    c. Ratio
    d. 130-30 fund

39. To _____ is to impose a financial charge or other levy upon a taxpayer by a state or the functional equivalent of a state.

    _____es are also imposed by many subnational entities. _____es consist of direct _____ or indirect _____, and may be paid in money or as its labour equivalent (often but not always unpaid.)

    a. 130-30 fund
    b. 1921 recession
    c. 100-year flood
    d. Tax

40. To tax is to impose a financial charge or other levy upon a taxpayer by a state or the functional equivalent of a state.

    _____ are also imposed by many subnational entities. _____ consist of direct tax or indirect tax, and may be paid in money or as its labour equivalent (often but not always unpaid.)

    a. Taxes
    b. 1921 recession
    c. 100-year flood
    d. 130-30 fund

41. The _____ or gross domestic income (GDI), a basic measure of an economy's economic performance, is the market value of all final goods and services produced within the borders of a nation in a year. _____ can be defined in three ways, all of which are conceptually identical. First, it is equal to the total expenditures for all final goods and services produced within the country in a stipulated period of time (usually a 365-day year.)
    a. Market structure
    b. Monopolistic competition
    c. Countercyclical
    d. Gross domestic product

42. The _____ or the output gap is the difference between potential GDP and actual GDP or actual output. The calculation for the output gap is Y-Y* where Y* is potential output and Y is actual output. If this calculation yields a positive number it is called an expansionary gap and indicates an economy in expansion; if the calculation yields a negative number it is called a recessionary gap and indicates an economy in recession.
    a. 130-30 fund
    b. 1921 recession
    c. 100-year flood
    d. GDP gap

43. In economics, the _____ also known as MPL or MPN is the change in output from hiring one additional unit of labor. It is the increase in output added by the last unit of labor. Assuming that no other inputs to production change, the marginal product of a given input (X) can be expressed as:

Chapter 25. The Demand for Resources 363

MP = ΔY/ΔX = (the change of Y)/(the change of X.)

a. Marginal product
c. Marginal product of labor
b. Production function
d. Product Pipeline

44. _____ is the difference between efficient behavior of firms assumed or implied by economic theory and their observed behavior in practice.

Economic theory assumes that the management of firms act to maximize owners' wealth by minimizing risk and maximizing economic profits -- which is accomplished by simultaneously maximizing revenues and minimizing costs, usually through the adjustment of output. In perfect competition, the free entry and exit of firms tends toward firms producing at the point where price equals long run average costs and long run average costs are minimized.

a. Revelation principle
c. X-efficiency
b. 100-year flood
d. X-inefficiency

45. In mathematics, an _____ is a statement about the relative size or order of two objects, or about whether they are the same or not

- The notation a < b means that a is less than b.
- The notation a > b means that a is greater than b.
- The notation a ≠ b means that a is not equal to b, but does not say that one is greater than the other or even that they can be compared in size.

In each statement above, a is not equal to b. These relations are known as strict inequalities. The notation a < b may also be read as 'a is strictly less than b'.

a. AD-IA Model
c. ACCRA Cost of Living Index
b. ACEA agreement
d. Inequality

46.

A _____ is a type of financial intermediary and a type of bank. Commercial banking is also known as business banking. It is a bank that provides checking accounts, savings accounts, and money market accounts and that accepts time deposits.

a. Daylight overdraft
c. Lombard banking
b. Bought deal
d. Commercial bank

47. A _____ is any systematic process enabling many market players to bid and ask: helping bidders and sellers interact and make deals. It is not just the price mechanism but the entire system of regulation, qualification, credentials, reputations and clearing that surrounds that mechanism and makes it operate in a social context.

Because a _____ relies on the assumption that players are constantly involved and unequally enabled, a _____ is distinguished specifically from a voting system where candidates seek the support of voters on a less regular basis.

a. Competitive equilibrium
b. Price mechanism
c. Market system
d. Contestable market

Chapter 26. Wage Determination

1. The supply of labor is the number of total hours that workers wish to work at a given real wage rate.

   _____ curves are derived from the 'labor-leisure' trade-off. More hours worked earn higher incomes but necessitate a cut in the amount of leisure that workers enjoy.

   a. Late capitalism
   b. Human trafficking
   c. Creative capitalism
   d. Labor supply

2. The _____ was an evolution of developed countries from an industrial/manufacturing-based wealth producing economy into a service sector asset based economy, brought about by globalization and currency manipulation by governments and their central banks. Some analysts claimed that this change in the economic structure of the United States had created a state of permanent steady growth, low unemployment, and immunity to boom and bust macroeconomic cycles. They believed that the change rendered obsolete many business practices.

   a. New Economy
   b. 1921 recession
   c. 130-30 fund
   d. 100-year flood

3. In economics, _____ is the total supply of goods and services produced by a national economy during a specific time period. It is the total amount of goods and services in the economy available at all possible price levels.

   a. Aggregate demand
   b. Aggregate expenditure
   c. Aggregate supply
   d. Aggregation problem

4. In a _____ there is both a monopoly (a single seller) and monopsony (a single buyer) in the same market.

   In such market price and output will be determined by the non economic forces like bargaining power of both buyer and seller. A _____ model is often used in situations where the switching costs of both sides are prohibitively high.

   a. Price takers
   b. Revenue-cap regulation
   c. Market concentration
   d. Bilateral monopoly

5. In economics, a _____ exists when a specific individual or enterprise has sufficient control over a particular product or service to determine significantly the terms on which other individuals shall have access to it. Monopolies are thus characterized by a lack of economic competition for the good or service that they provide and a lack of viable substitute goods. The verb 'monopolize' refers to the process by which a firm gains persistently greater market share than what is expected under perfect competition.

   a. 1921 recession
   b. 130-30 fund
   c. 100-year flood
   d. Monopoly

6. _____ and Keynesian Theory) is a macroeconomic theory based on the ideas of 20th-century British economist John Maynard Keynes. _____ argues that private sector decisions sometimes lead to inefficient macroeconomic outcomes and therefore advocates active policy responses by the public sector, including monetary policy actions by the central bank and fiscal policy actions by the government to stabilize output over the business cycle.

   The theories forming the basis of _____ were first presented in The General Theory of Employment, Interest and Money, published in 1936.

a. Market failure
b. Deflation
c. Rational choice theory
d. Keynesian economics

7. _____ in economics refers to metrics and measures of output from production processes, per unit of input. Labor _____, for example, is typically measured as a ratio of output per labor-hour, an input. _____ may be conceived of as a metrics of the technical or engineering efficiency of production.

a. Production-possibility frontier
b. Piece work
c. Fordism
d. Productivity

8. The term _____s refers to wages that have been adjusted for inflation. This term is used in contrast to nominal wages or unadjusted wages.

The use of adjusted figures is in undertaking some form of economic analysis.

a. Real wage
b. Living wage
c. Profit sharing
d. Federal Wage System

Chapter 26. Wage Determination

9. A _____ is:

   - Rewrite _____, in generative grammar and computer science
   - Standardization, a formal and widely-accepted statement, fact, definition, or qualification
   - Operation, a determinate _____ for performing a mathematical operation and obtaining a certain result (Mathematics, Logic)
     - Unary operation
     - Binary operation
   - _____ of inference, a function from sets of formulae to formulae (Mathematics, Logic)
   - _____ of thumb, principle with broad application that is not intended to be strictly accurate or reliable for every situation. Also often simply referred to as a _____
   - Moral, an atomic element of a moral code for guiding choices in human behavior
   - Heuristic, a quantized '_____' which shows a tendency or probability for successful function
   - A regulation, as in sports
   - A Production _____, as in computer science
   - Procedural law, a _____ set governing the application of laws to cases
     - A law, which may informally be called a '_____'
     - A court ruling, a decision by a court
   - In the U.S. Government, a regulation mandated by Congress, but written or expanded upon by the Executive Branch.
   - Norm (sociology), an informal but widely accepted _____, concept, truth, definition, or qualification (social norms, legal norms, coding norms)
   - Norm (philosophy), a kind of sentence or a reason to act, feel or believe
   - 'Rulership' is the concept of governance by a government:
     - Military _____, governance by a military body
     - Monastic _____, a collection of precepts that guides the life of monks or nuns in a religious order where the superior holds the place of Christ
   - Slide _____

   - '_____,' a song by Ayumi Hamasaki
   - '_____,' a song by rapper Nas
   - '_____s,' an album by the band The Whitest Boy Alive
   - _____s: Pyaar Ka Superhit Formula, a 2003 Bollywood film
   - ruler, an instrument for measuring lengths
   - _____, a component of an astrolabe, circumferator or similar instrument
   - The _____s, a bestselling self-help book
   - _____ Project (Run Up-to-date Linux Everywhere), a project that aims to use up-to-date Linux software on old PCs
   - _____ engine, a software system that helps managing business _____s
   - Ja _____, a hip hop artist
     - R.U.L.E., a 2005 greatest hits album by rapper Ja _____
   - '_____s,' a KMFDM song

a. Technocracy
b. Procter ' Gamble
c. Demand
d. Rule

10. In economics, _____ are the resources employed to produce goods and services. They facilitate production but do not become part of the product (as with raw materials) or significantly transformed by the production process (as with fuel used to power machinery.) To 19th century economists, the _____ were land (natural resources, gifts from nature), labor (the ability to work), and capital goods (human-made tools and equipment.)
   a. Hicks-neutral technical change
   b. Long-run
   c. Product Pipeline
   d. Factors of production

11. The _____ or gross domestic income (GDI), a basic measure of an economy's economic performance, is the market value of all final goods and services produced within the borders of a nation in a year. _____ can be defined in three ways, all of which are conceptually identical. First, it is equal to the total expenditures for all final goods and services produced within the country in a stipulated period of time (usually a 365-day year.)
   a. Market structure
   b. Countercyclical
   c. Monopolistic competition
   d. Gross domestic product

12. The _____ or the output gap is the difference between potential GDP and actual GDP or actual output. The calculation for the output gap is Y-Y* where Y* is potential output and Y is actual output. If this calculation yields a positive number it is called an expansionary gap and indicates an economy in expansion; if the calculation yields a negative number it is called a recessionary gap and indicates an economy in recession.
   a. GDP gap
   b. 100-year flood
   c. 1921 recession
   d. 130-30 fund

13. In microeconomics, _____ is quite simply the conversion of inputs into outputs. It is an economic process that uses resources to create a good or service that is suitable for exchange. This can include manufacturing, storing, shipping, and packaging.
   a. Solved
   b. MET
   c. Production
   d. Red Guards

14. In economics, the _____ is the wage rate that produces neither an access supply of workers nor an excess demand for workers and labor market. See economic equilibrium.
   a. International free trade agreement
   b. Effective unemployment rate
   c. Economic stability
   d. Equilibrium wage

15. Economics:

   - _____, the desire to own something and the ability to pay for it
   - _____ curve, a graphic representation of a _____ schedule
   - _____ deposit, the money in checking accounts
   - _____ pull theory, the theory that inflation occurs when _____ for goods and services exceeds existing supplies
   - _____ schedule, a table that lists the quantity of a good a person will buy it each different price
   - _____ side economics, the school of economics at believes government spending and tax cuts open economy by raising _____

Chapter 26. Wage Determination 369

a. Variability	b. McKesson ' Robbins scandal
c. Production	d. Demand

16. The _____ is 'the basic residential unit in which economic production, consumption, inheritance, child rearing, and shelter are organized and carried out'; [the _____] 'may or may not be synonomous with family'.

The _____ is the basic unit of analysis in many social, microeconomic and government models. The term refers to all individuals who live in the same dwelling.

a. 130-30 fund	b. Household
c. Family economics	d. 100-year flood

17. In economic models, the _____ time frame assumes no fixed factors of production. Firms can enter or leave the marketplace, and the cost (and availability) of land, labor, raw materials, and capital goods can be assumed to vary. In contrast, in the short-run time frame, certain factors are assumed to be fixed, because there is not sufficient time for them to change.

a. Price/performance ratio	b. Long-run
c. Diseconomies of scale	d. Productivity world

18. The _____ is the number of total hours that workers wish to work at a given real wage rate.

Labor supply curves are derived from the 'labor-leisure' trade-off. More hours worked earn higher incomes but necessitate a cut in the amount of leisure that workers enjoy.

a. Compound interest	b. Supply of labor
c. De minimis fringe benefits	d. Dual labor market

19. The term '_____' refers to the concept of collecting information and attempting to spot a pattern in the information. In some fields of study, the term '_____' has more formally-defined meanings.

In project management _____ is a mathematical technique that uses historical results to predict future outcome.

a. Probit model	b. Coefficient of determination
c. Quantile regression	d. Trend analysis

20. _____ is the a method of technical and economic research of the systems for purpose to optimize a parity between system's consumer functions or properties and expenses to achieve those functions or properties.

This methodology for continuous perfection of production, industrial technologies, organizational structures was developed by Juryj Sobolev in 1948 at the 'Perm telephone factory'

- 1948 Juryj Sobolev - the first success in application of a method analysis at the 'Perm telephone factory' .
- 1949 - the first application for the invention as result of use of the new method.

Chapter 26. Wage Determination

Today in economically developed countries practically each enterprise or the company use methodology of the kind of functional-cost analysis as a practice of the quality management, most full satisfying to principles of standards of series ISO 9000.

- Interest of consumer not in products itself, but the advantage which it will receive from its usage.
- The consumer aspires to reduce his expenses
- Functions needed by consumer can be executed in the various ways, and, hence, with various efficiency and expenses. Among possible alternatives of realization of functions exist such in which the parity of quality and the price is the optimal for the consumer.

The goal of _____ is achievement of the highest consumer satisfaction of production at simultaneous decrease in all kinds of industrial expenses Classical _____ has three English synonyms - Value Engineering, Value Management, Value Analysis.

a. Monopoly wage
c. Staple financing
b. Function cost analysis
d. Willingness to pay

21. In economics, _____ describes the state of a market with respect to competition.

- Perfect competition, in which the market consists of a very large number of firms producing a homogeneous product.
- Monopolistic competition where there are a large number of independent firms which have a very small proportion of the market share.
- Oligopoly, in which a market is dominated by a small number of firms which own more than 40% of the market share.
- Oligopsony, a market dominated by many sellers and a few buyers.
- Monopoly, where there is only one provider of a product or service.
- Natural monopoly, a monopoly in which economies of scale cause efficiency to increase continuously with the size of the firm. A firm is a natural monopoly if it is able to serve the entire market demand at a lower cost than any combination of two or more smaller, more specialized firms.
- Monopsony, when there is only one buyer in a market.

The imperfectly competitive structure is quite identical to the realistic market conditions where some monopolistic competitors, monopolists, oligopolists, and duopolists exist and dominate the market conditions. The elements of _____ include the number and size distribution of firms, entry conditions, and the extent of differentiation.

These somewhat abstract concerns tend to determine some but not all details of a specific concrete market system where buyers and sellers actually meet and commit to trade.

a. Labour economics
c. Market structure
b. Human capital
d. Monopolistic competition

22. In economics, a _____ 'purchase') is a market form in which only one buyer faces many sellers. It is an example of imperfect competition, similar to a monopoly, in which only one seller faces many buyers. As the only purchaser of a good or service, the 'monopsonist' may dictate terms to its suppliers in the same manner that a monopolist controls the market for its buyers.

Chapter 26. Wage Determination

a. 100-year flood
c. 130-30 fund

b. 1921 recession
d. Monopsony

23. _____ has several particular meanings:

- in mathematics
    - _____ function
    - Euler _____
    - _____
    - _____ subgroup
    - method of _____s (partial differential equations)
- in physics and engineering
    - any _____ curve that shows the relationship between certain input- and output parameters, e.g.
    - an I-V or current-voltage _____ is the current in a circuit as a function of the applied voltage
    - Receiver-Operator _____
- in fiction
    - in Dungeons ' Dragons, _____ is another name for ability score

a. Russian financial crisis
c. Demand

b. Technocracy
d. Characteristic

24. A _____ is a group of people who share or are motivated by at least one common issue or interest, or work together on a specific project(s) to achieve a common objective. _____s are also characterised by attempts to share and exercise political and social power and to make decisions on a consensus-driven and egalitarian basis. _____s differ from cooperatives in that they are not necessarily focused upon an economic benefit or saving (but can be that as well.)

a. 1921 recession
c. 100-year flood

b. 130-30 fund
d. Collective

25. In organized labor, _____ is the method whereby workers organize together (usually in unions) to meet, converse, and negotiate upon the work conditions with their employers normally resulting in a written contract setting forth the wages, hours, and other conditions to be observed for a stipulated period.It is the practice in which union and company representatives meet to negotiate a new labor contract. In various national labor and employment law contexts, _____ takes on a more specific legal meaning and so, in a broad sense, however, it is the coming together of workers to negotiate their employment.

A collective agreement is a labor contract between an employer and one or more unions.

a. Designated Suppliers Program
c. Demarcation dispute

b. Strikebreaker
d. Collective bargaining

26. A trade union or _____ is an organization of workers who have banded together to achieve common goals in key areas and working conditions. The trade union, through its leadership, bargains with the employer on behalf of union members (rank and file members) and negotiates labor contracts (Collective bargaining) with employers. This may include the negotiation of wages, work rules, complaint procedures, rules governing hiring, firing and promotion of workers, benefits, workplace safety and policies.

Chapter 26. Wage Determination

a. Demand-side technologies
b. Business valuation standards
c. Basis of futures
d. Labor union

27. _____ is the practice of influencing decisions made by government. It includes all attempts to influence legislators and officials, whether by other legislators, constituents or organized groups. A lobbyist is a person who tries to influence legislation on behalf of a special interest or a member of a lobby.
    a. Adam Smith
    b. Lobbying
    c. Adolph Fischer
    d. Adolf Hitler

28. A _____ or labor union is an organization of workers who have banded together to achieve common goals in key areas and working conditions. The _____, through its leadership, bargains with the employer on behalf of union members (rank and file members) and negotiates labor contracts (Collective bargaining) with employers. This may include the negotiation of wages, work rules, complaint procedures, rules governing hiring, firing and promotion of workers, benefits, workplace safety and policies.
    a. Trade union
    b. Case-Shiller Home Price Indices
    c. Consumer goods
    d. Guaranteed investment contracts

29. In economics and especially in the theory of competition, _____ are obstacles in the path of a firm that make it difficult to enter a given market.

    _____ are the source of a firm's pricing power - the ability of a firm to raise prices without losing all its customers.

    The term refers to hindrances that an individual may face while trying to gain entrance into a profession or trade.

    a. Barriers to entry
    b. Social dumping
    c. Limit price
    d. Group boycott

30. _____ is the term denoting either an entrance or changes which are inserted into a system and which activate/modify a process. It is an abstract concept, used in the modeling, system(s) design and system(s) exploitation. It is usually connected with other terms, e.g., _____ field, _____ variable, _____ parameter, _____ value, _____ signal, _____ device and _____ file.
    a. Input
    b. AD-IA Model
    c. ACCRA Cost of Living Index
    d. ACEA agreement

31. _____ is the requirement to hold a license issued by a regulatory body or professional organisation, before practising a trade, profession or other occupation. Such requirements are commonly defended as a form of consumer protection against the risk of loss from unqualified or incompetent service providers. Economists including Milton Friedman have criticised _____ as a restriction on competition.
    a. Occupational licensing
    b. Authorised capital
    c. Australian Financial Services Licence
    d. Investment goods

32. _____ refers to organizing a union in a manner that seeks to unify workers in a particular industry along the lines of the particular craft or trade that they work in by class or skill level. It contrasts with industrial unionism, in which all workers in the same industry are organized into the same union, regardless of differences in skill.

_____ is perhaps best exemplified by many of the construction unions that formed the backbone of the old American Federation of Labor (which later merged with the industrial unions of the Congress of Industrial Organizations to form the AFL-CIO.)

a. 100-year flood
b. Craft unionism
c. 130-30 fund
d. 1921 recession

33. _____ is a common market structure where many competing producers sell products that are differentiated from one another (ie. the products are substitutes, but are not exactly alike.) Many markets are monopolistically competitive, common examples include the markets for restaurants, cereal, clothing, shoes and service industries in large cities.

a. Perfect competition
b. Mathematical economics
c. Monopolistic competition
d. Financial crisis

34. _____ in economics and business is the result of an exchange and from that trade we assign a numerical monetary value to a good, service or asset. If Alice trades Bob 4 apples for an orange, the _____ of an orange is 4 apples. Inversely, the _____ of an apple is 1/4 oranges.

a. Price book
b. Price
c. Premium pricing
d. Price war

35. _____ is one of the four Ps of the marketing mix. The other three aspects are product, promotion, and place. It is also a key variable in microeconomic price allocation theory.

a. Premium pricing
b. Point of total assumption
c. Guaranteed Maximum Price
d. Pricing

36. _____s is the social science that studies the production, distribution, and consumption of goods and services. The term _____s comes from the Ancient Greek oá¼°κονομῖα from oá¼¶κος (oikos, 'house') + vÍŒμος (nomos, 'custom' or 'law'), hence 'rules of the house(hold)'. Current _____ models developed out of the broader field of political economy in the late 19th century, owing to a desire to use an empirical approach more akin to the physical sciences.

a. Energy economics
b. Opportunity cost
c. Inflation
d. Economic

37. _____ is the increase in the amount of the goods and services produced by an economy over time. It is conventionally measured as the percent rate of increase in real gross domestic product, or real GDP. Growth is usually calculated in real terms, i.e. inflation-adjusted terms, in order to net out the effect of inflation on the price of the goods and services produced.

a. Economic growth
b. ACCRA Cost of Living Index
c. AD-IA Model
d. ACEA agreement

38. In economics, _____ is the ratio of the percent change in one variable to the percent change in another variable. It is a tool for measuring the responsiveness of a function to changes in parameters in a relative way. Commonly analyzed are _____ of substitution, price and wealth.

a. Elasticity of demand
b. ACEA agreement
c. Elasticity
d. ACCRA Cost of Living Index

Chapter 26. Wage Determination

39. In economics and sociology, an _____ is any factor (financial or non-financial) that enables or motivates a particular course of action, or counts as a reason for preferring one choice to the alternatives. It is an expectation that encourages people to behave in a certain way. Since human beings are purposeful creatures, the study of _____ structures is central to the study of all economic activity (both in terms of individual decision-making and in terms of co-operation and competition within a larger institutional structure.)
   a. Epstein-Zin preferences
   b. Economic reform
   c. Incentive
   d. Isocost

40. The _____ of 1938 (_____, ch. 676, 52 Stat. 1060, June 25, 1938, 29 U.S.C.ch.8), also called the Wages and Hours Bill, is United States federal law that applies to employees engaged in interstate commerce or employed by an enterprise engaged in commerce or in the production of goods for commerce, unless the employer can claim an exemption from coverage.
   a. Hostile work environment
   b. Generalized System of Preferences
   c. Habitability
   d. Fair Labor Standards Act

41. A _____ is the lowest hourly, daily or monthly wage that employers may legally pay to employees or workers. Equivalently, it is the lowest wage at which workers may sell their labor. Although _____ laws are in effect in a great many jurisdictions, there are differences of opinion about the benefits and drawbacks of a _____.
   a. Permanent war economy
   b. Microfoundations
   c. Marginal propensity to consume
   d. Minimum wage

42. A _____ is a government- or group-imposed limit on how low a price can be charged for a product. In order for a _____ to be effective, it must be greater than the equilibrium price. An ineffective _____, below equilibrium price.

   A _____ can be set below the free-market equilibrium price.

   a. Price markdown
   b. Price floor
   c. Flat rate
   d. Two-part tariff

43. _____, or a _____ is the concept of a resulting effect (cf. cause and effect, arising from another action. In general terms, it is used to indicate that all human actions, particularly crime and sin, have profound effects.
   a. Rule
   b. Variability
   c. Solved
   d. Consequence

44. _____ is the body of law which prohibits employers from hiring employees or workers for less than a given hourly, daily or monthly minimum wage. More than 90% of all countries have some kind of minimum wage legislation.

   Until relatively recently, _____s were usually very tightly focused.

   a. Joint venture
   b. Minimum wage law
   c. Bankruptcy in Canada
   d. Home country control

45. A _____ is the transfer of wealth from one party (such as a person or company) to another. A _____ is usually made in exchange for the provision of goods, services or both, or to fulfill a legal obligation.

   The simplest and oldest form of _____ is barter, the exchange of one good or service for another.

a. Going concern
b. Social gravity
c. Soft count
d. Payment

46. In economics, the _____ can be defined as the graph depicting the relationship between the price of a certain commodity, and the amount of it that consumers are willing and able to purchase at that given price. It is a graphic representation of a demand schedule. The _____ for all consumers together follows from the _____ of every individual consumer: the individual demands at each price are added together.
    a. Cost curve
    b. Wage curve
    c. Kuznets curve
    d. Demand curve

47. _____ refers to the stock of skills and knowledge embodied in the ability to perform labor so as to produce economic value. It is the skills and knowledge gained by a worker through education and experience. Many early economic theories refer to it simply as labor, one of three factors of production, and consider it to be a fungible resource -- homogeneous and easily interchangeable. Other conceptions of labor dispense with these assumptions.
    a. Human capital
    b. Law of increasing costs
    c. Price theory
    d. General equilibrium

48. In economics, the people in the _____ are the suppliers of labor. The _____ is all the nonmilitary people who are employed or unemployed. In 2005, the worldwide _____ was over 3 billion people.
    a. Labor force
    b. Departmentalization
    c. Grenelle agreements
    d. Distributed workforce

49. In microeconomics, _____ is the extra revenue that an additional unit of product will bring. It is the additional income from selling one more unit of a good; sometimes equal to price. It can also be described as the change in total revenue/change in number of units sold.
    a. Long term
    b. Market demand schedule
    c. Reservation price
    d. Marginal revenue

50. The phrase _____, according to the Organization for Economic Co-operation and Development, refers to 'creative work undertaken on a systematic basis in order to increase the stock of knowledge, including knowledge of man, culture and society, and the use of this stock of knowledge to devise new applications [sic]'

New product design and development is more than often a crucial factor in the survival of a company. In an industry that is fast changing, firms must continually revise their design and range of products. This is necessary due to continuous technology change and development as well as other competitors and the changing preference of customers.

    a. 1921 recession
    b. 100-year flood
    c. 130-30 fund
    d. Research and development

51. _____ is a situation in which the limited resources of a firm are allocated in accordance with the wishes of consumers. An allocatively efficient economy produces an 'optimal mix' of commodities. A firm is allocatively efficient when its price is equal to its marginal costs (that is, P = MC) in a perfect market.
    a. ACCRA Cost of Living Index
    b. Economic efficiency
    c. ACEA agreement
    d. Allocative efficiency

52. _____ is a specific term used in companies' financial reporting from the company-whole point of view. Because that use excludes the effects of changing ownership interest, an economic measure of _____ is necessary for financial analysis from the shareholders' point of view

_____ is defined by the Financial Accounting Standards Board, or FASB, as e;the change in equity [net assets] of a business enterprise during a period from transactions and other events and circumstances from nonowner sources. It includes all changes in equity during a period except those resulting from investments by owners and distributions to owners.e;

_____ is the sum of net income and other items that must bypass the income statement because they have not been realized, including items like an unrealized holding gain or loss from available for sale securities and foreign currency translation gains or losses.

- a. Real income
- b. Windfall gain
- c. Net national income
- d. Comprehensive income

53. _____ was a survey conducted by the U.S. Department of Justice to gauge the prevalence of alcohol and illegal drug use among prior arrestees. It was a reformulation of the prior Drug Use Forecasting (DUF) program, focused on five drugs in particular: cocaine, marijuana, methamphetamine, opiates, and PCP.

Participants were randomly selected from arrest records in major metropolitan areas; because no personally identifying information is taken from each record chosen, the resulting data can be correlated to arrest rates, but not to the total population of persons charged.

- a. AD-IA Model
- b. ACEA agreement
- c. ACCRA Cost of Living Index
- d. Arrestee Drug Abuse Monitoring

54. In political science and economics, the _____ or agency dilemma treats the difficulties that arise under conditions of incomplete and asymmetric information when a principal hires an agent, such as the problem that the two may not have the same interests, while the principal is, presumably, hiring the agent to pursue the interests of the former.

Various mechanisms may be used to try to align the interests of the agent with those of the principal, such as piece rates/commissions, profit sharing, efficiency wages, performance measurement (including financial statements), the agent posting a bond, or fear of firing. The _____ is found in most employer/employee relationships, for example, when stockholders hire top executives of corporations.

- a. 1921 recession
- b. Principal-agent problem
- c. 100-year flood
- d. 130-30 fund

55. _____ was a Scottish moral philosopher and a pioneer of political economy. One of the key figures of the Scottish Enlightenment, Smith is the author of The Theory of Moral Sentiments and An Inquiry into the Nature and Causes of the Wealth of Nations. The latter, usually abbreviated as The Wealth of Nations, is considered his magnum opus and the first modern work of economics.

a. Alan Greenspan
c. Adolph Fischer
b. Adolf Hitler
d. Adam Smith

56. In labor economics, the _____ hypothesis argues that wages, at least in some markets, are determined by more than simply supply and demand. Specifically, it points to the incentive for managers to pay their employees more than the market-clearing wage in order to increase their productivity or efficiency. This increased labor productivity pays for the relatively higher wages.
   a. Exogenous growth model
   c. Inflatable rats
   b. Efficiency wage
   d. Earnings calls

57. _____, when used as a special term, refers to various incentive plans introduced by businesses that provide direct or indirect payments to employees that depend on company's profitability in addition to employees' regular salary and bonuses. In publicly traded companies these plans typically amount to allocation of shares to employees.

The _____ plans are based on predetermined economic sharing rules that define the split of gains between the company as a principal and the employee as an agent.

   a. Profit sharing
   c. Pension insurance contract
   b. Spiff
   d. Living wage

58. _____ is a fee paid on borrowed assets. It is the price paid for the use of borrowed money, or, money earned by deposited funds. Assets that are sometimes lent with _____ include money, shares, consumer goods through hire purchase, major assets such as aircraft, and even entire factories in finance lease arrangements.
   a. Asset protection
   c. Insolvency
   b. Internal debt
   d. Interest

Chapter 27. Rent, Interest, and Profit

1. _____ is a fee paid on borrowed assets. It is the price paid for the use of borrowed money, or, money earned by deposited funds. Assets that are sometimes lent with _____ include money, shares, consumer goods through hire purchase, major assets such as aircraft, and even entire factories in finance lease arrangements.
   a. Internal debt
   b. Insolvency
   c. Asset protection
   d. Interest

2. An _____ is the price a borrower pays for the use of money they do not own, for instance a small company might borrow from a bank to kick start their business, and the return a lender receives for deferring the use of funds, by lending it to the borrower. _____s are normally expressed as a percentage rate over the period of one year.

   _____s targets are also a vital tool of monetary policy and are used to control variables like investment, inflation, and unemployment.

   a. ACCRA Cost of Living Index
   b. Enterprise value
   c. Interest rate
   d. Arrow-Debreu model

3. _____ in economics and business is the result of an exchange and from that trade we assign a numerical monetary value to a good, service or asset. If Alice trades Bob 4 apples for an orange, the _____ of an orange is 4 apples. Inversely, the _____ of an apple is 1/4 oranges.
   a. Price war
   b. Price
   c. Premium pricing
   d. Price book

4. _____s is the social science that studies the production, distribution, and consumption of goods and services. The term _____s comes from the Ancient Greek oá¼°κονομῖα from oá¼¶κος (oikos, 'house') + vÏŒμος (nomos, 'custom' or 'law'), hence 'rules of the house(hold)'. Current _____ models developed out of the broader field of political economy in the late 19th century, owing to a desire to use an empirical approach more akin to the physical sciences.
   a. Inflation
   b. Economic
   c. Energy economics
   d. Opportunity cost

5. In economics supernormal profit _____ or pure profit or excess profits, is a profit exceeding the normal profit. Normal profit equals the opportunity cost of labour and capital, while supernormal profit is the amount exceeds the normal return from these input factors in production.

   _____ is usually generated by an oligopoly or a monopoly; however, these firms often try to hide this from the market to reduce risk of competition or antitrust investigation.

   a. Economic profit
   b. Accounting profit
   c. ACCRA Cost of Living Index
   d. Abnormal profit

6. The _____ is a term used in economics to describe a good that is not scarce. A _____ is available in as great a quantity as desired with zero opportunity cost to society.

   A good that is made available at zero price is not necessarily a _____.

   a. Durable good
   b. Giffen good
   c. Merit good
   d. Free good

Chapter 27. Rent, Interest, and Profit

7. The _____ or gross domestic income (GDI), a basic measure of an economy's economic performance, is the market value of all final goods and services produced within the borders of a nation in a year. _____ can be defined in three ways, all of which are conceptually identical. First, it is equal to the total expenditures for all final goods and services produced within the country in a stipulated period of time (usually a 365-day year.)
   a. Countercyclical
   b. Monopolistic competition
   c. Market structure
   d. Gross domestic product

8. In economics, the _____ of demand measures the responsiveness of the demand of a good to the change in the income of the people demanding the good. It is calculated as the ratio of the percent change in demand to the percent change in income. For example, if, in response to a 10% increase in income, the demand of a good increased by 20%, the _____ of demand would be 20%/10% = 2.
   a. AD-IA Model
   b. ACEA agreement
   c. ACCRA Cost of Living Index
   d. Income elasticity

9. In economics, the _____ measures the responsiveness of the demand of a good to the change in the income of the people demanding the good. It is calculated as the ratio of the percent change in demand to the percent change in income. For example, if, in response to a 10% increase in income, the demand of a good increased by 20%, the _____ would be 20%/10% = 2.
   a. Expenditure minimization problem
   b. Indifference map
   c. Elasticity of substitution
   d. Income elasticity of demand

10. In economics, _____ describes demand that is not very sensitive to a change in price.
    a. Inelastic
    b. Effective unemployment rate
    c. Export-led growth
    d. Inflation hedge

11. _____ is defined as the measure of responsiveness in the quantity demanded for a commodity as a result of change in price of the same commodity. It is a measure of how consumers react to a change in price. In other words, it is percentage change in quantity demanded as per the percentage change in price of the same commodity.
    a. 130-30 fund
    b. 100-year flood
    c. Price elasticity of demand
    d. 1921 recession

12. In economics, the _____ is defined as a numerical measure of the responsiveness of the quantity supplied of product (A) to a change in price of product (A) alone. It is the measure of the way quantity supplied reacts to a change in price.

For example, if, in response to a 10% rise in the price of a good, the quantity supplied increases by 20%, the _____ would be 20%/10% = 2.

   a. Price elasticity of supply
   b. Hedonimetry
   c. Demand shaping
   d. Passive income

Chapter 27. Rent, Interest, and Profit

13. Economics:

    - _____, the desire to own something and the ability to pay for it
    - _____ curve, a graphic representation of a _____ schedule
    - _____ deposit, the money in checking accounts
    - _____ pull theory, the theory that inflation occurs when _____ for goods and services exceeds existing supplies
    - _____ schedule, a table that lists the quantity of a good a person will buy it each different price
    - _____ side economics, the school of economics at believes government spending and tax cuts open economy by raising _____

    a. McKesson ' Robbins scandal
    b. Variability
    c. Production
    d. Demand

14. In economics, _____ is the ratio of the percent change in one variable to the percent change in another variable. It is a tool for measuring the responsiveness of a function to changes in parameters in a relative way. Commonly analyzed are _____ of substitution, price and wealth.

    a. ACEA agreement
    b. Elasticity of demand
    c. ACCRA Cost of Living Index
    d. Elasticity

15. Price _____ is defined as the measure of responsiveness in the quantity demanded for a commodity as a result of change in price of the same commodity. It is a measure of how consumers react to a change in price. In other words, it is percentage change in quantity demanded by the percentage change in price of the same commodity.

    a. Elasticity of demand
    b. ACCRA Cost of Living Index
    c. Elasticity
    d. ACEA agreement

16. A _____ is an object whose consumption increases the utility of the consumer, for which the quantity demanded exceeds the quantity supplied at zero price. _____s are usually modeled as having diminishing marginal utility. The first individual purchase has high utility; the second has less.

    a. Pie method
    b. Composite good
    c. Merit good
    d. Good

17. _____ in economics refers to metrics and measures of output from production processes, per unit of input. Labor _____, for example, is typically measured as a ratio of output per labor-hour, an input. _____ may be conceived of as a metrics of the technical or engineering efficiency of production.

    a. Production-possibility frontier
    b. Piece work
    c. Fordism
    d. Productivity

18. Economic _____ is defined as an excess distribution to any factor in a production process above that which is required to induce the factor into the process or any excess above that which is necessary to keep the factor in its current use..

Classical Factor _____ is primarily concerned with the fee paid for the use of fixed (e.g. natural) resources. The classical definition is expressed as any excess payment above that required to induce or provide for production.

a. 130-30 fund
b. Rent
c. 100-year flood
d. 1921 recession

19. _____ is an economic model based on price, utility and quantity in a market. It predicts that in a competitive market, price will function to equalize the quantity demanded by consumers, and the quantity supplied by producers, resulting in an economic equilibrium of price and quantity. The model incorporates other factors changing equilibrium as a shift of demand and/or supply.

   a. Deferred gratification
   b. Rational addiction
   c. Joint demand
   d. Supply and demand

20. A _____ product is a product designed for cheapness and short-term convenience rather than medium to long-term durability, with most products only intended for single use. The term is also sometimes used for products that may last several months (ex. _____ air filters) to distinguish from similar products that last indefinitely (ex.

   a. Disposable
   b. 100-year flood
   c. 1921 recession
   d. 130-30 fund

21. _____ is gross income minus income tax on that income.

Discretionary income is income after subtracting taxes and normal expenses (such as rent or mortgage, utilities, insurance, medical, transportation, property maintenance, child support, inflation, food and sundries, 'c.) to maintain a certain standard of living.

   a. Disposable personal income
   b. Stamp Act
   c. Taxation as theft
   d. Disposable income

22. In economics and sociology, an _____ is any factor (financial or non-financial) that enables or motivates a particular course of action, or counts as a reason for preferring one choice to the alternatives. It is an expectation that encourages people to behave in a certain way. Since human beings are purposeful creatures, the study of _____ structures is central to the study of all economic activity (both in terms of individual decision-making and in terms of co-operation and competition within a larger institutional structure.)

   a. Epstein-Zin preferences
   b. Economic reform
   c. Isocost
   d. Incentive

23. A variety of measures of _____ and output are used in economics to estimate total economic activity in a country or region, including gross domestic product (GDP), gross national product (GNP), and net _____

There are three main ways of calculating these numbers; the output approach, the income approach and the expenditure approach. In theory, the three must yield the same, because total expenditures on goods and services must equal the total income paid to the producers (Gnational income), and that must also equal the total value of the output of goods and services (GNP.)

   a. GNI per capita
   b. Volume index
   c. Gross world product
   d. National income

24. _____ is the shortage of common things such as food, clothing, shelter and safe drinking water, all of which determine the quality of life. It may also include the lack of access to opportunities such as education and employment which aid the escape from _____ and/or allow one to enjoy the respect of fellow citizens. According to Mollie Orshansky who developed the _____ measurements used by the U.S. government, 'to be poor is to be deprived of those goods and services and pleasures which others around us take for granted.' Ongoing debates over causes, effects and best ways to measure _____, directly influence the design and implementation of _____-reduction programs and are therefore relevant to the fields of public administration and international development.

   a. Liberal welfare reforms   b. Poverty
   c. Growth Elasticity of Poverty   d. Poverty map

25. _____ refers to income that is not a wage.

It includes interest, dividends or realized capital gains from investments, rent from land or property ownership, and any other income that does not derive from work.

_____ has often been treated differently for tax purposes than earned income, in order to redistribute income or to recognize its qualitative difference from income derived from work.

   a. Average propensity to save   b. Aggregate income
   c. Independent income   d. Unearned income

26. In economics and business, specifically cost accounting, the _____ point (BEP) is the point at which cost or expenses and revenue are equal: there is no net loss or gain, and one has 'broken even'. A profit or a loss has not been made, although opportunity costs have been paid, and capital has received the risk-adjusted, expected return.

For example, if the business sells less than 200 tables each month, it will make a loss, if it sells more, it will be a profit.

   a. Nonmarket   b. Break-even
   c. Small numbers game   d. Buffer stock scheme

27. A _____ is the transfer of wealth from one party (such as a person or company) to another. A _____ is usually made in exchange for the provision of goods, services or both, or to fulfill a legal obligation.

The simplest and oldest form of _____ is barter, the exchange of one good or service for another.

   a. Soft count   b. Social gravity
   c. Going concern   d. Payment

28. To _____ is to impose a financial charge or other levy upon a taxpayer by a state or the functional equivalent of a state.

_____es are also imposed by many subnational entities. _____es consist of direct _____ or indirect _____, and may be paid in money or as its labour equivalent (often but not always unpaid).

a. 100-year flood
c. 1921 recession
b. Tax
d. 130-30 fund

29. The _____ is 'the basic residential unit in which economic production, consumption, inheritance, child rearing, and shelter are organized and carried out'; [the _____] 'may or may not be synonomous with family'.

The _____ is the basic unit of analysis in many social, microeconomic and government models. The term refers to all individuals who live in the same dwelling.

a. Family economics
c. 100-year flood
b. 130-30 fund
d. Household

30. In economics, the _____ market is a hypothetical market that brings savers and borrowers together, also bringing together the money available in commercial banks and lending institutions available for firms and households to finance expenditures, either investments or consumption. Savers supply the _____; for instance, buying bonds will transfer their money to the institution issuing the bond, which can be a firm or government. In return, borrowers demand _____; when an institution sells a bond, it is demanding _____.

a. Spatial inequality
c. Loanable funds
b. Reservation wage
d. Buffer stock scheme

31. The _____ consists of a number of economic theories which describe the nature of the firm, company including its existence, its behaviour, and its relationship with the market.

In simplified terms, the _____ aims to answer these questions:

1. Existence - why do firms emerge, why are not all transactions in the economy mediated over the market?
2. Boundaries - why the boundary between firms and the market is located exactly there? Which transactions are performed internally and which are negotiated on the market?
3. Organization - why are firms structured in such specific way? What is the interplay of formal and informal relationships?

Despite looking simple, these questions are not answered by the established economic theory, which usually views firms as given, and treats them as black boxes without any internal structure.

The First World War period saw a change of emphasis in economic theory away from industry-level analysis which mainly included analysing markets to analysis at the level of the firm, as it became increasingly clear that perfect competition was no longer an adequate model of how firms behaved. Economic theory till then had focussed on trying to understand markets alone and there had been little study on understanding why firms or organisations exist.

a. Khazzoom-Brookes postulate
c. Policy Ineffectiveness Proposition
b. Technology gap
d. Theory of the firm

32. In finance, a _____ is a debt security, in which the authorized issuer owes the holders a debt and, depending on the terms of the _____, is obliged to pay interest (the coupon) and/or to repay the principal at a later date, termed maturity. A _____ is a formal contract to repay borrowed money with interest at fixed intervals.

Thus a _____ is like a loan: the issuer is the borrower (debtor), the holder is the lender (creditor), and the coupon is the interest.

a. Zero-coupon
b. Prize Bond
c. Callable
d. Bond

33. _____ is a life of security. It may also refer to the final payment date of a loan or other financial instrument, at which point all remaining interest and principal is due to be paid.

1, 3, 6 months _____ band can be calculated by using 30-day per month periods.

a. Refinancing risk
b. Future value
c. Future-oriented
d. Maturity

34. In economics, _____ is a measure of national income. Basically, it is an approach to measure GDP. It is defined as the value of planned goods and services produced in an economy.
a. Aggregate expenditure
b. Aggregate supply
c. Aggregate demand
d. Aggregation problem

35.

A _____ is a type of financial intermediary and a type of bank. Commercial banking is also known as business banking. It is a bank that provides checking accounts, savings accounts, and money market accounts and that accepts time deposits.

a. Bought deal
b. Commercial bank
c. Daylight overdraft
d. Lombard banking

36. _____ is money accepted for exchange of goods in an economy. The prevalence of one money over another arises, usually, when a government designates through decrees that the government shall accept only particular notes and coins in payment for taxes. Typically, money of _____ consists of stamped coins and minted paper bills.
a. Currency
b. Local currency
c. Totnes pound
d. Security thread

37. A security is a fungible, negotiable instrument representing financial value. _____ are broadly categorized into debt _____; equity _____, e.g., common stocks; and derivative (finance) contracts such as forwards, futures, options and swaps. The company or other entity issuing the security is called the issuer.
a. Securities
b. Pass-Through Certificates
c. Settlement risk
d. Red herring prospectus

38. In finance, _____ is a financial action that does not promise safety of the initial investment along with the return on the principal sum. _____ typically involves the lending of money or the purchase of assets, equity or debt but in a manner that has not been given thorough analysis or is deemed to have low margin of safety or a significant risk of the loss of the principal investment. The term, '_____,' which is formally defined as above in Graham and Dodd's 1934 text, Security Analysis, contrasts with the term 'investment,' which is a financial operation that, upon thorough analysis, promises safety of principal and a satisfactory return.
   a. Hybrid market
   b. Global Financial Centres Index
   c. Municipal Bond Arbitrage
   d. Speculation

39. The _____ or the output gap is the difference between potential GDP and actual GDP or actual output. The calculation for the output gap is Y-Y* where Y* is potential output and Y is actual output. If this calculation yields a positive number it is called an expansionary gap and indicates an economy in expansion; if the calculation yields a negative number it is called a recessionary gap and indicates an economy in recession.
   a. 100-year flood
   b. 1921 recession
   c. GDP gap
   d. 130-30 fund

40. The _____ is a measure of the size of firms in relation to the industry and an indicator of the amount of competition among them. Named after economists Orris C. Herfindahl and Albert O. Hirschman, it is an economic concept, widely applied in competition law, antitrust and also technology management. It is defined as the sum of the squares of the market shares of the 50 largest firms within the industry, where the market shares are expressed as percentages.
   a. Vector autoregression
   b. Reduced form
   c. Herfindahl index
   d. Panel data

41. In economics, _____ is a rise in the general level of prices of goods and services in an economy over a period of time. When the general price level rises, each unit of currency buys fewer goods and services; consequently, _____ is also a decline in the real value of money--a loss of purchasing power in the medium of exchange which is also the monetary unit of account in the economy. A chief measure of general price-level _____ is the general _____ rate, which is the percentage change in a general price index (normally the Consumer Price Index) over time.
   a. Energy economics
   b. Opportunity cost
   c. Economic
   d. Inflation

42. In economics, a _____ 'purchase') is a market form in which only one buyer faces many sellers. It is an example of imperfect competition, similar to a monopoly, in which only one seller faces many buyers. As the only purchaser of a good or service, the 'monopsonist' may dictate terms to its suppliers in the same manner that a monopolist controls the market for its buyers.
   a. 130-30 fund
   b. 1921 recession
   c. 100-year flood
   d. Monopsony

43. In finance and economics _____ or nominal rate of interest refers to the rate of interest before adjustment for inflation (in contrast with the real interest rate); or, for interest rates 'as stated' without adjustment for the full effect of compounding (also referred to as the nominal annual rate.) An interest rate is called nominal if the frequency of compounding (e.g. a month) is not identical to the basic time unit (normally a year.)

The real interest rate includes compensation for the lender's lost value due to inflation, whereas the _____ excludes inflation.

a. Nominal interest rate
b. Risk-free interest rate
c. London Interbank Offered Rate
d. Fixed interest

44. The '_____' is approximately the nominal interest rate minus the inflation rate Since the inflation rate over the course of a loan is not known initially, volatility in inflation represents a risk to both the lender and the borrower.

In economics and finance, an individual who lends money for repayment at a later point in time expects to be compensated for the time value of money, or not having the use of that money while it is lent.

a. Core inflation
b. Cost-push inflation
c. Real interest rate
d. Reflation

45. The phrase _____, according to the Organization for Economic Co-operation and Development, refers to 'creative work undertaken on a systematic basis in order to increase the stock of knowledge, including knowledge of man, culture and society, and the use of this stock of knowledge to devise new applications [sic]'

New product design and development is more than often a crucial factor in the survival of a company. In an industry that is fast changing, firms must continually revise their design and range of products. This is necessary due to continuous technology change and development as well as other competitors and the changing preference of customers.

a. 130-30 fund
b. 100-year flood
c. 1921 recession
d. Research and development

46. _____ has several particular meanings:

- in mathematics
    - _____ function
    - Euler _____
    - _____
    - _____ subgroup
    - method of _____s (partial differential equations)
- in physics and engineering
    - any _____ curve that shows the relationship between certain input- and output parameters, e.g.
    - an I-V or current-voltage _____ is the current in a circuit as a function of the applied voltage
    - Receiver-Operator _____
- in fiction
    - in Dungeons ' Dragons, _____ is another name for ability score

a. Demand
b. Russian financial crisis
c. Technocracy
d. Characteristic

47. In finance, _____ rate of profit or sometimes just return, is the ratio of money gained or lost on an investment relative to the amount of money invested. The amount of money gained or lost may be referred to as interest, profit/loss, gain/loss, or net income/loss. The money invested may be referred to as the asset, capital, principal, or the cost basis of the investment.
   a. Sortino ratio
   b. Cost accrual ratio
   c. Rate of return
   d. Current ratio

48. _____ is the controlled distribution of resources and scarce goods or services. _____ controls the size of the ration, one's allotted portion of the resources being distributed on a particular day or at a particular time.

In economics, it is often common to use the word '_____' to refer to one of the roles that prices play in markets, while _____ is called 'non-price _____.' Using prices to ration means that those with the most money (or other assets) and who want a product the most are first to receive it.

   a. 100-year flood
   b. 130-30 fund
   c. 1921 recession
   d. Rationing

49. _____ is a common concept in economics, and gives rise to derived concepts such as consumer debt. Generally _____ is defined by opposition to production. But the precise definition can vary because different schools of economists define production quite differently.
   a. Federal Reserve Bank Notes
   b. Consumption
   c. Foreclosure data providers
   d. Cash or share options

50. _____ refers to internal and external organizing and correcting factors that provide order to market and other types of societal institutions and organizations - economic, political, social and cultural - so that they may function efficiently and effectively as well as repair their failures.

The expression _____ is increasingly found in the title, abstract and text of articles, chapters and papers in the business, management, organization, strategy, social-issues, political-science and sociology literatures. The ABI/Inform Global source located 1748 such uses of both expressions in October 2008, compared with 31 in 1991 and 247 in 2002.

   a. Private Benefits of Control
   b. Total revenue
   c. Positive statement
   d. Nonmarket

51. A _____ is a government imposed limit on how high a price can be charged on a product. For a _____ to be effective, it must differ from the free market price. In the graph at right, the supply and demand curves intersect to determine the free-market quantity and price.
   a. Price ceiling
   b. Fire sale
   c. Product sabotage
   d. Pricing

52. The underground economy or _____ is a market where all commerce is conducted without regard to taxation, law or regulations of trade. The term is also often known as the underdog, shadow economy, black economy, parallel economy or phantom trades.

In modern societies the underground economy covers a vast array of activities.

Chapter 27. Rent, Interest, and Profit

a. Market economy
b. Social market economy
c. Black market
d. Protectionism

53. _____ is the structure and set of regulations in place to control activity, usually in large organizations and government. As opposed to adhocracy, it is represented by standardized procedure (rule-following) that dictates the execution of most or all processes within the body, formal division of powers, hierarchy, and relationships. In practice the interpretation and execution of policy can lead to informal influence.

a. 1921 recession
b. Bureaucracy
c. 130-30 fund
d. 100-year flood

54. A _____ is an expression that compares quantities relative to each other. The most common examples involve two quantities, but any number of quantities can be compared. _____s are represented mathematically by separating each quantity with a colon, for example the _____ 2:3, which is read as the _____ 'two to three'.

a. Ratio
b. 130-30 fund
c. 100-year flood
d. Y-intercept

55. The reserve requirement (or required _____) is a bank regulation that sets the minimum reserves each bank must hold to customer deposits and notes. It would normally be in the form of fiat currency stored in a bank vault (vault cash), or with a central bank.

The _____ is sometimes used as a tool in the monetary policy, influencing the country's economy, borrowing, and interest rates.

a. Bank-State-Branch
b. First player wins
c. Dividend unit
d. Reserve ratio

56. _____ is the difference between price and the costs of bringing to market whatever it is that is accounted as an enterprise (whether by harvest, extraction, manufacture, or purchase) in terms of the component costs of delivered goods and/or services and any operating or other expenses.

A key difficulty in measuring profit is in defining costs. Pure economic monetary profits can be zero or negative even in competitive equilibrium when accounted monetized costs exceed monetized price.

a. ACCRA Cost of Living Index
b. Accounting profit
c. Economic profit
d. Operating profit

57. In economics, _____ is the difference between a company's total revenue and its opportunity costs. It is the increase in wealth that an investor has from making an investment, taking into consideration all costs associated with that investment including the opportunity cost of capital.

Profit is the factor income of the entrepreneur.

a. Accounting profit
b. Operating profit
c. Economic profit
d. ACCRA Cost of Living Index

Chapter 27. Rent, Interest, and Profit

58. An _____ is a person who has possession of an enterprise and assumes significant accountability for the inherent risks and the outcome. It is an ambitious leader who combines land, labor, and capital to create and market new goods or services. The term is a loanword from French and was first defined by the Irish economist Richard Cantillon.
   a. ACEA agreement
   b. Entrepreneur
   c. ACCRA Cost of Living Index
   d. Expansionary policies

59. An _____ is an easy accounted cost, such as wage, rent and materials. It can be transacted in the form of money payment and is lost directly, as opposed to monetary implicit costs.
   a. Explicit cost
   b. Average variable cost
   c. Average fixed cost
   d. Inventory valuation

60. In economics, an _____ occurs when one foregoes an alternative action but does not make an actual payment. (For instance, the explicit cost of a night at the movies includes the moviegoer's ticket and soda, but the _____ includes the pay he would have earned if he had chosen to work instead.) _____s are related to forgone benefits of any single transaction.
   a. External sector
   b. Overnight trade
   c. Ostrich strategy
   d. Implicit cost

61. An _____ is a risk that meets the ideal criteria for efficient insurance. The concept of _____ underlies nearly all insurance decisions.

For a risk to be insurable, several things need to be true:

- The insurer must be able to charge a premium high enough to cover not only claims expenses, but also to cover the insurer's expenses. In other words, the risk cannot be catastrophic, or so large that no insurer could hope to pay for the loss.

- The nature of the loss must be definite and financially measurable. That is, there should not be room for argument as to whether or not payment is due, nor as to what amount the payment should be.

   a. Ogden tables
   b. Actuary
   c. Extreme value theory
   d. Insurable risk

62. _____ is a component of the firm's opportunity costs. The time that the owner spends running the firm could be spent on running another firm. This is _____: the return the entrepreneur can expect to earn or the profit that the business owners considers necessary to make running the business worth his/her while.
   a. Profit margin
   b. Profit maximization
   c. 100-year flood
   d. Normal profit

63. _____ or economic opportunity loss is the value of the next best alternative foregone as the result of making a decision. _____ analysis is an important part of a company's decision-making processes but is not treated as an actual cost in any financial statement. The next best thing that a person can engage in is referred to as the _____ of doing the best thing and ignoring the next best thing to be done.
   a. Opportunity cost
   b. Industrial organization
   c. Economic ideology
   d. Economic

64. In economics, the _____ is the agent who receives the net income (income after deducting all costs.)

Residual claimancy is generally required in order for there to be Moral Hazard, which is a problem typical of information asymmetry. This is specifically the case for the Principal-agent problem.

a. Horizontal merger
c. Residual claimant

b. Frontier markets
d. Free contract

65. A _____ refers to any type debt instrument, such as a loan, bond, mortgage that does not have a fixed rate of interest over the life of the instrument. Such debt typically uses an index or other base rate for establishing the interest rate for each relevant period. One of the most common rates to use as the basis for applying interest rates is the London Inter-bank Offered Rate, or LIBOR

a. Money market
c. Moneylender

b. Disposal tax effect
d. Floating interest rate

66. In finance, the _____s between two currencies specifies how much one currency is worth in terms of the other. It is the value of a foreign natione;s currency in terms of the home natione;s currency. For example an _____ of 102 Japanese yen to the United States dollar means that JPY 102 is worth the same as USD 1.

a. ACEA agreement
c. Exchange rate

b. Interbank market
d. ACCRA Cost of Living Index

67. A _____ is:

- Rewrite _____, in generative grammar and computer science
- Standardization, a formal and widely-accepted statement, fact, definition, or qualification
- Operation, a determinate _____ for performing a mathematical operation and obtaining a certain result (Mathematics, Logic)
    - Unary operation
    - Binary operation
- _____ of inference, a function from sets of formulae to formulae (Mathematics, Logic)
- _____ of thumb, principle with broad application that is not intended to be strictly accurate or reliable for every situation. Also often simply referred to as a _____
- Moral, an atomic element of a moral code for guiding choices in human behavior
- Heuristic, a quantized '_____' which shows a tendency or probability for successful function
- A regulation, as in sports
- A Production _____, as in computer science
- Procedural law, a _____ set governing the application of laws to cases
    - A law, which may informally be called a '_____'
    - A court ruling, a decision by a court
- In the U.S. Government, a regulation mandated by Congress, but written or expanded upon by the Executive Branch.
- Norm (sociology), an informal but widely accepted _____, concept, truth, definition, or qualification (social norms, legal norms, coding norms)
- Norm (philosophy), a kind of sentence or a reason to act, feel or believe
- 'Rulership' is the concept of governance by a government:
    - Military _____, governance by a military body
    - Monastic _____, a collection of precepts that guides the life of monks or nuns in a religious order where the superior holds the place of Christ
- Slide _____

- '_____,' a song by Ayumi Hamasaki
- '_____,' a song by rapper Nas
- '_____s,' an album by the band The Whitest Boy Alive
- _____s: Pyaar Ka Superhit Formula, a 2003 Bollywood film
- ruler, an instrument for measuring lengths
- _____, a component of an astrolabe, circumferator or similar instrument
- The _____s, a bestselling self-help book
- _____ Project (Run Up-to-date Linux Everywhere), a project that aims to use up-to-date Linux software on old PCs
- _____ engine, a software system that helps managing business _____s
- Ja _____, a hip hop artist
    - R.U.L.E., a 2005 greatest hits album by rapper Ja _____
- '_____s,' a KMFDM song

a. Demand
b. Technocracy
c. Procter ' Gamble
d. Rule

Chapter 27. Rent, Interest, and Profit

68. The terms _____ , nominal _____ , and effective _____ describe the interest rate for a whole year (annualized), rather than just a monthly fee/rate, as applied on a loan, mortgage, credit card, etc. It is a finance charge expressed as an annual rate. Those terms have formal, legal definitions in some countries or legal jurisdictions, but in general:

- The nominal _____ is the simple-interest rate (for a year.)
- The effective _____ is the fee+compound interest rate (calculated across a year.)

The nominal _____ is calculated as: the rate, for a payment period, multiplied by the number of payment periods in a year. However, the exact legal definition of 'effective _____', or EAR in short, can vary greatly in each jurisdiction, depending on the type of fees included, such as participation fees, loan origination fees, monthly service charges, or late fees. The effective _____ has been called the 'mathematically-true' interest rate for each year.

a. Arranger
b. Automatic transfer service account
c. Universal bank
d. Annual percentage rate

69. _____ is used to assign the available resources in an economic way. It is part of resource management.

In strategic planning, is a plan for using available resources, for example human resources, especially in the near term, to achieve goals for the future.

a. 130-30 fund
b. 1921 recession
c. 100-year flood
d. Resource allocation

70. A _____ is a low, adjustable introductory rate advertised for a loan or credit card in order to attract potential customers to obtain the service. The _____ s are normally too good to be true for the long term, and are far below the common realistic rate for the service. In a competitive market, many companies will compete with each other for the lower _____.

a. Teaser rate
b. Centralization
c. Personal offshoring
d. Product innovation

71. In economics, a _____ exists when a specific individual or enterprise has sufficient control over a particular product or service to determine significantly the terms on which other individuals shall have access to it. Monopolies are thus characterized by a lack of economic competition for the good or service that they provide and a lack of viable substitute goods. The verb 'monopolize' refers to the process by which a firm gains persistently greater market share than what is expected under perfect competition.

a. 130-30 fund
b. 1921 recession
c. Monopoly
d. 100-year flood

72. _____ is the a method of technical and economic research of the systems for purpose to optimize a parity between system's consumer functions or properties and expenses to achieve those functions or properties.

Chapter 27. Rent, Interest, and Profit

This methodology for continuous perfection of production, industrial technologies, organizational structures was developed by Juryj Sobolev in 1948 at the 'Perm telephone factory'

- 1948 Juryj Sobolev - the first success in application of a method analysis at the 'Perm telephone factory'.
- 1949 - the first application for the invention as result of use of the new method.

Today in economically developed countries practically each enterprise or the company use methodology of the kind of functional-cost analysis as a practice of the quality management, most full satisfying to principles of standards of series ISO 9000.

- Interest of consumer not in products itself, but the advantage which it will receive from its usage.
- The consumer aspires to reduce his expenses
- Functions needed by consumer can be executed in the various ways, and, hence, with various efficiency and expenses. Among possible alternatives of realization of functions exist such in which the parity of quality and the price is the optimal for the consumer.

The goal of _____ is achievement of the highest consumer satisfaction of production at simultaneous decrease in all kinds of industrial expenses Classical _____ has three English synonyms - Value Engineering, Value Management, Value Analysis.

a. Monopoly wage
c. Willingness to pay
b. Staple financing
d. Function cost analysis

Chapter 28. Government and Market Failure

1. In economics, a _____ exists when the production or use of goods and services by the market is not efficient. That is, there exists another outcome where all involved can be made better off. _____s can be viewed as scenarios where individuals' pursuit of pure self-interest leads to results that are not efficient - that can be improved upon from the societal point-of-view.
   a. General equilibrium
   b. Fixed exchange rate
   c. Market failure
   d. Financial economics

2. In economics, _____ is a measure of national income. Basically, it is an approach to measure GDP. It is defined as the value of planned goods and services produced in an economy.
   a. Aggregate demand
   b. Aggregate supply
   c. Aggregate expenditure
   d. Aggregation problem

3. _____s is the social science that studies the production, distribution, and consumption of goods and services. The term _____s comes from the Ancient Greek οἰκονομία from οἶκος (oikos, 'house') + νόμος (nomos, 'custom' or 'law'), hence 'rules of the house(hold)'. Current _____ models developed out of the broader field of political economy in the late 19th century, owing to a desire to use an empirical approach more akin to the physical sciences.
   a. Opportunity cost
   b. Energy economics
   c. Inflation
   d. Economic

4. _____ is a broad label that refers to any individuals or households that use goods and services generated within the economy. The concept of a _____ is used in different contexts, so that the usage and significance of the term may vary.

Typically when business people and economists talk of _____s they are talking about person as _____, an aggregated commodity item with little individuality other than that expressed in the buy/not-buy decision.

   a. 1921 recession
   b. 130-30 fund
   c. 100-year flood
   d. Consumer

5. _____ are final goods specifically intended for the mass market. For instance, _____ do not include investment assets, like precious antiques, even though these antiques are final goods.

Manufactured goods are goods that have been processed by way of machinery.

   a. Fiscal stimulus plans
   b. Bulgarian-American trade
   c. Consumer goods
   d. G-20 Leaders Summit on Financial Markets and the World Economy

6. A _____ is any systematic process enabling many market players to bid and ask: helping bidders and sellers interact and make deals. It is not just the price mechanism but the entire system of regulation, qualification, credentials, reputations and clearing that surrounds that mechanism and makes it operate in a social context.

Because a _____ relies on the assumption that players are constantly involved and unequally enabled, a _____ is distinguished specifically from a voting system where candidates seek the support of voters on a less regular basis.

a. Price mechanism
c. Market system
b. Competitive equilibrium
d. Contestable market

7. A _____ is defined in economics as a good that exhibits these properties:

- Excludable - it is reasonably possible to prevent a class of consumers (e.g. those who have not paid for it) from consuming the good.
- Rivalrous - consumptions by one consumer prevents simultaneous consumption by other consumers. _____s satisfies an individual want while public good satisfies a collective want of the society.

A _____ is the opposite of a public good, as they are almost exclusively made for profit.

An example of the _____ is bread: bread eaten by a given person cannot be consumed by another (rivalry), and it is easy for a baker to refuse to trade a loaf (excludable

a. Positional goods
c. Demerit good
b. Pie method
d. Private good

8. In economics, a _____ is a good that is non-rivaled and non-excludable. This means, respectively, that consumption of the good by one individual does not reduce availability of the good for consumption by others; and that no one can be effectively excluded from using the good. In the real world, there may be no such thing as an absolutely non-rivaled and non-excludable good; but economists think that some goods approximate the concept closely enough for the analysis to be economically useful.

a. Happiness economics
c. Public good
b. Neoclassical synthesis
d. Demand-pull theory

9. _____ has several particular meanings:

- in mathematics
    - _____ function
    - Euler _____
    - _____
    - _____ subgroup
    - method of _____s (partial differential equations)
- in physics and engineering
    - any _____ curve that shows the relationship between certain input- and output parameters, e.g.
    - an I-V or current-voltage _____ is the current in a circuit as a function of the applied voltage
    - Receiver-Operator _____
- in fiction
    - in Dungeons ' Dragons, _____ is another name for ability score

a. Characteristic
c. Demand
b. Technocracy
d. Russian financial crisis

10. _____ is a common concept in economics, and gives rise to derived concepts such as consumer debt. Generally _____ is defined by opposition to production. But the precise definition can vary because different schools of economists define production quite differently.
   a. Consumption
   b. Foreclosure data providers
   c. Federal Reserve Bank Notes
   d. Cash or share options

11. Economics:

   • _____, the desire to own something and the ability to pay for it
   • _____ curve, a graphic representation of a _____ schedule
   • _____ deposit, the money in checking accounts
   • _____ pull theory, the theory that inflation occurs when _____ for goods and services exceeds existing supplies
   • _____ schedule, a table that lists the quantity of a good a person will buy it each different price
   • _____ side economics, the school of economics at believes government spending and tax cuts open economy by raising _____

   a. Production
   b. Demand
   c. McKesson ' Robbins scandal
   d. Variability

12. A _____ is an object whose consumption increases the utility of the consumer, for which the quantity demanded exceeds the quantity supplied at zero price. _____s are usually modeled as having diminishing marginal utility. The first individual purchase has high utility; the second has less.
   a. Merit good
   b. Composite good
   c. Pie method
   d. Good

13. In economics, the _____ of a good or of a service is the utility of the specific use to which an agent would put a given increase in that good or service, or of the specific use that would be abandoned in response to a given decrease. In other words, _____ is the utility of the marginal use -- which, on the assumption of economic rationality, would be the least urgent use of the good or service, from the best feasible combination of actions in which its use is included. Under the mainstream assumptions, the _____ of a good or service is the posited quantified change in utility obtained by increasing or by decreasing use of that good or service.
   a. 1921 recession
   b. Marginal utility
   c. 130-30 fund
   d. 100-year flood

14. In economics, _____ is a measure of the relative satisfaction from consumption of various goods and services. Given this measure, one may speak meaningfully of increasing or decreasing _____, and thereby explain economic behavior in terms of attempts to increase one's _____. For illustrative purposes, changes in _____ are sometimes expressed in units called utils.
   a. Utility
   b. Expected utility hypothesis
   c. Utility function
   d. Ordinal utility

Chapter 28. Government and Market Failure

15. In law and economics, the _____, describes the economic efficiency of an economic allocation or outcome in the presence of externalities. The theorem states that when trade in an externality is possible and there are no transaction costs, bargaining will lead to an efficient outcome regardless of the initial allocation of property rights. In practice, obstacles to bargaining or poorly defined property rights can prevent Coasian bargaining.
    a. General Mining Act of 1872
    b. Prior appropriation water rights
    c. Coase theorem
    d. Means test

16. _____ is a term that refers both to:

    - a formal discipline used to help appraise, or assess, the case for a project or proposal, which itself is a process known as project appraisal; and
    - an informal approach to making decisions of any kind.

    Under both definitions the process involves, whether explicitly or implicitly, weighing the total expected costs against the total expected benefits of one or more actions in order to choose the best or most profitable option. The formal process is often referred to as either CBA (_____) or BCost-benefit analysis

    A hallmark of CBA is that all benefits and all costs are expressed in money terms, and are adjusted for the time value of money, so that all flows of benefits and flows of project costs over time (which tend to occur at different points in time) are expressed on a common basis in terms of their e;present value.e; Closely related, but slightly different, formal techniques include Cost-effectiveness analysis, Economic impact analysis, Fiscal impact analysis and Social Return on Investment(SROI) analysis. The latter builds upon the logic of _____, but differs in that it is explicitly designed to inform the practical decision-making of enterprise managers and investors focused on optimising their social and environmental impacts.

    a. 100-year flood
    b. Decision theory
    c. 130-30 fund
    d. Cost-benefit analysis

17. In economics and finance, _____ is the change in total cost that arises when the quantity produced changes by one unit. It is the cost of producing one more unit of a good. Mathematically, the _____ function is expressed as the first derivative of the total cost (TC) function with respect to quantity (Q.)
    a. Marginal cost
    b. Quality costs
    c. Khozraschyot
    d. Variable cost

18. In economics, a _____ is a graph of the costs of production as a function of total quantity produced. In a free market economy, productively efficient firms use these curves to find the optimal point of production, where they make the most profits. There are a few different types of _____s, each relevant to a different area of economics.
    a. Kuznets curve
    b. Demand curve
    c. Phillips curve
    d. Cost curve

398   *Chapter 28. Government and Market Failure*

19. A _____ is:

   - Rewrite _____, in generative grammar and computer science
   - Standardization, a formal and widely-accepted statement, fact, definition, or qualification
   - Operation, a determinate _____ for performing a mathematical operation and obtaining a certain result (Mathematics, Logic)
     - Unary operation
     - Binary operation
   - _____ of inference, a function from sets of formulae to formulae (Mathematics, Logic)
   - _____ of thumb, principle with broad application that is not intended to be strictly accurate or reliable for every situation. Also often simply referred to as a _____
   - Moral, an atomic element of a moral code for guiding choices in human behavior
   - Heuristic, a quantized '_____' which shows a tendency or probability for successful function
   - A regulation, as in sports
   - A Production _____, as in computer science
   - Procedural law, a _____ set governing the application of laws to cases
     - A law, which may informally be called a '_____'
     - A court ruling, a decision by a court
   - In the U.S. Government, a regulation mandated by Congress, but written or expanded upon by the Executive Branch.
   - Norm (sociology), an informal but widely accepted _____, concept, truth, definition, or qualification (social norms, legal norms, coding norms)
   - Norm (philosophy), a kind of sentence or a reason to act, feel or believe
   - 'Rulership' is the concept of governance by a government:
     - Military _____, governance by a military body
     - Monastic _____, a collection of precepts that guides the life of monks or nuns in a religious order where the superior holds the place of Christ
   - Slide _____

   - '_____,' a song by Ayumi Hamasaki
   - '_____,' a song by rapper Nas
   - '_____s,' an album by the band The Whitest Boy Alive
   - _____s: Pyaar Ka Superhit Formula, a 2003 Bollywood film
   - ruler, an instrument for measuring lengths
   - _____, a component of an astrolabe, circumferator or similar instrument
   - The _____s, a bestselling self-help book
   - _____ Project (Run Up-to-date Linux Everywhere), a project that aims to use up-to-date Linux software on old PCs
   - _____ engine, a software system that helps managing business _____s
   - Ja _____, a hip hop artist
     - R.U.L.E., a 2005 greatest hits album by rapper Ja _____
   - '_____s,' a KMFDM song

a. Technocracy   b. Demand
c. Procter ' Gamble   d. Rule

20. In economics, and cost accounting, _____ describes the total economic cost of production and is made up of variable costs, which vary according to the quantity of a good produced and include inputs such as labor and raw materials, plus fixed costs, which are independent of the quantity of a good produced and include inputs (capital) that cannot be varied in the short term, such as buildings and machinery. _____ in economics includes the total opportunity cost of each factor of production in addition to fixed and variable costs.

The rate at which _____ changes as the amount produced changes is called marginal cost.

a. 1921 recession
b. 130-30 fund
c. 100-year flood
d. Total cost

21. Many _____ are related to the environmental consequences of production and use

- Systemic risk describes the risks to the overall economy arising from the risks which the banking system takes. That the private costs of banking failure may be smaller than the social costs justifies banking regulations, although regulations could create a moral hazard.

- Anthropogenic climate change is attributed to greenhouse gas emissions from burning oil, gas, and coal. Global warming has been ranked as the #1 externality of all economic activity, in the magnitude of potential harms and yet remains unmitigated.

a. White certificates
b. Total Economic Value
c. Green certificate
d. Negative externalities

22. Examples of _____ include:

- A beekeeper keeps the bees for their honey. A side effect or externality associated with his activity is the pollination of surrounding crops by the bees. The value generated by the pollination may be more important than the value of the harvested honey.

- An individual planting an attractive garden in front of his house may provide benefits to others living in the area, and even financial benefits in the form of increased property values for all property owners.

- An individual buying a product that is interconnected in a network (e.g., a video cellphone) will increase the usefulness of such phones to other people who have a video cellphone. When each new user of a product increases the value of the same product owned by others, the phenomenon is called a network externality or a network effect. Network externalities often have 'tipping points' where, suddenly, the product reaches general acceptance and near-universal usage, a phenomenon which can be seen in the near universal take-up of cellphones in some Scandinavian countries.

- Knowledge spillover of inventions and information - once an invention (or most other forms of practical information) is discovered or made more easily accessible, others benefit by exploiting the invention or information. Copyright and intellectual property law are mechanisms to allow the inventor or creator to benefit from a temporary, state-protected monopoly in return for 'sharing' the information through publication or other means.

a. Total Economic Value
b. Negative externalities
c. Weighted average cost of carbon
d. Positive externalities

23. A _____ or labor union is an organization of workers who have banded together to achieve common goals in key areas and working conditions. The _____, through its leadership, bargains with the employer on behalf of union members (rank and file members) and negotiates labor contracts (Collective bargaining) with employers. This may include the negotiation of wages, work rules, complaint procedures, rules governing hiring, firing and promotion of workers, benefits, workplace safety and policies.
 a. Consumer goods
 b. Trade union
 c. Guaranteed investment contracts
 d. Case-Shiller Home Price Indices

24. _____ or economic opportunity loss is the value of the next best alternative foregone as the result of making a decision. _____ analysis is an important part of a company's decision-making processes but is not treated as an actual cost in any financial statement. The next best thing that a person can engage in is referred to as the _____ of doing the best thing and ignoring the next best thing to be done.
 a. Economic
 b. Industrial organization
 c. Economic ideology
 d. Opportunity cost

25. A _____ is the exclusive authority to determine how a resource is used, whether that resource is owned by government or by individuals. All economic goods have a _____s attribute. This attribute has three broad components

 1. The right to use the good
 2. The right to earn income from the good
 3. The right to transfer the good to others

The concept of _____s as used by economists and legal scholars are related but distinct. The distinction is largely seen in the economists' focus on the ability of an individual or collective to control the use of the good.

 a. Post-sale restraint
 b. Holder in due course
 c. High-reeve
 d. Property right

26. A _____ describes one of a number of pieces of legislation relating to the reduction of smog and air pollution in general. The use by governments to enforce clean air standards has contributed to an improvement in human health and longer life spans. Critics argue it has also sapped corporate profits and contributed to outsourcing, while defenders counter that improved environmental air quality has generated more jobs than it has eliminated.
 a. 130-30 fund
 b. Clean Air Act
 c. 100-year flood
 d. Smog

27. To _____ is to impose a financial charge or other levy upon a taxpayer by a state or the functional equivalent of a state.

_____es are also imposed by many subnational entities. _____es consist of direct _____ or indirect _____, and may be paid in money or as its labour equivalent (often but not always unpaid.)

a. 130-30 fund
b. Tax
c. 100-year flood
d. 1921 recession

28. To tax is to impose a financial charge or other levy upon a taxpayer by a state or the functional equivalent of a state. _____ are also imposed by many subnational entities. _____ consist of direct tax or indirect tax, and may be paid in money or as its labour equivalent (often but not always unpaid.)

a. 130-30 fund
b. 100-year flood
c. 1921 recession
d. Taxes

29. In economics, _____ is the total supply of goods and services produced by a national economy during a specific time period. It is the total amount of goods and services in the economy available at all possible price levels.

a. Aggregate expenditure
b. Aggregate demand
c. Aggregation problem
d. Aggregate supply

30. A _____ arises when one infers that something is true of the whole from the fact that it is true of some part of the whole (or even of every proper part.) For example: 'This fragment of metal cannot be broken with a hammer, therefore the machine of which it is a part cannot be broken with a hammer.' This is clearly fallacious, because many machines can be broken into their constituent parts without any of those parts being breakable.

This fallacy is often confused with the fallacy of hasty generalization, in which an unwarranted inference is made from a statement about a sample to a statement about the population from which it is drawn.

a. 130-30 fund
b. 1921 recession
c. 100-year flood
d. Fallacy of composition

31. _____ describes a deliberate attempt to interfere with the free and fair operation of the market and create artificial, false or misleading appearances with respect to the price of a security, commodity or currency. _____ is prohibited under Section 9(a)(2) of the Securities Exchange Act of 1934, and in Australia under Section s 1041A of the Corporations Act 2001. The Act defines _____ as transactions which create an artificial price or maintain an artificial price for a tradable security.

a. Net domestic product
b. Market manipulation
c. Legal monopoly
d. Managerial economics

32. In economics, an _____ or spillover of an economic transaction is an impact on a party that is not directly involved in the transaction. In such a case, prices do not reflect the full costs or benefits in production or consumption of a product or service. A positive impact is called an external benefit, while a negative impact is called an external cost.

a. Environmental impact assessment
b. Externality
c. Environmental tariff
d. Existence value

33. _____ is a practice of protecting the environment, on individual, organisational or governmental level, for the benefit of the natural environment and (or) humans.

Due to the pressures of population and technology the biophysical environment is being degraded, sometimes permanently. This has been recognised and governments began placing restraints on activities that caused environmental degradation.

a. AD-IA Model
b. ACCRA Cost of Living Index
c. ACEA agreement
d. Environmental Protection

34. A _____ refers to any type debt instrument, such as a loan, bond, mortgage that does not have a fixed rate of interest over the life of the instrument. Such debt typically uses an index or other base rate for establishing the interest rate for each relevant period. One of the most common rates to use as the basis for applying interest rates is the London Inter-bank Offered Rate, or LIBOR

a. Money market
b. Moneylender
c. Floating interest rate
d. Disposal tax effect

35. _____ in economics and business is the result of an exchange and from that trade we assign a numerical monetary value to a good, service or asset. If Alice trades Bob 4 apples for an orange, the _____ of an orange is 4 apples. Inversely, the _____ of an apple is 1/4 oranges.

a. Price book
b. Price
c. Premium pricing
d. Price war

36. _____ is any long-term change in the patterns of average weather of a specific region or the Earth as a whole. _____ reflects abnormal variations to the Earth's climate and subsequent effects on other parts of the Earth, such as in the ice caps over durations ranging from decades to millions of years.

In recent usage, especially in the context of environmental policy, _____ usually refers to changes in modern climate

a. 130-30 fund
b. Climate Change
c. 100-year flood
d. 1921 recession

37. Competition law, known in the United States as _____ law, has three main elements:

- prohibiting agreements or practices that restrict free trading and competition between business entities. This includes in particular the repression of cartels.
- banning abusive behaviour by a firm dominating a market, or anti-competitive practices that tend to lead to such a dominant position. Practices controlled in this way may include predatory pricing, tying, price gouging, refusal to deal, and many others.
- supervising the mergers and acquisitions of large corporations, including some joint ventures. Transactions that are considered to threaten the competitive process can be prohibited altogether, or approved subject to 'remedies' such as an obligation to divest part of the merged business or to offer licences or access to facilities to enable other businesses to continue competing.

The substance and practice of competition law varies from jurisdiction to jurisdiction. Protecting the interests of consumers (consumer welfare) and ensuring that entrepreneurs have an opportunity to compete in the market economy are often treated as important objectives. Competition law is closely connected with law on deregulation of access to markets, state aids and subsidies, the privatisation of state owned assets and the establishment of independent sector regulators. In recent decades, competition law has been viewed as a way to provide better public services.

a. Anti-Inflation Act
b. Intellectual property law
c. Antitrust
d. United Kingdom competition law

38. _____ is the increase in the average temperature of the Earth's near-surface air and oceans since the mid-twentieth century and its projected continuation. Global surface temperature increased 0.74 ± 0.18 °C (1.33 ± 0.32 °F) during the last century. The Intergovernmental Panel on Climate Change (IPCC) concludes that anthropogenic greenhouse gases are responsible for most of the observed temperature increase since the middle of the twentieth century, and that natural phenomena such as solar variation and volcanoes probably had a small warming effect from pre-industrial times to 1950 and a small cooling effect afterward.

a. Controlled Foreign Corporations
b. Dividend unit
c. Consumer goods
d. Global warming

39. _____, anti-selection insurance, statistics, and risk management. It refers to a market process in which 'bad' results occur when buyers and sellers have asymmetric information (i.e. access to different information): the 'bad' products or customers are more likely to be selected. A bank that sets one price for all its checking account customers runs the risk of being adversely selected against by its low-balance, high-activity (and hence least profitable) customers.

a. ACCRA Cost of Living Index
b. AD-IA Model
c. Adverse selection
d. ACEA agreement

40. The _____ is a protocol to the United Nations Framework Convention on Climate Change (UNFCCC or FCCC), an international environmental treaty produced at the United Nations Conference on treaty is intended to achieve 'stabilization of greenhouse gas concentrations in the atmosphere at a level that would prevent dangerous anthropogenic interference with the climate system.' The _____ establishes legally binding commitments for the reduction of four greenhouse gases (carbon dioxide, methane, nitrous oxide, sulphur hexafluoride), and two groups of gases (hydrofluorocarbons and perfluorocarbons) produced by 'Annex I' (industrialized) nations, as well as general commitments for all member countries. As of January 14 2009, 183 parties have ratified the protocol, which was initially adopted for use on 11 December 1997 in Kyoto, Japan and which entered into force on 16 February 2005. Under Kyoto, industrialized countries agreed to reduce their collective GHG emissions by 5.2% compared to the year 1990.

a. Greenhouse gases
b. Green New Deal
c. Carbon offset
d. Kyoto Protocol

41. An _____ is quite usually a standard guarantee from the seller of a product that specifies the extent to which the quality or performance of the product is assured and states the conditions under which the product can be returned, replaced, or repaired. It is often given in the form of a specific, written 'Warranty' document. However, a warranty may also arise by operation of law based upon the seller's description of the goods, and perhaps their source and quality, and any material deviation from that specification would violate the guarantee.

a. ACCRA Cost of Living Index
b. AD-IA Model
c. ACEA agreement
d. Express warranty

42. _____ is the prospect that a party insulated from risk may behave differently from the way it would behave if it were fully exposed to the risk. In insurance, _____ that occurs without conscious or malicious action is called morale hazard.

_____ is related to information asymmetry, a situation in which one party in a transaction has more information than another.

a. Moral hazard
b. 1921 recession
c. 100-year flood
d. 130-30 fund

43. _____, in law and economics, is a form of risk management primarily used to hedge against the risk of a contingent loss. _____ is defined as the equitable transfer of the risk of a loss, from one entity to another, in exchange for a premium, and can be thought of as a guaranteed small loss to prevent a large, possibly devastating loss. An insurer is a company selling the _____; an insured or policyholder is the person or entity buying the _____.

a. AD-IA Model
b. ACEA agreement
c. ACCRA Cost of Living Index
d. Insurance

44. _____ is the United States of America's federal assistance program, formerly known as 'welfare'. It began on July 1, 1997, and succeeded the Aid to Families with Dependent Children program, providing cash assistance to indigent American families with dependent children through the United States Department of Health and Human Services. Prior to 1997, the federal government designed the overall program requirements and guidelines, while states administered the program and determined eligibility for benefits.

a. Temporary Assistance for Needy Families
b. 1921 recession
c. 100-year flood
d. 130-30 fund

45. _____ and Keynesian Theory) is a macroeconomic theory based on the ideas of 20th-century British economist John Maynard Keynes. _____ argues that private sector decisions sometimes lead to inefficient macroeconomic outcomes and therefore advocates active policy responses by the public sector, including monetary policy actions by the central bank and fiscal policy actions by the government to stabilize output over the business cycle.

The theories forming the basis of _____ were first presented in The General Theory of Employment, Interest and Money, published in 1936.

a. Deflation
b. Rational choice theory
c. Market failure
d. Keynesian economics

46. _____ is a cross-disciplinary area concerned with protecting the safety, health and welfare of people engaged in work or employment. As a secondary effect, it may also protect co-workers, family members, employers, customers, suppliers, nearby communities, and other members of the public who are impacted by the workplace environment. It may involve interactions among many subject areas, including occupational medicine, occupational (or industrial) hygiene, public health, safety engineering, chemistry, health physics, ergonomics, toxicology, epidemiology, environmental health, industrial relations, public policy, sociology, and occupational health psychology.

a. Occupational Safety and Health
b. ACCRA Cost of Living Index
c. AD-IA Model
d. ACEA agreement

47. The United States _____ is an agency of the United States Department of Labor. It was created by Congress under the Occupational Safety and Health Act, signed by President Richard M. Nixon, on December 29, 1970. Its mission is to prevent work-related injuries, illnesses, and deaths by issuing and enforcing rules (called standards) for workplace safety and health.
a. AD-IA Model
b. ACCRA Cost of Living Index
c. ACEA agreement
d. Occupational Safety and Health Administration

Chapter 29. Public Choice Theory and the Economics of Taxation

1. _____ is the public sector analogy to market failure and occurs when a government intervention causes a more inefficient allocation of goods and resources than would occur without that intervention. Likewise, the government's failure to intervene in a market failure that would result in a socially preferable mix of output is referred to as passive _____ (Weimer and Vining, 2004.) Just as with market failures, there are many different kinds of _____s that describe corresponding distortions.
   a. Natural monopoly
   b. Government-granted monopoly
   c. Government failure
   d. Privatizing profits and socializing losses

2. In economics, a _____ exists when the production or use of goods and services by the market is not efficient. That is, there exists another outcome where all involved can be made better off. _____s can be viewed as scenarios where individuals' pursuit of pure self-interest leads to results that are not efficient - that can be improved upon from the societal point-of-view.
   a. Fixed exchange rate
   b. General equilibrium
   c. Market failure
   d. Financial economics

3. _____ in economic theory is the use of modern economic tools to study problems that are traditionally in the province of political science.

In particular, it studies the behavior of politicians and government officials as mostly self-interested agents and their interactions in the social system either as such or under alternative constitutional rules. These can be represented a number of ways, including standard constrained utility maximization, game theory, or decision theory.

   a. Public interest theory
   b. Rational ignorance
   c. Public choice
   d. Paradox of voting

4. _____ is the structure and set of regulations in place to control activity, usually in large organizations and government. As opposed to adhocracy, it is represented by standardized procedure (rule-following) that dictates the execution of most or all processes within the body, formal division of powers, hierarchy, and relationships. In practice the interpretation and execution of policy can lead to informal influence.
   a. 100-year flood
   b. 130-30 fund
   c. 1921 recession
   d. Bureaucracy

5. _____ is a fee paid on borrowed assets. It is the price paid for the use of borrowed money , or, money earned by deposited funds . Assets that are sometimes lent with _____ include money, shares, consumer goods through hire purchase, major assets such as aircraft, and even entire factories in finance lease arrangements.
   a. Asset protection
   b. Internal debt
   c. Insolvency
   d. Interest

6. _____ is the trading of favors or quid pro quo, such as vote trading by legislative members to obtain passage of actions of interest to each legislative member. It is also the 'cross quoting' of papers by academics in order to drive up reference counts. The Nuttall Encyclopedia describes log-rolling as 'mutual praise by authors of each other's work.' American frontiersman Davy Crockett was one of the first to apply the term to legislation:

Chapter 29. Public Choice Theory and the Economics of Taxation

The first known use of the term was by Congressman Davy Crockett, who said on the floor (of the U.S. House of Representatives) in 1835, 'my people don't like me to log-roll in their business, and vote away pre-emption rights to fellows in other states that never kindle a fire on their own land.'

The widest accepted origin is the old custom of neighbors assisting each other with the moving of logs.

a. 130-30 fund
c. 1921 recession
b. 100-year flood
d. Logrolling

7. The _____ is the apparent contradiction that although water is on the whole more useful, in terms of survival, than diamonds, diamonds command a higher price in the market. The economist Adam Smith is often considered to be the classic presenter of this paradox. Nicolaus Copernicus, John Locke, John Law and others had previously tried to explain the disparity.

a. 130-30 fund
c. 100-year flood
b. Paradox of value
d. St. Petersburg paradox

8. The _____, also referred to as Downs paradox, is that for a rational, self-interested voter the costs of voting will normally exceed the expected benefits. Because the chance of exercising a decisive vote (i.e. the chance of a tied election) is tiny compared to any realistic estimate of the private individual benefits of the different possible outcomes, the expected benefits of voting are less than the costs. The fact that people do vote is a major problem for public choice theory, first observed by Anthony Downs.

a. Public interest theory
c. Separability problem
b. Paradox of voting
d. Public choice

9. A _____ is defined in economics as a good that exhibits these properties:

- Excludable - it is reasonably possible to prevent a class of consumers (e.g. those who have not paid for it) from consuming the good.
- Rivalrous - consumptions by one consumer prevents simultaneous consumption by other consumers. _____s satisfies an individual want while public good satisfies a collective want of the society.

A _____ is the opposite of a public good, as they are almost exclusively made for profit.

An example of the _____ is bread: bread eaten by a given person cannot be consumed by another (rivalry), and it is easy for a baker to refuse to trade a loaf (excludable

a. Demerit good
c. Positional goods
b. Private good
d. Pie method

10. In economics, a _____ is a good that is non-rivaled and non-excludable. This means, respectively, that consumption of the good by one individual does not reduce availability of the good for consumption by others; and that no one can be effectively excluded from using the good. In the real world, there may be no such thing as an absolutely non-rivaled and non-excludable good; but economists think that some goods approximate the concept closely enough for the analysis to be economically useful.

a. Demand-pull theory
b. Public good
c. Happiness economics
d. Neoclassical synthesis

11. A _____ is an object whose consumption increases the utility of the consumer, for which the quantity demanded exceeds the quantity supplied at zero price. _____s are usually modeled as having diminishing marginal utility. The first individual purchase has high utility; the second has less.
   a. Composite good
   b. Good
   c. Merit good
   d. Pie method

12. The _____ is the part of economic and administrative life that deals with the delivery of goods and services by and for the government, whether national, regional or local/municipal.

Examples of _____ activity range from delivering social security, administering urban planning and organising national defenses.

The organization of the _____ can take several forms, including:

- Direct administration funded through taxation; the delivering organization generally has no specific requirement to meet commercial success criteria, and production decisions are determined by government.
- Publicly owned corporations (in some contexts, especially manufacturing, 'state-owned enterprises'); which differ from direct administration in that they have greater commercial freedoms and are expected to operate according to commercial criteria, and production decisions are not generally taken by government (although goals may be set for them by government.)
- Partial outsourcing (of the scale many businesses do, e.g. for IT services), is considered a _____ model.

A borderline form is

- Complete outsourcing or contracting out, with a privately owned corporation delivering the entire service on behalf of government. This may be considered a mixture of private sector operations with public ownership of assets, although in some forms the private sector's control and/or risk is so great that the service may no longer be considered part of the _____.

   a. Public sector
   b. 130-30 fund
   c. Policy cycle
   d. 100-year flood

13. In economics, _____ is a measure of national income. Basically, it is an approach to measure GDP. It is defined as the value of planned goods and services produced in an economy.
   a. Aggregate demand
   b. Aggregate expenditure
   c. Aggregation problem
   d. Aggregate supply

Chapter 29. Public Choice Theory and the Economics of Taxation

14. _____ has several particular meanings:

- in mathematics
    - _____ function
    - Euler _____
    - _____
    - _____ subgroup
    - method of _____s (partial differential equations)
- in physics and engineering
    - any _____ curve that shows the relationship between certain input- and output parameters, e.g.
    - an I-V or current-voltage _____ is the current in a circuit as a function of the applied voltage
    - Receiver-Operator _____
- in fiction
    - in Dungeons ' Dragons, _____ is another name for ability score

a. Demand
b. Technocracy
c. Russian financial crisis
d. Characteristic

15. Economics:

- _____, the desire to own something and the ability to pay for it
- _____ curve, a graphic representation of a _____ schedule
- _____ deposit, the money in checking accounts
- _____ pull theory, the theory that inflation occurs when _____ for goods and services exceeds existing supplies
- _____ schedule, a table that lists the quantity of a good a person will buy it each different price
- _____ side economics, the school of economics at believes government spending and tax cuts open economy by raising _____

a. Variability
b. Production
c. McKesson ' Robbins scandal
d. Demand

16. In law and economics, the _____, describes the economic efficiency of an economic allocation or outcome in the presence of externalities. The theorem states that when trade in an externality is possible and there are no transaction costs, bargaining will lead to an efficient outcome regardless of the initial allocation of property rights. In practice, obstacles to bargaining or poorly defined property rights can prevent Coasian bargaining.

a. General Mining Act of 1872
b. Prior appropriation water rights
c. Means test
d. Coase theorem

Chapter 29. Public Choice Theory and the Economics of Taxation

17. _____ is a term that refers both to:

- a formal discipline used to help appraise, or assess, the case for a project or proposal, which itself is a process known as project appraisal; and
- an informal approach to making decisions of any kind.

Under both definitions the process involves, whether explicitly or implicitly, weighing the total expected costs against the total expected benefits of one or more actions in order to choose the best or most profitable option. The formal process is often referred to as either CBA (_____) or BCost-benefit analysis

A hallmark of CBA is that all benefits and all costs are expressed in money terms, and are adjusted for the time value of money, so that all flows of benefits and flows of project costs over time (which tend to occur at different points in time) are expressed on a common basis in terms of their e;present value.e; Closely related, but slightly different, formal techniques include Cost-effectiveness analysis, Economic impact analysis, Fiscal impact analysis and Social Return on Investment(SROI) analysis. The latter builds upon the logic of _____, but differs in that it is explicitly designed to inform the practical decision-making of enterprise managers and investors focused on optimising their social and environmental impacts.

a. 130-30 fund
b. Decision theory
c. 100-year flood
d. Cost-benefit analysis

18. A _____ is any systematic process enabling many market players to bid and ask: helping bidders and sellers interact and make deals. It is not just the price mechanism but the entire system of regulation, qualification, credentials, reputations and clearing that surrounds that mechanism and makes it operate in a social context.

Because a _____ relies on the assumption that players are constantly involved and unequally enabled, a _____ is distinguished specifically from a voting system where candidates seek the support of voters on a less regular basis.

a. Competitive equilibrium
b. Price mechanism
c. Market system
d. Contestable market

19. The principle that taxes should vary according to an individual's level of wealth or income is the _____ principle.
a. ACCRA Cost of Living Index
b. ACEA agreement
c. AD-IA Model
d. Ability-to-pay

20. In economics, the _____ is used to illustrate the idea that increases in the rate of taxation do not necessarily increase tax revenue. (For instance, whereas a 0% income tax rate will generate no revenue, neither will a 100% rate, as citizens will have no incentive to make money.) Increasing taxes beyond the peak of the curve point will decrease tax revenue.
a. 100-year flood
b. 130-30 fund
c. 1921 recession
d. Laffer curve

21. To _____ is to impose a financial charge or other levy upon a taxpayer by a state or the functional equivalent of a state.

Chapter 29. Public Choice Theory and the Economics of Taxation

_____es are also imposed by many subnational entities. _____es consist of direct _____ or indirect _____, and may be paid in money or as its labour equivalent (often but not always unpaid.)

a. 100-year flood
c. 1921 recession
b. 130-30 fund
d. Tax

22. In economics, tax incidence is the analysis of the effect of a particular tax on the distribution of economic welfare. Tax incidence is said to 'fall' upon the group that, at the end of the day, bears the burden of the tax. The key concept is that the tax incidence or _____ does not depend on where the revenue is collected, but on the price elasticity of demand and price elasticity of supply.

a. 130-30 fund
c. 1921 recession
b. Tax burden
d. 100-year flood

23. In a company, _____ is the sum of all financial records of salaries, wages, bonuses and deductions.

A paycheck, is traditionally a paper document issued by an employer to pay an employee for services rendered. While most commonly used in the United States, recently the physical paycheck has been increasingly replaced by electronic direct deposit to bank accounts.

a. Tax expense
c. Total Expense Ratio
b. 100-year flood
d. Payroll

24. Total _____ is defined by the United States' Bureau of Economic Analysis as

income received by persons from all sources. It includes income received from participation in production as well as from government and business transfer payments. It is the sum of compensation of employees (received), supplements to wages and salaries, proprietors' income with inventory valuation adjustment (IVA) and capital consumption adjustment (CCAdj), rental income of persons with CCAdj, _____ receipts on assets, and personal current transfer receipts, less contributions for government social insurance.

a. Personal income
c. Greater fool theory
b. Bidding
d. Dividend Discount Model

25. A _____ is a tax by which the tax rate increases as the taxable amount increases. 'Progressive' describes a distribution effect on income or expenditure, referring to the way the rate progresses from low to high, where the average tax rate is less than the marginal tax rate. It can be applied to individual taxes or to a tax system as a whole; a year, multi-year, or lifetime.

a. Progressive tax
c. Proportional tax
b. 130-30 fund
d. 100-year flood

26. _____ is an ad valorem tax that an owner is required to pay on the value of the property being taxed. _____ can be defined as 'generally, tax imposed by municipalities upon owners of property within their jurisdiction based on the value of such property.' There are three species or types of property: Land, Improvements to Land (immovable manmade objects; i.e., buildings), and Personal (movable manmade objects.) Real estate, real property or realty are all terms for the combination of land and improvements.

a. Bank regulation
b. Community property
c. Property tax
d. Chief Financial Officers Act of 1990

27. A _____ is a tax imposed so that the tax rate is fixed as the amount subject to taxation increases. In simple terms, it imposes an equal burden (relative to resources) on the rich and poor. 'Proportional' describes a distribution effect on income or expenditure, referring to the way the rate remains consistent (does not progress from 'low to high' or 'high to low' as income or consumption changes), where the marginal tax rate is equal to the average tax rate.
a. 100-year flood
b. Regressive tax
c. 130-30 fund
d. Proportional tax

28. A _____ is a tax imposed in such a manner that the tax rate decreases as the amount subject to taxation increases. In simple terms, a _____ imposes a greater burden (relative to resources) on the poor than on the rich -- there is an inverse relationship between the tax rate and the taxpayer's ability to pay as measured by assets, consumption, or income. 'Regressive' describes a distribution effect on income or expenditure, referring to the way the rate progresses from high to low, where the average tax rate exceeds the marginal tax rate.
a. 130-30 fund
b. Proportional tax
c. Regressive tax
d. 100-year flood

29. A _____ is a consumption tax charged at the point of purchase for certain goods and services. The tax is usually set as a percentage by the government charging the tax. There is usually a list of exemptions.
a. 130-30 fund
b. 1921 recession
c. Sales tax
d. 100-year flood

30. An _____ is a tax levied on the financial income of people, corporations, or other legal entities. Various _____ systems exist, with varying degrees of tax incidence. Income taxation can be progressive, proportional, or regressive.
a. ACCRA Cost of Living Index
b. ACEA agreement
c. AD-IA Model
d. Income tax

31. To tax is to impose a financial charge or other levy upon a taxpayer by a state or the functional equivalent of a state.

_____ are also imposed by many subnational entities. _____ consist of direct tax or indirect tax, and may be paid in money or as its labour equivalent (often but not always unpaid.)

a. 1921 recession
b. 100-year flood
c. Taxes
d. 130-30 fund

32. In economics, _____ describes demand that is not very sensitive to a change in price.
a. Export-led growth
b. Inflation hedge
c. Effective unemployment rate
d. Inelastic

33. In economics, _____ is the analysis of the effect of a particular tax on the distribution of economic welfare. _____ is said to 'fall' upon the group that, at the end of the day, bears the burden of the tax. The key concept is that the _____ or tax burden does not depend on where the revenue is collected, but on the price elasticity of demand and price elasticity of supply.

Chapter 29. Public Choice Theory and the Economics of Taxation

a. 1921 recession
c. 100-year flood
b. 130-30 fund
d. Tax incidence

34. _____ in economics and business is the result of an exchange and from that trade we assign a numerical monetary value to a good, service or asset. If Alice trades Bob 4 apples for an orange, the _____ of an orange is 4 apples. Inversely, the _____ of an apple is 1/4 oranges.

   a. Price war
   c. Price book
   b. Premium pricing
   d. Price

35. In economics, a _____ is a loss of economic efficiency that can occur when equilibrium for a good or service is not Pareto optimal. In other words, either people who would have more marginal benefit than marginal cost are not buying the good or service, or people who would have more marginal cost than marginal benefit are buying the product.

Causes of _____ can include monopoly pricing, externalities, taxes or subsidies, and binding price ceilings or floors.

   a. Contract curve
   c. Deadweight loss
   b. Leapfrogging
   d. Distributive efficiency

36. _____ is an economic model based on price, utility and quantity in a market. It predicts that in a competitive market, price will function to equalize the quantity demanded by consumers, and the quantity supplied by producers, resulting in an economic equilibrium of price and quantity. The model incorporates other factors changing equilibrium as a shift of demand and/or supply.

   a. Joint demand
   c. Rational addiction
   b. Deferred gratification
   d. Supply and demand

37. In finance, a _____ is a debt security, in which the authorized issuer owes the holders a debt and, depending on the terms of the _____, is obliged to pay interest (the coupon) and/or to repay the principal at a later date, termed maturity. A _____ is a formal contract to repay borrowed money with interest at fixed intervals.

Thus a _____ is like a loan: the issuer is the borrower (debtor), the holder is the lender (creditor), and the coupon is the interest.

   a. Callable
   c. Prize Bond
   b. Zero-coupon
   d. Bond

38. _____ are the income that is gained by governments because of taxation of the people.

Just as there are different types of tax, the form in which _____ is collected also differs; furthermore, the agency that collects the tax may not be part of central government, but may be an alternative third-party licenced to collect tax which they themselves will use. For example:

- In the UK, the DVLA collects road tax, which is then passed on the treasury.

_____s on purchases can come from two forms: 'tax' itself is a percentage of the price added to the purchase (such as sales tax in US states, or VAT in the UK), while 'duty' is a fixed amount added to the purchase price (such as is commonly found on cigarettes.) In order to calculate the total tax raised from these sales, we must work out the effective tax rate multiplied by the quantity supplied.

a. Tax and spend
b. Taxable wage
c. Taxation as slavery
d. Tax revenue

39. In economics, _____ is the ratio of the percent change in one variable to the percent change in another variable. It is a tool for measuring the responsiveness of a function to changes in parameters in a relative way. Commonly analyzed are _____ of substitution, price and wealth.

a. Elasticity
b. ACCRA Cost of Living Index
c. Elasticity of demand
d. ACEA agreement

40. In economics, the _____ is defined as a numerical measure of the responsiveness of the quantity supplied of product (A) to a change in price of product (A) alone. It is the measure of the way quantity supplied reacts to a change in price.

For example, if, in response to a 10% rise in the price of a good, the quantity supplied increases by 20%, the _____ would be 20%/10% = 2.

a. Demand shaping
b. Hedonimetry
c. Passive income
d. Price elasticity of supply

41. In economics, _____ is the transfer of income, wealth or property from some individuals to others.

One premise of _____ is that money should be distributed to benefit the poorer members of society, and that the rich have an obligation to assist the poor, thus creating a more financially egalitarian society. Another argument is that the rich exploit the poor or otherwise gain unfair benefits.

a. 130-30 fund
b. 1921 recession
c. 100-year flood
d. Redistribution

42. Many _____ are related to the environmental consequences of production and use

- Systemic risk describes the risks to the overall economy arising from the risks which the banking system takes. That the private costs of banking failure may be smaller than the social costs justifies banking regulations, although regulations could create a moral hazard.

- Anthropogenic climate change is attributed to greenhouse gas emissions from burning oil, gas, and coal. Global warming has been ranked as the #1 externality of all economic activity, in the magnitude of potential harms and yet remains unmitigated.

a. Negative externalities
b. Green certificate
c. Total Economic Value
d. White certificates

43. A _____ is a counterfeit agreement among industries. It is an informal organization of producers that agree to coordinate prices and production. _____s usually occur in an oligopolistic industry, where there is a small number of sellers and usually involve homogeneous products.

a. Cartel
b. Shill
c. 100-year flood
d. Shanzhai

44. _____ is the transition of a national economy from monopoly control by groups of large businesses to a free market economy. This change rarely arises naturally, and is generally the result of regulation by a governing body.

A modern example of _____ is the economic restructuring of Germany after the fall of the Third Reich in 1945.

a. Complementary monopoly
b. Decartelization
c. Monopolization
d. Market power

45. A _____ refers to property being sold by a taxing authority or the court to recover delinquent taxes.

When property taxes are not paid, title gets transferred to the state. The owner will then have a period of time to redeem the property by paying the overdue taxes, including penalties and costs.

a. Tax wedge
b. Tax competition
c. Taxation as theft
d. Tax sale

46. A _____ is the transfer of wealth from one party (such as a person or company) to another. A _____ is usually made in exchange for the provision of goods, services or both, or to fulfill a legal obligation.

The simplest and oldest form of _____ is barter, the exchange of one good or service for another.

a. Soft count
b. Social gravity
c. Payment
d. Going concern

47. _____ is a practice of protecting the environment, on individual, organisational or governmental level, for the benefit of the natural environment and (or) humans.

Due to the pressures of population and technology the biophysical environment is being degraded, sometimes permanently. This has been recognised and governments began placing restraints on activities that caused environmental degradation.

a. ACEA agreement
b. Environmental Protection
c. ACCRA Cost of Living Index
d. AD-IA Model

Chapter 30. Antitrust Policy and Regulation

1. Competition law, known in the United States as _____ law, has three main elements:

   - prohibiting agreements or practices that restrict free trading and competition between business entities. This includes in particular the repression of cartels.
   - banning abusive behaviour by a firm dominating a market, or anti-competitive practices that tend to lead to such a dominant position. Practices controlled in this way may include predatory pricing, tying, price gouging, refusal to deal, and many others.
   - supervising the mergers and acquisitions of large corporations, including some joint ventures. Transactions that are considered to threaten the competitive process can be prohibited altogether, or approved subject to 'remedies' such as an obligation to divest part of the merged business or to offer licences or access to facilities to enable other businesses to continue competing.

   The substance and practice of competition law varies from jurisdiction to jurisdiction. Protecting the interests of consumers (consumer welfare) and ensuring that entrepreneurs have an opportunity to compete in the market economy are often treated as important objectives. Competition law is closely connected with law on deregulation of access to markets, state aids and subsidies, the privatisation of state owned assets and the establishment of independent sector regulators. In recent decades, competition law has been viewed as a way to provide better public services.

   a. Intellectual property law
   b. United Kingdom competition law
   c. Antitrust
   d. Anti-Inflation Act

2. The _____ is an independent agency of the United States government, established in 1914 by the _____ Act. Its principal mission is the promotion of 'consumer protection' and the elimination and prevention of what regulators perceive to be harmfully 'anti-competitive' business practices, such as coercive monopoly.

   The _____ Act was one of President Wilson's major acts against trusts.

   a. 1921 recession
   b. 100-year flood
   c. 130-30 fund
   d. Federal Trade Commission

3. The _____ of 1914 (15 U.S.C §§ 41-58, as amended) established the Federal Trade Commission (FTC), a bipartisan body of five members appointed by the President of the United States for seven year terms. This Commission was authorized to issue Cease and Desist orders to large corporations to curb unfair trade practices. This Act also gave more flexibility to the US congress for judicial matters.

   a. Federal Trade Commission Act
   b. Minimum wage law
   c. Competition law theory
   d. Buydown

4. An _____ is an equitable remedy in the form of a court order, whereby a party is required to do certain acts. The party that fails to adhere to the _____ faces civil or criminal penalties and may have to pay damages or accept sanctions for failing to follow the court's order. In some cases, breaches of _____s are considered serious criminal offences that merit arrest and possible prison sentences.

   a. ACCRA Cost of Living Index
   b. Injunction
   c. AD-IA Model
   d. ACEA agreement

5. The term _____ refers to an offense under Section 2 of the American Sherman Antitrust Act, passed in 1890. Section 2 states that any person 'who shall monopolize .

a. Complementary monopoly
b. Quasi-rent
c. Bilateral monopoly
d. Monopolization

6. In economics, a _____ occurs when, due to the economies of scale of a particular industry, the maximum efficiency of production and distribution is realized through a single supplier.

Natural monopolies arise where the largest supplier in an industry, often the first supplier in a market, has an overwhelming cost advantage over other actual or potential competitors. This tends to be the case in industries where capital costs predominate, creating economies of scale which are large in relation to the size of the market, and hence high barriers to entry; examples include water services and electricity.

a. Natural monopoly
b. Privatizing profits and socializing losses
c. Common-pool resource
d. Collective goods

7. _____ is a common law doctrine relating to the enforceability of contractual restrictions on freedom to conduct business. In an old leading case of Mitchell v. Reynolds (1711) Lord Smith L.C. said,

'it is the privilege of a trader in a free country, in all matters not contrary to law, to regulate his own mode of carrying it on according to his own discretion and choice.

a. Restraint of trade
b. Third line forcing
c. Group boycott
d. Conscious parallelism

8. _____ was a predominant American integrated oil producing, transporting, refining, and marketing company. Established in 1870 as an Ohio Corporation, it was the largest oil refiner in the world and operated as a major company trust and was one of the world's first and largest multinational corporations until it was broken up by the United States Supreme Court in 1911. John D. Rockefeller was a founder, chairman and major shareholder, and the company made him a billionaire and eventually the richest man in history.

a. 1921 recession
b. 130-30 fund
c. 100-year flood
d. Standard Oil

9. _____, in law, is a term that indicates that a statute permits a court to triple the amount of the actual/compensatory damages to be awarded to a prevailing plaintiff, generally in order to punish the losing party for willful conduct. _____ are a multiple of, and not an addition to, actual damages. Thus, where a person received an award of $100 for an injury, a court applying _____ would raise the award to $300.

a. Personal Responsibility and Work Opportunity Reconciliation Act of 1996
b. Treble damages
c. Property right
d. Directive 2006/54/EC

10. _____, known in the United States as antitrust law, has three main elements:

- prohibiting agreements or practices that restrict free trading and competition between business entities. This includes in particular the repression of cartels.
- banning abusive behaviour by a firm dominating a market, or anti-competitive practices that tend to lead to such a dominant position. Practices controlled in this way may include predatory pricing, tying, price gouging, refusal to deal, and many others.
- supervising the mergers and acquisitions of large corporations, including some joint ventures. Transactions that are considered to threaten the competitive process can be prohibited altogether, or approved subject to 'remedies' such as an obligation to divest part of the merged business or to offer licences or access to facilities to enable other businesses to continue competing.

The substance and practice of _____ varies from jurisdiction to jurisdiction. Protecting the interests of consumers (consumer welfare) and ensuring that entrepreneurs have an opportunity to compete in the market economy are often treated as important objectives. _____ is closely connected with law on deregulation of access to markets, state aids and subsidies, the privatisation of state owned assets and the establishment of independent sector regulators. In recent decades, _____ has been viewed as a way to provide better public services.

a. Hostile work environment
b. Fee simple
c. Due diligence
d. Competition law

11. In economics, a _____ exists when a specific individual or enterprise has sufficient control over a particular product or service to determine significantly the terms on which other individuals shall have access to it. Monopolies are thus characterized by a lack of economic competition for the good or service that they provide and a lack of viable substitute goods. The verb 'monopolize' refers to the process by which a firm gains persistently greater market share than what is expected under perfect competition.

a. 100-year flood
b. Monopoly
c. 1921 recession
d. 130-30 fund

Chapter 30. Antitrust Policy and Regulation 419

12. A _____ is:

   - Rewrite _____, in generative grammar and computer science
   - Standardization, a formal and widely-accepted statement, fact, definition, or qualification
   - Operation, a determinate _____ for performing a mathematical operation and obtaining a certain result (Mathematics, Logic)
     - Unary operation
     - Binary operation
   - _____ of inference, a function from sets of formulae to formulae (Mathematics, Logic)
   - _____ of thumb, principle with broad application that is not intended to be strictly accurate or reliable for every situation. Also often simply referred to as a _____
   - Moral, an atomic element of a moral code for guiding choices in human behavior
   - Heuristic, a quantized '_____' which shows a tendency or probability for successful function
   - A regulation, as in sports
   - A Production _____, as in computer science
   - Procedural law, a _____ set governing the application of laws to cases
     - A law, which may informally be called a '_____'
     - A court ruling, a decision by a court
   - In the U.S. Government, a regulation mandated by Congress, but written or expanded upon by the Executive Branch.
   - Norm (sociology), an informal but widely accepted _____, concept, truth, definition, or qualification (social norms, legal norms, coding norms)
   - Norm (philosophy), a kind of sentence or a reason to act, feel or believe
   - 'Rulership' is the concept of governance by a government:
     - Military _____, governance by a military body
     - Monastic _____, a collection of precepts that guides the life of monks or nuns in a religious order where the superior holds the place of Christ
   - Slide _____

   - '_____,' a song by Ayumi Hamasaki
   - '_____,' a song by rapper Nas
   - '_____s,' an album by the band The Whitest Boy Alive
   - _____s: Pyaar Ka Superhit Formula, a 2003 Bollywood film
   - ruler, an instrument for measuring lengths
   - _____, a component of an astrolabe, circumferator or similar instrument
   - The _____s, a bestselling self-help book
   - _____ Project (Run Up-to-date Linux Everywhere), a project that aims to use up-to-date Linux software on old PCs
   - _____ engine, a software system that helps managing business _____s
   - Ja _____, a hip hop artist
     - R.U.L.E., a 2005 greatest hits album by rapper Ja _____
   - '_____s,' a KMFDM song

a. Procter ' Gamble   b. Demand
c. Technocracy   d. Rule

13. The Celler-Derek Browne Act is a United States federal law passed in 1950 that reformed and strengthened the Clayton Antitrust Act of 1914 which had amended the Sherman Antitrust Act of 1890. The _____ was passed to close a loophole regarding certain asset acquisitions and acquisitions involving firms that were not direct competitors. While the Clayton Act prohibited stock purchase mergers that resulted in reduced competition, shrewd businessmen were able to find ways around the Clayton Act by simply buying up a competitor's assets.

   a. Leave of absence
   b. Patent
   c. Civil Rights Act of 1964
   d. Celler-Kefauver Act

14. _____ in economics and business is the result of an exchange and from that trade we assign a numerical monetary value to a good, service or asset. If Alice trades Bob 4 apples for an orange, the _____ of an orange is 4 apples. Inversely, the _____ of an apple is 1/4 oranges.

   a. Price book
   b. Price war
   c. Price
   d. Premium pricing

15. _____ exists when sales of identical goods or services are transacted at different prices from the same provider. In a theoretical market with perfect information, no transaction costs or prohibition on secondary exchange (or re-selling) to prevent arbitrage, _____ can only be a feature of monopoly and oligopoly markets, where market power can be exercised. Otherwise, the moment the seller tries to sell the same good at different prices, the buyer at the lower price can arbitrage by selling to the consumer buying at the higher price but with a tiny discount.

   a. Lerner Index
   b. Transfer pricing
   c. Price discrimination
   d. Loss leader

16. The _____ of 1938 is a United States federal law that amended the Federal Trade Commission Act to add the clause 'unfair or deceptive acts or practices in commerce are hereby declared unlawful' to the Section 5 prohibition of unfair methods of competition, in order to protect consumers as well as competition.

   1938 amendment to the federal trade commission act that authorized the FTC to restrict unfair or deceptive acts; also called the advertising act. Until this amendment was passed, the FTC could only restrict practices that were unfair to competitors.

   a. Fee simple
   b. Human rights in Brazil
   c. Merger guidelines
   d. Wheeler-Lea Act

17. The _____ consists of a number of economic theories which describe the nature of the firm, company including its existence, its behaviour, and its relationship with the market.

   In simplified terms, the _____ aims to answer these questions:

   1. Existence - why do firms emerge, why are not all transactions in the economy mediated over the market?
   2. Boundaries - why the boundary between firms and the market is located exactly there? Which transactions are performed internally and which are negotiated on the market?
   3. Organization - why are firms structured in such specific way? What is the interplay of formal and informal relationships?

   Despite looking simple, these questions are not answered by the established economic theory, which usually views firms as given, and treats them as black boxes without any internal structure.

The First World War period saw a change of emphasis in economic theory away from industry-level analysis which mainly included analysing markets to analysis at the level of the firm, as it became increasingly clear that perfect competition was no longer an adequate model of how firms behaved. Economic theory till then had focussed on trying to understand markets alone and there had been little study on understanding why firms or organisations exist.

a. Theory of the firm
c. Policy Ineffectiveness Proposition

b. Khazzoom-Brookes postulate
d. Technology gap

18. _____, in strategic management and marketing is, according to Carlton O'Neal, the percentage or proportion of the total available market or market segment that is being serviced by a company. It can be expressed as a company's sales revenue (from that market) divided by the total sales revenue available in that market. It can also be expressed as a company's unit sales volume (in a market) divided by the total volume of units sold in that market.

a. Product differentiation
c. Pricing science

b. Market share
d. Customer to customer

19. In competition law the _____ defines the market in which one or more goods compete. Therefore, the _____ defines whether two or more products can be considered substitute goods and whether they constitute a particular and separate market for competition analysis.

The _____ combines the product market and the geographic market, defined as follows:

1. A relevant product market comprises all those products and/or services which are regarded as interchangeable or substitutable by the consumer by reason of the products' characteristics, their prices and their intended use;
2. A relevant geographic market comprises the area in which the firms concerned are involved in the supply of products or services and in which the conditions of competition are sufficiently homogeneous.

The notion of _____ is used in order to identify the products and undertakings which are directly competing in a business. Therefore, the _____ is the market where the competition takes place.

a. Community property
c. Competition law

b. Greenfield agreement
d. Relevant market

20.

The _____ is a doctrine developed by the United States Supreme Court in its interpretation of the Sherman Antitrust Act. The rule, stated and applied in the case of Standard Oil Co. of New Jersey v. United States, 221 U.S. 1 (1911), is that only combinations and contracts unreasonably restraining trade are subject to actions under the anti-trust laws and that size and possession of monopoly power are not illegal.

a. Rule of reason
c. Pigford v. Glickman

b. Directive 2006/54/EC
d. Negligence in employment

Chapter 30. Antitrust Policy and Regulation

21. A _____ is an object whose consumption increases the utility of the consumer, for which the quantity demanded exceeds the quantity supplied at zero price. _____s are usually modeled as having diminishing marginal utility. The first individual purchase has high utility; the second has less.
    a. Good
    b. Merit good
    c. Pie method
    d. Composite good

22. The notion of _____ is found in the writings of Mikhail Bakunin, Friedrich Nietzsche, and in Werner Sombart's Krieg und Kapitalismus (War and Capitalism) (1913, p. 207), where he wrote: 'again out of destruction a new spirit of creativity arises'. In Capitalism, Socialism and Democracy, the Austrian economist Joseph Schumpeter popularized and used the term to describe the process of transformation that accompanies radical innovation.
    a. 100-year flood
    b. 1921 recession
    c. 130-30 fund
    d. Creative destruction

23. The _____ is a measure of the size of firms in relation to the industry and an indicator of the amount of competition among them. Named after economists Orris C. Herfindahl and Albert O. Hirschman, it is an economic concept, widely applied in competition law, antitrust and also technology management. It is defined as the sum of the squares of the market shares of the 50 largest firms within the industry, where the market shares are expressed as percentages.
    a. Reduced form
    b. Panel data
    c. Vector autoregression
    d. Herfindahl index

24. In economics, a _____ is the combination of two or more firms competing in the same market with the same good or service.See Horizontal integration.
    a. Federal Reserve districts
    b. Horizontal merger
    c. Market dominance
    d. Financial system

25. _____ is a term used to describe a policy of allowing events to take their own course. The term is a French phrase literally meaning 'let do'. It is a doctrine that states that government generally should not intervene in the marketplace.
    a. Heroic capitalism
    b. Theory of Productive Forces
    c. Laissez-faire
    d. Communization

26. The phrase _____ and acquisitions refers to the aspect of corporate strategy, corporate finance and management dealing with the buying, selling and combining of different companies that can aid, finance, or help a growing company in a given industry grow rapidly without having to create another business entity.

    An acquisition, also known as a takeover or a buyout, is the buying of one company (the 'target') by another. An acquisition may be friendly or hostile.

    a. Differential accumulation
    b. Peace dividend
    c. Mergers
    d. Political economy

27. The phrase _____ refers to the aspect of corporate strategy, corporate finance and management dealing with the buying, selling and combining of different companies that can aid, finance, or help a growing company in a given industry grow rapidly without having to create another business entity.

    An acquisition, also known as a takeover or a buyout, is the buying of one company (the 'target') by another. An acquisition may be friendly or hostile.

Chapter 30. Antitrust Policy and Regulation

a. Political economy
b. Peace dividend
c. Productive and unproductive labour
d. Mergers and acquisitions

28. In economics, _____ is a measure of national income. Basically, it is an approach to measure GDP. It is defined as the value of planned goods and services produced in an economy.

a. Aggregate demand
b. Aggregation problem
c. Aggregate supply
d. Aggregate expenditure

29. In economics and sociology, an _____ is any factor (financial or non-financial) that enables or motivates a particular course of action, or counts as a reason for preferring one choice to the alternatives. It is an expectation that encourages people to behave in a certain way. Since human beings are purposeful creatures, the study of _____ structures is central to the study of all economic activity (both in terms of individual decision-making and in terms of co-operation and competition within a larger institutional structure.)

a. Incentive
b. Isocost
c. Epstein-Zin preferences
d. Economic reform

30. A _____ is officially defined as being 'any merger that is not horizontal or vertical; in general, it is the combination of firms in different industries or firms operating in different geographic areas'. _____s can serve various purposes, including extending corporate territories and extending a product range. One example of a _____ was the merger between the Walt Disney Company and the American Broadcasting Company.

a. Cost-effectiveness analysis
b. Factor cost
c. Conglomerate merger
d. Borrowing base

31. In economics, market concentration is a function of the number of firms and their respective shares of the total production (alternatively, total capacity or total reserves) in a market. Alternative terms are _____ and Seller concentration.

Market concentration is related to the concept of industrial concentration, which concerns the distribution of production within an industry, as opposed to a market.

a. ACCRA Cost of Living Index
b. Industry concentration
c. AD-IA Model
d. ACEA agreement

32. The _____ are a set of internal rules promulgated by the Antitrust Division of the United States Department of Justice (DOJ) in conjunction with the Federal Trade Commission (FTC.) These rules, which have been revised a number of times in the past four decades, govern the extent to which these two regulatory bodies will scrutinize and/or challenge a potential merger on grounds of market concentration or threat to competition within a relevant market.

The _____ have sections governing both horizontal integration and vertical integration.

a. No-FEAR Act
b. Law of increasing relative cost
c. Business valuation
d. Merger guidelines

33. _____ is an agreement between business competitors to sell the same product or service at the same price. In general, it is an agreement intended to ultimately push the price of a product as high as possible, leading to profits for all the sellers. Price-fixing can also involve any agreement to fix, peg, discount or stabilize prices.

a. Cut-throat competition
b. Moral victory
c. Non-price competition
d. Price fixing

34.

The _____ is an independent agency of the United States government, created, directed, and empowered by Congressional statute , and with the majority of its commissioners appointed by the current President. The _____ works towards six strategic goals in the areas of broadband, competition, the spectrum, the media, public safety and homeland security, and modernizing the _____.

a. Federal Communications Commission
b. 130-30 fund
c. 1921 recession
d. 100-year flood

35. The _____ is the United States federal agency with jurisdiction over interstate electricity sales, wholesale electric rates, hydroelectric licensing, natural gas pricing, and oil pipeline rates. _____ also reviews and authorizes liquefied natural gas (LNG) terminals, interstate natural gas pipelines and non-federal hydropower projects.

A predecessor agency, the Federal Power Commission, was founded in 1920 to allow cabinet members to coordinate federal hydropower development.

a. Commodity trading advisors
b. Demographics of India
c. Constrained Pareto optimality
d. Federal Energy Regulatory Commission

36. _____ and Keynesian Theory) is a macroeconomic theory based on the ideas of 20th-century British economist John Maynard Keynes. _____ argues that private sector decisions sometimes lead to inefficient macroeconomic outcomes and therefore advocates active policy responses by the public sector, including monetary policy actions by the central bank and fiscal policy actions by the government to stabilize output over the business cycle.

The theories forming the basis of _____ were first presented in The General Theory of Employment, Interest and Money, published in 1936.

a. Keynesian economics
b. Deflation
c. Rational choice theory
d. Market failure

37. The _____ refers to the 'common well-being' or 'general welfare.' The _____ is central to policy debates, politics, democracy and the nature of government itself. While nearly everyone claims that aiding the common well-being or general welfare is positive, there is little, if any, consensus on what exactly constitutes the _____.

There are different views on how many members of the public must benefit from an action before it can be declared to be in the _____: at one extreme, an action has to benefit every single member of society in order to be truly in the _____; at the other extreme, any action can be in the _____ as long as it benefits some of the population and harms none.

a. Public interest
b. Power Elite
c. Second-class citizen
d. Stealth tax

38. _____ is an economic theory holding that regulation is supplied in response to the demand of the public for the correction of inefficient or inequitable market practices. Regulation is assumed initially to benefit society as a whole rather than particular vested interests. The regulatory body is considered to represent the interest of the society in which it operates rather than the private interests of the regulators.
a. Public choice
b. Rational ignorance
c. Paradox of voting
d. Public interest theory

39. The _____ is a federally owned corporation in the United States created by congressional charter in May 1933 to provide navigation, flood control, electricity generation, fertilizer manufacturing, and economic development in the Tennessee Valley, a region particularly impacted by the Great Depression. The _____ was envisioned not only as an electricity provider, but also as a regional economic development agency that would use federal experts and electricity to rapidly modernize the region's economy and society.

The _____'s jurisdiction covers most of Tennessee, parts of Alabama, Mississippi, and Kentucky, and small slices of Georgia, North Carolina, and Virginia.

a. 1921 recession
b. 130-30 fund
c. 100-year flood
d. Tennessee Valley Authority

40. _____ is a fee paid on borrowed assets. It is the price paid for the use of borrowed money, or, money earned by deposited funds. Assets that are sometimes lent with _____ include money, shares, consumer goods through hire purchase, major assets such as aircraft, and even entire factories in finance lease arrangements.
a. Asset protection
b. Insolvency
c. Interest
d. Internal debt

41. A _____ is the transfer of wealth from one party (such as a person or company) to another. A _____ is usually made in exchange for the provision of goods, services or both, or to fulfill a legal obligation.

The simplest and oldest form of _____ is barter, the exchange of one good or service for another.

a. Social gravity
b. Soft count
c. Going concern
d. Payment

42. In economics, _____ is a measure of the relative satisfaction from consumption of various goods and services. Given this measure, one may speak meaningfully of increasing or decreasing _____, and thereby explain economic behavior in terms of attempts to increase one's _____. For illustrative purposes, changes in _____ are sometimes expressed in units called utils.
a. Expected utility hypothesis
b. Utility function
c. Utility
d. Ordinal utility

43. A _____ is a counterfeit agreement among industries. It is an informal organization of producers that agree to coordinate prices and production. _____s usually occur in an oligopolistic industry, where there is a small number of sellers and usually involve homogeneous products.

a. 100-year flood
c. Cartel
b. Shanzhai
d. Shill

44. _____ is the transition of a national economy from monopoly control by groups of large businesses to a free market economy. This change rarely arises naturally, and is generally the result of regulation by a governing body.

A modern example of _____ is the economic restructuring of Germany after the fall of the Third Reich in 1945.

a. Market power
c. Complementary monopoly
b. Monopolization
d. Decartelization

45. In 1940, President Franklin Roosevelt split the authority into two agencies, the Civil Aeronautics Administration (CAA) and the _____ The CAA was responsible for air traffic control, safety programs, and airway development. The _____ was entrusted with safety rulemaking, accident investigation, and economic regulation of the airlines.

a. 130-30 fund
c. 100-year flood
b. Civil Aeronautics Board
d. 1921 recession

46. The _____ was a regulatory body in the United States created by the Interstate Commerce Act of 1887, which was signed into law by President Grover Cleveland. The agency was abolished in 1995, and the agency's remaining functions were transferred to the Surface Transportation Board.

The Commission's five members were appointed by the President with the consent of the United States Senate.

a. ACEA agreement
c. Office of Thrift Supervision
b. Interstate Commerce Commission
d. ACCRA Cost of Living Index

47. _____ is a component of the firm's opportunity costs. The time that the owner spends running the firm could be spent on running another firm. This is _____: the return the entrepreneur can expect to earn or the profit that the business owners considers necessary to make running the business worth his/her while.

a. Profit margin
c. Normal profit
b. Profit maximization
d. 100-year flood

48. _____ is the difference between efficient behavior of firms assumed or implied by economic theory and their observed behavior in practice.

Economic theory assumes that the management of firms act to maximize owners' wealth by minimizing risk and maximizing economic profits -- which is accomplished by simultaneously maximizing revenues and minimizing costs, usually through the adjustment of output. In perfect competition, the free entry and exit of firms tends toward firms producing at the point where price equals long run average costs and long run average costs are minimized.

a. 100-year flood
c. X-efficiency
b. Revelation principle
d. X-inefficiency

Chapter 30. Antitrust Policy and Regulation

49. _____ is the structure and set of regulations in place to control activity, usually in large organizations and government. As opposed to adhocracy, it is represented by standardized procedure (rule-following) that dictates the execution of most or all processes within the body, formal division of powers, hierarchy, and relationships. In practice the interpretation and execution of policy can lead to informal influence.
   a. 1921 recession
   b. Bureaucracy
   c. 100-year flood
   d. 130-30 fund

50. _____ is an agreement, usually secretive, which occurs between two or more persons to deceive, mislead or to obtain an objective forbidden by law typically involving fraud or gaining an unfair advantage. It is an agreement among firms to divide the market, set prices kickbacks, or misrepresenting the independence of the relationship between the colluding parties.' All acts effected by _____ are considered void.
   a. Net Book Agreement
   b. Bid rigging
   c. Collusion
   d. Dividing territories

51. _____ is the removal or simplification of government rules and regulations that constrain the operation of market forces. _____ does not mean elimination of laws against fraud, but eliminating or reducing government control of how business is done, thereby moving toward a more free market.

The stated rationale for '_____' is often that fewer and simpler regulations will lead to a raised level of competitiveness, therefore higher productivity, more efficiency and lower prices overall.

   a. Deregulation
   b. Fundamental psychological law
   c. Secular basis
   d. Macroeconomic policy instruments

52. _____ is a broad label that refers to any individuals or households that use goods and services generated within the economy. The concept of a _____ is used in different contexts, so that the usage and significance of the term may vary.

Typically when business people and economists talk of _____s they are talking about person as _____, an aggregated commodity item with little individuality other than that expressed in the buy/not-buy decision.

   a. 130-30 fund
   b. 100-year flood
   c. 1921 recession
   d. Consumer

53. _____ is the requirement to hold a license issued by a regulatory body or professional organisation, before practising a trade, profession or other occupation. Such requirements are commonly defended as a form of consumer protection against the risk of loss from unqualified or incompetent service providers. Economists including Milton Friedman have criticised _____ as a restriction on competition.
   a. Australian Financial Services Licence
   b. Occupational licensing
   c. Investment goods
   d. Authorised capital

54. An _____ is any great bottleneck (or price rise) in the supply of energy resources to an economy. It usually refers to the shortage of oil and additionally to electricity or other natural resources. An _____ may be referred to as an oil crisis, petroleum crisis, energy shortage, electricity shortage or electricity crisis.

a. Oil depletion
b. Oil reserves in the United States
c. Olduvai theory
d. Energy crisis

55. The _____ of 1990 (ADA) is the short title of United States (Pub.L. 101-336, 104 Stat. 327, enacted July 26, 1990), codified at 42 U.S.C.
   a. Employment discrimination law in the United Kingdom
   b. International commercial law
   c. Expedited Funds Availability Act
   d. Americans with Disabilities Act

56. _____ is a practice of protecting the environment, on individual, organisational or governmental level, for the benefit of the natural environment and (or) humans.

Due to the pressures of population and technology the biophysical environment is being degraded, sometimes permanently. This has been recognised and governments began placing restraints on activities that caused environmental degradation.

   a. AD-IA Model
   b. ACEA agreement
   c. Environmental Protection
   d. ACCRA Cost of Living Index

57. The U.S. _____ is a federal agency whose goal is ending employment discrimination. The _____ investigates discrimination complaints based on an individual's race, color, national origin, religion, sex, age, disability and retaliation for reporting and/or opposing a discriminatory practice. The Commission is also tasked with filing suits on behalf of alleged victim(s) of discrimination against employers and as an adjudicatory for claims of discrimination brought against federal agencies.
   a. ACCRA Cost of Living Index
   b. AD-IA Model
   c. ACEA agreement
   d. Equal Employment Opportunity Commission

58. _____ is a cross-disciplinary area concerned with protecting the safety, health and welfare of people engaged in work or employment. As a secondary effect, it may also protect co-workers, family members, employers, customers, suppliers, nearby communities, and other members of the public who are impacted by the workplace environment. It may involve interactions among many subject areas, including occupational medicine, occupational (or industrial) hygiene, public health, safety engineering, chemistry, health physics, ergonomics, toxicology, epidemiology, environmental health, industrial relations, public policy, sociology, and occupational health psychology.
   a. ACCRA Cost of Living Index
   b. AD-IA Model
   c. Occupational Safety and Health
   d. ACEA agreement

59. The United States _____ is an agency of the United States Department of Labor. It was created by Congress under the Occupational Safety and Health Act, signed by President Richard M. Nixon, on December 29, 1970. Its mission is to prevent work-related injuries, illnesses, and deaths by issuing and enforcing rules (called standards) for workplace safety and health.
   a. ACEA agreement
   b. Occupational Safety and Health Administration
   c. AD-IA Model
   d. ACCRA Cost of Living Index

Chapter 30. Antitrust Policy and Regulation

60. In economics, and cost accounting, _____ describes the total economic cost of production and is made up of variable costs, which vary according to the quantity of a good produced and include inputs such as labor and raw materials, plus fixed costs, which are independent of the quantity of a good produced and include inputs (capital) that cannot be varied in the short term, such as buildings and machinery. _____ in economics includes the total opportunity cost of each factor of production in addition to fixed and variable costs.

The rate at which _____ changes as the amount produced changes is called marginal cost.

a. 100-year flood
c. 130-30 fund
b. 1921 recession
d. Total cost

61. A _____ is expenditure of time or money in conforming with government requirements such as legislation or regulation. For example, people or organizations registered for value added tax have the extra burden of having to keep detailed records of all input tax and output tax to facilitate the completion of VAT returns. This may necessitate them having to employ someone skilled in this field, which would be regarded a _____.

a. Labor mobility
c. Culture of capitalism
b. Neofeudalism
d. Compliance cost

Chapter 31. Agriculture: Economics and Policy

1. _____s is the social science that studies the production, distribution, and consumption of goods and services. The term _____s comes from the Ancient Greek oá¼°κovoµῑα from oá¼¶κoς (oikos, 'house') + vÍŒµoς (nomos, 'custom' or 'law'), hence 'rules of the house(hold)'. Current _____ models developed out of the broader field of political economy in the late 19th century, owing to a desire to use an empirical approach more akin to the physical sciences.
   a. Inflation
   b. Economic
   c. Energy economics
   d. Opportunity cost

2. In economic theory, _____ is the competitive situation in any market where the conditions necessary for perfect competition are not satisfied. It is a market structure that does not meet the conditions of perfect competition.

   Forms of _____ include:

   - Monopoly, in which there is only one seller of a good.
   - Oligopoly, in which there is a small number of sellers.
   - Monopolistic competition, in which there are many sellers producing highly differentiated goods.
   - Monopsony, in which there is only one buyer of a good.
   - Oligopsony, in which there is a small number of buyers.

   There may also be _____ in markets due to buyers or sellers lacking information about prices and the goods being traded.

   There may also be _____ due to a time lag in a market.

   a. AD-IA Model
   b. ACCRA Cost of Living Index
   c. ACEA agreement
   d. Imperfect competition

3. In economics, _____ describes demand that is not very sensitive to a change in price.
   a. Effective unemployment rate
   b. Inelastic
   c. Inflation hedge
   d. Export-led growth

4. In economics, _____ describes the state of a market with respect to competition.

   - Perfect competition, in which the market consists of a very large number of firms producing a homogeneous product.
   - Monopolistic competition where there are a large number of independent firms which have a very small proportion of the market share.
   - Oligopoly, in which a market is dominated by a small number of firms which own more than 40% of the market share.
   - Oligopsony, a market dominated by many sellers and a few buyers.
   - Monopoly, where there is only one provider of a product or service.
   - Natural monopoly, a monopoly in which economies of scale cause efficiency to increase continuously with the size of the firm. A firm is a natural monopoly if it is able to serve the entire market demand at a lower cost than any combination of two or more smaller, more specialized firms.
   - Monopsony, when there is only one buyer in a market.

The imperfectly competitive structure is quite identical to the realistic market conditions where some monopolistic competitors, monopolists, oligopolists, and duopolists exist and dominate the market conditions. The elements of _____ include the number and size distribution of firms, entry conditions, and the extent of differentiation.

These somewhat abstract concerns tend to determine some but not all details of a specific concrete market system where buyers and sellers actually meet and commit to trade.

   a. Market structure
   c. Labour economics
   b. Monopolistic competition
   d. Human capital

5. _____ in economics and business is the result of an exchange and from that trade we assign a numerical monetary value to a good, service or asset. If Alice trades Bob 4 apples for an orange, the _____ of an orange is 4 apples. Inversely, the _____ of an apple is 1/4 oranges.
   a. Premium pricing
   c. Price book
   b. Price war
   d. Price

6. _____ is defined as the measure of responsiveness in the quantity demanded for a commodity as a result of change in price of the same commodity. It is a measure of how consumers react to a change in price. In other words, it is percentage change in quantity demanded as per the percentage change in price of the same commodity.
   a. 100-year flood
   c. Price elasticity of demand
   b. 1921 recession
   d. 130-30 fund

7. In economics, the _____ and cross price elasticity of demand measures the responsiveness of the demand of a good to a change in the price of another good.

It is measured as the percentage change in demand for the first good that occurs in response to a percentage change in price of the second good. For example, if, in response to a 10% increase in the price of fuel, the demand of new cars that are fuel inefficient decreased by 20%, the _____ would be −20%/10% = −2.

   a. Snob effect
   c. Convex preferences
   b. Quality bias
   d. Cross elasticity of demand

8. Economics:

- _____ ,the desire to own something and the ability to pay for it
- _____ curve,a graphic representation of a _____ schedule
- _____ deposit, the money in checking accounts
- _____ pull theory,the theory that inflation occurs when _____ for goods and services exceeds existing supplies
- _____ schedule,a table that lists the quantity of a good a person will buy it each different price
- _____ side economics,the school of economics at believes government spending and tax cuts open economy by raising _____

   a. Demand
   c. Production
   b. McKesson ' Robbins scandal
   d. Variability

9. In economics, _____ is the ratio of the percent change in one variable to the percent change in another variable. It is a tool for measuring the responsiveness of a function to changes in parameters in a relative way. Commonly analyzed are _____ of substitution, price and wealth.
   a. ACEA agreement
   b. Elasticity
   c. Elasticity of demand
   d. ACCRA Cost of Living Index

10. Price _____ is defined as the measure of responsiveness in the quantity demanded for a commodity as a result of change in price of the same commodity. It is a measure of how consumers react to a change in price. In other words, it is percentage change in quantity demanded by the percentage change in price of the same commodity.
    a. ACCRA Cost of Living Index
    b. Elasticity of demand
    c. ACEA agreement
    d. Elasticity

11. In economics, the concept of the _____ refers to the decision-making time frame of a firm in which at least one factor of production is fixed. Costs which are fixed in the _____ have no impact on a firms decisions. For example a firm can raise output by increasing the amount of labour through overtime.
    a. Hicks-neutral technical change
    b. Productivity model
    c. Short-run
    d. Product Pipeline

12. In economics, the _____ can be defined as the graph depicting the relationship between the price of a certain commodity, and the amount of it that consumers are willing and able to purchase at that given price. It is a graphic representation of a demand schedule. The _____ for all consumers together follows from the _____ of every individual consumer: the individual demands at each price are added together.
    a. Kuznets curve
    b. Wage curve
    c. Demand curve
    d. Cost curve

13. In economics, _____ are business expenses that are not dependent on the activities of the business They tend to be time-related, such as salaries or rents being paid per month. This is in contrast to variable costs, which are volume-related (and are paid per quantity.)

In management accounting, _____ are defined as expenses that do not change in proportion to the activity of a business, within the relevant period or scale of production.

    a. Cost of poor quality
    b. Fixed costs
    c. Cost-Volume-Profit Analysis
    d. Quality costs

14. In economics, the _____ of demand measures the responsiveness of the demand of a good to the change in the income of the people demanding the good. It is calculated as the ratio of the percent change in demand to the percent change in income. For example, if, in response to a 10% increase in income, the demand of a good increased by 20%, the _____ of demand would be 20%/10% = 2.
    a. ACCRA Cost of Living Index
    b. Income elasticity
    c. AD-IA Model
    d. ACEA agreement

15. In economics, the _____ measures the responsiveness of the demand of a good to the change in the income of the people demanding the good. It is calculated as the ratio of the percent change in demand to the percent change in income. For example, if, in response to a 10% increase in income, the demand of a good increased by 20%, the _____ would be 20%/10% = 2.

a. Elasticity of substitution
b. Expenditure minimization problem
c. Indifference map
d. Income elasticity of demand

16. _____s are expenses that change in proportion to the activity of a business. In other words, _____ is the sum of marginal costs. It can also be considered normal costs.
   a. Cost allocation
   b. Quality costs
   c. Cost-Volume-Profit Analysis
   d. Variable cost

17. In economics, an _____ is any good or commodity, transported from one country to another country in a legitimate fashion, typically for use in trade. _____ goods or services are provided to foreign consumers by domestic producers. _____ is an important part of international trade.
   a. ACEA agreement
   b. ACCRA Cost of Living Index
   c. AD-IA Model
   d. Export

18. A _____ product is a product designed for cheapness and short-term convenience rather than medium to long-term durability, with most products only intended for single use. The term is also sometimes used for products that may last several months (ex. _____ air filters) to distinguish from similar products that last indefinitely (ex.
   a. 1921 recession
   b. 130-30 fund
   c. Disposable
   d. 100-year flood

19. _____ is gross income minus income tax on that income.

Discretionary income is income after subtracting taxes and normal expenses (such as rent or mortgage, utilities, insurance, medical, transportation, property maintenance, child support, inflation, food and sundries, 'c.) to maintain a certain standard of living.

   a. Stamp Act
   b. Disposable personal income
   c. Taxation as theft
   d. Disposable income

20. A variety of measures of _____ and output are used in economics to estimate total economic activity in a country or region, including gross domestic product (GDP), gross national product (GNP), and net _____

There are three main ways of calculating these numbers; the output approach, the income approach and the expenditure approach. In theory, the three must yield the same, because total expenditures on goods and services must equal the total income paid to the producers (Gnational income), and that must also equal the total value of the output of goods and services (GNP.)

   a. Volume index
   b. Gross world product
   c. GNI per capita
   d. National income

21. _____ is the identification, assessment, and prioritization of risks followed by coordinated and economical application of resources to minimize, monitor, and control the probability and/or impact of unfortunate events.. Risks can come from uncertainty in financial markets, project failures, legal liabilities, credit risk, accidents, natural causes and disasters as well as deliberate attacks from an adversary. Several _____ standards have been developed including the Project Management Institute, the National Institute of Science ' Technology, actuarial societies, and ISO standards.

Chapter 31. Agriculture: Economics and Policy

a. Kanban
b. Regression toward the mean
c. Penny stock
d. Risk management

22. _____, anti-selection insurance, statistics, and risk management. It refers to a market process in which 'bad' results occur when buyers and sellers have asymmetric information (i.e. access to different information): the 'bad' products or customers are more likely to be selected. A bank that sets one price for all its checking account customers runs the risk of being adversely selected against by its low-balance, high-activity (and hence least profitable) customers.

a. ACEA agreement
b. AD-IA Model
c. ACCRA Cost of Living Index
d. Adverse selection

23. In economics and business, specifically cost accounting, the _____ point (BEP) is the point at which cost or expenses and revenue are equal: there is no net loss or gain, and one has 'broken even'. A profit or a loss has not been made, although opportunity costs have been paid, and capital has received the risk-adjusted, expected return.

For example, if the business sells less than 200 tables each month, it will make a loss, if it sells more, it will be a profit.

a. Break-even
b. Nonmarket
c. Buffer stock scheme
d. Small numbers game

24. _____, in law and economics, is a form of risk management primarily used to hedge against the risk of a contingent loss. _____ is defined as the equitable transfer of the risk of a loss, from one entity to another, in exchange for a premium, and can be thought of as a guaranteed small loss to prevent a large, possibly devastating loss. An insurer is a company selling the _____; an insured or policyholder is the person or entity buying the _____.

a. ACEA agreement
b. AD-IA Model
c. ACCRA Cost of Living Index
d. Insurance

25. In economic models, the _____ time frame assumes no fixed factors of production. Firms can enter or leave the marketplace, and the cost (and availability) of land, labor, raw materials, and capital goods can be assumed to vary. In contrast, in the short-run time frame, certain factors are assumed to be fixed, because there is not sufficient time for them to change.

a. Productivity world
b. Diseconomies of scale
c. Long-run
d. Price/performance ratio

26. In statistics and image processing, to smooth a data set is to create an approximating function that attempts to capture important patterns in the data, while leaving out noise or other fine-scale structures/rapid phenomena. Many different algorithms are used in _____. One of the most common algorithms is the 'moving average', often used to try to capture important trends in repeated statistical surveys.

a. X-bar chart
b. Partial regression plot
c. Partial residual plot
d. Smoothing

27. _____, as defined by the _____ Association of America (Information technologyAA), is 'the study, design, development, implementation, support or management of computer-based information systems, particularly software applications and computer hardware.' _____ deals with the use of electronic computers and computer software to convert, store, protect, process, transmit, and securely retrieve information.

Today, the term _____ has ballooned to encompass many aspects of computing and technology, and the term has become very recognizable. The _____ umbrella can be quite large, covering many fields.

a. ACCRA Cost of Living Index
b. Information technology
c. AD-IA Model
d. ACEA agreement

28. _____ is the change in population over time, and can be quantified as the change in the number of individuals in a population using 'per unit time' for measurement. The term _____ can technically refer to any species, but almost always refers to humans, and it is often used informally for the more specific demographic term _____ rate , and is often used to refer specifically to the growth of the population of the world.

Simple models of _____ include the Malthusian Growth Model and the logistic model.

a. Population dynamics
b. 130-30 fund
c. Population growth
d. 100-year flood

29. The _____ is 'the basic residential unit in which economic production, consumption, inheritance, child rearing, and shelter are organized and carried out'; [the _____] 'may or may not be synonymous with family'.

The _____ is the basic unit of analysis in many social, microeconomic and government models. The term refers to all individuals who live in the same dwelling.

a. 100-year flood
b. Family economics
c. 130-30 fund
d. Household

30. In economics, the people in the _____ are the suppliers of labor. The _____ is all the nonmilitary people who are employed or unemployed. In 2005, the worldwide _____ was over 3 billion people.
a. Grenelle agreements
b. Departmentalization
c. Distributed workforce
d. Labor force

31. In a _____ there is both a monopoly (a single seller) and monopsony (a single buyer) in the same market.

In such market price and output will be determined by the non economic forces like bargaining power of both buyer and seller. A _____ model is often used in situations where the switching costs of both sides are prohibitively high.

a. Price takers
b. Bilateral monopoly
c. Market concentration
d. Revenue-cap regulation

32. _____, or a _____ is the concept of a resulting effect (cf. cause and effect, arising from another action. In general terms, it is used to indicate that all human actions, particularly crime and sin, have profound effects.
a. Variability
b. Consequence
c. Solved
d. Rule

33. In economics, the _____ market is a hypothetical market that brings savers and borrowers together, also bringing together the money available in commercial banks and lending institutions available for firms and households to finance expenditures, either investments or consumption. Savers supply the _____; for instance, buying bonds will transfer their money to the institution issuing the bond, which can be a firm or government. In return, borrowers demand _____; when an institution sells a bond, it is demanding _____.
   a. Buffer stock scheme
   b. Spatial inequality
   c. Loanable funds
   d. Reservation wage

34. In economics, a _____ exists when a specific individual or enterprise has sufficient control over a particular product or service to determine significantly the terms on which other individuals shall have access to it. Monopolies are thus characterized by a lack of economic competition for the good or service that they provide and a lack of viable substitute goods. The verb 'monopolize' refers to the process by which a firm gains persistently greater market share than what is expected under perfect competition.
   a. 130-30 fund
   b. 100-year flood
   c. 1921 recession
   d. Monopoly

35. _____ and Keynesian Theory) is a macroeconomic theory based on the ideas of 20th-century British economist John Maynard Keynes. _____ argues that private sector decisions sometimes lead to inefficient macroeconomic outcomes and therefore advocates active policy responses by the public sector, including monetary policy actions by the central bank and fiscal policy actions by the government to stabilize output over the business cycle.

The theories forming the basis of _____ were first presented in The General Theory of Employment, Interest and Money, published in 1936.

   a. Keynesian economics
   b. Deflation
   c. Market failure
   d. Rational choice theory

36. _____ is a type of inflation caused by substantial increases in the cost of important goods or services where no suitable alternative is available. A situation that has been often cited of this was the oil crisis of the 1970s, which some economists see as a major cause of the inflation experienced in the Western world in that decade. It is argued that this inflation resulted from increases in the cost of petroleum imposed by the member states of OPEC.
   a. Chronic inflation
   b. Headline inflation
   c. Mundell-Tobin effect
   d. Cost-push inflation

37. In economics, _____ is a rise in the general level of prices of goods and services in an economy over a period of time. When the general price level rises, each unit of currency buys fewer goods and services; consequently, _____ is also a decline in the real value of money--a loss of purchasing power in the medium of exchange which is also the monetary unit of account in the economy. A chief measure of general price-level _____ is the general _____ rate, which is the percentage change in a general price index (normally the Consumer Price Index) over time.
   a. Economic
   b. Opportunity cost
   c. Inflation
   d. Energy economics

38. _____ is a broad label that refers to any individuals or households that use goods and services generated within the economy. The concept of a _____ is used in different contexts, so that the usage and significance of the term may vary.

Chapter 31. Agriculture: Economics and Policy

Typically when business people and economists talk of _____s they are talking about person as _____, an aggregated commodity item with little individuality other than that expressed in the buy/not-buy decision.

a. 100-year flood
b. 130-30 fund
c. 1921 recession
d. Consumer

39. In economics, a _____ may be either a subsidy or a price control, both with the intended effect of keeping the market price of a good higher than the competitive equilibrium level.

In the case of a price control, a _____ is the minimum legal price a seller may charge, typically placed above equilibrium. It is the support of certain price levels at or above market values by the government.

a. Payment schedule
b. Price support
c. Labor intensity
d. Marginal profit

40. To _____ is to impose a financial charge or other levy upon a taxpayer by a state or the functional equivalent of a state.

_____es are also imposed by many subnational entities. _____es consist of direct _____ or indirect _____, and may be paid in money or as its labour equivalent (often but not always unpaid.)

a. Tax
b. 1921 recession
c. 100-year flood
d. 130-30 fund

41. In economics, tax incidence is the analysis of the effect of a particular tax on the distribution of economic welfare. Tax incidence is said to 'fall' upon the group that, at the end of the day, bears the burden of the tax. The key concept is that the tax incidence or _____ does not depend on where the revenue is collected, but on the price elasticity of demand and price elasticity of supply.

a. 1921 recession
b. 130-30 fund
c. 100-year flood
d. Tax burden

42. In microeconomics, _____ is quite simply the conversion of inputs into outputs. It is an economic process that uses resources to create a good or service that is suitable for exchange. This can include manufacturing, storing, shipping, and packaging.

a. MET
b. Red Guards
c. Solved
d. Production

43. A _____ is an expression that compares quantities relative to each other. The most common examples involve two quantities, but any number of quantities can be compared. _____s are represented mathematically by separating each quantity with a colon, for example the _____ 2:3, which is read as the _____ 'two to three'.

a. Y-intercept
b. 130-30 fund
c. Ratio
d. 100-year flood

44. A _____ is:

- Rewrite _____, in generative grammar and computer science
- Standardization, a formal and widely-accepted statement, fact, definition, or qualification
- Operation, a determinate _____ for performing a mathematical operation and obtaining a certain result (Mathematics, Logic)
    - Unary operation
    - Binary operation
- _____ of inference, a function from sets of formulae to formulae (Mathematics, Logic)
- _____ of thumb, principle with broad application that is not intended to be strictly accurate or reliable for every situation. Also often simply referred to as a _____
- Moral, an atomic element of a moral code for guiding choices in human behavior
- Heuristic, a quantized '_____' which shows a tendency or probability for successful function
- A regulation, as in sports
- A Production _____, as in computer science
- Procedural law, a _____ set governing the application of laws to cases
    - A law, which may informally be called a '_____'
    - A court ruling, a decision by a court
- In the U.S. Government, a regulation mandated by Congress, but written or expanded upon by the Executive Branch.
- Norm (sociology), an informal but widely accepted _____, concept, truth, definition, or qualification (social norms, legal norms, coding norms)
- Norm (philosophy), a kind of sentence or a reason to act, feel or believe
- 'Rulership' is the concept of governance by a government:
    - Military _____, governance by a military body
    - Monastic _____, a collection of precepts that guides the life of monks or nuns in a religious order where the superior holds the place of Christ
- Slide _____

- '_____,' a song by Ayumi Hamasaki
- '_____,' a song by rapper Nas
- '_____s,' an album by the band The Whitest Boy Alive
- _____s: Pyaar Ka Superhit Formula, a 2003 Bollywood film
- ruler, an instrument for measuring lengths
- _____, a component of an astrolabe, circumferator or similar instrument
- The _____s, a bestselling self-help book
- _____ Project (Run Up-to-date Linux Everywhere), a project that aims to use up-to-date Linux software on old PCs
- _____ engine, a software system that helps managing business _____s
- Ja _____, a hip hop artist
    - R.U.L.E., a 2005 greatest hits album by rapper Ja _____
- '_____s,' a KMFDM song

a. Procter ' Gamble
c. Demand
b. Technocracy
d. Rule

Chapter 31. Agriculture: Economics and Policy

45. In economics, and cost accounting, _____ describes the total economic cost of production and is made up of variable costs, which vary according to the quantity of a good produced and include inputs such as labor and raw materials, plus fixed costs, which are independent of the quantity of a good produced and include inputs (capital) that cannot be varied in the short term, such as buildings and machinery. _____ in economics includes the total opportunity cost of each factor of production in addition to fixed and variable costs.

The rate at which _____ changes as the amount produced changes is called marginal cost.

- a. 130-30 fund
- b. 100-year flood
- c. 1921 recession
- d. Total cost

46. _____ is a term in economics, where demand for one good or service occurs as a result of demand for another. This may occur as the former is a part of production of the second. For example, demand for coal leads to _____ for mining, as coal must be mined for coal to be consumed.

- a. Days Sales Outstanding
- b. Derived demand
- c. Rate risk
- d. Leontief production function

47. _____ is the economic policy of restraining trade between states, through methods such as tariffs on imported goods, restrictive quotas, and a variety of other restrictive government regulations designed to discourage imports, and prevent foreign take-over of local markets and companies. This policy is closely aligned with anti-globalization, and contrasts with free trade, where government barriers to trade are kept to a minimum. The term is mostly used in the context of economics, where _____ refers to policies or doctrines which 'protect' businesses and workers within a country by restricting or regulating trade with foreign nations.

- a. Digital economy
- b. Google economy
- c. Knowledge economy
- d. Protectionism

48. A _____ is a general term that describes any government policy or regulation that restricts international trade. The barriers can take many forms, including the following terms that include many restrictions in international trade within multiple countries that import and export any items of trade.

- Import duty
- Import licenses
- Export licenses
- Import quotas
- Tariffs
- Subsidies
- Non-tariff barriers to trade
- Voluntary Export Restraints
- Local Content Requirements
- Embargo

Most _____s work on the same principle: the imposition of some sort of cost on trade that raises the price of the traded products. If two or more nations repeatedly use _____s against each other, then a trade war results.

a. Global financial system
b. Certificate of origin
c. Trade barrier
d. National Foreign Trade Council

49. _____ is the trading of favors or quid pro quo, such as vote trading by legislative members to obtain passage of actions of interest to each legislative member. It is also the 'cross quoting' of papers by academics in order to drive up reference counts. The Nuttall Encyclopedia describes log-rolling as 'mutual praise by authors of each other's work.' American frontiersman Davy Crockett was one of the first to apply the term to legislation:

The first known use of the term was by Congressman Davy Crockett, who said on the floor (of the U.S. House of Representatives) in 1835, 'my people don't like me to log-roll in their business, and vote away pre-emption rights to fellows in other states that never kindle a fire on their own land.'

The widest accepted origin is the old custom of neighbors assisting each other with the moving of logs.

a. 130-30 fund
b. 100-year flood
c. 1921 recession
d. Logrolling

50. _____ in economic theory is the use of modern economic tools to study problems that are traditionally in the province of political science.

In particular, it studies the behavior of politicians and government officials as mostly self-interested agents and their interactions in the social system either as such or under alternative constitutional rules. These can be represented a number of ways, including standard constrained utility maximization, game theory, or decision theory.

a. Paradox of voting
b. Rational ignorance
c. Public choice
d. Public interest theory

51. _____ is a fee paid on borrowed assets. It is the price paid for the use of borrowed money , or, money earned by deposited funds . Assets that are sometimes lent with _____ include money, shares, consumer goods through hire purchase, major assets such as aircraft, and even entire factories in finance lease arrangements.

a. Asset protection
b. Internal debt
c. Insolvency
d. Interest

52. _____ is the a method of technical and economic research of the systems for purpose to optimize a parity between system's consumer functions or properties and expenses to achieve those functions or properties.

This methodology for continuous perfection of production, industrial technologies, organizational structures was developed by Juryj Sobolev in 1948 at the 'Perm telephone factory'

- 1948 Juryj Sobolev - the first success in application of a method analysis at the 'Perm telephone factory' .
- 1949 - the first application for the invention as result of use of the new method.

Chapter 31. Agriculture: Economics and Policy 441

Today in economically developed countries practically each enterprise or the company use methodology of the kind of functional-cost analysis as a practice of the quality management, most full satisfying to principles of standards of series ISO 9000.

- Interest of consumer not in products itself, but the advantage which it will receive from its usage.
- The consumer aspires to reduce his expenses
- Functions needed by consumer can be executed in the various ways, and, hence, with various efficiency and expenses. Among possible alternatives of realization of functions exist such in which the parity of quality and the price is the optimal for the consumer.

The goal of _____ is achievement of the highest consumer satisfaction of production at simultaneous decrease in all kinds of industrial expenses Classical _____ has three English synonyms - Value Engineering, Value Management, Value Analysis.

a. Monopoly wage
c. Staple financing
b. Willingness to pay
d. Function cost analysis

53. The _____ is an economic and political union of 27 member states, located primarily in Europe. It was established by the Treaty of Maastricht on 1 November 1993, upon the foundations of the pre-existing European Economic Community. With a population of almost 500 million, the _____ generates an estimated 30% share (US$18.4 trillion in 2008) of the nominal gross world product.

a. ACEA agreement
c. European Union
b. ACCRA Cost of Living Index
d. European Court of Justice

54. In economics, _____ refers to the ability of a party to produce a good or service using fewer real resources than another entity producing the same good or service..A party has an _____ when using the same input as another party, it can produce a greater output. Since _____ is determined by a simple comparison of labor productivities, it is possible for a a party to have no _____ in anything. It can be contrasted with the concept of comparative advantage which refers to the ability to produce a particular good at a lower opportunity cost.

a. ACCRA Cost of Living Index
c. Index number
b. International economics
d. Absolute advantage

55. _____ is a term used in economics to describe how an economic quantity is related to economic fluctuations. It is the opposite of procyclical. However, it has more than one meaning.

a. Mathematical economics
c. Law of comparative advantage
b. Price revolution
d. Countercyclical

56. A _____ is the transfer of wealth from one party (such as a person or company) to another. A _____ is usually made in exchange for the provision of goods, services or both, or to fulfill a legal obligation.

The simplest and oldest form of _____ is barter, the exchange of one good or service for another.

a. Social gravity
c. Soft count
b. Going concern
d. Payment

Chapter 32. Income Inequality and Poverty

1. The _____ is 'the basic residential unit in which economic production, consumption, inheritance, child rearing, and shelter are organized and carried out'; [the _____] 'may or may not be synonomous with family'.

   The _____ is the basic unit of analysis in many social, microeconomic and government models. The term refers to all individuals who live in the same dwelling.

   a. 100-year flood
   c. 130-30 fund
   b. Family economics
   d. Household

2. _____ is the shortage of common things such as food, clothing, shelter and safe drinking water, all of which determine the quality of life. It may also include the lack of access to opportunities such as education and employment which aid the escape from _____ and/or allow one to enjoy the respect of fellow citizens. According to Mollie Orshansky who developed the _____ measurements used by the U.S. government, 'to be poor is to be deprived of those goods and services and pleasures which others around us take for granted.' Ongoing debates over causes, effects and best ways to measure _____, directly influence the design and implementation of _____-reduction programs and are therefore relevant to the fields of public administration and international development.

   a. Liberal welfare reforms
   c. Growth Elasticity of Poverty
   b. Poverty map
   d. Poverty

3. _____ is a common concept in economics, and gives rise to derived concepts such as consumer debt. Generally _____ is defined by opposition to production. But the precise definition can vary because different schools of economists define production quite differently.

   a. Federal Reserve Bank Notes
   c. Foreclosure data providers
   b. Cash or share options
   d. Consumption

4. Economics:

   - _____, the desire to own something and the ability to pay for it
   - _____ curve, a graphic representation of a _____ schedule
   - _____ deposit, the money in checking accounts
   - _____ pull theory, the theory that inflation occurs when _____ for goods and services exceeds existing supplies
   - _____ schedule, a table that lists the quantity of a good a person will buy it each different price
   - _____ side economics, the school of economics at believes government spending and tax cuts open economy by raising _____

   a. Variability
   c. McKesson ' Robbins scandal
   b. Production
   d. Demand

Chapter 32. Income Inequality and Poverty 443

5. In mathematics, an _____ is a statement about the relative size or order of two objects, or about whether they are the same or not

- The notation a < b means that a is less than b.
- The notation a > b means that a is greater than b.
- The notation a ≠ b means that a is not equal to b, but does not say that one is greater than the other or even that they can be compared in size.

In each statement above, a is not equal to b. These relations are known as strict inequalities. The notation a < b may also be read as 'a is strictly less than b'.

a. AD-IA Model
b. ACEA agreement
c. Inequality
d. ACCRA Cost of Living Index

6. In economics, the _____ market is a hypothetical market that brings savers and borrowers together, also bringing together the money available in commercial banks and lending institutions available for firms and households to finance expenditures, either investments or consumption. Savers supply the _____; for instance, buying bonds will transfer their money to the institution issuing the bond, which can be a firm or government. In return, borrowers demand _____; when an institution sells a bond, it is demanding _____.

a. Loanable funds
b. Spatial inequality
c. Reservation wage
d. Buffer stock scheme

7. _____ is the a method of technical and economic research of the systems for purpose to optimize a parity between system's consumer functions or properties and expenses to achieve those functions or properties.

This methodology for continuous perfection of production, industrial technologies, organizational structures was developed by Juryj Sobolev in 1948 at the 'Perm telephone factory'

- 1948 Juryj Sobolev - the first success in application of a method analysis at the 'Perm telephone factory'.
- 1949 - the first application for the invention as result of use of the new method.

Today in economically developed countries practically each enterprise or the company use methodology of the kind of functional-cost analysis as a practice of the quality management, most full satisfying to principles of standards of series ISO 9000.

- Interest of consumer not in products itself, but the advantage which it will receive from its usage.
- The consumer aspires to reduce his expenses
- Functions needed by consumer can be executed in the various ways, and, hence, with various efficiency and expenses. Among possible alternatives of realization of functions exist such in which the parity of quality and the price is the optimal for the consumer.

The goal of _____ is achievement of the highest consumer satisfaction of production at simultaneous decrease in all kinds of industrial expenses Classical _____ has three English synonyms - Value Engineering, Value Management, Value Analysis.

Chapter 32. Income Inequality and Poverty

a. Monopoly wage
c. Willingness to pay
b. Staple financing
d. Function cost analysis

8. In economics, _____ is how a natione;s total economy is distributed among its population. ._____ has always been a central concern of economic theory and economic policy. Classical economists such as Adam Smith, Thomas Malthus and David Ricardo were mainly concerned with factor _____, that is, the distribution of income between the main factors of production, land, labour and capital.
   a. Equipment trust certificate
   c. Eco commerce
   b. Authorised capital
   d. Income distribution

9. In economics, the _____ is a graphical representation of the cumulative distribution function of a probability distribution; it is a graph showing the proportion of the distribution assumed by the bottom y% of the values. It is a curve that illustrates income distribution. It is often used to represent income distribution, where it shows for the bottom x% of households, what percentage y% of the total income they have.
   a. Demand curve
   c. Phillips curve
   b. Kuznets curve
   d. Lorenz curve

10. A _____ is an expression that compares quantities relative to each other. The most common examples involve two quantities, but any number of quantities can be compared. _____s are represented mathematically by separating each quantity with a colon, for example the _____ 2:3, which is read as the _____ 'two to three'.
    a. 100-year flood
    c. 130-30 fund
    b. Y-intercept
    d. Ratio

11. A _____ is the procedure of systematically acquiring and recording information about the members of a given population. It is a regularly occurring and official count of a particular population. The term is used mostly in connection with national 'population and door to door _____es' (to be taken every 10 years according to United Nations recommendations), agriculture, and business _____es.
    a. 130-30 fund
    c. 1921 recession
    b. Census
    d. 100-year flood

12. A _____ is any systematic process enabling many market players to bid and ask: helping bidders and sellers interact and make deals. It is not just the price mechanism but the entire system of regulation, qualification, credentials, reputations and clearing that surrounds that mechanism and makes it operate in a social context.

Because a _____ relies on the assumption that players are constantly involved and unequally enabled, a _____ is distinguished specifically from a voting system where candidates seek the support of voters on a less regular basis.

a. Contestable market
c. Competitive equilibrium
b. Price mechanism
d. Market system

13. Necessary _____s:

If x is a necessary _____ of y, then the presence of y necessarily implies the presence of x. The presence of x, however, does not imply that y will occur.

Chapter 32. Income Inequality and Poverty

Sufficient _____s:

If x is a sufficient _____ of y, then the presence of x necessarily implies the presence of y.

a. Cause
c. Political philosophy
b. Philosophy of economics
d. Materialism

14. In economics, _____ is the transfer of income, wealth or property from some individuals to others.

One premise of _____ is that money should be distributed to benefit the poorer members of society, and that the rich have an obligation to assist the poor, thus creating a more financially egalitarian society. Another argument is that the rich exploit the poor or otherwise gain unfair benefits.

a. 1921 recession
c. 100-year flood
b. Redistribution
d. 130-30 fund

15. To _____ is to impose a financial charge or other levy upon a taxpayer by a state or the functional equivalent of a state.

_____es are also imposed by many subnational entities. _____es consist of direct _____ or indirect _____, and may be paid in money or as its labour equivalent (often but not always unpaid.)

a. 100-year flood
c. 130-30 fund
b. 1921 recession
d. Tax

16. To tax is to impose a financial charge or other levy upon a taxpayer by a state or the functional equivalent of a state.

_____ are also imposed by many subnational entities. _____ consist of direct tax or indirect tax, and may be paid in money or as its labour equivalent (often but not always unpaid.)

a. 1921 recession
c. 130-30 fund
b. Taxes
d. 100-year flood

17. A _____ is a group of people who share or are motivated by at least one common issue or interest, or work together on a specific project(s) to achieve a common objective. _____s are also characterised by attempts to share and exercise political and social power and to make decisions on a consensus-driven and egalitarian basis. _____s differ from cooperatives in that they are not necessarily focused upon an economic benefit or saving (but can be that as well.)

a. 100-year flood
c. 130-30 fund
b. 1921 recession
d. Collective

18. In organized labor, _____ is the method whereby workers organize together (usually in unions) to meet, converse, and negotiate upon the work conditions with their employers normally resulting in a written contract setting forth the wages, hours, and other conditions to be observed for a stipulated period. It is the practice in which union and company representatives meet to negotiate a new labor contract. In various national labor and employment law contexts, _____ takes on a more specific legal meaning and so, in a broad sense, however, it is the coming together of workers to negotiate their employment.

A collective agreement is a labor contract between an employer and one or more unions.

a. Demarcation dispute
b. Strikebreaker
c. Designated Suppliers Program
d. Collective bargaining

19. A _____ product is a product designed for cheapness and short-term convenience rather than medium to long-term durability, with most products only intended for single use. The term is also sometimes used for products that may last several months (ex. _____ air filters) to distinguish from similar products that last indefinitely (ex.

a. Disposable
b. 100-year flood
c. 1921 recession
d. 130-30 fund

20. _____ is gross income minus income tax on that income.

Discretionary income is income after subtracting taxes and normal expenses (such as rent or mortgage, utilities, insurance, medical, transportation, property maintenance, child support, inflation, food and sundries, 'c.) to maintain a certain standard of living.

a. Disposable personal income
b. Disposable income
c. Taxation as theft
d. Stamp Act

21. A trade union or _____ is an organization of workers who have banded together to achieve common goals in key areas and working conditions. The trade union, through its leadership, bargains with the employer on behalf of union members (rank and file members) and negotiates labor contracts (Collective bargaining) with employers. This may include the negotiation of wages, work rules, complaint procedures, rules governing hiring, firing and promotion of workers, benefits, workplace safety and policies.

a. Business valuation standards
b. Demand-side technologies
c. Basis of futures
d. Labor union

22. In economics, _____ is the ability of a firm to alter the market price of a good or service. A firm with _____ can raise prices without losing all customers to competitors.

When a firm has _____ it faces a downward-sloping demand curve.

a. Pacman conjecture
b. Revenue-cap regulation
c. Price makers
d. Market power

23. A variety of measures of _____ and output are used in economics to estimate total economic activity in a country or region, including gross domestic product (GDP), gross national product (GNP), and net _____.

Chapter 32. Income Inequality and Poverty 447

There are three main ways of calculating these numbers; the output approach, the income approach and the expenditure approach. In theory, the three must yield the same, because total expenditures on goods and services must equal the total income paid to the producers (Gnational income), and that must also equal the total value of the output of goods and services (GNP.)

a. Volume index
b. Gross world product
c. National income
d. GNI per capita

24. _____ is a mechanism that allows people easily to buy and sell products. Services are often included in the scope of the term. _____ regulation is an economic term that describes restrictions in the market.
a. Financialization
b. Market dominance
c. Fixed exchange rate system
d. Product market

25. In economics and business, specifically cost accounting, the _____ point (BEP) is the point at which cost or expenses and revenue are equal: there is no net loss or gain, and one has 'broken even'. A profit or a loss has not been made, although opportunity costs have been paid, and capital has received the risk-adjusted, expected return.

For example, if the business sells less than 200 tables each month, it will make a loss, if it sells more, it will be a profit.

a. Small numbers game
b. Nonmarket
c. Buffer stock scheme
d. Break-even

26. _____ is money accepted for exchange of goods in an economy. The prevalence of one money over another arises, usually, when a government designates through decrees that the government shall accept only particular notes and coins in payment for taxes. Typically, money of _____ consists of stamped coins and minted paper bills.
a. Local currency
b. Currency
c. Security thread
d. Totnes pound

27. In algebra, a _____ is a function depending on n that associates a scalar, det(A), to an n×n square matrix A. The fundamental geometric meaning of a _____ is a scale factor for measure when A is regarded as a linear transformation. _____s are important both in calculus, where they enter the substitution rule for several variables, and in multilinear algebra.

For a fixed nonnegative integer n, there is a unique _____ function for the n×n matrices over any commutative ring R. In particular, this function exists when R is the field of real or complex numbers.

a. 1921 recession
b. 130-30 fund
c. 100-year flood
d. Determinant

28. _____s is the social science that studies the production, distribution, and consumption of goods and services. The term _____s comes from the Ancient Greek oá¼°κονομῖα from oá¼¶κος (oikos, 'house') + vÏŒμος (nomos, 'custom' or 'law'), hence 'rules of the house(hold)'. Current _____ models developed out of the broader field of political economy in the late 19th century, owing to a desire to use an empirical approach more akin to the physical sciences.

a. Economic
b. Opportunity cost
c. Energy economics
d. Inflation

29. _____ is the increase in the amount of the goods and services produced by an economy over time. It is conventionally measured as the percent rate of increase in real gross domestic product, or real GDP. Growth is usually calculated in real terms, i.e. inflation-adjusted terms, in order to net out the effect of inflation on the price of the goods and services produced.
   a. ACCRA Cost of Living Index
   b. ACEA agreement
   c. AD-IA Model
   d. Economic growth

30. In finance, _____ is a financial action that does not promise safety of the initial investment along with the return on the principal sum. _____ typically involves the lending of money or the purchase of assets, equity or debt but in a manner that has not been given thorough analysis or is deemed to have low margin of safety or a significant risk of the loss of the principal investment. The term, '_____,' which is formally defined as above in Graham and Dodd's 1934 text, Security Analysis, contrasts with the term 'investment,' which is a financial operation that, upon thorough analysis, promises safety of principal and a satisfactory return.
   a. Hybrid market
   b. Global Financial Centres Index
   c. Municipal Bond Arbitrage
   d. Speculation

31. A _____ or labor union is an organization of workers who have banded together to achieve common goals in key areas and working conditions. The _____, through its leadership, bargains with the employer on behalf of union members (rank and file members) and negotiates labor contracts (Collective bargaining) with employers. This may include the negotiation of wages, work rules, complaint procedures, rules governing hiring, firing and promotion of workers, benefits, workplace safety and policies.
   a. Guaranteed investment contracts
   b. Case-Shiller Home Price Indices
   c. Trade union
   d. Consumer goods

32. A _____ is any worker who has some special skill, knowledge, or (usually acquired) ability in his work. A _____ may have attended a college, university or technical school. Or, a _____ may have learned his skills on the job.
   a. Time and attendance
   b. Skilled worker
   c. Global Career Development Facilitator
   d. Timebar scheduling

33. In a _____ there is both a monopoly (a single seller) and monopsony (a single buyer) in the same market.

In such market price and output will be determined by the non economic forces like bargaining power of both buyer and seller. A _____ model is often used in situations where the switching costs of both sides are prohibitively high.

   a. Market concentration
   b. Bilateral monopoly
   c. Revenue-cap regulation
   d. Price takers

34. In economics, a _____ exists when a specific individual or enterprise has sufficient control over a particular product or service to determine significantly the terms on which other individuals shall have access to it. Monopolies are thus characterized by a lack of economic competition for the good or service that they provide and a lack of viable substitute goods. The verb 'monopolize' refers to the process by which a firm gains persistently greater market share than what is expected under perfect competition.

   a. 100-year flood   b. 1921 recession
   c. 130-30 fund   d. Monopoly

450 Chapter 32. Income Inequality and Poverty

35. A _____ is:

- Rewrite _____, in generative grammar and computer science
- Standardization, a formal and widely-accepted statement, fact, definition, or qualification
- Operation, a determinate _____ for performing a mathematical operation and obtaining a certain result (Mathematics, Logic)
    - Unary operation
    - Binary operation
- _____ of inference, a function from sets of formulae to formulae (Mathematics, Logic)
- _____ of thumb, principle with broad application that is not intended to be strictly accurate or reliable for every situation. Also often simply referred to as a _____
- Moral, an atomic element of a moral code for guiding choices in human behavior
- Heuristic, a quantized '_____' which shows a tendency or probability for successful function
- A regulation, as in sports
- A Production _____, as in computer science
- Procedural law, a _____ set governing the application of laws to cases
    - A law, which may informally be called a '_____'
    - A court ruling, a decision by a court
- In the U.S. Government, a regulation mandated by Congress, but written or expanded upon by the Executive Branch.
- Norm (sociology), an informal but widely accepted _____, concept, truth, definition, or qualification (social norms, legal norms, coding norms)
- Norm (philosophy), a kind of sentence or a reason to act, feel or believe
- 'Rulership' is the concept of governance by a government:
    - Military _____, governance by a military body
    - Monastic _____, a collection of precepts that guides the life of monks or nuns in a religious order where the superior holds the place of Christ
- Slide _____

- '_____,' a song by Ayumi Hamasaki
- '_____,' a song by rapper Nas
- '_____s,' an album by the band The Whitest Boy Alive
- _____s: Pyaar Ka Superhit Formula, a 2003 Bollywood film
- ruler, an instrument for measuring lengths
- _____, a component of an astrolabe, circumferator or similar instrument
- The _____s, a bestselling self-help book
- _____ Project (Run Up-to-date Linux Everywhere), a project that aims to use up-to-date Linux software on old PCs
- _____ engine, a software system that helps managing business _____s
- Ja _____, a hip hop artist
    - R.U.L.E., a 2005 greatest hits album by rapper Ja _____
- '_____s,' a KMFDM song

a. Rule
c. Demand
b. Technocracy
d. Procter ' Gamble

Chapter 32. Income Inequality and Poverty

36. _____ data refers to selected population characteristics as used in government, marketing or opinion research, or the _____ profiles used in such research. Note the distinction from the term 'demography' Commonly-used _____s include race, age, income, disabilities, mobility (in terms of travel time to work or number of vehicles available), educational attainment, home ownership, employment status, and even location.
   a. NEET
   b. Generation Z
   c. Demographic warfare
   d. Demographic

37. In economics, the people in the _____ are the suppliers of labor. The _____ is all the nonmilitary people who are employed or unemployed. In 2005, the worldwide _____ was over 3 billion people.
   a. Grenelle agreements
   b. Distributed workforce
   c. Departmentalization
   d. Labor force

38. In finance, the _____s between two currencies specifies how much one currency is worth in terms of the other. It is the value of a foreign natione;s currency in terms of the home natione;s currency. For example an _____ of 102 Japanese yen to the United States dollar means that JPY 102 is worth the same as USD 1.
   a. ACCRA Cost of Living Index
   b. Exchange rate
   c. ACEA agreement
   d. Interbank market

39. A _____, sometimes called a pegged exchange rate, is a type of exchange rate regime wherein a currency's value is matched to the value of another single currency or to a basket of other currencies such as gold.

    A _____ is usually used to stabilize the value of a currency, vis-a-vis the currency it is pegged to. This facilitates trade and investments between the two countries, and is especially useful for small economies where external trade forms a large part of their GDP.

   a. Law of supply
   b. Leading indicators
   c. Monetary economics
   d. Fixed exchange rate

40. In macroeconomics, _____ is a condition of the national economy, where all or nearly all persons willing and able to work at the prevailing wages and working conditions are able to do so. It is defined either as 0% unemployment, literally, no unemployment (the rate of unemployment is the fraction of the work force unable to find work), as by James Tobin, or as the level of employment rates when there is no cyclical unemployment. It is defined by the majority of mainstream economists as being an acceptable level of natural unemployment above 0%, the discrepancy from 0% being due to non-cyclical types of unemployment.
   a. Harrod-Johnson diagram
   b. Marginal propensity to consume
   c. Demand shock
   d. Full employment

41. _____ to the arrival of new individuals into a habitat or population. It is a biological concept and is important in population ecology, differentiated from emigration and migration.

    _____ is a modern phenomenon.

   a. AD-IA Model
   b. ACCRA Cost of Living Index
   c. ACEA agreement
   d. Immigration

42. _____ is exchange of capital, goods, and services across international borders or territories. In most countries, it represents a significant share of gross domestic product (GDP.) While _____ has been present throughout much of history, its economic, social, and political importance has been on the rise in recent centuries.
    a. Incoterms
    b. Intra-industry trade
    c. Import license
    d. International trade

43. In economics, _____ is a measure of the relative satisfaction from consumption of various goods and services. Given this measure, one may speak meaningfully of increasing or decreasing _____, and thereby explain economic behavior in terms of attempts to increase one's _____. For illustrative purposes, changes in _____ are sometimes expressed in units called utils.
    a. Utility function
    b. Ordinal utility
    c. Expected utility hypothesis
    d. Utility

44. The _____ or gross domestic income (GDI), a basic measure of an economy's economic performance, is the market value of all final goods and services produced within the borders of a nation in a year. _____ can be defined in three ways, all of which are conceptually identical. First, it is equal to the total expenditures for all final goods and services produced within the country in a stipulated period of time (usually a 365-day year.)
    a. Countercyclical
    b. Monopolistic competition
    c. Market structure
    d. Gross domestic product

45. The _____ or the output gap is the difference between potential GDP and actual GDP or actual output. The calculation for the output gap is Y-Y* where Y* is potential output and Y is actual output. If this calculation yields a positive number it is called an expansionary gap and indicates an economy in expansion; if the calculation yields a negative number it is called a recessionary gap and indicates an economy in recession.
    a. GDP gap
    b. 100-year flood
    c. 1921 recession
    d. 130-30 fund

46. In economics and sociology, an _____ is any factor (financial or non-financial) that enables or motivates a particular course of action, or counts as a reason for preferring one choice to the alternatives. It is an expectation that encourages people to behave in a certain way. Since human beings are purposeful creatures, the study of _____ structures is central to the study of all economic activity (both in terms of individual decision-making and in terms of co-operation and competition within a larger institutional structure.)
    a. Economic reform
    b. Epstein-Zin preferences
    c. Incentive
    d. Isocost

47. _____ and Keynesian Theory) is a macroeconomic theory based on the ideas of 20th-century British economist John Maynard Keynes. _____ argues that private sector decisions sometimes lead to inefficient macroeconomic outcomes and therefore advocates active policy responses by the public sector, including monetary policy actions by the central bank and fiscal policy actions by the government to stabilize output over the business cycle.

The theories forming the basis of _____ were first presented in The General Theory of Employment, Interest and Money, published in 1936.

    a. Rational choice theory
    b. Deflation
    c. Market failure
    d. Keynesian economics

Chapter 32. Income Inequality and Poverty

48. A _____ is a situation that involves losing one quality or aspect of something in return for gaining another quality or aspect. It implies a decision to be made with full comprehension of both the upside and downside of a particular choice.

In economics the term is expressed as opportunity cost, referring the most preferred alternative given up.

a. Whitemail
b. Nonmarket
c. Friedman-Savage utility function
d. Trade-off

49. The _____ was an evolution of developed countries from an industrial/manufacturing-based wealth producing economy into a service sector asset based economy, brought about by globalization and currency manipulation by governments and their central banks. Some analysts claimed that this change in the economic structure of the United States had created a state of permanent steady growth, low unemployment, and immunity to boom and bust macroeconomic cycles. They believed that the change rendered obsolete many business practices.

a. New Economy
b. 130-30 fund
c. 100-year flood
d. 1921 recession

50. The _____ is the minimum level of income deemed necessary to achieve an adequate standard of living in a given country. In practice, like the definition of poverty, the official or common understanding of the poverty line is significantly higher in developed countries than in developing countries.

The common international poverty line has been roughly $1 a day, or more precisely $1.08 at 1993 purchasing-power parity (PPP.)

a. Poverty threshold
b. Poverty reduction
c. Poverty
d. Poverty map

51. In economics, _____ is a measure of national income. Basically, it is an approach to measure GDP. It is defined as the value of planned goods and services produced in an economy.

a. Aggregate supply
b. Aggregate demand
c. Aggregation problem
d. Aggregate expenditure

52. _____ has several particular meanings:

- in mathematics
    - _____ function
    - Euler _____
    - _____
    - _____ subgroup
    - method of _____s (partial differential equations)
- in physics and engineering
    - any _____ curve that shows the relationship between certain input- and output parameters, e.g.
    - an I-V or current-voltage _____ is the current in a circuit as a function of the applied voltage
    - Receiver-Operator _____
- in fiction
    - in Dungeons ' Dragons, _____ is another name for ability score

a. Russian financial crisis   b. Demand
c. Characteristic   d. Technocracy

53. The term '_____' refers to the concept of collecting information and attempting to spot a pattern in the information. In some fields of study, the term '_____' has more formally-defined meanings.

In project management _____ is a mathematical technique that uses historical results to predict future outcome.

a. Probit model   b. Trend analysis
c. Quantile regression   d. Coefficient of determination

54. _____ or government expenditure is classified by economists into three main types. Government purchases of goods and services for current use are classed as government consumption. Government purchases of goods and services intended to create future benefits, such as infrastructure investment or research spending, are classed as government investment.

a. 1921 recession   b. 100-year flood
c. Government spending   d. 130-30 fund

55. _____, in law and economics, is a form of risk management primarily used to hedge against the risk of a contingent loss. _____ is defined as the equitable transfer of the risk of a loss, from one entity to another, in exchange for a premium, and can be thought of as a guaranteed small loss to prevent a large, possibly devastating loss. An insurer is a company selling the _____; an insured or policyholder is the person or entity buying the _____.

a. Insurance   b. ACCRA Cost of Living Index
c. ACEA agreement   d. AD-IA Model

Chapter 32. Income Inequality and Poverty

56. _____ is a voluntary transfer of resources from one country to another, given at least partly with the objective of benefiting the recipient country. It may have other functions as well: it may be given as a signal of diplomatic approval, or to strengthen a military ally, to reward a government for behaviour desired by the donor, to extend the donor's cultural influence, to provide infrastructure needed by the donor for resource extraction from the recipient country, or to gain other kinds of commercial access. Humanitarianism and altruism are, nevertheless, significant motivations for the giving of _____.

a. ACEA agreement
c. ACCRA Cost of Living Index
b. AD-IA Model
d. Aid

57. _____ was a federal assistance program in effect from 1935 to 1997, which was administered by the United States Department of Health and Human Services. This program provided financial assistance to children whose families had low or no income.

The program was created under the name Aid to Dependent Children (ADC) by the Social Security Act of 1935 as part of the New Deal; the words 'families with' were added to the name in 1960, partly due to concern that the program's rules discouraged marriage.

a. ACEA agreement
c. Aid to Families with Dependent Children
b. AD-IA Model
d. ACCRA Cost of Living Index

58. In statistics, _____ has two related meanings:

- the arithmetic _____
- the expected value of a random variable, which is also called the population _____.

It is sometimes stated that the '_____' _____s average. This is incorrect if '_____' is taken in the specific sense of 'arithmetic _____' as there are different types of averages: the _____, median, and mode. Other simple statistical analyses use measures of spread, such as range, interquartile range, or standard deviation. For a real-valued random variable X, the _____ is the expectation of X. Note that not every probability distribution has a defined _____ (or variance); see the Cauchy distribution for an example.

a. 100-year flood
c. 130-30 fund
b. 1921 recession
d. Mean

59. The term _____ refers to an investigative process undertaken to determine whether or not an individual or family is eligible to qualify for help from the government.

Resentment over a _____ was among the factors giving rise to the National Unemployed Workers' Movement in the United Kingdom. Pension Credit payments by the government are means-tested, meaning that the entitlement to it is affected by the amount of income and savings.

a. Coase theorem
c. Means test
b. Compulsory arbitration
d. Lawrence textile strike

60. In a company, _____ is the sum of all financial records of salaries, wages, bonuses and deductions.

A paycheck, is traditionally a paper document issued by an employer to pay an employee for services rendered. While most commonly used in the United States, recently the physical paycheck has been increasingly replaced by electronic direct deposit to bank accounts.

a. 100-year flood
b. Total Expense Ratio
c. Tax expense
d. Payroll

61. _____ is the United States of America's federal assistance program, formerly known as 'welfare'. It began on July 1, 1997, and succeeded the Aid to Families with Dependent Children program, providing cash assistance to indigent American families with dependent children through the United States Department of Health and Human Services. Prior to 1997, the federal government designed the overall program requirements and guidelines, while states administered the program and determined eligibility for benefits.

a. 100-year flood
b. 130-30 fund
c. Temporary Assistance for Needy Families
d. 1921 recession

62. A _____ refers to any type debt instrument, such as a loan, bond, mortgage that does not have a fixed rate of interest over the life of the instrument. Such debt typically uses an index or other base rate for establishing the interest rate for each relevant period. One of the most common rates to use as the basis for applying interest rates is the London Inter-bank Offered Rate, or LIBOR

a. Money market
b. Disposal tax effect
c. Moneylender
d. Floating interest rate

63. A _____ is a place of residence or refuge and comfort. It is usually a place in which an individual or a family can rest and be able to store personal property. Most modern-day households contain sanitary facilities and a means of preparing food.

a. Home
b. 130-30 fund
c. 100 year flood
d. 1921 recession

64. The term _____ describes two different concepts:

- The first is a recognition of partial payment already made towards taxes due.
- The second is a state benefit paid to workers through the tax system, which has the effect of increasing (rather than reducing) net income.

Within the Australian, Canadian, United Kingdom, and United States tax systems, a _____ is a recognition of partial payment already made towards taxes due. A similar concept exists (fr:Avoir fiscal) in the French tax system. This situation arises, for example, when standard rate tax has been deducted at source , but the tax-payer is subject to further taxation at a higher rate. It also applies in dividend imputation systems.

a. 1921 recession
b. 100-year flood
c. 130-30 fund
d. Tax credit

65. _____ is a broad label that refers to any individuals or households that use goods and services generated within the economy. The concept of a _____ is used in different contexts, so that the usage and significance of the term may vary.

Typically when business people and economists talk of _____s they are talking about person as _____, an aggregated commodity item with little individuality other than that expressed in the buy/not-buy decision.

a. 100-year flood
c. 130-30 fund
b. 1921 recession
d. Consumer

66. In statistics, the _____ problem occurs when one considers a set of statistical inferences simultaneously. Errors in inference, including confidence intervals that fail to include their corresponding population parameters are more likely to occur when one considers the family as a whole. Several statistical techniques have been developed to prevent this from happening, allowing significance levels for single and _____ to be directly compared.
a. Familywise error rate
c. Hypotheses suggested by the data
b. False discovery rate
d. Multiple comparisons

67. In probability theory and statistics, a _____ is described as the number separating the higher half of a sample, a population from the lower half. The _____ of a finite list of numbers can be found by arranging all the observations from lowest value to highest value and picking the middle one. If there is an even number of observations, the _____ is not unique, so one often takes the mean of the two middle values.
a. Fiscal stimulus plans
c. Labour vouchers
b. First player wins
d. Median

68. In business, _____ is the total liabilitiess minus total outside assets of an individual or a company. For a company, this is called shareholders' prefernce and may be referred to as book value. _____ is stated as at a particular year in time.
a. Sinking fund
c. Bond credit rating
b. Post earnings announcement drift
d. Net worth

69. _____ or economic opportunity loss is the value of the next best alternative foregone as the result of making a decision. _____ analysis is an important part of a company's decision-making processes but is not treated as an actual cost in any financial statement. The next best thing that a person can engage in is referred to as the _____ of doing the best thing and ignoring the next best thing to be done.
a. Economic
c. Economic ideology
b. Industrial organization
d. Opportunity cost

Chapter 33. The Economics of Health Care

1. The _____ or gross domestic income (GDI), a basic measure of an economy's economic performance, is the market value of all final goods and services produced within the borders of a nation in a year. _____ can be defined in three ways, all of which are conceptually identical. First, it is equal to the total expenditures for all final goods and services produced within the country in a stipulated period of time (usually a 365-day year.)
   a. Countercyclical
   b. Market structure
   c. Monopolistic competition
   d. Gross domestic product

2. The _____ or the output gap is the difference between potential GDP and actual GDP or actual output. The calculation for the output gap is Y-Y* where Y* is potential output and Y is actual output. If this calculation yields a positive number it is called an expansionary gap and indicates an economy in expansion; if the calculation yields a negative number it is called a recessionary gap and indicates an economy in recession.
   a. 1921 recession
   b. GDP gap
   c. 130-30 fund
   d. 100-year flood

3. _____ in economics and business is the result of an exchange and from that trade we assign a numerical monetary value to a good, service or asset. If Alice trades Bob 4 apples for an orange, the _____ of an orange is 4 apples. Inversely, the _____ of an apple is 1/4 oranges.
   a. Price book
   b. Premium pricing
   c. Price war
   d. Price

4. A _____ is a normalized average (typically a weighted average) of prices for a given class of goods or services in a given region, during a given interval of time. It is a statistic designed to help to compare how these prices, taken as a whole, differ between time periods or geographical locations.

   Price indices have several potential uses.

   a. Price index
   b. Transactional Net Margin Method
   c. Product sabotage
   d. Two-part tariff

5. _____ is a common concept in economics, and gives rise to derived concepts such as consumer debt. Generally _____ is defined by opposition to production. But the precise definition can vary because different schools of economists define production quite differently.
   a. Federal Reserve Bank Notes
   b. Foreclosure data providers
   c. Cash or share options
   d. Consumption

6. In an insurance policy, the _____ or excess (UK term) is the portion of any claim that is not covered by the insurance provider. It is the amount of expenses that must be paid out of pocket before an insurer will cover any expenses. It is normally quoted as a fixed quantity and is a part of most policies covering losses to the policy holder.
   a. PVNBP
   b. Double indemnity
   c. Dual trigger insurance
   d. Deductible

7. _____ is the United States of America's federal assistance program, formerly known as 'welfare'. It began on July 1, 1997, and succeeded the Aid to Families with Dependent Children program, providing cash assistance to indigent American families with dependent children through the United States Department of Health and Human Services. Prior to 1997, the federal government designed the overall program requirements and guidelines, while states administered the program and determined eligibility for benefits.

a. 1921 recession
b. Temporary Assistance for Needy Families
c. 100-year flood
d. 130-30 fund

8. In a _____ there is both a monopoly (a single seller) and monopsony (a single buyer) in the same market.

In such market price and output will be determined by the non economic forces like bargaining power of both buyer and seller. A _____ model is often used in situations where the switching costs of both sides are prohibitively high.

a. Revenue-cap regulation
b. Price takers
c. Market concentration
d. Bilateral monopoly

9. _____, in law and economics, is a form of risk management primarily used to hedge against the risk of a contingent loss. _____ is defined as the equitable transfer of the risk of a loss, from one entity to another, in exchange for a premium, and can be thought of as a guaranteed small loss to prevent a large, possibly devastating loss. An insurer is a company selling the _____; an insured or policyholder is the person or entity buying the _____.

a. ACCRA Cost of Living Index
b. AD-IA Model
c. ACEA agreement
d. Insurance

10. In economics, a _____ exists when a specific individual or enterprise has sufficient control over a particular product or service to determine significantly the terms on which other individuals shall have access to it. Monopolies are thus characterized by a lack of economic competition for the good or service that they provide and a lack of viable substitute goods. The verb 'monopolize' refers to the process by which a firm gains persistently greater market share than what is expected under perfect competition.

a. Monopoly
b. 1921 recession
c. 100-year flood
d. 130-30 fund

11. Economics:

- _____, the desire to own something and the ability to pay for it
- _____ curve, a graphic representation of a _____ schedule
- _____ deposit, the money in checking accounts
- _____ pull theory, the theory that inflation occurs when _____ for goods and services exceeds existing supplies
- _____ schedule, a table that lists the quantity of a good a person will buy it each different price
- _____ side economics, the school of economics at believes government spending and tax cuts open economy by raising _____

a. Production
b. Demand
c. McKesson ' Robbins scandal
d. Variability

12. _____ is a voluntary transfer of resources from one country to another, given at least partly with the objective of benefiting the recipient country. It may have other functions as well: it may be given as a signal of diplomatic approval, or to strengthen a military ally, to reward a government for behaviour desired by the donor, to extend the donor's cultural influence, to provide infrastructure needed by the donor for resource extraction from the recipient country, or to gain other kinds of commercial access. Humanitarianism and altruism are, nevertheless, significant motivations for the giving of _____.

   a. AD-IA Model   b. ACEA agreement
   c. AID   d. ACCRA Cost of Living Index

13. _____ describes the relocation by a company of a business process from one country to another -- typically an operational process, such as manufacturing such as accounting. Even state governments employ _____.

The term is in use in several distinct but closely related ways.

   a. Offshore outsourcing   b. ACEA agreement
   c. ACCRA Cost of Living Index   d. Offshoring

14. _____ is subcontracting a process, such as product design or manufacturing, to a third-party company. The decision to outsource is often made in the interest of lowering cost or making better use of time and energy costs, redirecting or conserving energy directed at the competencies of a particular business, or to make more efficient use of land, labor, capital, (information) technology and resources. _____ became part of the business lexicon during the 1980s.

   a. Additional Funds Needed   b. Averch-Johnson effect
   c. Electronic business   d. Outsourcing

15. _____ or financing is to provide capital (funds), which means money for a project, a person, a business or any other private or public institutions.

Those funds can be allocated for either short term or long term purposes. The health fund is a new way of _____ private healthcare centers.

   a. Business transformation   b. Funding
   c. Customer retention   d. No-bid contract

16. _____ is a legally declared inability or impairment of ability of an individual or organization to pay its creditors. Creditors may file a _____ petition against a debtor ('involuntary _____') in an effort to recoup a portion of what they are owed or initiate a restructuring. In the majority of cases, however, _____ is initiated by the debtor (a 'voluntary _____' that is filed by the insolvent individual or organization.)

   a. Bankruptcy in the United Kingdom   b. Petition mill
   c. Liquidation   d. Bankruptcy

17. In law and economics, the _____, describes the economic efficiency of an economic allocation or outcome in the presence of externalities. The theorem states that when trade in an externality is possible and there are no transaction costs, bargaining will lead to an efficient outcome regardless of the initial allocation of property rights. In practice, obstacles to bargaining or poorly defined property rights can prevent Coasian bargaining.

   a. General Mining Act of 1872   b. Prior appropriation water rights
   c. Means test   d. Coase theorem

Chapter 33. The Economics of Health Care

18. _____ is a term that refers both to:

- a formal discipline used to help appraise, or assess, the case for a project or proposal, which itself is a process known as project appraisal; and
- an informal approach to making decisions of any kind.

Under both definitions the process involves, whether explicitly or implicitly, weighing the total expected costs against the total expected benefits of one or more actions in order to choose the best or most profitable option. The formal process is often referred to as either CBA (_____) or BCost-benefit analysis

A hallmark of CBA is that all benefits and all costs are expressed in money terms, and are adjusted for the time value of money, so that all flows of benefits and flows of project costs over time (which tend to occur at different points in time) are expressed on a common basis in terms of their e;present value.e; Closely related, but slightly different, formal techniques include Cost-effectiveness analysis, Economic impact analysis, Fiscal impact analysis and Social Return on Investment(SROI) analysis. The latter builds upon the logic of _____, but differs in that it is explicitly designed to inform the practical decision-making of enterprise managers and investors focused on optimising their social and environmental impacts.

a. 100-year flood
b. Decision theory
c. 130-30 fund
d. Cost-benefit analysis

19. _____ is the shortage of common things such as food, clothing, shelter and safe drinking water, all of which determine the quality of life. It may also include the lack of access to opportunities such as education and employment which aid the escape from _____ and/or allow one to enjoy the respect of fellow citizens. According to Mollie Orshansky who developed the _____ measurements used by the U.S. government, 'to be poor is to be deprived of those goods and services and pleasures which others around us take for granted.' Ongoing debates over causes, effects and best ways to measure _____, directly influence the design and implementation of _____-reduction programs and are therefore relevant to the fields of public administration and international development.

a. Poverty map
b. Growth Elasticity of Poverty
c. Liberal welfare reforms
d. Poverty

20. In economics, _____ is a measure of national income. Basically, it is an approach to measure GDP. It is defined as the value of planned goods and services produced in an economy.

a. Aggregate supply
b. Aggregation problem
c. Aggregate demand
d. Aggregate expenditure

21. Competition law, known in the United States as _____ law, has three main elements:

- prohibiting agreements or practices that restrict free trading and competition between business entities. This includes in particular the repression of cartels.
- banning abusive behaviour by a firm dominating a market, or anti-competitive practices that tend to lead to such a dominant position. Practices controlled in this way may include predatory pricing, tying, price gouging, refusal to deal, and many others.
- supervising the mergers and acquisitions of large corporations, including some joint ventures. Transactions that are considered to threaten the competitive process can be prohibited altogether, or approved subject to 'remedies' such as an obligation to divest part of the merged business or to offer licences or access to facilities to enable other businesses to continue competing.

The substance and practice of competition law varies from jurisdiction to jurisdiction. Protecting the interests of consumers (consumer welfare) and ensuring that entrepreneurs have an opportunity to compete in the market economy are often treated as important objectives. Competition law is closely connected with law on deregulation of access to markets, state aids and subsidies, the privatisation of state owned assets and the establishment of independent sector regulators. In recent decades, competition law has been viewed as a way to provide better public services.

a. Intellectual property law
b. United Kingdom competition law
c. Antitrust
d. Anti-Inflation Act

22. _____s is the social science that studies the production, distribution, and consumption of goods and services. The term _____s comes from the Ancient Greek οἰκονομία from οἶκος (oikos, 'house') + νόμος (nomos, 'custom' or 'law'), hence 'rules of the house(hold)'. Current _____ models developed out of the broader field of political economy in the late 19th century, owing to a desire to use an empirical approach more akin to the physical sciences.

a. Opportunity cost
b. Energy economics
c. Inflation
d. Economic

23. A _____ is the transfer of wealth from one party (such as a person or company) to another. A _____ is usually made in exchange for the provision of goods, services or both, or to fulfill a legal obligation.

The simplest and oldest form of _____ is barter, the exchange of one good or service for another.

a. Payment
b. Soft count
c. Going concern
d. Social gravity

24. _____ is the concept or idea of fairness in economics, particularly as to taxation or welfare economics.

In welfare economics, _____ may be distinguished from economic efficiency in overall evaluation of social welfare. Although '_____' has broader uses, it may be posed as a counterpart to economic inequality in yielding a 'good' distribution of welfare.

a. ACEA agreement
b. AD-IA Model
c. ACCRA Cost of Living Index
d. Equity

25. Examples of _____ include:

- A beekeeper keeps the bees for their honey. A side effect or externality associated with his activity is the pollination of surrounding crops by the bees. The value generated by the pollination may be more important than the value of the harvested honey.

- An individual planting an attractive garden in front of his house may provide benefits to others living in the area, and even financial benefits in the form of increased property values for all property owners.

- An individual buying a product that is interconnected in a network (e.g., a video cellphone) will increase the usefulness of such phones to other people who have a video cellphone. When each new user of a product increases the value of the same product owned by others, the phenomenon is called a network externality or a network effect. Network externalities often have 'tipping points' where, suddenly, the product reaches general acceptance and near-universal usage, a phenomenon which can be seen in the near universal take-up of cellphones in some Scandinavian countries.

- Knowledge spillover of inventions and information - once an invention (or most other forms of practical information) is discovered or made more easily accessible, others benefit by exploiting the invention or information. Copyright and intellectual property law are mechanisms to allow the inventor or creator to benefit from a temporary, state-protected monopoly in return for 'sharing' the information through publication or other means.

a. Weighted average cost of carbon
b. Total Economic Value
c. Positive externalities
d. Negative externalities

26. In economics, the _____ of demand measures the responsiveness of the demand of a good to the change in the income of the people demanding the good. It is calculated as the ratio of the percent change in demand to the percent change in income. For example, if, in response to a 10% increase in income, the demand of a good increased by 20%, the _____ of demand would be 20%/10% = 2.
a. ACCRA Cost of Living Index
b. ACEA agreement
c. AD-IA Model
d. Income elasticity

27. In economics, the _____ measures the responsiveness of the demand of a good to the change in the income of the people demanding the good. It is calculated as the ratio of the percent change in demand to the percent change in income. For example, if, in response to a 10% increase in income, the demand of a good increased by 20%, the _____ would be 20%/10% = 2.
a. Expenditure minimization problem
b. Indifference map
c. Elasticity of substitution
d. Income elasticity of demand

28. _____ is defined as the measure of responsiveness in the quantity demanded for a commodity as a result of change in price of the same commodity. It is a measure of how consumers react to a change in price. In other words, it is percentage change in quantity demanded as per the percentage change in price of the same commodity.
a. 1921 recession
b. 100-year flood
c. 130-30 fund
d. Price elasticity of demand

29. In economics, _____ is the ratio of the percent change in one variable to the percent change in another variable. It is a tool for measuring the responsiveness of a function to changes in parameters in a relative way. Commonly analyzed are _____ of substitution, price and wealth.
   a. ACEA agreement
   b. Elasticity
   c. ACCRA Cost of Living Index
   d. Elasticity of demand

30. Price _____ is defined as the measure of responsiveness in the quantity demanded for a commodity as a result of change in price of the same commodity. It is a measure of how consumers react to a change in price. In other words, it is percentage change in quantity demanded by the percentage change in price of the same commodity.
   a. ACEA agreement
   b. ACCRA Cost of Living Index
   c. Elasticity
   d. Elasticity of demand

31. In calculus, a function f defined on a subset of the real numbers with real values is called _____, if for all x and y such that x >≤ y one has f(x) >≤ f(y), so f preserves the order. In layman's terms, the sign of the slope is always positive (the curve tending upwards) or zero (i.e., non-decreasing, or asymptotic, or depicted as a horizontal, flat line) Likewise, a function is called monotonically decreasing (non-increasing) if, whenever x >≤ y, then f(x) >≥ f(y), so it reverses the order.
   a. 130-30 fund
   b. 1921 recession
   c. 100-year flood
   d. Monotonic

32. In economics, the _____ of a good or of a service is the utility of the specific use to which an agent would put a given increase in that good or service, or of the specific use that would be abandoned in response to a given decrease. In other words, _____ is the utility of the marginal use -- which, on the assumption of economic rationality, would be the least urgent use of the good or service, from the best feasible combination of actions in which its use is included. Under the mainstream assumptions, the _____ of a good or service is the posited quantified change in utility obtained by increasing or by decreasing use of that good or service.
   a. 1921 recession
   b. Marginal utility
   c. 100-year flood
   d. 130-30 fund

33. In economics, _____ is a measure of the relative satisfaction from consumption of various goods and services. Given this measure, one may speak meaningfully of increasing or decreasing _____, and thereby explain economic behavior in terms of attempts to increase one's _____. For illustrative purposes, changes in _____ are sometimes expressed in units called utils.
   a. Ordinal utility
   b. Expected utility hypothesis
   c. Utility function
   d. Utility

34. _____ is the prospect that a party insulated from risk may behave differently from the way it would behave if it were fully exposed to the risk. In insurance, _____ that occurs without conscious or malicious action is called morale hazard.

_____ is related to information asymmetry, a situation in which one party in a transaction has more information than another.

   a. 130-30 fund
   b. 100-year flood
   c. 1921 recession
   d. Moral hazard

Chapter 33. The Economics of Health Care

35. _____ is an economic model based on price, utility and quantity in a market. It predicts that in a competitive market, price will function to equalize the quantity demanded by consumers, and the quantity supplied by producers, resulting in an economic equilibrium of price and quantity. The model incorporates other factors changing equilibrium as a shift of demand and/or supply.

   a. Rational addiction
   b. Joint demand
   c. Supply and demand
   d. Deferred gratification

36. To _____ is to impose a financial charge or other levy upon a taxpayer by a state or the functional equivalent of a state.

   _____es are also imposed by many subnational entities. _____es consist of direct _____ or indirect _____, and may be paid in money or as its labour equivalent (often but not always unpaid.)

   a. 100-year flood
   b. Tax
   c. 130-30 fund
   d. 1921 recession

37. _____ is a situation in which the limited resources of a firm are allocated in accordance with the wishes of consumers. An allocatively efficient economy produces an 'optimal mix' of commodities. A firm is allocatively efficient when its price is equal to its marginal costs (that is, P = MC) in a perfect market.

   a. ACCRA Cost of Living Index
   b. ACEA agreement
   c. Economic efficiency
   d. Allocative efficiency

38. In economics, _____ is the total supply of goods and services produced by a national economy during a specific time period. It is the total amount of goods and services in the economy available at all possible price levels.

   a. Aggregate expenditure
   b. Aggregation problem
   c. Aggregate supply
   d. Aggregate demand

39. In finance, a _____ is a debt security, in which the authorized issuer owes the holders a debt and, depending on the terms of the _____, is obliged to pay interest (the coupon) and/or to repay the principal at a later date, termed maturity. A _____ is a formal contract to repay borrowed money with interest at fixed intervals.

   Thus a _____ is like a loan: the issuer is the borrower (debtor), the holder is the lender (creditor), and the coupon is the interest.

   a. Bond
   b. Zero-coupon
   c. Prize Bond
   d. Callable

40. In economics, the _____ is defined as a numerical measure of the responsiveness of the quantity supplied of product (A) to a change in price of product (A) alone. It is the measure of the way quantity supplied reacts to a change in price.

For example, if, in response to a 10% rise in the price of a good, the quantity supplied increases by 20%, the _____ would be 20%/10% = 2.

a. Price elasticity of supply
b. Demand shaping
c. Hedonimetry
d. Passive income

41. _____ is the increase in the amount of the goods and services produced by an economy over time. It is conventionally measured as the percent rate of increase in real gross domestic product, or real GDP. Growth is usually calculated in real terms, i.e. inflation-adjusted terms, in order to net out the effect of inflation on the price of the goods and services produced.

a. ACCRA Cost of Living Index
b. AD-IA Model
c. Economic growth
d. ACEA agreement

42. _____ in economics refers to metrics and measures of output from production processes, per unit of input. Labor _____, for example, is typically measured as a ratio of output per labor-hour, an input. _____ may be conceived of as a metrics of the technical or engineering efficiency of production.

a. Production-possibility frontier
b. Fordism
c. Piece work
d. Productivity

43. _____ is an urban planning and transportation theory that concentrates growth in the center of a city to avoid urban sprawl; and advocates compact, transit-oriented, walkable, bicycle-friendly land use, including neighborhood schools, complete streets, mixed-use development with a range of housing choices.

_____ values long-range, regional considerations of sustainability over a short-term focus. Its goals are to achieve a unique sense of community and place; expand the range of transportation, employment, and housing choices; equitably distribute the costs and benefits of development; preserve and enhance natural and cultural resources; and promote public health.

a. Smart growth
b. 100-year flood
c. 130-30 fund
d. 1921 recession

44. _____ is a fee paid on borrowed assets. It is the price paid for the use of borrowed money, or, money earned by deposited funds. Assets that are sometimes lent with _____ include money, shares, consumer goods through hire purchase, major assets such as aircraft, and even entire factories in finance lease arrangements.

a. Asset protection
b. Internal debt
c. Insolvency
d. Interest

45. The term _____ describes two different concepts:

- The first is a recognition of partial payment already made towards taxes due.
- The second is a state benefit paid to workers through the tax system, which has the effect of increasing (rather than reducing) net income.

Within the Australian, Canadian, United Kingdom, and United States tax systems, a _____ is a recognition of partial payment already made towards taxes due. A similar concept exists (fr:Avoir fiscal) in the French tax system. This situation arises, for example, when standard rate tax has been deducted at source, but the tax-payer is subject to further taxation at a higher rate. It also applies in dividend imputation systems.

Chapter 33. The Economics of Health Care

a. Tax credit
b. 100-year flood
c. 130-30 fund
d. 1921 recession

46. A _____ is a bond which is worth a certain monetary value and which may only be spent for specific reasons or on specific goods. Examples include -- but are not limited to -- housing, travel and food _____s. The term _____ is also a synonym for receipt, and is often used to refer to receipts used as evidence of, for example, the declaration that a service has been performed or that an expenditure has been made.
   a. 130-30 fund
   b. 1921 recession
   c. 100-year flood
   d. Voucher

47. A _____ refers to any type debt instrument, such as a loan, bond, mortgage that does not have a fixed rate of interest over the life of the instrument. Such debt typically uses an index or other base rate for establishing the interest rate for each relevant period. One of the most common rates to use as the basis for applying interest rates is the London Inter-bank Offered Rate, or LIBOR
   a. Floating interest rate
   b. Disposal tax effect
   c. Moneylender
   d. Money market

48. In economics, an _____ is any good or commodity, transported from one country to another country in a legitimate fashion, typically for use in trade. _____ goods or services are provided to foreign consumers by domestic producers. _____ is an important part of international trade.
   a. Export
   b. ACEA agreement
   c. AD-IA Model
   d. ACCRA Cost of Living Index

49. _____ is the public sector analogy to market failure and occurs when a government intervention causes a more inefficient allocation of goods and resources than would occur without that intervention. Likewise, the government's failure to intervene in a market failure that would result in a socially preferable mix of output is referred to as passive _____ (Weimer and Vining, 2004.) Just as with market failures, there are many different kinds of _____s that describe corresponding distortions.
   a. Government-granted monopoly
   b. Privatizing profits and socializing losses
   c. Natural monopoly
   d. Government failure

50. In health insurance in the United States, a _____ is a managed care organization of medical doctors, hospitals, and other health care providers who have covenanted with an insurer or a third-party administrator to provide health care at reduced rates to the insurer's or administrator's clients.

A _____ is a subscription-based medical care arrangement. A membership allows a substantial discount below their regularly-charged rates from the designated professionals partnered with the organization.

   a. Mortality drag
   b. Self insurance
   c. Statutory accounting principles
   d. Preferred provider organization

51. _____s are accounts maintained by retail financial institutions that pay interest but can not be used directly as money (for example, by writing a cheque.) These accounts let customers set aside a portion of their liquid assets while earning a monetary return.

_____s are offered by commercial banks, savings and loan associations, credit unions, building societies and mutual savings banks.

a. Savings account
b. Fractional-reserve banking
c. Lombard Club
d. Fair Finance Watch

52. _____ is the name given to practices of law surrounding insurance, including insurance policies and claims. It can be broadly broken into two categories - regulation of the business of insurance and regulation of claim handling.

As a preliminary matter, insurance companies are generally required to follow all of the same laws and regulations as any other type of business.

a. Occupational Safety and Health Act
b. Electronic Commerce Protection Act
c. Importation right
d. Insurance law

Chapter 34. Labor Market Institutions and Issues: Unionism, Discrimination, Immigration 469

1. The American Federation of Labor and Congress of Industrial Organizations, commonly _____, is a national trade union center, the largest federation of unions in the United States, made up of 65 national and international unions (including Canadian), together representing more than 10 million workers. It was formed in 1955 when the AFL and the CIO merged after a long estrangement. From 1955 until 2005, the _____'s member unions represented nearly all unionized workers in the United States.
   a. AFL-CIO
   b. AD-IA Model
   c. ACEA agreement
   d. ACCRA Cost of Living Index

2. The _____ was one of the first federations of labor unions in the United States. It was founded in Columbus, Ohio in 1886 by Samuel Gompers as a reorganization of its predecessor, the Federation of Organized Trades and Labor Unions. Gompers became president of the AFL in 1886 and was reelected every year except one until his death on December 13, 1924.
   a. American Federation of Labor
   b. ACCRA Cost of Living Index
   c. AD-IA Model
   d. ACEA agreement

3. A _____ is a group of people who share or are motivated by at least one common issue or interest, or work together on a specific project(s) to achieve a common objective. _____s are also characterised by attempts to share and exercise political and social power and to make decisions on a consensus-driven and egalitarian basis. _____s differ from cooperatives in that they are not necessarily focused upon an economic benefit or saving (but can be that as well.)
   a. 100-year flood
   b. 1921 recession
   c. 130-30 fund
   d. Collective

4. In organized labor, _____ is the method whereby workers organize together (usually in unions) to meet, converse, and negotiate upon the work conditions with their employers normally resulting in a written contract setting forth the wages, hours, and other conditions to be observed for a stipulated period. It is the practice in which union and company representatives meet to negotiate a new labor contract. In various national labor and employment law contexts, _____ takes on a more specific legal meaning and so, in a broad sense, however, it is the coming together of workers to negotiate their employment.

A collective agreement is a labor contract between an employer and one or more unions.

   a. Strikebreaker
   b. Designated Suppliers Program
   c. Demarcation dispute
   d. Collective bargaining

5. The _____ proposed by John L. Lewis in 1932, was a federation of unions that organized workers in industrial unions in the United States and Canada from 1935 to 1955. The Taft-Hartley Act of 1947 required union leaders to swear that they were not Communists. Many CIO leaders refused to obey that requirement, later found unconstitutional.
   a. Multinational corporation
   b. Congress of Industrial Organizations
   c. Chinese correction
   d. Foreign direct investment

6. _____ is a field of economics that studies the strategic behavior of firms, the structure of markets and their interactions. The study of _____ adds to the perfectly competitive model real-world frictions such as limited information, transaction cost, cost of adjusting prices, government actions, and barriers to entry by new firms into a market. It then considers how firms are organized and how they compete.
   a. Economic ideology
   b. Economic
   c. Inflation
   d. Industrial Organization

Chapter 34. Labor Market Institutions and Issues: Unionism, Discrimination, Immigration

7. A trade union or _____ is an organization of workers who have banded together to achieve common goals in key areas and working conditions. The trade union, through its leadership, bargains with the employer on behalf of union members (rank and file members) and negotiates labor contracts (Collective bargaining) with employers. This may include the negotiation of wages, work rules, complaint procedures, rules governing hiring, firing and promotion of workers, benefits, workplace safety and policies.
   a. Labor union
   b. Basis of futures
   c. Business valuation standards
   d. Demand-side technologies

8. The _____ is a labor union in the United States and Canada. Formed in 1903 by the merger of several local and regional locals of teamsters, the union now represents a diverse membership of blue-collar and professional workers in both the public and private sectors. The union had approximately 1.4 million members in 2007.
   a. International Brotherhood of Teamsters
   b. ACCRA Cost of Living Index
   c. AD-IA Model
   d. ACEA agreement

9. The International Union, United Automobile, Aerospace and Agricultural Implement Workers of America, better known as the _____ , is a labor union which represents workers in the United States and Puerto Rico. Founded in order to represent workers in the automobile manufacturing industry, _____ members in the 21st century work in industries as diverse as health care, casino gaming and higher education. Headquartered in Detroit, Michigan, the union has approximately 800 local unions, which negotiated 3,100 contracts with some 2,000 employers.
   a. ACEA agreement
   b. AD-IA Model
   c. ACCRA Cost of Living Index
   d. United Auto Workers

10. In economics, the concept of the _____ refers to the decision-making time frame of a firm in which at least one factor of production is fixed. Costs which are fixed in the _____ have no impact on a firms decisions. For example a firm can raise output by increasing the amount of labour through overtime.
    a. Short-run
    b. Productivity model
    c. Product Pipeline
    d. Hicks-neutral technical change

11. A _____ or labor union is an organization of workers who have banded together to achieve common goals in key areas and working conditions. The _____, through its leadership, bargains with the employer on behalf of union members (rank and file members) and negotiates labor contracts (Collective bargaining) with employers. This may include the negotiation of wages, work rules, complaint procedures, rules governing hiring, firing and promotion of workers, benefits, workplace safety and policies.
    a. Case-Shiller Home Price Indices
    b. Guaranteed investment contracts
    c. Consumer goods
    d. Trade union

12. _____ is a broad label that refers to any individuals or households that use goods and services generated within the economy. The concept of a _____ is used in different contexts, so that the usage and significance of the term may vary.

Typically when business people and economists talk of _____s they are talking about person as _____, an aggregated commodity item with little individuality other than that expressed in the buy/not-buy decision.

Chapter 34. Labor Market Institutions and Issues: Unionism, Discrimination, Immigration 471

a. 100-year flood
b. 130-30 fund
c. 1921 recession
d. Consumer

13. In economics, the _____ of demand measures the responsiveness of the demand of a good to the change in the income of the people demanding the good. It is calculated as the ratio of the percent change in demand to the percent change in income. For example, if, in response to a 10% increase in income, the demand of a good increased by 20%, the _____ of demand would be 20%/10% = 2.
   a. AD-IA Model
   b. ACEA agreement
   c. ACCRA Cost of Living Index
   d. Income elasticity

14. In economics, the _____ measures the responsiveness of the demand of a good to the change in the income of the people demanding the good. It is calculated as the ratio of the percent change in demand to the percent change in income. For example, if, in response to a 10% increase in income, the demand of a good increased by 20%, the _____ would be 20%/10% = 2.
   a. Elasticity of substitution
   b. Income elasticity of demand
   c. Expenditure minimization problem
   d. Indifference map

15. _____ and Keynesian Theory) is a macroeconomic theory based on the ideas of 20th-century British economist John Maynard Keynes. _____ argues that private sector decisions sometimes lead to inefficient macroeconomic outcomes and therefore advocates active policy responses by the public sector, including monetary policy actions by the central bank and fiscal policy actions by the government to stabilize output over the business cycle.

The theories forming the basis of _____ were first presented in The General Theory of Employment, Interest and Money, published in 1936.

   a. Deflation
   b. Market failure
   c. Rational choice theory
   d. Keynesian economics

16. _____ in economics and business is the result of an exchange and from that trade we assign a numerical monetary value to a good, service or asset. If Alice trades Bob 4 apples for an orange, the _____ of an orange is 4 apples. Inversely, the _____ of an apple is 1/4 oranges.
   a. Price war
   b. Price
   c. Price book
   d. Premium pricing

17. _____ is defined as the measure of responsiveness in the quantity demanded for a commodity as a result of change in price of the same commodity. It is a measure of how consumers react to a change in price. In other words, it is percentage change in quantity demanded as per the percentage change in price of the same commodity.
   a. 130-30 fund
   b. 1921 recession
   c. 100-year flood
   d. Price elasticity of demand

18. A _____ is a person who works despite an ongoing strike. _____s are usually individuals who are not employed by the company prior to the trade union dispute, but rather hired prior to or during the strike to keep production or services going. '_____s' may also refer to be workers who cross picket lines to work.
   a. Division of labour
   b. Work-life balance
   c. Strikebreaker
   d. Designated Suppliers Program

472 *Chapter 34. Labor Market Institutions and Issues: Unionism, Discrimination, Immigration*

19. In a _____ there is both a monopoly (a single seller) and monopsony (a single buyer) in the same market.

In such market price and output will be determined by the non economic forces like bargaining power of both buyer and seller. A _____ model is often used in situations where the switching costs of both sides are prohibitively high.

   a. Revenue-cap regulation
   b. Market concentration
   c. Price takers
   d. Bilateral monopoly

20. Economics:

   - _____, the desire to own something and the ability to pay for it
   - _____ curve, a graphic representation of a _____ schedule
   - _____ deposit, the money in checking accounts
   - _____ pull theory, the theory that inflation occurs when _____ for goods and services exceeds existing supplies
   - _____ schedule, a table that lists the quantity of a good a person will buy it each different price
   - _____ side economics, the school of economics at believes government spending and tax cuts open economy by raising _____

   a. Variability
   b. McKesson ' Robbins scandal
   c. Production
   d. Demand

21. In economics, _____ is the ratio of the percent change in one variable to the percent change in another variable. It is a tool for measuring the responsiveness of a function to changes in parameters in a relative way. Commonly analyzed are _____ of substitution, price and wealth.
   a. Elasticity of demand
   b. ACEA agreement
   c. ACCRA Cost of Living Index
   d. Elasticity

22. Price _____ is defined as the measure of responsiveness in the quantity demanded for a commodity as a result of change in price of the same commodity. It is a measure of how consumers react to a change in price. In other words, it is percentage change in quantity demanded by the percentage change in price of the same commodity.
   a. ACCRA Cost of Living Index
   b. Elasticity of demand
   c. ACEA agreement
   d. Elasticity

23. A _____ is an object whose consumption increases the utility of the consumer, for which the quantity demanded exceeds the quantity supplied at zero price. _____s are usually modeled as having diminishing marginal utility. The first individual purchase has high utility; the second has less.
   a. Pie method
   b. Composite good
   c. Merit good
   d. Good

Chapter 34. Labor Market Institutions and Issues: Unionism, Discrimination, Immigration 473

24. In economics, a _____ exists when a specific individual or enterprise has sufficient control over a particular product or service to determine significantly the terms on which other individuals shall have access to it. Monopolies are thus characterized by a lack of economic competition for the good or service that they provide and a lack of viable substitute goods. The verb 'monopolize' refers to the process by which a firm gains persistently greater market share than what is expected under perfect competition.

    a. 1921 recession
    b. Monopoly
    c. 100-year flood
    d. 130-30 fund

25. An _____ is a place of employment where workers must pay union dues whether they are a member of a labor union or not. This mandatory payment is sometimes called the Rand formula. The first _____ was established at the Ford Motor Company plant in Ontario, Canada, in 1946.

    a. Indivisibility of labor
    b. Agency shop
    c. Industrial manslaughter
    d. Entry-level job

26. _____ is the period of time that an individual spends at paid occupational labor. Unpaid labors such as housework are not considered part of the working week. Many countries regulate the work week by law, such as stipulating minimum daily rest periods, annual holidays and a maximum number of working hours per week.

    a. 100-year flood
    b. 130-30 fund
    c. 1921 recession
    d. Working time

27. _____ are statutes enforced in twenty-two U.S. states, mostly in the southern or western U.S., allowed under provisions of the Taft-Hartley Act, which prohibit agreements between trade unions and employers making membership or payment of union dues or 'fees' a condition of employment, either before or after hiring.

Prior to the passage of the Taft-Hartley Act by Congress over President Harry S. Truman's veto in 1947, unions and employers covered by the National Labor Relations Act could lawfully agree to a 'closed shop,' in which employees at unionized workplaces are required to be members of the union as a condition of employment. Under the law in effect before the Taft-Hartley amendments, an employee who ceased being a member of the union for whatever reason, from failure to pay dues to expulsion from the union as an internal disciplinary punishment, could also be fired even if the employee did not violate any of the employer's rules.

    a. Chief Financial Officers Act of 1990
    b. Community property
    c. Fee simple
    d. Right-to-work laws

28. The supply of labor is the number of total hours that workers wish to work at a given real wage rate.

_____ curves are derived from the 'labor-leisure' trade-off. More hours worked earn higher incomes but necessitate a cut in the amount of leisure that workers enjoy.

    a. Human trafficking
    b. Labor supply
    c. Creative capitalism
    d. Late capitalism

29. In economics, _____ is the total supply of goods and services produced by a national economy during a specific time period. It is the total amount of goods and services in the economy available at all possible price levels.

474 Chapter 34. Labor Market Institutions and Issues: Unionism, Discrimination, Immigration

a. Aggregation problem
b. Aggregate expenditure
c. Aggregate supply
d. Aggregate demand

30. _____ in economics refers to metrics and measures of output from production processes, per unit of input. Labor _____, for example, is typically measured as a ratio of output per labor-hour, an input. _____ may be conceived of as a metrics of the technical or engineering efficiency of production.
   a. Fordism
   b. Productivity
   c. Piece work
   d. Production-possibility frontier

31. _____ is a pejorative term for the practice of hiring more workers than are needed to perform a given job complex and time-consuming merely to employ additional workers. The term 'make-work' is sometimes used as a synonym for _____.

The term '_____' is usually used by management to describe behaviors and rules sought by workers.

   a. Channel coordination
   b. Featherbedding
   c. Foreign ownership
   d. Cultural synergy

32. The _____ or gross domestic income (GDI), a basic measure of an economy's economic performance, is the market value of all final goods and services produced within the borders of a nation in a year. _____ can be defined in three ways, all of which are conceptually identical. First, it is equal to the total expenditures for all final goods and services produced within the country in a stipulated period of time (usually a 365-day year.)
   a. Gross domestic product
   b. Market structure
   c. Countercyclical
   d. Monopolistic competition

33. The _____ or the output gap is the difference between potential GDP and actual GDP or actual output. The calculation for the output gap is Y-Y* where Y* is potential output and Y is actual output. If this calculation yields a positive number it is called an expansionary gap and indicates an economy in expansion; if the calculation yields a negative number it is called a recessionary gap and indicates an economy in recession.
   a. 1921 recession
   b. 130-30 fund
   c. 100-year flood
   d. GDP gap

34. In microeconomics, _____ is the extra revenue that an additional unit of product will bring. It is the additional income from selling one more unit of a good; sometimes equal to price. It can also be described as the change in total revenue/change in number of units sold.
   a. Reservation price
   b. Market demand schedule
   c. Long term
   d. Marginal revenue

35. The marginal revenue productivity theory of wages, also referred to as the _____ of labor, is the change in total revenue earned by a firm that results from employing one more unit of labor. It is a neoclassical model that determines, under some conditions, the optimal number of workers to employ at an exogenously determined market wage rate.

The _____ of a worker is equal to the product of the marginal product of labor (MP) and the marginal revenue (MR), given by MR×MP = _____.

a. Marginal revenue product
b. Real prices and ideal prices
c. Coal depletion
d. Marginal revenue productivity theory of wages

36. _____s is the social science that studies the production, distribution, and consumption of goods and services. The term _____s comes from the Ancient Greek οá¼°κονομῖα from οá¼¶κος (oikos, 'house') + vÏŒμος (nomos, 'custom' or 'law'), hence 'rules of the house(hold)'. Current _____ models developed out of the broader field of political economy in the late 19th century, owing to a desire to use an empirical approach more akin to the physical sciences.
a. Energy economics
b. Opportunity cost
c. Inflation
d. Economic

476 Chapter 34. Labor Market Institutions and Issues: Unionism, Discrimination, Immigration

37. A _____ is:

- Rewrite _____, in generative grammar and computer science
- Standardization, a formal and widely-accepted statement, fact, definition, or qualification
- Operation, a determinate _____ for performing a mathematical operation and obtaining a certain result (Mathematics, Logic)
    - Unary operation
    - Binary operation
- _____ of inference, a function from sets of formulae to formulae (Mathematics, Logic)
- _____ of thumb, principle with broad application that is not intended to be strictly accurate or reliable for every situation. Also often simply referred to as a _____
- Moral, an atomic element of a moral code for guiding choices in human behavior
- Heuristic, a quantized '_____' which shows a tendency or probability for successful function
- A regulation, as in sports
- A Production _____, as in computer science
- Procedural law, a _____ set governing the application of laws to cases
    - A law, which may informally be called a '_____'
    - A court ruling, a decision by a court
- In the U.S. Government, a regulation mandated by Congress, but written or expanded upon by the Executive Branch.
- Norm (sociology), an informal but widely accepted _____, concept, truth, definition, or qualification (social norms, legal norms, coding norms)
- Norm (philosophy), a kind of sentence or a reason to act, feel or believe
- 'Rulership' is the concept of governance by a government:
    - Military _____, governance by a military body
    - Monastic _____, a collection of precepts that guides the life of monks or nuns in a religious order where the superior holds the place of Christ
- Slide _____

- '_____,' a song by Ayumi Hamasaki
- '_____,' a song by rapper Nas
- '_____s,' an album by the band The Whitest Boy Alive
- _____s: Pyaar Ka Superhit Formula, a 2003 Bollywood film
- ruler, an instrument for measuring lengths
- _____, a component of an astrolabe, circumferator or similar instrument
- The _____s, a bestselling self-help book
- _____ Project (Run Up-to-date Linux Everywhere), a project that aims to use up-to-date Linux software on old PCs
- _____ engine, a software system that helps managing business _____s
- Ja _____, a hip hop artist
    - R.U.L.E., a 2005 greatest hits album by rapper Ja _____
- '_____s,' a KMFDM song

a. Technocracy
c. Demand

b. Procter ' Gamble
d. Rule

Chapter 34. Labor Market Institutions and Issues: Unionism, Discrimination, Immigration 477

38. A _____ product is a product designed for cheapness and short-term convenience rather than medium to long-term durability, with most products only intended for single use. The term is also sometimes used for products that may last several months (ex. _____ air filters) to distinguish from similar products that last indefinitely (ex.
   a. 130-30 fund
   b. 100-year flood
   c. 1921 recession
   d. Disposable

39. _____ is gross income minus income tax on that income.

Discretionary income is income after subtracting taxes and normal expenses (such as rent or mortgage, utilities, insurance, medical, transportation, property maintenance, child support, inflation, food and sundries, 'c.) to maintain a certain standard of living.

   a. Disposable income
   b. Stamp Act
   c. Taxation as theft
   d. Disposable personal income

40. _____ refers to discriminatory employment practices such as bias in hiring, promotion, job assignment, termination, and compensation, and various types of harassment.

In many countries, laws prohibit employers from discriminating on the basis of race, color, sex, religion, national origin, physical or mental disability, or age. There is also a growing body of law preventing or occasionally justifying _____ based on sexual orientation or gender identity.

   a. Irish competition law
   b. Employment discrimination
   c. Energy Independence and Security Act of 2007
   d. Impotent poor

41. _____ refers to the stock of skills and knowledge embodied in the ability to perform labor so as to produce economic value. It is the skills and knowledge gained by a worker through education and experience. Many early economic theories refer to it simply as labor, one of three factors of production, and consider it to be a fungible resource -- homogeneous and easily interchangeable. Other conceptions of labor dispense with these assumptions.
   a. General equilibrium
   b. Law of increasing costs
   c. Price theory
   d. Human capital

42. In economics, the people in the _____ are the suppliers of labor. The _____ is all the nonmilitary people who are employed or unemployed. In 2005, the worldwide _____ was over 3 billion people.
   a. Grenelle agreements
   b. Distributed workforce
   c. Departmentalization
   d. Labor force

43. A variety of measures of _____ and output are used in economics to estimate total economic activity in a country or region, including gross domestic product (GDP), gross national product (GNP), and net _____

There are three main ways of calculating these numbers; the output approach, the income approach and the expenditure approach. In theory, the three must yield the same, because total expenditures on goods and services must equal the total income paid to the producers (Gnational income), and that must also equal the total value of the output of goods and services (GNP.)

a. GNI per capita
b. National income
c. Gross world product
d. Volume index

44. In economics and business, specifically cost accounting, the _____ point (BEP) is the point at which cost or expenses and revenue are equal: there is no net loss or gain, and one has 'broken even'. A profit or a loss has not been made, although opportunity costs have been paid, and capital has received the risk-adjusted, expected return.

For example, if the business sells less than 200 tables each month, it will make a loss, if it sells more, it will be a profit.

a. Small numbers game
b. Break-even
c. Buffer stock scheme
d. Nonmarket

45. _____ is the increase in the amount of the goods and services produced by an economy over time. It is conventionally measured as the percent rate of increase in real gross domestic product, or real GDP. Growth is usually calculated in real terms, i.e. inflation-adjusted terms, in order to net out the effect of inflation on the price of the goods and services produced.

a. Economic growth
b. ACEA agreement
c. ACCRA Cost of Living Index
d. AD-IA Model

46. In microeconomics, _____ is quite simply the conversion of inputs into outputs. It is an economic process that uses resources to create a good or service that is suitable for exchange. This can include manufacturing, storing, shipping, and packaging.

a. Solved
b. Red Guards
c. MET
d. Production

47. In mathematics, a _____ is a constant multiplicative factor of a certain object. For example, in the expression $9x^2$, the _____ of x^2 is 9.

The object can be such things as a variable, a vector, a function, etc.

a. 1921 recession
b. 130-30 fund
c. 100-year flood
d. Coefficient

48. In economics, _____ refers to the ability of a person or a country to produce a particular good at a lower marginal cost and opportunity cost than another person or country. It is the ability to produce a product most efficiently given all the other products that could be produced. It can be contrasted with absolute advantage which refers to the ability of a person or a country to produce a particular good at a lower absolute cost than another.

a. Gravity model of trade
b. Triffin dilemma
c. Hot money
d. Comparative advantage

49. In economic theory, _____ is the competitive situation in any market where the conditions necessary for perfect competition are not satisfied. It is a market structure that does not meet the conditions of perfect competition.

Chapter 34. Labor Market Institutions and Issues: Unionism, Discrimination, Immigration

Forms of _____ include:

- Monopoly, in which there is only one seller of a good.
- Oligopoly, in which there is a small number of sellers.
- Monopolistic competition, in which there are many sellers producing highly differentiated goods.
- Monopsony, in which there is only one buyer of a good.
- Oligopsony, in which there is a small number of buyers.

There may also be _____ in markets due to buyers or sellers lacking information about prices and the goods being traded.

There may also be _____ due to a time lag in a market.

a. Imperfect competition
c. ACEA agreement
b. AD-IA Model
d. ACCRA Cost of Living Index

50. In economics, _____ describes the state of a market with respect to competition.

- Perfect competition, in which the market consists of a very large number of firms producing a homogeneous product.
- Monopolistic competition where there are a large number of independent firms which have a very small proportion of the market share.
- Oligopoly, in which a market is dominated by a small number of firms which own more than 40% of the market share.
- Oligopsony, a market dominated by many sellers and a few buyers.
- Monopoly, where there is only one provider of a product or service.
- Natural monopoly, a monopoly in which economies of scale cause efficiency to increase continuously with the size of the firm. A firm is a natural monopoly if it is able to serve the entire market demand at a lower cost than any combination of two or more smaller, more specialized firms.
- Monopsony, when there is only one buyer in a market.

The imperfectly competitive structure is quite identical to the realistic market conditions where some monopolistic competitors, monopolists, oligopolists, and duopolists exist and dominate the market conditions. The elements of _____ include the number and size distribution of firms, entry conditions, and the extent of differentiation.

These somewhat abstract concerns tend to determine some but not all details of a specific concrete market system where buyers and sellers actually meet and commit to trade.

a. Monopolistic competition
c. Human capital
b. Market structure
d. Labour economics

51. A _____ is an expression that compares quantities relative to each other. The most common examples involve two quantities, but any number of quantities can be compared. _____s are represented mathematically by separating each quantity with a colon, for example the _____ 2:3, which is read as the _____ 'two to three'.

Chapter 34. Labor Market Institutions and Issues: Unionism, Discrimination, Immigration

a. Y-intercept
c. 100-year flood

b. 130-30 fund
d. Ratio

52. _____ to the arrival of new individuals into a habitat or population. It is a biological concept and is important in population ecology, differentiated from emigration and migration.

_____ is a modern phenomenon.

a. AD-IA Model
c. Immigration

b. ACCRA Cost of Living Index
d. ACEA agreement

53. _____ is the change in population over time, and can be quantified as the change in the number of individuals in a population using 'per unit time' for measurement. The term _____ can technically refer to any species, but almost always refers to humans, and it is often used informally for the more specific demographic term _____ rate , and is often used to refer specifically to the growth of the population of the world.

Simple models of _____ include the Malthusian Growth Model and the logistic model.

a. 130-30 fund
c. Population growth

b. Population dynamics
d. 100-year flood

54. In economics a _____ is an entity that owes a debt to someone else. The entity may be an individual, a firm, a government, a company or other legal person. The counterparty is called a creditor.

a. Duration gap
c. Debtor

b. Senior stretch loan
d. Decision process tool

55. In macroeconomics, _____ is a condition of the national economy, where all or nearly all persons willing and able to work at the prevailing wages and working conditions are able to do so. It is defined either as 0% unemployment, literally, no unemployment (the rate of unemployment is the fraction of the work force unable to find work), as by James Tobin, or as the level of employment rates when there is no cyclical unemployment. It is defined by the majority of mainstream economists as being an acceptable level of natural unemployment above 0%, the discrepancy from 0% being due to non-cyclical types of unemployment.

a. Harrod-Johnson diagram
c. Marginal propensity to consume

b. Demand shock
d. Full employment

56. A _____ is a transfer of money by a foreign worker to his home country.

Money sent home by migrants constitutes the second largest financial inflow to many developing countries, exceeding international aid. Latest estimates vary between IFAD estimates of US$401 billion and the World Bank information from central banks at a more conservative US$250 billion for 2006 and these figures are increasing by almost 30% year on year.

a. 1921 recession
c. Remittance

b. 100-year flood
d. 130-30 fund

Chapter 34. Labor Market Institutions and Issues: Unionism, Discrimination, Immigration 481

57. In law and economics, the _____, describes the economic efficiency of an economic allocation or outcome in the presence of externalities. The theorem states that when trade in an externality is possible and there are no transaction costs, bargaining will lead to an efficient outcome regardless of the initial allocation of property rights. In practice, obstacles to bargaining or poorly defined property rights can prevent Coasian bargaining.
   a. Prior appropriation water rights
   b. Means test
   c. Coase theorem
   d. General Mining Act of 1872

58. _____ is a term that refers both to:

   - a formal discipline used to help appraise, or assess, the case for a project or proposal, which itself is a process known as project appraisal; and
   - an informal approach to making decisions of any kind.

Under both definitions the process involves, whether explicitly or implicitly, weighing the total expected costs against the total expected benefits of one or more actions in order to choose the best or most profitable option. The formal process is often referred to as either CBA (_____) or BCost-benefit analysis

A hallmark of CBA is that all benefits and all costs are expressed in money terms, and are adjusted for the time value of money, so that all flows of benefits and flows of project costs over time (which tend to occur at different points in time) are expressed on a common basis in terms of their e;present value.e; Closely related, but slightly different, formal techniques include Cost-effectiveness analysis, Economic impact analysis, Fiscal impact analysis and Social Return on Investment(SROI) analysis. The latter builds upon the logic of _____, but differs in that it is explicitly designed to inform the practical decision-making of enterprise managers and investors focused on optimising their social and environmental impacts.

   a. Decision theory
   b. 100-year flood
   c. 130-30 fund
   d. Cost-benefit analysis

59. _____ or government expenditure is classified by economists into three main types. Government purchases of goods and services for current use are classed as government consumption. Government purchases of goods and services intended to create future benefits, such as infrastructure investment or research spending, are classed as government investment.
   a. 100-year flood
   b. 1921 recession
   c. 130-30 fund
   d. Government spending

60. The term _____ refers to government debt, expenditures and revenues, or to finance (particularly financial revenue) in general.

   - _____ deficit is the budget deficit of federal or local government
   - _____ policy is the discretionary spending of governments. Contrasts with monetary policy.
   - _____ year and _____ quarter are reporting periods for firms and other agencies.

a. Procter ' Gamble
c. Drawdown

b. Bucket shop
d. Fiscal

61. _____ is a common concept in economics, and gives rise to derived concepts such as consumer debt. Generally _____ is defined by opposition to production. But the precise definition can vary because different schools of economists define production quite differently.

a. Federal Reserve Bank Notes
c. Cash or share options

b. Foreclosure data providers
d. Consumption

Chapter 35. International Trade

1. _____s is the social science that studies the production, distribution, and consumption of goods and services. The term _____s comes from the Ancient Greek oá¼°κονομῖα from oá¼¶κος (oikos, 'house') + vÏŒμος (nomos, 'custom' or 'law'), hence 'rules of the house(hold)'. Current _____ models developed out of the broader field of political economy in the late 19th century, owing to a desire to use an empirical approach more akin to the physical sciences.
   a. Opportunity cost
   b. Inflation
   c. Energy economics
   d. Economic

2. The _____ or gross domestic income (GDI), a basic measure of an economy's economic performance, is the market value of all final goods and services produced within the borders of a nation in a year. _____ can be defined in three ways, all of which are conceptually identical. First, it is equal to the total expenditures for all final goods and services produced within the country in a stipulated period of time (usually a 365-day year.)
   a. Countercyclical
   b. Monopolistic competition
   c. Market structure
   d. Gross domestic product

3. _____ is exchange of capital, goods, and services across international borders or territories. In most countries, it represents a significant share of gross domestic product (GDP.) While _____ has been present throughout much of history, its economic, social, and political importance has been on the rise in recent centuries.
   a. Import license
   b. Incoterms
   c. Intra-industry trade
   d. International trade

4. _____ in economics and business is the result of an exchange and from that trade we assign a numerical monetary value to a good, service or asset. If Alice trades Bob 4 apples for an orange, the _____ of an orange is 4 apples. Inversely, the _____ of an apple is 1/4 oranges.
   a. Price war
   b. Premium pricing
   c. Price book
   d. Price

5. A _____ is a normalized average (typically a weighted average) of prices for a given class of goods or services in a given region, during a given interval of time. It is a statistic designed to help to compare how these prices, taken as a whole, differ between time periods or geographical locations.

   Price indices have several potential uses.

   a. Price index
   b. Transactional Net Margin Method
   c. Two-part tariff
   d. Product sabotage

6. In economics, an _____ is any good or commodity, transported from one country to another country in a legitimate fashion, typically for use in trade. _____ goods or services are provided to foreign consumers by domestic producers. _____ is an important part of international trade.
   a. AD-IA Model
   b. ACEA agreement
   c. ACCRA Cost of Living Index
   d. Export

7. The _____ was an evolution of developed countries from an industrial/manufacturing-based wealth producing economy into a service sector asset based economy, brought about by globalization and currency manipulation by governments and their central banks. Some analysts claimed that this change in the economic structure of the United States had created a state of permanent steady growth, low unemployment, and immunity to boom and bust macroeconomic cycles. They believed that the change rendered obsolete many business practices.

a. New Economy
b. 100-year flood
c. 130-30 fund
d. 1921 recession

8. A _____ is a general term that describes any government policy or regulation that restricts international trade. The barriers can take many forms, including the following terms that include many restrictions in international trade within multiple countries that import and export any items of trade.

- Import duty
- Import licenses
- Export licenses
- Import quotas
- Tariffs
- Subsidies
- Non-tariff barriers to trade
- Voluntary Export Restraints
- Local Content Requirements
- Embargo

Most _____s work on the same principle: the imposition of some sort of cost on trade that raises the price of the traded products. If two or more nations repeatedly use _____s against each other, then a trade war results.

a. Global financial system
b. Trade barrier
c. National Foreign Trade Council
d. Certificate of origin

9. The balance of trade (or net exports, sometimes symbolized as NX) is the difference between the monetary value of exports and imports in an economy over a certain period of time. It is the relationship between a nation's imports and exports. A favorable balance of trade is known as a trade surplus and consists of exporting more than is imported; an unfavorable balance of trade is known as a _____ or, informally, a trade gap.

a. Demographics of India
b. Computational economic
c. Trade deficit
d. Complementary asset

10. The balance of trade (or net exports, sometimes symbolized as NX) is the difference between the monetary value of exports and imports in an economy over a certain period of time. It is the relationship between a nation's imports and exports. A favorable balance of trade is known as a _____ and consists of exporting more than is imported; an unfavorable balance of trade is known as a trade deficit or, informally, a trade gap.

a. Black-Scholes
b. Business valuation standards
c. Dividend unit
d. Trade surplus

11. In economics, _____ refers to the ability of a party to produce a good or service using fewer real resources than another entity producing the same good or service..A party has an _____ when using the same input as another party, it can produce a greater output. Since _____ is determined by a simple comparison of labor productivities, it is possible for a a party to have no _____ in anything. It can be contrasted with the concept of comparative advantage which refers to the ability to produce a particular good at a lower opportunity cost.

a. International economics
c. Index number
b. ACCRA Cost of Living Index
d. Absolute advantage

12. _____ is a term used in accounting, economics and finance to spread the cost of an asset over the span of several years.

In simple words we can say that _____ is the reduction in the value of an asset due to usage, passage of time, wear and tear, technological outdating or obsolescence, depletion, inadequacy, rot, rust, decay or other such factors.

In accounting, _____ is a term used to describe any method of attributing the historical or purchase cost of an asset across its useful life, roughly corresponding to normal wear and tear.

a. Salvage value
c. Historical cost
b. Net income per employee
d. Depreciation

13. In finance, the _____s between two currencies specifies how much one currency is worth in terms of the other. It is the value of a foreign natione;s currency in terms of the home natione;s currency. For example an _____ of 102 Japanese yen to the United States dollar means that JPY 102 is worth the same as USD 1.

a. ACCRA Cost of Living Index
c. Interbank market
b. ACEA agreement
d. Exchange rate

14. A _____, sometimes called a pegged exchange rate, is a type of exchange rate regime wherein a currency's value is matched to the value of another single currency or to a basket of other currencies such as gold.

A _____ is usually used to stabilize the value of a currency, vis-a-vis the currency it is pegged to. This facilitates trade and investments between the two countries, and is especially useful for small economies where external trade forms a large part of their GDP.

a. Law of supply
c. Monetary economics
b. Leading indicators
d. Fixed exchange rate

15. The _____ is 'the basic residential unit in which economic production, consumption, inheritance, child rearing, and shelter are organized and carried out'; [the _____] 'may or may not be synonymous with family'.

The _____ is the basic unit of analysis in many social, microeconomic and government models. The term refers to all individuals who live in the same dwelling.

a. Household
c. Family economics
b. 130-30 fund
d. 100-year flood

16. _____ to the arrival of new individuals into a habitat or population. It is a biological concept and is important in population ecology, differentiated from emigration and migration.

_____ is a modern phenomenon.

a. Immigration
b. ACCRA Cost of Living Index
c. ACEA agreement
d. AD-IA Model

17. In economics, an _____ is any good (e.g. a commodity) or service brought into one country from another country in a legitimate fashion, typically for use in trade. It is a good that is brought in from another country for sale. _____ goods or services are provided to domestic consumers by foreign producers. An _____ in the receiving country is an export to the sending country.

a. Incoterms
b. Import
c. Economic integration
d. Import quota

18. _____ is the a method of technical and economic research of the systems for purpose to optimize a parity between system's consumer functions or properties and expenses to achieve those functions or properties.

This methodology for continuous perfection of production, industrial technologies, organizational structures was developed by Juryj Sobolev in 1948 at the 'Perm telephone factory'

- 1948 Juryj Sobolev - the first success in application of a method analysis at the 'Perm telephone factory'.
- 1949 - the first application for the invention as result of use of the new method.

Today in economically developed countries practically each enterprise or the company use methodology of the kind of functional-cost analysis as a practice of the quality management, most full satisfying to principles of standards of series ISO 9000.

- Interest of consumer not in products itself, but the advantage which it will receive from its usage.
- The consumer aspires to reduce his expenses
- Functions needed by consumer can be executed in the various ways, and, hence, with various efficiency and expenses. Among possible alternatives of realization of functions exist such in which the parity of quality and the price is the optimal for the consumer.

The goal of _____ is achievement of the highest consumer satisfaction of production at simultaneous decrease in all kinds of industrial expenses Classical _____ has three English synonyms - Value Engineering, Value Management, Value Analysis.

a. Staple financing
b. Monopoly wage
c. Willingness to pay
d. Function cost analysis

19. _____ is a broad label that refers to any individuals or households that use goods and services generated within the economy. The concept of a _____ is used in different contexts, so that the usage and significance of the term may vary.

Typically when business people and economists talk of _____s they are talking about person as _____, an aggregated commodity item with little individuality other than that expressed in the buy/not-buy decision.

a. 1921 recession
c. Consumer
b. 130-30 fund
d. 100-year flood

20. _____ are final goods specifically intended for the mass market. For instance, _____ do not include investment assets, like precious antiques, even though these antiques are final goods.

Manufactured goods are goods that have been processed by way of machinery.

a. Consumer goods
c. Bulgarian-American trade
b. G-20 Leaders Summit on Financial Markets and the World Economy
d. Fiscal stimulus plans

21. In economics, _____ are the resources employed to produce goods and services. They facilitate production but do not become part of the product (as with raw materials) or significantly transformed by the production process (as with fuel used to power machinery.) To 19th century economists, the _____ were land (natural resources, gifts from nature), labor (the ability to work), and capital goods (human-made tools and equipment.)
  a. Long-run
  b. Product Pipeline
  c. Hicks-neutral technical change
  d. Factors of production

22. In microeconomics, _____ is quite simply the conversion of inputs into outputs. It is an economic process that uses resources to create a good or service that is suitable for exchange. This can include manufacturing, storing, shipping, and packaging.
  a. Production
  b. Solved
  c. MET
  d. Red Guards

23. In economics, _____ refers to the ability of a person or a country to produce a particular good at a lower marginal cost and opportunity cost than another person or country. It is the ability to produce a product most efficiently given all the other products that could be produced. It can be contrasted with absolute advantage which refers to the ability of a person or a country to produce a particular good at a lower absolute cost than another.
  a. Triffin dilemma
  b. Hot money
  c. Gravity model of trade
  d. Comparative advantage

24. _____ is the increase in the amount of the goods and services produced by an economy over time. It is conventionally measured as the percent rate of increase in real gross domestic product, or real GDP. Growth is usually calculated in real terms, i.e. inflation-adjusted terms, in order to net out the effect of inflation on the price of the goods and services produced.
  a. ACCRA Cost of Living Index
  b. ACEA agreement
  c. AD-IA Model
  d. Economic growth

25. A _____ is an object whose consumption increases the utility of the consumer, for which the quantity demanded exceeds the quantity supplied at zero price. _____s are usually modeled as having diminishing marginal utility. The first individual purchase has high utility; the second has less.
  a. Composite good
  b. Merit good
  c. Pie method
  d. Good

26. _____ refers to the distribution of resources, including land, water, minerals, fuel and wealth in general among corresponding geographic entities (states, countries, etc.).

The most common use of this concept has historically been in examining the unequal distribution of resources among nation states. Such unequal distribution of resources was commonly related to land for agriculture, necessary for population growth.

   a. 130-30 fund
   c. 100-year flood
   b. Resource distribution
   d. 1921 recession

27. _____ was a survey conducted by the U.S. Department of Justice to gauge the prevalence of alcohol and illegal drug use among prior arrestees. It was a reformulation of the prior Drug Use Forecasting (DUF) program, focused on five drugs in particular: cocaine, marijuana, methamphetamine, opiates, and PCP.

Participants were randomly selected from arrest records in major metropolitan areas; because no personally identifying information is taken from each record chosen, the resulting data can be correlated to arrest rates, but not to the total population of persons charged.

   a. Arrestee Drug Abuse Monitoring
   c. AD-IA Model
   b. ACEA agreement
   d. ACCRA Cost of Living Index

28. _____ was a Scottish moral philosopher and a pioneer of political economy. One of the key figures of the Scottish Enlightenment, Smith is the author of The Theory of Moral Sentiments and An Inquiry into the Nature and Causes of the Wealth of Nations. The latter, usually abbreviated as The Wealth of Nations, is considered his magnum opus and the first modern work of economics.

   a. Adam Smith
   c. Adolf Hitler
   b. Adolph Fischer
   d. Alan Greenspan

29. _____ refers to the state of not requiring any outside aid, support for survival; it is therefore a type of personal or collective autonomy. On a large scale, a totally self-sufficient economy that does not trade with the outside world is called an autarky.

The term _____ is usually applied to varieties of sustainable living in which nothing is consumed outside of what is produced by the self-sufficient individuals.

   a. Sustainable forest management
   c. Sustainability science
   b. Global Reporting Initiative
   d. Self-sufficiency

30. A _____ is an expression that compares quantities relative to each other. The most common examples involve two quantities, but any number of quantities can be compared. _____s are represented mathematically by separating each quantity with a colon, for example the _____ 2:3, which is read as the _____ 'two to three'.
   a. Y-intercept
   c. 100-year flood
   b. 130-30 fund
   d. Ratio

31. _____ and Keynesian Theory) is a macroeconomic theory based on the ideas of 20th-century British economist John Maynard Keynes. _____ argues that private sector decisions sometimes lead to inefficient macroeconomic outcomes and therefore advocates active policy responses by the public sector, including monetary policy actions by the central bank and fiscal policy actions by the government to stabilize output over the business cycle.

The theories forming the basis of _____ were first presented in The General Theory of Employment, Interest and Money, published in 1936.

    a. Rational choice theory   b. Deflation
    c. Market failure   d. Keynesian economics

32. _____ or economic opportunity loss is the value of the next best alternative foregone as the result of making a decision. _____ analysis is an important part of a company's decision-making processes but is not treated as an actual cost in any financial statement. The next best thing that a person can engage in is referred to as the _____ of doing the best thing and ignoring the next best thing to be done.

    a. Economic ideology   b. Economic
    c. Opportunity cost   d. Industrial organization

33. In international economics and international trade, _____ or _____ is the relative prices of a country's export to import. '_____' are sometimes used as a proxy for the relative social welfare of a country, but this heuristic is technically questionable and should be used with extreme caution. An improvement in a nation's _____ is good for that country in the sense that it has to pay less for the products it import.

    a. Terms of trade   b. Kennedy Round
    c. Commercial invoice   d. Common market

34. _____ is a situation in which the limited resources of a firm are allocated in accordance with the wishes of consumers. An allocatively efficient economy produces an 'optimal mix' of commodities. A firm is allocatively efficient when its price is equal to its marginal costs (that is, P = MC) in a perfect market.

    a. ACEA agreement   b. Economic efficiency
    c. ACCRA Cost of Living Index   d. Allocative efficiency

35. In calculus, a function f defined on a subset of the real numbers with real values is called _____, if for all x and y such that $x \gtreqless y$ one has $f(x) \gtreqless f(y)$, so f preserves the order. In layman's terms, the sign of the slope is always positive (the curve tending upwards) or zero (i.e., non-decreasing, or asymptotic, or depicted as a horizontal, flat line) Likewise, a function is called monotonically decreasing (non-increasing) if, whenever $x \gtreqless y$, then $f(x) \lesseqgtr f(y)$, so it reverses the order.

    a. Monotonic   b. 100-year flood
    c. 130-30 fund   d. 1921 recession

36. _____ is a type of trade policy that allows traders to act and transact without interference from government. Thus, the policy permits trading partners mutual gains from trade, with goods and services produced according to the theory of comparative advantage.

Under a _____ policy, prices are a reflection of true supply and demand, and are the sole determinant of resource allocation.

a. 130-30 fund
b. 100-year flood
c. Free trade
d. 1921 recession

37. _____ is an economic model based on price, utility and quantity in a market. It predicts that in a competitive market, price will function to equalize the quantity demanded by consumers, and the quantity supplied by producers, resulting in an economic equilibrium of price and quantity. The model incorporates other factors changing equilibrium as a shift of demand and/or supply.

a. Rational addiction
b. Supply and demand
c. Deferred gratification
d. Joint demand

38. In finance, a _____ is a debt security, in which the authorized issuer owes the holders a debt and, depending on the terms of the _____, is obliged to pay interest (the coupon) and/or to repay the principal at a later date, termed maturity. A _____ is a formal contract to repay borrowed money with interest at fixed intervals.

Thus a _____ is like a loan: the issuer is the borrower (debtor), the holder is the lender (creditor), and the coupon is the interest.

a. Bond
b. Callable
c. Zero-coupon
d. Prize Bond

39. Economics:

- _____,the desire to own something and the ability to pay for it
- _____ curve,a graphic representation of a _____ schedule
- _____ deposit, the money in checking accounts
- _____ pull theory,the theory that inflation occurs when _____ for goods and services exceeds existing supplies
- _____ schedule,a table that lists the quantity of a good a person will buy it each different price
- _____ side economics,the school of economics at believes government spending and tax cuts open economy by raising _____

a. McKesson ' Robbins scandal
b. Production
c. Variability
d. Demand

40. In economics, the _____ can be defined as the graph depicting the relationship between the price of a certain commodity, and the amount of it that consumers are willing and able to purchase at that given price. It is a graphic representation of a demand schedule. The _____ for all consumers together follows from the _____ of every individual consumer: the individual demands at each price are added together.

a. Demand curve
b. Wage curve
c. Kuznets curve
d. Cost curve

41. A _____ is a duty imposed on goods when they are moved across a political boundary. They are usually associated with protectionism, the economic policy of restraining trade between nations. For political reasons, _____s are usually imposed on imported goods, although they may also be imposed on exported goods.

a. Tariff
b. 1921 recession
c. 100-year flood
d. 130-30 fund

42. _____ is the economic policy of restraining trade between states, through methods such as tariffs on imported goods, restrictive quotas, and a variety of other restrictive government regulations designed to discourage imports, and prevent foreign take-over of local markets and companies. This policy is closely aligned with anti-globalization, and contrasts with free trade, where government barriers to trade are kept to a minimum. The term is mostly used in the context of economics, where _____ refers to policies or doctrines which 'protect' businesses and workers within a country by restricting or regulating trade with foreign nations.
a. Google economy
b. Knowledge economy
c. Digital economy
d. Protectionism

43. To _____ is to impose a financial charge or other levy upon a taxpayer by a state or the functional equivalent of a state.

_____es are also imposed by many subnational entities. _____es consist of direct _____ or indirect _____, and may be paid in money or as its labour equivalent (often but not always unpaid.)

a. 100-year flood
b. Tax
c. 1921 recession
d. 130-30 fund

44. To tax is to impose a financial charge or other levy upon a taxpayer by a state or the functional equivalent of a state.

_____ are also imposed by many subnational entities. _____ consist of direct tax or indirect tax, and may be paid in money or as its labour equivalent (often but not always unpaid.)

a. 100-year flood
b. Taxes
c. 1921 recession
d. 130-30 fund

45. _____ is a common concept in economics, and gives rise to derived concepts such as consumer debt. Generally _____ is defined by opposition to production. But the precise definition can vary because different schools of economists define production quite differently.
a. Federal Reserve Bank Notes
b. Consumption
c. Foreclosure data providers
d. Cash or share options

46. An _____ is a document issued by a national government authorizing the importation of certain goods into its territory. _____s are considered to be non-tariff barriers to trade when used as a way to discriminate against another country's goods in order to protect a domestic industry from foreign competition. Each license specifies the volume of imports allowed, and the total volume allowed should not exceed the quota.
a. Export function
b. Effective rate of protection
c. Import
d. Import license

47. An _____ is a type of protectionist trade restriction that sets a physical limit on the quantity of a good that can be imported into a country in a given period of time. Quotas, like other trade restrictions, are used to benefit the producers of a good in a domestic economy at the expense of all consumers of the good in that economy.

Critics say quotas often lead to corruption (bribes to get a quota allocation), smuggling (circumventing a quota), and higher prices for consumers.

a. International Monetary Systems
b. Economic integration
c. Agreement on Agriculture
d. Import quota

48. _____s are limitations on the quantity of goods exported to a specific country or countries by a government.

An _____ may be imposed:

- To prevent a shortage of goods in the domestic market because it is more profitable to export
- To manage the effect on the domestic market of the importing country, which may otherwise impose antidumping duties on the imported goods
- As part of foreign policy, for example as a component of trade sanctions
- To limit or restrict arms or dual-use items that may be used in proliferation, terrorism chemical, or biological warfare.
- To limit or restrict trade to embargoed nations.

a. Export restriction
b. ACCRA Cost of Living Index
c. ACEA agreement
d. AD-IA Model

49. The _____ is an economic reason for protectionism. The crux of the argument is that nascent industries often do not have the economies of scale that their older competitors from other countries may have, and thus need to be protected until they can attain similar economies of scale. It was first used by Alexander Hamilton in 1790 and later by Friedrich List, in 1841, to support protection for German manufacturing against British industry.

a. ACEA agreement
b. ACCRA Cost of Living Index
c. Infant industry argument
d. AD-IA Model

50. _____ exists when sales of identical goods or services are transacted at different prices from the same provider. In a theoretical market with perfect information, no transaction costs or prohibition on secondary exchange (or re-selling) to prevent arbitrage, _____ can only be a feature of monopoly and oligopoly markets, where market power can be exercised. Otherwise, the moment the seller tries to sell the same good at different prices, the buyer at the lower price can arbitrage by selling to the consumer buying at the higher price but with a tiny discount.

a. Loss leader
b. Lerner Index
c. Transfer pricing
d. Price discrimination

51. A _____ arises when one infers that something is true of the whole from the fact that it is true of some part of the whole (or even of every proper part.) For example: 'This fragment of metal cannot be broken with a hammer, therefore the machine of which it is a part cannot be broken with a hammer.' This is clearly fallacious, because many machines can be broken into their constituent parts without any of those parts being breakable.

This fallacy is often confused with the fallacy of hasty generalization, in which an unwarranted inference is made from a statement about a sample to a statement about the population from which it is drawn.

a. 130-30 fund
b. 1921 recession
c. 100-year flood
d. Fallacy of composition

52. In economic theory, _____ is the competitive situation in any market where the conditions necessary for perfect competition are not satisfied. It is a market structure that does not meet the conditions of perfect competition.

Forms of _____ include:

- Monopoly, in which there is only one seller of a good.
- Oligopoly, in which there is a small number of sellers.
- Monopolistic competition, in which there are many sellers producing highly differentiated goods.
- Monopsony, in which there is only one buyer of a good.
- Oligopsony, in which there is a small number of buyers.

There may also be _____ in markets due to buyers or sellers lacking information about prices and the goods being traded.

There may also be _____ due to a time lag in a market.

a. ACCRA Cost of Living Index
b. AD-IA Model
c. ACEA agreement
d. Imperfect competition

53. In economics, _____ describes the state of a market with respect to competition.

- Perfect competition, in which the market consists of a very large number of firms producing a homogeneous product.
- Monopolistic competition where there are a large number of independent firms which have a very small proportion of the market share.
- Oligopoly, in which a market is dominated by a small number of firms which own more than 40% of the market share.
- Oligopsony, a market dominated by many sellers and a few buyers.
- Monopoly, where there is only one provider of a product or service.
- Natural monopoly, a monopoly in which economies of scale cause efficiency to increase continuously with the size of the firm. A firm is a natural monopoly if it is able to serve the entire market demand at a lower cost than any combination of two or more smaller, more specialized firms.
- Monopsony, when there is only one buyer in a market.

The imperfectly competitive structure is quite identical to the realistic market conditions where some monopolistic competitors, monopolists, oligopolists, and duopolists exist and dominate the market conditions. The elements of _____ include the number and size distribution of firms, entry conditions, and the extent of differentiation.

These somewhat abstract concerns tend to determine some but not all details of a specific concrete market system where buyers and sellers actually meet and commit to trade.

a. Market structure
b. Monopolistic competition
c. Human capital
d. Labour economics

54. The _____ was an act signed into law on June 17, 1930, that raised U.S. tariffs on over 20,000 imported goods to record levels. In the United States 1,028 economists signed a petition against this legislation, and after it was passed, many countries retaliated with their own increased tariffs on U.S. goods, and American exports and imports were reduced by more than half.

Although rated capacity had increased tremendously, actual output, income, and expenditure had not.

a. Loss of use
b. Judgment summons
c. Smoot-Hawley Tariff Act
d. Patent Law Treaty

55. _____ is a program of the United States Department of Labor that provides a variety of reemployment services and benefits to workers who have lost their jobs or suffered a reduction of hours and wages as a result of increased imports or shifts in production outside the United States. The _____ program aims to help program participants obtain new jobs, ensuring they retain employment and earn wages comparable to their prior employment.

_____ was established as part of the Trade Expansion Act in 1962, during the Presidency of John F. Kennedy.

a. Delancey Street Foundation
b. New Economic Policy
c. Financial Crimes Enforcement Network
d. Trade adjustment assistance

56. _____ describes the relocation by a company of a business process from one country to another -- typically an operational process, such as manufacturing such as accounting. Even state governments employ _____.

The term is in use in several distinct but closely related ways.

a. Offshoring
b. ACEA agreement
c. ACCRA Cost of Living Index
d. Offshore outsourcing

57. _____ is subcontracting a process, such as product design or manufacturing, to a third-party company. The decision to outsource is often made in the interest of lowering cost or making better use of time and energy costs, redirecting or conserving energy directed at the competencies of a particular business, or to make more efficient use of land, labor, capital, (information) technology and resources. _____ became part of the business lexicon during the 1980s.

a. Electronic business
b. Averch-Johnson effect
c. Additional Funds Needed
d. Outsourcing

58. _____, in law and economics, is a form of risk management primarily used to hedge against the risk of a contingent loss. _____ is defined as the equitable transfer of the risk of a loss, from one entity to another, in exchange for a premium, and can be thought of as a guaranteed small loss to prevent a large, possibly devastating loss. An insurer is a company selling the _____; an insured or policyholder is the person or entity buying the _____.

a. ACEA agreement
b. ACCRA Cost of Living Index
c. AD-IA Model
d. Insurance

59. The _____ movement is movement of movements which are critical of the globalization of capitalism. Participants base their criticisms on a number of related ideas. What is shared is that participants stand in opposition to the unregulated political power of large, multi-national corporations and to the powers exercised through trade agreements.

a. Overcapitalisation
b. Asset price inflation
c. Anti-globalization
d. Anti-consumerism

60. A _____ is a group of people who share or are motivated by at least one common issue or interest, or work together on a specific project(s) to achieve a common objective. _____s are also characterised by attempts to share and exercise political and social power and to make decisions on a consensus-driven and egalitarian basis. _____s differ from cooperatives in that they are not necessarily focused upon an economic benefit or saving (but can be that as well.)

a. 1921 recession
b. 130-30 fund
c. 100-year flood
d. Collective

61. In organized labor, _____ is the method whereby workers organize together (usually in unions) to meet, converse, and negotiate upon the work conditions with their employers normally resulting in a written contract setting forth the wages, hours, and other conditions to be observed for a stipulated period. It is the practice in which union and company representatives meet to negotiate a new labor contract. In various national labor and employment law contexts, _____ takes on a more specific legal meaning and so, in a broad sense, however, it is the coming together of workers to negotiate their employment.

A collective agreement is a labor contract between an employer and one or more unions.

a. Collective bargaining
b. Strikebreaker
c. Designated Suppliers Program
d. Demarcation dispute

62. A trade union or _____ is an organization of workers who have banded together to achieve common goals in key areas and working conditions. The trade union, through its leadership, bargains with the employer on behalf of union members (rank and file members) and negotiates labor contracts (Collective bargaining) with employers. This may include the negotiation of wages, work rules, complaint procedures, rules governing hiring, firing and promotion of workers, benefits, workplace safety and policies.

a. Demand-side technologies
b. Basis of futures
c. Business valuation standards
d. Labor union

63. The _____ is an important selective, mainly private, international organization designed by its founders to supervise and liberalize international trade. The organization officially commenced on 1 January 1995, under the Marrakesh Agreement, succeeding the 1947 General Agreement on Tariffs and Trade (GATT.)

The _____ deals with regulation of trade between participating countries; it provides a framework for negotiating and formalising trade agreements, and a dispute resolution process aimed at enforcing participants' adherence to _____ agreements which are signed by representatives of member governments and ratified by their parliaments.

a. Backus-Kehoe-Kydland consumption correlation puzzle
b. Bio-energy village
c. 2009 G-20 London summit protests
d. World Trade Organization

64. A _____ or labor union is an organization of workers who have banded together to achieve common goals in key areas and working conditions. The _____, through its leadership, bargains with the employer on behalf of union members (rank and file members) and negotiates labor contracts (Collective bargaining) with employers. This may include the negotiation of wages, work rules, complaint procedures, rules governing hiring, firing and promotion of workers, benefits, workplace safety and policies.
   a. Consumer goods
   b. Case-Shiller Home Price Indices
   c. Guaranteed investment contracts
   d. Trade union

Chapter 36. Exchange Rates, the Balance of Payments, and Trade Deficits

1. The _____ is published by The Economist as an informal way of measuring the purchasing power parity (PPP) between two currencies and provides a test of the extent to which market exchange rates result in goods costing the same in different countries. It 'seeks to make exchange-rate theory a bit more digestible'.

The index takes its name from the Big Mac, a hamburger sold at McDonald's restaurants.

   a. Deindexation
   b. Cost-weighted activity index
   c. Rank mobility index
   d. Big Mac index

2. In finance, the _____s between two currencies specifies how much one currency is worth in terms of the other. It is the value of a foreign natione;s currency in terms of the home natione;s currency. For example an _____ of 102 Japanese yen to the United States dollar means that JPY 102 is worth the same as USD 1.
   a. ACEA agreement
   b. ACCRA Cost of Living Index
   c. Interbank market
   d. Exchange rate

3. In economics, the _____ measures the payments that flow between any individual country and all other countries. It is used to summarize all international economic transactions for that country during a specific time period, usually a year. The _____ is determined by the country's exports and imports of goods, services, and financial capital, as well as financial transfers.
   a. Gross domestic product per barrel
   b. Balance of payments
   c. Gross world product
   d. Skyscraper Index

4. The _____ of monetary management established the rules for commercial and financial relations among the world's major industrial states in the mid 20th Century. The _____ was the first example of a fully negotiated monetary order intended to govern monetary relations among independent nation-states.

Preparing to rebuild the international economic system as World War II was still raging, 730 delegates from all 44 Allied nations gathered at the Mount Washington Hotel in Bretton Woods, New Hampshire, United States, for the United Nations Monetary and Financial Conference.

   a. 1921 recession
   b. Bretton Woods system
   c. 100-year flood
   d. 130-30 fund

5. _____ is money accepted for exchange of goods in an economy. The prevalence of one money over another arises, usually, when a government designates through decrees that the government shall accept only particular notes and coins in payment for taxes. Typically, money of _____ consists of stamped coins and minted paper bills.
   a. Totnes pound
   b. Local currency
   c. Security thread
   d. Currency

6. In economics, an _____ is any good or commodity, transported from one country to another country in a legitimate fashion, typically for use in trade. _____ goods or services are provided to foreign consumers by domestic producers. _____ is an important part of international trade.
   a. ACEA agreement
   b. Export
   c. ACCRA Cost of Living Index
   d. AD-IA Model

7. The _____ is where currency trading takes place. It is where banks and other official institutions facilitate the buying and selling of foreign currencies. FX transactions typically involve one party purchasing a quantity of one currency in exchange for paying a quantity of another.
   a. Currency swap
   b. Foreign exchange market
   c. Floating currency
   d. Covered interest arbitrage

8. In economics, an _____ is any good (e.g. a commodity) or service brought into one country from another country in a legitimate fashion, typically for use in trade. It is a good that is brought in from another country for sale. _____ goods or services are provided to domestic consumers by foreign producers. An _____ in the receiving country is an export to the sending country.
   a. Economic integration
   b. Import quota
   c. Import
   d. Incoterms

9. A _____ is a general term that describes any government policy or regulation that restricts international trade. The barriers can take many forms, including the following terms that include many restrictions in international trade within multiple countries that import and export any items of trade.

   - Import duty
   - Import licenses
   - Export licenses
   - Import quotas
   - Tariffs
   - Subsidies
   - Non-tariff barriers to trade
   - Voluntary Export Restraints
   - Local Content Requirements
   - Embargo

   Most _____s work on the same principle: the imposition of some sort of cost on trade that raises the price of the traded products. If two or more nations repeatedly use _____s against each other, then a trade war results.

   a. Global financial system
   b. Certificate of origin
   c. National Foreign Trade Council
   d. Trade barrier

10. In economics, _____ refers to the ability of a party to produce a good or service using fewer real resources than another entity producing the same good or service..A party has an _____ when using the same input as another party, it can produce a greater output. Since _____ is determined by a simple comparison of labor productivities, it is possible for a a party to have no _____ in anything. It can be contrasted with the concept of comparative advantage which refers to the ability to produce a particular good at a lower opportunity cost.
    a. ACCRA Cost of Living Index
    b. Index number
    c. International economics
    d. Absolute advantage

11. The _____ is 'the basic residential unit in which economic production, consumption, inheritance, child rearing, and shelter are organized and carried out'; [the _____] 'may or may not be synonomous with family'.

Chapter 36. Exchange Rates, the Balance of Payments, and Trade Deficits 499

The _____ is the basic unit of analysis in many social, microeconomic and government models. The term refers to all individuals who live in the same dwelling.

a. Family economics
c. 130-30 fund
b. 100-year flood
d. Household

12. A variety of measures of _____ and output are used in economics to estimate total economic activity in a country or region, including gross domestic product (GDP), gross national product (GNP), and net _____

There are three main ways of calculating these numbers; the output approach, the income approach and the expenditure approach. In theory, the three must yield the same, because total expenditures on goods and services must equal the total income paid to the producers (Gnational income), and that must also equal the total value of the output of goods and services (GNP.)

a. Gross world product
c. Volume index
b. GNI per capita
d. National income

13. A _____ is the transfer of wealth from one party (such as a person or company) to another. A _____ is usually made in exchange for the provision of goods, services or both, or to fulfill a legal obligation.

The simplest and oldest form of _____ is barter, the exchange of one good or service for another.

a. Soft count
c. Going concern
b. Social gravity
d. Payment

14. _____ is the a method of technical and economic research of the systems for purpose to optimize a parity between system's consumer functions or properties and expenses to achieve those functions or properties.

This methodology for continuous perfection of production, industrial technologies, organizational structures was developed by Juryj Sobolev in 1948 at the 'Perm telephone factory'

- 1948 Juryj Sobolev - the first success in application of a method analysis at the 'Perm telephone factory' .
- 1949 - the first application for the invention as result of use of the new method.

Today in economically developed countries practically each enterprise or the company use methodology of the kind of functional-cost analysis as a practice of the quality management, most full satisfying to principles of standards of series ISO 9000.

- Interest of consumer not in products itself, but the advantage which it will receive from its usage.
- The consumer aspires to reduce his expenses
- Functions needed by consumer can be executed in the various ways, and, hence, with various efficiency and expenses. Among possible alternatives of realization of functions exist such in which the parity of quality and the price is the optimal for the consumer.

The goal of _____ is achievement of the highest consumer satisfaction of production at simultaneous decrease in all kinds of industrial expenses Classical _____ has three English synonyms - Value Engineering, Value Management, Value Analysis.

a. Willingness to pay
b. Staple financing
c. Monopoly wage
d. Function cost analysis

15. The _____ is the difference between the monetary value of exports and imports in an economy over a certain period of time. It is the relationship between a nation's imports and exports. A positive _____ is known as a trade surplus and consists of exporting more than is imported; a negative _____ is known as a trade deficit or, informally, a trade gap.

a. Balance of trade
b. Rational expectations
c. Marginal propensity to import
d. SIMIC

16. A _____ refers to any type debt instrument, such as a loan, bond, mortgage that does not have a fixed rate of interest over the life of the instrument. Such debt typically uses an index or other base rate for establishing the interest rate for each relevant period. One of the most common rates to use as the basis for applying interest rates is the London Inter-bank Offered Rate, or LIBOR

a. Floating interest rate
b. Disposal tax effect
c. Moneylender
d. Money market

17. In economics, the _____ is one of the two primary components of the balance of payments, the other being the capital account. It is the sum of the balance of trade (exports minus imports of goods and services), net factor income (such as interest and dividends) and net transfer payments (such as foreign aid.)

$$\text{Current account} = \text{Balance of trade} \\ + \text{Net factor income from abroad} \\ + \text{Net unilateral transfers from abroad}$$

The _____ balance is one of two major metrics of the nature of a country's foreign trade (the other being the net capital outflow.)

a. Compensation of employees
b. Gross private domestic investment
c. National Income and Product Accounts
d. Current account

18. _____s is the social science that studies the production, distribution, and consumption of goods and services. The term _____s comes from the Ancient Greek oá¼°κονομῖα from oá¼¶κος (oikos, 'house') + vΐŒμος (nomos, 'custom' or 'law'), hence 'rules of the house(hold)'. Current _____ models developed out of the broader field of political economy in the late 19th century, owing to a desire to use an empirical approach more akin to the physical sciences.

a. Inflation
b. Opportunity cost
c. Energy economics
d. Economic

19. A _____ is an object whose consumption increases the utility of the consumer, for which the quantity demanded exceeds the quantity supplied at zero price. _____s are usually modeled as having diminishing marginal utility. The first individual purchase has high utility; the second has less.

a. Composite good
b. Pie method
c. Merit good
d. Good

20. In financial accounting, the _____ is one of the accounts in shareholders' equity. Sole proprietorships have a single _____ in the owner's equity. Partnerships maintain a _____ for each of the partners.
   a. Compensation of employees
   b. Current account
   c. Net national product
   d. Capital account

21. In economics, _____ refers to an activity of spending which increases the availability of fixed capital goods or means of production. It is the total spending on new fixed investment minus replacement investment, which simply replaces depreciated capital goods.
   a. Lehman Formula
   b. Greenfield investment
   c. Tangible investments
   d. Net investment

22. The balance of trade (or net exports, sometimes symbolized as NX) is the difference between the monetary value of exports and imports in an economy over a certain period of time. It is the relationship between a nation's imports and exports. A favorable balance of trade is known as a trade surplus and consists of exporting more than is imported; an unfavorable balance of trade is known as a _____ or, informally, a trade gap.
   a. Complementary asset
   b. Computational economic
   c. Demographics of India
   d. Trade deficit

23. The balance of trade (or net exports, sometimes symbolized as NX) is the difference between the monetary value of exports and imports in an economy over a certain period of time. It is the relationship between a nation's imports and exports. A favorable balance of trade is known as a _____ and consists of exporting more than is imported; an unfavorable balance of trade is known as a trade deficit or, informally, a trade gap.
   a. Business valuation standards
   b. Dividend unit
   c. Trade surplus
   d. Black-Scholes

24. In economics, economic output is divided into physical goods and intangible services. Consumption of _____ is assumed to produce utility. It is often used when referring to a _____ Tax.
   a. Manufactured goods
   b. Goods and services
   c. Private good
   d. Composite good

25. The Federal Reserve System (also the Federal Reserve; informally The Fed) is the central banking system of the United States. Created in 1913 by the enactment of the Federal Reserve Act (signed by Woodrow Wilson), it is a quasi-public and quasi-private (government entity with private components) banking system that comprises (1) the presidentially appointed Board of Governors of the Federal Reserve System in Washington, D.C.; (2) the Federal Open Market Committee; (3) twelve regional _____ located in major cities throughout the nation acting as fiscal agents for the U.S. Treasury, each with its own nine-member board of directors; (4) numerous other private U.S. member banks, which subscribe to required amounts of non-transferable stock in their regional _____; and (5) various advisory councils. Since February 2006, Ben Bernanke has served as the Chairman of the Board of Governors of the Federal Reserve System.
   a. Federal funds
   b. Federal Reserve Banks
   c. Fed Funds Probability
   d. Federal Open Market Committee

26. The _____ is an international organization that oversees the global financial system by following the macroeconomic policies of its member countries, in particular those with an impact on exchange rates and the balance of payments. It is an organization formed to stabilize international exchange rates and facilitate development. It also offers financial and technical assistance to its members, making it an international lender of last resort.

   a. ACCRA Cost of Living Index
   b. ACEA agreement
   c. Office of Thrift Supervision
   d. International Monetary Fund

27. The _____ was an evolution of developed countries from an industrial/manufacturing-based wealth producing economy into a service sector asset based economy, brought about by globalization and currency manipulation by governments and their central banks. Some analysts claimed that this change in the economic structure of the United States had created a state of permanent steady growth, low unemployment, and immunity to boom and bust macroeconomic cycles. They believed that the change rendered obsolete many business practices.

   a. 100-year flood
   b. 130-30 fund
   c. 1921 recession
   d. New Economy

28. A _____, reserve bank, or monetary authority is the entity responsible for the monetary policy of a country or of a group of member states. It is a bank that can lend money to other banks in times of need. Its primary responsibility is to maintain the stability of the national currency and money supply, but more active duties include controlling subsidized-loan interest rates, and acting as a lender of last resort to the banking sector during times of financial crisis (private banks often being integral to the national financial system.)

   a. 100-year flood
   b. 130-30 fund
   c. 1921 recession
   d. Central bank

29. A _____, sometimes called a pegged exchange rate, is a type of exchange rate regime wherein a currency's value is matched to the value of another single currency or to a basket of other currencies such as gold.

A _____ is usually used to stabilize the value of a currency, vis-a-vis the currency it is pegged to. This facilitates trade and investments between the two countries, and is especially useful for small economies where external trade forms a large part of their GDP.

   a. Leading indicators
   b. Fixed exchange rate
   c. Monetary economics
   d. Law of supply

30. _____ is a broad label that refers to any individuals or households that use goods and services generated within the economy. The concept of a _____ is used in different contexts, so that the usage and significance of the term may vary.

Typically when business people and economists talk of _____s they are talking about person as _____, an aggregated commodity item with little individuality other than that expressed in the buy/not-buy decision.

   a. 130-30 fund
   b. 100-year flood
   c. Consumer
   d. 1921 recession

31. _____ is a term used in accounting, economics and finance to spread the cost of an asset over the span of several years.

Chapter 36. Exchange Rates, the Balance of Payments, and Trade Deficits

In simple words we can say that _____ is the reduction in the value of an asset due to usage, passage of time, wear and tear, technological outdating or obsolescence, depletion, inadequacy, rot, rust, decay or other such factors.

In accounting, _____ is a term used to describe any method of attributing the historical or purchase cost of an asset across its useful life, roughly corresponding to normal wear and tear.

a. Salvage value
c. Net income per employee
b. Depreciation
d. Historical cost

32. A _____ product is a product designed for cheapness and short-term convenience rather than medium to long-term durability, with most products only intended for single use. The term is also sometimes used for products that may last several months (ex. _____ air filters) to distinguish from similar products that last indefinitely (ex.

a. 100-year flood
c. 1921 recession
b. 130-30 fund
d. Disposable

33. _____ is gross income minus income tax on that income.

Discretionary income is income after subtracting taxes and normal expenses (such as rent or mortgage, utilities, insurance, medical, transportation, property maintenance, child support, inflation, food and sundries, 'c.) to maintain a certain standard of living.

a. Stamp Act
c. Disposable personal income
b. Taxation as theft
d. Disposable income

34. A _____ or a flexible exchange rate is a type of exchange rate regime wherein a currency's value is allowed to fluctuate according to the foreign exchange market. A currency that uses a _____ is known as a floating currency. The opposite of a _____ is a fixed exchange rate.

a. Floating currency
c. Floating exchange rate
b. Foreign exchange market
d. Trade Weighted US dollar Index

35. _____ is a term used in accounting relating to the increase in value of an asset. In this sense it is the reverse of depreciation, which measures the fall in value of assets over their normal life-time.

_____ is a rise of a currency in a floating exchange rate.

a. Appreciation
c. ACCRA Cost of Living Index
b. ACEA agreement
d. AD-IA Model

36. In economics and business, specifically cost accounting, the _____ point (BEP) is the point at which cost or expenses and revenue are equal: there is no net loss or gain, and one has 'broken even'. A profit or a loss has not been made, although opportunity costs have been paid, and capital has received the risk-adjusted, expected return.

For example, if the business sells less than 200 tables each month, it will make a loss, if it sells more, it will be a profit.

a. Break-even
b. Nonmarket
c. Buffer stock scheme
d. Small numbers game

37. Economics:

- _____, the desire to own something and the ability to pay for it
- _____ curve, a graphic representation of a _____ schedule
- _____ deposit, the money in checking accounts
- _____ pull theory, the theory that inflation occurs when _____ for goods and services exceeds existing supplies
- _____ schedule, a table that lists the quantity of a good a person will buy it each different price
- _____ side economics, the school of economics at believes government spending and tax cuts open economy by raising _____

a. Variability
b. Production
c. McKesson ' Robbins scandal
d. Demand

38. In algebra, a _____ is a function depending on n that associates a scalar, det(A), to an n×n square matrix A. The fundamental geometric meaning of a _____ is a scale factor for measure when A is regarded as a linear transformation. _____s are important both in calculus, where they enter the substitution rule for several variables, and in multilinear algebra.

For a fixed nonnegative integer n, there is a unique _____ function for the n×n matrices over any commutative ring R. In particular, this function exists when R is the field of real or complex numbers.

a. 100-year flood
b. 130-30 fund
c. 1921 recession
d. Determinant

39. _____ in economics and business is the result of an exchange and from that trade we assign a numerical monetary value to a good, service or asset. If Alice trades Bob 4 apples for an orange, the _____ of an orange is 4 apples. Inversely, the _____ of an apple is 1/4 oranges.

a. Price book
b. Premium pricing
c. Price
d. Price war

40. A _____ is a hypothetical measure of overall prices for some set of goods and services, in a given region during a given interval, normalized relative to some base set. Typically, a _____ is approximated with a price index.

The classical dichotomy is the assumption that there is a relatively clean distinction between overall increases or decreases in prices and underlying, e;reale; economic variables.

a. Price level
b. Discouraged worker
c. Discretionary spending
d. Price elasticity of supply

41. _____ refers to a business or organization attempting to acquire goods or services to accomplish the goals of the enterprise. Though there are several organizations that attempt to set standards in the _____ process, processes can vary greatly between organizations. Typically the word '_____' is not used interchangeably with the word 'procurement', since procurement typically includes Expediting, Supplier Quality, and Traffic and Logistics (T'L) in addition to _____.
a. Purchasing
b. Free port
c. 130-30 fund
d. 100-year flood

42. _____ is the number of goods/services that can be purchased with a unit of currency. For example, if you had taken one dollar to a store in the 1950s, you would have been able to buy a greater number of items than you would today, indicating that you would have had a greater _____ in the 1950s. Currency can be either a commodity money, like gold or silver, or fiat currency like US dollars.
a. Human Poverty Index
b. Compliance cost
c. Purchasing power
d. Genuine progress indicator

43. The _____ theory uses the long-term equilibrium exchange rate of two currencies to equalize their purchasing power. Developed by Gustav Cassel in 1920, it is based on the law of one price: the theory states that, in ideally efficient markets, identical goods should have only one price.

This purchasing power SEM rate equalizes the purchasing power of different currencies in their home countries for a given basket of goods.

a. Bureau of Labor Statistics
b. Measures of national income and output
c. Gross national product
d. Purchasing power parity

44. _____ describes a deliberate attempt to interfere with the free and fair operation of the market and create artificial, false or misleading appearances with respect to the price of a security, commodity or currency. _____ is prohibited under Section 9(a)(2) of the Securities Exchange Act of 1934, and in Australia under Section s 1041A of the Corporations Act 2001. The Act defines _____ as transactions which create an artificial price or maintain an artificial price for a tradable security.
a. Managerial economics
b. Market manipulation
c. Legal monopoly
d. Net domestic product

45. _____ is a fee paid on borrowed assets. It is the price paid for the use of borrowed money , or, money earned by deposited funds . Assets that are sometimes lent with _____ include money, shares, consumer goods through hire purchase, major assets such as aircraft, and even entire factories in finance lease arrangements.
a. Asset protection
b. Interest
c. Internal debt
d. Insolvency

46. An _____ is the price a borrower pays for the use of money they do not own, for instance a small company might borrow from a bank to kick start their business, and the return a lender receives for deferring the use of funds, by lending it to the borrower. _____s are normally expressed as a percentage rate over the period of one year.

_____s targets are also a vital tool of monetary policy and are used to control variables like investment, inflation, and unemployment.

a. Enterprise value
c. Arrow-Debreu model
b. ACCRA Cost of Living Index
d. Interest rate

47. In finance, _____ is a financial action that does not promise safety of the initial investment along with the return on the principal sum. _____ typically involves the lending of money or the purchase of assets, equity or debt but in a manner that has not been given thorough analysis or is deemed to have low margin of safety or a significant risk of the loss of the principal investment. The term, '_____,' which is formally defined as above in Graham and Dodd's 1934 text, Security Analysis, contrasts with the term 'investment,' which is a financial operation that, upon thorough analysis, promises safety of principal and a satisfactory return.
   a. Global Financial Centres Index
   c. Municipal Bond Arbitrage
   b. Hybrid market
   d. Speculation

48. The _____ or Aggregate Demand-Aggregate Supply model is a macroeconomic model that explains price level and output through the relationship of aggregate demand and aggregate supply. It was first put forth by John Maynard Keynes in his work The General Theory of Employment, Interest, and Money. It is the foundation for the modern field of macroeconomics, and is accepted by a broad array of economists, from Libertarian, Monetarist supporters of laissez-faire, such as Milton Friedman to Socialist, Post-Keynesian supporters of economic interventionism, such as Joan Robinson.
   a. IS/LM model
   c. Adaptive expectations
   b. Economic interdependence
   d. AD-AS

49. A fixed exchange rate, sometimes called a _____, is a type of exchange rate regime wherein a currency's value is matched to the value of another single currency or to a basket of other currencies such as gold.

A fixed exchange rate is usually used to stabilize the value of a currency, vis-a-vis the currency it is pegged to. This facilitates trade and investments between the two countries, and is especially useful for small economies where external trade forms a large part of their GDP.

a. Pegged exchange rate
c. Recession
b. Mainstream economics
d. Leading indicators

50. In international economics and international trade, _____ or _____ is the relative prices of a country's export to import. '_____' are sometimes used as a proxy for the relative social welfare of a country, but this heuristic is technically questionable and should be used with extreme caution. An improvement in a nation's _____ is good for that country in the sense that it has to pay less for the products it import.
   a. Terms of trade
   c. Kennedy Round
   b. Commercial invoice
   d. Common market

51. Necessary _____s:

If x is a necessary _____ of y, then the presence of y necessarily implies the presence of x. The presence of x, however, does not imply that y will occur.

Sufficient _____s:

If x is a sufficient _____ of y, then the presence of x necessarily implies the presence of y.

a. Political philosophy
b. Philosophy of economics
c. Materialism
d. Cause

52. _____ is the electoral problem resulting from competition between two or more candidates or political parties from the same or approximate location in the political ideological spectrum or space against an opposing candidate or political party from the other side of the political ideological spectrum or space. The resulting fragmentation of political support may result in electoral defeat. _____s, and thus political calculations attempting to avoid them, appear most frequently in elections involving executives and representatives from single member districts.

a. 100-year flood
b. 1921 recession
c. Coordination failure
d. 130-30 fund

53. In economics, _____ is the difference between a company's total revenue and its opportunity costs. It is the increase in wealth that an investor has from making an investment, taking into consideration all costs associated with that investment including the opportunity cost of capital.

Profit is the factor income of the entrepreneur.

a. ACCRA Cost of Living Index
b. Accounting profit
c. Operating profit
d. Economic profit

54. The underground economy or _____ is a market where all commerce is conducted without regard to taxation, law or regulations of trade. The term is also often known as the underdog, shadow economy, black economy, parallel economy or phantom trades.

In modern societies the underground economy covers a vast array of activities.

a. Market economy
b. Protectionism
c. Social market economy
d. Black market

55. _____ is the controlled distribution of resources and scarce goods or services. _____ controls the size of the ration, one's allotted portion of the resources being distributed on a particular day or at a particular time.

In economics, it is often common to use the word '_____' to refer to one of the roles that prices play in markets, while _____ is called 'non-price _____.' Using prices to ration means that those with the most money (or other assets) and who want a product the most are first to receive it.

a. 130-30 fund
b. 100-year flood
c. Rationing
d. 1921 recession

56. The _____ is a monetary system in which a region's common medium of exchange are paper notes that are normally freely convertible into pre-set, fixed quantities of gold. The _____ is not currently used by any government, having been replaced completely by fiat currency. Gold certificates were used as paper currency in the United States from 1882 to 1933, these certificates were freely convertable into gold coins.

In the 1790s Britain suffered a massive shortage of silver coinage and ceased to mint larger silver coins.

- a. 1921 recession
- b. Gold standard
- c. 100-year flood
- d. 130-30 fund

57. _____ and Keynesian Theory) is a macroeconomic theory based on the ideas of 20th-century British economist John Maynard Keynes. _____ argues that private sector decisions sometimes lead to inefficient macroeconomic outcomes and therefore advocates active policy responses by the public sector, including monetary policy actions by the central bank and fiscal policy actions by the government to stabilize output over the business cycle.

The theories forming the basis of _____ were first presented in The General Theory of Employment, Interest and Money, published in 1936.

- a. Keynesian economics
- b. Market failure
- c. Rational choice theory
- d. Deflation

58. _____ is a reduction in the value of a currency with respect to other monetary units. In common modern usage, it specifically implies an official lowering of the value of a country's currency within a fixed exchange rate system, by which the monetary authority formally sets a new fixed rate with respect to a foreign reference currency. In contrast, (currency) depreciation is used for the unofficial decrease in the exchange rate in a floating exchange rate system.

- a. Devaluation
- b. Petrodollar recycling
- c. Texas redbacks
- d. Reserve currency

59. The _____ was a worldwide economic downturn starting in most places in 1929 and ending at different times in the 1930s or early 1940s for different countries. It was the largest and most important economic depression in the 20th century, and is used in the 21st century as an example of how far the world's economy can fall. The _____ originated in the United States; historians most often use as a starting date the stock market crash on October 29, 1929, known as Black Tuesday.

- a. Jarrow March
- b. British Empire Economic Conference
- c. Wall Street Crash of 1929
- d. Great Depression

60. _____ is the process by which the government, central bank (ii) availability of money, and (iii) cost of money or rate of interest, in order to attain a set of objectives oriented towards the growth and stability of the economy. Monetary theory provides insight into how to craft optimal _____.

_____ is referred to as either being an expansionary policy where an expansionary policy increases the total supply of money in the economy, and a contractionary policy decreases the total money supply.

- a. 130-30 fund
- b. 1921 recession
- c. 100-year flood
- d. Monetary policy

Chapter 36. Exchange Rates, the Balance of Payments, and Trade Deficits

61. In economics, _____ is the total amount of money available in an economy at a particular point in time. There are several ways to define 'money', but standard measures usually include currency in circulation and demand deposits.

_____ data are recorded and published, usually by the government or the central bank of the country.

a. Money supply
c. Veil of money
b. Neutrality of money
d. Velocity of money

62. The term _____ refers to government debt, expenditures and revenues, or to finance (particularly financial revenue) in general.

- _____ deficit is the budget deficit of federal or local government
- _____ policy is the discretionary spending of governments. Contrasts with monetary policy.
- _____ year and _____ quarter are reporting periods for firms and other agencies.

a. Fiscal
c. Procter ' Gamble
b. Drawdown
d. Bucket shop

63. In economics, _____ is the use of government spending and revenue collection to influence the economy.

_____ can be contrasted with the other main type of economic policy, monetary policy, which attempts to stabilize the economy by controlling interest rates and the supply of money. The two main instruments of _____ are government spending and taxation.

a. Fiscalism
c. Sustainable investment rule
b. 100-year flood
d. Fiscal policy

64. In cases of extreme appreciation or depreciation, a central bank will normally intervene to stabilize the currency. Thus, the exchange rate regimes of floating currencies may more technically be known as a _____. A central bank might, for instance, allow a currency price to float freely between an upper and lower bound, a price 'ceiling' and 'floor'.

a. Continuous linked settlement
c. Managed float
b. Foreign exchange reserves
d. Triangular arbitrage

65. A currency crisis, which is also called a balance-of-payments crisis, occurs when the value of a currency changes quickly, undermining its ability to serve as a medium of exchange or a store of value. It is a type of financial crisis and is often associated with a real economic crisis. _____ can be especially destructive to small open economies or bigger, but not sufficiently stable ones.

a. 100-year flood
c. Currency crises
b. 130-30 fund
d. 1921 recession

66. The _____ or gross domestic income (GDI), a basic measure of an economy's economic performance, is the market value of all final goods and services produced within the borders of a nation in a year. _____ can be defined in three ways, all of which are conceptually identical. First, it is equal to the total expenditures for all final goods and services produced within the country in a stipulated period of time (usually a 365-day year).

a. Monopolistic competition
c. Market structure

b. Countercyclical
d. Gross domestic product

67. A _____ is a normalized average (typically a weighted average) of prices for a given class of goods or services in a given region, during a given interval of time. It is a statistic designed to help to compare how these prices, taken as a whole, differ between time periods or geographical locations.

Price indices have several potential uses.

a. Product sabotage
c. Transactional Net Margin Method

b. Price index
d. Two-part tariff

68. A _____ is:

- Rewrite _____, in generative grammar and computer science
- Standardization, a formal and widely-accepted statement, fact, definition, or qualification
- Operation, a determinate _____ for performing a mathematical operation and obtaining a certain result (Mathematics, Logic)
    - Unary operation
    - Binary operation
- _____ of inference, a function from sets of formulae to formulae (Mathematics, Logic)
- _____ of thumb, principle with broad application that is not intended to be strictly accurate or reliable for every situation. Also often simply referred to as a _____
- Moral, an atomic element of a moral code for guiding choices in human behavior
- Heuristic, a quantized '_____' which shows a tendency or probability for successful function
- A regulation, as in sports
- A Production _____, as in computer science
- Procedural law, a _____ set governing the application of laws to cases
    - A law, which may informally be called a '_____'
    - A court ruling, a decision by a court
- In the U.S. Government, a regulation mandated by Congress, but written or expanded upon by the Executive Branch.
- Norm (sociology), an informal but widely accepted _____, concept, truth, definition, or qualification (social norms, legal norms, coding norms)
- Norm (philosophy), a kind of sentence or a reason to act, feel or believe
- 'Rulership' is the concept of governance by a government:
    - Military _____, governance by a military body
    - Monastic _____, a collection of precepts that guides the life of monks or nuns in a religious order where the superior holds the place of Christ
- Slide _____

- '_____,' a song by Ayumi Hamasaki
- '_____,' a song by rapper Nas
- '_____s,' an album by the band The Whitest Boy Alive
- _____s: Pyaar Ka Superhit Formula, a 2003 Bollywood film
- ruler, an instrument for measuring lengths
- _____, a component of an astrolabe, circumferator or similar instrument
- The _____s, a bestselling self-help book
- _____ Project (Run Up-to-date Linux Everywhere), a project that aims to use up-to-date Linux software on old PCs
- _____ engine, a software system that helps managing business _____s
- Ja _____, a hip hop artist
    - R.U.L.E., a 2005 greatest hits album by rapper Ja _____
- '_____s,' a KMFDM song

a. Procter ' Gamble
b. Technocracy
c. Demand
d. Rule

69. _____ is a common concept in economics, and gives rise to derived concepts such as consumer debt. Generally _____ is defined by opposition to production. But the precise definition can vary because different schools of economists define production quite differently.
    a. Foreclosure data providers
    b. Federal Reserve Bank Notes
    c. Consumption
    d. Cash or share options

70. In economics a _____ is an entity that owes a debt to someone else. The entity may be an individual, a firm, a government, a company or other legal person. The counterparty is called a creditor.
    a. Duration gap
    b. Senior stretch loan
    c. Decision process tool
    d. Debtor

ANSWER KEY

Chapter 1
1. b	2. d	3. d	4. b	5. d	6. d	7. d	8. d	9. b	10. d
11. d	12. c	13. d	14. d	15. d	16. d	17. d	18. d	19. c	20. a
21. a	22. d	23. c	24. d	25. d	26. a	27. d	28. d	29. d	30. a
31. d	32. d	33. d	34. b	35. b	36. d	37. d	38. d	39. d	40. b
41. d	42. c	43. a	44. b	45. d	46. a	47. a	48. d	49. b	50. d
51. a	52. d	53. d	54. d	55. c	56. d	57. b	58. b	59. c	60. d
61. d	62. b	63. d	64. d	65. b	66. d	67. b	68. d	69. c	70. b
71. d	72. a	73. d	74. b	75. a	76. d	77. c	78. d		

Chapter 2
1. d	2. d	3. d	4. a	5. c	6. d	7. d	8. b	9. d	10. a
11. d	12. d	13. d	14. c	15. b	16. d	17. d	18. d	19. b	20. d
21. d	22. a	23. d	24. a	25. d	26. d	27. a	28. d	29. b	30. d
31. d	32. b	33. d	34. a	35. a	36. b	37. d	38. d	39. d	40. d
41. c	42. c	43. d	44. d	45. d	46. d	47. d	48. a	49. d	50. d
51. c	52. b	53. c	54. c	55. d	56. b	57. d	58. b	59. d	60. d
61. b	62. a	63. d	64. d	65. d	66. a	67. c	68. d	69. d	70. b
71. a	72. d	73. d	74. a						

Chapter 3
1. a	2. d	3. b	4. d	5. d	6. d	7. d	8. b	9. d	10. d
11. d	12. d	13. d	14. d	15. b	16. c	17. d	18. a	19. a	20. d
21. d	22. b	23. d	24. d	25. a	26. b	27. a	28. d	29. d	30. b
31. d	32. b	33. d	34. d	35. d	36. b	37. a	38. a	39. a	40. c
41. d	42. d	43. d	44. d	45. d	46. a	47. a	48. a	49. d	50. c
51. d	52. c	53. d	54. a	55. d	56. d	57. a	58. d	59. a	60. a
61. d	62. d	63. d	64. d	65. d	66. b				

Chapter 4
1. c	2. d	3. a	4. d	5. d	6. d	7. d	8. a	9. d	10. d
11. b	12. a	13. d	14. d	15. a	16. d	17. c	18. d	19. c	20. c
21. b	22. a	23. d	24. d	25. a	26. c	27. b	28. d	29. a	30. c
31. c	32. d	33. d	34. a	35. d	36. a	37. b	38. d	39. d	40. a
41. b	42. c	43. c	44. c	45. d	46. d	47. d	48. a	49. d	50. a
51. c	52. a	53. a	54. d	55. b	56. d	57. d	58. b	59. d	60. c
61. c	62. d	63. d	64. d	65. d	66. a	67. d	68. b	69. d	70. c
71. d	72. d	73. d	74. a	75. b	76. d	77. d	78. a	79. b	80. d
81. d	82. b	83. b	84. d	85. b	86. c	87. d	88. d	89. c	90. b
91. d	92. d	93. d	94. d	95. b	96. d	97. d	98. d		

Chapter 5

1. c	2. d	3. b	4. d	5. b	6. a	7. c	8. a	9. d	10. d
11. c	12. a	13. d	14. c	15. d	16. b	17. d	18. b	19. b	20. c
21. a	22. b	23. c	24. d	25. d	26. b	27. d	28. b	29. c	30. d
31. d	32. b	33. d	34. d	35. d	36. d	37. c	38. c	39. a	40. d
41. d	42. d	43. d	44. d	45. d	46. d	47. b	48. b	49. d	50. d
51. c	52. d	53. c	54. d	55. b	56. b	57. d	58. d	59. d	60. c
61. d	62. c	63. d	64. c	65. d	66. d	67. c	68. d	69. b	

Chapter 6

1. a	2. c	3. d	4. d	5. d	6. d	7. d	8. c	9. d	10. d
11. d	12. c	13. d	14. d	15. a	16. a	17. d	18. a	19. c	20. b
21. b	22. b	23. d	24. d	25. a	26. d	27. d	28. d	29. a	30. c
31. d	32. d	33. d	34. c	35. b	36. c	37. d	38. a	39. d	40. d
41. d	42. b	43. c	44. b	45. d	46. d	47. d	48. b	49. b	50. d
51. d	52. a	53. c	54. a	55. d	56. d	57. d	58. d	59. c	60. d
61. a	62. b	63. c	64. d	65. b	66. b	67. a	68. d	69. d	70. d
71. d	72. d	73. d	74. d	75. d	76. d	77. d	78. a	79. a	

Chapter 7

1. c	2. a	3. a	4. b	5. d	6. d	7. b	8. c	9. d	10. d
11. c	12. d	13. d	14. d	15. b	16. b	17. a	18. c	19. b	20. d
21. d	22. b	23. d	24. b	25. b	26. d	27. a	28. d	29. d	30. c
31. d	32. b	33. a	34. d	35. c	36. c	37. c	38. d	39. d	40. a
41. d	42. c	43. d	44. d	45. d	46. d	47. d	48. d	49. a	50. d
51. a	52. b	53. c	54. d	55. c	56. c	57. d	58. a	59. a	60. d
61. b	62. a	63. b	64. d	65. d	66. d	67. b	68. d	69. d	70. d
71. a	72. d	73. d	74. c	75. d	76. a	77. a	78. b	79. a	80. d
81. a	82. a	83. d	84. b	85. d	86. c	87. d	88. b	89. d	90. b
91. b	92. d	93. a	94. b	95. d	96. a	97. c	98. a	99. b	100. c
101. d	102. d								

Chapter 8

1. b	2. a	3. b	4. d	5. a	6. d	7. b	8. b	9. d	10. d
11. d	12. d	13. c	14. d	15. b	16. a	17. d	18. d	19. c	20. d
21. a	22. a	23. c	24. d	25. d	26. d	27. d	28. c	29. d	30. d
31. c	32. d	33. d	34. b	35. b	36. d	37. d	38. d	39. c	40. d
41. c	42. d	43. d	44. d	45. d	46. d	47. c	48. b	49. a	50. d
51. b	52. c	53. d	54. d	55. d	56. d	57. c	58. d	59. d	60. d
61. a	62. d	63. c							

ANSWER KEY

Chapter 9

1. b	2. a	3. c	4. c	5. d	6. c	7. b	8. d	9. d	10. a
11. d	12. b	13. d	14. d	15. b	16. d	17. d	18. b	19. a	20. d
21. c	22. d	23. d	24. d	25. b	26. d	27. d	28. d	29. b	30. b
31. b	32. b	33. d	34. b	35. d	36. d	37. a	38. d	39. d	40. b
41. d	42. b	43. b	44. d	45. d	46. d	47. d	48. a	49. a	50. a
51. c	52. d	53. a	54. d	55. c	56. d	57. b			

Chapter 10

1. d	2. a	3. b	4. d	5. c	6. b	7. a	8. a	9. a	10. d
11. d	12. b	13. d	14. c	15. d	16. b	17. d	18. d	19. d	20. c
21. c	22. a	23. b	24. d	25. d	26. c	27. c	28. c	29. b	30. a
31. d	32. a	33. d	34. d	35. d	36. b	37. d	38. b	39. a	40. b
41. d	42. d	43. d	44. c	45. c	46. d	47. d	48. d	49. d	50. d
51. d	52. d	53. d	54. d	55. b	56. d	57. d	58. a	59. a	60. a
61. d	62. d	63. a	64. d	65. d	66. b	67. d	68. b	69. d	70. d
71. a	72. d	73. d	74. a	75. d	76. d	77. d	78. d	79. d	80. d
81. b	82. b	83. d	84. a	85. b					

Chapter 11

1. d	2. d	3. a	4. b	5. c	6. d	7. a	8. d	9. b	10. d
11. a	12. d	13. a	14. a	15. d	16. d	17. d	18. d	19. d	20. b
21. d	22. a	23. b	24. b	25. a	26. a	27. d	28. d	29. c	30. d
31. d	32. d	33. a	34. b	35. b	36. b	37. d	38. c	39. d	40. d
41. d	42. d	43. d	44. d	45. c	46. d	47. a	48. d	49. c	50. d
51. b	52. c	53. a	54. c	55. a	56. c	57. d	58. d	59. a	60. c
61. c	62. a	63. b	64. d	65. c	66. a	67. a	68. b	69. c	70. d

Chapter 12

1. d	2. d	3. d	4. d	5. d	6. d	7. d	8. c	9. d	10. b
11. d	12. d	13. c	14. d	15. d	16. a	17. d	18. d	19. a	20. d
21. b	22. d	23. c	24. a	25. d	26. c	27. d	28. d	29. d	30. a
31. d	32. c	33. d	34. d	35. a	36. c	37. d	38. b	39. d	40. c
41. b	42. d	43. a	44. c	45. c	46. a	47. d	48. b	49. b	50. a
51. d	52. d	53. d	54. c	55. d	56. d	57. c	58. a	59. c	60. d
61. b	62. c	63. d	64. b	65. d	66. d	67. b	68. d	69. b	70. b
71. d	72. a	73. b	74. c	75. d	76. d	77. b	78. c	79. d	80. c
81. d	82. b	83. d							

Chapter 13

1. a	2. d	3. d	4. b	5. d	6. c	7. d	8. b	9. d	10. a
11. d	12. b	13. d	14. c	15. d	16. a	17. c	18. d	19. b	20. a
21. d	22. c	23. d	24. d	25. a	26. a	27. d	28. d	29. d	30. b
31. c	32. c								

Chapter 14

1. a	2. a	3. d	4. d	5. d	6. c	7. c	8. c	9. a	10. d
11. c	12. d	13. d	14. b	15. d	16. d	17. c	18. b	19. d	20. d
21. c	22. d	23. d	24. b	25. c	26. d	27. d	28. d	29. d	30. d
31. d	32. c	33. d	34. b	35. d	36. b	37. d	38. d	39. c	40. d
41. b	42. d	43. d	44. a	45. d	46. d	47. c	48. d	49. a	50. a
51. d	52. b	53. c	54. a	55. d	56. d	57. d	58. d	59. d	60. c
61. d	62. c	63. d	64. d	65. c	66. a	67. d	68. c	69. c	70. d
71. b	72. d	73. c	74. c						

Chapter 15

1. c	2. c	3. d	4. b	5. d	6. b	7. d	8. d	9. d	10. a
11. d	12. d	13. a	14. d	15. d	16. d	17. a	18. d	19. c	20. d
21. c	22. d	23. d	24. a	25. c	26. c	27. d	28. a	29. d	30. a
31. d	32. d	33. d	34. d	35. a	36. c	37. a	38. d	39. d	40. b
41. c	42. c	43. b	44. c						

Chapter 16

1. d	2. c	3. d	4. d	5. c	6. d	7. d	8. a	9. a	10. d
11. a	12. d	13. c	14. b	15. a	16. a	17. d	18. d	19. c	20. a
21. d	22. d	23. d	24. d	25. b	26. d	27. d	28. c	29. b	30. b
31. c	32. d	33. d	34. d	35. d	36. d	37. a	38. b	39. a	40. a
41. d	42. b	43. d	44. c	45. c	46. a	47. a	48. d	49. a	50. c
51. a	52. d	53. d	54. d	55. a	56. a	57. b	58. d	59. d	60. d
61. d	62. b								

Chapter 17

1. d	2. d	3. d	4. b	5. b	6. b	7. d	8. c	9. d	10. d
11. d	12. d	13. d	14. a	15. d	16. d	17. d	18. c	19. b	20. a
21. d	22. d	23. d	24. d	25. d	26. a	27. d	28. d	29. c	30. d
31. c	32. d	33. b	34. d	35. d	36. d	37. d	38. b	39. b	40. d
41. d	42. a	43. d	44. c	45. d	46. d	47. a	48. d	49. d	50. b
51. d	52. d	53. a	54. c	55. d	56. d	57. d	58. d	59. d	60. d

Chapter 18

1. a	2. d	3. d	4. d	5. d	6. d	7. c	8. c	9. a	10. d
11. c	12. a	13. a	14. c	15. d	16. a	17. b	18. a	19. d	20. d
21. c	22. d	23. d	24. c	25. d	26. c	27. d	28. d	29. d	30. b
31. c	32. d	33. b	34. c	35. a	36. b	37. a	38. d	39. d	40. d
41. d	42. d	43. c	44. d	45. a	46. b	47. d	48. b	49. b	50. a
51. d	52. d	53. b	54. c	55. c	56. b	57. b	58. d		

ANSWER KEY

Chapter 19

1. c	2. d	3. d	4. d	5. c	6. a	7. d	8. d	9. d	10. c
11. c	12. d	13. d	14. d	15. d	16. a	17. d	18. d	19. d	20. d
21. c	22. b	23. b	24. a	25. b	26. c	27. d	28. a	29. c	30. d
31. a	32. d	33. d	34. d	35. a	36. d	37. d	38. a	39. d	

Chapter 20

1. c	2. d	3. d	4. d	5. c	6. d	7. d	8. d	9. a	10. a
11. d	12. d	13. b	14. d	15. d	16. d	17. b	18. c	19. d	20. a
21. a	22. d	23. b	24. a	25. d	26. d	27. c	28. d	29. c	30. a
31. c	32. d	33. d	34. d	35. b	36. b	37. d	38. b	39. d	40. d

Chapter 21

1. d	2. b	3. c	4. b	5. a	6. c	7. d	8. a	9. d	10. d
11. c	12. d	13. d	14. d	15. d	16. b	17. d	18. b	19. d	20. b
21. d	22. d	23. a	24. d	25. a	26. d	27. d	28. d	29. d	30. d
31. b	32. d	33. d	34. d	35. b	36. d	37. b	38. d	39. d	40. d
41. d	42. d	43. a	44. d	45. d	46. d	47. d	48. a	49. d	50. b
51. c	52. a	53. b	54. d	55. a	56. c	57. c	58. b	59. b	60. c
61. a	62. b	63. d							

Chapter 22

1. d	2. d	3. c	4. c	5. b	6. b	7. d	8. d	9. d	10. b
11. a	12. d	13. a	14. d	15. d	16. c	17. d	18. a	19. b	20. b
21. b	22. a	23. d	24. d	25. d	26. c	27. d	28. d	29. c	30. d
31. d	32. b	33. d	34. c	35. a	36. b	37. b	38. d	39. d	40. c
41. a	42. d	43. d	44. d	45. d	46. d	47. d	48. b	49. d	50. d
51. d	52. d	53. d	54. d	55. d	56. c	57. d	58. d	59. d	60. d
61. d	62. d	63. a	64. a	65. d	66. b				

Chapter 23

1. d	2. d	3. d	4. d	5. d	6. b	7. d	8. c	9. d	10. b
11. d	12. b	13. d	14. b	15. b	16. d	17. d	18. d	19. c	20. a
21. d	22. d	23. a	24. d	25. b	26. a	27. d	28. d	29. d	30. d
31. b	32. c	33. c	34. c	35. a	36. d	37. d	38. d	39. d	40. d
41. c	42. d	43. d	44. a	45. a	46. d	47. d	48. b	49. d	50. a
51. a	52. a	53. c	54. d	55. c	56. d	57. a	58. d	59. d	60. d
61. d	62. d	63. d	64. a	65. b	66. d	67. d	68. b	69. d	70. d
71. d	72. a	73. d	74. d						

Chapter 24

1. c	2. c	3. d	4. d	5. d	6. c	7. d	8. d	9. d	10. a
11. b	12. d	13. d	14. c	15. d	16. d	17. c	18. d	19. c	20. c
21. d	22. d	23. d	24. d	25. b	26. d	27. d	28. c	29. c	30. d
31. b	32. d	33. b	34. d	35. d	36. d	37. d	38. d	39. a	40. d
41. d	42. d	43. d	44. b	45. a	46. c	47. d	48. b	49. d	50. b
51. d	52. c	53. d	54. d	55. d					

Chapter 25

1. a	2. d	3. a	4. d	5. b	6. c	7. a	8. a	9. d	10. d
11. d	12. d	13. d	14. d	15. a	16. a	17. d	18. c	19. c	20. d
21. b	22. d	23. b	24. d	25. d	26. d	27. d	28. d	29. b	30. b
31. d	32. a	33. a	34. b	35. b	36. b	37. c	38. c	39. d	40. a
41. d	42. d	43. c	44. d	45. d	46. d	47. c			

Chapter 26

1. d	2. a	3. c	4. d	5. d	6. d	7. d	8. a	9. d	10. d
11. d	12. a	13. c	14. d	15. d	16. b	17. b	18. b	19. d	20. b
21. c	22. d	23. d	24. d	25. d	26. d	27. b	28. a	29. a	30. a
31. a	32. b	33. c	34. b	35. d	36. d	37. a	38. c	39. c	40. d
41. d	42. b	43. d	44. b	45. d	46. d	47. a	48. a	49. d	50. d
51. d	52. d	53. d	54. b	55. d	56. b	57. a	58. d		

Chapter 27

1. d	2. c	3. b	4. b	5. d	6. d	7. d	8. d	9. d	10. a
11. c	12. a	13. d	14. d	15. a	16. d	17. d	18. b	19. d	20. a
21. d	22. d	23. d	24. b	25. d	26. b	27. d	28. b	29. d	30. c
31. d	32. d	33. d	34. a	35. b	36. a	37. a	38. d	39. c	40. c
41. d	42. d	43. a	44. c	45. d	46. d	47. c	48. d	49. b	50. d
51. a	52. c	53. b	54. a	55. d	56. b	57. c	58. b	59. a	60. d
61. d	62. d	63. a	64. c	65. d	66. c	67. d	68. d	69. d	70. a
71. c	72. d								

Chapter 28

1. c	2. c	3. d	4. d	5. c	6. c	7. d	8. c	9. a	10. a
11. b	12. d	13. b	14. a	15. c	16. d	17. a	18. d	19. d	20. d
21. d	22. d	23. b	24. d	25. d	26. b	27. b	28. d	29. d	30. d
31. b	32. b	33. d	34. c	35. b	36. b	37. c	38. d	39. c	40. d
41. d	42. a	43. d	44. a	45. d	46. a	47. d			

ANSWER KEY

Chapter 29

1. c	2. c	3. c	4. d	5. d	6. d	7. b	8. b	9. b	10. b
11. b	12. a	13. b	14. d	15. d	16. d	17. d	18. c	19. d	20. d
21. d	22. b	23. d	24. a	25. a	26. c	27. d	28. c	29. c	30. d
31. c	32. d	33. d	34. d	35. c	36. d	37. d	38. d	39. a	40. d
41. d	42. a	43. a	44. b	45. d	46. c	47. b			

Chapter 30

1. c	2. d	3. a	4. b	5. d	6. a	7. a	8. d	9. b	10. d
11. b	12. d	13. d	14. c	15. c	16. d	17. a	18. b	19. d	20. a
21. a	22. d	23. d	24. b	25. c	26. c	27. d	28. c	29. a	30. c
31. b	32. d	33. d	34. a	35. d	36. a	37. a	38. d	39. d	40. c
41. d	42. c	43. c	44. d	45. b	46. b	47. c	48. d	49. b	50. c
51. a	52. d	53. b	54. d	55. d	56. c	57. d	58. c	59. b	60. d
61. d									

Chapter 31

1. b	2. d	3. b	4. a	5. d	6. c	7. d	8. a	9. b	10. b
11. c	12. c	13. b	14. b	15. d	16. d	17. d	18. c	19. d	20. d
21. d	22. d	23. a	24. d	25. c	26. d	27. b	28. c	29. d	30. d
31. b	32. b	33. c	34. d	35. a	36. d	37. c	38. d	39. b	40. a
41. d	42. d	43. c	44. d	45. d	46. b	47. d	48. c	49. d	50. c
51. d	52. d	53. c	54. d	55. d	56. d				

Chapter 32

1. d	2. d	3. d	4. d	5. c	6. a	7. d	8. d	9. d	10. d
11. b	12. d	13. a	14. b	15. d	16. b	17. d	18. d	19. a	20. b
21. d	22. d	23. c	24. d	25. d	26. b	27. d	28. a	29. d	30. d
31. c	32. b	33. b	34. d	35. a	36. d	37. d	38. b	39. d	40. d
41. d	42. d	43. d	44. d	45. a	46. c	47. d	48. d	49. a	50. a
51. d	52. c	53. b	54. c	55. a	56. d	57. c	58. d	59. c	60. d
61. c	62. d	63. a	64. d	65. d	66. d	67. d	68. d	69. d	

Chapter 33

1. d	2. b	3. d	4. a	5. d	6. d	7. b	8. d	9. d	10. a
11. b	12. c	13. d	14. d	15. b	16. d	17. d	18. d	19. d	20. d
21. c	22. d	23. a	24. d	25. c	26. d	27. d	28. d	29. b	30. d
31. d	32. b	33. d	34. d	35. c	36. b	37. d	38. c	39. a	40. a
41. c	42. d	43. a	44. d	45. a	46. d	47. a	48. a	49. d	50. d
51. a	52. d								

Chapter 34

1. a	2. a	3. d	4. d	5. b	6. d	7. a	8. a	9. d	10. a
11. d	12. d	13. d	14. b	15. d	16. b	17. d	18. c	19. d	20. d
21. d	22. b	23. d	24. b	25. b	26. d	27. d	28. b	29. c	30. b
31. b	32. a	33. d	34. d	35. a	36. d	37. d	38. d	39. a	40. b
41. d	42. d	43. b	44. b	45. a	46. d	47. d	48. d	49. a	50. b
51. d	52. c	53. c	54. c	55. d	56. c	57. c	58. d	59. d	60. d
61. d									

Chapter 35

1. d	2. d	3. d	4. d	5. a	6. d	7. a	8. b	9. c	10. d
11. d	12. d	13. d	14. d	15. a	16. a	17. b	18. d	19. c	20. a
21. d	22. a	23. d	24. d	25. d	26. b	27. a	28. a	29. d	30. d
31. d	32. c	33. a	34. d	35. a	36. c	37. b	38. a	39. d	40. a
41. a	42. d	43. b	44. b	45. b	46. d	47. d	48. a	49. c	50. d
51. d	52. d	53. a	54. c	55. d	56. a	57. d	58. d	59. c	60. d
61. a	62. d	63. d	64. d						

Chapter 36

1. d	2. d	3. b	4. b	5. d	6. b	7. b	8. c	9. d	10. d
11. d	12. d	13. d	14. d	15. a	16. a	17. d	18. d	19. d	20. d
21. d	22. d	23. c	24. b	25. b	26. d	27. d	28. d	29. b	30. c
31. b	32. d	33. d	34. c	35. a	36. a	37. d	38. d	39. c	40. a
41. a	42. c	43. d	44. b	45. b	46. d	47. d	48. d	49. a	50. a
51. d	52. c	53. d	54. d	55. c	56. b	57. a	58. a	59. d	60. d
61. a	62. a	63. d	64. c	65. c	66. d	67. b	68. d	69. c	70. d